Forensic Recovery of Human Remains

Forensic Recovery of Human Remains: Archaeological Approaches provides a comprehensive and updated guide to the search, recovery, documentation, and excavation of human remains in forensic contexts.

Recognizing that many crime scene and law enforcement personnel lack formal training in archaeological techniques and skeletal biology, this book equips readers with practical methods for processing scenes with skeletal remains and decomposing bodies, while documenting context. Coverage includes new case studies, expanded figures and tables, updated citations, and two new chapters. One chapter now focuses solely on taphonomic modifications, while the final chapter highlights how research has advanced forensic archaeology practice.

While complex scenarios such as mass burials or water recoveries should be handled by specialists, this book prepares readers to manage less complex cases, such as single burials and surface recoveries, competently. It also outlines how professionals can apply proper search and recovery techniques, ensuring that critical evidence is preserved and that forensic investigations are conducted with rigor and accuracy, from field to courtroom.

This third edition serves as an essential resource for undergraduates, graduate students, law enforcement and death scene personnel, forensic anthropology practitioners, and forensic archaeologists.

Forensic Recovery of Human Remains

Archaeological Approaches

Third Edition

John J. Schultz, Lana J. Williams, James T. Pokines,
Tosha L. Dupras, and Sandra M. Wheeler

CRC Press
Taylor & Francis Group
Boca Raton London New York

CRC Press is an imprint of the
Taylor & Francis Group, an **informa** business

Designed cover image: Shutterstock

Third edition published 2027
by CRC Press
2385 NW Executive Center Drive, Suite 320, Boca Raton FL 33431

and by CRC Press
4 Park Square, Milton Park, Abingdon, Oxon, OX14 4RN

CRC Press is an imprint of Taylor & Francis Group, LLC

First edition published by CRC Press 2005
Second edition published by CRC Press 2012

Library of Congress Cataloging-in-Publication Data
Names: Schultz, John J. author | Williams, Lana J. author | Pokines, James T. author |
Dupras, Tosha L. author | Wheeler, Sandra M. author
Title: Forensic recovery of human remains: archaeological approaches / John J. Schultz,
Lana J. Williams, James T. Pokines, Tosha L. Dupras and Sandra M. Wheeler.
Description: Third edition. | Boca Raton, FL: CRC Press, 2026. |
"First edition published by CRC Press 2005; Second edition published by CRC Press 2021"
Title page verso. | Includes bibliographical references and index. |
Identifiers: LCCN 2026005652 (print) | LCCN 2026005653 (ebook) |
ISBN 9781138706729 hardback | ISBN 9781032748214 paperback | ISBN 9781315201658 ebook
Subjects: LCSH: Forensic anthropology | Archaeology | Human remains (Archaeology) | Criminal investigation
Classification: LCC GN69.8 .F695 2026 (print) | LCC GN69.8 (ebook)
LC record available at https://lccn.loc.gov/2026005652
LC ebook record available at https://lccn.loc.gov/2026005653

ISBN: 9781138706729 (hbk)
ISBN: 9781032748214 (pbk)
ISBN: 9781315201658 (ebk)

DOI: 10.4324/9781315201658

Typeset in Berling
by codeMantra

This book is dedicated to the law enforcement officers, fire investigators, crime scene personnel, death investigators, cemetery personnel, and forensic specialists whose tireless efforts bring truth to light and resolution to those left behind. The emotional toll of this work is profound, yet with every individual who is recovered and remembered for who they were – not merely for the circumstances of their death – the burden is eased by the solace it brings to grieving families.

CONTENTS

I first encountered *Forensic Recovery of Human Remains: Archaeological Approaches* as a graduate student more than a decade ago. At the time, I was just beginning to understand what it meant to move from reading about forensic recovery to actually practicing it. Field methods felt abstract and intimidating in the way many new skills do: you know they matter, you know you'll be responsible for them someday, but you don't yet have the experience to picture yourself carrying them out with confidence. This book changed that for me. It made recovery approachable, presenting archaeological principles clearly and practically, with explanations and illustrations that turned complex processes into something I could visualize and understand.

Since then, this book has followed me throughout my career. I've taught these methods to undergraduate and graduate students since 2013, and I've used the text to help guide students through their first attempts at gridding a scene, mapping remains or thinking critically about context. Some of my favorite moments as an instructor come from watching students realize that these methods aren't just academic – *they actually work.* They bring order to chaotic scenes. They help answer questions. They give clarity to situations that, at first glance, can feel overwhelming. This book helped me see that for myself as a student, and it continues to help the students I teach today.

My connection to the material deepened even further during my years as a forensic anthropologist with the Defense POW/MIA Accounting Agency. There, I applied these same archaeological methods in some of the most challenging environments imaginable – from remote jungles to steep mountainsides – while excavating historic aircraft losses. Those recoveries demanded patience, precision, and a deep respect for context. The scene might begin with only a few fragments of evidence or a single piece of wreckage exposed at the surface, but the recovery required the same discipline taught in this book: establish a grid, identify stratigraphy, document everything, understand the taphonomy, and recover remains with the utmost care and deliberation. The principles in these chapters proved invaluable. They translated seamlessly to real-world missions where the stakes were incredibly high.

Today, in my role as a forensic anthropologist for the Georgia Bureau of Investigation, I apply these methods on a near-daily basis. Every recovery – whether a surface scatter hidden in heavy vegetation, a partially exposed burial, or a multi-component scene with commingling and animal activity – begins with the same questions I first learned from this text: What is the context? What came first? What disturbances are present? And what is the most methodical, respectful way to proceed? This book continues to be the resource that grounds those decisions. It provides structure when a scene feels complex and reinforces best practices when time pressures or environmental challenges make the work difficult.

That consistent relevance is exactly why this third edition matters. The field has grown significantly since the previous editions, and the authors have clearly worked hard to make this volume reflect the realities of modern forensic work. They have added a significant amount of new material with more than 30 new figures, tables, and teaching visuals; three new case studies; expanded appendices; and updated review materials. Each chapter now includes clear learning objectives and outcomes that instructors, students, and agencies will appreciate.

Two new chapters in particular stand out as major contributions. The new chapter on taphonomy provides an accessible, practical overview of how bodies and surrounding environments change over time – and why those changes matter during search and recovery. Subtle shifts in color, sediment patterns, dispersal distances, moisture, plant activity, and scavenging inform everything from where a search begins to how an excavation proceeds. This chapter encourages readers to slow down, observe carefully, and ground their decisions in what the scene is actually telling them.

The new chapter on research and teaching highlights the evidence-based foundation behind today's methods. Controlled studies of GPR detection, surface recovery rates, soil interference, and search techniques demonstrate how far the field has come. Equally important, the teaching activities in this chapter showcase realistic, hands-on learning scenarios that educators and practitioners can use immediately. They bridge the gap between conceptual understanding and field-ready competence, which is essential for a discipline as applied and meticulous as ours.

The improvements throughout the book are thoughtful and intentional. The writing is clear and direct. The visuals do exactly what they should: make concepts easier to understand and apply. The examples span a wide range of environments and conditions, which reflects the reality that forensic scenes do not occur in controlled, predictable settings. The addition of "How To" boxes – sharpening trowels, constructing grids, handling soil samples, and more – captures the kinds of practical skills that students and early-career practitioners often struggle with. These details may seem small, but they are the kinds of things that build confidence in the field.

What makes this book so enduring is its broad usefulness. Undergraduates encountering forensic archaeology for the first time find it approachable. Graduate students appreciate its depth. Crime scene investigators and death investigators rely on its clarity and value its thoroughness. And practitioners – those of us responsible for recovering remains with accuracy and care – trust it because the methods work. No matter where someone enters the field, this book meets them there.

But beyond technique, this edition reinforces something essential: recovery work is not just a technical task and does not exist in a vacuum. It is a scientific process, a legal obligation, and, most importantly, a responsibility to the individuals whose remains we are recovering and to the families awaiting answers. The way we search, excavate, document, and interpret has profound consequences. This book prepares readers for that responsibility with both skill and humility.

I've carried this book with me for years – both mentally and physically, and sometimes literally in my backpack on missions or casework. It has shaped how I teach, how I think, and how I practice. And I know it will continue to guide the next generation of forensic archaeologists, anthropologists, and investigators who will use these methods in classrooms, in training grounds, and at forensic scenes.

It is a privilege to introduce this third edition. I hope it serves you as well as it has served me.

Brittany S. Walter, PhD, D-ABFA, RPA
Georgia Bureau of Investigation,
Medical Examiner's Office

PREFACE

Processing forensic scenes involving human remains can be very complex. Unfortunately, standard training for many crime scene and law enforcement personnel typically does not include methods for search and recovery of human remains and associated evidence. In many cases, investigators receive their initial training at the time when human remains are discovered. Insufficient prior knowledge of archaeological techniques and skeletal biology can result in improperly processed scenes, where vital evidence may be destroyed or overlooked.

Certain skeletal elements may be missed because the individual performing the recovery lacks a framework for identifying or locating human remains and associated evidence. Alternatively, inappropriate search or excavation techniques may be used. The third edition of this book is intended to fill the need for an updated, comprehensive reference pertaining to the search, recovery, documentation, and excavation of human remains and associated evidence from forensic contexts.

This book is intended for advanced undergraduates and graduate students, law enforcement and death scene personnel, forensic anthropology practitioners, and forensic archaeologists. In an ideal world, individuals with expertise in forensic anthropology and forensic archaeology would be present at every crime scene that involved the search for and recovery of human remains. However, we recognize that it is not possible in every situation for law enforcement agencies to call upon these experts or have them employed in-house. Therefore, our aim is to equip readers with the knowledge necessary to apply proper search, excavation, and recovery techniques in the absence of specialized personnel. The techniques described in this book are best suited for less complex scenes such as single burials. More complicated scenarios – including multiple or mass burials, water recoveries, or cremations – should be handled by experienced professionals when possible.

Published more than a decade after the second edition in 2012, the third edition has been significantly updated to highlight the many advances and developments in forensic archaeology and includes the addition of a fifth co-author, James T. Pokines. We revised and expanded the content in each chapter, incorporating recent citations, suggested readings, and relevant research, along with newly integrated case study examples. Each chapter now opens with clearly defined learning objectives and outcomes, and the key terms, review, and discussion sections have been revised to improve usability and engagement in training. The third edition also introduces two new chapters (Chapters 5 and 13), focusing on taphonomic modifications and research and training in forensic archaeology. The tables, figures, and images in this edition have been substantially expanded to enhance clarity and instructional value. New sidebars have also been added to highlight key skills essential for conducting forensic searches and archaeological recovery.

The chapters in this edition are organized as follows:

- Chapter 1 differentiates between forensic archaeology and forensic anthropology and guides readers on locating experts in these fields.
- Chapter 2 describes the equipment needed for searches, recoveries, and excavations of human skeletal remains.
- Chapter 3 introduces human skeletal terminology that assists investigators to adequately describe the scene and remains in their reports and to understand biological terminology used in other death investigation reports.
- Chapter 4 focuses on how to distinguish forensic from non-forensic scenes using contextual information and specific criteria.
- Chapter 5 discusses common taphonomic changes to bones, including color changes and dispersal, and explains the importance of these modifications to bones regarding search and recovery methods, as well as using this information for site reconstruction.
- Chapter 6 details search methods and criteria for locating surface deposits and burials.
- Chapter 7 highlights different types of geophysical technologies that can be used in searches involving metallic evidence, graves, and submerged bodies.
- Chapter 8 provides step-by-step instructions for surveying and mapping techniques used to document scenes.
- Chapter 9 outlines procedures for recognizing and collecting associated botanical and entomological evidence at scenes.
- Chapter 10 provides step-by-step instructions on recovering surface site remains and evidence and excavating buried remains and evidence from a variety of contexts.
- Chapter 11 covers skeletal and evidence collection and addresses challenges in distinguishing human from nonhuman skeletal remains.
- Chapter 12 highlights the components of a final forensic archaeological report and the key information that it should contain.
- Chapter 13 highlights how research has advanced forensic archaeology practice and includes classroom exercises and mock teaching scenarios to improve field proficiency and scene documentation.

The authors would like to extend our thanks to the students, colleagues, and field practitioners who provided valuable comments that greatly improved the previous second edition and the current third edition. We would also like to thank the following individuals and agencies for inviting us to work with them: Orange County Sheriff's Office, Orlando Police Department, Seminole County Sheriff's Office, Lake Mary Police Department, Dr. Michael Spence (Western University), Ontario Provincial Police, Royal Canadian Mounted Police, Ontario Coroner's Office, Shoals Marine Laboratory, Boston University's Chobanian and Avedisian School of Medicine, and the Office of the Chief Medical Examiner, Massachusetts. Thanks also to the following individuals and agencies for graciously allowing us to use their artwork, images, and/or likenesses: Fanny Bocquentin (French National Centre for Scientific Research), Dave Clarke, Kelly Wood, William Hawkins, Gene Ralston, Mary Peter, Mike Warren, S. "Stacy" Barber, Jeff Brzezinski, Orange County Sheriff's Office, Seminole County Sheriff's Office, and André Strauss (Lapa do Santo/MAE-USP). Special thanks to Dr. Brittany S. Walter (D-ABFA, RPA, Georgia Bureau of Investigation, Medical Examiner's Office) for her willingness to write the foreword for this edition.

John J. Schultz is a Professor and Department Chair at the University of Kentucky and a Fellow of the American Academy of Forensic Sciences. He earned a BA in Anthropology from SUNY at Stony Brook, an MS in Human Biology from the University of Indianapolis, and a PhD in Anthropology from the University of Florida. Formerly a Department Chair at the University of Central Florida, he conducted forensic anthropology casework for approximately 20 years at the local medical examiner's office. His primary research interests include biological profile methods and forensic archaeology methods that emphasize forensic scene reconstruction and search techniques.

Lana J. Williams is a Senior Lecturer at the University of Central Florida. She earned her MA from the University of Central Florida and PhD in Anthropology from The University of Western Ontario, where she received the Governor General's Award for research. She specializes in biochemical analysis of human remains, mortuary and forensic archaeology, and human osteology. She has conducted fieldwork in Greece, Belize, Türkiye, and is currently the lead bioarchaeologist with two field projects in Egypt. She has over 20 years of experience in forensic archaeology casework assisting law enforcement in Florida, Pennsylvania, and Ontario, Canada.

James T. Pokines is an Associate Professor in the Forensic Anthropology Program at the Boston University School of Medicine. He received a BA degree in Anthropology/Archaeology from Cornell University, MA and PhD degrees in Anthropology from the University of Chicago, and ABFA Board certification. He is a former Board Member and Vice President of the ABFA and a Fellow of the American Academy of Forensic Sciences. He has over 25 years of experience as a forensic anthropologist and forensic archaeologist, including 12 years at the Central Identification Laboratory, Hawaii. He is also the forensic anthropologist for the Commonwealth of Massachusetts.

Tosha L. Dupras is a Professor of Anthropology and Dean of the College of Arts and Sciences at Texas Tech University. She earned a BA in Archaeology from Simon Fraser University, an MSc in Human Biology from the University of Guelph, and a PhD in Anthropology from McMaster University. She specializes in bioarchaeology and is a member of the Dakhleh Oasis Project in Egypt and member of the Sai Island Archaeological Mission in Sudan. She has also assisted local law enforcement with the search for, excavation, and analysis of human remains.

Sandra M. Wheeler is an Assistant Dean in the College of Sciences and a Senior Lecturer in the Department of Anthropology at the University of Central Florida. She earned an MA from the University of Central Florida and a PhD in Anthropology from The University of Western Ontario. She is a bioarchaeologist specializing in mortuary archaeology, juvenile osteology, and forensic archaeology. She has conducted fieldwork in Belize, Mexico, and Egypt. She has also assisted local law enforcement agencies with the search for and archaeological recovery of human remains in Florida and Ontario, Canada.

Learning Objectives

- Summarize the development of forensic archaeology.
- Define forensic anthropology and forensic archaeology within the medicolegal process.
- Outline the skill sets of forensic anthropologists and forensic archaeologists.

Learning Connections

- Establish the main tasks of the forensic archaeologist that will be expanded upon through the book.
- Introduce the interconnectedness of forensic anthropology and forensic archaeology.

The application of forensic archaeology methods began through forensic anthropologists understanding the benefits of incorporating an archaeological perspective when processing forensic scenes involving human remains that would require forensic anthropology analysis. The roots and proponents of forensic archaeology as an emerging discipline began in the 1970s with publications discussing the benefits and contributions of incorporating standard archaeological techniques to crime scene and death investigations (Bass and Birkby, 1978; Kerley, 1978; Morse et al., 1976). During the 1980s, there was a growing emphasis on the use of proper archaeological field methods when recovering and excavating human remains from forensic contexts (e.g., Berryman and Lahren, 1984; Morse et al., 1983; Sigler-Eisenberg, 1985; Skinner and Lazenby, 1983; Wolf, 1986). These early proponents of forensic archaeology recognized the legal importance of both the utilization of proper collection techniques for human remains and precise documentation of associated contextual information from crime scenes.

Throughout the 1990s, the forensic archaeology emphasis continued with proponents using a multidisciplinary approach for detection of graves and collection of evidence, as well as improved field methods for the recovery of remains within a forensic context (e.g., Dirkmaat and Adovasio, 1997; France et al., 1992; Hunter et al., 1994; Scott and Connor, 1997). At the same time, forensic anthropologists began embracing taphonomic data collection and analyses for both the recovery and laboratory analysis phases of forensic anthropology (e.g., Haglund and Sorg, 1997a; Micozzi, 1991; Ubelaker, 1991). **Forensic taphonomy** analyses focus on interpreting the depositional context, discriminating between **antemortem**, **perimortem**, and **postmortem** modifications of the remains, and estimating **postmortem interval (PMI)** (Haglund and Sorg, 1997b; refer to Chapter 5). Forensic taphonomy provided a scientific basis for scene and laboratory interpretations because the ideal process for taphonomic analysis involves recovering remains using archaeological methods, techniques, and principles (Dirkmaat and Cabo, 2012).

Forensic archaeology has been recognized as its own discipline within academic programs, by professional and international organizations, and by the law enforcement community (e.g., Dirkmaat and Cabo, 2012; Hanson, 2008; Pokines et al., 2022; Schultz and Dupras, 2008). However, many personnel involved with the practical aspects of recovering human remains still have not been trained in or do not universally practice proper archaeological methods to conduct searches successfully, document recovery scenes, excavate graves, and collect and transport evidence.

Although the focus of this book is forensic archaeology, a brief introduction to **forensic anthropology** is warranted. While both disciplines are highly specialized and sometimes thought of as synonymous, there are distinct differences between forensic anthropology and forensic archaeology. In North America, it is common for forensic archaeology to be encompassed within the discipline of forensic anthropology, and in such cases, it may be referred to as forensic bioarchaeology (Skinner et al., 2003). However, in other locations, such as in the United Kingdom and Australia, forensic anthropology and forensic archaeology are viewed as two distinct disciplines. To understand the differences between forensic anthropology and forensic archaeology and the contributions that each can make to crime scene investigation, it is important to start with a discussion of anthropology in general.

Broadly defined, anthropology is the study of humans. The word anthropology derives from the Greek *anthros* (man) and *logos* (the study of). Anthropologists use a holistic or biocultural approach (i.e., modeling the influences of biological and cultural environments on human physiology and wellbeing) to understand the many facets of human behavior, both past and present. In North America, anthropology is commonly divided into four areas of study, including cultural (social) anthropology, archaeology, linguistics, and biological (physical) anthropology. Cultural anthropology is the study of people's lifeways – what they do, believe, experience, and create. Cultural anthropologists mostly work with living societies. Archaeology is the study of the human past through material culture (e.g., pottery, stone tools, art, and architecture), debris, landscapes, and physical remains. Linguistics studies language structure, use, and change in the ways we communicate and relate to each other. In most cases, linguistics is an important aspect of the other areas of anthropology. **Biological anthropology** studies the behavioral and biological aspects of humans, their extinct ancestors, and related nonhuman primates such as chimpanzees, gorillas, and monkeys. Some of the more specialized areas covered by biological anthropology include:

- Primatology – the study of the behavior, biology, evolution, and taxonomy of nonhuman primates.
- Paleoanthropology – the study of the origins and evolution of early humans and their behavior through fossil and archaeological records.
- Human biology – the study of modern human population variations and adaptations.
- Human growth and development – the study of how humans grow and develop throughout the lifespan from conception through senescence and death.
- Nutrition – the study of human diet and nutrition from social, biological, and evolutionary perspectives.
- Genetics – the study of human DNA, heredity, and the variation of inherited characteristics.
- Osteology – the anatomical study of the structure and function of the human skeleton including individualized traits and pathology.

So where do forensic anthropology and forensic archaeology fit into all of this?

ANTHROPOLOGY IN THE MEDICOLEGAL PROCESS

In the United States, death investigations and investigator certifications are part of a formalized medicolegal process undertaken by either a coroner or medical examiner. There is a major difference between the two positions: a **coroner** is an elected official, and a **medical examiner (ME)** is an appointed position. Since a coroner is an elected position, the chief coroner is usually not a forensic pathologist, and their background and experience vary. The coroner decides when an autopsy, which must be performed by a forensic pathologist, is needed. Conversely, a chief ME is a board-certified forensic pathologist who is appointed to a government office. The role of the coroner or ME is to determine cause and manner of death, as well as to identify the deceased.

When human remains are found, the law enforcement agency controls the scene, and the coroner or ME controls the body or skeletal remains. The law enforcement agency or medicolegal system involved in a death investigation has jurisdictional authority to involve or invite other experts in a death investigation as consultants or through formal appointments. For example, since the complexity of outdoor scenes involving skeletal remains can vary, the coroner, ME, or law enforcement agency involved can invite experts to assist with the recovery of the skeletal remains, such as a forensic anthropologist or forensic archaeologist, and with the recovery of evidence, such as a forensic entomologist or forensic botanist. In some instances, personnel with specialized skills not normally required during most body searches may be invited to participate on-site when machinery or technology is required, such as a backhoe operator or a ground-penetrating radar (GPR) specialist.

While numerous experts are frequently involved as medicolegal team members, forensic anthropologists have become integral team members for death investigations involving decomposing bodies, fragmentary remains, and skeletal remains, because they provide a unique skill set in both the laboratory and the field. It is common for forensic anthropologists to be employed at universities, colleges, or museums and consult on an as-needed basis for coroner and ME offices, because a full-time anthropologist is generally not needed daily. However, there are several ME offices throughout the United States that employ forensic anthropologists as full-time or half-time employees due to caseload, mass fatality preparedness, and shared expertise as an investigator or autopsy technician (Austin and Fulginiti, 2008).

WHAT DO FORENSIC ANTHROPOLOGISTS DO?

Traditionally, forensic anthropologists have been requested to assist local law enforcement agencies and coroner or ME offices with the identification of human skeletal remains. It is becoming more likely, however, that the forensic anthropologist will be asked to assist in other capacities. Table 1.1 includes a list of skills that the forensic anthropologist should be experienced in or knowledgeable about.

In the laboratory, forensic anthropologists provide important osteology skills that are pertinent to a death investigation. When the anthropologist is presented with evidence collected from a scene, the first task is to differentiate bone from non-bone material. Once the material is identified as bone, the next task is to differentiate human bone from nonhuman bone. If the bone is identified as being human, the next task is to determine if the skeletal material is from a modern medicolegal context, more commonly referred to as a forensic context, or from a non-forensic (i.e., non-medicolegal) context, such as archaeological remains or discarded anatomical teaching materials. If the material is from a forensic context, the anthropologist's next task is to sort the remains to determine the **minimum number of individuals (MNI)**. In some instances, the forensic context could involve a grave containing several individuals, or a plane crash involving extreme fragmentation of multiple people. After MNI is determined, the next task in osteological analysis is to construct a **biological profile** (e.g., age, sex, population affinity, stature, and individualizing traits), determine the presence of antemortem and perimortem trauma, and interpret possible postmortem modifications. The osteological analysis could also include interpreting indications of time since death and individual identification if requested.

In addition to the skills listed in Table 1.1, the forensic anthropologist, regardless of archaeological knowledge, may also be able to assist in searching crime scenes and recovering skeletal remains. Of particular importance is the fact that forensic anthropologists are also trained in recognizing patterns of **taphonomy** (i.e., what happens to a body after the individual dies; refer to Chapter 5), and they may be able to help locate remains based on these processes. Forensic anthropologists can also readily identify fetal, infant, and child skeletal remains, which often look very different from adult human skeletal remains and can be easily overlooked by the untrained eye (refer to Chapter 3). As previously mentioned, many forensic anthropologists are knowledgeable and trained in archaeological methods, so their expertise can also be extremely beneficial during recovery.

Table 1.1 Skills and Knowledge Areas Associated with Forensic Anthropology

- Knowledge of and familiarity with:
  - Human soft tissue anatomy
  - Burnt and cremated remains
  - Fetal, infant, and juvenile skeletal remains (growth and development)
  - Dental development, morphology, and variation
  - Skeletal and dental pathology
- Identify human versus nonhuman skeletal remains
- Assist in determining context of human remains (e.g., forensic, anatomical, historical, archaeological)
- Understand and recognize taphonomic processes (e.g., decomposition, weathering, animal activity) and information needed for determining time since death
- Develop biological profile: skeletal indications of sex, age at death, population affinity, and stature
- Distinguish antemortem, perimortem, and postmortem skeletal modification and/or trauma
- Identify unique skeletal traits or variations (genetic and acquired)
- Use radiologic images of dentition and skeletal remains for identification
- Understand methodology and use of mitochondrial and nuclear DNA for identification
- Understand use of facial reproduction and superimposition identification techniques
- Provide law enforcement officials with a written report of all activities

Source: Modified from Skinner et al. (2003); and Snow (1982).

WHAT DO FORENSIC ARCHAEOLOGISTS DO?

As a separate discipline, or as a set of skills that the forensic anthropologist may possess, forensic archaeology involves applying archaeological techniques to the crime scene. It is important to recognize that there are fundamental differences between traditional academic archaeology and forensic archaeology (Hunter, 2002). Traditional academic archaeology is research-based and question-driven, where certain methodological steps are consistently followed. The forensic archaeologist, however, in addition to applying methodological steps, must deal with law enforcement and legal procedures, major time constraints, the media, the occasional presence of soft tissues, and situations in which traditional archaeological methods will not work. Forensic archaeologists also have the goal of full recovery of entire scenes. Academic archaeology frequently only samples portions of sites, as research questions can be answered with smaller amounts of data. Forensic archaeologists must also be much more flexible in their approach and adapt their methods to each case at hand (Hoshower, 1998).

Forensic archaeologists should be proficient in all the skills associated with traditional archaeology and know how to apply this expertise in a forensic context. A list of skills, drawn from the authors' experience and modified from Skinner et al. (2003), can be found in Table 1.2. It is important to recognize that, during a forensic investigation, there are five primary responsibilities directly associated with the forensic archaeologist: locating or eliminating areas of interest, interpreting scene context, mapping the scene, excavating remains, and collecting remains and associated evidence (Figure 1.1). All five responsibilities include accurate and detailed recording and reporting of information.

Locating and Eliminating Areas of Interest

Locating sites of deposition and eliminating sites as areas of interest are primary aspects of any forensic investigation. Many searches in forensic investigations begin with someone randomly finding a bone, while others are initiated with a tip from an informant. Both instances are followed by a visual search of the area to locate evidence associated with a missing individual or their remains. At times, the initial search may indicate the possible presence of remains and require further investigation. For example, authors John Schultz and Lana Williams assisted with a search in a Central Florida commercial development lot, an area of interest indicated by an informant and previously searched using cadaver dogs. Time constraints and the size of the area to be exposed required heavy equipment to assist with the search. After consulting with the heavy equipment operator, the area was exposed by scraping away thin layers of soil so any changes in the layers or patterns of disturbance would be recognizable. Throughout the process, notes were kept on soil characteristics, elevation of layers, and any inclusions and disturbances. Digging continued until the entire area was exposed and all possible means of detection had been exhausted. Although no evidence of remains was found, the expertise of the forensic archaeologists in this investigation assisted with the equally important elimination of a site as an area of further interest.

Table 1.2 Skills and Knowledge Areas Associated with Forensic Archaeology

- Knowledge and recognition of:
  - Basic human soft tissue anatomy and decomposition process
  - Basic nonhuman and human (adult and juvenile) skeletal remains
  - Burnt and cremated remains
  - Associated forensic evidence (e.g., tool marks, surgical implants, bullets)
- Assist with visual and intrusive method ground searches
- Assist in determining context of human remains (e.g., forensic, anatomical, historical, archaeological)
- Direct any heavy equipment use during a ground search
- Understand and recognize taphonomic processes (e.g., decomposition, weathering, animal activity) and environmental changes associated with the burial process
- Conduct or assist with geophysical search methods (e.g., GPR, electromagnetic survey)
- Analyze site formation processes and provide detailed descriptions of soils
- Perform survey and mapping at various levels of the search and recovery process
- Establish spatial controls (e.g., GPS data, gridding, datum points)
- Excavate and record site using archaeological methods specifically adapted to each case
- Collect, document, and preserve sediment, botanical, and entomological evidence
- Collect, document, and preserve human remains and associated evidence
- Provide law enforcement officials with a written report of all activities

Source: Modified from Skinner et al. (2003) and Snow (1982).

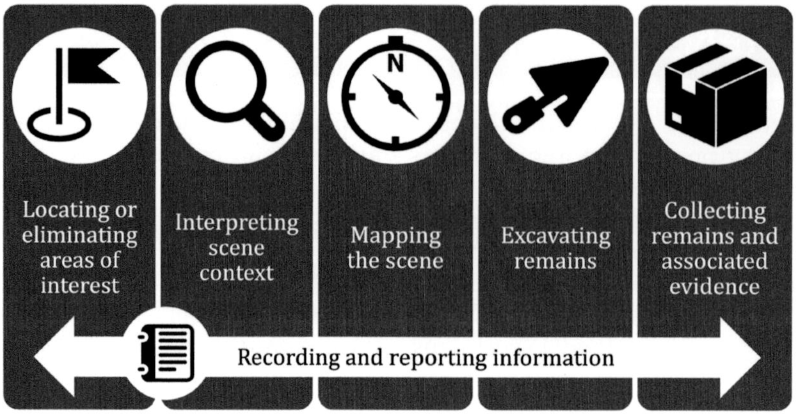

Figure 1.1 Five primary responsibilities directly associated with the forensic archaeologist during a forensic investigation.

Interpreting Scene Context

The second role of the forensic archaeologist includes the skills and techniques needed to understand and interpret the initial context and prolonged history of crime scene transformation. The results of **postdepositional** (i.e., after remains are deposited) events will be the first thing encountered by the team of investigators, and the interpretation of these transformations can be vital during the search and recovery process. For example, scene context can be important when determining medicolegal significance of human remains (e.g., forensic, anatomical, historical, or archaeological). In addition, documenting scene context is a necessity when understanding post-depositional processes during the recovery, and information about scene context is essential when assessing taphonomic modifications (refer to Chapter 5). In one instance, author Tosha Dupras realized firsthand the intensity of taphonomic processes during her involvement in a skeletal recovery near Niagara Falls. In this example, the individual was discovered on a steep slope at the base of a cliff face. It was soon recognized that this site was annually exposed to excessive water runoff from melting snow, continual falling rock from the cliff face, and landscape alteration from a combination of water and falling rock. As a result, the skeleton was dispersed from the top of the slope to the bottom, with the cranial and upper body elements near the top, and the lower body deposited toward the bottom of the slope. As the body decomposed, various parts were shifted down the slope as the terrain changed each year due to taphonomic dispersal processes. An understanding of the taphonomic processes at this scene aided in developing the search and excavation techniques employed to recover this individual.

Mapping the Scene

Mapping techniques commonly used in forensic archaeology allow investigators to maintain an exact record of where every item of evidence was located at the scene. These techniques can also assist investigators in reconstructing the order of events that took place prior to recovery. An example of this occurred in Canada when author Sandra Wheeler assisted with the mapping and recovery of an individual found among tall reeds along a canal embankment. The embankment slope caused the cranium to slide away from the body during the decomposition process and become lodged in the reeds further downhill. To aid the mapping and recovery of evidence from the slope, the crime scene unit carefully trimmed the reeds surrounding the cranium and the additional remains. During autopsy, the forensic anthropologist working with investigators identified a possible perimortem fracture in two of the facial bones of the cranium. However, the forensic anthropologist and investigating detective needed to eliminate the possibility of the fracture being caused by the postmortem movement of the cranium. The investigators examined the original scene map to evaluate the slope of the hill and distance that the cranium traveled (Figure 1.2). The map shows the cranium did not travel far from the body, and the reeds blocked it from rolling further down the slope. It was determined that the skull's postmortem movement could not have caused the force needed to result in the type of fracture identified by the forensic anthropologist. Although crime scene photographs were taken, the level of detail needed to reconstruct and evaluate the exact location of the cranium on the embankment in relation to the body at the time of recovery was not possible. In this instance, proper mapping techniques used in forensic archaeology, which included plan and section drawings, assisted with the reconstruction of events, and provided support for the identification of perimortem trauma to the individual.

Excavating Remains

Forensic archaeologists also play a key role in the reconstruction and interpretation of events occurring during scene creation and deposition of the evidence or body.

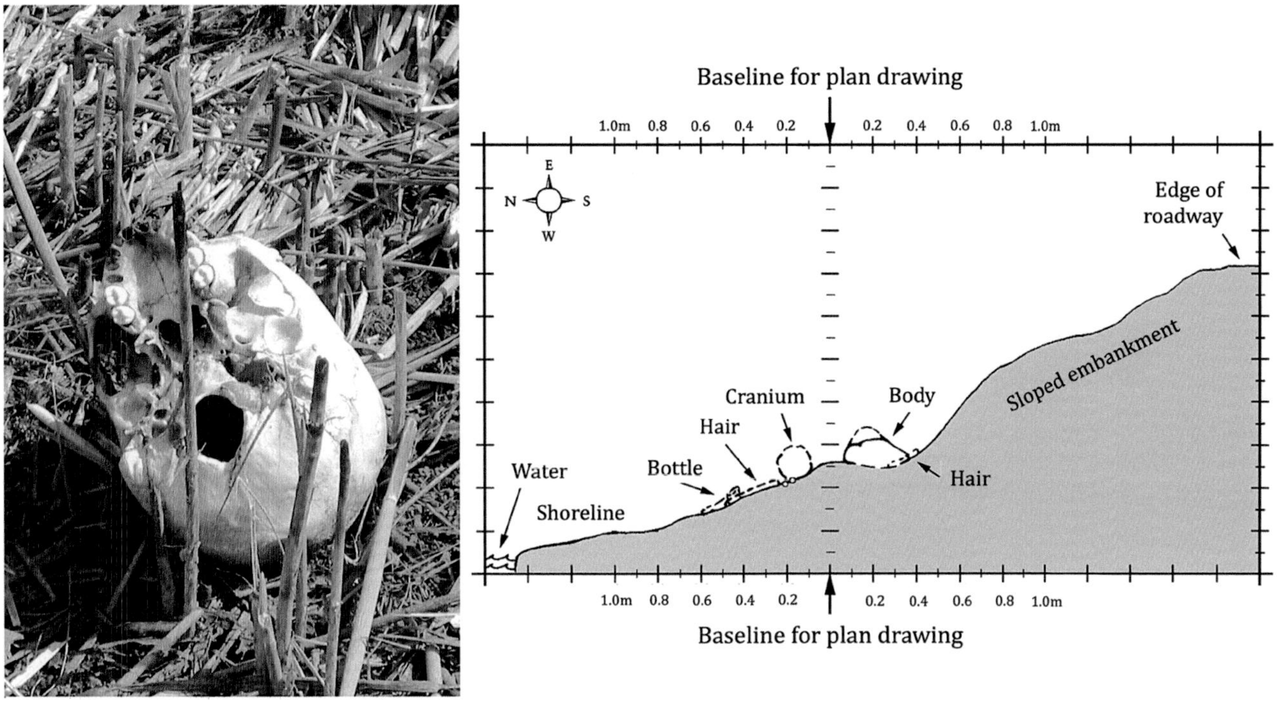

Figure 1.2 Field photograph of the cranium (left) taken downhill to show its position among reeds, which were cut to aid in the recovery of the remains. The embankment's section drawing (right) shows the cranium's position on the slope in relation to the body at the time of recovery.

Meticulous archaeological techniques can also be used to corroborate or disprove assailant stories about what happened at a particular scene. For example, authors Sandra Wheeler and Lana Williams assisted in the recovery of an individual in Ontario, who was placed in a hole in a cement pad initially intended for the installation of a water pump. During burial, the assailants undercut the cement pad and removed enough soil to accommodate the body. The assailants then used the loose sediment and large fragments of the cement pad, which were removed earlier for water pump installation, to backfill over the victim's body. During forensic archaeological excavation, everything was meticulously mapped and recorded, with top and bottom elevations noted for each object and layer encountered. The victim's head was positioned in the undercut with no other debris or cement fragments in the vicinity. During the coroner investigation, multiple fractures to the victim's skull were discovered, likely sustained through being beaten at the time of death. The assailants, however, claimed that the fractures were caused during burial, when fragments of cement were tossed in over the body. When records from the excavation were consulted, it was evident that the victim's head was covered with a sediment layer and located approximately 15 cm (about 5.9 in.) below the elevation of the nearest cement fragment. Moreover, it was evident that any material used to backfill the hole could not have been dropped directly on the victim's head. By using proper excavation, mapping, and recording techniques throughout recovery, the coroner and the investigating detectives were able to eliminate any damage to the victim's skull during burial and attribute the fractures to injuries sustained during the last moments of the individual's life.

Collecting Remains and Associated Evidence

Because forensic anthropologists are trained in recognizing human skeletal remains, they may be able to provide valuable assistance in locating missing skeletal elements. This was true in a Central Florida case where authors Tosha Dupras and Lana Williams assisted in analyzing human skeletal remains recovered during a forensic investigation without the assistance of a forensic anthropologist. After inventorying the recovered remains, which were intermingled with a matting of plant roots and the individual's clothing, examination of the scene photographs revealed several bones that should have been present were missing. Upon revisiting the site, several additional bones were recovered (Figure 1.3). To the layperson, it may seem that missing a few bones would be inconsequential, but these bones could hold the key to the individual's identification and aid in reconstructing events surrounding the individual's death. In addition, it may also save time, money, and resources in the future by avoiding a situation where the missing bones are discovered well after the initial case is closed and mistakenly identified as a new case.

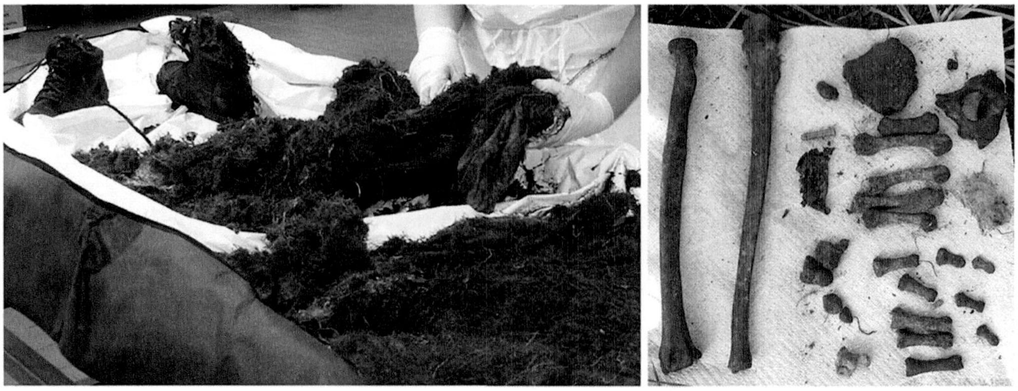

Figure 1.3 Sorting through plant materials and remains removed from a crime scene (left). Remains were recovered from the scene without the help of a forensic anthropologist or forensic archaeologist. Author Tosha Dupras later recovered missing bones and evidence (right) when she assisted the homicide detective at the site.

EDUCATION AND TRAINING

In North America, a forensic archaeologist is expected to be trained in archaeological techniques and human osteology. Typically, forensic archaeologists will begin their education in biological anthropology and specialize in human osteology or human skeletal biology. Once the skills of human osteology are mastered, the methods and techniques of analyzing skeletal remains can be applied to cases of legal importance.

In recent years, the number of forensic anthropologists receiving training in archaeological field methods has increased. This increase, in part, is due to many graduate students in forensic anthropology understanding the importance of receiving training in archaeological methods and taking advantage of training in both areas in the same academic department. However, at times, the training of the forensic anthropologist will not include the skills associated with proper archaeological techniques, nor will the forensic archaeologist necessarily have knowledge of human osteology. Therefore, when searching for the appropriate individual to assist in crime scene excavations, local law enforcement agencies should be aware of an individual's skill set before asking for that individual's assistance.

There are numerous short courses offered around the country that include training in archaeological methods. Although this text is written to assist law enforcement personnel, death investigation personnel, anthropology students, and professional forensic anthropologists and archaeologists, it is not meant to replace training in these methods. If an individual with skills in forensic archaeology is not available to assist with a case, at minimum, one, if not all, personnel involved with field collection, search, or recovery should attend a forensic archaeology short course. Information on these courses can be found by doing an Internet search, or through the website for the American Board of Forensic Anthropology (ABFA) (https://www.theabfa.org/). Once at this site, select the 'More' button at the top of the screen, and then 'Students – Other opportunities' from the pull-down menu to find a list of upcoming short courses, internships, and field schools. You can also find short courses announced through the American Academy of Forensic Sciences (AAFS) (http://www.aafs.org) Anthropology news feed on their website.

EMPLOYMENT IN ACADEMIC AND NON-ACADEMIC SETTINGS

In most instances, forensic archaeologists do not have full-time positions in which they actively work on forensic cases. Most of the practicing forensic anthropologists and forensic archaeologists in North America are employed as professors at universities or other academic institutes. When their field or laboratory skills are needed, law enforcement agencies, medical examiners, and coroners consult practicing forensic anthropologists. In addition, forensic anthropologists are employed in jobs outside of academics. As mentioned earlier, coroner or ME offices occasionally hire forensic anthropologists for additional roles in the office and to work on forensic anthropology casework when the need arises. They may also be hired full time by coroner or ME offices if they are in regions that support a heavy caseload. The single largest employer of forensic anthropologists and forensic archaeologists in the United States is the **Defense POW/MIA Accounting Agency** (http://www.dpaa.mil), located on the island of Oahu in Hawaii. The DPAA was formed in January 2015 and had been formerly the Joint POW/MIA Accounting Command (JPAC). One of the missions of the DPAA is to account for all Americans missing due to any conflicts involving the United States. As a result, forensic anthropologists and forensic archaeologists perform searches and recoveries in countries where there are reports of remains belonging to American servicemembers (Figure 1.4).

Forensic anthropologists and forensic archaeologists are also recognized for their participation in disaster responses to mass fatality contexts, including plane crashes (e.g., TWA Flight 800 in 1996), earthquakes, floods, and bombings (e.g., Oklahoma City Federal Building in 1995), as well as large-scale terrorist incidents such as the September 11 attacks in 2001. As a discipline, forensic anthropologists are uniquely trained for participation in the disaster response to mass fatality incidents because of their expertise in the recovery and triage of human remains, identification of victims, and interpretation of skeletal trauma (Wiersema and Woody, 2016). In the United States, most state and federal mass disaster teams, known as the **Disaster Mortuary Operational Response Teams** (http://www.dmort.org), have several forensic anthropologists and forensic archaeologists on their rosters. In addition, other government agencies that employ forensic anthropologists in a full-time capacity include the Federal Bureau of Investigation (http://www.fbi.gov), National Transportation and Safety Board (http://www.ntsb.gov), and the Armed Forces Institute of Pathology (http://www.afip.org).

Since the 1980s, forensic anthropologists and forensic archaeologists have become vital team members in the search, recovery, and identification of victims of human rights violations around the world. Agencies such as **Physicians for Human Rights (PHR)**, the **International Commission on Missing Persons (ICMP)**, and the United Nations International Criminal Tribunals routinely employ forensic anthropologists and forensic archaeologists in locations such as Guatemala, Argentina, Bosnia, Rwanda, and East Timor to assist in the identification of individuals who have died because of their ethnicity, political affiliation, or religious beliefs. In 2000, initial scientific investigation of Spanish Civil War (1936–1939) mass graves took place, and by 2020, over 850 mass graves have been excavated in Spain, resulting in almost 11,000 victims recovered (Etxeberria et al., 2021). This increase in the search and identification of 20th-century conflict casualties also includes search and recovery of WWI and WWII military casualties in Europe and elsewhere (Márquez-Grant and Errickson, 2021).

Figure 1.4 Members from the Defense POW/MIA Accounting Agency (DPAA) conducting search and recovery efforts in the Himalayan Mountains in the Arunachal Pradesh region, India, in search of Army Air Corps members who went down in a U.S. aircraft in 1944.

Source: Figure 1.4 by U.S. Air Force SSgt Erik Cardenas is within Public Domain (US Dept of Defense), adapted from https://www.dpaa.mil/News-Stories/Our-Stories/Article/630302/dpaa-conducts-recovery-operations-in-india/; the appearance of U.S. Department of Defense (DoD) visual information does not imply or constitute DoD endorsement.

LOCATING A FORENSIC ANTHROPOLOGIST OR FORENSIC ARCHAEOLOGIST

The **American Academy of Forensic Sciences (AAFS)** is a nonprofit organization comprising forensic specialists in the following 12 sections: Anthropology, Criminalistics, Digital and Multimedia Sciences, Engineering & Applied Sciences, Forensic Nursing Science, General, Jurisprudence, **Odontology**, **Pathology**/Biology, Psychiatry and Behavioral Sciences, Questioned Documents, and Toxicology (Table 1.3). The AAFS has members representing all the United States and over 70 countries worldwide. To achieve recognition within the broader discipline of forensic sciences in North America, most forensic anthropologists belong to the anthropology section of the AAFS. There are certain qualifications that must be met to become a member of the Academy. For the anthropology section, members must demonstrate through casework, teaching, or research that they are active in the discipline. Please note, however, that this does not mean that the individual has been certified as an expert in forensic anthropology.

A growing number of members of the anthropology section of the AAFS have received certification from the **American Board of Forensic Anthropology (ABFA)**. Traditionally, Diplomate (D-ABFA) status has been the only recognized form of certification for forensic anthropology practitioners in the United States and Canada. In 2025, the ABFA implemented a multilevel certification program of two sequential levels that test competencies at each level: **Analyst (A-ABFA)** and **Diplomate (D-ABFA)**. The examination for the analyst certification is designed to evaluate laboratory skills and fundamental knowledge, and applicants must possess at least an appropriate master's degree. After earning an analyst certification, individuals with a relevant doctoral degree can apply to take the Diplomate exam. The Diplomate exam further evaluates advanced knowledge, synthesis, and interpretation of relevant information expected beyond analyst competencies. Currently, there are over 110 active members listed as board-certified Diplomates. For a list of active forensic anthropologists with Diplomate status and their contact information, visit the American Board of Forensic Anthropology website (http://www.theabfa.org) to search by state or name.

Unfortunately, there are no currently recognized associations or boards specifically for forensic archaeology in North America, and because of this, there are no easy ways to find individuals who have skills in forensic archaeology. The **Society for American Archaeology (SAA)** does keep a forensic archaeology recovery roster, but this information can only be accessed on their website (http://www.saa.org) if you are a member of the organization. The best way to find these specialists, particularly in North America, is to contact individuals who identify themselves as forensic anthropologists and inquire as to their skills in the realm of forensic archaeology. Another option, if forensic specialists are not available in your area, is to contact local universities with field archaeologists on staff. Even though these individuals may not be trained in the **forensic context**, they will possess all the necessary archaeological skills to conduct excavations.

Table 1.3 Brief Description of AAFS Sections (Includes Education and/or Specialty of Forensic Scientists for Each Section)

Anthropology
- Aid death investigations from various contexts by applying theories and methods from anthropology
- Biological anthropologists and archaeologists with advanced degrees in anthropology-related disciplines

Criminalists
- Examine physical evidence by applying standard techniques of natural and physical sciences
- Criminalists typically have degrees in forensic science, chemistry, biology, molecular biology, and physics

Digital & Multimedia Sciences
- Examine digital and multimedia evidence by applying industry standard and scientific processing techniques
- Digital evidence examiners typically have degrees in computer science, information technology, engineering, as well as specialized degrees in digital forensics, computer forensics, and media forensics

Engineering & Applied Sciences
- Engineering scientists apply techniques of science and engineering to address questions relating to criminal, civil, and regulatory issues
- Scientists specializing across the engineering fields, in addition to physicists and chemists

Forensic Nursing Science
- Combine principles of forensic sciences with those of nursing in clinical investigation of liability issues, medical deaths, and crime-related trauma
- Experienced nursing professionals interested in forensic health science

General
- Most diverse section of AAFS; includes forensic science specialties not included in other sections
- Examples of forensic specialties include crime scene investigator, firearms analyst, accounting, medicolegal death investigator, coroner (non-medical degree), photography, and veterinary science.

Jurisprudence
- Primarily concerned with admissibility of forensic science evidence in civil and criminal court proceedings and applying Daubert standards
- Judges and lawyers involved professionally in forensic science issues

Odontology
- Identify human remains using dental evidence and provide assessments of patterned injuries, age assessments, and abuse and neglect cases
- Doctor of Dental Surgery or Doctor of Dental Medicine

Pathology/Biology
- Forensic pathologists apply principles of medicine in general and pathology to death investigations, perform autopsies to determine cause of death, involved with circumstances surrounding death; Forensic biology applies life sciences to death investigations to determine body location, postmortem interval, and body identification
- Forensic pathologists are medical doctors that receive pathology training through a residency and a one-year fellowship in forensic pathology. Forensic biologists typically have a graduate degree in a biological science, and include fields such as botany, ecology, entomology, genetics, and microbiology

Psychiatry & Behavioral Sciences
- Focus on a range of legal issues involving civil cases, criminal cases, and other areas including family/domestic relations law
- Psychiatrists (medical doctors) and forensic psychologists (PhD in psychology) with specialized training

Questioned Documents
- Examine and evaluate documents regarding their source or authenticity
- Degrees in forensic science, sciences, or related subjects, and completion of a training program (minimum 24 months) under the supervision of a qualified primary training officer

Toxicology
- Analysis of drugs in legal setting involving cases where there were impairing, adverse, or toxic effects of drugs
- Toxicologists have degrees in life or physical sciences, including backgrounds in chemistry and coursework in pharmacology

Source: Information derived from individual section pages found at https://aafs.org

CASE STUDY #1: THE FLEXIBLE APPROACH

Two of the authors, Tosha Dupras and John Schultz, were asked to assist in a case involving the search for a missing adult female. She had been missing for approximately 12 years, and police received a tip that she may have been deposited in an unused subterranean city sewage-holding tank that was not easily accessible. One suspect in this case was previously employed by the city and worked at the treatment facility when the holding tank was in use. Shortly after the woman's disappearance, this holding tank was sealed off and no longer used.

This case truly was a challenge, and there was no viable way to apply traditional archaeological techniques throughout the recovery process, so an adaptable and flexible approach was required. The first obstacle was gaining access to the small entrance opening for the large subterranean sewage-holding tank, which required city workers to remove part of a small structure wall located directly above the tank (Figure 1.5). A sturdy tripod was set up over the opening to safely lower individuals into the tank, and exhaust tubes were inserted into the tank to provide ventilation.

Representatives from environmental health and safety deemed this a hazardous site due to the material in the holding tank, particularly due to lethal gases that were present. The potential lethal nature of this site required the material first to be removed from the holding tank before it could be thoroughly examined. This was accomplished by lowering heavily protected individuals into the tank, who were outfitted with oxygen so they would not succumb to deadly gases (Figure 1.6).

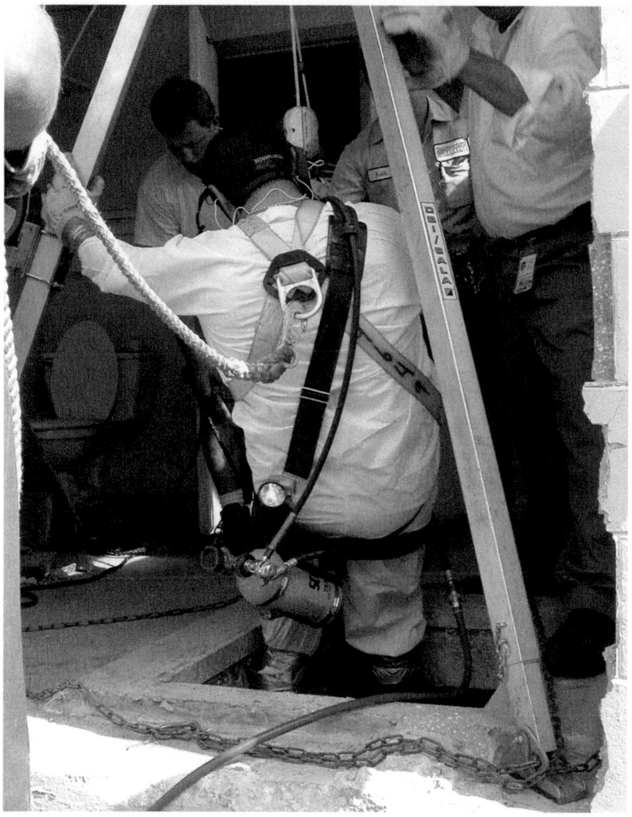

Figure 1.6 Lowering a well-protected city worker, wearing a biohazard suit and oxygen tank with mask, through the sewage-holding tank entrance.

Figure 1.5 Search at the sewage-holding tank with outer wall removed to gain access to the holding tank entrance (left), and tripod with safety lines set up over entrance along with exhaust vent tubes (right).

Once in the tank, workers used a large vacuum to suction material into the tank of an industrial vacuum truck. When filled, the vacuum trucks separated the sediment from the liquid and moved the material to a large dumping area constructed for the drained material and lined with heavy plastic (Figure 1.7). Large screens were set up in the bucket of a backhoe to sieve the sediment and recover any remains (Figure 1.8). The thick, wet nature of the material required us to use a wet screening method (refer to Chapter 9) (Figure 1.9). It took three days to remove and process all the material from the holding tank, and no evidence of human remains was recovered. If this missing individual was placed in the holding tank, in all probability, the 12 years in this environment destroyed any traces of her remains. To date, she remains a missing person.

Figure 1.7 Large vacuum truck dumping sediment materials from the sewage-holding tank into a prepared area lined with heavy plastic.

Figure 1.8 Author Tosha Dupras (center), Orange County, Florida crime scene investigator Kelly Wood (back), and Orange County homicide detective Dave Clarke (right) sieving sediment materials removed from the sewage-holding tank.

Figure 1.9 Crime scene investigator Kelly Wood (right) uses water to flush sediment material carefully when sieving, while author Tosha Dupras (left) thoroughly examines all fragments retained by the screen.

Key Terms

AAFS
ABFA (A-ABFA, D-ABFA)
ante-, peri-, and postmortem
biological anthropology
biological profile
coroner
DMORT
DPAA
forensic anthropology
forensic archaeology
forensic context
forensic odontology
forensic pathology
forensic taphonomy
ICMP
medical examiner (ME)
minimum number of individuals (MNI)
osteology
PHR
postdepositional
postmortem interval (PMI)
SAA

REVIEW AND DISCUSSION QUESTIONS

1. In the following circumstances, would it be appropriate to request assistance from a forensic archaeologist? What specialized skills or knowledge would they provide in the recovery of the remains?
   - Utility workers uncover five large bones while digging a trench for a new electrical line.
   - Partially skeletonized human remains were recovered from an abandoned warehouse, but during pre-autopsy preparation, the forensic technician determined that the remains were incomplete.
   - The neighbor's dog, Marley, left a pile of dirt-covered, chewed bones on your front porch, one of which resembles a human femur.
   - During installation of a burial vault, workers discover skeletonized remains of an individual buried in the cemetery plot, which according to records should have been empty.
   - While digging the foundation for a backyard shed, a neighbor uncovers a group of cut and chipped burnt bones.
   - During a preliminary police inquiry, investigators received a tip that an individual in an advanced state of soft tissue decomposition is buried under a concrete slab in a suspect's backyard.
   - A hunter finds what may be portions of a child's skull and some additional small bones sticking out of the ground in the woods.
2. Relate the skills and knowledge areas listed in Table 1.2 to each of the five primary responsibilities directly associated with the forensic archaeologist during an investigation.
3. Forensic archaeologists have become vital team members in disaster response to mass fatality incidents and the search, recovery, and identification of remains belonging to American servicemembers as well as victims of human rights violations around the world. What organizations would they be working with in these cases? What are similarities or differences in mission focus for these organizations?

Suggested Readings

Austin, D., Fulginiti, L. 2008. The forensic anthropology laboratory in a medical examiner setting. In: Warren, M.W., Walsh-Haney, H.A., Freas, L.E., eds. *Forensic Anthropology Laboratory*, pp. 23–46. Boca Raton, FL: CRC Press.

Dirkmaat, D.C., Adovasio, J.M. 1997. The role of archaeology in the recovery and interpretation of human remains from an outdoor forensic setting. In: Haglund, W.D., Sorg, M.H., eds. *Forensic Taphonomy: The Postmortem Fate of Human Remains*, pp. 39–64. Boca Raton, FL: CRC Press.

Dirkmaat, D.C., Cabo, L.L., Ousley, S.D., Symes, S.A. 2008. New perspectives in forensic anthropology. *Yearbook of Physical Anthropology* 51:33–52. DOI:10.1002/ajpa.20948

Mann, R.W., Anderson, B.E., Holland, T.H., Webb Jr, J.E. 2009. Unusual 'crime' scenes: the role of forensic anthropology in recovering and identifying American MIAs. In: Steadmann, D.W., ed. *Hard Evidence: Case Studies in Forensic Anthropology*, 2nd ed., pp. 133–140. Upper Saddle River, NJ: Prentice Hall.

Schultz, J.J., Dupras, T.L. 2008. The contribution of forensic archaeology to homicide investigations. *Homicide Studies* 12:399–413. DOI:10.1177/1088767908324430

Skinner, M.F., Alempijevic, D., Djuruc-Srejic, M. 2003. Guidelines for international forensic bioarchaeology monitors of mass grave exhumations. *Forensic Science International* 134:81–92. DOI:10.1016/S0379-0738(03)00124-5

Steadman, D.W., Haglund, W.D. 2005. The scope of anthropological contributions to human rights investigations. *Journal of Forensic Sciences* 50:23–30. DOI:10.1520/JFS2004214

Wiersema, J.M., Woody, A. 2016. The forensic anthropologist in the mass fatality context. *Academic Forensic Pathology* 6(3):455–462. DOI:10.23907/2016.046

References

Austin, D., Fulginiti, L. 2008. The forensic anthropology laboratory in a medical examiner setting. In: Warren, M. W., Walsh-Haney, H. A., Freas, L. E., eds. *Forensic Anthropology Laboratory*, pp. 23–46. Boca Raton, FL: CRC Press.

Bass, W.M., Birkby, W.H. 1978. Exhumation: The method could make the difference. *FBI Law Enforcement Bulletin* 47:6–11.

Berryman, H.E., Lahren, C.H. 1984. The advantages of simulated crime scenes in teaching forensic anthropology. *Journal of Forensic Sciences* 20:699–700.

Dirkmaat, D.C., Adovasio, J.M. 1997. The role of archaeology in the recovery and interpretation of human remains from an outdoor forensic setting. In: Haglund, W.D., Sorg, M.H., eds. *Forensic Taphonomy: The Postmortem Fate of Human Remains*, pp. 39–64. Boca Raton, FL: CRC Press.

Dirkmaat, D.C., Cabo, L.L. 2012. Forensic anthropology: Embracing the new paradigm. In: Dirkmaat, D.C., ed. *A Companion to Forensic Taphonomy*, pp. 3–40. Malden, MA: Blackwell.

Etxeberria, F., González-Ruibal, A., Herrasti, L., Márquez-Grant, N., Muñoz-Encinar, L., Ramos, J., 2021. Twenty years of forensic archaeology and anthropology of the Spanish Civil War (1936–1939) and Francoist Regime. *Forensic Science International: Synergy* 3:100159. DOI:10.1016/j.fsisyn.2021.100159

France, D.L., Griffin, T.J., Swanburg, J.G., Lindemann, J.W., Davenport, G.C., Tramell, V., Travis, C.T., Kondratieff, R., Nelson, A., Castellano, K., Hopkins D. 1992. A multidisciplinary approach to the detection of clandestine graves. *Journal of Forensic Sciences* 37:1145–1458. DOI:10.1520/JFS13337J

Haglund, W.D., Sorg, M.H. (eds). 1997a. *Forensic Taphonomy: The Postmortem Fate of Human Remains*. Boca Raton, FL: CRC Press.

Haglund, W.D., Sorg, M.H. 1997b. Method and theory of forensic taphonomy research. In: Haglund, W.D., Sorg, M.H., eds. *Forensic Taphonomy: The Postmortem Fate of Human Remains*, pp. 13–26. Boca Raton, FL: CRC Press.

Hanson, I. 2008. Forensic archaeology: Approaches to international investigations. In: Oxenham, M., ed. *Forensic Approaches to Death, Disaster and Abuse*, pp. 17–28. Brisbane: Australia Academic Press.

Hoshower, L.M. 1998. Forensic archaeology and the need for flexible excavation strategies: A case study. *Journal of Forensic Sciences* 43:53–56. DOI:10.1520/JFS16089J

Hunter, J.R. 2002. Foreword: A pilgrim in forensic archaeology – A personal view. In: Haglund, W.D., Sorg, M.H., eds. *Advances in Forensic Taphonomy: Method, Theory, and Archaeological Perspectives*, pp. xxv–xxxii. Boca Raton, FL: CRC Press.

Hunter, J.R., Heron, C., Janaway, R.C., Martin, A.L., Pollard, A.M., Roberts, C.A. 1994. Forensic archaeology in Britain. *Antiquity* 68:758–769. DOI:10.1017/S0003598X00047451

Kerley, E.R. 1978. Recent developments in forensic anthropology. *Yearbook of Physical Anthropology* 21:160–173.

Márquez-Grant, N., Errickson, D. 2021. The legislation, search, recovery, identification, and repatriation of conflict casualties worldwide: Introducing the WWI and WWII Special Issue. *Forensic Science International* 320:110716. DOI:10.1016/j.forsciint.2021.110716

Micozzi, M.S. 1991. *Postmortem Change in Human and Animal Remains: A Systematic Approach*. Springfield, Illinois: Charles C Thomas.

Morse, D., Crusoe, D., Smith, H.G. 1976. Forensic archaeology. *Journal of Forensic Sciences* 21:323–332. DOI:10.1520/JFS10500J

Morse, D., Duncan, J., Stoutamire, J. 1983. *Handbook of Forensic Archaeology and Anthropology*. Tallahassee, FL: Rose Printing.

Pokines, J.T., L'Abbé, E.N., Symes, S.A. (eds). 2022. *Manual of Forensic Taphonomy*, 2nd ed., Boca Raton, FL: CRC Press. DOI:10.4324/9781003171492

Schultz, J.J., Dupras, T.L. 2008. The contribution of forensic archaeology to homicide investigations. *Homicide Studies* 12:399–413. DOI:10.1177/1088767908324430

Scott, D.D., Connor, M. 1997. Context delecti: Archaeological context in forensic work. In: Haglund, W.D., Sorg, M.H., eds. *Forensic Taphonomy: The Postmortem Fate of Human Remains*, pp. 27–38. Boca Raton, FL: CRC Press.

Sigler–Eisenberg, B. 1985. Forensic research: Expanding the concept of applied archaeology. *American Antiquity* 50:650–655. DOI:10.1017/S0002731600086467

Skinner, M.F., Alempijevic, D., Djuruc-Srejic, M. 2003. Guidelines for international forensic bioarchaeology monitors of mass grave exhumations. *Forensic Science International* 134:81–92. DOI:10.1016/S0379–0738(03)00124-5

Skinner, M., Lazenby, R.A. 1983. *Found! Human Remains: A Field Manual for the Recovery of the Recent Human Skeleton*. Burnaby, BC: Archaeology Press Simon Fraser University.

Snow, C.C. 1982. Forensic anthropology. *Annual Review of Anthropology* 11:97–131.

Ubelaker, D.H. 1991. Perimortem and postmortem modification of human bone: Lessons from forensic anthropology. *Anthropologie* 29:171–174. https://www.jstor.org/stable/26295566

Wiersema, J.M., Woody, A. 2016. The forensic anthropologist in the mass fatality context. *Academic Forensic Pathology* 6(3):455–462. DOI:10.23907/2016.046

Wolf, D.J. 1986. Forensic anthropology scene investigations. In: Reichs, K., ed. *Forensic Osteology: Advances in the Identification of Human Remains*, pp. 3–23. Springfield, IL: Charles C Thomas.

CHAPTER 2

TOOLS AND EQUIPMENT

Learning Objectives

- Describe examples of personal safety equipment and explain its importance.
- List and identify examples from a forensic archaeology tool kit used in searches, excavations, and recoveries.
- Determine types of packing materials needed to store and transport evidence.
- Apply best practices for cleaning field equipment.

Learning Connections

- Introduce tools and equipment discussed in future chapters on specific methods in searches, excavations, and recoveries.

Forensic archaeologists should be well prepared to perform searches, excavations, and recoveries and should not rely on local law enforcement to provide the necessary tools and equipment. Since the search and recovery of human remains is not a common type of crime scene for most law enforcement agencies, it is not surprising that most agencies will not include most of the specialized equipment in this chapter in their field kits. The variety of tools and equipment used by forensic archaeologists during excavations is practically limitless, but the following content provides descriptions of the most helpful tools commonly used in the forensic recovery of human remains. The tools and equipment shown in the chapter images are not endorsed or promoted; these are examples from the authors' personal search and recovery kits.

Many of the suggested tools and disposable supplies are available at local hardware and home improvement stores. However, metric measurement tools, personal protective equipment, and more specialized items may not be readily available locally. If this is the case, they can easily be obtained through online specialty stores, some of which are listed in Table 2.1. An example checklist of search and recovery equipment is located at the end of this chapter in Table 2.2. More specialized search equipment is discussed in Chapters 6 and 7, and equipment and supplies needed for the collection and preservation of entomological and botanical evidence is discussed in Chapter 10.

Table 2.1 Companies Selling Equipment Used in Forensic Archaeology

Company and Contact Information	Equipment Available
Forestry Suppliers, Inc. http://www.forestry-suppliers.com/ 205 West Franklin Street, Jackson, MS 39201 Customer service: 1-800-647-5368 Email: online contact service	Survey equipment Chaining pins and meter rods Metric measuring tapes Compasses and GPS Probes and sifting screens Trowels and small tools Soil charts and sampling supplies
Evident Inc. Crime Scene Products http://www.shopevident.com/ 739 Brooks Mill Road, Union Hall, VA 24176 Customer service: 1-800-576-7606 Email: online contact service	Photo scales and arrows Body bags and tags Evidence markers and tape Protective clothing (PPE) Entomology collection kits
Lynn Peavey Company http://www.lynnpeavey.com/ P.O. Box 14100, Lenexa, KS 66214-3612 Customer service: 1-800-255-6499 Email: online contact service	Barrier tape and privacy shields Metal detecting equipment Protective clothing (PPE) Sifting screens and small tools Photo equipment and kits

(Continued)

DOI: 10.4324/9781315201658-2

Table 2.1 ***(Continued)*** Companies Selling Equipment Used in Forensic Archaeology

Company and Contact Information	Equipment Available
Sirchie http://www.sirchie.com/ 100 Hunter Place, Youngsville, NC 27596 Customer service: 1-800-356-7311 Email: online contact service	Entomology collection kits Protective clothing (PPE) Evidence marker kits Evidence packaging and tape Casting materials
Forensics Source http://www.forensicssource.com 13386 Intl Parkway Jacksonville, FL 32218 Customer service: 1-800-347-1200 Email: online contact service	Casting supplies and kits Photographic scale kits Evidence markers and flags Evidence packaging and tape Scene drawing templates
Stoney Knoll Archaeological Supplies, Inc. http://www.stoneyknoll.com P.O. Box 493, Stockton Springs, ME 04981 Customer service: 207-548-0080 Email: online contact service	Sifting screens and wire mesh Field excavation tools and kits Chaining pins and pin flags Soil texture charts Photographic supplies
Tri-Tech Forensics http://tritechforensics.com 3811 Intl Blvd NE #100, Leland, NC 28451 Customer service: 1-800-438-7884 Email: online contact service	Protective clothing (PPE) Odor perception inhibitors Photographic scales and markers Body bags and tags

PERSONAL SAFETY EQUIPMENT

Forensic archaeologists face several safety concerns, including exposure to biological or chemical hazards and working under hazardous conditions; therefore, personal safety is of utmost concern when performing recoveries and excavations. During the initial briefing for any investigation, it is important that all team members are informed of any risks to health and safety resulting from the environment of the scene or search conditions (e.g., biohazards). If there are any specific risks associated with the archaeological work, appropriate advice should be provided and documented. Forensic archaeologists should be prepared to provide themselves with appropriate **personal protective equipment (PPE)** (Figure 2.1).

In addition to providing personal safety, disposable coveralls, boot covers, and nitrile gloves also protect against contamination of recovered materials and within the scene in general. Safety glasses are recommended for any activities requiring tool use and when working within excavations; disposable face shields should be used when there is a risk of contamination from chemicals or biohazards such as body fluids. Respiratory face masks, including an N95 respirator, should have a close facial fit and are intended for efficient filtration of airborne particles. Some models have exhalation valves that can make breathing easier and help reduce heat build-up, but these should not be used when sterile conditions are needed (i.e., presence of harmful bacterial or viral conditions is suspected on scene). Filter breathing masks are also helpful when encountering odorous conditions as well as in cases with heavy infestations of insects. Extreme unpleasant odors may inhibit performance in the recovery of remains. Odor perception inhibitor balms and nose plugs neutralize odors without affecting breathing capacity.

With field conditions varying from scene to scene, it is always best to keep a few optional items available, such as sunscreen and insect repellent, in case any adverse conditions or special circumstances arise. An LED headlamp is often used to highlight immediate work areas, and certain materials such as broken glass or metal pieces will reflect light, possibly preventing injury. Work gloves are needed when working with tools, screening materials, and excavating. Knee pads or kneeling pads are also helpful when clearing plant growth and excavating. A first aid kit is a necessity in the field, as any cuts or scrapes should be attended to as soon as possible to prevent infections.

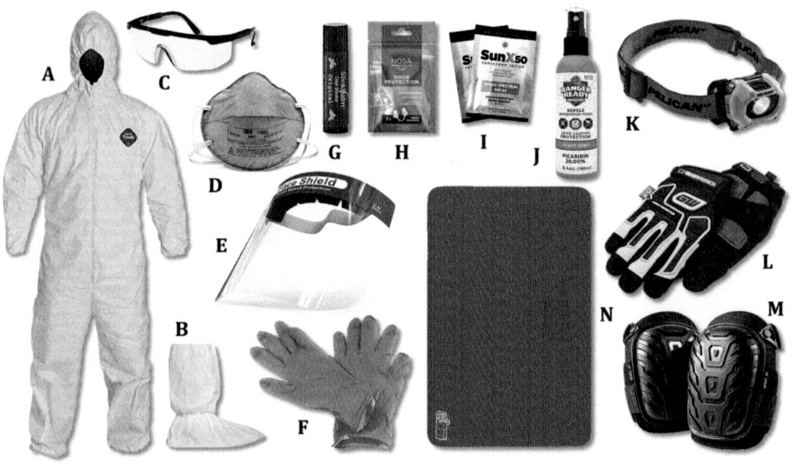

Figure 2.1 Equipment for personal safety: (a) Tyvek disposable coverall; (b) Tyvek disposable boot covers; (c) safety glasses; (d) N95 respirator mask; (e) disposable face shield; (f) 6 mil nitrile gloves; (g) odor perception inhibitor balm; (h) odor perception inhibitor nose plugs; (i) sunscreen; (j) insect repellent; (k) LED headlamp; (l) work gloves; (m) work knee pads; and (n) kneeling pad.

SEARCH AND SITE PREPARATION EQUIPMENT

Certain tools are necessary during a search (Figure 2.2) and site preparation (Figure 2.3). When beginning a search, all personnel should be equipped with a bundle of brightly colored survey flags used to mark the locations of scattered evidence. These flags usually have metal posts; however, if a geophysical survey is being conducted, or will be conducted after a foot search, it is best to use flags with a fiberglass post to avoid interfering with geophysical signals. Survey flags and survey flagging tape may also be used to mark the entrance and exit locations to the site, and barrier tape may be used to mark larger evidentiary areas where unwarranted foot traffic should be avoided. A utility knife or multi-function tool is often necessary for cutting flagging or barrier tapes, and a small LED flashlight is useful when examining animal burrows or heavy plant growth, such as thickets.

When specifically searching for buried bodies or evidence, a variety of probes can be used and should be included as standard field equipment. The most common probe used is the basic **T-bar probe** to detect soil disturbances. If the search is being conducted in an area with any possibility of encountering buried utility lines, an insulated T-bar soil probe is necessary for safety purposes. Detailed descriptions of different types of probes, and their proper uses, can be found in Chapter 6.

Figure 2.2 Equipment for searching the site: (a) metal staff marking flags; (b) fiberglass staff marking flags; (c) LED flashlight; (d) barrier tape; (e) survey flagging tape; (f) multi-function tool; (g) utility knife; (h) insulated T-bar soil probe; and (i) small cordless circular saw.

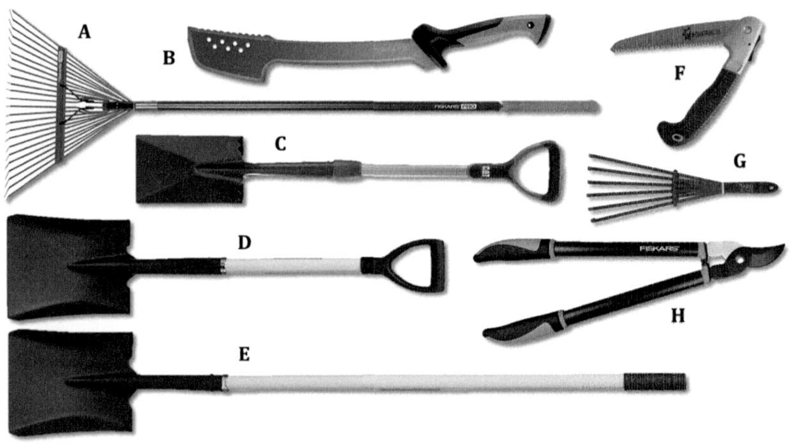

Figure 2.3 Equipment for site preparation: (a) fan rake; (b) hand machete/hatchet; (c) D-handle edge spade; (d) D-handle flat-blade transfer shovel; (e) long handle flat-blade transfer shovel; (f) folding hand saw; (g) hand rake; and (h) hand loppers.

Small hand machetes and handsaws are helpful in clearing plant growth from the surrounding work areas and around any associated evidence. A small handheld circular saw is helpful when larger treefall branches or other materials are blocking the clear view of suspect areas. When removing surface debris such as leaf litter and vegetation, a fan rake (plastic preferred) should be used. Investigators should be especially vigilant when clearing underbrush or leaf cover with fan or hand rakes since evidence can be lodged at the base of trees or in other plant materials. Hand loppers are useful for cutting thick underbrush or branches, fencing wire or landscaping cables, and any other heavy materials that impede investigation or obstruct the work area.

Site preparation may also require removing or transferring sediment heaps for further investigation through a screening process. Shovels are useful when working with larger quantities of soil, but they should never be used as excavation tools. All materials removed from a site should be sifted with a screen, and smaller items can be sorted by using stacked sieves (refer to Figure 2.8). Short-handle, square-point **edge spades** are typically used for removing very thin layers of soil from surface areas or to cut and remove sod from yards or fields. Flat-blade **transfer shovels** should only be used to move sediment that has already been screened from one location to another or when backfilling holes. Transfer shovels may also be used in removing very thin layers of soil from surface areas, but they are not as precise as using an edge spade.

MAPPING, MEASURING, AND SURVEY EQUIPMENT

As presented in Chapter 1, all five responsibilities directly associated with the forensic archaeologist include accurate and detailed recording and reporting of information. Metric measuring tapes are indispensable tools during the mapping and excavation processes, and the more different kinds are available, the better (Figure 2.4). A 3-, 5- or 8-m steel tape that can be clipped to a belt or small tool bag is one of the most fundamental pieces of equipment used in search and recovery. At least two 20- to 50-m fiberglass **reel measuring tapes** should also be included, as these are needed for laying out grids in geophysical survey (refer to Chapter 7) and when mapping larger areas of search and recovery. Metric folding meter sticks are also handy when drawing features and recording elevation measurements. Nylon plastic meter sticks are recommended, as they do not absorb fluids and are easier to clean. A flexible fiberglass metric tailor's tape is handy for measuring irregular surfaces or diameters. An azimuth board, or compass rose, is typically used in mapping and recording surface-scattered remains. It is securely fastened to a central location at the scene, and corresponding distances are measured with angles taken from this board. Galvanized nails and plastic landscaping stakes are used for holding measuring tapes in place, marking specific locations when mapping, and setting up grids over areas to be mapped or excavated (refer to Chapter 8).

A transit is used with a stadia rod for measuring precise angles and distances from fixed points. These points are used to plot the survey map, plan, and section drawings

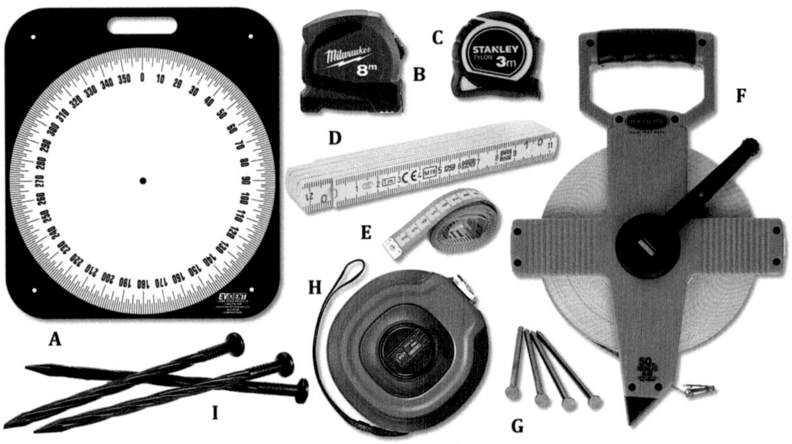

Figure 2.4 Equipment for mapping and measuring the site: (a) azimuth board; (b) 8-m steel measuring tape; (c) 3-m steel measuring tape; (d) nylon plastic folding meter stick; (e) fiberglass metric tailor's tape; (f) 50-m fiberglass reel measuring tape; (g) galvanized 4-inch nails; (h) 20-m fiberglass measuring tape; and (i) 12-inch plastic landscaping stakes.

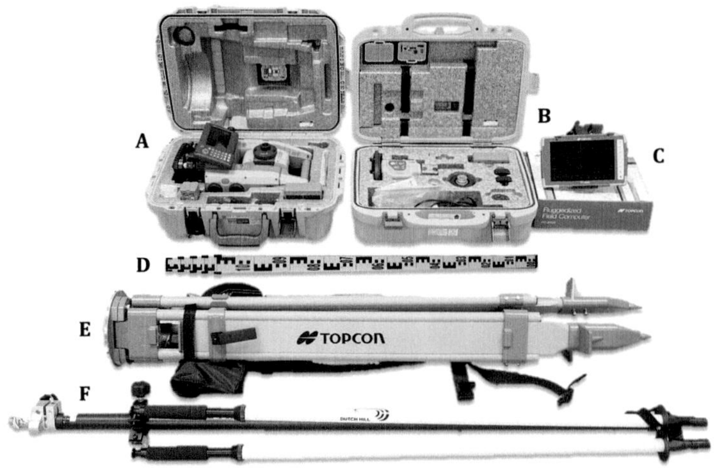

Figure 2.5 Equipment for surveying the site: (a) robotic total station with batteries and charger; (b) 360° prism and remote controller; (c) data collector; (d) telescoping 4-m stadia rod; (e) surveying tripod for total station; and (f) prism pole and data collector bipod.

of the site. A **total station** (Figure 2.5) can also be used for this purpose; however, it is an expensive piece of equipment and requires a trained operator to work with the prism, remote controller, and data collector.

A handheld GPS (Figure 2.6) may also be useful to record site location and data points for evidence. Keep spare batteries for the GPS unit on hand, and it is always recommended to test any electronic equipment before going to the field. A handheld precision or **orienteering (baseplate) compass** is also useful for determining directionality when conducting a search over a large area and can also be useful for recording the orientation of evidence, including graves and body position, relative to other features, such as posts, trees, or buildings.

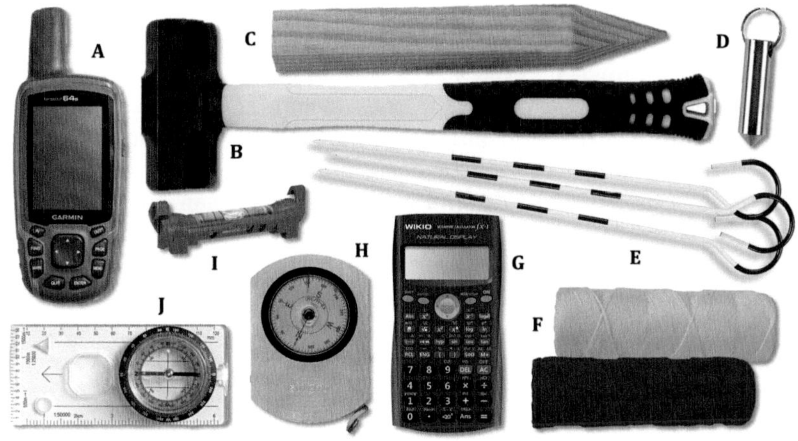

Figure 2.6 Equipment for mapping and establishing a grid: (a) handheld GPS; (b) mallet; (c) wood survey hub stake; (d) plumb bob; (e) chaining pins; (f) fluorescent nylon mason line; (g) calculator; (h) precision compass; (i) line level; and (j) baseplate (orienteering) compass.

PHOTOGRAPHY EQUIPMENT

Photography equipment (Figure 2.7) is an essential part of every field kit for recording and reporting information. Most DSLR cameras come with accessories, such as a battery and charger, neck strap, camera bag, tripod or monopod, and an 18–55 mm lens. Additional batteries and memory cards are recommended. A regular flash unit may also be included among those accessories, and this can be linked to a lens-mount LED ring flash to create even and shadow-free lighting in close-up photographs and to cast light from specific directions to capture intricate details.

Every photograph should be associated with contextual information, such as the date, time, site location, and identification of objects. A simple, small erasable whiteboard and marker can be used in recording this information and may be included in the photograph or used as a content header for a group of photographs. Photographic markers, such as lettered and numbered **evidence-marking tents** can be used in reference to specific objects but also used to establish references for grid squares. **North arrows** should be used in all photography to note scale and orientation of any evidence. If one is not readily available, a pointed trowel oriented toward the north can be substituted. Fluorescent evidence markers can be used to indicate smaller objects or outline features that may be difficult to see in contrast to their surroundings. Color and size **photographic scales** should be included in all photographs with smaller objects, while larger, break-apart centimeter and meter scale rods are used when photographing larger objects and ground features.

Additional equipment needed to record site data properly (Figure 2.8) includes notepads, various color pens, permanent markers, and all necessary blank recording forms (refer to Appendices A through F). A waterproof field notebook can also be very useful in bad weather conditions. Depending on the methods used in mapping and surveying, a cross-section survey book may also be necessary. A magnifying lens and an LED pocket magnifying loupe can be used to identify tiny objects or materials during search and recovery. For detailed drawings of excavations or other pertinent features, metric 1:10 or 1:5 graph paper, a clipboard or drawing board, a small straight-edge ruler, large binder clips, and mechanical pencils with extra leads and drawing erasers will be required.

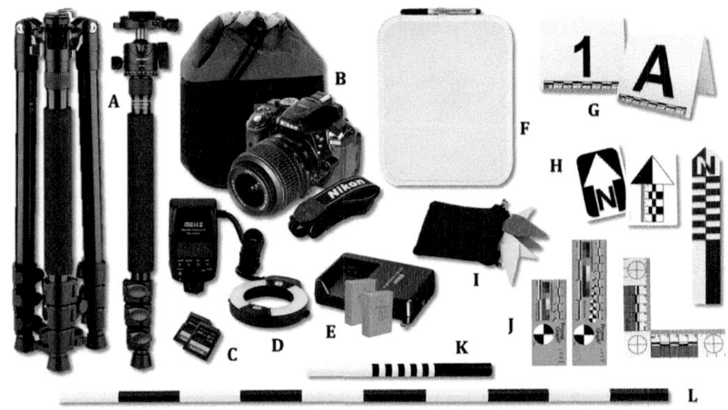

Figure 2.7 Equipment for site photography: (a) camera tripod and monopod; (b) DSLR camera, neck strap, and bag; (c) memory cards; (d) lens-mount LED ring flash; (e) camera batteries and charger; (f) 8 × 10 inch white board and marker; (g) evidence-marking tents; (h) north arrows; (i) fluorescent first-response evidence markers; (j) color and size photography scales; (k) break-apart magnetic centimeter scale rod; and (l) break-apart magnetic meter scale rod.

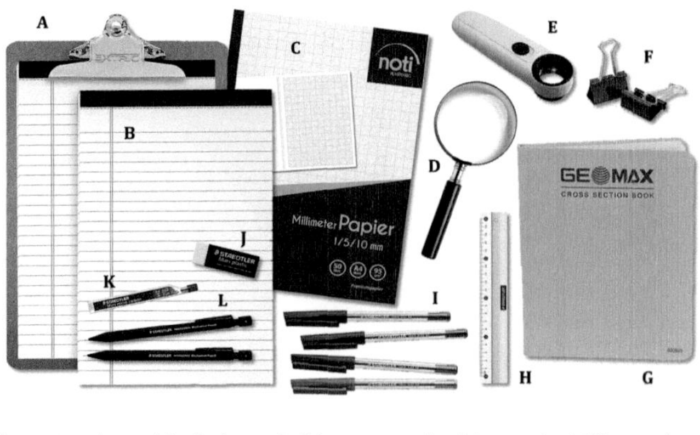

Figure 2.8 Equipment for recording site data: (a) clipboard; (b) note pads; (c) metric 1:10 graph paper; (d) magnifying lens; (e) LED pocket magnifying loupe; (f) large binder clips; (g) cross-section survey book; (h) small straight-edge ruler; (i) various color pens; (j) drawing eraser; (k) pencil leads; and (l) mechanical pencils.

FIELD EXCAVATION EQUIPMENT

Before excavation begins, a grid is usually constructed (refer to Chapter 8). The size of the grid depends on the area to be excavated, and a calculator can be useful for determining the dimensions of the grid. The equipment necessary to construct a grid (refer to Figure 2.6) consists of **chaining pins** or wood survey hub stakes to establish the perimeter, and a mallet is used to secure the stakes into the ground. A brightly colored nylon cord or mason line is used to establish the internal and external grid lines, and a line level is used to assure that the grid lines are level. **Plumb bobs** (plummets) with a 2- to 5-ounce (50- to 140-g) weight are crucial for measuring surface and excavation elevations from a set datum point at the site and plotting the exact elevation of evidence within the grid.

Initial steps in excavation usually entail the removal of grave fill or surface debris for screening and require larger tools for this purpose (Figure 2.9). When collecting loose sediment from larger cleared spaces within the excavation or surface debris in the surrounding area, use heavy-duty plastic or metal dust pans, plastic scoop cutting boards, and plastic kitchen utility and hand scoops. Avoid the use of flimsy metal or plastic dustpans that will bend or break when they are used in heavy soils. Sturdy metal or plastic buckets, such as large spackle and paint buckets, can be easily labeled and used to transport sediment for screening.

Large brushes and whisk brooms are useful in removing loose dirt from surrounding areas but should never be used directly on the remains, as they may become displaced or damaged. **Natural bristle brushes** made of animal hair or hog bristles, often referred to as China bristle paint brushes, are recommended to clear loose sediment from the immediate area being excavated and around remains before photographing or drawing. Natural bristle brushes tend to last longer than synthetic bristle brushes and tend not to clump up in sandy or wet clay soils. These brushes are also less likely to lose bristles. A variety of different-sized brushes should be included in the excavation kit.

Box screens with 1/4-inch (6.4 mm) mesh are typically used for sifting through sediment removed from the excavation to recover materials that may otherwise be overlooked. Collapsible sawhorses are an excellent platform for screening materials. When screens are placed across the sawhorses, a relatively flat, level, working surface allows for more control over the materials being screened and a clear view of any objects that may be recovered in the process. A set of nested sifting screens should be used for screening smaller elements, such as fetal bones or insect casings, which would normally be missed using the larger gauge screens. If nested sifting screens are not available, smaller gauge screens, such as 1/16-inch (1.6 mm) mesh, may be attached to an 8 × 10 inch (20 × 25 cm) wooden picture frame and used in the same manner. Screen mesh can be either metal or plastic; however, metal is recommended for larger screens, as it is more durable, especially when working with heavier or damp sediments. Plastic sheeting or tarps (refer to Figure 2.12) should be placed beneath the screens to catch the screened sediment. This method also allows for the screened material to be kept separate in cases where finer screening is necessary. After each bucket of sediment is completely screened, simply change out the plastic sheeting or tarp from under the work area. The tarp or sheeting can be used to keep the sediment separate for further screening or to move the sediment to a collection pile.

Smaller and finer tools are used once more precise excavation begins (Figure 2.10). Margin and **pointing**

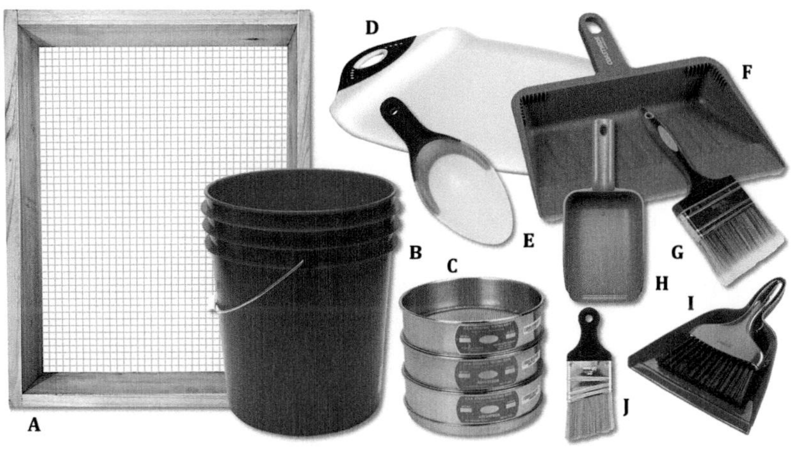

Figure 2.9 Larger tools for materials screening and excavation: (a) ¼-inch galvanized wire mesh box screen; (b) 5-gallon bucket; (c) nested sifting screens; (d) 9 × 13-inch plastic scoop cutting board; (e) plastic kitchen utility scoop; (f) heavy-duty dustpan; (g) 4-inch paint brush; (h) square plastic hand scoop; (i) small dustpan and hand broom; and (j) short-handle angled sash paint brush.

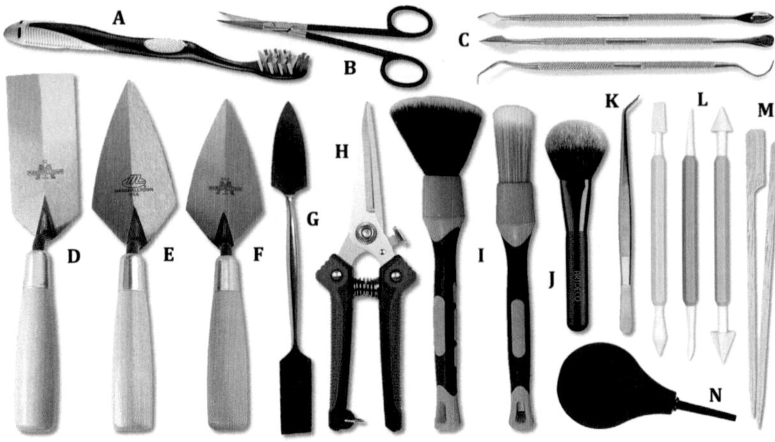

Figure 2.10 Small hand tools for excavation: (a) toothbrush; (b) Mayo dissecting scissors; (c) leaf and point dental tools; (d) 5½-inch margin trowel; (e) 5½-inch pointing trowel; (f) 4½-inch pointing trowel; (g) leaf-and-square trowel; (h) bypass pruning shears; (i) round trim paint brushes; (j) cosmetic powder brush; (k) dissecting tweezers; (l) plastic sculpting tools; (m) bamboo paddle skewers; and (n) small bulb syringe.

cement trowels with 4½- or 5½-inch blades are used for precise excavation, especially when removing sediment surrounding bones or objects where larger tools would damage or displace evidence. With a bit of practice, a pointed hand trowel with a sharpened blade can be used for extremely delicate work and may prove to be the most effective tool in the excavation kit. Square-edged margin trowels are excellent for excavating in sandy or wet sediments, and the smaller leaf-and-square trowels as well as leaf and point dental tools are ideal for detailing around smaller objects and bone in heavier sediments; however, great care should be taken to avoid scratching, nicking, or damaging any surfaces. Trowels made of drop-forged steel are recommended as the handles, blade welds, and points are more resistant to breakage. Some of the more popular brands of trowels used by archaeologists include Marshalltown or Goldblatt. Cheaply constructed trowels will bend or break and can put an end to any excavation quickly if the site is miles from the nearest hardware store. Garden-variety trowels with curved blades are not suited for excavation and should not be used in recovery of human remains. In addition, garden claw tools should never be used for excavating.

Root clippers or bypass pruning shears are needed for trimming roots and small ground cover, while dissecting scissors can be used on cloth, heavy tape, or other materials associated with the remains that might hinder the recovery process. Wood or plastic sculpting tools, toothbrushes, round trim paint brushes, and cosmetic powder brushes are smaller, softer alternatives for very delicate excavation. Leaf and point dental tools may also be used, but again only with extreme care to avoid producing any misleading or erroneous marks on the bone surfaces. Small tweezers are useful for removing small items or for evidence collection. Bulb syringes may also be useful for blowing away dirt particles, particularly when preparing for photography in excavations. In some cases, it may be preferable to use disposable bamboo skewers or various sizes of plastic spoons when detailing remains in extremely wet conditions or when soft tissue is still present.

SOILS DATA EQUIPMENT

At times, it may be necessary to collect soil data for the site or excavation, and it is expected that the forensic archaeologist would have this equipment (Figure 2.11) as part of their field kit. A T-bar soil corer is used for collecting compressed core samples for soil profile descriptions. Plastic coffee scoops are useful in collecting loose sediment samples, which are stored in sample bags or aluminum sample tins. Often a small rock hammer may be needed to collect samples in clay or rocky soils. It is recommended that standardized soil color charts, such as a **Munsell soil color book**, and soil texture charts be used in soils data collection and reporting. This is a common practice used by field archaeologists and the **United States Geological Survey (USGS)**, a non-regulatory science bureau within the U.S. Department of the Interior, for all soils research.

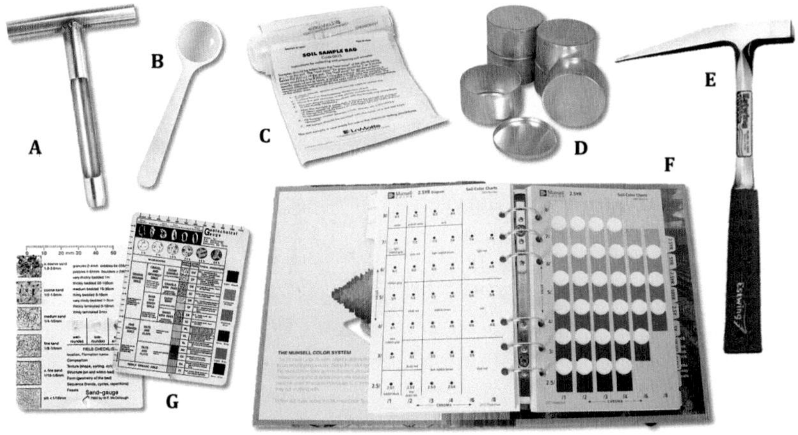

Figure 2.11 Equipment for collecting soils data: (a) 6-inch T-bar soil corer; (b) plastic coffee scoop; (c) soil sample bags; (d) aluminum soil sample tins with lids; (e) small rock hammer; (f) soil color charts; and (g) soil texture guides.

ENTOMOLOGICAL AND BOTANICAL DATA EQUIPMENT

Entomological and botanical data is quite often collected at the scene for further analysis by forensic specialists. This process requires some specialty equipment (Figures 2.12 and 2.13) that should be considered as part of a forensic archaeologist's field kit, or available for use through crime scene personnel field kits. Chapter 9 provides information on collection and preservation of entomological and botanical evidence.

For entomological samples, a set of featherweight tweezers and forceps are necessary during collection to avoid crushing insects or larvae. A disposable scalpel may be needed to create a small access point for when using a probe thermometer to measure the temperature in maggot masses. A plastic hand trowel, plastic spoons, a spooned spatula, and a larval handing brush are all used for collecting larvae from maggot masses and migrating larvae. A telescoping insect net is used to capture flying insects, which are then placed in a prepared insect kill jar. Entomological samples are preserved in smaller glass vials using various preservation solutions, such as 80% ethyl alcohol or KAA fixative. A maggot box containing vermiculite is used to collect a sample of maggots for rearing, while small disposable plastic food containers can also be altered for use in live insect collection.

Botanical evidence is most often preserved by simply using a field plant press made from corrugated cardboard and newsprint paper tied between two wooden frames. Since botanicals are highly susceptible to degradation and decomposition, especially in hot conditions, a portable cooler protects the evidence until samples can be refrigerated. Long-edge pruning shears should be used to cleanly cut samples. Whole plants or larger plant evidence may also be stored in large kraft paper bags, while seeds, flowers, and leaves can be stored in small kraft paper envelopes. Fungi are collected and stored in pasteboard boxes to preserve their shape. Samples that are watery or juicy (e.g., fruits or succulents) can be wrapped in waxed paper prior to being placed in kraft paper or a pasteboard box. If pollen is to be collected from nearby plants, sterile foam swabs with sample tubes work well. Any water samples taken for algal or diatom analysis should be collected in wide-mouth HDPE containers.

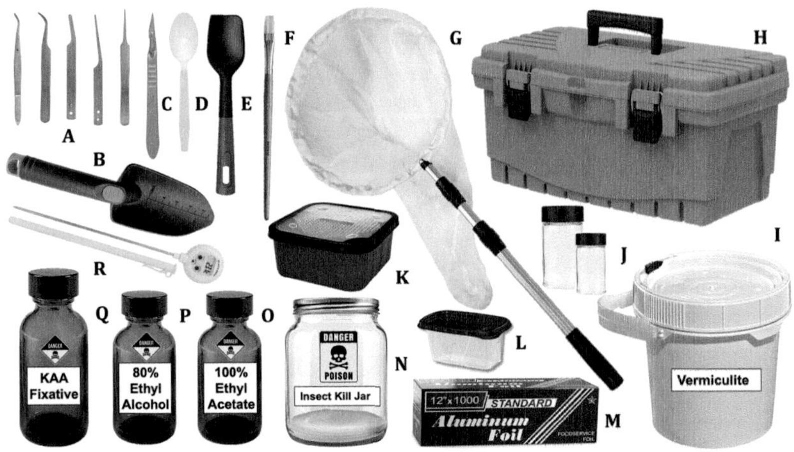

Figure 2.12 Equipment for collecting and preserving entomological evidence: (a) featherweight tweezers and forceps; (b) plastic hand trowel; (c) disposable scalpel; (d) plastic spoon; (e) silicone-spooned spatula; (f) larvae handling brush; (g) telescoping insect net; (h) equipment carry case; (i) ½-gallon (2 liter) bucket of vermiculite; (j) 2-ounce (30 dram) and 4-oz (60 dram) glass vials; (k) 24-ounce (0.7 liter) maggot box; (l) small disposable plastic food containers; (m) aluminum foil; (n) insect kill jar; (o) 8-ounce (0.2 liter) 100% ethyl acetate; (p) 8-ounce (0.2 liter) 80% ethyl alcohol solution; (q) 10-ounce (0.3 liter) KAA fixative; (r) digital bimetal probe thermometer.

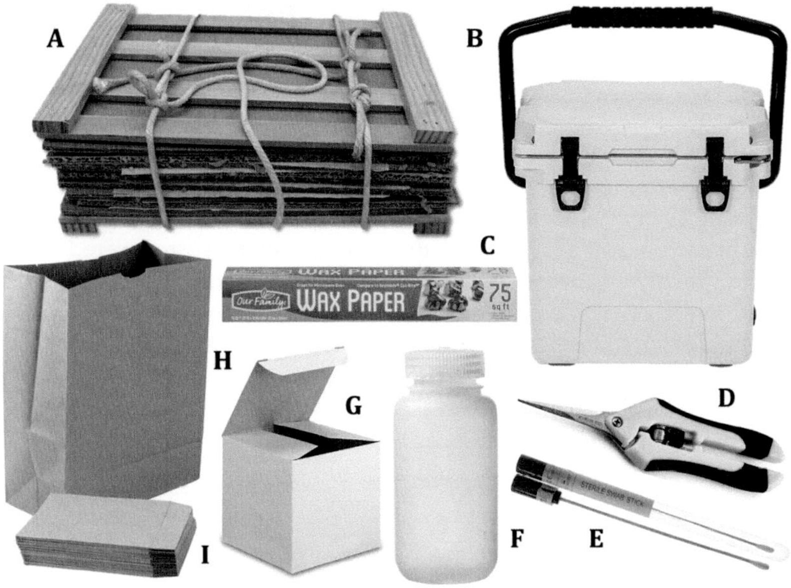

Figure 2.13 Equipment for collecting and preserving botanical evidence: (a) field plant press; (b) portable cooler; (c) wax paper; (d) long-edge pruning shears; (e) sterile foam-tip sample swab; (f) wide-mouth 16-ounce (500 ml) HDPE plastic sample container; (g) pasteboard sample box; (h) large kraft paper bag; (i) small kraft paper envelopes.

PACKAGING FOR RECOVERED MATERIALS

Materials that need to be collected from the site should be stored properly and securely for transport (Figure 2.14). Smaller items may be stored in 4-mil zip-close bags. In regions of high heat and humidity or in instances where the items may retain some moisture, it is recommended that a rolled section of cotton medical gauze is included to absorb condensation or moisture when the bag is sealed. Small paper bags should be used for dry bone and other items where specific labeling and separation by context is warranted. These may be gathered and placed into reusable shopping bags or poly material cadaver bags for secure transport. Poly material **cadaver bags** should always be used with remains where soft tissue is present and for partial or complete remains recovered from graves. At times, it may be necessary for a section of buried remains to be removed with surrounding sediment intact, and these recovered materials should be placed in larger reusable shopping bags or smaller poly material cadaver bags to retain their cohesion and integrity during transport. Tarps and plastic sheeting are used in the screening process, but they can also be used to cover an excavation in case of rain, protect the excavation overnight, or wrap very large objects for transport.

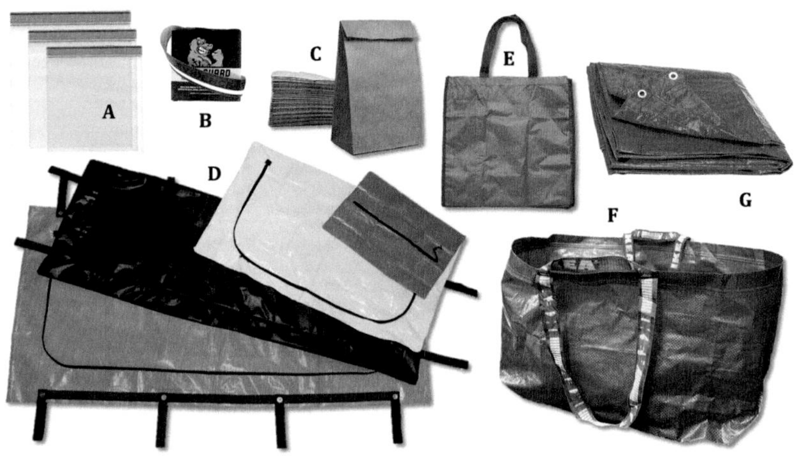

Figure 2.14 Equipment for packaging recovered materials: (a) various size 4-mil zip-close bags; (b) tamper-proof evidence tape; (c) small paper bags; (d) various cadaver/remains bags; (e) small reusable shopping bags; (f) large reusable shopping bags; and (g) 6 × 8-foot waterproof tarp.

CARING FOR YOUR EQUIPMENT

Field equipment can be exposed to various environments and taking proper care of your equipment is vital to extend its lifespan. Time should be budgeted after each excavation to clean and disinfect all tools and prepare them for storage (Figure 2.15). All tools should be thoroughly cleaned using hot water and antibacterial dish soap. A steel wire brush or wire scrub cloth should be used to remove all dirt and residues. It is recommended that all brushes and smaller hand tools be disinfected with a 2% bleach-to-water solution after each excavation to avoid any possibility of contamination and transfer of materials to the next recovery scene. Depending on field conditions, larger tools such as screens, shovels, buckets, utility scoops, and dustpans may need disinfecting after cleaning. A non-corrosive cleaner and degreaser may be necessary after using tools in recoveries involving soft tissue preservation. Keep in mind that decomposition molecules can permanently attach themselves to any organic component in tools such as wood handles, brush fibers, kneeling pads, paper, or any fabric items. One of the authors spent over a week tracking down an item in a tool kit that was carrying a decomposition odor. After repeatedly cleaning all tools in the kit, it was finally discovered that a simple pad of notepaper was the culprit. In cases where the smell of decomposition is especially pungent even after cleaning, you may want to replace these tools with ones that are easier to clean and maintain. Special commercial odor inhibitor sprays, soaps, and disinfectants are available to treat tools for extreme decomposition smell.

Forensic contexts with moist or wet soils can have deleterious effects on tools particularly those with metal components such as trowels, shovels, and screens. If left wet, these tools will rust and corrode. To prevent this, tools should be left to completely air dry or dried with a cotton shop towel after cleaning and disinfecting. If rust does form, it should be removed as soon as possible by washing the tool with hot water and dish detergent to remove any heavily adhered grit or staining. After this, use a steel wire brush or scrub cloth on the metal surface until all rust is removed and rinse again with hot water. Silicone rust inhibitor spray can help remove light rust and corrosion by applying it to the metal surface and rubbing it with a steel wire scrubbing cloth or medium-grain sandpaper. If there is extensive rust present, the use of a commercial rust remover spray or gel may be necessary.

Before storing tools, standard lubricating oil or silicone rust inhibitor spray should be applied to any metal surface and then wiped down with a cotton shop towel. Tools should be stored in a dry place. If your toolkit must be stored in a humid area, reusable commercial desiccant packages can be added, or, if these are not available, uncooked rice placed into a porous drawstring bag can serve as an improvised desiccant package. Desiccant bags should be replaced regularly to keep the humidity down and prevent rust and corrosion build-up.

Tools with a sharp edge, such as shovels, trowels, machetes, pruning shears, and root clippers, can become dull with use and should be sharpened on a regular basis with a flat hand file or a honing stone that can be kept in the toolkit (refer to Box 1). A sharp-edged spade or trowel can aid in removing sod or thin soil layers and cutting small roots when excavating. You may also consider bringing your tools into a tool shop to have them professionally sharpened.

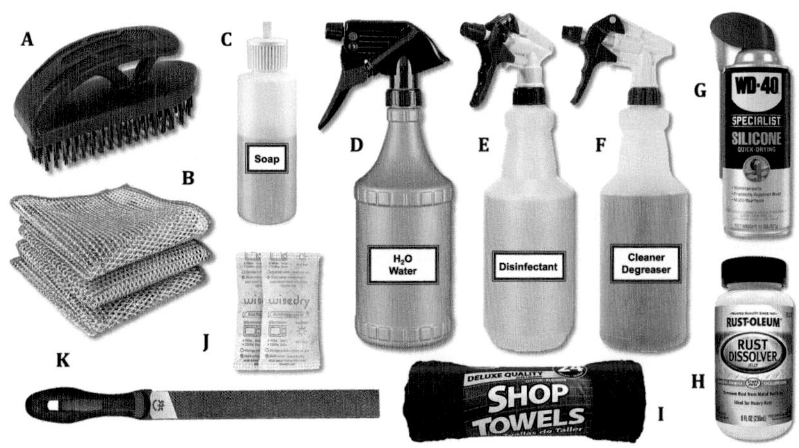

Figure 2.15 Equipment for tool cleaning and storage: (a) steel wire brush; (b) steel wire scrub cloths; (c) bottle with liquid soap; (d) spray bottle with water; (e) spray bottle with disinfectant; (f) spray bottle with cleaner and degreaser; (g) silicone spray; (h) rust remover gel; (i) cotton work towels; (j) reusable desiccant packs; and (k) 6-inch flat metal hand file.

Box #1: How to Sharpen a Spade or Trowel

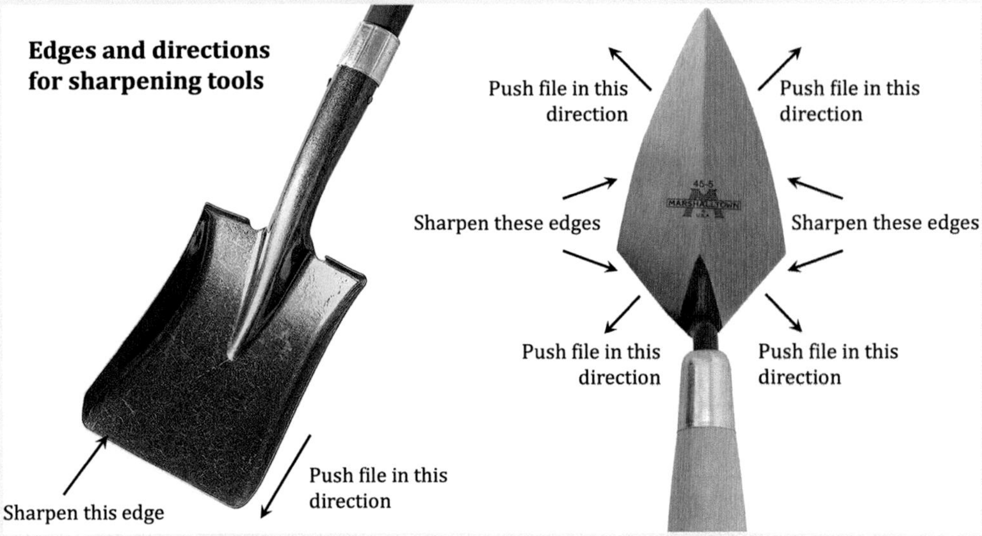

Figure 2.16

TO SHARPEN AN EDGE SPADE, TRANSFER SHOVEL, OR TROWEL:

1. Clean off any dirt or residue from the blade with a steel wire brush or steel wire scrubbing cloth.
2. Position the blade edge facing up and secure it in place using a clamp or vise for stability.
3. To sharpen the edge, you will need to use a hand file or coarse abrasive stone.
4. Use the angle that is already on your tool's blade as a guide. If the blade is too dull to find the original angle, a 45-degree angle is appropriate for most digging tools. Sharpen the inside (upward facing) edge of the tool. (Spades, shovels, and trowels are single-beveled tools. Do not sharpen the opposite side of the edge.)
5. Push the sharpener forward in even passes along the entire length of the blade. It is safer to sharpen moving in the direction away from the handle in case you would happen to slip.
6. The dullness of your tool's edge will dictate how many strokes you need to take with the sharpener before you see a shiny beveled edge appear. When sharpened at a proper angle, about 1/8-in (3 mm) of the blade will be visibly shiny from sharpening, and you should notice a slight burr forming on the back of the edge.
7. Continue to sharpen until you feel a burr along the entire backside of cutting edge. Once you have the burr running across the entire edge, make a few light strokes along the backside that will remove the burr and then go back to the beveled side and make a few light strokes on the cutting edge for final sharpening.
8. Apply a light layer of silicone spray to prevent rust and wipe down before storing.

Key Terms

box screen
cadaver bag
chaining pin
edge spade
evidence-marking tents
folding meter stick
Munsell soil color book
natural bristle brush
North arrow
orienteering (baseplate) compass
personal protective equipment (PPE)
photography scales
plumb bob (plummet)
pointing trowel
reel measuring tape
T-bar probe
total station
transfer shovel
USGS

Table 2.2 Example Checklist of Equipment Used in Search and Recovery

Items	Number
Field Equipment and Packaging	
Transfer shovel, L	2
Transfer shovel, S	1
Edge spade	1
Fan rake	1
Bucket	3
Screen, 1/4-inch mesh	1
Screen, 1/8-inch mesh	1
Chaining pins	50+
Marking flags	100+
Survey flagging tape	2
Azimuth board	1
Hand compass	2
Handheld GPS	1
5-m steel tape	1
30-m fiberglass tape	3
Trowel	2
Brushes	4
Line level	2
Mason line	2
Sculpting tools	1
Tweezers	1
Plastic bags, L	50+
Plastic bags, M	50+
Plastic bags, S	50+
Evidence tape	2
Cadaver bags, adult	2
Cadaver bags, juvenile	2
Cadaver bags, infant	2
Shopping bags, L	12
Shopping bags, S	12
Tarp	2
T-bar probe	1
Metal detector	1
Portable cordless saw	1
Multi-use tool	1
Hand loppers	1
Dust pans	2
T-bar probe	1
Metal detector	1
Portable cordless saw	1
Multi-use tool	1
Hand loppers	1
Dust pans	2
Utility scoops	6
Galvanized nails	10+
Portable stadia rod	1
Soil corer	1
Root clippers	1

(*Continued*)

Table 2.2 *(Continued)* Example Checklist of Equipment Used in Search and Recovery

Items	Number
Photography and Office Supplies	
Camera and accessories	1
Memory cards	4
White board, markers	1
Note pads	2
Clip board	1
Pens	10+
Binder clips	10+
Evidence-marking tents	1-50, A-Z
North arrow	1
Color and size scales	2
1:10 scale graph paper	1
Mechanical pencils	2
Magnifying loupe	1
Straight-edge ruler	1
Survey Equipment	
Total station in case	1
Batteries	2
Battery charger	1
Total station tripod	1
360° prism in case	1
Prism pole	1
Data logger	1
Data logger charger	1
Field Data Collection Kits	
Soils collection kit	1
Botanical collection kit	1
Entomology collection kit	1
Portable cooler	1
Personal Safety Equipment	
Disposable coverall	2
Disposable boot covers	4
Respirator masks	4
Disposable face shields	2
Work gloves, pair	2
Knee pads, pair	1
Kneeling pad	3
Nitrile gloves, L	50+
Nitrile gloves, M	50+
Safety glasses	1
Spare boots	1
Spare pants	1
Spare T-shirt	1
Sunscreen	2
Insect repellent	2
Headlamp	1
Flashlight	1
Dry snacks	2

REVIEW AND DISCUSSION QUESTIONS

1. Forensic archaeologists face several safety concerns, including exposure to biological or chemical hazards, which are often not known until encountered during search and recovery. Under the following circumstances, what PPE would be recommended for use?
   - A body was buried with a layer of quicklime (calcium oxide), which is thought to speed up decomposition and destroy evidence.
   - Bones were discovered when cleaning muck from a hog pen that was in use.
   - When investigating a large fire pit, detectives come across heavy concentrations of burnt bone fragments.
   - During a search, remains found on the ground surface still retain decomposing soft tissues.
2. The practice of correctly using specific tools for a field case prevents injury and unnecessary loss or destruction of critical information in a forensic context. Under the following circumstances, which tool(s) would be appropriate for the task described? Are there any safety concerns or issues with evidence recovery associated with using tools in these tasks?
   - A bucket of loose debris from the surface of a grid area needs to be examined.
   - Heavy underbrush and a layer of leaf cover is to be removed from a search area.
   - The locations of cut and chipped bone fragments, found in an open field, need to be marked for mapping.
   - The location of burnt remains, found scattered across the cement floor of a warehouse, need to be marked for mapping.
   - The position and orientation of an old shed, relative to a tree line within a search area, need to be determined.
   - A thin layer of surface soil needs to be removed from a suspected burial site and a hole from a previous test excavation needs to be backfilled.
   - During excavation of a grave, a group of small bones need to be detail outlined in place before being photographed.
   - A small area with city utility lines and landscaped bushes needs to be examined for possible soil disturbances.
3. Forensic archaeologists depend on their tools for every aspect of their work. What types of maintenance should be performed on digging and cutting equipment after every use? Why is it important to clean each of your tools carefully after every use?

CHAPTER 3

HUMAN SKELETAL TERMINOLOGY

Learning Objectives

- Define and introduce terminology of the juvenile and adult skeletons.
- Recognize and describe bone segments, major bones, and bony features of the human skeleton.

Learning Connections

- Introduce the bone names, terminology, and descriptions used in forensic reports when describing skeletal elements.
- Establish the interconnectedness of future chapters that use skeletal terminology during stages of recovery, including search, discovery, excavation, mapping, and collection of remains.

Identification of human remains should be performed by personnel proficient in human osteology, and we advocate that it is preferable to include an osteology expert such as a forensic anthropologist when processing scenes involving human skeletal remains. There are several advantages when including an osteology expert as a team member at scenes involving the recovery of human skeletal remains. The osteologist can first recognize and identify whole bones in the field and exclude nonhuman bones that are commonly encountered during outdoor recoveries (refer to Chapter 11 for a discussion of nonhuman bones.) At the same time, properly recognizing and identifying smaller-sized juvenile remains can be difficult with unfused bone sections (Figure 3.1). In addition, it can be difficult to recognize fragmented and weathered bones. In most instances, only an osteology expert can recognize bones that have been modified and distinguish modified human bones and fragments from modified nonhuman bones. Another advantage for including an osteologist as a team member is the ability to inventory in the field which bones are present (and missing). A forensic anthropologist can then develop search strategies to locate additional bones after identifying which bones have been recovered (refer to Chapter 6). When it is not possible to include a forensic anthropologist in the field during a search, investigators can send images to the medical examiner or a forensic anthropologist to identify human and nonhuman bones. This is particularly helpful when a case initially involves locating several bones, and investigators need to know whether they are dealing with nonhuman or human remains.

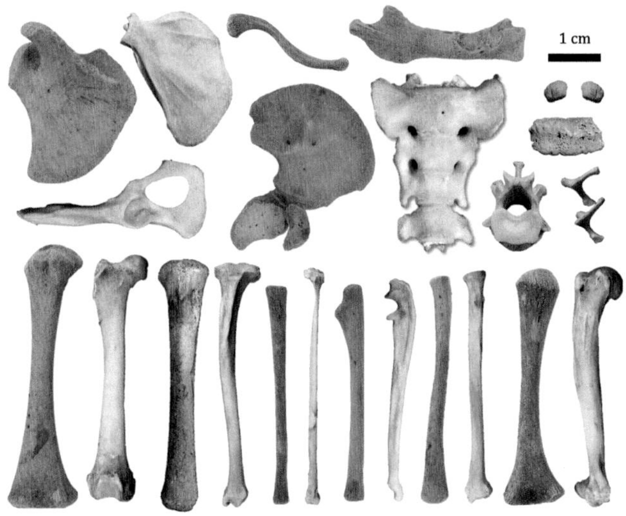

Figure 3.1 Examples of human fetal remains and raccoon (*Procyon lotor*) recovered during site search. Elements with darker coloration and staining are fetal remains; note the lack of fused bone sections at the ends of the fetal long bones (bottom row).

While investigators are generally expected to write detailed reports and construct scene maps for all types of crime scenes, investigators should also be expected to keep detailed notes and construct well-documented maps for scenes that involve human skeletal remains. As the purpose of this book is to provide investigators with a guide to process scenes properly involving human skeletal remains, we recognize that most field investigators, whether homicide detectives or crime scene personnel, will not have a basic osteology background. The reason for

DOI: 10.4324/9781315201658-3

including information on human skeletal terminology is not that the reader will become an expert in human osteology who can identify individual characteristics of bones of the skeleton. This chapter is designed instead to help the reader construct scene maps in which bones are illustrated and describe specifics in scene notes about the body position, any dispersal of remains (refer to Chapter 6), and the condition of bones (refer to Chapter 5). In addition, processing of a scene involving skeletal remains does not end after the remains are collected or excavated, particularly with a homicide investigation. This chapter is also designed to provide a better understanding of terminology used in forensic reports on describing skeletal material that may be provided by a medical examiner, coroner, or forensic anthropologist.

The authors strongly caution that this chapter is not to be used as a definitive guide for bone identification, as only very basic information on the human skeleton is provided. Information such as sex, age at death, population affinity, stature, pathology, and trauma should only be determined by a qualified expert; therefore, the methods required for determining this information are not included here. A qualified forensic anthropologist or medical examiner should handle final identification of all skeletal material. If further references are needed for documentation, several human anatomy books contain excellent skeletal descriptions, and there are also books written by biological anthropologists and anatomists that deal specifically with the human skeleton. These include *Human Osteology and Skeletal Radiology: An Atlas and Guide* by Evan Matshes and colleagues (2005), *Human Osteology: A Laboratory and Field Manual* (5th edition) by William Bass (2005), *Skeleton Keys* by Jeffrey Schwartz (2006), *Human Osteology* by Tim White, Michael Black and Pieter Folkens (2011), and the condensed version of the previous book, *The Human Bone Manual* by Tim White and Pieter Folkens (2005). Also, since these texts are mainly concerned with adult skeletal morphology, the following can be used as reference for juvenile skeletal remains: *The Osteology of Infants and Children* by Brenda Baker, Tosha Dupras and Matthew Tocheri (2005), *Juvenile Osteology: A Laboratory and Field Manual* by Maureen Schaefer, Sue Black and Louise Scheuer (2009), *Developmental Juvenile Osteology* (2nd edition) by Craig Cunningham, Louise Scheuer and Sue Black (2016), and, the condensed version of the previous book, *The Juvenile Skeleton* also by Louise Scheuer and Sue Black (2004).

TERMS ASSOCIATED WITH BONE MORPHOLOGY

When human skeletal remains are processed at a crime scene, specific bone identification, including siding, can be provided onsite when an osteology expert is part of the recovery team. When this is not possible, however, scene investigators still need to provide a description of the types of bones recovered, and a well-documented map can still be constructed even without using the proper bone names or bone sides. If a specific bone is not readily identifiable, investigators should document the bone based on its shape and size (e.g., maximum length of the bone). Bones have several different shapes, such as **long**, **short**, **flat**, **tubular**, **sesamoid**, and **irregular**, that can be used as general identifiers in notes and map legends (Figure 3.2). Table 3.1 provides a description

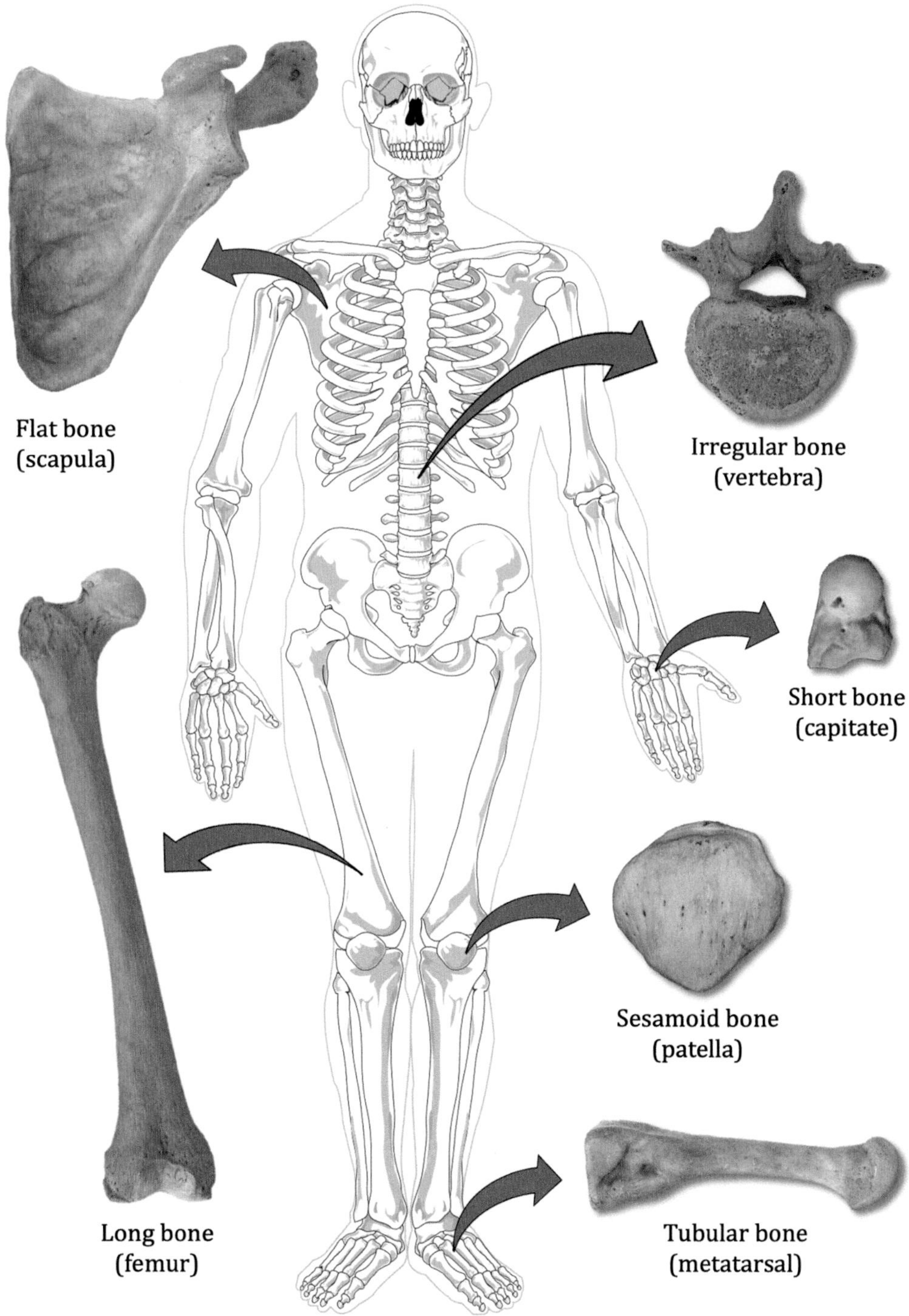

Figure 3.2 Examples of basic bone shapes in the human skeleton.

Table 3.1 Common Descriptive Bone Identifiers Based on Shape

Long	Considerably longer than they are wide with an elongated diaphysis and larger diameter epiphyses at both ends, such as the humerus and femur
Tubular	Shaped like long bones but significantly smaller in size, such as the metacarpals and metatarsals
Short	Roughly cube-shaped, lacking a diaphysis, and contain mostly trabecular bone, such as the carpals and tarsals
Sesamoid	Smaller, rounded bones that form within a tendon, such as the patella, and vary greatly in size
Flat	Thin, flat, usually somewhat curved, lacking a diaphysis and medullary cavity, such as cranial bones of the skull, ribs, sternum, and scapula
Irregular	More complex shapes that are not easily characterized in other classifications, such as the vertebrae, sacrum, and mandible

Table 3.2 Terms Used to Describe External Features of Bones

Projections	
Ala	Wing-like structure
Articular surface	Surface that comes into contact with another bone
Condyle	Large, rounded articular projection
Crest	Sharp border or ridge
Dens	Tooth-shaped projection
Epicondyle	Small projection superior to a condyle
Facet	Smooth, flattened articular surface
Line (ridge)	Long, thin elevation with roughened surface
Process	Bony projection
Ramus	Arm-like bar of bone
Spine	Relatively long, slender projection
Trochanter	Large, blunt elevation for muscle attachment
Tubercle	Small, round elevation with roughened surface
Tuberosity	Large, round elevation with roughened surface
Depressions and Holes	
Alveolus	Angular cavity or pit
Canal	Tunnel-like channel
Foramen	Opening or hole passing through bone
Fossa	Shallow depression
Groove (sulcus)	Furrow on bone surface
Notch	Indentation at an edge
Pit	Tiny pocket or depression
Sinus	Hollow area within a cranial bone
Suture	Joint between cranial bones

of these common bone identifiers based on shape. Each bone of the skeleton also has numerous visible external features that are named according to their appearance. Many of the terms used to describe these features commonly appear in forensic reports. Table 3.2 provides a summary and description of terms associated with external bone features. If needed, the scene investigator can later work with an osteology expert to provide the specific names of each bone and its external features if the scene was documented properly. For example, the osteology expert would need scene photographs of each bone or grouping of bones, and this information can then be added to the scene notes, map legend, and corresponding evidence descriptions. All bones can be numbered following the mapping system used and identified later in the laboratory. If some remains need to be collected prior to the availability of a forensic anthropologist to visit the scene, these bone locations can be marked with numbered pin flags with each bone placed into a correspondingly numbered bag. The bones from these locations can be mapped with bones that are recovered later.

Osteologists use broad terms to describe the gross morphological portions of the long bones (Figures 3.3 and 3.4). During the growth and development phase of mammalian bone, bones do not grow as one unit. For example, long bones, such as those of the arms and legs, will ultimately form from multiple bony elements. Each of the growth components has a specific name. The portion that makes up the shaft of the bone is referred to as the **diaphysis**, while the expanded ends of the shaft are called **metaphyses**, and the ends of the long bones, which exist as separate bones until fusion occurs, are called

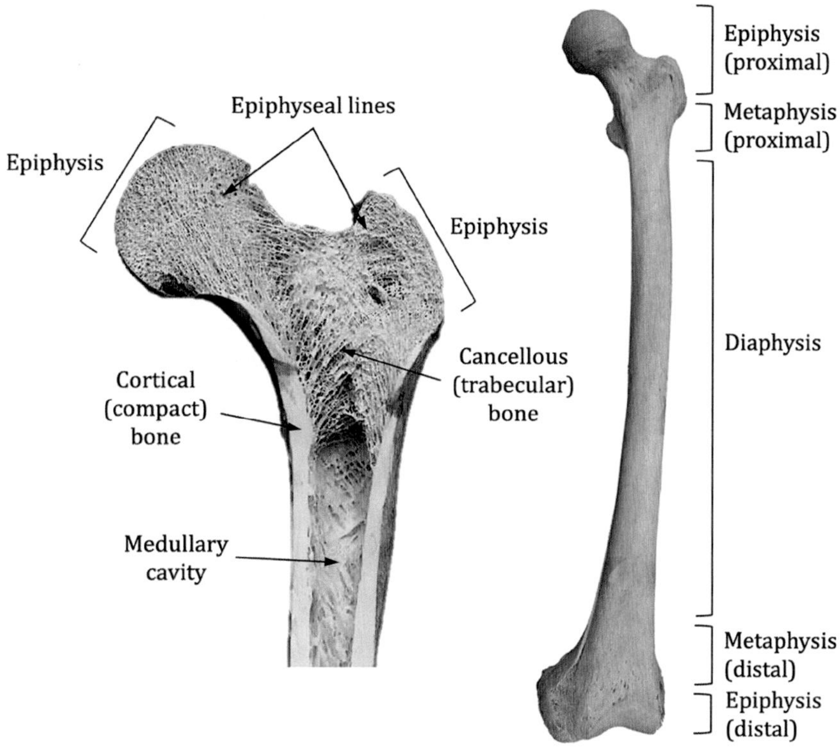

Figure 3.3 Gross morphology of dry adult long bone: (left) cross section and (right) anterior view of a left femur.

Source: Figure 3.3 is adapted from Bone cross-section no text.svg by Pbroks13, licensed under CC BY 3.0 Unported; modified, and labeled structures (https://commons.wikimedia.org/wiki/File:Bone_cross-section_no_text.svg).

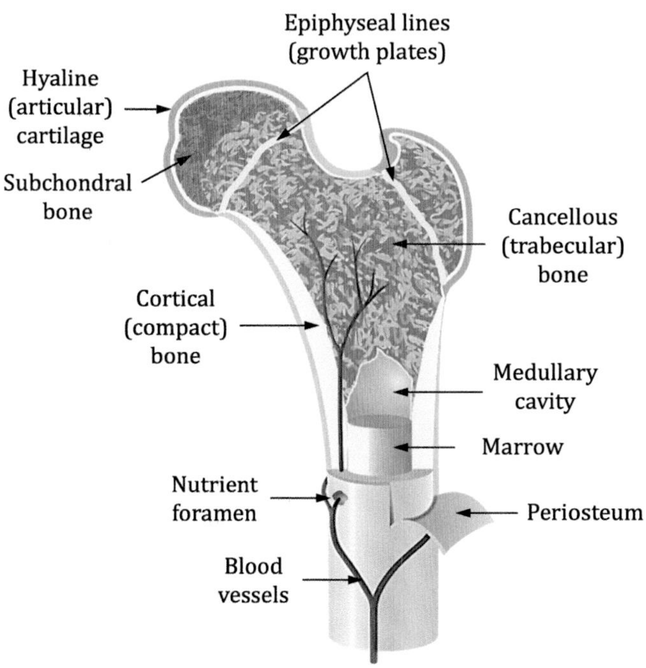

Figure 3.4 Gross morphology of tissues in adult long bone (anterior view of proximal end of a left femur).

epiphyses. During development, there are cartilaginous soft tissue layers between the metaphyses and the epiphyses, known as **epiphyseal growth plates**, which allow for growth near the ends of long bones. When growth ceases in adulthood, these growth plates become bony remnants known as **epiphyseal lines**. When long bones are articulated, the articular surface is covered with **hyaline cartilage**, and the bone surface under this cartilage is referred to as **subchondral bone**. The diaphysis of the long bone is made up of thick, dense **cortical (compact) bone**, while the ends are composed of **cancellous (trabecular) bone**. Cortical bone is covered by a fibrous soft tissue called the **periosteum**. The diaphysis of the long bone also has a feature called the **nutrient foramen**, which allows for the passage of bloods vessels and nerves into the bone. Each long bone also has a hollow center referred to as the **medullary cavity**. During life, this cavity is filled with yellow **marrow**, which consists mainly of fat cells, and red marrow, which consists of tissues involved in the formation of red and white blood cells. Table 3.3 provides a summary of the terminology associated with the gross morphology of the long bones.

Table 3.3 Terms Used to Describe Gross Morphology of Long Bones

Diaphysis	Shaft of a long bone
Metaphysis	Expanded, growth portion of a long bone located between diaphysis and epiphysis
Epiphysis	End of bone separate from metaphysis during development; becomes fused when growth has ceased
Epiphyseal growth plate	Layer of cartilage between metaphysis and epiphysis that allows for growth in bone
Epiphyseal line	Remnant of epiphyseal growth plate in adult bones
Hyaline cartilage	Cartilage tissue covering external articular surface of bone
Subchondral bone	Area of bone at joint covered by hyaline cartilage
Cortical (compact) bone	Smooth, dense outer layer of bone
Cancellous (trabecular) bone	Light, porous interior structure of short bones, irregular bones, and ends of long and tubular bones
Medullary cavity	Central cavity of diaphysis that holds bone marrow
Marrow	Soft, fatty tissue found at the center of most bones
Periosteum	Fibrous connective tissue covering outer surface of bone
Nutrient foramen	External opening of nutrient canal in diaphysis; facilitates blood and nerve supply

ANATOMICAL OR RELATIVE POSITION

When presenting the human skeleton in reports, the forensic anthropologist will describe the skeleton and its components in relation to the **standard anatomical position** (Figure 3.5). In standard anatomical position, the human body is standing erect, facing forward with feet together, arms extended, and raised slightly out from the body, and with the hands supinated so the palms are facing forward with the thumb bones outward. In this position almost all the bones are visible, and none are crossed over one another. Most skeletal data recording sheets will include a drawing of a skeleton in the standard anatomical position, and this may be a common inclusion in reports by medical examiners, coroners, or forensic anthropologists (refer to Appendix A). These drawings may be used to indicate the absence or presence of skeletal elements or may also be used to illustrate pathology or trauma.

The skeleton and independent skeletal elements may be described in reference to anatomical planes (Figure 3.6). The **median (sagittal) plane** runs through the center of the body from the head to the feet and divides the body into right and left halves, while the **frontal (coronal) plane** divides the body into front and back halves. The **horizontal (transverse) plane** passes through the body perpendicular to the median and frontal planes and is used to divide the body at any level into upper and lower sections. An **oblique plane** is any plane passing through the body that is not parallel or perpendicular to the other three planes and is used to divide the body at any angle other than horizontal or vertical at any level.

The skeleton also may be divided into particular regions (Figure 3.7). The skull (i.e., cranium plus the mandible) and the hyoid are usually treated as one complex structure referred to as the **cranial skeleton**. The **infracranial skeleton** is the entire region below the skull. While the investigator may come across the term **postcranial** to describe the skeleton located below the skull, this term is more accurately used to describe the skeleton of a quadrupedal animal as it literally translates to 'behind the cranium' (refer to Figure 3.5). The human skeleton can also be divided into two further areas, the axial skeleton, and the appendicular skeleton. The **axial skeleton** is found at the midline of the body and consists of 80 bones, including the skull, the auditory ossicles, the hyoid, the vertebral column, and the ribs. The **appendicular skeleton** is composed of 126 bones, including all the bones of the shoulder girdle, pelvic girdle, the limbs, and the hands and feet.

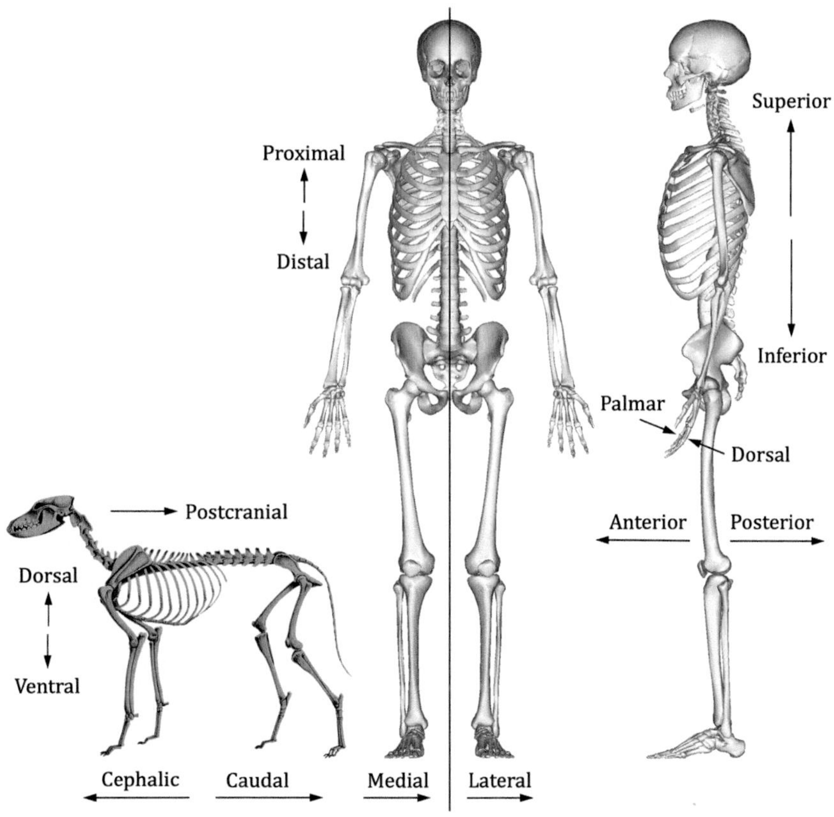

Figure 3.5 The human skeleton illustrating standard anatomical position and terms commonly used to describe the relative position in anterior view (center) and lateral view (right). The canine skeleton (left) illustrates positional terms that are more suited for describing the quadrupedal skeleton.

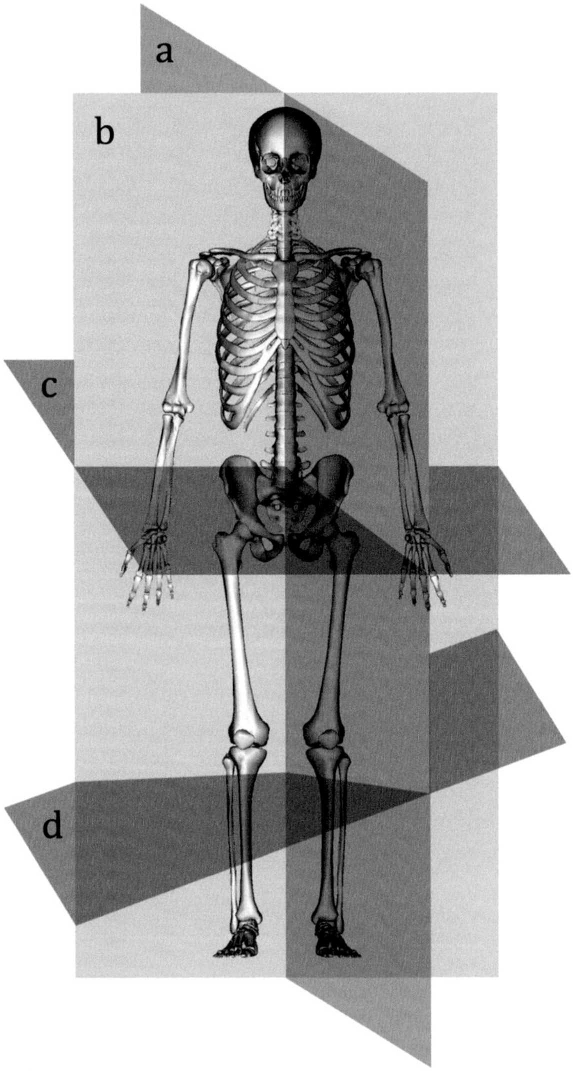

Figure 3.6 The anatomical planes of reference for the human skeleton are the (a) median or sagittal plane, dividing the body into right and left halves; (b) the frontal or coronal plane dividing the body into front and back halves; (c) horizontal or transverse plane, dividing the body into upper and lower sections at any level; and (d) the oblique plane, which divides the body at any angle other than horizontal or vertical.

There are several other terms that may appear in relation to the anatomical and positional description of the skeleton, or even in descriptions of a skeleton in relation to additional evidence at the scene (e.g., carnivore gnawing), pathology (e.g., healed fractures), trauma (e.g., a gunshot wound or sharp-force trauma), or taphonomy (refer to Chapter 5). These terms may also be used in field reports to describe the relative position of particular skeletal elements or to describe the spatial relationship between objects and the skeleton. When referring to the limbs, the end of a long bone closest to the axial skeleton is referred to as the **proximal** end of the bone, while the end of a long bone furthest from the axial skeleton is referred to as the **distal** end (refer to Figure 3.5). For example, a bullet found beside the upper portion of the humerus may be described as being located near the proximal end of the humerus. **Superior** and **inferior** may also be used to describe portions of bones in relation to where they are positioned within the skeleton. For example, the surface of the vertebra that is toward the cranium is the superior surface, while the surface that is toward the feet is the inferior surface. Any part of the skeleton or bone that is found toward the middle of the body, or midline, is referred to as **medial**, while any part of the body that is away from the midline is called **lateral**. Any portion of the skeleton or bone located toward the front of the body is described as **anterior**, while anything toward the back is described as **posterior**. Anything located on the sole of the foot is described as **plantar**, while anything located on the palm of the hand is described as **palmar**. The top of the foot or back of the hand is referred to as **dorsal**. The directional terms **cephalic** (i.e., toward the head), **caudal** (i.e., toward the tail), **ventral** (i.e., toward the chest), and **dorsal** (i.e., toward the back) are better used to describe quadrupedal skeletons; however, some medical examiners may use these terms when describing the human skeleton. See Table 3.4 for a summary of the terms commonly used in forensic reports to describe anatomical and relative position.

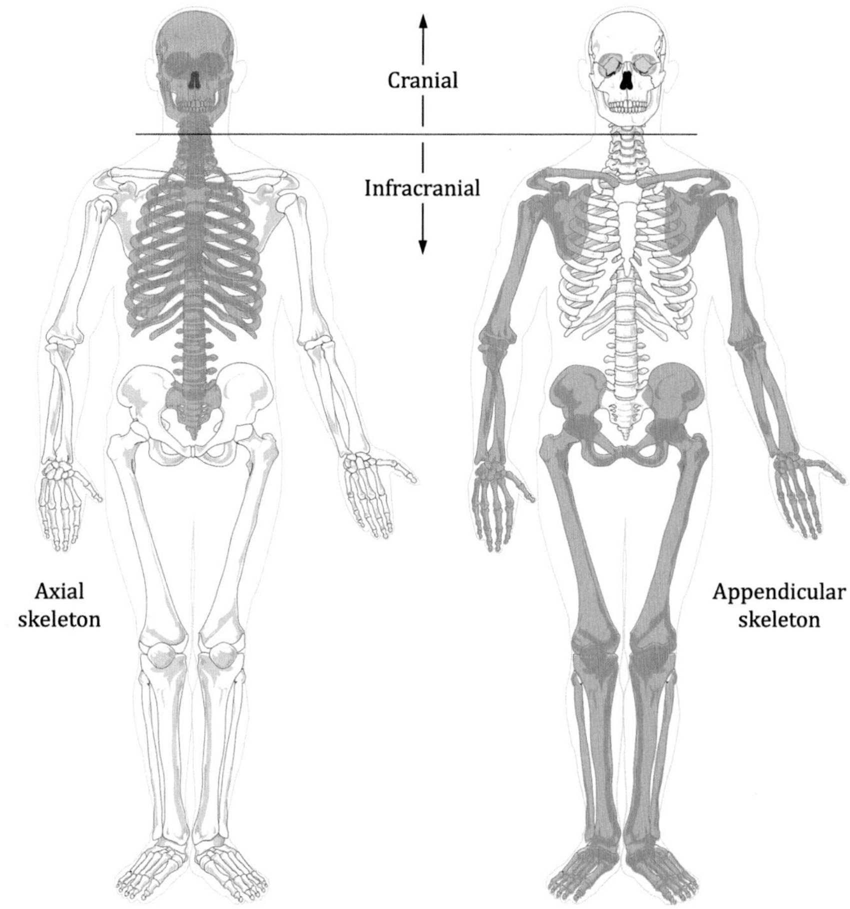

Figure 3.7 The anatomical regions of reference for the human skeleton.

Table 3.4 Terms Used to Describe Anatomical and Relative Positions

Anatomical Position	
Standard anatomical position	Body standing erect, face forward, feet together, arms slightly raised, palms of hands facing anteriorly
Supination	Rotation of hand so palm faces anteriorly
Pronation	Rotation of hand so palm faces posteriorly
Median (sagittal) plane	Plane runs through body from head to feet, dividing body into left and right halves
Frontal (coronal) plane	Plane runs through body from head to feet, dividing body into front and back halves
Horizontal (transverse) plane	Plane perpendicular to median and frontal planes; divides body into upper and lower sections at any level
Oblique plane	Any plane through the body not parallel or perpendicular to the other planes; divides body at any angle other than horizontal or vertical at any level
Cranial skeleton	The skull (cranium and mandible) and hyoid
Infracranial skeleton	All skeletal elements below the skull and hyoid
Axial skeleton	Bones of the midline (includes skull, auditory ossicles, hyoid, ribs, and vertebral column)
Appendicular skeleton	Bones of the shoulder girdle, pelvic girdle, and limbs
Relative Position	
Superior	Upper or above; toward the head
Inferior	Lower or below; toward the feet
Anterior	Toward the front

(Continued)

Table 3.4 *(Continued)* Terms Used to Describe Anatomical and Relative Positions

Anatomical Position	
Posterior	Toward the back
Proximal	End of bone closest to axial skeleton
Distal	End of bone furthest from the axial skeleton
Medial	Toward the midline
Lateral	Away from the midline
Dorsal	On the back of the hand or top of the foot
Palmar	On the palm of the hand
Plantar	On the sole of the foot
Bilateral	On both sides
Unilateral	On one side
Nonhuman Anatomical and Relative Position	
Postcranial skeleton	All bones of quadrupedal skeleton except the skull
Cephalic	Toward the head of a quadruped
Caudal	Toward the tail of a quadruped
Dorsal	Toward the back of a quadruped
Ventral	Toward the chest of a quadruped

BASIC ADULT HUMAN SKELETON

The average adult human skeleton contains 206 bones (Figure 3.8). Take note, however, that human variation may exist in the number of skeletal elements that each person has, so there may be more or less than 206 bones, depending on genetics, development, and life history. For example, one common area of the human skeleton where variation may occur is in the number of specific types of vertebrae within the spinal column. Table 3.5 contains common names of bones and areas of the human body, while Table 3.6 contains an inventory of the average adult human skeleton. Appendix A includes a visual inventory sheet that can be used for the documentation of adult skeletal elements at the scene.

The adult skull contains an average of 28 bones and it is sometimes listed as 29 bones when including the hyoid in the skull bone inventory (Figure 3.9). Although there are

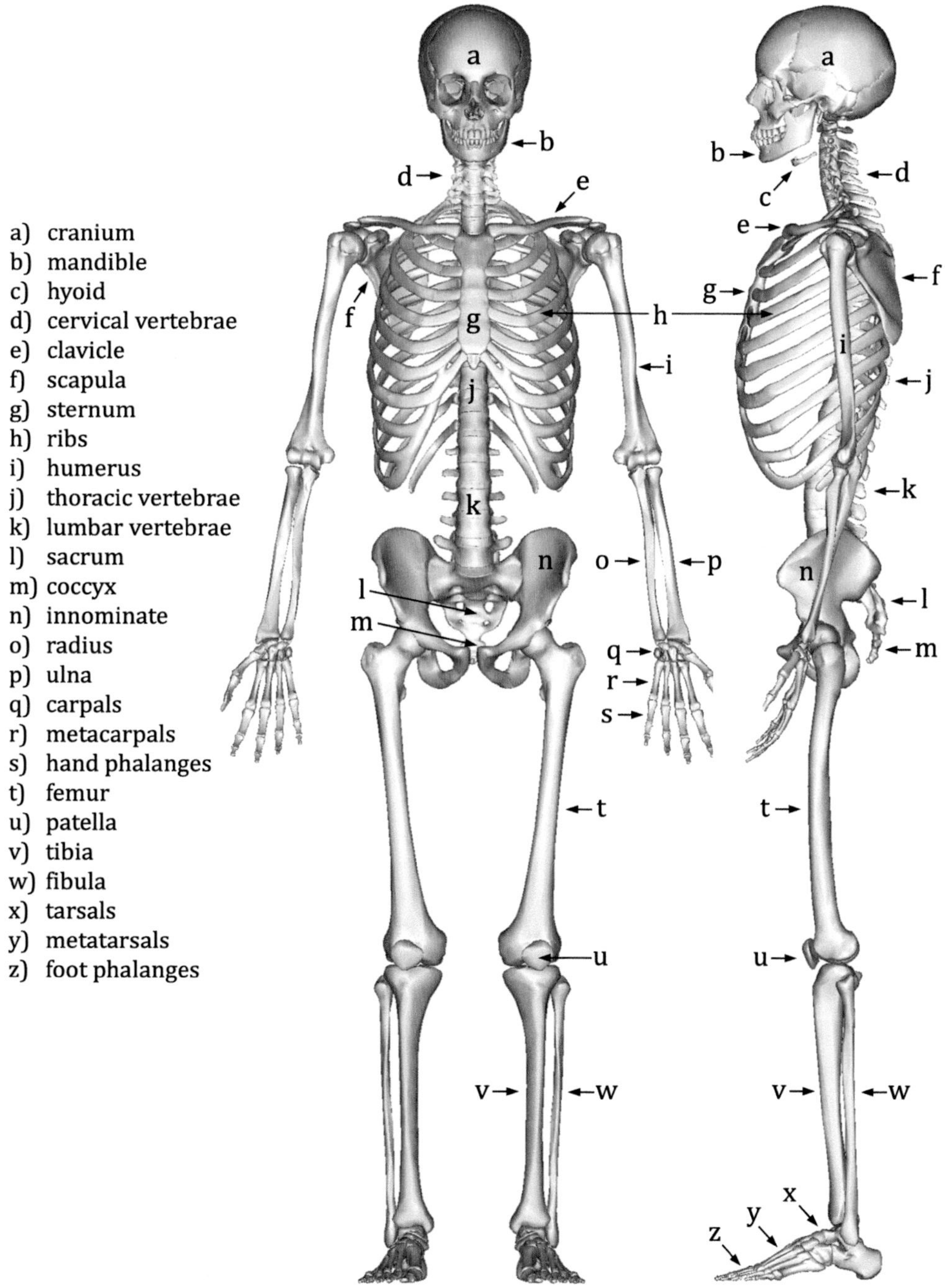

Figure 3.8 Elements of the human skeleton shown in their anatomical position.

Table 3.5 Common and Scientific Names for Bones and Areas of Human Skeleton

Common Name	Scientific Name
Upper jaw	Maxilla
Lower jaw	Mandible
Head	Skull (cranium and mandible)
Neck	Cervical vertebrae (7) and hyoid
Upper back	Thoracic vertebrae (12) and ribs (12 pair)
Lower back	Lumbar vertebrae (5)
Tailbone	Coccyx
Breastbone	Sternum
Collarbone	Clavicle
Scapula	Shoulder blade
Shoulder girdle	Left and right proximal humerus, scapula, and clavicle
Shoulder joint (ball and socket)	Humeral head and glenoid fossa of scapula
Upper arm	Humerus
Elbow joint	Distal humerus, proximal radius, and proximal ulna
Forearm	Ulna and radius
Hand	Carpals, metacarpals, and hand phalanges
Wrist	Carpals (8)
Fingers	Hand phalanges (14)
Thumb	1st proximal hand phalanx and 1st distal hand phalanx
Hip bone	Innominate (os coxa)
Pelvic girdle	Sacrum, coccyx, and left and right innominate (os coxa)
Hip joint	Acetabulum of innominate (os coxa) and head of femur
Thigh	Femur
Kneecap	Patella
Knee bones	Distal femur, proximal tibia, and patella
Shin	Tibia
Foot	Tarsals, metatarsals, and foot phalanges
Ankle bones	Distal tibia, distal fibula, and talus (tarsal)
Heel bone	Calcaneus
Toes	Foot phalanges (14)
Big toe	1st proximal foot phalanx and 1st distal foot phalanx
Baby teeth	Deciduous dentition
Wisdom teeth	Permanent third molars

Table 3.6 Inventory of Bones in the Average Adult Human Skeleton

Axial Skeleton			
Facial Bones (Splanchnocranium)			
Mandible	1	Nasal	2
Vomer	1	Lacrimal	2
Maxilla	2	Palatine	2
Zygomatic	2	Inferior nasal concha	2
Cranial Vault Bones (Calvarium)			
Frontal	1	Sphenoid	1
Occipital	1	Temporal	2
Ethmoid	1	Parietal	2
Auditory ossicles	6		

(Continued)

Table 3.6 *(Continued)* Inventory of Bones in the Average Adult Human Skeleton

Axial Skeleton				
Other Axial Bones				
Hyoid	1	Sacrum	1	
Cervical vertebra	7	Coccyx	1	
Thoracic vertebra	12	Sternum *	1	
Lumbar vertebra	5	Ribs	24	
Total bones in axial skeleton				***80***
Appendicular Skeleton				
Clavicle	2	Scapula	2	
Humerus	2	Carpals	16	
Ulna	2	Metacarpals	10	
Radius	2	Hand phalanges	28	
Femur	2	Patella	2	
Tibia	2	Tarsals	14	
Fibula	2	Metatarsals	10	
Innominate (os coxa)	2	Foot phalanges	28	
Total bones in appendicular skeleton				***126***
Total bones in adult human skeleton				**206**

*While considered one bone, the sternum is often recovered in two pieces, the wider manubrium (superior) and the narrower body (inferior).

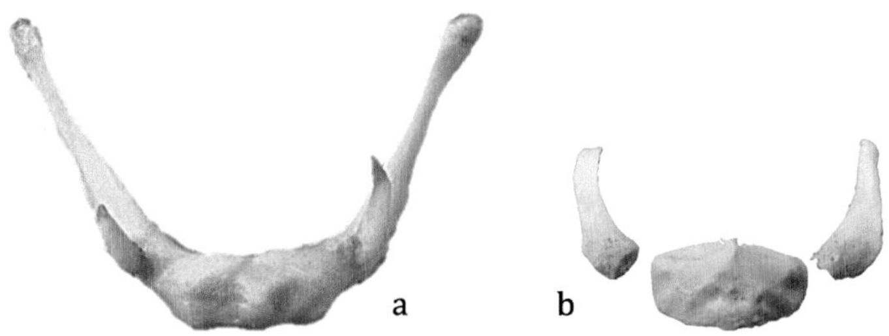

Figure 3.9 Superior view of the hyoid bone: (a) fused and (b) unfused.

many situations in which the cranial bones may become separated (e.g., in unfused juvenile remains, during exposure to high temperature fires, in cases of high impact blunt force trauma, or a gunshot wound), normally the majority of the cranial elements will be found articulated. The exception to this would be the mandible, the hyoid, and the auditory ossicles, all of which may easily become disarticulated after soft tissue decomposes. Figure 3.10 shows the skull and hyoid in four views with all the different bones identified. It is useful to be familiar with the different bones of the skull, as both medical examiners and forensic anthropologists will refer to the separate bones of the skull when documenting the location of pathology or trauma.

For the purposes of mapping and greater understanding of field and forensic reports, we have provided illustrations of articulated portions of the human skeleton as well as singular bones, since it is just as likely to find dispersed bones as it is to find a fully articulated skeleton in a forensic case. The vertebral column (Figure 3.11) and the thoracic area (Figure 3.12) make up the axial skeleton, which is an area of the body that is most likely to bear evidence of sharp-force trauma (i.e., stab wounds), and therefore it is important that all bones be collected from the scene if possible. The **shoulder girdle** (Figure 3.12) and the **pelvic girdle** (Figure 3.13) form the attachments between the axial and appendicular skeleton. The bones of the arm (Figure 3.14) consist of the humerus, the ulna, and the radius. The hand is made up of eight carpals, five metacarpals, five proximal phalanges, four intermediate phalanges (the first digit, or thumb, does not have an intermediate phalanx), and five distal phalanges (Figure 3.15). The bones of the leg (Figure 3.16) consist of the femur, patella, tibia, and fibula. Each foot consists of seven tarsals, five metatarsals, five proximal phalanges, four intermediate phalanges (the first digit, or big toe, also does not have an intermediate phalanx), and five distal phalanges (Figure 3.17). Although the hand

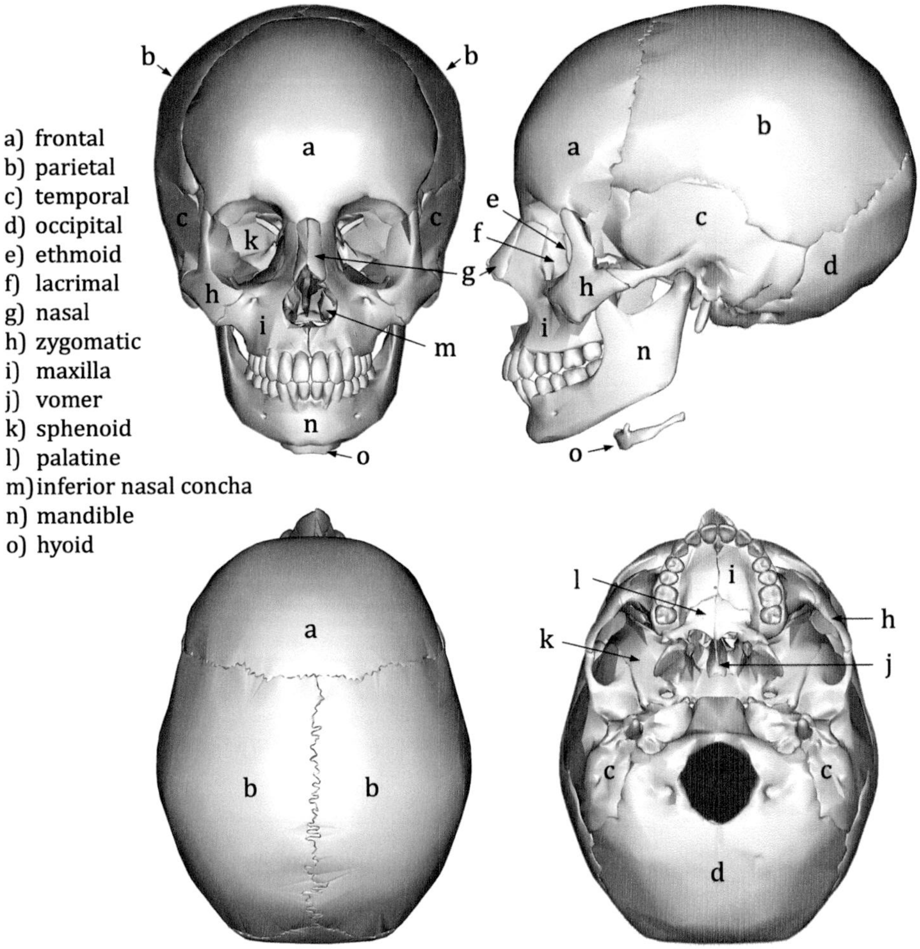

Figure 3.10 Bones of the skull shown from the anterior view (upper left), lateral view (upper right), superior view (lower left), and inferior view (lower right).

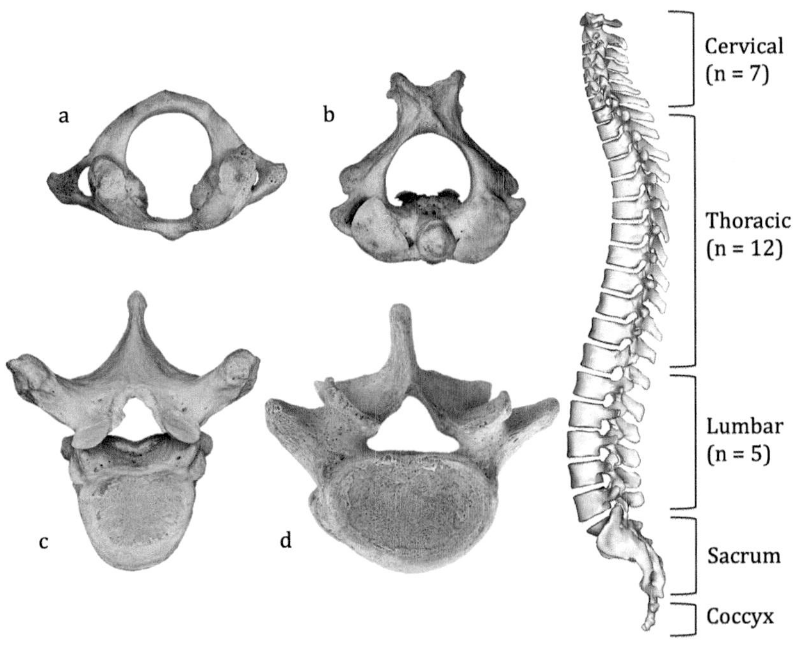

Figure 3.11 Articulated bones of the vertebral column are shown on the right with the number of elements assigned to each category. Superior views of individual vertebra illustrate some of the differences between categories: (a) first cervical vertebra (C1 or atlas); (b) second cervical vertebra (C2 or axis); (c) thoracic vertebra #7 (T7); and (d) lumbar vertebra #3 (L3).

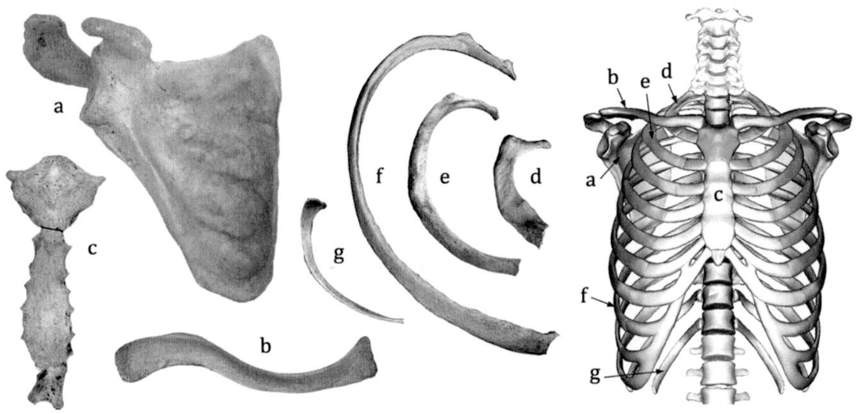

Figure 3.12 Bones of the shoulder girdle (proximal humerus not included) and thoracic area are shown articulated on the right. The shoulder girdle is composed of the scapulae and clavicles, with the right scapula (a) shown in anterior view and the right clavicle (b) shown in superior view. The thoracic area is composed of the sternum (c), ribs (d–g), and thoracic vertebrae (shown in Figure 3.11). From the superior view, most ribs can be distinguished by their morphology: rib #1 (d); rib #2 (e); rib #8 (f); and rib #12 (g).

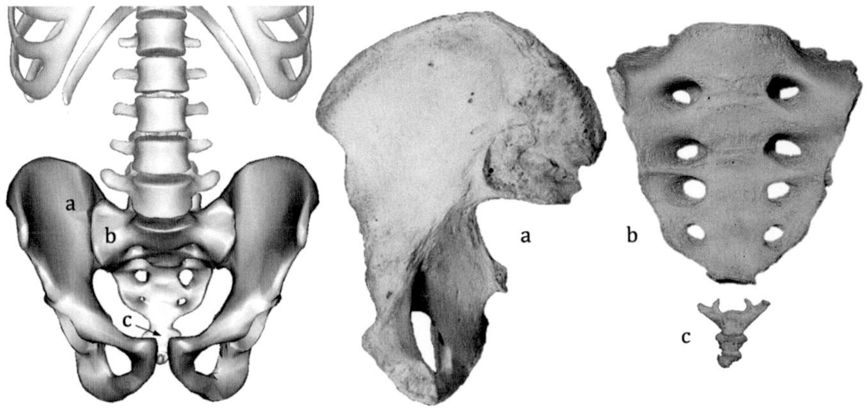

Figure 3.13 Bones of the lower portion of the vertebral column and the pelvic girdle are shown articulated on the left. The pelvic girdle is composed of the left and right innominates (os coxae). The right innominate (os coxa) (a) is shown in medial view, while the sacrum (b) and coccyx (c) are shown in anterior view.

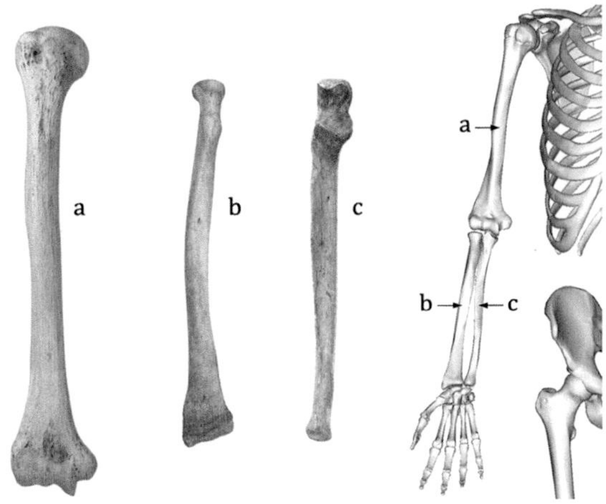

Figure 3.14 Bones of the arm are shown articulated on the right. The right humerus (a), right radius (b) and right ulna (c) are all shown in anterior view on the left.

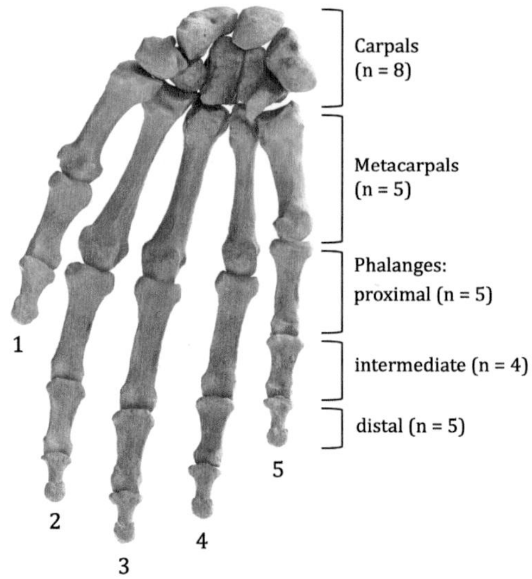

Figure 3.15 Articulated bones of the right wrist and hand shown in standard anatomical position (palm facing forward). Digits are numbered starting with the thumb (1) through the little finger (5).

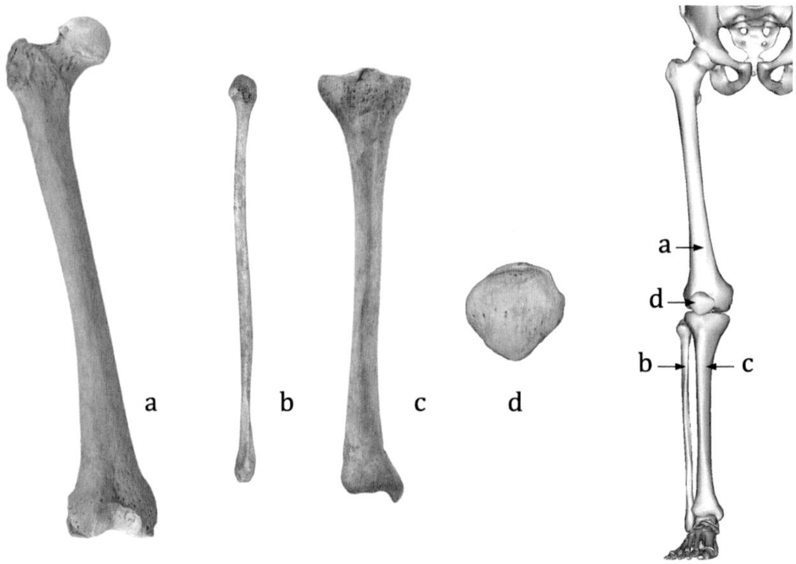

Figure 3.16 Bones of the leg are shown articulated on the right. The right femur (a), fibula (b), tibia (c) and patella (d) are all shown in anterior view on the left.

and foot bones are small, it is important that they are recognized and collected from a scene. Forensically relevant information such as defense wounds to the hands may be present on these small bones and may be vital for reconstructing the events surrounding an individual's death. Fortunately, foot bones or even whole feet are often recovered still in footwear. Table 3.7 provides a list of the separate hand and foot bones.

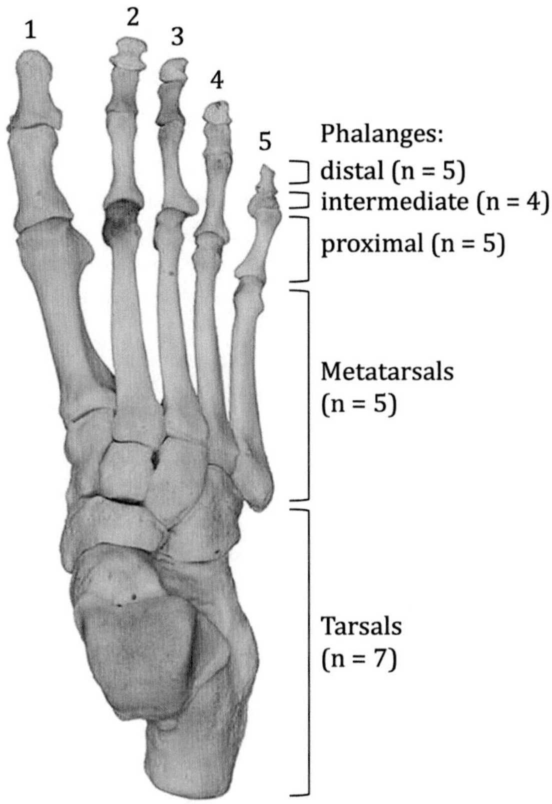

Figure 3.17 Articulated bones of the ankle (without tibia) and right foot shown in superior view. Digits are numbered starting with the big toe (1) through the little toe (5).

Table 3.7 Inventory of Bones in the Average Adult Hands and Feet

Hands and Wrists		Feet and Ankles	
Carpals		**Tarsals**	
Lunate	2	Calcaneus	2
Scaphoid	2	Talus	2
Triquetral	2	Navicular	2
Pisiform	2	Cuboid	2
Trapezium	2	1st cuneiform	2
Trapezoid	2	2nd cuneiform	2
Capitate	2	3rd cuneiform	2
Hamate	2		
Metacarpals (Palms of hands)		**Metatarsals (Arches of feet)**	
Metacarpal #1	2	Metatarsal #1	2
Metacarpal #2	2	Metatarsal #2	2
Metacarpal #3	2	Metatarsal #3	2
Metacarpal #4	2	Metatarsal #4	2
Metacarpal #5	2	Metatarsal #5	2
Phalanges (Fingers)		**Phalanges (Toes)**	
Proximal	10	Proximal	10
Intermediate	8	Intermediate	8
Distal	10	Distal	10
Total bones in hands and wrists	**64**	**Total bones in feet and ankles**	**62**

BASIC JUVENILE HUMAN SKELETON

It should be noted that the fetal, infant, child, and teenage or adolescent skeleton has a significantly different morphological appearance and can contain far more bones than the adult skeleton (Figures 3.18 and 3.19). Appendix A includes visual inventory sheets that can be used for the documentation of adolescent, younger child, and perinate/infant skeletal elements at the scene. At 11 weeks before birth, there are usually about 800 bony elements of the skeleton, and at birth, there are about 450 (Baker et al., 2005). As an individual grows, more skeletal elements will develop, and eventually all these elements will fuse together to form the adult skeleton (Figures 3.20 and 3.21). By adulthood, normally between the ages of 21 and 25, all of the epiphyses have fused in the skeleton (White and Folkens, 2005). Table 3.8 provides ranges of age estimates based on non-fusion and fusion of epiphyses in various infracranial skeletal elements.

Bones of an infant or fetal skeleton are commonly light brown in color after decomposition has stained them and may appear to the untrained eye as small twigs, debris, or be mistaken as the skeleton of a nonhuman animal (refer to Figure 3.1). As a result, they are easily missed at the scene. Occasionally, it may be necessary to identify fetal bones in a field situation if a female victim was pregnant, or in a case where a fetus or infant is the focus of a scene. Although it may seem like this would be a rarity, the authors have participated in forensic cases in which the identification and estimation of fetal age greatly assisted in the identification of the victim. Care should be taken when removing dirt and debris from the pelvic area of any human skeleton, as this would be the most likely location of fetal remains, if they were present (refer to Chapter 11 for more information on the recovery of juvenile human skeletal remains).

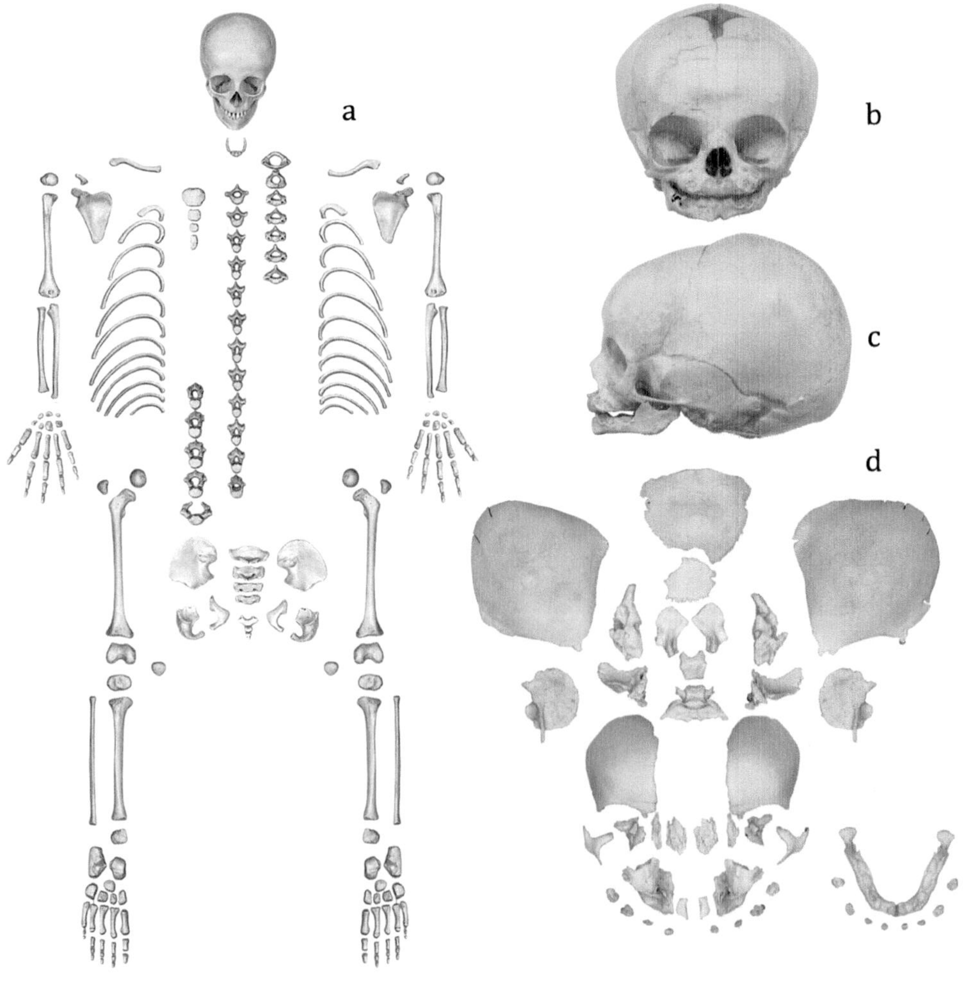

Figure 3.18 Bones of the juvenile skeleton: (a) shows the disarticulated skeleton of a six-year-old child, demonstrating that there are many more skeletal elements at this stage of development when compared with an adult. The fetal skull, (b) in anterior view and (c) lateral view, is also not fused (d) and consists of more elements than found in an adult skull.

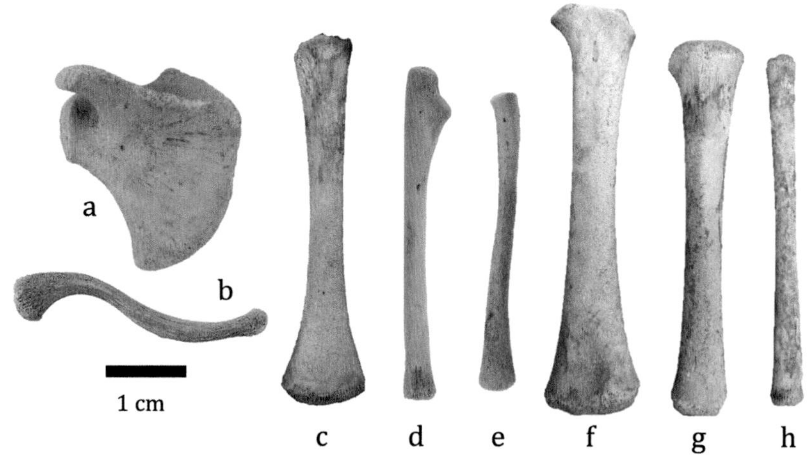

Figure 3.19 Bones of the fetal skeleton: (a) scapula in posterior view; (b) clavicle in superior view; and (c) humerus, (d) ulna, (e) radius, (f) femur, (g) tibia, and (h) fibula in anterior view.

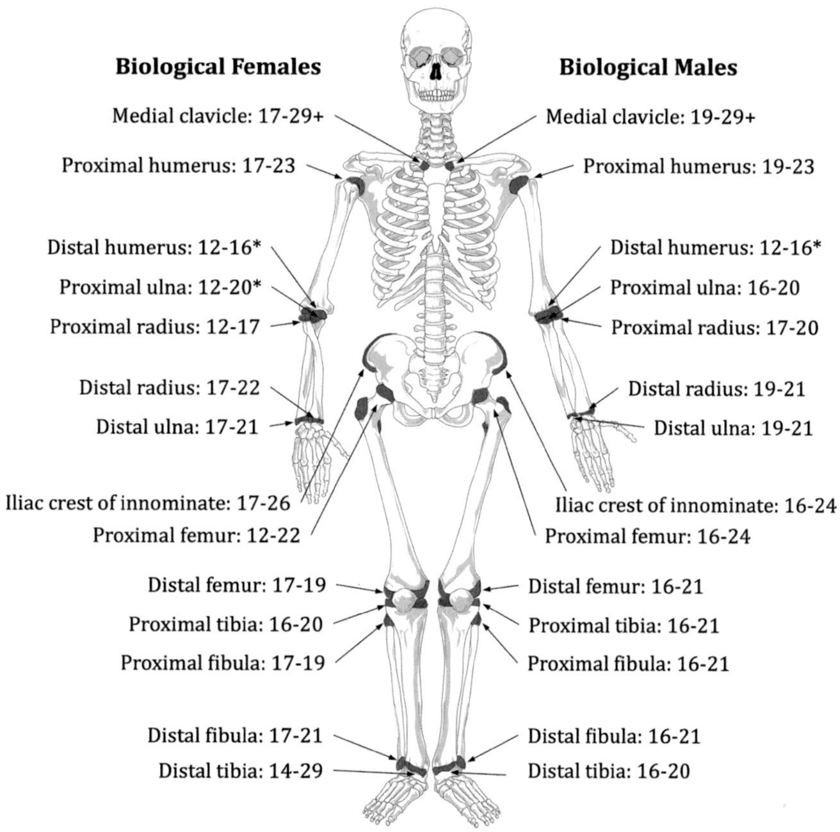

Figure 3.20 Age of epiphyseal fusion for various infracranial skeletal elements in biological females (left) and biological males (right) (*range estimate based on small sample size [e.g., <10] for partial and complete union).

Source: Data derived from Coqueugniot and Weaver (2007)

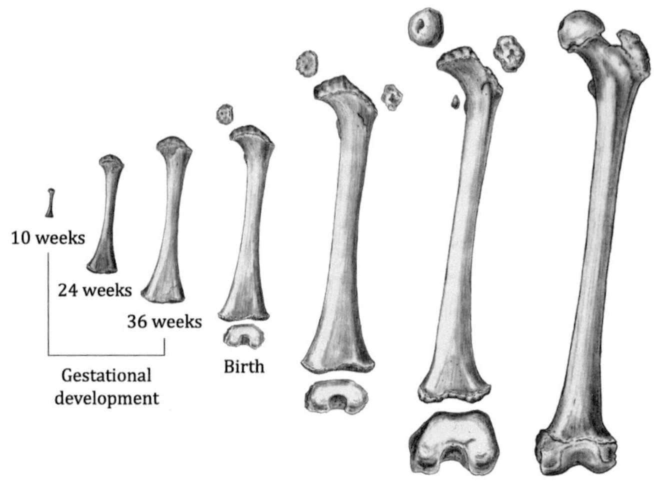

Figure 3.21 Comparison of various stages of growth of the human femur. The anterior view of the left femur illustrates the appearance and development of the diaphysis and epiphyses during development.

Table 3.8 Age of Epiphyseal Fusion for Various Appendicular Skeletal Elements

	Biological Females Age (yrs)		Biological Males Age (yrs)	
Region	***Open (No Fusion)***	***Fusion Range***	***Open (No Fusion)***	***Fusion Range***
Medial clavicle	≤24	17–29+	≤24	19–29+
Proximal humerus	≤20	17–23	≤19	19–23
Distal humerus	≤12	12–16*	≤15	12–16*
Proximal radius	≤12	12–17	≤16	17–20
Distal radius	≤19	17–22	≤21	19–21
Proximal ulna	≤12	12–20*	≤16	16–20
Distal ulna	≤19	17–21	≤21	19–21
Proximal femur	≤17	12–22	≤20	16–24
Distal femur	≤19	17–19	≤20	16–21
Proximal tibia	≤19	16–20	≤20	16–21
Distal tibia	≤17	14–29	≤19	16–20
Proximal fibula	≤19	17–19	≤20	16–21
Distal fibula	≤17	17–21	≤20	16–21
Iliac crest of innominate	≤19	17–26	≤20	16–24

Source: Derived from Coqueugniot and Weaver (2007)
* Range estimate based on small sample size (e.g., <10) for partial and complete union

BASIC HUMAN DENTITION

Humans typically have two sets of teeth, the **deciduous**, also called the primary, baby, or milk teeth, and the **permanent**, also called the secondary or adult teeth. Teeth can be a very important part of a forensic investigation, as positive identification of the individual can be made with comparisons to dental records. The dentition is the only part of the human skeleton that comes into regular contact with the environment during a person's life. As a result, teeth can retain modifications that occur during the life of the individual, be it intentional or unintentional. For example, trips to the dentist may alter the teeth (e.g., fillings, tooth extraction, root canals) in a way that can be used to identify the person after death.

Terms Associated with Dental Morphology and Position

Each tooth is made up of a crown, root, pulp cavity, and a root canal (Figure 3.22). The structural components of a tooth include **enamel, dentin**, and **cementum**. The area where the enamel and cementum of a tooth meet, marking the boundary between the crown and root, is referred to as the **cementoenamel junction (CEJ)**. A soft, connective tissue, known as the **periodontal ligament (PDL)**, attaches the tooth to the tooth socket. The blood and nerve supply for the tooth enters through the **apical foramen**, found at the tip of the root, and continues through the **root canal** into the **pulp chamber**.

Four morphological tooth types are found in human dentition: incisors, canines, premolars, and molars (Figure 3.23). **Incisors** are so named because of their chisel-like appearance and sharp cutting edges. **Canines** are typically longer than incisors and have a cone-shaped appearance; however, over time, their tips can become flattened due to wear or chipping. **Premolars** are smaller and shorter than canines and have two pointed cusps on their chewing surface, which is why they are sometimes referred to as 'bicuspids.' **Molars** are the largest teeth and have broad chewing surfaces adapted for grinding food.

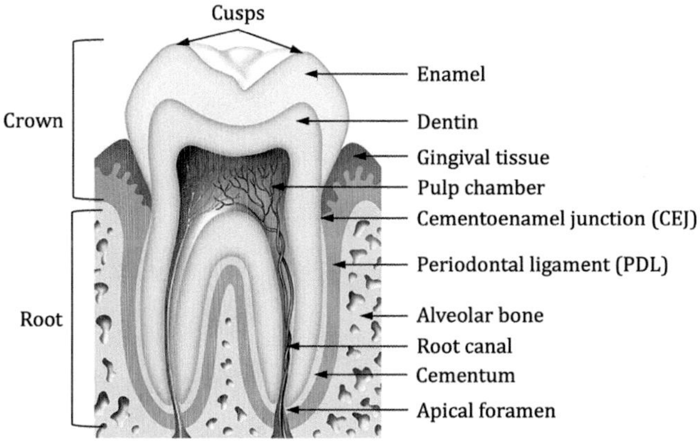

Figure 3.22 Gross morphology of tissues in a tooth.

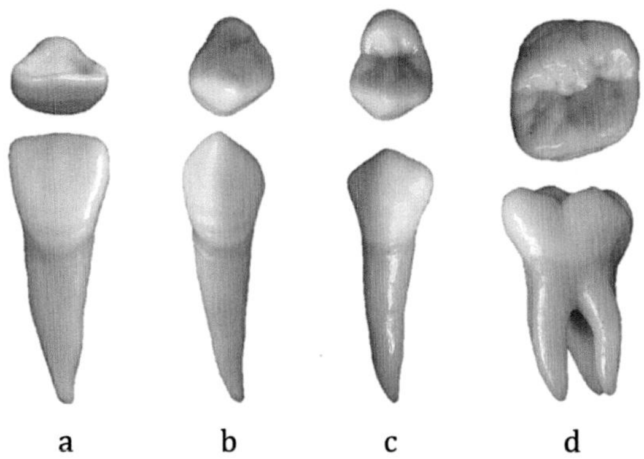

Figure 3.23 Comparison of the four basic tooth types in human dentition. The occlusal surface of each tooth type is shown in the upper row, while the lower row shows the incisor (a) and canine (b) in labial view and the premolar (c) and molar (d) in buccal view.

When describing the dentition, the teeth are separated into four quadrants by dividing the mouth into an upper and lower half (i.e., the maxilla and the mandible), and left and right halves at the median plane. This creates upper right, upper left, lower right, and lower left quadrants (Figure 3.24). The deciduous dentition is made up of five teeth in each of the four dental quadrants for a total of 20 teeth. In each deciduous quadrant there are two incisors, one canine, no premolars, and two primary molars. The permanent dentition is made up of eight teeth in each of the four dental quadrants for a total of 32 teeth. In each permanent quadrant, there are two incisors, one canine, two premolars, and three molars. During middle childhood, an individual will have mixed dentition, or both deciduous and permanent teeth, until all of the deciduous teeth are pushed out.

As with the skeleton, there are directional and descriptor terms that are used by the forensic odontologist, medical examiner, and forensic anthropologist to describe teeth and any remarkable modification of them. Each tooth has six directional planes (Figure 3.25) that are commonly used to describe the location of modifications such as cavities or fillings. The chewing surface of the tooth is called the **occlusal** surface (this may be called the **incisal** surface on incisors). The surface or direction toward the tip of the tooth root is referred to as the **apical** surface. The surface of premolars and molars facing the anterior of the mouth and the surface of the canines and incisors facing the midline of the mouth is called the **mesial** surface, while the opposite surface is called the **distal** surface. The surface of the tooth adjacent to the tongue is called the **lingual** surface, while the opposite side on molars and premolars is referred to as the **buccal** surface, and on the canines and incisors, this is called the **labial** surface. Refer to Table 3.9 for a summary of terms associated with human dentition that may be used in forensic reports.

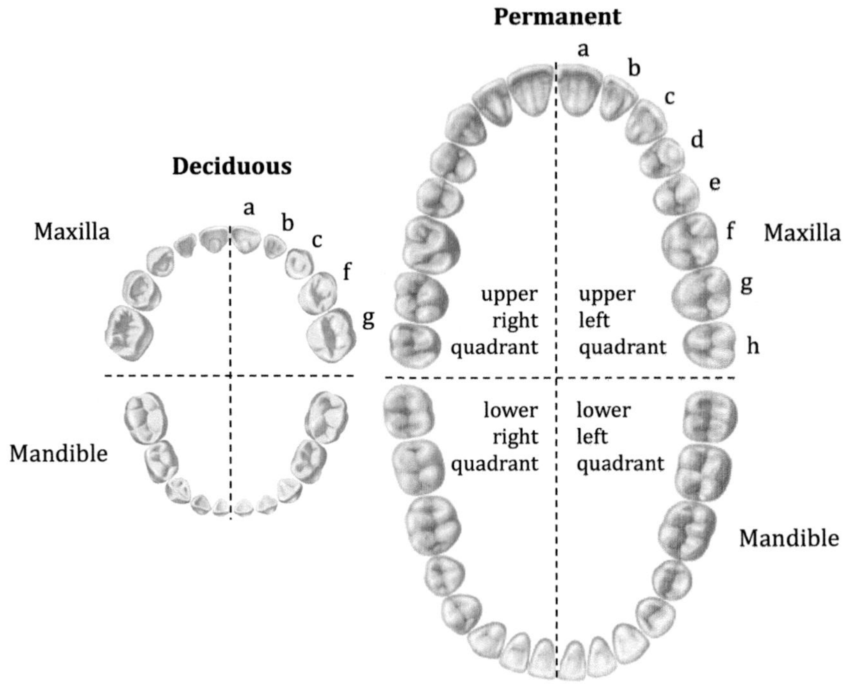

Figure 3.24 Comparison of deciduous (left) and permanent (right) dentition. Permanent dentition has eight teeth in each quadrant (32 teeth): (a) 1st incisor, (b) 2nd incisor, (c) canine, (d) 1st premolar, (e) 2nd premolar, (f) 1st molar, (g) 2nd molar, and (h) 3rd molar. Deciduous dentition has five teeth in each quadrant (20 teeth) and follows the same general tooth type pattern as permanent dentition but lacks premolars.

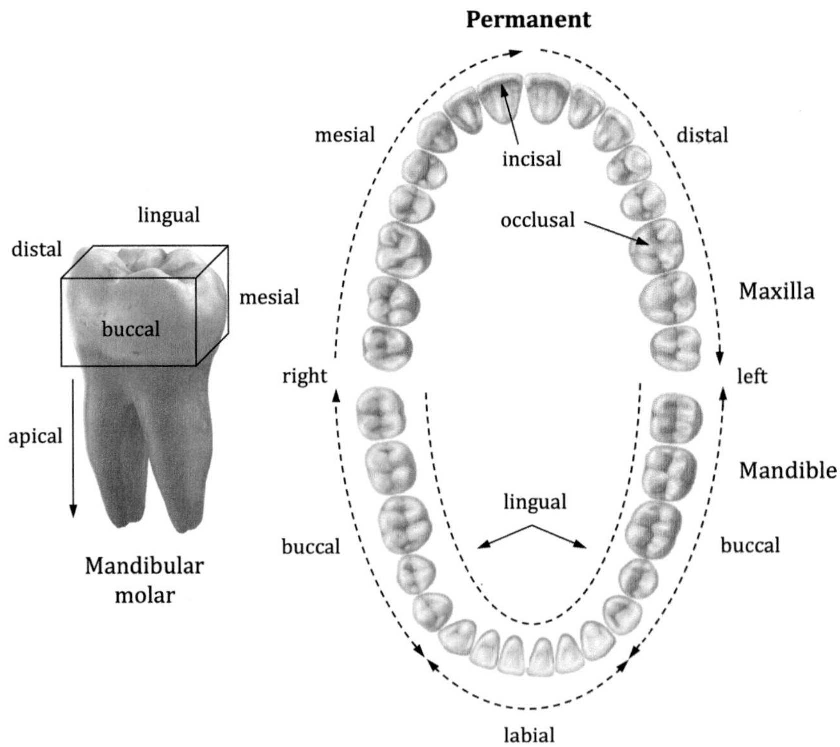

Figure 3.25 Directional terms associated with dentition are illustrated on permanent dentition.

Table 3.9 Terms Used to Describe Gross Morphology and Relative Position of Human Dentition

Gross Morphology	
Crown	Visible portion of the tooth; covered by enamel
Cusp	Elevation on occlusal surface of tooth; primarily found on premolars and molars
Root	Portion of tooth embedded in jaw covered by cementum
Enamel	Hard, white mineral portion of tooth; makes up majority of tooth crown
Dentin	Softer core tissue of crown and root of tooth; surrounds pulp chamber
Cementum	Hard tissue covering tooth root; provides attachment surface for periodontal ligament
Cementoenamel junction (CEJ)	Area where the enamel and cementum of a tooth meet; marks boundary between crown and root
Pulp chamber	Inner portion of crown containing blood and nerve supply
Root canal	Narrow end of pulp chamber at root end of tooth
Periodontal ligament (PDL)	Soft tissue ligament holding tooth in tooth socket
Apical foramen	Small opening at tip of tooth root that allows blood and nerve supply to pass into root canal and pulp chamber
Relative Position	
Occlusal	Chewing or grinding surface of premolars and molars
Incisal	Biting and cutting surface of incisors and canines
Labial	Surface of incisors and canines adjacent to the lips
Buccal	Surface of premolars and molars adjacent to the cheek
Lingual	Surface of tooth adjacent to the tongue
Mesial	Toward anterior of the mouth for premolars and molars or median plane for incisors and canines
Distal	Toward posterior of the mouth for premolars and molars or lateral side for incisors and canines
Apical	Toward tip of the tooth root

Dental Numbering Systems

Worldwide there are many different systems that dentists use to assign identity to each tooth. Here we present the two most widely used systems so that investigators can interpret which teeth are being discussed in a report. For example, if a forensic odontologist uses the dentition to make a positive identification, they will commonly discuss singular teeth used to make the match, and these teeth will be referred to according to a dental numbering system. In North America, the standard system used by dentists to number teeth is called the **Universal (National) system**. The alternate standard system accepted worldwide is called the **International (FDI, Fédération Dentaire Internationale) system**.

In the Universal system (Figure 3.26), dentists use a simple number or letter to identify each tooth. The

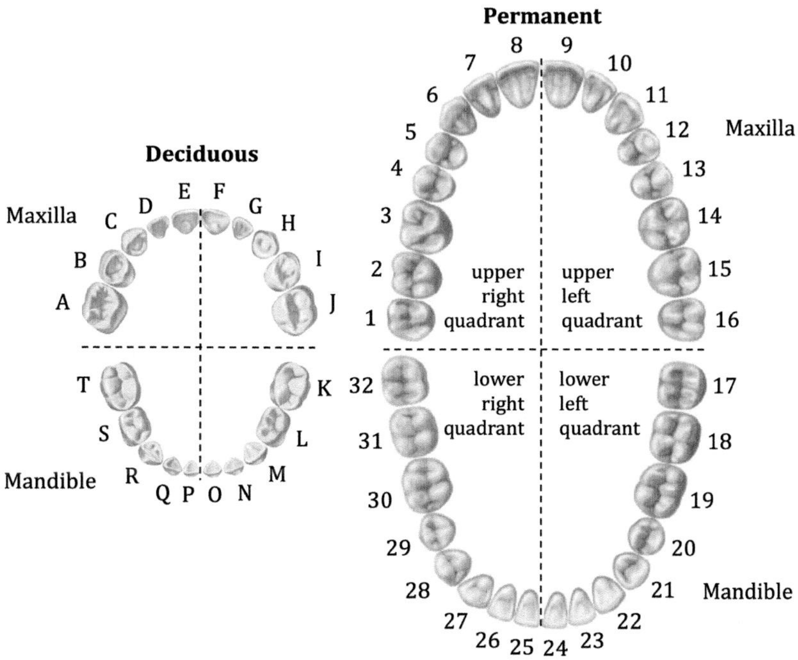

Figure 3.26 Comparison of deciduous (left) and permanent (right) dentition using the Universal (or National) numbering system.

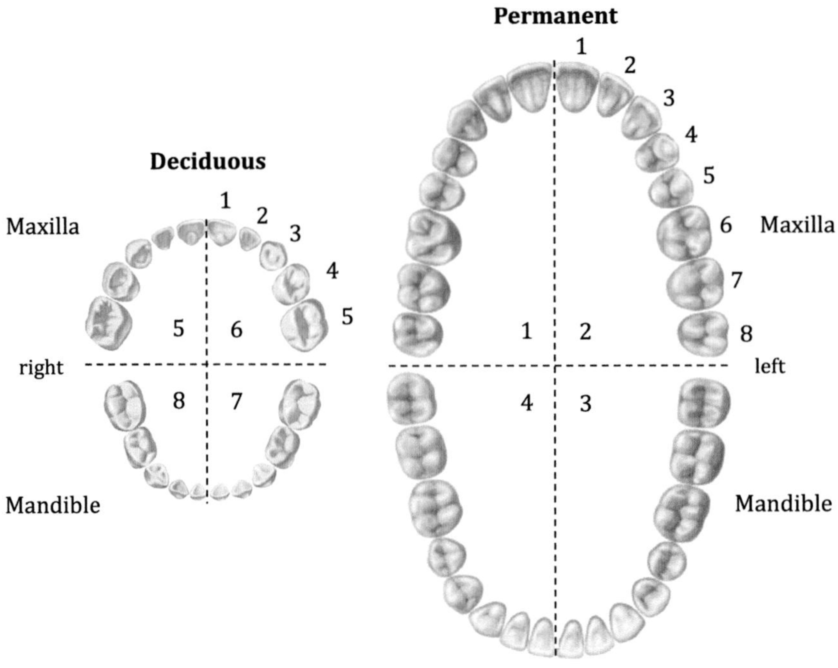

Figure 3.27 Comparison of deciduous (left) and permanent (right) dentition using the International (or FDI) numbering system.

deciduous dentition is identified using letter identifiers, A through T, starting with the upper right second deciduous molar labeled as 'A' and the lower right second molar labeled as 'T.' The permanent dentition is identified using numerical identifiers, 1 through 32, starting with the upper right third permanent molar labeled as '1,' and the lower right third molar labeled as '32.'

The International system (Figure 3.27) is a little more complicated, using a double-digit numbering system that considers both the quadrant and the specific tooth type. In some respects, it is easier to start the description of this system with the permanent teeth. When identifying a tooth using this system, the first number represents the quadrant where the tooth is located. Quadrants for the permanent teeth are numbered as follows:

- Upper right quadrant – 1
- Upper left quadrant – 2
- Lower left quadrant – 3
- Lower right quadrant – 4.

The second number in this system identifies specific tooth types, which are numbered as follows:

- first incisor – 1
- second incisor – 2
- canine – 3
- first premolar – 4
- second premolar – 5
- first molar – 6
- second molar – 7
- third molar – 8.

Thus, a tooth labeled as '36' would be a permanent lower left first molar, while a tooth labeled as 14 would represent a permanent upper right first premolar. The deciduous dentition follows a similar pattern, with the first number identifying the quadrant, and the second number identifying the specific tooth type. The quadrant designations for the deciduous teeth are a continuation of the permanent dentition, and are numbered as follows:

- Upper right quadrant – 5
- Upper left quadrant – 6
- Lower left quadrant – 7
- Lower right quadrant – 8.

Since there are only five teeth in each of the deciduous quadrants, they are numbered as:

- first incisor – 1
- second incisor – 2
- canine – 3
- first molar – 4
- second molar – 5.

Therefore, a tooth labeled '73' would represent a deciduous lower left canine, and one designated as '55' would be a deciduous upper right second molar.

Key Terms

anterior/posterior
appendicular skeleton
axial skeleton
buccal/labial/lingual
cranial skeleton
crown
deciduous teeth
diaphysis
epiphysis
flat bone
frontal plane
horizontal plane
infracranial skeleton
irregular bone
long bone
medial/lateral
median plane
mesial/distal
metaphysis
oblique plane
occlusal (incisal)/apical
palmar/plantar/dorsal
pelvic girdle
permanent teeth
proximal/distal
root
sesamoid bone
short bone
shoulder girdle
standard anatomical position
superior/inferior
tubular bone

REVIEW AND DISCUSSION QUESTIONS

1. You are asked to take notes on a group of bones located during a search, but you have no osteological training. How would you describe the bones (a–f) in Figure 3.28?
2. How many bones are there in the average adult human skeleton? How many bones are there in the average human skeleton at birth?
3. The upper limbs of the human skeleton are composed of which three paired long bones? The lower limbs are composed of which three paired long bones?
4. How many bones are there in the human hand and wrist? How many bones are there in the human foot and ankle?
5. What are the four types of teeth found in the human mouth? How many teeth are there in a complete set of permanent dentition? And in a complete set of deciduous dentition?
6. It is important to learn and use proper terms for anatomical and relative position in the human skeleton and dentition. Using the terms presented in the chapter, how would you describe the following when found in standard anatomical position?
   - Lumbar vertebrae in relation to the sacrum
   - Thoracic vertebrae in relation to the sternum
   - Metatarsals in relation to the foot phalanges
   - Radius in relation to the ulna
   - Sacrum in relation to the right femur
   - Lower deciduous incisors in relation to the lower deciduous molars
   - Lower left permanent 2nd molar in relation to a lower left permanent canine
7. When reading a report concerning remains recovered from a crime scene in Europe, you find that the dental anthropologist has used the International (FDI) system for recording dental information. You need to include this information when writing a report for a North American medical examiner office. Transcribe the following International (FDI) system identifications to Universal (National) system identifications and list the tooth each one represents:
   - 48
   - 63
   - 14
   - 21
   - 72

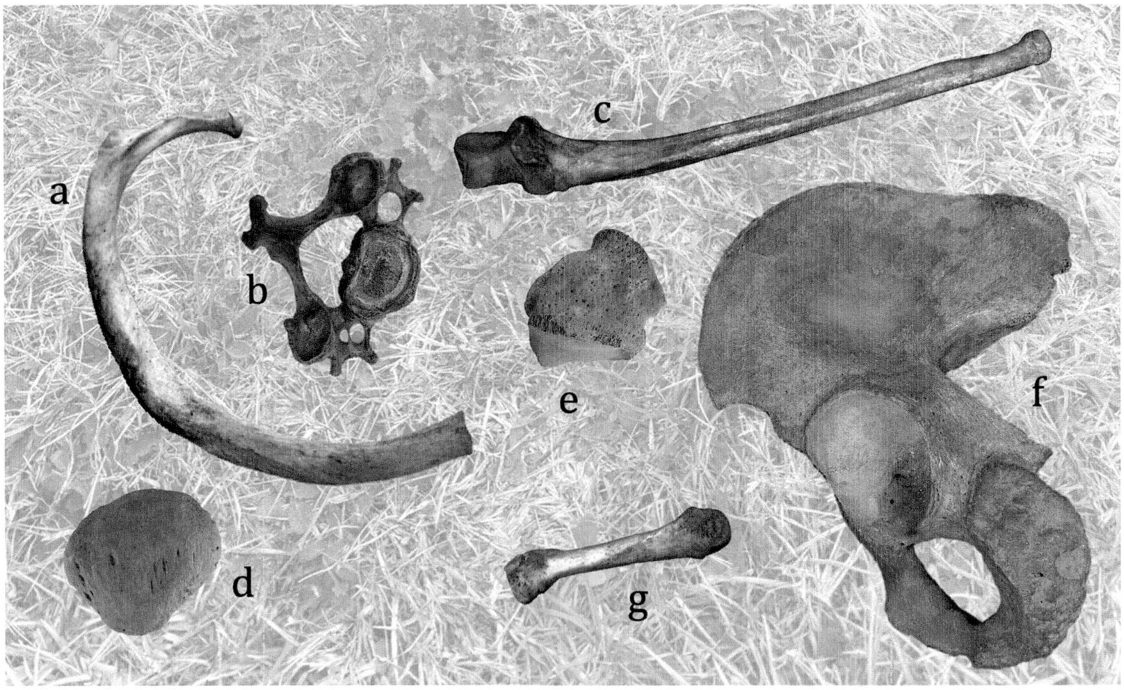

Figure 3.28 Describe the shapes of bones (a) through (f) using terminology presented in Chapter 3.

Suggested Readings

Bass, W.M. 2005. *Human Osteology: A Laboratory and Field Manual*, 5th ed., Columbia: Missouri Archaeological Society.

Matshes, E., Burbridge, B., Sher, B., Mohamed, A., Juurlink, B. 2005. *Human Osteology and Skeletal Radiology: An Atlas and Guide*. Boca Raton, FL: CRC Press. DOI:10.1201/9780203492147

Schaefer, M., Black, S., Scheuer, L. 2009. *Juvenile Osteology: A Laboratory and Field Manual*. San Diego, CA: Elsevier Academic Press. DOI:10.1016/B978-0-12–374635-1.X0001-X

White, T.D., Folkens, P.A. 2005. *The Human Bone Manual*. San Diego, CA: Elsevier Academic Press. DOI: 10.1016.C2009-0-00102-0

References

Baker, B.J., Dupras, T.L., Tocheri, M.W. 2005. *The Osteology of Infants and Children*. College Station: Texas A&M University Press.

Bass, W.M. 2005. *Human Osteology: A Laboratory and Field Manual*, 5th ed., Columbia: Missouri Archaeological Society.

Coqueugniot, H., Weaver, T. 2007. Brief communication: Infracranial maturation in the skeletal collection from Coimbra, Portugal: New aging standards for epiphyseal union. *American Journal of Physical Anthropology* 134(3):424–437. DOI:10.1002/ajpa.20683

Cunningham, C., Scheuer, L., Black, S. 2016. *Developmental Juvenile Osteology*, 2nd ed., San Diego, CA: Elsevier Academic Press.

Matshes, E., Burbridge, B., Sher, B., Mohamed, A., Juurlink, B. 2005. *Human Osteology and Skeletal Radiology: An Atlas and Guide*. Boca Raton, FL: CRC Press. DOI:10.1201/9780203492147

Scheuer, L., Black, S. 2004. *The Juvenile Skeleton*. San Diego, CA: Elsevier Academic Press.

Schaefer, M., Black, S., Scheuer, L. 2009. *Juvenile Osteology: A Laboratory and Field Manual*. San Diego, CA: Elsevier Academic Press. DOI:10.1016/B978-0-12–374635-1.X0001-X

Schwartz, J. 2006. *Skeleton Keys: An Introduction to Human Skeletal Morphology, Development, and Analysis*, 2nd ed., New York: Oxford University Press.

White, T.D., Black, M.T., Folkens, P.A. 2011. *Human Osteology*, 3rd ed., San Diego, CA: Elsevier Academic Press. DOI:10.1016/C2009-0-03221-8

White, T.D., Folkens, P.A. 2005. *The Human Bone Manual*. San Diego, CA: Elsevier Academic Press. DOI:10.1016.C2009-0-00102-0

Learning Objectives

- Define a forensic context.
- Summarize the different categories of non-forensic skeletal remains.
- Recognize how contextual information is used to determine forensic and non-forensic contexts.

Learning Connections

- Establish the interconnectedness of future chapters that outline proper archaeological methods, so contextual information is preserved and documented.
- Determine how contextual information is incorporated in the field when applying proper archaeological methods to distinguish between a forensic and non-forensic context.

Recognizing contextual information in the field when applying proper archaeological methods is essential when distinguishing between a forensic and non-forensic context. Every potential forensic scene with human bones is unique. When bones are discovered, regardless of context, it is not unusual for law enforcement or the medical examiner's/coroner's office to become involved. Upon arrival at a scene, one of the important tasks of the investigators, in conjunction with the forensic archaeologist, is to establish whether or not the scene is of forensic significance. There are many potential contexts in which human remains may be found, and the preservation and documentation of these contexts can significantly aid in determining jurisdiction of the scene and remains, as well as final disposition of the remains. It is very important during the initial assessment of the site, and subsequent processing and procurement of evidence, to note all the characteristics of the site. What is the site's location? Where are the remains? How are they positioned? What is the associated contextual evidence? All of these pieces of information can help investigators determine the context of the scene, and whether it is forensic, archaeological, historical, or other type of non-forensic context involving human remains.

Contextual information such as location, body position, associated artifacts, and taphonomic modifications to the remains will assist in determining whether the scene and remains are of recent and forensic significance. Forensic archaeologists might be involved in recovering buried remains that have been disturbed by a variety of processes (e.g., gravesite erosion or backhoe use during construction) that can destroy contextual evidence and make it difficult to determine forensic significance. In some instances, recovered remains may require full examination by a forensic anthropologist or medical examiner in the laboratory before forensic significance can be determined. No matter what the initial setting may present, the scene should be treated as being medicolegally significant until determined otherwise.

Even when not medicolegally significant, the forensic anthropologist often must examine the remains and produce a report to expedite the case to its final disposition. General categories used by forensic archaeologists and forensic anthropologists for non-forensic skeletal remains (Figure 4.1) include archaeological prehistoric,

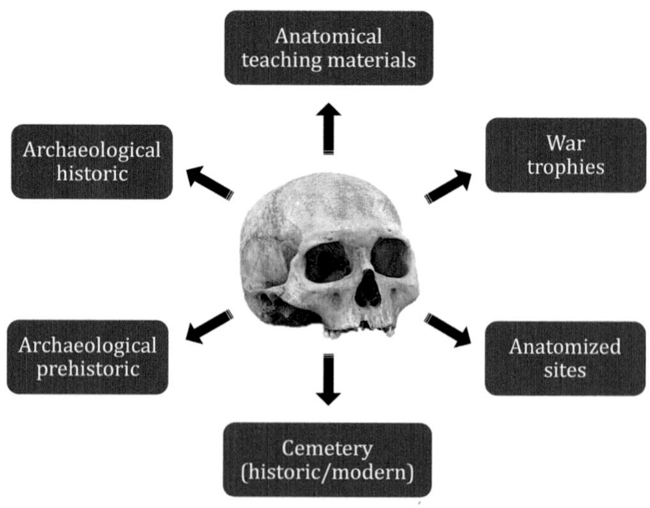

Figure 4.1 General categories of non-forensic skeletal remains used by forensic archaeologists and forensic anthropologists when determining forensic context.

DOI: 10.4324/9781315201658-4

archaeological historic, cemetery (historic or modern), war trophies, anatomized sites (i.e., body parts disposed of after dissection and surgical training), and anatomical specimens used as teaching material, which includes commercially prepared specimens and autopsied material (Bruwelheide et al., 2023; Pokines, 2018; Schultz, 2012). Before considering the scene context, the various types of deposition, body position, process of decomposition, and different types of non-forensic remains will be discussed.

DEFINING A FORENSIC CONTEXT AND JURISDICTION

Context can be referred to as an object's exact place in time and space and its association and relationship with other items. A forensic context differs from what we consider to be an archaeological context, with depth of time and intent of placement being the primary variables. When defining a **forensic context**, investigators must consider the interrelated circumstances in which something of medicolegal significance occurs or is found, such as the association and relationship between skeletal remains, personal possessions, location of burial site, environment, and sometimes population affinity.

Depending on the circumstances, a forensic context or setting can be officially determined by the local law enforcement, medical examiner, or coroner's office, and discovery of unmarked graves and out-of-context remains may fall under jurisdiction of the State Archaeologist if they are determined to be non-forensic and originate from an archaeological and/or cemetery context. For example, Section 872.05 of the Florida Statutes (2023) recognizes two common scenarios involving the discovery and reporting of unmarked graves to the State Archaeologist: the inadvertent discovery of remains that are reported to local enforcement, and discovery of remains by a professional archaeologist while involved in archaeological research. The district medical examiner is required to refer unmarked graves and associated remains that are not part of a crime scene and are greater than 75 years old to the State Archaeologist. According to Wheeler (2013), between 1987 and 2010, nearly 70% of cases indicating discovery of an unmarked grave received by the State Archaeologist in Florida were reported by either a medical examiner or professional archaeologist. In many instances, the forensic archaeologist and anthropologist are invaluable in determining the proper context of unmarked graves so they can be correctly referred to the jurisdiction of the State Archaeologist. It is also important to note that while jurisdiction of disturbed graves that are not part of a crime scene and greater than 75 years involves the State Archaeologist, the time period requiring notification of the State Archaeologist may be greater than 75 years for some states (e.g., in Massachusetts, where the law is 100 years). In addition, in the state of Florida, it is a third-degree felony if a grave with human remains or associated burial artifacts is willfully mutilated, destroyed, injured, or removed (Section 872.02 of the Florida Statutes, 2023). In this instance, law enforcement will be involved in an investigation, because the burial site becomes a crime scene.

INDICATIONS OF A FORENSIC CONTEXT

Location of Remains

Because of the nature of bodies disposed as the result of criminal activity, the location of forensic contexts can be extremely varied. Outside of surface-scatter scenes, primary graves are one of the most common types encountered in a forensic setting (Killam, 2004). Although multiple burials are occasionally found in a forensic context, the most common occurrence is in cases of human rights violations where many individuals will be deposited into one large grave (Haglund, 2002; Schmitt, 2002; Simmons, 2002; Skinner et al., 2002; Stover and Ryan, 2001).

What Are Surface Scatters?

Surface scatters include remains situated either completely on the ground surface or partly exposed, typically with little to no effort of concealment. In most cases, surface depositions retain some soft tissues (e.g., skin, hair, or nails), indicating a more recent disposal, as taphonomic processes will usually destroy soft tissues in a given period of time. Due to the likelihood that remains in surface depositions will be disturbed (Dirkmaat and Adovasio, 1997), they are usually recorded in relation to a primary or secondary scatter scene. A **primary surface scatter** is the location where the body was originally placed, which may include an abundance of skeletal remains still in relative anatomical position and the presence of a **cadaver decomposition island** (soil stained by decomposition fluids and often containing fly larvae casings) (Figure 4.2). A **secondary surface scatter** can result from many different types of taphonomic processes, such as movement of the remains by natural environmental forces, the perpetrator, or by animals. In most cases, secondary surface scatters are often marked by the presence of partial elements or smaller proportions of skeletal remains.

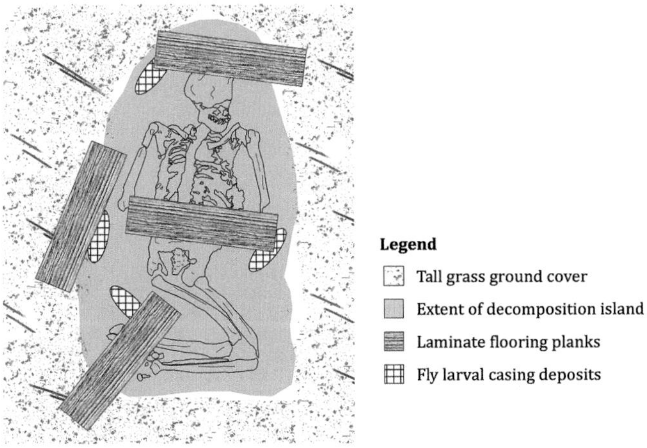

Figure 4.2 Primary surface scatter with scalp hair and some soft tissue still present; note cadaver decomposition island within tall grass ground cover and deposits of fly larval casings associated with decomposition process.

What Is a Burial versus a Grave?

In archaeology, **burial** is the process of deliberately placing a body in the ground and covering it, while a **grave** is a feature or location in the ground where a body has been buried (Sprague, 2005). Determining forensic significance of an unmarked grave becomes more difficult when postdepositional disturbances occur, as these disturbances may result in the loss of valuable contextual evidence. A **disturbed grave** is one that has been altered at some point after the initial burial but not necessarily moved to a new location (Hester et al., 2008). Burrowing animals, gravesite erosion, heavy equipment, or human activity are common causes of grave disturbance. In most cases, a few skeletal elements may be disarticulated or missing, while the remaining elements are preserved in their original anatomical position. Missing skeletal elements, either due to erosion or animal activity, may be recovered by tracing the routes of removal. Identification of human activity, such as someone returning to the burial site to remove or add specific items, may play a crucial role in later legal aspects of the investigation. The following descriptions of the main types of graves encountered can provide useful information when trying to determine context.

In a **primary grave**, the body remains in the location where it was originally deposited, and the context of burial has not been disturbed (i.e., all skeletal remains are in anatomical order) (Hester et al., 2008; Sprague, 2005). When excavated, the bones will appear to be articulated; that is, most of the bones will remain in correct anatomical position in relation to one another as if soft tissues were still present (Figure 4.3). Some settling of bones may occur, causing some misalignment, and rodents and other burrowing species can disturb remains (examples of a process called **bioturbation**). The presumption is that the relationships of the skeletal articulations have not been altered significantly since the decomposition of the soft tissue.

A **secondary grave** consists of skeletal elements that have been removed from their original location by human activity and deposited in another location, thus significantly disturbing the original grave context (Hester et al., 2008; Sprague, 2005). If sufficient time has elapsed to allow for complete decomposition of the soft tissue, the bones removed from the primary grave will not remain in an articulated or anatomical position unless purposefully placed in this fashion. Consequently, a secondary grave commonly consists of a jumbled arrangement of skeletal remains (Figure 4.4). In addition, it is not unusual for skeletal elements to be missing, as most secondary graves contain skulls and larger long and flat bones such as those found in the pelvis and limbs.

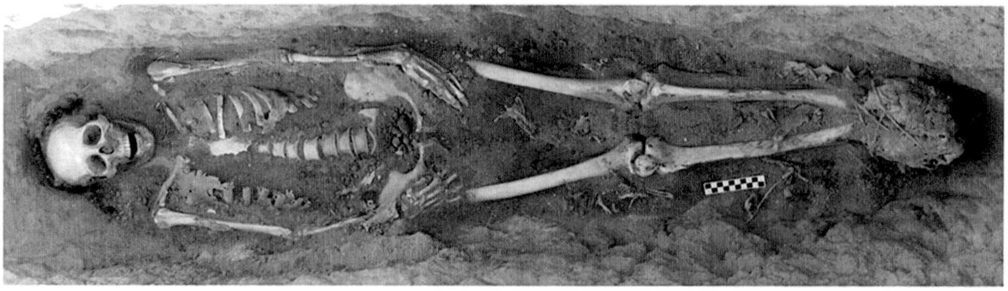

Figure 4.3 Primary grave found in an archaeological context in Egypt.

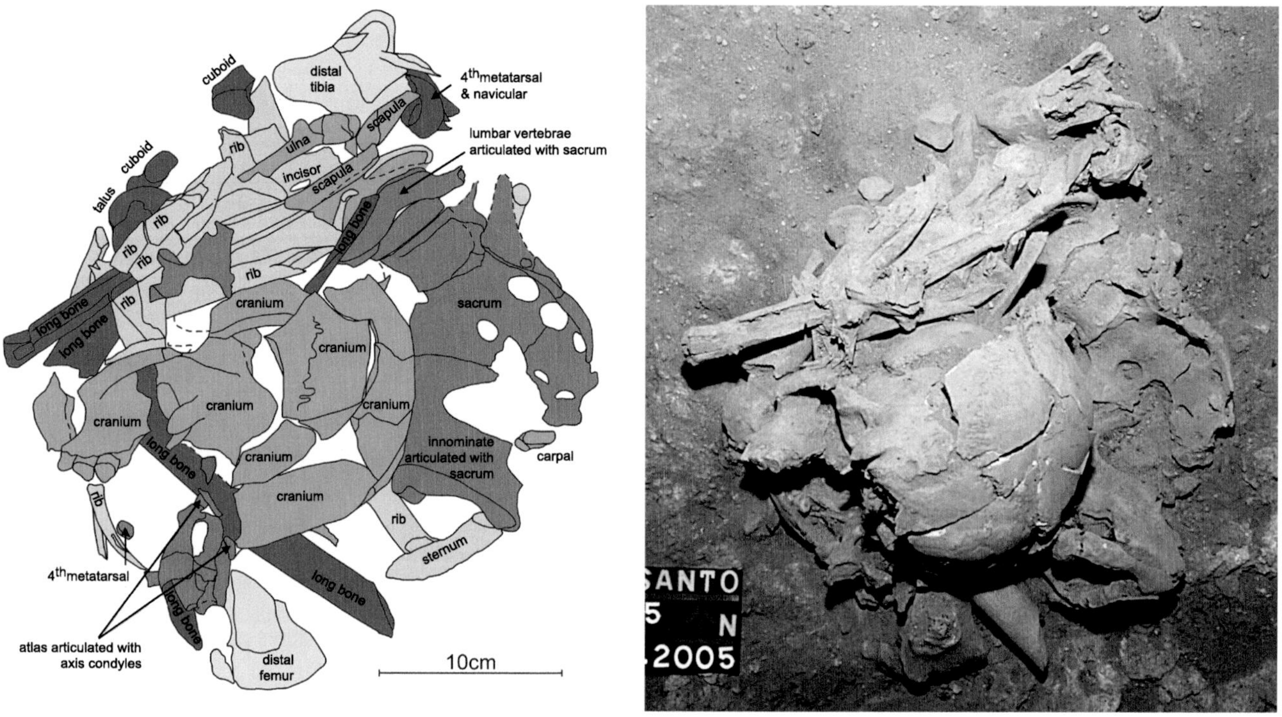

Figure 4.4 Secondary grave found in an archaeological context in Brazil *(Photograph by MAE-USP/Andre Strauss)*

Source: Figure 4.4 is adapted from Lapa do Santo – Sepultamento 15 – Foto de Campo da Exposição 7.jpg (https://commons.wikimedia.org/wiki/File:Lapa_do_Santo_-_Sepultamento_15_-_Foto_de_Campo_da_Exposi%C3%A7%C3%A3o_7.jpg) and Lapa do Santo – Sepulamento 15 – Croqui de escavacao de sepultamento vetorizado Exposição 07.jpg (https://commons.wikimedia.org/wiki/File:Lapa_do_Santo_-_Sepultamento_15_-_Croqui_de_escavacao_de_sepultamento_vetorizado_Exposicao_07.jpg) by MAE-USP/André Strauss, used under CC BY-SA 4.0 International/cropped image, labeled and shaded structures in drawing

A **multiple grave** contains the remains of two or more individuals buried in the same feature at different times (Sprague, 2005). A multiple grave contains the combination of primary articulated remains and disturbed remains due to the process of reentering an existing grave to deposit additional remains (Sprague, 2005). Although commonly confused in archaeological literature, a multiple grave can be differentiated from a mass grave based on the level of articulation. While a multiple grave consists of articulated and disarticulated remains, a **mass grave** consists of disarticulated remains or only articulated fragments (Sprague, 2005). However, when referring to mass graves in forensic contexts, including human rights investigations, remains are often articulated due to less bioturbation and other forms of taphonomic disturbance over a shorter period when compared to archaeological contexts.

What Are Cremains?

In a forensic investigation, cremated remains, or **cremains**, may originate as the result of criminal activity or due to normal cultural funerary practices through thermal damage (Figure 4.5). In the case where remains are subjected to thermal damage due to a perpetrator deliberately trying to dispose of a body through a fire context, the condition of the remains will most likely range from charred to incompletely burnt as it takes extremely high temperatures (above 1600°C/2912°F) to destroy bone (Iserson, 2001). Conversely, **cremation** is a process that uses intense

Figure 4.5 Fragmentary human bone cremains recovered from an archaeological context.

heat to reduce a body rapidly to ashes and small bone fragments (Iserson, 2001). Further, modern cremations from crematoriums are normally reduced to very small and non-distinguishable particles using current processing equipment, known as a **cremulator**, designed to reduce the volume of the cremains for **inurnment** (process of burying or entombing cremated remains in an urn) or scattering after the remains are removed from the cremation oven (Schultz et al., 2015).

In forensic contexts, bodies are often burned prior to burial or within the grave and may be classified as charred, partially cremated, incompletely cremated, or completely cremated depending on the intensity of the fire to which the body was exposed (Pope et al., 2022). It is almost impossible to destroy all evidence of a body completely through burning. The body may only be partially burnt, and areas of the body can be protected due to tissue shielding. After the burnt tissue is removed from the bone, it may be possible to ascertain biological and traumatic information about the decedent, in addition to conducting a DNA analysis. Completely burnt and fragmented human remains usually involve purposeful fragmentation and/or sustained high temperatures. When a forensic anthropologist analyzes completely fragmented burnt remains, it is usually still possible to determine that the remains are human. Based on the size of the fragments, it may be possible to discern identifiable biological features that allow the medical examiner to make positive identification of the decedents. Histological methods also can be applied, even on small fragments to potentially differentiate human from nonhuman bone fragments (Mulhern et al., 2012) and to provide an age-at-death estimation (Streeter, 2012) by evaluating the bone microstructure.

Position and Orientation of the Body

In a forensic context, the body may be found in any position, and in many cases, the position is directly related to the size of the grave. Position is best described through the relationship of legs, arms, and head to each other and to the trunk of the body (Hester et al., 2008; Sprague, 2005). The description should relate only to the body

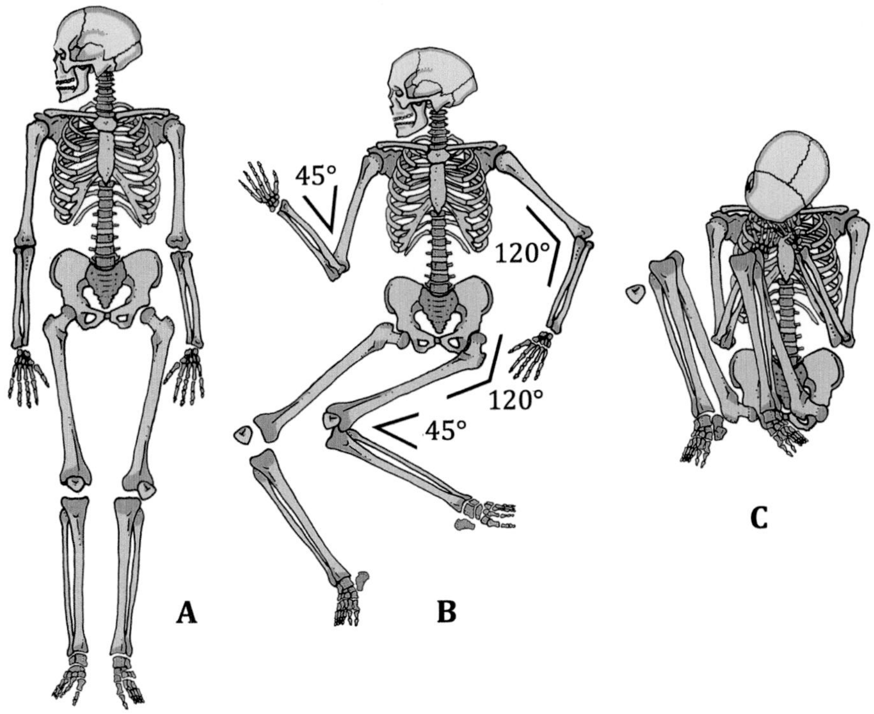

Figure 4.6 Examples of a primary burial placement in: (a) extended position, (b) semi-flexed position, and (c) flexed position. The semi-flexed position (b) shows an example of differing angles for the left and right arms and superior and inferior joints in the left leg.

with no reference to the grave, compass directions, or any other natural features. In other words, "it should be as if the body is floating in space" (Ubelaker, 1999:16). **Orientation** is the cardinal direction in which the head lies in relation to the body's central axis and should be recorded in directional terms using a compass, natural features, or human-made structures, but preferably in some combination of these reference points (Hester et al., 2008; Sprague, 2005). For example, an individual placed north of a nearby barn with their head to the east and feet to the west, would be oriented east-west outside the northern wall of the structure.

In a primary grave, the body may be in an extended, flexed, or semi-flexed position as shown in Figure 4.6. An extended position indicates that the legs are straight, forming a 180° angle with the trunk. The body can either be supine (i.e., lying on back) or prone (i.e., lying face down). An **extended position** is a common formal burial position, particularly with cemetery remains, where the hands are crossed over the chest or pelvis. A **flexed position** signifies that the body is at an angle of 90° or less between the legs and the trunk, while a **semi-flexed position** refers to burials in which the angle of the legs is between 90° and 180° from the trunk. In forensic contexts, bodies are usually placed within a hole that is dug quickly and may not be large enough to place the body neatly within the grave. As a result, bodies are found in many different positions with limbs situated in directions consistent with tossing or rolling a body rather than formally positioning a body prior to filling in the grave.

It is extremely important to note how the arms and legs are positioned in relation to the rest of the body. For instance, arm and hand bones found to be positioned behind the body might indicate that the individual's hands had been bound behind the back when placed in the grave, even though traces of a ligature may have long since disintegrated. Noting these details in positioning might assist in determining the context of the burial. The position of the body may also provide indications of postmortem state when it was placed in the grave. If the body was in full rigor (i.e., temporary stiffness of muscles after death), it is unlikely that the individual would be placed in a grave in a tightly flexed position. A tightly flexed position would indicate that the individual was placed in the grave prior to the onset of full rigor mortis (stiffening of the muscles after death) or after rigor mortis had dissipated. The onset and length of time that rigor mortis lasts are dependent on multiple variables (such as age, sex, physical condition, and musculature) but is particularly influenced by the ambient temperature (Adams, 2009; Clark et al., 1997).

Preservation of the Remains

When determining the context of human remains, it is important to consider preservation and taphonomic conditions. The state of decomposition or preservation can contribute significant information regarding the **postmortem interval (PMI)**. In many cases, the presence of soft tissue such as remnants of desiccated skin, ligaments, and tendons, as well as costal cartilage, hyaline cartilage on joint surfaces, intervertebral discs, tracheal rings, and thyroid cartilage are consistent with a short PMI and therefore indicate a forensic context. In the absence of soft tissue structures, other evidence such as the smell of decomposition or a yellowish-hue and greasy texture due to the retention of fats, fluid, and collagen may also indicate a short PMI. However, retention of soft tissue through mummification or build-up and retention of fats during decomposition can preserve soft tissue for significant periods of time in the right environment (Clark et al., 1997; Hester et al., 2008). As a result, the presence of soft tissue by itself cannot be used as an indicator of forensic context. At the same time, preservation of soft tissue remnants due to the process of embalming would need to be excluded when determining a forensic context. For these reasons, it is useful to have some background on the process of decomposition.

What Is the State of Preservation?

Decomposition is the process of decay, and it is commonly scored as a four- or five-stage process in forensic anthropology literature, with slight variation between the stages. Additionally, a quantitative framework for estimating **time since death (TSD)** in human cadavers has also been developed for forensic anthropology because of the association between temperature and decomposition. This method predicts the number of accumulated degree days, which account for time and temperature, using a total body score (TBS) that is generated by summing decomposition of three major areas of the body (head, trunk, and limbs) to provide an estimate of TSD (Megyesi et al., 2005; Moffatt et al., 2016).

A popular five-stage protocol for scoring decomposition and associated gross changes has been provided by Marks et al. (2009): fresh, discoloration, bloat, skeletonization, and skeletal decay. Refer to Clark et al. (1997), Emmons et al. (2022), Gunn (2019), and Marks et al. (2009) for detailed descriptions of decomposition processes. While an extensive description of decomposition is beyond the scope of this chapter, a brief overview will be provided, because it is beneficial to understand basic characteristics of decomposition stages when describing the remains in a field report and when reading forensic pathology and anthropology reports (Table 4.1). Stage 1 is the Fresh stage occurring immediately after death and includes **algor mortis** (cooling of the body), **livor mortis** (gravitational pooling of the blood), and **rigor mortis** (stiffening of muscles in the limbs) (Marks et al., 2009). Stage 2 is Discoloration, which includes **marbling** (greenish-blue discoloration of blood vessels visible through the skin) of the body and **skin slippage** (separation of skin layers), while Stage 3 is Bloat, marked by distention of the body and leaching of body fluids (Marks

Table 4.1 General Characteristics in Five-Stages of Decomposition following Marks et al. (2009)

Stage 1: Fresh
- Presence of algor mortis (cooling of the body), livor mortis (gravitational pooling of the blood), and rigor mortis (stiffening of muscles in the limbs)

Stage 2: Discoloration
- Marbling (greenish-blue discoloration of blood vessels visible through the skin), especially at the abdomen
- Skin slippage (separation of skin layers)

Stage 3: Bloat
- Distention of the body due to production and accumulation of gases
- Leaching of body fluids

Stage 4: Skeletonization
- Large-scale purging of body fluids and desiccation
- Exposure of skeletal elements

Stage 5: Skeletal Decay
- Complete loss of residual soft tissues and weathering of bone surface
- Disarticulation of bones

et al., 2009). **Bloating** is the result of the production and accumulation of gases due to the uncontrolled growth of endogenous bacteria and fungi in the body (Clark et al., 1997). Bloating is a recognizable byproduct of decomposition and occurs more slowly or is delayed in colder climates. During progression to Stage 4, depending on the environmental conditions, the skin can desiccate and mummify, while internal organs and muscle tissue will still decompose. Furthermore, adipocere development may occur when bodies are deposited in moist environments or submersed in water (Gunn, 2019). However, in a review of the literature, Ubelaker and Zarenko (2011) note that adipocere can occur in dry environments, and moisture can be from the body or environment (Clark et al., 1997). **Adipocere** can be defined as a soap-like decomposition product that forms from adipose tissue with a grayish-white coloration that varies in consistency from crumbly to paste-like (Forbes et al., 2004). While adipocere is noted on remains from forensic contexts, adipocere can be preserved for extended periods and persist in cemetery graves.

What Is Taphonomy?

When the term **taphonomy** is used in forensic archaeology, it is in reference to the postmortem period and the changes or modifications that occur to bodies and skeletal remains. Taphonomic agents can include scavengers, bacteria, chemicals, geological processes, humans, plants, and moving water (Haglund and Sorg, 1997; Pokines et al., 2022). A solid understanding and detailed documentation of these processes may help to determine the context of the remains and understand how postdepositional process may have altered the scene and remains. Refer to Chapter 5 for a more comprehensive discussion concerning common taphonomic processes encountered in forensic archaeology.

Associated Artifacts and Evidence

Associated artifacts are those that have some direct association with the body, and they may vary significantly in type and number. Evidence of modern surgical procedures, dental work, clothing, and other personal possessions can assist in determining the forensic context of the remains. Items related to the potential crime, or the process of burial, may also be present as associated artifacts or as indirect evidence, providing indications of a forensic context. These can include weapons, disposal artifacts (e.g., digging tools, tarps), and natural (e.g., tree limbs) or cultural (e.g., concrete blocks) materials used to cover the remains.

Are Personal Belongings or Cultural Materials Associated with the Remains?

Personal belongings or cultural materials can help to give some context to the skeletal remains. Personal belongings would be those items associated with an individual on a regular basis (Figure 4.7). These can include items, such as clothing, eyeglasses, wallets, and jewelry, and may belong to either the suspect or the victim. Styles and brands of clothing (e.g., Adidas), dates found on tags or on other associated artifacts (e.g., tool patents or years on coins), or certain kinds of materials (e.g., PVC plastic) could be used to indicate a forensic context simply by the period of time that these items have been in production. Other cultural items, such as a coffin, might indicate a modern or historic context, but may also signify that the remains are not of a forensic nature. However, it is always wise to remember that over time, anything, and everything has been used to conceal a body. Even though a style of clothing or a coffin may indicate that the remains of an individual are not of forensic significance, one can never be sure and should treat each case as if it were a forensic context.

Figure 4.7 Personal belongings recovered from remains recovered from an unmarked cemetery plot thought to be unused. The style of glasses, wallet, wedding ring, and lighter patent were all dated to the 1950s.

Are There Medical, Dental, or Cultural Modifications to the Body?

Modifications to the body or skeleton that were made during life can also help to indicate context. Skin or dental tattoos, prosthetic devices (e.g., artificial joints or limbs, and glass eyes), surgical implants (e.g., pacemakers), birth control devices (e.g., IUDs), dental work (e.g., restorations, crowns, false teeth, and bridges), skeletal alterations (e.g., cultural cranial or foot modification), and other medical procedures are all modifications that can be used to indicate cultural affiliation and time period of that individual (Figures 4.8 and 4.9).

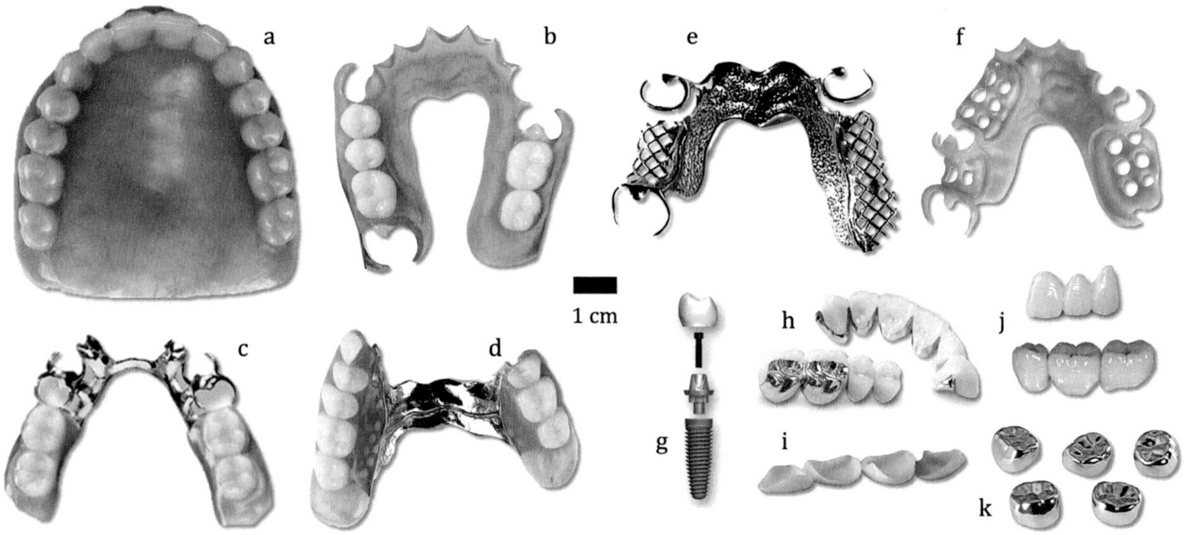

Figure 4.8 Examples of dental prosthetics: (a) full acrylic denture plate, (b) partial flexible dental plate, (c) partial wire bridge, (d) partial plate bridge, (e) metal bridge plate, (f) resin bridge plate, (g) dental implant with crown, stem, abutment, and screw, (h) fused porcelain teeth on gold armature, (i) porcelain dental veneers, (j) fused porcelain teeth, and (k) base metal crowns.

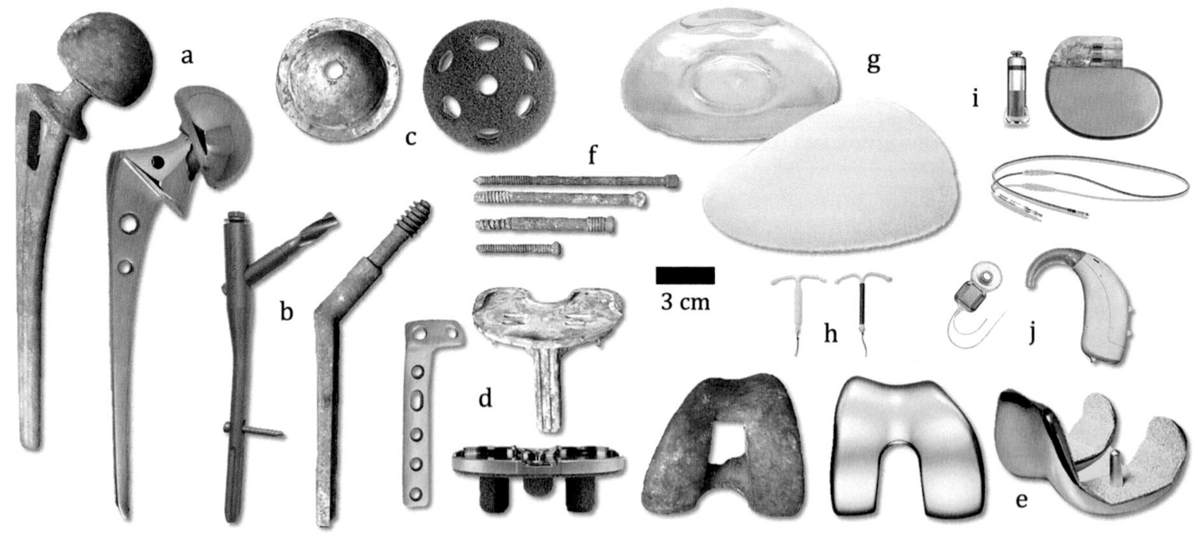

Figure 4.9 Examples of surgical and medical prosthetics: (a) hip joint replacement implants, (b) proximal femoral fracture nails, (c) acetabular cup implants, (d) proximal tibia baseplates and tibia support plate, (e) femoral component of knee replacements, (f) internal fixation (i.e., fracture) screws, (g) silicone and saline breast implants, (h) intrauterine devices, (i) leadless and wired pacemakers with pacemaker wire, and (j) cochlear implant and hearing aid.

COMMON NON-FORENSIC CONTEXTS

Archaeological Prehistoric Context

Archaeology is the study of past human societies through the recovery and analysis of material culture, physical remains, and evidence of environmental interactions that they have left behind. Common criteria that can indicate an archaeological prehistoric context include proximity of burial sites to known prehistoric features (e.g., middens, cairns), the position of the skeleton, and associated artifacts. The placement of remains across the landscape in prehistoric contexts usually follows some kind of pattern, such as those seen in cemeteries or burial grounds, or social arrangement, for instance using natural caves or crevasses for disposal (Ucko, 1969). Although primary graves are common, prehistoric skeletons may also be found in secondary, multiple, and mass graves. Skeletons from primary graves in prehistoric contexts are commonly found in a flexed or semi-flexed position (Roberts, 2009; Ubelaker, 1999), although this is highly dependent on the culture and time being investigated. In most instances, grouped prehistoric graves also follow patterns of orientation, possibly toward a specific feature or event such as a body of water or the rising of the sun (Ucko, 1969).

Associated burial artifacts can include lithics (e.g., chipped stone tools and debitage) as well as ceramic vessels and sherds. Skeletal and dental alterations may also be present, such as artificial cranial modifications, dental inlays, or filing of teeth. These practices are usually culture-specific and normally indicate an archaeological context. Taphonomic modifications of prehistoric skeletons include bones that are lighter in weight, and the overall quality of the bone surface may be eroded, cracked, and chalky rather than smooth and greasy in texture. Prehistoric bones generally display a uniform staining ranging from light tan to darker colors, dependent on the type of soil and moisture leaching from the surrounding area. In some cases, however, it must also be noted that cultural treatment of the body during funerary preparation may lead to purposeful preservation of soft tissues. In this case, all contextual information must be weighed together to form an opinion of context.

Archaeological Historic and Cemetery Contexts

Identification of skeletal remains belonging to the historic period is easily performed if skeletal remains can be analyzed ***in situ*** (in their original, undisturbed location or position). Historic remains are found in a variety of marked and unmarked locations including pioneer graves, small family cemeteries, small community cemeteries, graves within the documented boundaries of an existing cemetery, and graves in proximity to an existing cemetery. In cemetery burials, individuals are usually placed in an extended position with their hands at the side or placed over the chest or abdomen. It should be noted, however, that certain cultural customs might influence body position and orientation. For example, many burials of enslaved persons from the middle 1700s to late 1800s are positioned facing a body of water in a west-east orientation to ensure that the soul of the deceased will follow the water to the seas and eventually return to Africa (Handler, 1994).

Historic period burials with associated items are also very telling (Pokines and Baker, 2022; Schultz et al., 2003). These can include remnants of coffin wood, coffin hardware and adornment, evidence of embalming, adhered fabric from the coffin lining or pillow, period jewelry or clothing artifacts (e.g., buttons, textiles, clasps, and pins) that are either adhered to the remains or are in direct association. As mentioned above, clothing, clothing artifacts (e.g., buttons), and personal items are very useful in estimating a general time frame, as most textiles and fashions can be dated to different time periods.

Historic period and/or cemetery remains that are not *in situ* may be identified through several characteristics. Many taphonomic indicators will also help to determine if remains are from an historical cemetery (Berryman et al., 1997; Pokines and Baker, 2022; Pokines et al., 2016; Schultz, 2012; Schultz et al., 2003), and these should be incorporated into any osteological analysis. For example, several taphonomic changes associated with burial in a casket involving soil staining and erosion of bone are consistent with historic period skeletal remains. Evidence of historic period dental work and evidence of autopsy and preparation for example, cut ribs and medial clavicles, in addition to removing the upper portion of the cranial vault of the skull, are common locations that would indicate that remains had previously been autopsied (Schultz, 2003, 2012). In addition, cultural modifications made to the body during funerary preparations for an open casket (e.g., trocar plugs, eye caps, mouth former, calvaria clamps, and remnants of injectors), as well as mummified tissues due to embalming would indicate a historic and/or cemetery context (Berryman et al., 1997; Schultz, 2012; Schultz et al., 2003).

Anatomical and Commercially Prepared Use of Human Skeletal Remains

Discarded human bones and fragments originating from anatomy laboratories and commercially prepared teaching specimens will have specific modifications related to preparation and use of the material for instructional purposes. For example, wires for holding elements together, drill holes or cuts, markings to demonstrate muscle attachments, glued teeth, writing on the bones, and a dark patina due to handling are all modifications that indicate remains used in teaching anatomy (Schultz, 2012; Yucha et al., 2022) (Figures 4.10 and 4.11). Remains discarded

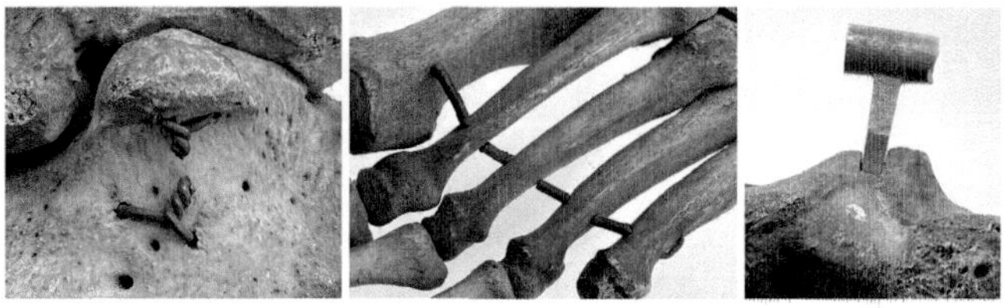

Figure 4.10 Examples of wires, drill holes, springs, and hinge armatures used in a commercially prepared teaching skeleton.

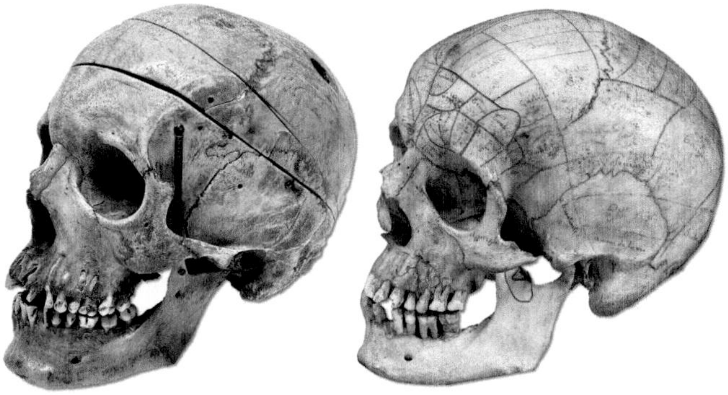

Figure 4.11 Example of anatomically prepared skull (left) originally obtained from autopsy and used in teaching, and a commercially prepared skull (right) with markings used in pseudoscientific practice of phrenology.

from historic medical schools and hospitals will also be very specific in their nature (refer to Case Study #4). These remains will usually possess cut marks, and the elements discarded will most likely be associated with amputated limbs. One of the best indicators of the context of these remains will be historic documentation of building locations such as a hospital or university.

Ritual Use of Human Skeletal Remains

It is also important to consider that there may be non-forensic contexts where skeletal remains are procured for specific uses, such as a scene in which skeletal remains have been used in ritual ceremonies and the remains are not forensic in nature (e.g., Schultz et al., 2020; Winburn et al., 2017; Yucha et al., 2022). In these instances, the location, position, orientation, preservation, and other taphonomic modifications, and associated evidence will be very important when determining forensic or non-forensic remains. Remains associated with rituals are usually found in telling locations (e.g., on an altar, associated with a cauldron, or in a charm fetish), and/or will also be associated with very specific items that are indicative of ritual use. For example, while not being exclusive to Florida, human remains associated with a ritual context that are brought to Florida medical examiner's offices are commonly associated with Palo (e.g., Schultz et al., 2020; Wetli and Martinez, 1983; Winburn et al., 2017).

Palo is an Afro-Caribbean syncretic (blending of two or more belief systems) religion, and while Palo is like Santeria, only Palo routinely incorporates human skeletal remains in its rituals (Wetli and Martinez, 1983). The Palo ritual involving human skeletal remains is associated with a cauldron, known as a ***nganga***, that contains various items to direct the intentions of the spirit *nganga*, including a skull or cranium at the center of the cauldron with tibiae, ribs, and finger and toe bones (Canizares, 2002). While the construction of the *nganga* is described as including skeletal remains looted from a cemetery (Canizares, 2002), it is also common to find commercially prepared bones for teaching purposes associated with Palo rituals (Schultz et al., 2020; Wetli and Martinez, 1983; Winburn et al., 2017). In rare instances, owners of the skeletal remains have left the tags on the crania/skulls, and retained the receipts, to document that the commercially prepared teaching material was purchased legally over the internet (Schultz et al., 2020). While the sacred space that contains the *nganga* is usually found in a backyard shed, garage, or business warehouse (Kail, 2008; Schultz et al., 2020; Winburn et al., 2017), *nganga* are occasionally discarded outdoors (Schultz et al., 2020; Wetli and Martinez, 1983; Winburn et al., 2017), at times buried or next to bodies of water and may involve a forensic archaeologist or anthropologist during recovery of the remains.

CASE STUDY #2: 'NOT A BURIAL' FORENSIC SITES

The term "forensic site" at times has been used synonymously with "burial," but in practice, this may be largely incorrect. Forensic anthropologists respond to and collect remains from many kinds of scenes. In some cases, sediments and other materials containing remains from scenes are even collected in the field then transported to the laboratory for additional processing, including wet screening to recover delicate remains (Bunch, 2010). One author, James T. Pokines, tabulated the types of outdoor scenes responded to (n = 75) while employed at the Office of the Chief Medical Examiner (OCME), Massachusetts (Table 4.2). These cases were tabulated from January 2012 through May 2024 and included every type of field response where a report needed to be generated. Cases where no searching or recovery turned out to be needed, such as where suspected human remains were instead nonhuman, or in one case what turned out to be a plastic skull, were not included in the sample. Indoor cases or those involving the interior of burned automobiles were also not included.

Surface

The most numerous case type (n = 40; 53.3%) was surface (usually referred to as terrestrial) remains (Table 4.2). In Massachusetts, nearly all of these cases involved forests or otherwise wooded areas, although wetlands and urban or suburban scenes did occur. These cases can involve large amounts of bone dispersal (refer to Chapter 5) and require intensive searching methods. Mapping efforts also must cover a wider area, and a variety of techniques will be relevant (refer to Chapter 8). The skeletal remains also may have taken on staining from their environment (Pokines, 2016; Pollock et al., 2018; Schultz and Dupras, 2022) that makes them less visible to searchers (refer to Chapter 5). All forensic archaeological training therefore should include a heavy component of surface recoveries, as these may outnumber burials in a given caseload.

Table 4.2 Types of Forensic Scenes Involving Forensic Anthropological Search at the Office of the Chief Medical Examiner (OCME), Massachusetts, 2012 through May 2024

Type	n =	%
Surface	40	53.3
Burial	23	30.7
Burial and surface	1	1.3
Exhumation	7	9.3
Freshwater	2	2.7
Mausoleum	2	2.7
Total	**75**	**100%**

Burial

Burials of all configurations (n = 23; 30.7%) were the next most common type (Table 4.2). These included a large variety among burial contexts. Temporally, variation included recent remains, where an intact and only slightly decomposed body was recovered, and a large-scale excavation of a pit feature used to dispose of anatomized remains (those elements used for anatomical and surgical training) and related medical and laboratory artifacts suspected to date back to as early as the 1850s (currently under analysis) (Figure 4.12). Other cases were also of historical origin, as with the partial disturbance of an unmarked extension of a known cemetery. Other burial types included modern homicides where the remains had enough time to skeletonize, one case of a trophy skull from WWII (Yucha et al., 2022) being buried in a backyard, a body likely buried by natural river action, and test pits in reported modern burial locations that yielded no finds.

Excavation in many cases proceeded in conjunction with a field representative from the Massachusetts Historical Commission (MHC), i.e., the state historical preservation office as they are often termed. This situation occurs when it is unclear under whose temporal jurisdiction a case lies. In Massachusetts, the cutoff point is 100 years, with younger cases being the jurisdiction of the OCME. Multiple scenes involved Native American burials exposed accidentally through construction activities or naturally through erosion. The preferred option in these cases, in conjunction with the Massachusetts Commission on Indian Affairs and the given landowner, is to leave the remains in place and rebury any disturbed bones, provided that the burial can be sealed off from

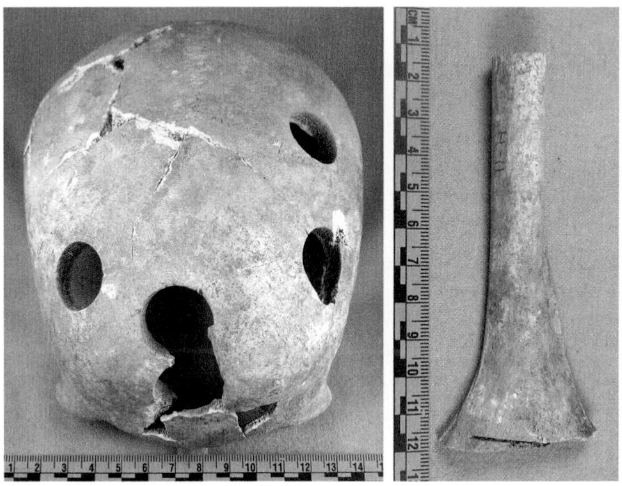

Figure 4.12 Anatomized remains of a skull (left) and humerus (right) recovered with related medical and laboratory artifacts suspected to date back to as early as the 1850s.

further disturbance. More recent cemeteries also have required excavation, in cases where unmarked burials were disturbed, cemetery fill had been dumped in a different location, and known cemeteries had been moved in the past, but some graves had been left behind.

One additional case (1.3%) was classified as both burial and surface since a shallow burial had been disturbed by heavy machinery and spread over a wide area in a construction yard. This situation necessitated excavation of the burial and visual survey over a wide area to collect the dispersed remains. There proved to be no overlap in the bones, and the articulation and pair-matching was consistent with all of them being from the same individual.

Exhumations

Exhumations (the legal recovery of remains from their official place of burial, often to identify unknown remains, recover a DNA sample from identified remains to identify a different set of unknown remains, or for further analysis, including trauma) made up 9.3% (n = 7) of the total OCME sample (Table 4.2). James T. Pokines was the attending anthropologist at a further seven U.S. military exhumations while he was employed at the Central Identification Laboratory in Oahu, Hawaii. Of note, exhumations in general may be on the increase in many jurisdictions due to changes in DNA technology and database analysis, making it possible to identify remains from cold cases dating back decades. The role of the forensic anthropologist in these cases is normally not the excavation itself, as these are typically carried out by the cemetery personnel using heavy machinery, followed by shoveling. A forensic anthropologist may perform some excavation in cases where the coffin has degraded or otherwise been compromised, and there is the possibility of losing some of its contents. The forensic anthropologist also may wish to gather data on field conditions (e.g., burial depth, presence of a vault, type of coffin, condition of the coffin, height of the water table, soil characteristics) to inform expectations about what possible conditions may be encountered with future exhumed remains. It also may be that person's role to perform the actual removal of the remains from the coffin, whether in the field or back in the laboratory if the entire coffin is being transported. The forensic anthropologist also may be charged with only the removal of bone or tooth specimens for DNA analysis in cases where the rest of the remains are to be immediately reburied. Members of law enforcement are typically quite grateful for assistance in the latter situations, as the jurisdiction of the case may no longer lie with the medical examiner's office, and the forensic anthropologist is performing this service out of professional courtesy.

Cases where exhumations require some direct forensic anthropological assistance are likely due to coffin or other container degradation in the years or decades since interment. In some cases of unidentified remains, burial may not have included a formal coffin at all and may consist of as little as a body bag inside a cardboard box. The latter of these will not survive multiple years of burial and may only persist as small remnants or soil stains indicating its former presence. Even well-protected coffins may let in water, which also can pool in vaults that have no drainage outlet. Soft tissue remains, even after decades, may be largely composed of adipocere in cases where burial depth was at or near the water line. In short, it has been difficult to predict the condition of coffins and/or remains prior to their exhumation, and the recovery team should be prepared for a variety of situations. Concrete vault lids require heavy machinery to lift, and this may be accomplished by the same backhoe that did the excavating, using suspended chains. Equipment to open corroded coffin seals should be on hand, and these may need to be cordless due to the distances from electrical supplies. The cemetery personnel may or may not have such equipment available. At a minimum, pry-bars may be needed. If the coffin or other container has degraded heavily, the forensic anthropologist may have to excavate the loose deposits at the bottom of the burial, so complete excavation equipment (including screens) should be on hand. The same processes that degraded the coffin may have degraded the remains (Pokines and Baker, 2022a), so the skeleton may be in a delicate state.

In some cases, burial records are still obtainable from the cemetery, including which funeral home was involved, what type of coffin or other container was used, and if a concrete vault was used. This information may give the recovery team useful information regarding what equipment may be necessary and a range of possible conditions for the remains, although preparations should be made for anything from a complete body that can be put into a body bag to fully skeletonized bones that require individual handling. Some coffins also may be in such poor condition that they cannot be lifted out of the burial with heavy equipment, so it may be necessary to excavate additional space next to the coffin so that the forensic anthropologist can process the scene while working at the burial depth. This can include, in one case example, excavating deeper than a corroded metal coffin so that the lid could be pried back, one long side cut vertically at both ends, and the long side bent downward so that the contents (still in their mostly intact original but not fully cohesive body bag) could be slid down into a new body bag opened on top of a body board. The backhoe chains were then attached to the body board, and the entire mass could be lifted onto the ground surface with no loss of remains.

In author James T. Pokines' experience, obtaining court orders to exhume remains (essentially a search warrant conveying the power to remove the body or portions of it from the grave) has not been a rapid process and is initiated by law enforcement investigating a cold case. Generally, weeks may be available for planning, scheduling of personnel, and accommodating changes in weather.

Large amounts of time therefore have been available to obtain all recovery equipment needed, most of which should overlap with the equipment recommended for more typical field recoveries (refer to Chapter 2).

Other Types

Two cases (2.7%) consisted of searches for skeletonized remains in freshwater, which in both cases involved a submerged automobile. Police divers did the actual recoveries, and only one of the cases had remains and associated artifacts. The author Pokines provided field identification of the bones on shore. Two cases (2.7%) involved recoveries inside mausoleums that had been vandalized to provide bones for Palo ritual use (Yucha et al., 2022). The recoveries involved identifying the skeletal elements left behind inside the mausoleum chambers or spread about so that the removed remains could be matched to their source. DNA samples also were obtained. The methods included the simple collection of remains and recording their burial chamber provenience from removed coffins to screening of remains where coffins at the ground level had remained so wet over time that the wood had broken down into humus. Recovery also included climbing inside the damaged coffin chambers, there being no other way to proceed without significant additional demolition of the stonework (Figure 4.13). No actual excavation therefore was involved, as all remains were above-ground. Jurisdiction in these cases lie with the local police department, since, as identified and interred individuals, they were no longer under the jurisdiction of the OCME. In this case, the forensic anthropologist assisted the local police department with their investigations, again as a professional courtesy.

Figure 4.13 Vandalized mausoleum vault encountered during a forensic case in Massachusetts where the remains had to be examined by crawling inside. *(Image used with permission)*

CASE STUDY #3: DOG DAYS

In July of 2006, investigators received information that there may have been a possible unattended death and burial of a child. The supposed burial site was located on a wooded residential property, and the informants indicated that the grave had been marked with a wooden cross. Investigators arrived to find a small grave that had been marked with a wooden cross (Figure 4.14), which had a piece of purple, black, and white material draped around it. There were also two sets of artificial flowers on the ground in front of the cross. The ground around the cross did not appear to be disturbed, and vegetation around the cross and surrounding area was consistent. The current residents of the property had only lived there for four months and indicated the cross was there when they moved in. Permission was given by the residents to excavate the grave.

Crime scene analysts began to process the scene by probing the area to locate the limits of the burial scene. A grid was constructed around the area, and all vegetation was cleared from the grid (Figure 4.15). Grave fill was removed layer by layer, and, at an elevation of approximately 38 cm (15 in.), a degraded black plastic bag was

Figure 4.14 Makeshift wooden cross wrapped with fabric and used to mark the location of a grave. (*Photograph courtesy of Seminole County Sheriff's Office)*

Figure 4.15 Grave and surrounding area gridded and cleared for excavation. (*Photograph courtesy of Seminole County Sheriff's Office*)

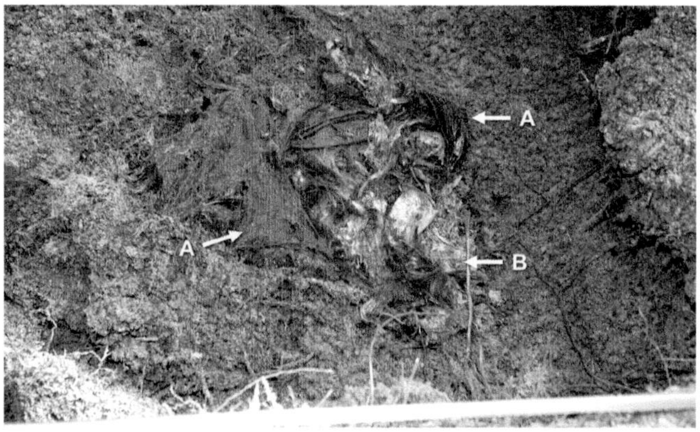

Figure 4.16 Degraded plastic bag (a) and remains of an elderly pet dog (b). (*Photograph courtesy of Seminole County Sheriff's Office*)

discovered (Figure 4.16). Once masses of fur were discovered, it became evident that the grave contained someone's pet. Authors Tosha Dupras and John Schultz later confirmed that the skeletal remains were those of an elderly dog.

CASE STUDY #4: FENCE LINE FORENSICS

In July 2008, authors Lana Williams and Sandra Wheeler assisted in the excavation and recovery of skeletal elements found while digging postholes for a new fence on the property of a children's daycare center. Some of the displaced bones were identified as being human, and a few of the remains displayed cut marks. Law enforcement and the coroner's office requested assistance for the recovery of the remaining skeletal elements. Upon arrival at the scene, the area that was cleared for the new fence and the holes dug for the fence posts were recorded. Although some skeletal elements had been displaced, it was evident that the area in and around the post holes still held more buried bones.

After photographing the site, the limits of the burial feature containing the partially exposed skeletal elements were defined (Figure 4.17). Several antique glass medicine bottles were recovered from the fill (Figure 4.18). After clearing the fill around the remaining skeletal elements, two nearly complete and fully articulated limbs were exposed: a left foot, leg, and hip (including the left innominate, the left half of the sacrum, and the left halves of three lower lumbar vertebrae), and a right hand, arm, and shoulder (including the right scapula and lateral half of the right clavicle) (Figure 4.19). The foot and lower leg were tightly flexed beneath the femur, while the lower arm and hand were tightly flexed beneath the humerus. The skeletal remains of a small mammal, likely a cat, were also recovered from the same excavated area as the human skeletal remains. Two corroded metal nails were also found in association with the human remains.

Figure 4.17 Author Lana Williams defines the limits of a burial feature along a fence line by removing thin layers of soil and ground cover with a flat-blade transfer shovel.

Figure 4.18 Antique glass medicine bottles recovered from the fill above human remains most likely buried to dispose of medical school specimens illegally acquired through grave robbing.

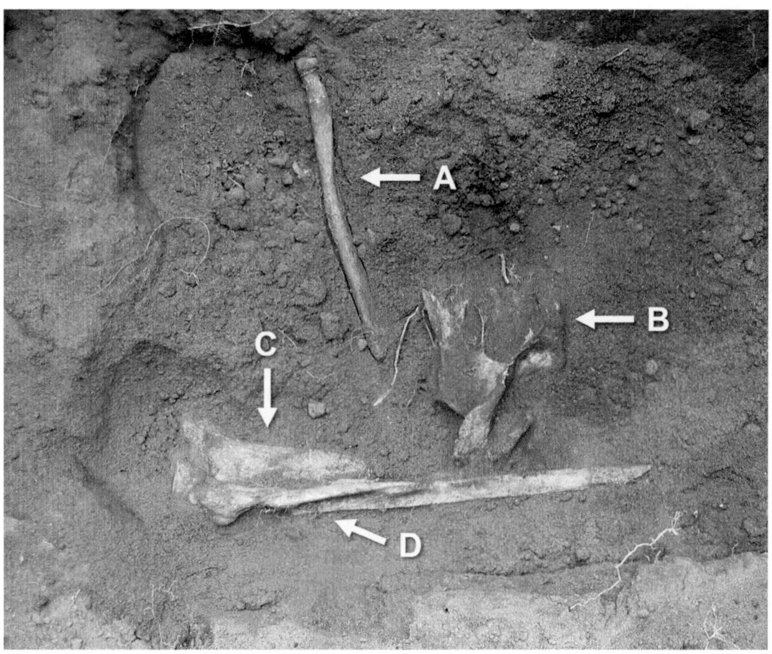

Figure 4.19 Human remains found during excavation of the burial feature along fence line: (a) radius, (b) scapula, (c) tibia, and (d) fibula (misaligned fracture at arrow).

All fill was screened, including any initially removed while digging new postholes, to ensure full recovery of all skeletal elements and associated evidence. After photographing and mapping all remains (Figure 4.20), field notes included descriptions of dark staining on remains, saw marks and discoloration of cut surfaces, and surface deterioration of cortical bone, all of which suggested that the deposition was not recent. When removing the leg, it was noted that this individual had suffered a severe fracture of the tibia and fibula with evidence of an active infection at the time of death. The taphonomic condition of the bones, presence of healed, nonaligned fractures, and association of the antique glass bottles led us to believe that this was not a case of forensic significance.

Further skeletal analyses indicated the pelvis and articulated leg were from an adult male; however, it was not possible to say whether the arm was from the same person. The right arm and shoulder had been detached by sawing through the midpoint of the clavicle, and the left leg and hip had been detached by sawing through the lumbar vertebrae and the sacrum. Analyses of the cut surfaces indicated that a straight blade hand saw with alternate-set teeth was used in dismemberment. Placement of the saw cuts was consistent with 18th- and 19th-century medical school dissections. The recovered nails were identified as 19th-century machine-cut nails, and the glass bottles were identified as a type commonly used in the 19th century for medical tinctures. It was also determined that the plot of land was located near the site of a 19th-century medical school and held a boarding house at that time. All evidence indicated that the recovered remains were likely buried in an attempt to dispose of medical school specimens illegally acquired through grave robbing, a common method of obtaining cadavers for medical schools during this time. Therefore, this was an anatomized site, and the remains were deemed as historic anatomical specimens rather than forensic in nature.

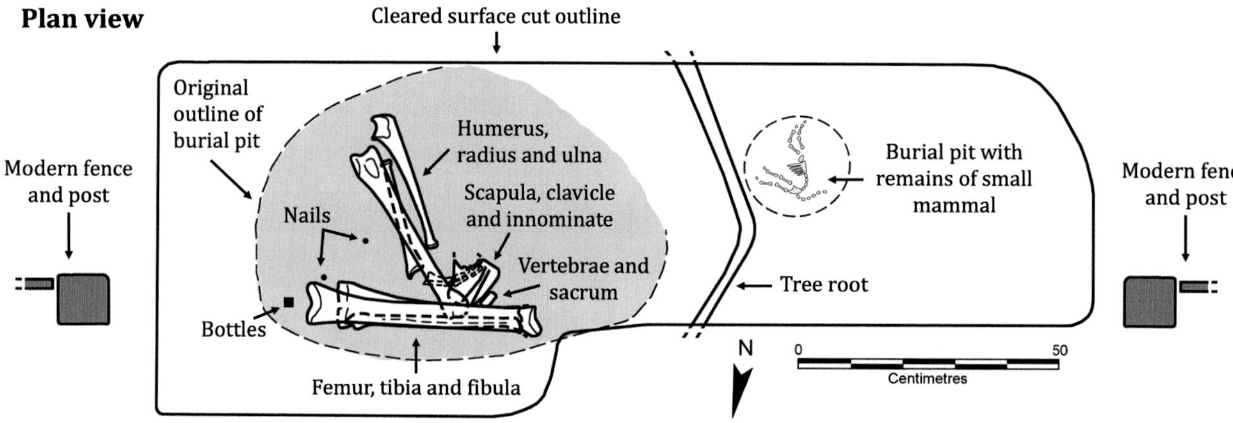

Figure 4.20 Plan view map of the recovery area and burial feature along the fence line.

Key Terms

adipocere
algor mortis
archaeology
bioturbation
bloating
burial
cadaver decomposition island
context
cremains
cremation
cremulator
disturbed grave
exhumation
extended position
flexed position
forensic context
grave
in situ
inurnment
livor mortis
marbling
mass grave
multiple grave
nganga
orientation
Palo
postmortem interval (PMI)
primary grave
primary surface scatter
rigor mortis
secondary grave
secondary surface scatter
semi-flexed position
skeletonization
skin slippage
surface scatter
taphonomy
time since death (TSD)

REVIEW AND DISCUSSION QUESTIONS

1. What are the laws in your jurisdiction regarding time, unmarked burial, and the jurisdiction of the State Archaeology office?
2. You are asked to take notes on a group of bones located during a search near a suburban nature park, all of which appear to be piled on the ground surface. You recognize that many of the skeletal elements are missing, especially the smaller bones of the skeleton. What additional indications would you look for in determining the context of these remains?
3. Does the presence of soft tissue always indicate you are working with remains in a forensic context? Explain your reasoning using information about decomposition and burial contexts.
4. How does body position assist with determining the context of remains? Why is it important to note the details of hand and foot position for an individual prior to removing the remains for further analyses?
5. What is adipocere? In what way(s) is relevant to forensic and taphonomic descriptions of context?
6. Remains of an individual were recovered from a shallow grave located near a river. The individual was in an extended position and oriented west-east. Explain how the following artifacts found in direct association with human remains could indicate the remains are potentially of forensic significance:
   - Leather shoes with nailed soles
   - Wire-rimmed eyeglasses
   - U.S. quarter with Washington's profile
   - Glass eye and hearing aid
   - Sterling silver belt buckle with 'BB-39' engraved over an anchor
7. Using the information from Question 5, explain how the position, orientation and associated artifacts could potentially indicate the remains are from a historical context.

Suggested Readings

Clark, M.A., Worrell, M.B., Pless, J.E. 1997. Postmortem changes in soft tissues. In: Haglund, W.D., Sorg, M.H., eds. *Forensic Taphonomy: The Postmortem Fate of Human Remains*, pp. 151–164. Boca Raton, FL: CRC Press.

Kail, T.M. 2008. *Magico-Religious Groups and Ritualistic Activities: A Guide for First Responders*. Boca Raton, FL: CRC Press.

Marks, M.J., Love, J.C., Dadour, I.R. 2009. Taphonomy and time: Estimating the postmortem interval. In: Steadmann, D.W., ed. *Hard Evidence: Case Studies in Forensic Anthropology*, 2nd ed., pp. 165–178. Upper Saddle River, NJ: Prentice Hall.

Pokines, J.T. 2018. Differential diagnosis of the taphonomic histories of common types of forensic osseous remains. *Journal of Forensic Identification* 68(1):68–145.

Schultz, J.J. 2012. Determining the forensic significance of skeletal remains. In: Dirkmaat, D.C., ed. *A Companion to Forensic Anthropology*, pp. 66–84. Hoboken, NJ: Blackwell Publishing Company.

Schultz, J.J., Warren, M.W., Krigbaum, J.S. 2015. Analysis of human cremains: Gross and chemical methods. In: Schmidt, C., Symes, S., eds. *The Analysis of Burned Human Remains*, 2nd ed., pp. 83–103. San Diego, CA: Academic Press.

Wetli, C.A., Martinez, R. 1983. Brujeria: Manifestations of Palo Mayombe in South Florida. *Journal of the Florida Medical Association* 70(8):629–634.

Yucha, J.M., Klales, A.R., Bartelink, E.J., Pokines, J.T. 2022. Contemporary cultural alteration to bone: Anatomical, ritual, and trophy. In: Pokines, J.T., L'Abbé, E.N., Symes, S.A., eds. *Manual of Forensic Taphonomy*, 2nd ed., pp. 251–293. Boca Raton, FL: CRC Press.

References

Adams, V.I. 2009. Medicolegal autopsy and postmortem toxicology. In: Waters, B.L., ed. *Handbook of Autopsy Practice*, pp. 7–20. Totowa, NJ: Humana Press.

Berryman, H.E., Bass, W.M., Symes, S.A., Smith, O.C. 1997. Recognition of cemetery remains in the forensic setting. In: Haglund, W.D., Sorg, M.H., eds. *Forensic Taphonomy: The Postmortem Fate of Human Remains*, pp. 165–170. Boca Raton, FL: CRC Press.

Bruwelheide, K.S., Owsley, D.W., Barca, K.G., Schlachtmeyer, S.S., France, C.A., Burgess Jr, J.M., Bies, B.S., Orrence, K.L., Creveling, M.C., Potter, S.R. 2023. A Civil War surgeon's pit at Manassas National Battlefield Park, Virginia. *Historical Archaeology*, Nov 29:1–26. DOI:10.1007/s41636-023-00436-w

Bunch, A 2010. Indoor wet screening of exhumed skeletal remains: A suggested procedure for the preparation of fragile evidence for anthropological analysis. *Journal of Forensic Sciences* 55(4):1102–1104. DOI: 10.1111/j.1556-4029.2010.01398.x

Canizares, B.R. 2002. *The Book on Palo: Deities, Initiatory Rituals, and Ceremonies*. Old Bethpage, NY: Original Publications.

Clark, M.A., Worrell, M.B., Pless, J.E. 1997. Postmortem changes in soft tissues. In: Haglund, W.D., Sorg, M.H., eds. *Forensic Taphonomy: The Postmortem Fate of Human Remains*, pp. 151–164. Boca Raton, FL: CRC Press.

Dirkmaat, D.C., Adovasio, J.M. 1997. The role of archaeology in the recovery and interpretation of human remains from an outdoor forensic setting. In: Haglund, W.D., Sorg, M.H., eds. *Forensic Taphonomy: The Postmortem Fate of Human Remains*, pp. 39–64. Boca Raton, FL: CRC Press.

Emmons, A.L., Deel, H., Davis, M., Metcalf, J.L. 2022. Soft tissue decomposition in terrestrial ecosystems. In: Pokines, J.T., L'Abbé, E.N., Symes, S.A., eds. *Manual of Forensic Taphonomy*, 2nd ed., pp. 41–77. Boca Raton, FL: CRC Press.

Florida Statutes § 872.02 and 872.05. 2023. Offenses Concerning Dead Bodies and Graves.

Forbes, S.L., Stuart, I.R., Dadour, I.R., Dent, B.B. 2004. A preliminary investigation of the stages of adipocere formation. *Journal of Forensic Sciences* 49:566–574. DOI:10.1520/JFS2002230

Gunn, A. 2019. *Essential Forensic Biology*, 3rd ed. Hoboken, NJ: Wiley.

Haglund, W.D. 2002. Recent mass graves, an introduction. In: Haglund, W.D., Sorg, M.H., eds. *Advances in Forensic Taphonomy: Method, Theory, and Archaeological Perspectives*, pp. 243–262. Boca Raton, FL: CRC Press.

Haglund, W.D. Sorg, M.H. 1997. Method and theory of forensic taphonomy research. In: Haglund, W.D., Sorg, M.H., eds. *Forensic Taphonomy: The Postmortem Fate of Human Remains*, pp. 13–26. Boca Raton, FL: CRC Press.

Handler, J.S. 1994. Update # 4: New York's African Burial ground. *African-American Archaeology Newsletter* 12:1–2.

Hester, T.J., Shafer, H., Feder, K. 2008. *Field Methods in Archaeology*, 7th ed., Walnut Creek, CA: Left Coast Press, Inc.

Iserson, K.V. 2001. *Death to Dust: What Happens to Dead Bodies?* 2nd ed., Tucson, AZ: Galen Press, Ltd.

Kail, T.M. 2008. *Magico-Religious Groups and Ritualistic Activities: A Guide for First Responders*. Boca Raton, FL: CRC Press.

Killam, E.W. 2004. *The Detection of Human Remains*, 2nd ed., Springfield, IL: Charles C. Thomas.

Marks, M.J., Love, J.C., Dadour, I.R. 2009. Taphonomy and time: Estimating the postmortem interval. In: Steadmann, D.W., ed. *Hard Evidence: Case Studies in Forensic Anthropology*, 2nd ed., pp. 165–178. Upper Saddle River, NJ: Prentice Hall.

Megyesi, M.S., Nawrocki, S.P., Haskell, N.H. 2005. Using accumulated degree days to estimate the postmortem interval from decomposed human remains. *Journal of Forensic Sciences* 50:618–626. DOI:10.1520/JFS2004017

Moffatt, C., Simmons, T., Lynch-Aird, J. 2016. An improved equation for TBS and ADD: Establishing a reliable postmortem interval framework for casework and experimental studies. *Journal of Forensic Sciences* 61(S1):S201–S207. DOI: 10.1111/1556-4029.12931

Mulhern, D.W., Ubelaker, D.H. 2012. Differentiating human from nonhuman bone microstructure. In: Crowder, C., Stout, S., eds. Bone Histology*: An Anthropological Perspective*, pp. 109–134. Boca Raton, FL: CRC Press.

Pokines, J.T. 2018. Differential diagnosis of the taphonomic histories of common types of forensic osseous remains. *Journal of Forensic Identification* 68(1):68–145.

Pokines, J.T. 2022. Introduction: The importance and use of forensic taphonomic data. In: Pokines, J.T., L'Abbé, E.N., Symes, S.A., eds. *Manual of Forensic Taphonomy*, 2nd ed., pp. 1–21. Boca Raton, FL: CRC Press.

Pokines, J.T., Baker, J.E. 2022. Effects of burial environment on osseous remains. In: Pokines, J.T., L'Abbé, E.N., Symes, S.A., eds. *Manual of Forensic Taphonomy*, 2nd ed., pp. 103–161. Boca Raton, FL: CRC Press.

Pokines, J.T., L'Abbé, E.N., Symes, S.A. (eds). 2022. *Manual of Forensic Taphonomy*, 2nd ed., Boca Raton, FL: CRC Press. DOI:10.4324/9781003171492

Pokines, J.T., Zinni, D.P., Crowley, K. 2016. Taphonomic patterning of cemetery remains received at the Office of the Chief Medical Examiner, Boston, Massachusetts. *Journal of Forensic Sciences* 61(S1):S71–S81. DOI: 10.1111/1556-4029.12902

Pollock, C., Pokines, J.T., Bethard, J. 2018. Organic staining on bone from exposure to wood and other plant materials. *Forensic Science International* 283:200–210. DOI:10.1016/j.forsciint.2017.12.021

Pope, E., Juarez, C.A., Galloway, A. 2022. Refined classification system for thermally damaged human remains by body segment. *Forensic Anthropology* 5(1):57–72. DOI:10.5744/fa.2021.0008

Roberts, C.A. 2009. *Human Remains in Archaeology: A Handbook*. York: Council for British Archaeology.

Schmitt, S. 2002. Mass graves and the collection of forensic evidence: Genocide, war crimes, and crimes against humanity. In: Haglund, W.D., Sorg, M.H., eds. *Advances in Forensic Taphonomy: Method, Theory, and Archaeological Perspectives*, pp. 277–292. Boca Raton, FL: CRC Press.

Schultz, J.J. 2012. Determining the forensic significance of skeletal remains. In: Dirkmaat, D.C., ed. *A Companion to Forensic Anthropology*, pp. 66–84. Hoboken, NJ: Blackwell Publishing Company.

Schultz, J.J., Dupras, T.L. 2022. Identifying the origin of taphonomic bone staining and color changes in forensic contexts. In: Pokines, J.T., L'Abbé, E.N., Symes, S.A., eds. *Manual of Forensic Taphonomy* 2nd ed., pp. 443–472. Boca Raton, FL: CRC Press.

Schultz, J.J., Warren, M.W., Krigbaum, J.S. 2015. Analysis of human cremains: Gross and chemical methods. In: Schmidt, C., Symes, S., eds. *The Analysis of Burned Human Remains*, 2nd ed., pp. 83–103. San Diego, CA: Academic Press.

Schultz, J.J., Williamson, M.A., Nawrocki, S.P., Falsetti, A.B., Warren, M.W. 2003. A taphonomic profile to aid in the recognition of human remains from historic and/or cemetery contexts. *Florida Anthropologist* 56:141–147.

Schultz, J.J., Green, A.E., Murdock, R.A., Hansen, M.H., Stephany, M.H., Garavaglia, J.C. 2020. The use of human skeletal remains in Palo rituals in Orange County, Florida. In: Garvin, J., Langley, N., eds. *Case Studies in Forensic Anthropology: Bonified Skeletons*, 1st ed., pp. 255–268. Boca Raton, FL: CRC Press.

Simmons, T. 2002. Taphonomy of a karstic cave execution site at Hrgar, Bosnia-Herzegovina. In: Haglund, W.D., Sorg, M.H., eds. *Advances in Forensic Taphonomy: Method, Theory, and Archaeological Perspectives*, pp. 263–276. Boca Raton, FL: CRC Press.

Skinner, M., York, H.P., Connor, M.A. 2002. Postburial disturbance of graves in Bosnia-Herzegovina. In: Haglund, W.D., Sorg, M.H., eds. *Advances in Forensic Taphonomy: Method, Theory, and Archaeological Perspectives*, pp. 293–308. Boca Raton, FL: CRC Press.

Sprague, R. 2005. *Burial Terminology*. Oxford: Altamira Press.

Stover, E., Ryan, M. 2001. Breaking bread with the dead. *Historical Archaeology* 35(1):7–25. DOI:10.1007/BF03374523

Streeter, M. 2012. Histological age-at-death estimation. In: Crowder, C., Stout, S., eds. Bone Histology*: An Anthropological Perspective*, pp. 135–152. Boca Raton, FL: CRC Press.

Ubelaker, D.H. 1999. *Human Skeletal Remains: Excavation, Analysis, Interpretation.* 3rd ed., Washington, DC: Taraxcum.

Ubelaker, D.H., Zarenko, K.M., 2011. Adipocere: What is known after over two centuries of research. *Forensic Science International* 208:167–172. DOI:10.1016/j.forsciint.2010.11.024

Ucko, P. 1969. Ethnography and archaeological interpretation of funerary remains. *World Archaeology* 1:262–280. DOI:10.1080/00438243.1969.9979444

Wetli, C.A., Martinez, R. 1983. Brujeria: Manifestations of Palo Mayombe in South Florida. *Journal of the Florida Medical Association* 70(8):629–634.

Wheeler, R.J. 2013. Florida's unmarked human burial law: A retrospective 1987–2010. *The Florida Anthropologist* 66(3):75–88.

Winburn, A.P., Martinez, R., Schoff, D. 2017. Afro-Cuban ritual use of human remains: Medicolegal considerations. *Journal of Forensic Identification* 67(1):1–30.

Yucha, J.M., Klales, A.R., Bartelink, E.J., Pokines, J.T. 2022. Contemporary cultural alteration to bone: Anatomical, ritual, and trophy. In: Pokines, J.T., L'Abbé, E.N., Symes, S.A., eds. *Manual of Forensic Taphonomy*, 2nd ed., pp. 251–293. Boca Raton, FL: CRC Press.

Learning Objectives

- Recognize common taphonomic changes to bones, including color changes and dispersal, and explain the importance of these changes to bones regarding search and recovery methods.
- Analyze taphonomic changes on recovered remains.
- Assist with reconstructing the postdepositional history of a forensic site from the time of deposition until the time of recovery.

Learning Connections

- Apply knowledge of bone dispersal distances to utilize appropriate methods during search and field recovery processes.
- Evaluate the effectiveness of the search and recovery methods used.

Taphonomy is the study of changes that biological organisms undergo between the time of death and the time of the discovery of their remains (Efremov, 1940; Lyman, 1994; Pokines et al., 2022b). One also may include changes that happen to remains during and after their recovery, including the loss of some remains due to the limitations of the recovery methods themselves (Pokines and Baker, 2022). Paleontologists tend to think of taphonomy as spanning millions of years (Martin, 1999), and this is often the case where fossilized specimens are being examined. To reach that fossilized state, however, the remains of all recently deceased organisms must survive multiple destructive forces, known as **taphonomic agencies**, that tend to alter them early in this process, including decomposition and consumption by larger organisms. Forensic anthropologists and paleontologists therefore are both interested in these early changes that occur in the tissues of the body after death, the study of which is **necrology**. Long-term survival of remains is greatly enhanced by their rapid burial, and the study of the environmental factors that affect organic remains between death and the final burial of the remains is called **biostratinomy**. As discussed in this book, there are multiple techniques that should be followed to excavate buried remains. Remains exposed on the ground surface tend to have much poorer preservation, easily undergoing the process of **dispersal** where remains are spread widely away from the point of original deposition through a variety of taphonomic agencies, and often can disappear completely over multiple years. The present chapter focuses upon those taphonomic effects likely to appear on remains in ways that generally decrease the potential for their recovery from terrestrial scenes. These include especially the actions of scavengers, mostly mammals and birds, that often destroy bones or portions of bones and disperse them away from a centralized concentration. Other common taphonomic agencies, including decomposing plants and topsoil, stain bones in ways that act as natural camouflage, thus decreasing their visibility to forensic searchers. An understanding of the common changes to a set of remains deposited in each terrestrial environment can greatly increase the effectiveness of search and recovery methods (Young et al., 2015, 2016) and should be a part of the training of anyone leading or participating in forensic recoveries.

Some taphonomic data must be collected in the field, as it is necessary to record the spatial relationship of the human remains along with aspects of the local environment, including tree canopy and understory species, **leaf litter** (the accumulating and decomposing plant parts on the ground surface), and levels of ongoing arthropod activity, which cannot be collected later during skeletal analysis. Spatial data are particularly important, as surface-scatter remains are frequently affected by dispersal, including most frequently by nonhuman animal activity. In addition, when dispersal patterns are correctly interpreted, there is a higher probability of delineating surface site boundaries and locating additional skeletal elements, the initial depositional site of dispersed remains, and secondary depositional sites of dispersed remains, such as when carnivores have dragged a limb or torso some

DOI: 10.4324/9781315201658-5

distance. The more common natural postmortem processes that can disarticulate, modify, damage, and disperse skeletal remains include subaerial weathering, carnivore activity, rodent gnawing, and botanical activity. These taphonomic processes are described in more detail in the following section to assist the forensic archaeologist in interpreting and reconstructing scenes. A complete analysis of direct modifications to bones, however, should be completed in the laboratory setting as a part of skeletal analysis.

TAPHONOMIC AGENCIES AND THEIR EFFECTS

Taphonomic agencies, such as vertebrate scavengers, invertebrates, gravity, solar radiation, tree roots, precipitation, etc., produce **taphonomic effects**, or the actual alterations occurring to the remains. These often can be classified and identified as to the source, which gives important information regarding the postmortem history of a set of remains and the depositional context(s) in which they resided. Dispersed remains, for example, often have carnivores gnawing on them and were likely moved substantial distances by these species. This movement can have an extensive direct effect upon subsequent searches for remains, especially in environments where plant cover is extensive, and visibility is poor. Conversely, the discovery of some remains with carnivore gnawing damage forewarns the field recovery personnel to be prepared for high degrees of dispersal.

Common Taphonomic Effects in Terrestrial Surface Environments

Subaerial Weathering

After skeletonization, the exposed bones often undergo a process known as **subaerial weathering**, where they become sun-bleached from UV light and crack apart slowly over the course of years, with the timing dependent upon many local environmental factors (Lyman, 1994; Pokines and Spiegel, 2022). These changes are often accompanied by other taphonomic effects, including algae, moss, and lichens growth on the exposed surfaces, and soil staining, soil adherence, acidic soil corrosion, and plant root infiltration and etching on the surface in contact with the ground (Pokines, 2016). While other researchers had mentioned subaerial weathering previously, Behrensmeyer (1978) organized these changes into a six-stage system that is still standard today, describing bones from fresh and unweathered (Stage 0), to fine surface cracking (Stage 1), delamination of the surface (Stage 2), exposure of coarsely textured bone underneath the delaminated areas (Stage 3), deeper cracking that penetrates the marrow cavity and has some splintering (Stage 4), and cracking and falling apart (Stage 5) (Figure 5.1). When assigning a weathering stage, each bone should be categorized in the most advanced stage that has covered at least 1 cm^2 of the bone surface, avoiding edges or borders and not applying the system to small fauna or any teeth (Behrensmeyer, 1978). It is also common for bones to display multiple subaerial weathering stages at once, highlighting how minor variations in the environmental setting can affect the rate of stage advancement.

Bone bleaching from UV light can develop rapidly in some environments with intense sun and a lack of shade (Pokines and Spiegel, 2022). Schultz et al. (2018) found that experimental pig bones left exposed in Florida over the course of nine months developed variable sun bleaching. For example, signs of sun bleaching appeared first in exposed bones, averaging approximately two months to reach Stage 1 (≤25% of surface bleached) and three months to reach Stage 2 (26–50% of surface bleached). In contrast, bones protected by shade took around three months to reach Stage 1 and five months to reach Stage 2. The percentages of surface bleaching of the bones increased with greater exposure times.

The causes of subaerial weathering have received some research attention (Pokines and Spiegel, 2022), and variations in these can greatly affect the rate of weathering and hence any estimations of the postmortem interval (PMI) that are based upon it. Any forces that cause bone to expand and contract repeatedly seem to have an effect upon surface cracking. These forces include cycles of

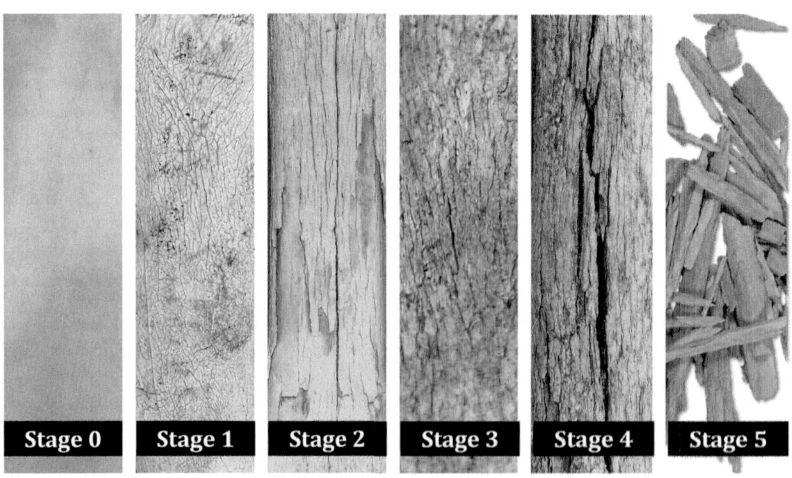

Figure 5.1 Bones demonstrating weathering stages (WS): Stage 0 (unweathered) to Stage 5 (falling apart), following Behrensmeyer (1978).

thermal expansion and contraction (Pal and Saha, 1989), freezing and thawing of ice forcing cracks apart (Pokines et al., 2016), and perhaps most importantly wetting and drying (Pokines et al., 2018a). Salt crystallization within a bone (Ouacha et al., 2013) and dissolution and replacement by minerals from the soil (Trueman et al., 2004) are also factors in subaerial weathering degradation of bones. Weathering is mostly to advance where these changes are cycled through repeatedly, as in temperate environments with many major changes in weather and local environment throughout the day. Bones undergoing advanced weathering are incorporated back into the sediment as they flake apart, thus giving a ceiling on the amount of time (decades or longer; Miller, 2011) that bones can persist in an environment.

Carnivore Activity

Mammalian carnivore alterations are common on human remains in many outdoor environments, and sometimes indoors (Pokines, 2022a), and their teeth and other mouth structures have evolved for this task (Figure 5.2). Bones are gnawed upon for many reasons, including as a byproduct of predation, dismembering of prey, removal of exterior soft tissue, accessing the internal fat content of bones, and sometimes from boredom, especially among domestic or zoo animals. Carnivore activity results in modifications and consumption of soft tissue and bone, as well as significant disarticulation and dispersal of body parts. Direct damage to bones (Figures 5.3–5.6) has been classified into multiple types (Binford, 1981; Fisher, 1995; Haynes, 1980; Lyman, 1994:205–214; Pokines, 2022a; Pokines and Kerbis Peterhans, 2007). These include **crenulated margins** (jagged or irregular edges) where carnivores have removed bone. Repeated gnawing in the same location, especially where exposed cortical bone is thicker, can take on a rounded appearance known as **edge polish**. **Tooth pits** are defined as marks that do not penetrate the cortical bone and have dimensions where their length is no more than three times their width (i.e., smaller, rounded, irregular marks). **Tooth punctures**, in contrast, have the same dimension restrictions as pits but do penetrate the cortical bone. Areas of cortical bone already exposed by gnawing that have deeper marks in them also can be classified as punctures. **Tooth scores (or striations)**, like pits, do not penetrate the cortical bone but are more than three times as long as they are wide (and are often much longer). **Tooth furrows**, like punctures, penetrate the cortical bone and, like, scores or striations, are more than three times as long as they are wide. As with punctures, furrows also can be found in areas of exposed cortical bone where gouging goes deeper. Carnivores generally can scoop out areas of cancellous bone, and this can be observed on butchered non-human bones where they have gnawed on the ends. They also tend to attack weaker portions of bones first, where the ends of long bones are gnawed and removed in order to access the marrow cavity. If both ends of a long bone have been removed, the resulting modified bone shape is referred to as a **cylinder**. Small bones or fragments of larger bones, especially ribs, vertebrae, and long bone ends, can be consumed entirely.

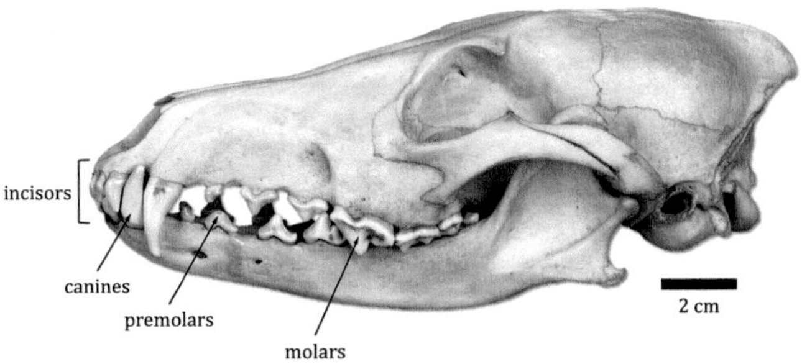

Figure 5.2 Skull of coyote (*Canis latrans*) showing incisors evolved for shearing, canines evolved for gripping and incapacitating prey, premolars for shredding soft tissue, and molars for crushing.

In North American environments, canids are responsible for much scavenging and dispersal of human remains (Haglund, 1997b; Haglund et al., 1988), and the species in this carnivore family include domestic dogs (*Canis familiaris*), coyotes (*C. latrans*), wolves (*C. lupus*), and multiple species of fox. Other mammalian carnivore scavengers include ursids (bears) (Udoni et al., 2021) and

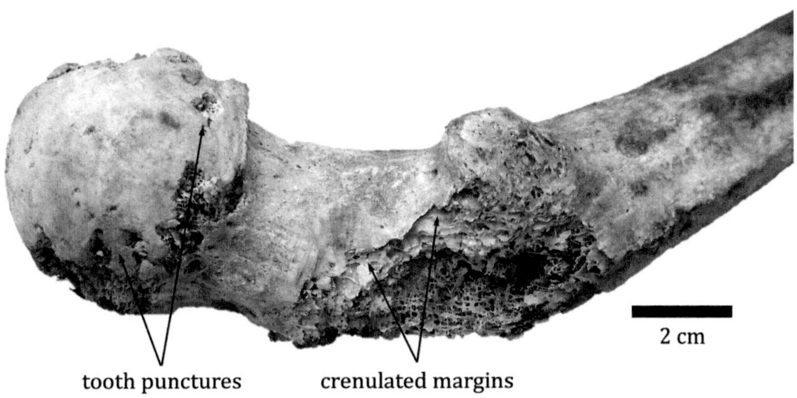

Figure 5.3 Carnivore-caused tooth punctures and crenulated margins on a proximal femur.

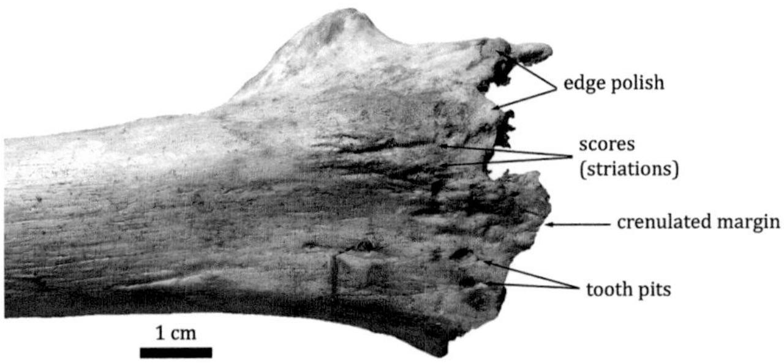

Figure 5.4 Carnivore-caused pits, scores (striations), crenulated margins, and edge polish on a proximal femur.

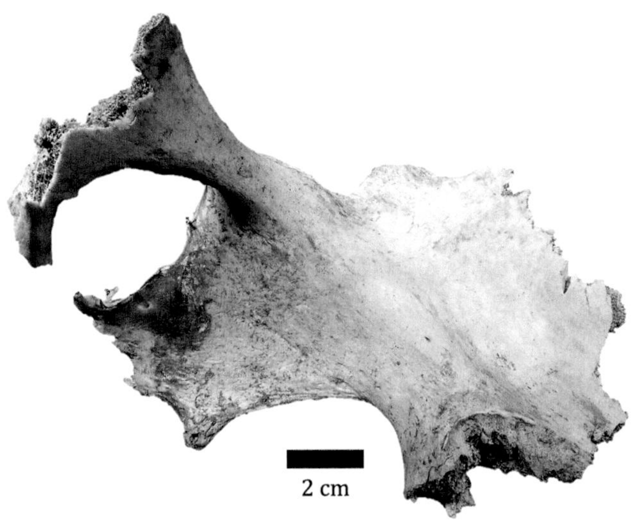

Figure 5.5 Carnivore-caused crenulated margins on an innominate (os coxa).

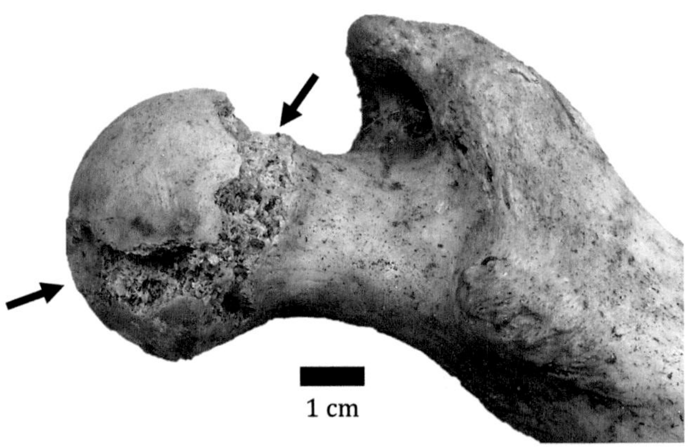

Figure 5.6 Carnivore-caused furrows into cancellous bone of a femoral head.

felids, including mountain lions (*Puma concolor*) (Stiner et al. 2012) and bobcats (*Felis rufus*). Pigs (*Sus scrofa*), while not carnivores in the taxonomic sense, are also known to scavenge human remains (Berryman, 2001; Pokines, 2022a) and exist in domesticated and feral or wild forms. Alligators and their relatives (Harding and Wolf, 2006; Schneider et al., 2022) and sharks (Işcan and McCabe, 1995; Pokines and Higgs, 2022) are also significant taphonomic agencies in their respective environments and can leave distinctive tooth marks. Birds are also important scavengers, though they tend not to alter bone as pervasively as carnivores (Komar and Beattie, 1998; Pokines et al., 2022a).

Rodent Activity

Rodent effects upon human skeletal remains are common and distinctive (Haglund, 1997a). There are over 2,200 named species of rodents (Wilson and Reeder, 2005), and many of them will enter buildings where humans are present and access spaces that other vertebrate scavengers cannot. Rodents gnaw bones in two different ways, with two different goals and types of taphonomic effects, termed **wet-bone** and **dry-bone gnawing**. All rodents have a pair of upper and a pair of lower incisors, and these grow continuously (Figure 5.7). To keep their incisors sharp and at a usable length, rodents frequently

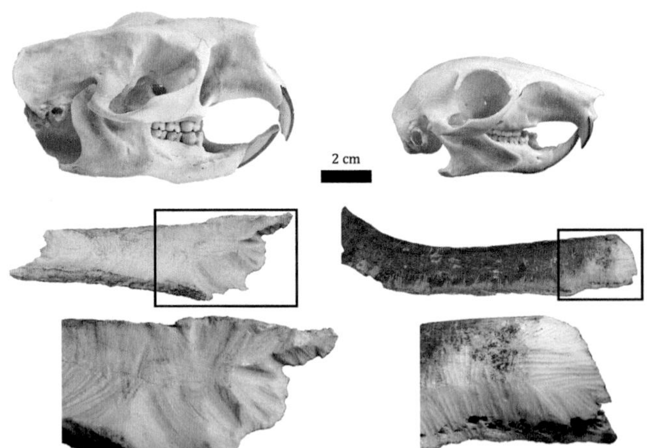

Figure 5.7 Examples of rodent skulls from North American porcupine (*Erethizon dorsatum*, left) and eastern gray squirrel (*Sciurus carolinensis*, right), each exhibiting pairs of large, ever-growing incisors in the maxilla and mandible (four total) with which they can cause extensive gnawing damage to bone and other materials. The size of the parallel rows of rodent gnaw marks can indicate the general size of rodent (larger rodent gnaw marks shown lower left, and those of a smaller rodent shown on the lower right).

Figure 5.8 Rodent dry-bone gnawing on a tibia shaft; note the parallel striations along the margins.

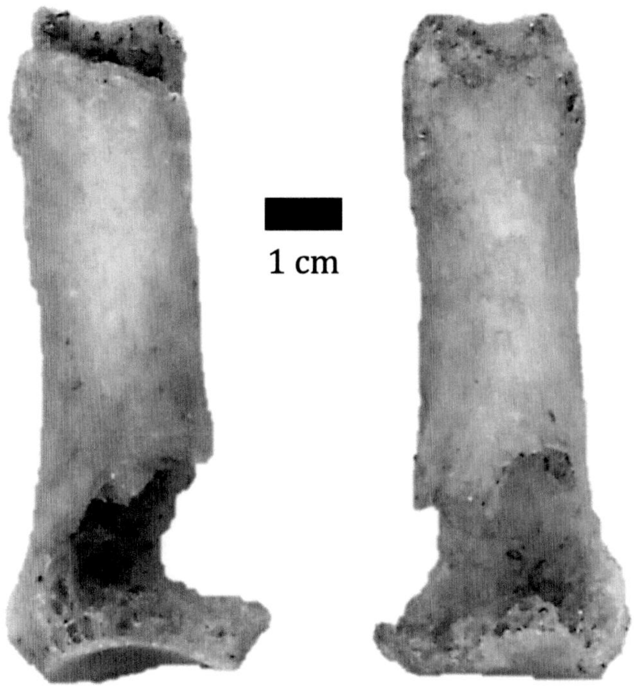

Figure 5.9 Rodent wet-bone gnawing on hand phalanges.

gnaw upon hard objects, including dry bone (Figure 5.8). This type of gnawing preferentially occurs on dry, cortical bone, especially margins that fit easily into a rodent's mouth. Broad, flat areas are more difficult to gnaw. Dry-bone gnawing leaves behind sets of short, often overlapping, striations with U-shaped profiles. The width of the markings varies proportionally with rodent body (and hence, incisor) size, but a large amount of overlap exists among species (Pokines, 2022a). With extended periods of gnawing, rodents can heavily remodel bone.

Omnivorous rodents, including house mice (*Mus musculus*) and Norway rats (*Rattus norvegicus*), also consume fresh remains and gnaw into fresh bone (wet-bone gnawing), while doing so to obtain fat inside of bones (Figures 5.9 and 5.10). These gnawed areas present a scooped-out appearance into cancellous areas and can grow quite large over time, even removing most of a proximal tibia or distal femur. Rodents are also known to nest inside human skeletal remains, as the bodies are both shelter and food supply (Haglund, 1997b; Pokines, 2022a).

Bone Damage and Loss

With exceptions of antemortem events (e.g., tooth loss, amputation, natural human variation), bones or portions of bones not recovered with a skeleton are missing due to four possible reasons: (1) the bones were purposefully removed during the postmortem period, (2) the bones or portions of them still existed but were not recovered, (3) they were destroyed prior to the recovery efforts by taphonomic agencies, or (4) they were recovered but were in an unidentifiable state. For bones that still existed but were not recovered, these were either within the searched area but were not found or were outside of the searched area and could not be found. Both of the latter situations may be fixable through modified search methods, as dispersal past a reasonable search area can be a common occurrence.

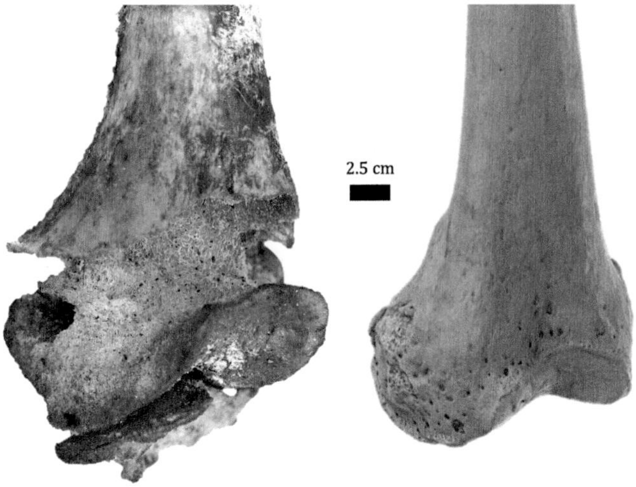

Figure 5.10 Rodent wet-bone gnawing on a distal femur (left) compared with complete distal femur (right).

Botanical Effects

Plants are an additional common taphonomic agency that produce changes to bones in terrestrial surface and burial environments. Roots frequently penetrate into buried bones (Figure 5.11), and care must be taken during excavation not to damage bones that are held in place in this manner. Tree roots also develop countable rings like the trunk and branches do, and this information can be used to establish a minimum time since burial. Cross-sections of roots growing through or above buried remains therefore should be retained for analysis (refer to Chapter 10). Plant roots also can infiltrate when bones are lying on the ground surface, so the appearance of plant roots or patterns of branching staining left by them (particularly when appearing on only one side of a bone and in conjunction with areas of soil staining) is not an automatic indicator of previous burial.

Bones lying on the ground surface often get stained various shades of brown by their contact with decomposing leaf litter and topsoil (Figure 5.12) (Pollock et al., 2018; Schultz and Dupras, 2022). Sometimes pine needles can cause distinctive patterns as they decompose in contact with bones (Figure 5.13). Diffuse green algae and/or moss staining on bones is also common in moist terrestrial environments (Pokines, 2016; Schultz and Dupras, 2022). These color changes may make bones more difficult to locate during visual surface searches.

Bone Camouflage

Multiple taphonomic agencies alter the surface color of bones in ways that change the level of difficulty in locating them using standard surface search methods (Schultz and Dupras, 2022). The natural color of bone is beige, but as indicated in the previous section, this color frequently becomes altered during the postmortem period. Therefore, search investigators should be trained regarding colors that naturally develop to aid their search methods. Any color change causing a bone to closely resemble a location's ground surface may make that bone contrast less against that background, making it more difficult to spot. Variable color changes may also form naturally occurring camouflage patterns and break up the visible outline of the bone, thus changing its apparent shape into something less recognizable. In contrast, sun bleaching may make bones more visible to searchers in environments where the paleness of the bone provides a greater contrast to the background surface. In many environments, however, bones exposed over the course of years are being slowly buried by the annual cycle of leaf fall and subsequent decomposition into hummus at the topsoil horizon. In such situations, sun-bleached or other-colored bones may not be visible from a distance due to their coverage in other materials. For example, McCallister (2025) experimented using nonhuman bones (white-tailed deer [*Odocoileus virginianus*] postcranial elements and pig [*Sus scrofa*] crania) that had three color states: natural control bones (minimum decomposition staining), stained (heavy

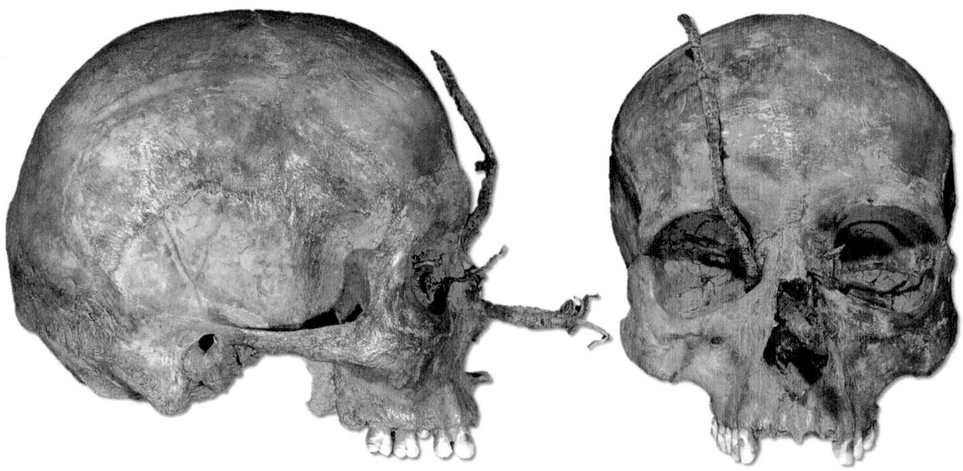

Figure 5.11 Root growth through the nasal cavity and eye orbits.

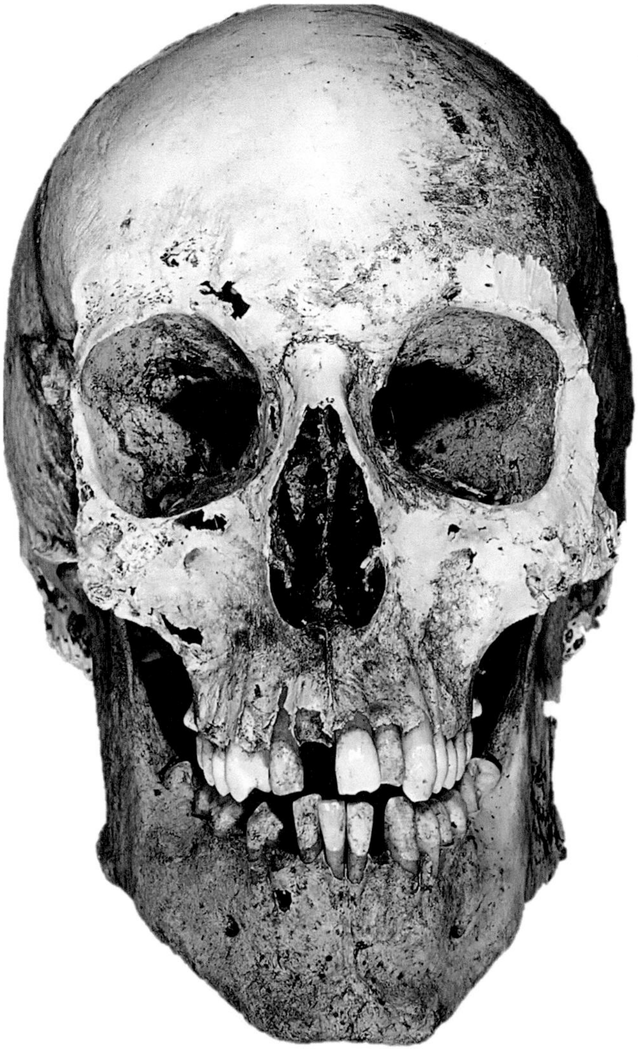

Figure 5.12 Variable surface staining on a cranial vault. The right side was in contact with the ground surface and became stained dark by decomposing plant matter and topsoil, while the left side has some diffuse green algae staining and sun bleaching. The mandible has the opposite pattern with staining on the left and sun bleaching on the right, indicating these skeletal elements became disarticulated during decomposition. Note the rodent gnaw marks around the lateral rim of the right eye orbit that occurred after staining.

decomposition with soil staining), and sun-bleached from weathering. The results indicated taphonomic color changes in the test environment had an effect on both the rate and distance at which bones were located (refer to Chapter 13).

Bone Dispersal Distances

Carnivores, and, in many contexts, members of the dog family (Canidae), are often the most destructive force to bones and also lead to their greatest dispersal in a variety of environments. In Massachusetts, coyotes in particular are pervasive and frequent even in urban areas and in increasing numbers (Pokines et al., 2021). A large amount of research has addressed the question of how far various scavenging species will disperse the remains of large vertebrates around human in size, including experiments with fresh remains in a variety of locations and scavenger communities (Pokines, 2022a). Researchers have also collected dispersal distances of human remains from actual forensic cases and made observational studies of natural nonhuman behavior dispersing the remains of other large vertebrates. Haynes (1980, 1981), for example, noted the ubiquitous dispersal of bones by wolves in North America when feeding upon white-tailed deer carcasses. Dispersal up to 30 m was common as a part of normal wolf feeding behavior. Pack animals are in competition with each other at kill sites, and movement of bone may come about by the desire to feed on portions of a carcass distantly enough to reduce immediate competition but also keep the carcass in sight.

Multiple studies that included bone dispersal distances have been compiled in Table 5.1 and Figure 5.14. These include observational studies of natural nonhuman animal behavior and experimental studies where carcasses or body parts were left as baits in order to study scavenging under more controlled conditions. In each case, the

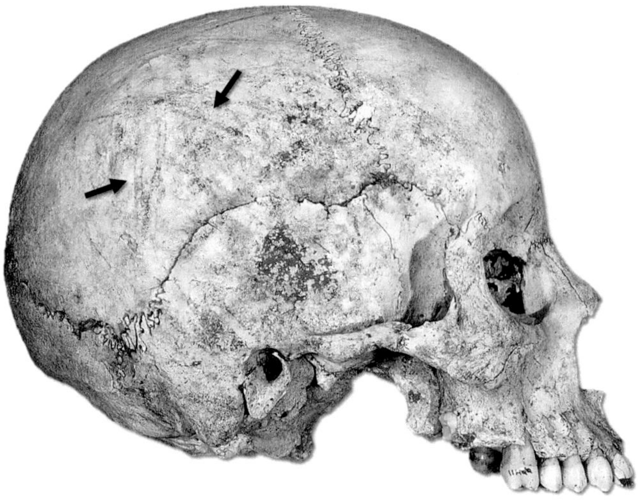

Figure 5.13 Linear staining caused by the decomposition of adhering pine needles (arrows) on the lateral surface of a cranial vault.

maximum dispersal distance reported is listed, although most dispersed remains were recovered far closer to their initial starting points. The primary species doing the dispersal was also recorded, although in most cases, there is likely input from multiple other species. The dispersing species include hyenas; other large mammals (canids in most of the environments examined); small mammals (mostly small carnivores such as raccoons [*Procyon lotor*]), foxes, and smaller cat species, including bobcats [*Felis rufus*]; rodents as a separate category from small mammal; and birds (including vultures [Cathartidae] and crows [Corvidae]). Methods often included camera setups in order to determine which species did at least the initial feeding and dispersal, and mapping of dispersed elements. Haglund's (1991) early research on this topic examined the dispersal of human remains from forensic cases in Washington state, United States, primarily by large canids (dogs and coyotes).

Among terrestrial dispersers, hyenas may be in a class by themselves. Striped hyenas (*Hyaena hyaena*), for example, transported bones in Israel up to 25 km from their likely source, disturbed modern graves from a modern hospital (Horwitz and Smith, 1988). Hyenas, both extant and extinct, are avid bone collectors and transporters, and they have evolved to be highly efficient bone-crushers (Pokines, 2022a). These species are found today only in Africa and southern Asia, but an increasing focus upon forensic taphonomy in these areas (e.g., Keyes et al., 2021; Spies et al., 2018) may encompass the activities of these species.

Large mammals besides hyenas consistently produced large maximum dispersal distances, ranging from 85 m to 500 m, primarily from experimental settings using pig remains. As noted above, Haglund (1991) found high

Table 5.1 Maximum Dispersal Distances of Large Vertebrate Remains by Different Scavenger Types

Primary Dispersing Species	Study Type	Max. Dispersal Distance (m)	Source(s)
Hyena	Observational	25,000	Horwitz and Smith (1988)
Bird	Experimental	600	Komar and Beattie (1998)
Large mammal	Experimental	500	King et al. (2016)
Large mammal	Observational	365	Haglund (1991)
Bird	Experimental	150	Pokines (2022b)
Large mammal	Experimental	130.9	Bright (2011)
Small mammal	Experimental	103.5	Young et al. (2015)
Bird	Observational	100	Stolen (2000)
Large mammal	Experimental	93	Ricketts (2013)
Large mammal	Experimental	85	Kjorlien (2004), Kjorlien et al. (2009)
Small mammal	Experimental	73.7	Keyes et al. (2021)
Small mammal	Experimental	55	Arilla et al. (2019)
Small mammal	Experimental	41	Arilla et al. (2020)
Bird	Experimental	31.6	Ballejo et al. (2015)
Bird	Experimental	20	Dabbs et al. (2013)
Small mammal	Experimental	18.3	Morton and Lord (2006)
Bird	Experimental	15	Schultz and Mitchell (2018)
Small mammal/bird	Experimental	13.3	Moss (2012)
Small mammal	Experimental	12.7	Spies et al. (2018)
Rodent	Experimental	12.5	Pokines et al. (2021)
Small mammal	Experimental	10	King et al. (2016)
Bird	Experimental	6	Demo et al. (2013)
Rodent	Experimental	5	Hoffman and Hays (1987)
Rodent	Observational	3.5	Hockett (1989)

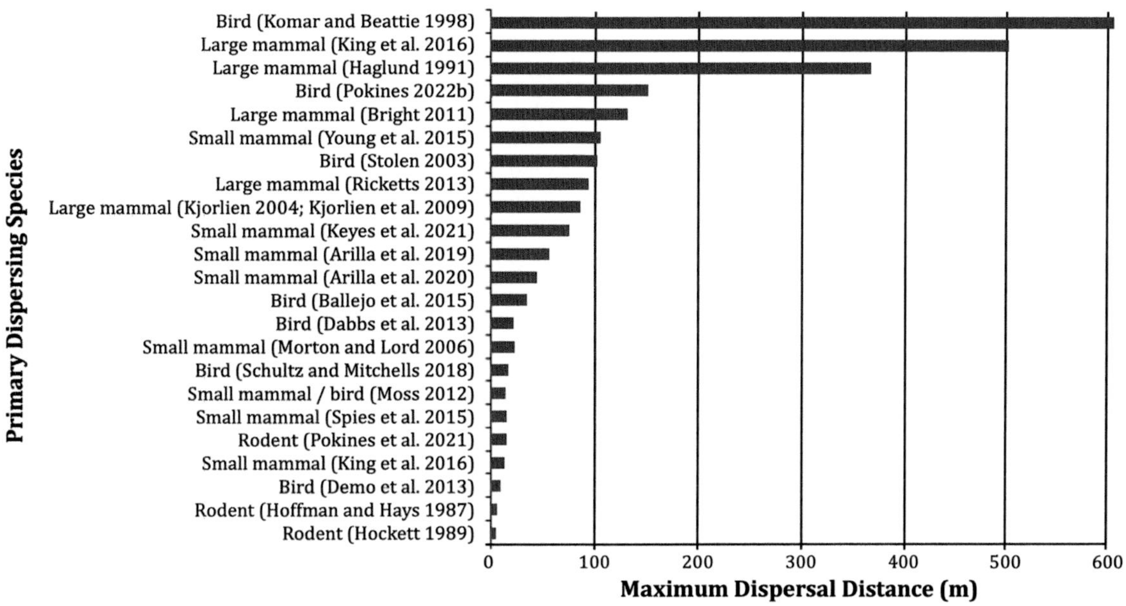

Figure 5.14 Maximum dispersal distances caused by scavenging species, including studies of birds, large mammals (carnivores), small mammals (primarily carnivores), and rodents. Studies include experimental and observational data.

degrees of dispersal by dogs and coyotes, including some bones up to 365 m away from their original location at 53 study sites. Dispersal over 30 m was common. King et al. (2016) found dispersal by coyotes of experimental pig remains to extend as far as 500 m, while dispersal by opossum (*Didelphis virginiana*) during the same experiment was under 10 m. Other researchers found substantial but smaller maximum dispersal distances by large mammals. Bright (2011) found black bears (*Ursus americanus*) to disperse experimental pig remains up to 130.9 m. Ricketts (2013) and Kjorlien (2004) and Kjorlien et al. (2009) noted large maximum dispersal distances of experimental pig remains by scavengers that included coyote.

Birds can cause direct damage to bone during feeding and also can disperse bones over long distances (Pokines et al., 2022a; Reeves, 2009; Spradley et al., 2012). The maximum dispersal distances in these studies were highly variable, ranging from 6 m to 600 m. The smaller distances appear to be more typical of normal feeding dispersing bones around their original location, while the larger distances appear to be less frequent cases of remains being transported for feeding in another location entirely. Komar and Beattie (1998) noted magpie (*Pica*; a member of the crow family) dispersing two small pig bones to a nest 600 m away from their source, although this was not typical of the dispersal noted in that experiment. Similarly, Stolen (2000) observed turkey vultures (*Cathartes aura*) transport small items of carrion up to 100 m (then further in one case after being disturbed while feeding). Pokines (2022b) observed gulls (*Larus* spp.) to transport a partial cow (*Bos taurus*) cervical vertebra 85 m, although most dispersal in this experiment averaged 10 m; scavenged bones from local trash sources were transported at least 150 m. Gulls are known to fly long distances to find food, often swallowing small bones of their prey or scavenged items, so it is possible that distances of multiple kilometers of dispersal can occur for small elements of large vertebrates. Other researchers found smaller maximal bone dispersal distances during experiments using pig (Ballejo et al., 2015; Dabbs et al., 2013; Schultz and Mitchell, 2018) or sheep (*Ovis aries*) carcasses (Demo et al., 2013), frequently by vulture species. While not measuring dispersal radius, Spradley et al. (2012) found black vultures (*Coragyps atratus*) feeding upon an experimentally placed human cadaver to cause significant dispersal. The maximum distance between body parts was 15.8 m, and the total surface area with dispersed remains was 83.6 m^2. Black vultures are common throughout much of southern United States, and their range extends throughout most of South America.

Small mammals in these studies were found to have maximum dispersal distances of 10 m to 103.5 m. Young et al. (2015) experimented with deer remains and found that red fox (*Vulpes vulpes*) and badger (*Meles meles*) dispersed them up to 103.5 m. These species or their close relatives are found throughout much of the world. Keyes et al. (2021) found that a small canid, black-backed jackal (*Canis mesomelas*), among other small species dispersed experimental pig bones up to 73.7 m in South Africa. Arilla et al. (2019, 2020) experimented with multiple common large vertebrate species and found that red fox, among other small species, dispersed bones up to 55 m during experiments in the Spanish Pyrenees. Arilla et al. (2019) also found that a large number (47.3%) of the 3,332 skeletal elements included in the experiment were not recovered at all, and a further 34.0% were recovered within 10 m. Other researchers found lower distances of dispersal by small mammals (King et al., 2016; Morton and Lord, 2006; Moss, 2012; Spies et al., 2018).

Rodents acting as primary dispersal agencies appear to produce the lowest distances, although relatively little research has been done on this topic. Many rodents gnaw on bones, either to extract soft tissue contained in wet bones or to wear down their teeth and extract mineral nutrients from dry bones (Pokines, 2022a). Maximum dispersal distances ranged from only 3.5 to 12.5 m, which is not surprising given that many individual large vertebrate bones outweigh many individual rodents. Pokines et al. (2021) found dispersal of dry white-tailed deer bones of up to 12.5 m in an urban park environment, with most dispersal likely due to rodents, including eastern gray squirrel (*Sciurus carolinensis*). Hoffman and Hays (1987) found wood rats (*Neotoma floridana*) to move experimentally placed, large and small vertebrate bones up to 5 m to a nest, with most bones dispersed at least 1 m. Hockett (1989) examined the nests of another species of wood rat (*Neotoma cinerea*) and found that bones must have been transported a minimum of 3.5 m up a steep slope; in this observational study, the maximum dispersal distance could not be discerned. Other, larger rodents are known to transport large bones, as with porcupines (*Hystrix* spp.) in Africa and southern Asia, and maximum distances of this behavior should be examined. These species also can transport large bones, including rhinoceros-sized tibias (Pokines et al., 2022a), but North American porcupines (*Erethizon dorsatum*) are both smaller and not known to be avid bone collectors.

Other Sources of Dispersal

Gravity, in conjunction with other forces such as trampling, rockfall, or precipitation, can aid in the dispersal of remains downslope from their point of deposition (Pokines et al., 2011). Plowing (Newcomb et al., 2017) can disperse shallowly buried remains, and some bones get churned to the surface. Repeated passes by plows can disperse bone several meters, with most dispersal in the direction parallel to the plow movement. Although the recovery of remains from water contexts is not the direct focus of this chapter, running water has a high potential to transport and otherwise alter remains (Evans, 2022), and these could later be deposited along a shore.

BONE DISPERSAL EFFECTS UPON SEARCH AND RECOVERY

Searching versus Processing

It is important to note that procedures used in searching for a forensic site are not the same as procedures used once a site is found. Visual searching (refer to Chapter 6) often involves multiple personnel spaced at intervals over a wide area and proceeding in formation. When objects are located, they are marked with pin flags, and searching continues. This form of searching may include the discovery of a concentration of remains with elements dispersed more distantly around it; however, this is insufficient by itself to locate all of the relevant evidence on the scene. Once concentrations have been located, the methods change from searching to processing. The latter involves a hands-and-knees crawl over the entire scene, moving at a much slower rate and with no gapping between searched areas (Pokines, 2015; Pokines et al., 2018b, 2019b). All living foliage and accumulated leaf litter must be removed to expose evidence, then sorted through before being dumped outside of the search area. Areas around dispersed remains should also be processed in this manner.

Success Rates during Bone Search and Scene Processing

As indicated in the section on bone camouflage, taphonomic color changes can affect the recovery rates of bones during experimental broad surface search (McCallister, 2025). Previous research using the same forested outdoor grid location found that element type also affected recovery rates, with some elements typically harder to spot, including isolated ribs (Pokines et al., 2019a). Experimentation also found differences in recovery rates based upon bone type when processing small areas by sorting through all leaf litter and removing all understory, as on a surface scene. This includes larger (Pokines et al., 2018b) and human-infant-sized (Pokines et al., 2019b) pig bones that had natural environmental staining (refer to Chapter 13). Sorting leaf litter twice (once on the ground and also after dumping the leaf litter on a tarp) also increased recovery rates, likely due to the contrasting color of the tarp making it easier to spot bones (Pokines et al., 2019b). In most actual surface-scatter cases, undecomposed leaf litter is not amenable to screening during recovery efforts, since very little of the leaf litter passes through the screen mesh. This results in the recovery team plucking through individual leaves and sticks and removing these from the screen by hand. Screening is, however, useful for processing leaf litter once it has broken down partially into **humus** (dark, organic material that forms in soil when plants and animal matter decays), as the smaller pieces may pass through screens through normal shaking or can be pushed through manually. This is especially important where bones and associated evidence have worked their way down into this layer within the soil horizon. As noted earlier, dumping the plant matter onto tarps for additional searching was found to increase bone recovery rates. Large shopping bags made of polypropylene (IKEA, 2025; refer to Chapter 2) hold enough dead plant matter (19 gal. [72 L]) to expedite efficient scene processing, are not too heavy for most adults to lift when full, and fold for easy storage. Multiple bags can be kept in a small space in a vehicle with other archaeological equipment and are not difficult to be transported to a site away from roads.

CASE STUDY #5 OUTDOOR SCENE DISPERSAL DISTANCES IN MASSACHUSETTS, UNITED STATES

Dispersal Data

Author James T. Pokines collected data on the dispersal of remains from forensic cases throughout Massachusetts, United States, spanning from January 2012 through May 2024 (Table 5.2). All of these cases were processed in conjunction with the Office of the Chief Medical Examiner (OCME) and multiple local and State law enforcement agencies. The 38 cases all came from outdoor surface contexts. In all cases where cadaver dogs were used, these were operated directly by Massachusetts State Police personnel. The environments included one urban site, one site in a freshwater marsh within forests, rural forested areas, and forested portions of suburban areas.

Mapping methods varied by context, logistics, and site complexity and ranged from radial coordinates using a compass and measuring tape or baseline methods to the frequent use of a total station and data logger system (refer to Chapter 8 for a discussion of these methods). (The variable precision of these methods is indicated in Table 5.2, where different measurements display different numbers of significant figures.) In cases of widely dispersed remains with many obstacles (usually trees) in between, mapping of remains distant from a main cluster could occur only using a GPS unit. The unit was only accurate to within ± 4 m (13 ft.) at best, so less precision is possible in these situations. Given the larger dispersal distances involved, the effects of using GPS coordinates for some more dispersed remains, upon the analysis of the results, were minimal and did not affect the broader patterns present. Coordinates in these cases were converted to Military Grid Reference System (MGRS) format using the World Geodetic System 1984 (WGS84) mapping datum so that distances between objects could be calculated. Postmortem intervals (PMIs) were determined to the nearest half month. In many cases, the date of death was thought to be the same as the time declared missing, depending upon the circumstances of the death. Cases with uncertain PMIs were rejected from the sample. Multiple cases did not have suitable dispersal data, so these were included only for purposes of comparing skeletal completeness vs. time. The presence or absence of carnivore and rodent gnawing was recorded for every case, as an indicator of what might be causing the dispersal.

Site Size over Time

The sizes of the sites over time were calculated in two different ways. Maximum width was the widest distance between any two portions of remains. In some cases, the approximate center of dispersal could be determined or estimated accurately enough for a broad analysis. Maximum site radius was measured from this point to the farthest recovered remains. In cases with partially intact decomposed bodies or skeletons that did not appear to have been moved prior to dispersal, the center of the scene was set as the location of the sacrum. When there was no longer any clear concentration of remains, the center of any visible decomposition stain with fly casings was used as the starting point for the body. In two cases, the site center was estimated to be a noose still in position on a tree with remains dispersed around it. Multiple scenes lacked any clear indication of a center, so maximum radius could not be calculated. In scenes where dispersal occurred only in one direction, the maximum width and maximum radius were the same. Differences in elevation were ignored for the purposes of this analysis.

Results are presented in Table 5.2 and Figures 5.15 and 5.16. The average PMI ($n = 38$) was 18.5 ± 24.8 months, ranging from 1 to 106 months. The average width of sites for which this could be calculated ($n = 24$) was 28.8 ± 33.8 m, ranging from (essentially) 0 m to 155 m. The site with 0 m dispersal was a unique occurrence in an island environment lacking most large scavengers, such as raccoons and coyotes in particular. The skeleton was mostly articulated but not 100% complete, with some small elements not recovered. Rodent gnawing was present, so some non-recovered elements could have been dispersed but not recovered. This skeleton was in a dense brush environment, impossible to detect until very close, and had the longest PMI (106 months). Cases with negligible dispersal therefore can occur under specialized circumstances but are atypical in most terrestrial surface environments.

The average radius of sites ($n = 16$) was 24.3 ± 37.7 m, also ranging from 0 m to 155 m. The similarity between the width and radius of sites is due to the commonness of most dispersal being in one direction: remains did not tend to be spread randomly in any direction. This directionality may be due to nonhuman animal behavior and the choice to move remains away from human habitations, along game trails, or to more sheltered locations where feeding could take place with less interruption, including dens. Since directionality of dispersal cannot be assumed, once maximum radius has been noted in one direction, this distance at minimum should be searched in all directions if the center of the site is known.

Utilizing cases for which width could be calculated and omitting two outliers ($n = 22$), a Spearman's r analysis found no significant correlation between time and site width ($r = -0.047$; one-tailed $p = 0.4179$) (Figure 5.15).

Table 5.2 Dispersal Site Data for a Sample (N = 38) of Terrestrial Forensic Scenes in Massachusetts, United States

Case #	Skeletal Completeness	Cadaver Dog Used	Environment	Gnawing Carnivore	Gnawing Rodent	Max Radius (m)	Max Width (m)	PMI (months)
1	1	Y	Marsh in forest	Y	Y	—	4.22	38
2	4	N	Forest	Y	N	22.99	27.67	6
3	5	N	Forest	Y	N	23.05	23.05	6
4	3	Y	Forest	Y	N	27.20	31.54	5
5	4	Y	Forest/suburban	Y	N	—	4.71	19
6	4	N	Forest/suburban	Y	Y	13.88	18.95	27
7	4	N	Forest/suburban	Y	N	23.31	23.31	7
8	5	N	Forest	Y	N	2.31	2.54	4
9	2	Y	Forest	Y	Y	—	39.13	12
10	4	N	Forest/suburban	Y	N	—	4.32	10
11	4	Y	Forest/suburban	Y	N	14.73	14.73	32
12	4	Y	Forest	Y	N	—	51.50	10
13	5	Y	Forest/suburban	N	N	8.99	10.51	14
14	3	Y	Forest/suburban	Y	N	1.07	1.81	11
15	5	N	Forest/suburban	Y	Y	13	13	69
16	3	Y	Forest	Y	N	59.43	63.51	1.5
17	3	N	Forest/suburban	Y	N	6.35	9.40	1.5
18	5	Y	Forest/suburban	Y	N	9.34	10.49	22
19	4	N	Forest/suburban	N	N	7.37	11.02	4
20	1	N	Forest	Y	Y	155	155	47
21	5	Unk	Forest/suburban	N	N	—	—	5
22	5	Unk	Marsh/suburban	Y	N	—	—	3.5
23	5	Y	Forest/suburban	N	N	—	—	1
24	5	Y	Forest	N	N	—	—	2
25	5	Unk	Urban	N	N	—	—	1.5
26	1	Y	Forest	N	Y	—	—	65
27	5	Unk	Urban	N	N	—	—	5
28	5	Unk	Forest/suburban	N	N	—	—	1
29	5	Unk	Forest/suburban	Y	Y	—	—	7
30	1	Y	Forest/suburban	Y	Y	—	—	82
31	5	Unk	Forest/suburban	Y	Y	—	—	20.5
32	5	Unk	Forest/suburban	Y	N	—	—	10
33	4	Unk	Forest/suburban	Y	N	—	—	2
34	2	Y	Forest	Y	N	—	51.79	4
35	1	Y	Forest	Y	N	—	—	3
36	3	Y	Forest	Y	N	—	59.68	7
37	5	N	Forest	N	Y	0	—	106
38	1	Y	Forest/suburban	Y	N	—	60	31.5

Skeletal completeness: 5 = complete or nearly complete; 4 = ~75% complete; 3 = ~50% complete; 2 = ~25% complete; 1 = <10% complete

Similarly, utilizing cases for which the radius could be calculated and omitting two outliers (n = 14), a Spearman's r analysis found no significant correlation between time and site width (r = 0.1676; one-tailed p = 0.2831) (Figure 5.16). These results indicate that sites in this environment are not showing a trend toward getting larger over time, but more data from other environments and taking such factors as season into consideration are needed. Sites may get dispersed quickly if scavengers are active in the environment. It is also likely that much dispersal does not get detected for older sites, since heavily dispersed remains might not be located at all, in part due to the color changes discussed earlier or due to dispersal distances beyond search radii. This factor may give the appearance of lesser degrees of dispersal, while in fact the opposite has occurred.

Skeletal Completeness over Time

In order to examine for variation in skeletal completeness over time, a five-point scale was implemented on the remains recovered from the same case sample from the OCME, Massachusetts (Table 5.2). This scale range followed: (1) ~10% complete, (2) ~25% complete, (3)

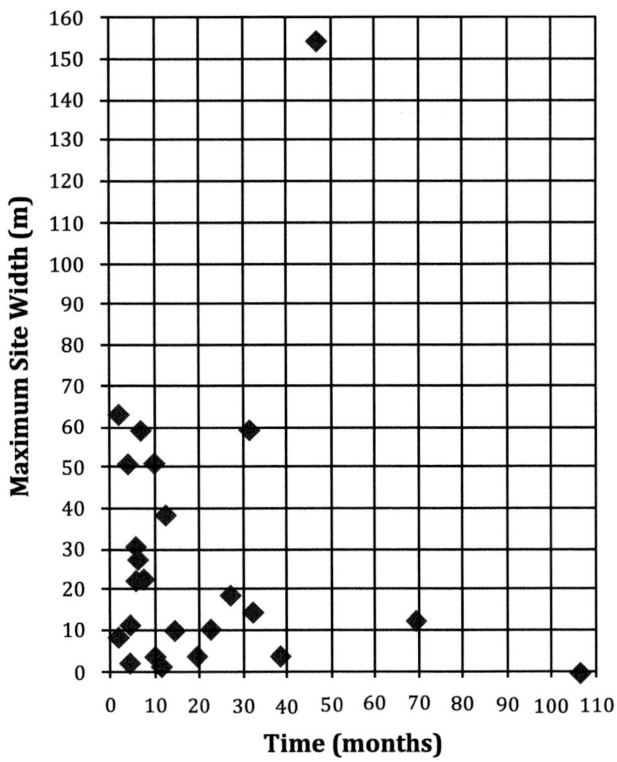

Figure 5.15 Outdoor terrestrial surface site maximum width compared with time between death and recovery; data are derived from forensic archaeological case data in Massachusetts, United States.

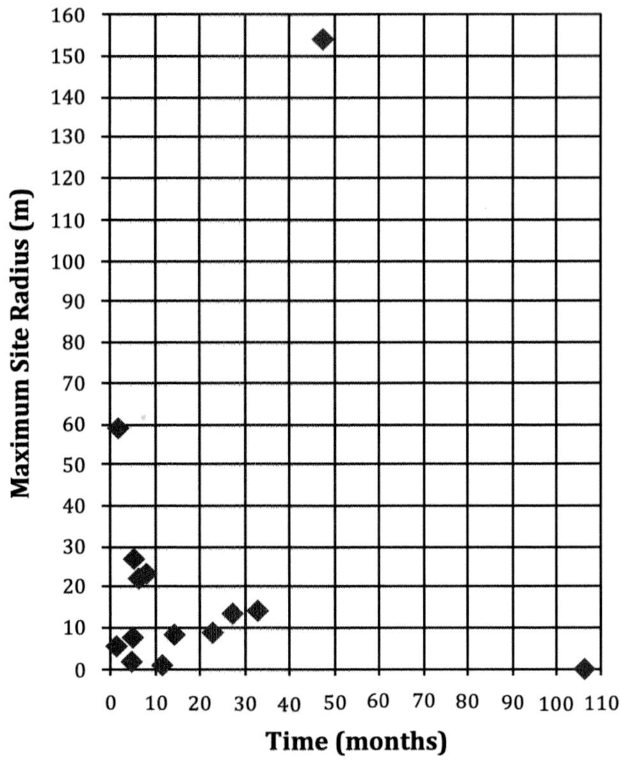

Figure 5.16 Outdoor terrestrial surface site maximum radius compared with time between death and recovery; data are derived from forensic archaeological case data in Massachusetts, United States.

~50% complete, (4) ~75% complete, and (5) complete or nearly complete sets of remains. These were plotted in time in months vs. completeness of the remains (Figure 5.17). One outlier case persisted as complete/nearly complete as late as 69 months, but this outdoor surface case involved remains recovered from a tent that protected them over much of that interval. Another case involved two different phases of recovery years apart and was omitted from correlation calculations. The non-dispersed island case, described above, also was omitted. Utilizing the remaining (n = 35) cases, a Spearman's r correlation analysis found a significant negative correlation between time and completeness (r = −0.325; one-tailed p = 0.02746). It was noted that three of the cases with the lowest recovery amounts (scores of 1) had undergone some of the longest amounts of exposure (38, 65, and 82 months). It is possible that with larger sample sizes, a more significant negative correlation could emerge between completeness and duration of the PMI. However, completeness of recovery may be affected by the thoroughness of searching methods, so any relationship may be subject to other factors besides time.

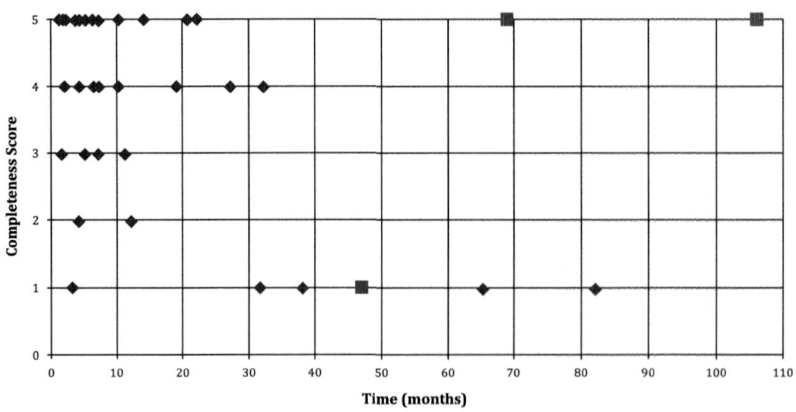

Figure 5.17 Skeletal completeness over time: 5 = complete/~complete; 4 = ~75% complete; 3 = ~50% complete; 2 = ~25% complete; 1 = <10% complete (diamond = one observation, square = two observations). Data are derived from forensic archaeological case data in Massachusetts, United States.

Sites with fewer surviving remains are less easy to locate, so these scenes may never make up a large portion of a surface remains case sample. Conversely, remains persisted in the highest category of completeness (5) as late as 22 months and the second-highest category (4) as late as 32 months in this environment.

Conclusions: Outdoor Search Procedure Recommendations

Outdoor search parameters (refer to Chapter 6) should be tailored to the search environments usually encountered and the nonhuman dispersal patterns found there. Forensic practitioners working in more open, semi-arid environments may encounter different patterns than those working in forested temperate environments. In practice, this means accumulating data over time from forensic scenes in a specific environment in order to understand variation in dispersal distances and why these occur. Search and recovery methods also may vary based upon such factors as the presence of significant leaf litter on the ground surface and the type of topsoil usually encountered and how difficult it is to screen. All field recovery reports should therefore include information on distances of bone dispersal for later analysis. The methods used, including cadaver dogs, should be included so that their possible effects upon bone recovery can be analyzed.

Nonhuman vertebrates routinely disperse bones as a part of their feeding activity, and this taphonomic agency has the greatest effect upon subsequent site size in terrestrial environments. Author James T. Pokines often uses a tiered system for outdoor recoveries (Pokines, 2015). After preliminary searching, the central site area and any visible bone clusters are processed in an inward direction. Direction of searching is then reversed, and the site boundaries are expanded, while the central portion is assessed, and mapping begins. This system allows the searchers to know which elements are missing from the skeleton while the search is still in progress. The area around the site center can undergo additional searching if needed using standard methods (Chapter 6), and cadaver dogs can also search for more highly dispersed elements.

Key Terms

biostratinomy
crenulated margin
cylinder
dispersal
dry-bone rodent gnawing
edge polish
humus
leaf litter
necrology
subaerial weathering
taphonomic agencies
taphonomic effects
taphonomy
tooth furrows
tooth pits
tooth punctures
tooth scores (striations)
wet-bone rodent gnawing

REVIEW AND DISCUSSION QUESTIONS

1. What is taphonomy? Why is it important regarding the recovery of human remains from forensic scenes?
2. What are some of the key species responsible for bone dispersal?
3. How does bone dispersal affect scene recovery methods?
4. How does bone natural camouflage affect bone recovery rates?
5. Research the predominate scavenging species where you work and/or study and describe the effects they may have on human remains.

Suggested Readings

Behrensmeyer, A.K. 1978. Taphonomic and ecologic information from bone weathering. *Paleobiology* 4:150–162. DOI:10.1017/S0094837300005820

Haglund, W.D., Sorg, M.H. (eds). 1997. *Forensic Taphonomy: The Postmortem Fate of Human Remains*. Boca Raton, FL: CRC Press. DOI:10.1201/9781439821923

Lyman, R.L. 1994. *Vertebrate Taphonomy*. New York: Cambridge University Press. DOI:10.1017/CBO9781139878302

Pokines, J.T., L'Abbé, E.N., S.A. Symes, S. A. (eds). 2022. *Manual of Forensic Taphonomy*, 2nd ed., Boca Raton, FL: CRC Press. DOI:10.4324/9781003171492

Sorg, M.H., ed. In press. *Haglund and Sorg's Forensic Taphonomy: 21st Century Advances and Regional Variation*. Boca Raton, FL: CRC Press.

References

Arilla, M., Rosell, J., Blasco, R. 2019. Contributing to characterise wild predator behaviour: consumption pattern, spatial distribution and bone damage on ungulate carcasses consumed by red fox (*Vulpes vulpes*). *Archaeological and Anthropological Sciences* 11(5):2271–2291. DOI:10.1007/s12520-018-0675-x

Arilla, M., Rosell, J., Blasco, R. 2020. A neo-taphonomic approach to human campsites modified by carnivores. *(Nature) Scientific Reports* 10:6659. DOI:10.1038/s41598-020-63431-8

Ballejo, F., Fernández, F.J., Montalvo, C.I., De Santis, L.J.M. 2015. Taphonomy and dispersion of bones scavenged by New World vultures and caracaras in Northwestern Patagonia: implications for the formation of archaeological sites. *Archaeological and Anthropological Sciences* 8(2):305–315. DOI:10.1007/s12520-015-0277–9

Berryman, H.E. 2001. Disarticulation pattern and tooth mark artifacts associated with pig scavenging of human remains: a case study. In: Haglund, W.D., Sorg, M.H., eds. *Advances in Forensic Taphonomy: Method, Theory, and Archaeological Perspectives*, pp. 487-495. Boca Raton, FL: CRC Press.

Binford, L. 1981. *Bones: Ancient Men and Modern Myths*. New York: Academic Press.

Bright, L.N. 2011. Taphonomic signatures of animal scavenging in Northern California: A forensic anthropological analysis. M.A. Thesis. Chico: California State University. https://hdl.handle.net/10211.3/10211.4_284

Dabbs, G.R., Martin, D.C. 2013. Geographic variation in the taphonomic effect of vulture scavenging: The case for southern Illinois. *Journal of Forensic Sciences* 58(S1):S20–S25. DOI:10.1111/1556–4029.12025

Demo, C., Rogério Cansi, E., Kosmann, C., Pujol-Luz, J.R. 2013. Vultures and others scavenger vertebrates associated with man-sized pig carcasses: A perspective in forensic taphonomy. *Zoologia (Curitiba)* 30(5):574–576. DOI:10.1590/S1984-46702013000500010

Efremov, J.A. 1940. Taphonomy: New branch of paleontology. *Pan-American Geologist* 74(2):81–93.

Evans, T. 2022. Fluvial taphonomy. In: Pokines, J.T., L'Abbé, E.N., Symes, S.A., eds. *Manual of Forensic Taphonomy*, 2nd ed., pp. 163–191. Boca Raton, FL: CRC Press.

Fisher, J.W. 1995. Bone surface modifications in zooarchaeology. *Journal of Archaeological Method and Theory* 2(1):7–68. DOI:10.1007/BF02228434

Haglund, W.D. 1991. Applications of taphonomic models to forensic applications. Ph.D. Dissertation. Seattle: University of Washington. https://www.proquest.com/dissertations-theses/applications-taphonomic-models-forensic/docview/304019483/se-2

Haglund, W.D. 1997a. Rodents and human remains. In: Haglund, W.D., Sorg, M.H., eds. *Forensic Taphonomy: The Postmortem Fate of Human Remains*, pp. 405–414. Boca Raton, FL: CRC Press.

Haglund, W.D. 1997b. Scattered skeletal human remains: search strategy considerations for locating missing teeth. In: Haglund, W.D., Sorg, M.H., eds. *Forensic Taphonomy: The Postmortem Fate of Human Remains*, pp. 383–394. Boca Raton, FL: CRC Press.

Haglund, W.D., Reay, D.T., Swindler, D. R. 1988. Tooth mark artifacts and survival of bones in animal scavenged human skeletons. *Journal of Forensic Sciences*, 33: 985–997.

Harding, B.E., Wolf, B.C. 2006. Alligator attacks in southwest Florida. *Journal of Forensic Sciences*, 51: 674–677. DOI:10.1111/j.1556-4029.2006.00135.x

Haynes, G. 1980. Prey bones and predators: Potential ecologic information from analysis of bone sites. *Ossa* 7:75–97.

Haynes, G. 1981. Bone modifications and skeletal disturbances by natural agencies: Studies in North America. Ph.D. Dissertation. Washington, DC: Catholic University of America. DOI:10.13140/RG.2.1.4561.8085

Hockett, B.S. 1989. The concept of "carrying range": A method for determining the role played by woodrats in contribution bones to archeological sites. *Nevada Archaeologist* 7(1):28–35.

Hoffman, R., Hays, C. 1987. The eastern wood rat (*Neotoma floridana*) as a taphonomic factor in archaeological sites. *Journal of Archaeological Science* 14(3):325–337. DOI:10.1016/0305-4403(87)90020-3

Horwitz, L., Smith, P. 1988. The effects of striped hyaena activity on human remains. *Journal of Archaeological Science* 15(5):471–481. DOI:10.1016/0305-4403(88)90077-5

IKEA 2025. FRAKTA Shopping bag, large, blue [online]. Available from: https://www.ikea.com/us/en/p/frakta-shopping-bag-large-blue-17228340/. Accessed 2025, January 01.

Işcan, M.Y., McCabe, B.Q. 1995. Analysis of human remains recovered from a shark. *Forensic Science International* 72:15–23. DOI: 10.1016/0379-0738(94)01643-J

Keyes, C.A., Myburgh, J., Brits, D. 2021. Scavenger activity in a peri-urban agricultural setting in the Highveld of South Africa. *International Journal of Legal Medicine* 135:979–991. DOI:10.1007/s00414-020-02413-x

King, K.A., Lord, W.D., Ketchum, H.R., O'Brien, R.C. 2016. Postmortem scavenging by the Virginia opossum (*Didelphis virginiana*): Impact on taphonomic assemblages and progression. *Forensic Science International* 266:576.e1–576.e6. DOI:10.1016/j.forsciint.2016.06.021

Kjorlien, Y.P. 2004. Patterns in the scattering of remains due to scavenger activity. M.A. Thesis. Edmonton: University of Alberta. https://www.proquest.com/dissertations-theses/patterns-scattering-remains-due-scavenger/docview/305095295/se-2

Kjorlien, Y.P., Beattie, O.B., Peterson, A.E. 2009. Scavenging activity can produce predictable patterns in surface skeletal remains scattering: Observations and comments from two experiments. *Forensic Science International* 188:103–106. DOI:10.1016/j.forsciint.2009.03.022

Komar, D., Beattie, O. 1998. Identifying bird scavenging in fleshed and dry remains. *Canadian Society of Forensic Science Journal* 31(3):177–188. DOI:10.1080/00085030.1998.10757117

Lyman, R.L. 1994. *Vertebrate Taphonomy*. Cambridge: Cambridge University Press. DOI:10.1017/CBO9781139878302

Martin, R.E. 1999. *Taphonomy: A Process Approach*. Cambridge: Cambridge University Press. DOI:10.1017/CBO9780511612381

McCallister, D. 2025. Recovery rates of osseous materials with variable taphonomic color change. M.S. Thesis. Boston, MA: Boston University School of Medicine.

Miller, J.H. 2011. Ghosts of Yellowstone: Multi-decadal histories of wildlife populations captured by bones on a modern landscape. *PLoS ONE* 6(3):e18057. DOI:10.1371/journal.pone.0018057

Morton, R.J., Lord, W. D. 2006. Taphonomy of child-sized remains: A study of scattering and scavenging in Virginia, USA. *Journal of Forensic Sciences* 51(3):475–479. DOI:10.1111/j.1556-4029.2006.00134.x

Moss, K.E. 2012. The effects of avian and terrestrial scavenger activity on human remains and decomposition in Southeast Texas during an 18 month study. M.A. Thesis. Houston, TX: University of Houston. https://www.proquest.com/dissertations-theses/effects-avian-terrestrial-scavenger-activity-on/docview/1283178681/se-2

Newcomb, A., Pokines, J.T., Moore, T.E. 2017. Taphonomic effects of mechanical plowing on buried juvenile remains. *Journal of Forensic Sciences* 62(1):67–73. DOI:10.1111/1556-4029.13259

Ouacha, H., Ben Moussa, A., Simao, J. 2013. The salt crystallization weathering of building rocks of the archaeological sites calcarenites of north-western Morocco (Lixus, Banasa and Thamusida). *European Scientific Journal* 9(18):282–290. DOI:10.1007/s41024-022-00237-3

Pal, S., Saha, S. 1989. Coefficient of thermal expansion of bone. In: Sahay, K.B., Saxena, R.K., eds. *Biomechanics*, pp. 52–60. New York: Wiley.

Pokines, J.T. 2015. A procedure for processing outdoor surface forensic scenes yielding skeletal remains among leaf litter. *Journal of Forensic Identification* 65(2):161–172. DOI:10.1080/0046813X.2015.1037437

Pokines, J.T. 2016. Taphonomic alterations to terrestrial surface-deposited human osseous remains in a New England environment. *Journal of Forensic Identification* 66(1):59–78.

Pokines, J.T. 2022a. Faunal dispersal, reconcentration, and gnawing damage to bone in terrestrial environments. In: Pokines, J.T., L'Abbé, E.N., Symes, S.A., eds. *Manual of Forensic Taphonomy*, 2nd ed., pp. 295–359. Boca Raton, FL: CRC Press.

Pokines, J.T. 2022b. Preliminary study of gull (Laridae) scavenging and dispersal of vertebrate remains, Shoals Marine Laboratory, coastal New England. *Journal of Forensic Sciences* 67(3):1149–1156. DOI:10.1111/1556-4029.14986

Pokines, J.T., Baker, J.E. 2022. Effects of burial environment on osseous remains. In: Pokines, J.T., L'Abbé, E.N., Symes, S.A., eds. *Manual of Forensic Taphonomy*, 2nd ed., pp. 103–161. Boca Raton, FL: CRC Press.

Pokines, J.T., Baker, S.E., Pollock, C. 2022a. Avian taphonomy. In: Pokines, J.T., L'Abbé, E.N., Symes, S.A., eds. *Manual of Forensic Taphonomy*, 2nd ed., pp. 581–604. Boca Raton, FL: CRC Press.

Pokines, J.T., L'Abbé, E.N., Symes, S. A. (eds). 2022b. *Manual of Forensic Taphonomy*, 2nd ed., Boca Raton, FL: CRC Press. DOI:10.4324/9781003171492

Pokines, J.T., Faillace, K., Berger, J., Pirtle, D., Sharpe, M., Curtis, A., Lombardi, K., Admans, J. 2018a. The effects of repeated wet-dry cycles as a component of bone weathering. *Journal of Archaeological Science: Reports* 17:433–441. DOI:10.1016/j.jasr.2017.08.002

Pokines, J.T., Mammano, K., Studebaker-Reed, M., Mowery, J., Patterson, M., Schneider, C., Trapp, B., Mincher, C. 2018b. Success rates of recovering dispersed bones among leaf litter. *Forensic Anthropology* 1(4):189–200. DOI:10.5744/fa.2018.0021

Pokines, J.T., Higgs, N.D. 2022. Marine environmental alterations to bone. In: Pokines, J.T., L'Abbé, E.N., Symes, S.A., eds. *Manual of Forensic Taphonomy*, 2nd ed., pp. 193–249. Boca Raton, FL: CRC Press.

Pokines, J.T., Kelley, S., Muschal, A., Liggett, I., Zamora, A., Hill, M., Sater, S., Shamlou, A., O'Brien, M. 2021. Bone dispersal by vertebrate taxa in an urban park environment in New England, USA. *Forensic Science International* 327:110982. DOI:10.1016/j.forsciint.2021.110982

Pokines, J.T., Kerbis Peterhans, J.C. 2007. Spotted hyena (*Crocuta crocuta*) den use and taphonomy in the Masai Mara National Reserve, Kenya. *Journal of Archaeological Science* 34(11):1914–1931. DOI:10.1016/j.jas.2007.01.012

Pokines, J.T., King, R.E., Graham, D.D., Costello, A.K., Adams, D.M., Pendray, J.M., Rao, K., Siwek, D. 2016. The effects of experimental freeze-thaw cycles to bone as a component of subaerial weathering. *Journal of Archaeological Science: Reports* 6:594–602. DOI:10.1016/j.jasrep.2016.03.019

Pokines, J.T., Nowell, A., Bisson, M.S., Cordova, C.E., Ames, C.J.H. 2011. The functioning of a natural faunal trap in a semi-arid environment: Preliminary investigations of WZM-1, a limestone sinkhole site near Wadi Zarqa Ma'in, Hashemite Kingdom of Jordan. *Journal of Taphonomy* 9(2):89–115. DOI:10.1676/07-121.1

Pokines, J.T., Robinson, S., Mansz, J., Heidel, N., Jasny, K., Gilligan, J., Carmona, A., Kroll, J., Lavigne, S., Calle, S. 2019a. Success rates of forensic surface search for osseous remains in a New England, U.S.A. environment. *Forensic Anthropology* 2(1):9–20. DOI:10.5744/fa.2018.1029

Pokines, J.T., Udoni, M.M., Sanders Stark, S., Cassidy, S., Atkinson, M.L., Church, E., File, C. L., Green, M.K., Herrera, M.D., Kilroy, G.S., Peace, B.N., Purcell, B.J., Reinman, A.S., Sanchez, A.M., Springman, S.J. 2019b. Success rates of recovering teeth and infant-sized bones dispersed among leaf litter. *Forensic Anthropology* 2(3):168–177. DOI:10.5744/fa.2019.1033

Pokines, J.T., Spiegel, C. 2022. Subaerial weathering and other terrestrial surface taphonomic processes. In: Pokines, J.T., L'Abbé, E.N., Symes, S.A., eds. *Manual of Forensic Taphonomy*, 2nd ed., pp. 403–441. Boca Raton, FL: CRC Press.

Pollock, C., Pokines, J.T., Bethard, J. 2018. Organic staining on bone from exposure to wood and other plant materials. *Forensic Science International* 283:200–210. DOI: 10.1016/j.forsciint.2017.12.021

Reeves, N.M. 2009. Taphonomic effects of vulture scavenging. *Journal of Forensic Sciences* 54(3):523–528. DOI:10.1111/j.1556-4029.2009.01020.x

Ricketts, D.R. 2013. Scavenging effects and scattering patterns on Porcine Carcasses in Eastern Massachusetts. M.S. Thesis. Boston, MA: Boston University School of Medicine. https://hdl.handle.net/2144/17143

Schneider, C., Pokines, J.T., L'Abbé, E.N., Pobiner, B. 2022. Reptile taphonomy. In: Pokines, J.T., L'Abbé, E.N., Symes, S.A., eds. *Manual of Forensic Taphonomy*, 2nd ed., pp. 667–693. Boca Raton, FL: CRC Press.

Schultz, J.J., Dupras, T.L. 2022. Identifying the origin of taphonomic bone staining and color changes in forensic contexts. In: Pokines, J.T., L'Abbé, E.N., Symes S.A., eds. *Manual of Forensic Taphonomy*, 2nd ed., pp. 443–472. Boca Raton, FL: CRC Press. DOI:10.4324/9781003171492-12

Schultz, J.J., Hawkins, M.M., Mitchell, A.T. 2018. Skeletal weathering in central Florida: A preliminary approach for developing a scoring protocol to estimate time since death. *Forensic Science International* 290:85–93. DOI:10.1016/j.forsciint.2018.06.017

Schultz, J.J., Mitchell, A.T. 2018. Avian scavenging of small-sized pig carcasses in Central Florida: Utilizing GIS to analyze site variables affecting skeletal dispersal. *Journal of Forensic Sciences* 63(4):1021–1032. DOI:10.1111/1556-4029.13694

Spies, M.J., Finaughty, D.A., Gibbon, V.E. 2018. Forensic taphonomy: Scavenger-induced scattering patterns in the temperate southwestern Cape, South Africa—A first look. *Forensic Science International* 290:29–35. DOI:10.1016/j.forsciint.2018.06.015

Spradley, M.K., Hamilton, M.D., Giordano, A. 2012. Spatial patterning of vulture scavenged human remains. *Forensic Science International* 219:57–63. DOI:10.1016/j.forsciint.2011.11.030

Stiner, M., Munro, N.D., Sanz, M. 2012. Carcass damage and digested bone from mountain lions (*Felis concolor*): Implications for carcass persistence on landscapes as a function of prey age. *Journal of Archaeological Science* 39(4):896–907. DOI:10.1016/j.jas.2011.10.020

Stolen, E.D. 2000. Foraging behavior of vultures in central Florida. *Florida Field Naturalist* 28(4):173–181.

Trueman, C.N.G., Behrensmeyer, A. K., Tuross, N., Weiner, S. 2004. Mineralogical and compositional changes in bones exposed on soil surfaces in Amboseli National Park, Kenya: Diagenetic mechanisms and the role of sediment pore fluids. *Journal of Archaeological Science* 31(6):721–739. DOI:10.1016/j.jas.2003.11.003

Udoni, M.M., Pokines, J.T., Moore, T.L. 2021. Experimental study of black bear (*Ursus americanus*) and grizzly bear (*U. arctos*) tooth marks and other gnawing damage on bone. *Forensic Anthropology* 4(2):71–87. DOI:10.5744/fa.2020.0035

Wilson, D. E., Reeder, D. M. (eds). 2005. *Mammal Species of the World*, 3rd ed., Baltimore, MD: The Johns Hopkins University.

Young, A., Márquez-Grant, N., Stillman, R., Smith, M.J., Korstjens, A.H. 2015. An investigation of red fox (*Vulpes vulpes*) and Eurasian badger (*Meles meles*) scavenging, scattering, and removal of deer remains: Forensic implications and applications. *Journal of Forensic Sciences* 60(S1):S39–S55. DOI:10.1111/1556-4029.12554

Young, A., Stillman, R., Smith, M. J., Korstjens, A. H. 2016. Applying knowledge of species-typical scavenging behavior to the search and recovery of mammalian skeletal remains. *Journal of Forensic Sciences* 61(2):458–456. DOI:10.1111/1556-4029.12974

SEARCH TECHNIQUES FOR LOCATING HUMAN REMAINS

Learning Objectives

- Introduce search methods used to locate human remains and associated evidence on the ground surface.
- Introduce search methods for locating clandestine graves and burial sites, including locating smaller areas or potential features that require more detailed searches.
- Provide casework examples that are useful for the reader to understand how to apply search methods in multiple contexts.

Learning Connections

- Employing proper field methods for recovering human remains are presented throughout this book and begin with proper search methods.
- Establish the interconnectedness of the skills and guidelines presented throughout this book that start with searches and discovery of human remains so forensic scenes can be properly processed, documented, and interpreted.

In forensic investigations, searches are performed to locate hidden **graves**, bodies deposited on the ground surface, and associated evidence. Searches are also commonly employed when searching for dispersed and missing body parts or skeletal elements. At the same time, searches also can be utilized to rule out areas so investigations can continue at additional suspected areas. Before conducting a search, a search plan should be formulated that identifies the personnel and equipment needed and the specific search techniques to be used.

The purpose of this chapter is to focus on search methods used to locate human remains and associated evidence on the surface, as well as strategies for locating missing and dispersed remains to identify the parameters for processing the scene. At the same time, methods for locating **clandestine graves** will be discussed, including locating smaller areas or potential features that require more detailed searches. It is important to note that the methods used when searching for a site are distinct from the methods used to process a site once it has been located. **Searching** implies utilizing broad search methods during attempts at locating a site or scattered remains, while **site processing** involves detailed searching *after* locating a site or scattered remains to delineate the extent of the site and to locate additional bones and associated evidence. Site processing often involves detailed clearing of the scene, mapping, and collection of remains and associated evidence, and excavation of remains if needed.

In addition to involving a forensic archaeologist in searches, including a forensic anthropologist on-site during the search phase can also be beneficial for identifying potentially significant physical evidence in situ. Often, the forensic anthropologist may serve as the on-site forensic archaeologist as well. Forensic anthropologists can provide a quick evaluation of remains to determine the following:

- Bone vs. non-bone material
- Human vs. nonhuman bones
- Forensic vs. non-forensic skeletal remains (e.g., historic, and prehistoric)
- Missing human skeletal elements and teeth that may still be within the search area
- Typical taphonomic alterations encountered on bones deposited in that environment and how this might affect recovery and subsequent analysis.

Most searches will have a greater rate of success when employing multiple methods (France et al., 1992, 1997). Search techniques can be either nonintrusive or intrusive. **Nonintrusive searches** are primarily performed by looking for remains and associated evidence deposited on the ground surface and searching for surface changes

DOI: 10.4324/9781315201658-6

consistent with a clandestine grave. Nonintrusive searches use nondestructive methods, which include visual surface searches, **human remains detection (HRD)** dogs and the majority of geophysical prospecting methods as discussed in Chapter 7. Conversely, **intrusive searches** use destructive methods with the potential to damage human remains and evidence; therefore, they should only be used as a follow-up to visual surface search methods or when nonintrusive methods are not successful. Intrusive searches include probing and coring the soil, digging test excavations, **shovel shining**, and the use of heavy equipment.

TYPES OF SEARCH AREAS

There are three basic types of areas that can be defined when searching for human remains: open, obstructed, and submerged (Killam, 2004). **Open areas** can be searched using aerial reconnaissance, walking grids, or remote sensing techniques. These areas include fields, flatlands, backyards, or any area that is primarily open to a 360° field of vision. Searchers tend to have the most success in locating remains in open areas. Urban developments, wooded areas, caves, and any other landscape features that impede search techniques are defined as **obstructed areas**, where it becomes more difficult to locate remains. Searches in **submerged areas**, or those underwater on a regular or seasonal basis, require specialized equipment and personnel. Search and mapping techniques used in submerged areas are specific to each individual case and are less commonly utilized.

PLANNING THE SEARCH

Preparation for a search is just as important as the search itself. The planning phase should include a preliminary physical reconnaissance of the search area to learn more about the terrain, the different search methods that can be used, and any specialized equipment that may be necessary. Prior to beginning every search, carefully determine the boundaries of the area to be searched and the different methods that will be used. If a large area is to be searched, geographic or topographic maps and aerial photographs can be helpful in providing specific information about the terrain and area to be searched (refer to Chapter 8 for various photographic and map resources). Maps and aerial photographs are typically used to determine how the area can be divided for the search and which search methods may produce the best results. While aerial photographs can be obtained commonly from online mapping sources, law enforcement also may collect aerial images of potential search areas using a helicopter or drone. Maps and photographs are also used to show any changes in the terrain that may have occurred since the body was buried. For example, an aerial photograph of the proposed search area from the estimated or reported date of **burial** and an aerial photograph from present day should be compared to determine any changes in the landscape and whether the suspected **burial site** is still intact and accessible (Figure 6.1). If a structure, pavement, or roadway was placed over the body after it was buried, traditional visual search methods will not work. However, it may still be possible to conduct a non-invasive search by conducting a geophysical survey over pavement or blacktop (refer to Chapter 7 on geophysical survey). During the planning phase, search leaders also can decide if there will be a need to track the search in real time. For example, it is possible to use a mapping program such as Google Earth and a GPS unit so that the extent of the search coverage can be plotted while the search is conducted, and these can be traced in real time with multiple searchers.

The planning phase also should entail learning as much as possible about the disposal of the body or burial process. Many offenders undertake extensive measures to dispose of their victims in a manner designed to evade detection. However, according to Killam (2004), most individuals will dispose of bodies in one of two ways: those that are dumped quickly within an area little-known or unknown to the perpetrator; and those that are deposited in an area where the landscape is well-known through ownership, holidays, or frequent visits. Killam (2004) also states that some 90% of victims are recovered downhill from roadways to facilitate carrying or deposition from vehicular access points. Specific information obtained about the disposal process may dictate which search methods will be appropriate. For instance, when planning a search for a buried homicide victim, detectives and other investigators should strive to develop a comprehensive understanding of the burial process while conducting interviews with informants and perpetrators. See Table 6.1 for specific questions to ask in a forensic context about bodies that have been buried to conceal their location. Finally, on the day of the search, ensure that sufficient personnel are available to conduct the search in the designated area and that all necessary equipment and experts arrive as scheduled. In addition, make sure that refreshments are provided for the personnel involved in the search. Providing water, snacks, and hot or cold drinks can help the search team to avoid many instances of heat stroke or overexposure to cold depending on the weather. Additional resources to provide search personnel include bug spray, sunscreen, a popup tent with chairs, as well as a command center with a bathroom. Refer to Chapter 2 for detailed lists of tools and equipment needed for searches and recoveries.

Figure 6.1 Aerial photographs of demarcated area of interest in 2012 (left), when body was deposited in forested area east of a small lake, and the same area of interest in 2018 (right) when forensic search was conducted. While a significant amount of construction had occurred in the interim, combined visual and geophysical search methods still produced positive results in locating the remains.

Table 6.1 Questions Investigators Should Ask Suspects/Informants about a Burial Prior to Conducting a Search

- When did the event occur?
- How large (i.e., height and weight) was the missing individual?
- How deep was the body buried?
- How long and wide was the grave? What was used to dig the grave?
- Were large tree roots encountered when digging? Were they cut, and if so, with what?
- In what position/direction was the body placed?
- Was the body wrapped in anything (e.g., tarp, rug, plastic sheeting) or placed in a container (e.g., storage bin, suitcase, large cooler)?
- Was the body clothed when it was buried? What type of clothing?
- Were any metal objects present with the body?
- Was anything placed over the body (e.g., boards, concrete, metal debris, or even a pet or a second individual) before the grave was filled?
- What were the local conditions of the area (e.g., dry or moist ground, open or wooded area)?
- Was anything placed over the grave after it was filled (e.g., brush, trash, tree limbs) to conceal its location?
- Were there any unique landmarks near the grave that may be helpful in locating the burial site during the search?
- Has the landscape changed since the body was buried?

VISUAL SURFACE SEARCHES

A **visual surface search** in forensic investigations typically involves lines of personnel who search an area to locate various types of forensic evidence on the ground surface or surface changes that could indicate a clandestine grave. Effective surface searches must utilize several common practices to prevent visual coverage gaps (Pokines and Baker, 2022). First, spacing between searchers must be appropriate for the terrain so that there is 100% visual coverage on a **search sweep**. It is recommended to use narrow spacing between searchers, because controlled research has shown that exposed skeletal elements on the ground surface can be missed by personnel even when proper search procedures are utilized (Pokines et al., 2019a). Second, the limits of coverage for swept areas must be marked visually to prevent gaps when setting the spacing for the next search sweep. Lastly, searches should attempt to devise plans that involve searching areas containing all or most of the surface remains. For example, there are instances when it is easier to estimate the last search sweep area and pattern when there is a partial skeleton dispersed over a limited area and investigators continue to search for the missing elements. However, it may be difficult to locate all of the remains when dealing with scavenged remains, and a forensic archaeologist may have to decide on a reasonable search area, because remains may have been consumed or dispersed beyond this radius.

When searching large areas or areas with obstructions, the quadrant or **zone search** method should be used by dividing the total search area into smaller zones that are easily managed in a day or less (Figure 6.2). These smaller manageable areas could follow existing boundaries formed by natural and cultural (i.e., human-constructed) obstructions or features. For example, natural obstructions can include streams, other bodies of water, hills, and cliffs. Cultural obstructions can include buildings, fences, clearings, roads, and parking lots. After boundaries of the search area have been determined, a pattern must be chosen for an effective and thorough search of the defined area. The pattern should maximize available personnel for the most efficient results, and corners of smaller search areas can be marked using a GPS to ensure 100% coverage of the entire search area. Three of the most effective patterns for visually searching the surface of an area on foot are a **strip (line) pattern**, a **grid pattern**, and a **spiral pattern**. Further, searches may also combine two visual methods such as a strip and spiral pattern.

Strip (Line) Pattern

The most frequently used search pattern is undertaken in a **strip (line) pattern** (Figure 6.3) through a preplanned area that provides 100% coverage if performed properly. Search team members line up in a straight line and are positioned close enough to one another so that their fields of view overlap (Figure 6.4) in strips (also known as **transects**). Depending on the size of the search team and the area to be searched, the individuals will search an area by walking a strip, first in one direction, and then walking in the opposite direction, completing a sweep in the strip adjacent to the first. This is repeated until the entire search area has been covered. Using flagging tape or survey flags, the end persons in the search line should mark the boundaries of the strip being searched in each sweep. Each line also can be spatially documented so that provenience information for the search lines and evidence is documented. Each search line should be directed by a

Figure 6.2 Aerial photograph of community farm used in planning stages when searching for remains that were buried in a tilled field. The zone method was used to divide larger area into smaller controlled search areas. Some zones were further divided into subsections that were more manageable using visual and geophysical search methods.

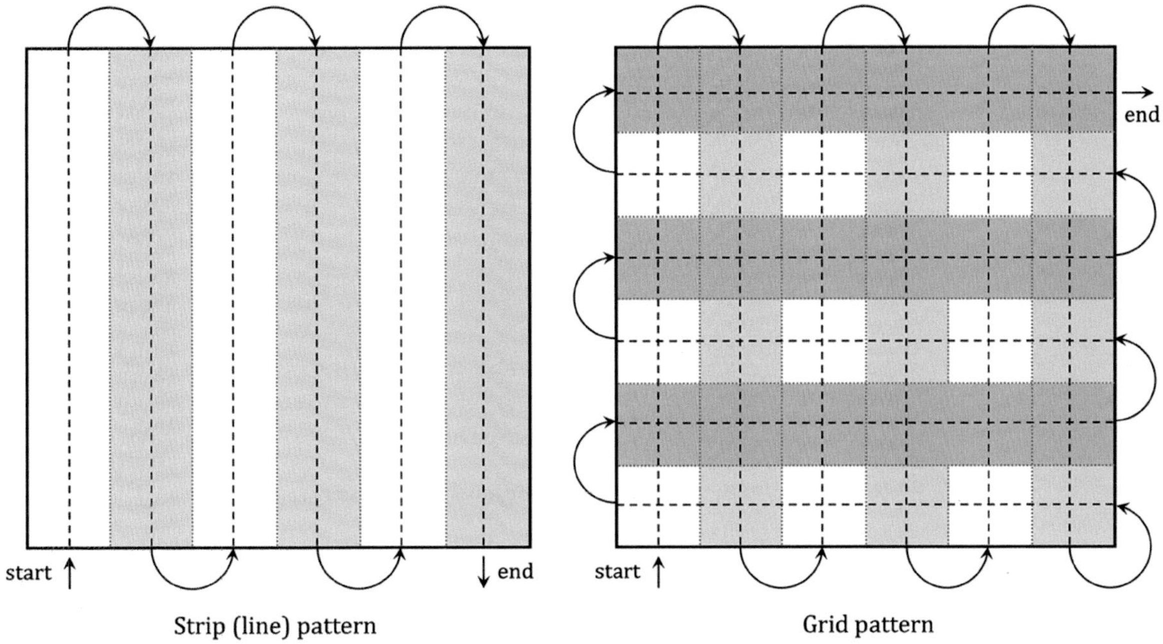

Figure 6.3 Two of the most effective patterns for visually searching the surface of a larger area on foot: a strip (line) pattern (left) and a grid pattern (right), both marked with directional pathways.

Figure 6.4 Author Sandra Wheeler (far left) working as team leader in a strip (line) search. Note that team members are carrying survey flags for use in marking boundaries and any potential evidence found during the search sweep.

team leader who is positioned in the middle of or behind the search line to maintain the pace of the search. If the search team is looking for human remains or evidence of burial, a forensic anthropologist and/or forensic archaeologist can follow behind the line and inspect any item that a searcher thinks might be bone or help identify suspicious surface changes that could be related to burial.

The line should move at a pace that is slow enough to allow all of the searchers ample time to view the ground in their line of sight. The team leader is responsible for ensuring that individual personnel remain within the designated search perimeter and do not advance beyond the established line. If members of the search line move too far ahead, the leader should regulate the pace to maintain formation, either by instructing personnel to reform a straight line or pausing the search to allow slower-moving team members to catch up. If the search line is stopped, only the leader can direct the line to resume the search. Team members should carry survey flags and mark any potential evidence in their respective lanes. When one team member locates potential evidence, he or she should call out to the team leader, and everyone in the line should stop for a detailed search of the immediate area. After everyone has finished the detailed search, the team leader can then direct the line to resume the search.

Grid Pattern

A more time-consuming variation of the line search is called a **grid pattern** (Figure 6.3). Once the line search pattern is completed, the team will search the same area a second time in a direction perpendicular (shifting 90°) to the first search. This pattern provides 200% spatial coverage, because the ground is visually searched twice. The main advantages of this method include searching the ground from two directions at multiple angles, and the same ground will be viewed a second time by different personnel. Experimental research on the success rates of locating nonhuman surface remains in forested environments has shown a higher rate of recovery following a second sweep of the area (Pokines et al., 2019a). In particular, the grid pattern should be utilized in areas with uneven terrain, heavy brush, or ground cover, when it may be difficult to inspect visually every angle of the ground when moving in only one direction across the landscape. In addition, depending on the amount of sunlight, certain surface changes related to burial may be more evident from a different angle of approach in the search line. Therefore, using this pattern increases the potential for discovering skeletal material or evidence that was not possible to locate from another angle.

Spiral Pattern

A **spiral pattern** (Figure 6.5) is most effective when both the search team and designated search area are small, or when the search begins at the top of a hill. Killam (2004) suggests using the spiral pattern as a one-person search method in which the searcher moves in decreasing concentric circles within a small search area (i.e., moving from the outer edges toward the center). This method is commonly used to ensure that evidence is not inadvertently trampled during the initial search. However, there are instances when it is more appropriate to reverse this pattern, starting the search initially inside and moving in a spiral pattern toward the outside. This reversed spiral pattern is often used when searching for bones that might have been dispersed from a known primary deposition site by carnivores or other taphonomic processes. In this instance, the pattern would begin at the location of the primary deposition site and continue outward in increasing concentric circles, as more bones are located.

Inside-Out Pattern

A key challenge with spiral pattern searches involves maintaining an expanding spiral that results in coverage gaps and difficulty maintaining 100% coverage (Pokines and Baker, 2022). An alternate method for processing a scene with a known concentration of bones has been suggested by Pokines (2015) as an **inside-out pattern** (Figure 6.6). This method is employed after a scene has already been discovered through other means, and select areas require additional processing. In these cases, sometimes a partial skeleton is already visible, partially obscured by leaf litter depending upon the seasons that have passed since deposition. Leaf litter is first cleared toward the main concentration of remains to determine their spatial extent and completeness, followed by reversing the direction outward to expand the search area for additional bones. Once additional evidence and bones have been identified, they should be flagged for recovery and documentation. The search perimeter should be expanded to locate additional bones, beginning at the locations where bones were already recovered. This method also has the benefit of allowing the forensic archaeologist to begin mapping the

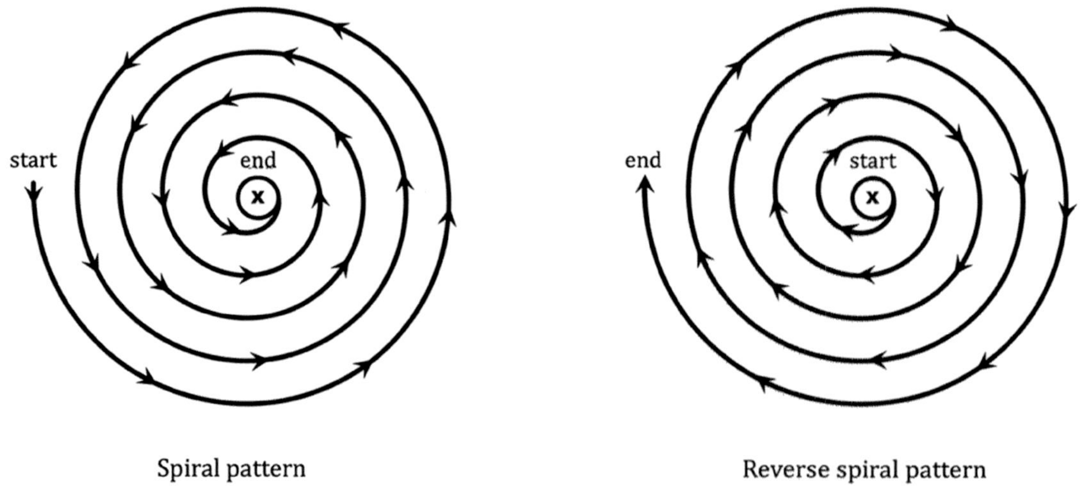

Figure 6.5 Two effective patterns for one-person or small team visual search of a smaller surface area, which are marked with directional pathways: a spiral pattern (left) to avoid inadvertent trampling of evidence in an initial search, and a reverse spiral pattern (right), used when searching for bones that might have been dispersed from a known primary deposition site.

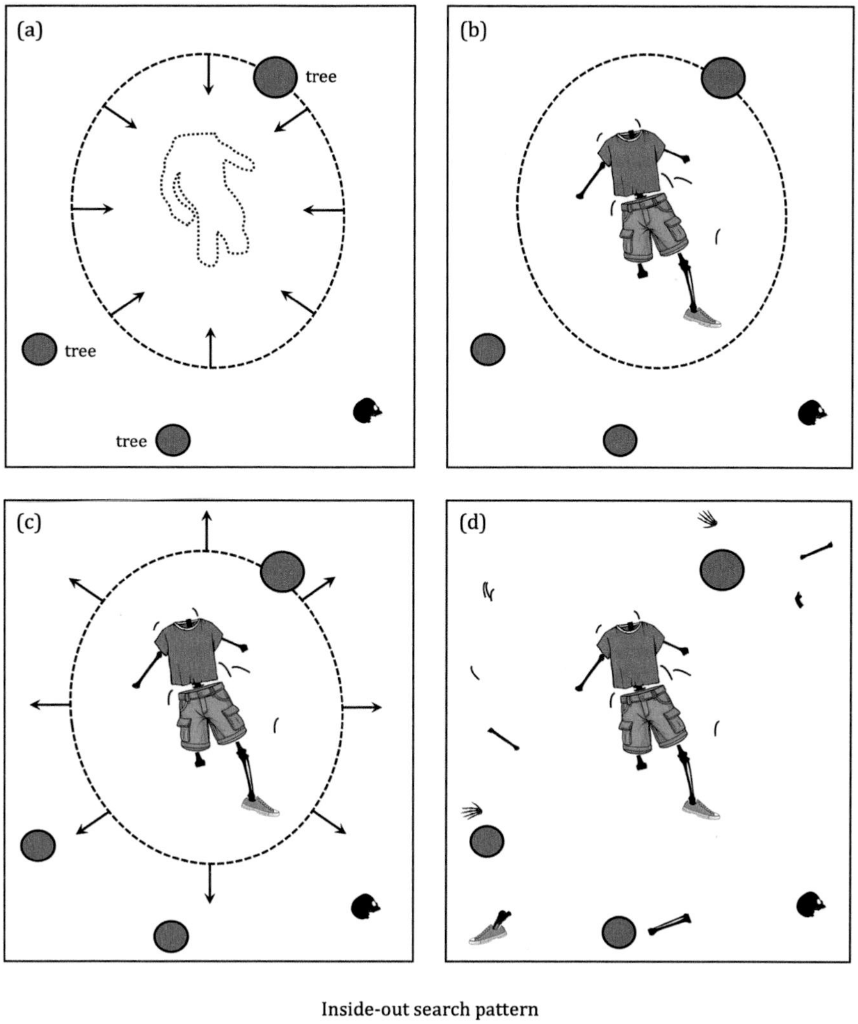

Figure 6.6 Inside-out search pattern is an effective method for searching a scene with a known concentration of bones: (a) search team forms around concentrated remains with cranium noted a few meters away, and proceeds to work inward; (b) central deposition is exposed and completeness of remains evaluated; (c) search team then reverses direction and works outward and around trees (indicated by dark circles) to uncover dispersed remains; (d) additional scattered remains and evidence (e.g., shoe) are uncovered and flagged with search perimeter being expanded in all directions as needed. Anthropologist may begin mapping the site core while the outer search zone continues to be expanded by search team. *Image:* adapted from Pokines (2015:165)

core area of the scene, while other personnel continue searching for more distantly dispersed elements. The wider perimeter simultaneously can be searched by an HRD dog team to locate more widely dispersed remains. In addition, this later, wider search benefits from determining which remains are still missing from the main concentration that may have already been documented.

Other Recommendations for Visual Searches

The degree of difficulty in conducting a visual search is directly related to the landscape features. An open field provides ideal landscape conditions for searching. However, as the number of obstructions increase in the search area, it becomes more difficult to locate bones and associated evidence. In search areas with scrub brush or other forms of ground cover, team members should be placed closer together to allow for more detailed searching in and around undergrowth. In addition, when detailed searching is required, the leader should instruct team members to search on hands and knees. The leader should slow the pace of the search in areas of dense undergrowth to increase the amount of time that the team is searching in each area. It is also important to remember that crime scenes can be three-dimensional. Bones and associated evidence can be found in other locations in addition to being deposited on the ground. In forested areas, it is sometimes helpful to look up, since remains can be deposited in trees by various means. For example, when searching a scene involving a plane crash in a wooded area, it is recommended that a visual search of the forest canopy is included to locate evidence that may be lodged in the tree limbs. Bones on the ground surface also could have derived from a hanged body, and a portion of the body still may be suspended.

BRIEFING TEAM MEMBERS PRIOR TO SEARCH

After the search plan is devised, all team members must be briefed on the procedures for the search. It should not be assumed that all team members have prior experience in conducting visual surface searches. When large searches are conducted, there could be numerous volunteers with no experience in searching for bones or burial sites. As a result, they would not be familiar with indicators that would signify a possible clandestine grave or recognize evidence of dispersed remains. If a search line consists of experienced and inexperienced personnel, they should be intermixed along the line so that the personnel with experience can help the inexperienced. Prior to starting the search, all search team members should be fully briefed on the following:

- Areas and types of terrain to be covered
- Patterns to use for the search
- Specific directions for the visual search
- Possible visual indicators
- Time constraints and local weather
- Time since death/body deposition.

INDICATORS OF SURFACE DEPOSITION

A body deposited on the ground surface will usually be easier to locate than a body that was buried to hide its location. However, there are numerous helpful indicators to look for when searching for remains deposited on the ground surface. Surface deposition will be identified by visually locating bones and soft tissue, clothing and personal possessions, and other forms of evidence that are associated with the remains such as material used to wrap a body (e.g., rugs, tarps, plastic sheeting, plastic bags). It is also important to search through piles of trash and natural brush, as these are quite often placed over a body to conceal it. Search teams also should look for any evidence of animal activity and scavenging, which may indicate scattering of a surface deposition over a larger area. Recent surface depositions also can be located via decomposition scent using HRD dogs (refer to HRD Dogs section in this chapter). However, depositions that have remained on the surface for multiple years can be difficult to recognize. Over time, clothing and other evidence can deteriorate from weathering, become slowly buried by leaf litter build-up, and impacted by plant growth, becoming difficult to recognize on the ground surface (Figure 6.7). The natural beige color of bone changes due to various taphonomic modifications (refer to Chapter 5), and, as a result, can become more difficult to locate over time as they become covered by fallen leaf litter or partially buried due to soil erosion, decay of organic material, and other environmental variables. When bones become partially buried, searchers may need to remove all organic material from the ground surface to locate bones and associated evidence. Table 6.2 provides a summary of indicators that are used to locate surface depositions.

Figure 6.7 Resulting degradation of fabrics from the front pocket and waist of men's trousers after a two-month period of exposure to weather, animal activity, and a covering layer of leaf litter. The darker tan linen waist fabric (a) was extremely faded from exposure to sunlight, while the white cotton pocket fabric (b) was stained a dark brown color by the leaf litter and wet ground conditions.

Table 6.2 Summary of Indicators Used to Locate Surface Depositions

- Skeletal remains and soft tissue
- Clothing, personal effects, and weapons
- Decomposition odor and staining
- Insect activity
- Animal activity and scavenging
- Loose trash or brush heaps
- Materials used for wrapping or transporting the body

Taphonomic Considerations in Locating Dispersed Remains

Remains deposited in outdoor environments usually exhibit some degree of dispersal of skeletal elements. Some common causes of dispersal of surface skeletal remains include taphonomic processes such as nonhuman animal or human activity, gravity, and fluvial transport (e.g., rivers, streams, and slope wash). Buried remains also can undergo disturbance even while staying buried. These processes include burrowing animals, plant root growth, tree falls, frost heaving, mud slides, and slumping of soil horizons. Therefore, proper search strategies are important in delineating site boundaries, locating primary and secondary deposition sites, determining the original position of the remains, and locating scattered skeletal elements and associated evidence.

In many instances, dispersal of skeletal remains results from carnivores, scavenging birds, and large omnivores scattering skeletal elements over a large area (refer to Chapter 5). It is therefore important to focus visual surface searches on areas with the highest concentration of skeletal elements as well as outlying zones where fewer scattered elements may exist. When searching for missing bones, the search team should be thorough and adapt their search methods to the particulars of the site. For example, since scavenged skeletal remains may be dispersed and deposited under thick brush by animals, team members need to search on their hands and knees when thick brush or heavy groundcover is encountered. Rodent burrows found within the search area should be thoroughly and carefully examined. If birds have scavenged the remains, nests in the proximity of the scatter could potentially be searched for smaller bones.

When skeletal remains are located, the ground surface should be carefully searched to ensure that small bones, bone fragments, teeth, and associated evidence are not missed. Using proper tools and methods, all organic material and debris in the primary site must be removed from the ground surface and screened. Experimental research involving success rates of locating nonhuman surface deposition obscured by leaf litter has provided additional search considerations. These studies were undertaken using pig (*Sus scrofa*) teeth and infant-sized remains

(Pokines et al., 2019b), as well as skeletal remains comparable in size to intact human juvenile remains or partial adult remains, and elements that overlap in size with adult remains (Pokines et al., 2018). Overall, careful searching by hand is recommended to reduce loss of bones, particularly of teeth and infant-sized bones. At the same time, it is recommended to perform a secondary search through the leaf litter to increase the overall recovery rate.

Directional Pathways in Locating Dispersed Remains

After cleaning the site of debris and mapping the location of known skeletal elements, it may be possible to infer the directional pathway that missing bones might have been dispersed from the primary deposition. For instance, if there are missing elements and it is noted that the dispersal of bones occurs in one direction from the primary deposition, the analyst would then know what direction to begin searching for missing elements or a possible secondary deposition of bones. This is most helpful to search teams in wooded environments with thick underbrush or heavy groundcover. As additional bones are located along the directional path of dispersal, team members can spread out into a directed search pattern if needed or HRD dog efforts could be concentrated in this direction. Natural landscape features, such as inclines or tree lines, may also direct dispersal patterns and should be considered when searching for missing elements. For example, if a body was deposited

Box #2: How to Screen Materials

Source: Image by Denise Kammerer-Cody is within Public Domain (US Army Corps of Engineers), adapted from 160628-A-ME637-001.JPG (https://www.nad.usace.army.mil/Media/Images/igphoto/2001625520/); cropped image.

USING A BOX SCREEN

1. Place a small load of sediment or surface debris onto the center of the box screen. Smaller amounts of materials improve level of recovery before and during sifting.
2. Shake the box screen so the materials are distributed across the mesh, with smaller-sized materials falling through the mesh openings.
3. While wearing gloves to prevent injury, move materials around, on the mesh, to sort through the larger materials retained during screening.
4. If larger clods of sediments are still intact, carefully use a wooden or plastic tool to break them up. If necessary, gently push the pieces into the mesh to evaluate if there are any evidence inclusions. Use a trowel with extreme caution to avoid damaging or destroying evidence.
5. Once all materials have been sorted, dump the remaining materials into a designated area for a screened materials heap.
6. Clean any adhered materials from the box screen mesh with a gloved hand, larger brush, or hand trowel before adding more materials for screening.

SCREENING TIPS

- Choice of screen size is dependent on soil texture and consistency. The standard screen size for archaeology is ¼-inch (6 mm) mesh; smaller screen size of ⅛-inch (3 mm) mesh should be used when recovering juvenile remains or other small-sized forms of evidence (e.g., jewelry beads or links, zipper teeth).
- Water screening may be necessary when breaking down problem sediments (e.g., heavy clays, muddy sediments). This can be done with one person using a hose or buckets of water while another person carefully monitors the mesh surface.

on the ground surface or buried on or near an incline, then gravity, wind, and water flow could move skeletal elements further down the hill to a lower level (Figure 6.8). In this instance, locating missing elements would require searching downhill from the primary deposition site. Urban landscaping and structural divisions, such as hedges, fencing or walled areas, also may influence dispersal patterns in unexpected ways when holes or burrows lead out from one seemingly enclosed area into another (Figure 6.9). It is important to note that proper search patterns and recovery methods remain essential when investigating directional pathways and surface-scattered remains, regardless of the location or environment.

After the primary deposition site has been properly cleaned of debris to expose the ground surface and all exposed skeletal elements and evidence have been mapped and collected (refer to Chapter 9 for stages involved with recovery of surface remains), the organic layer of the ground surface should be scraped with a trowel. The loose sediment should then be screened to locate any remaining small bones, fragments, teeth, or evidence that might have slumped or been trampled into the soil horizons over time.

The most difficult skeletal elements to locate in the field are the teeth because of their small size and ease of separation. For example, incisors and canines normally separate from their sockets early in the decomposition process, because they have single roots, as opposed to first maxillary premolars and molars, which typically have two or more roots (refer to Figure 3.19 for an example). It is important to locate as many teeth as possible for identification purposes, and this can be accomplished using

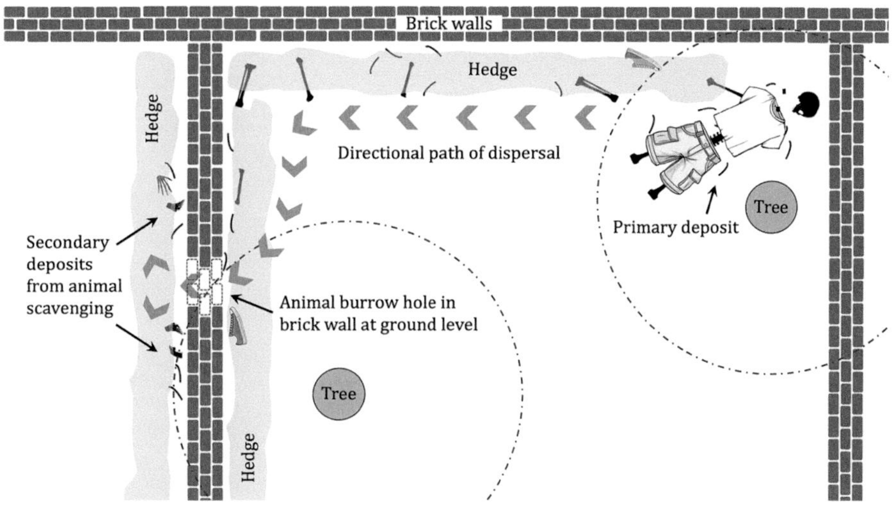

Figure 6.9 Surface deposition recovery site showing mapped dispersal path of skeletal elements from primary deposition to secondary surface-scatter features formed from animal scavenging. Note the animal burrow under the wall and in the path of dispersal leading to the secondary surface-scatter remains.

Figure 6.8 Cross-section showing body initially deposited in a grave that is now eroding. The skeletal remains are being dispersed downhill over time by soil erosion and waterflow. Additionally, elements at the base of the incline become covered by sediment, while smaller-sized and lighter-weight elements, such as ribs, may become entangled in new plant growth along the incline surface.

appropriate search strategies. Haglund (1997a) outlines search strategies used in locating missing teeth associated with remains scattered by medium-sized canids. Teams should search the primary deposition site for teeth, but also along any directional pathways that skeletal elements may have traveled, secondary deposition sites, and possibly areas containing animal scat. Haglund (1997b) also brings attention to special circumstances that might bias predictable patterns of canid bone dispersal, such as preexisting facial trauma, terrain, or purposeful dismemberment by humans. In these circumstances, it may not be possible to predict the correct location of missing teeth, and an extended and thorough search must be conducted.

SURFACE INDICATORS OF BURIED REMAINS

A **grave** is much more difficult to locate than a surface deposition because in most cases, a body is buried to conceal its location. In many instances, locating a clandestine grave may be impossible without prior information from an informant who provides the exact location of where the **burial** occurred. When searching for buried remains, surface indicators may be the best clues for locating a grave. A variety of surface changes occur during the disposal process, some of which may still be present long after burial (Figure 6.10). During the initial digging of a grave, the soil that is removed will normally be placed adjacent to the grave and on top of any associated vegetation. Soils are typically layered and vary in color and texture in relation to depth (i.e., **soil horizons**; refer to Chapter 9 on soils). The soil horizons removed from the grave during burial become intermixed with each other and with existing topsoil, plants, and other surface materials (e.g., crushed rock, landscaping mulch, trash items). On average, assuming that the original intent is to bury the body in an extended position, the dimensions of the disturbed area may be approximately the same length as the body and at least twice as wide as the body, due to the displaced sediments next to the grave. This entire area is referred to as the **burial site**. The terrain, type of soil, and effort expended in digging a grave will influence how deep the grave will be and how much soil is displaced. In general, hand-dug graves are only as deep as necessary to conceal the body, as digging a hole of this size is physically demanding and time-consuming.

When backfilling a grave, some of the original fill typically cannot be returned to the grave because the sediment becomes less compact, and the body's volume displaces a portion of the original fill. Excess sediment is usually scattered around the edges of the grave, or **grave outline**, and often left with no attempt to level the surface with the surrounding area, resulting in a small mound next to (Figure 6.10a) or over the grave (Figure 6.11). In addition, the surface of the grave fill covering the body will typically have a different color and texture than the surrounding surface soil due to the intermixing of the soil horizons during digging and backfilling. Soil beneath the topsoil tends to be much lighter in color, since the topsoil composition usually has higher amounts of carbon from decomposing plant matter on the ground surface. In cases where a body is buried at a shallow depth or placed in a natural depression, extra holes may be dug around the burial site to gather enough soil to completely or partially conceal the body.

Naturally, there is a high probability that surface changes will occur at the site, making the appearance of the grave differ significantly over time. These changes include depressions that form over the body, variations in localized areas of plant growth and plant composition, and variations in topsoil around the grave outline (Figure 6.12). A **primary grave depression** will normally occur as a result of compaction of the loose fill that was placed over the body and the collapsing of the thorax and abdominal areas of the body during decomposition (Figures 6.10b and 6.12b). Furthermore, smaller **secondary grave depressions** may form within the primary depression due to additional sediment compaction and soft tissue decomposition (Figure 6.12c). Depending on the length of time that the body has been buried and the regional landscape being searched, seasonal leaf litter may naturally build up in the primary depression and indicate the surface of the grave outline (Figures 6.10b and 6.13).

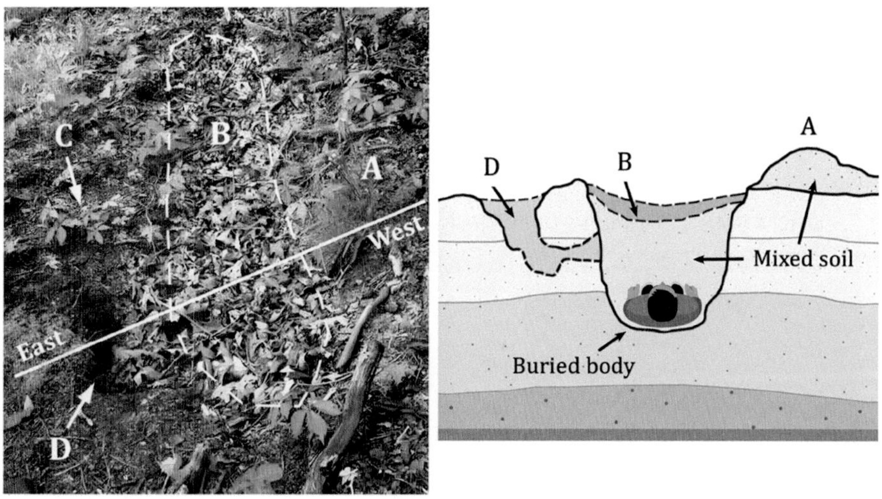

Figure 6.10 Image (left) showing (a) mounding of excess dirt remaining after backfilling process; (b) the primary grave depression filled with leaf litter; (c) ground cover that varies from surrounding plant growth due to disturbance of topsoil; and (d) a burrow possibly from a scavenging animal. The east-west transect line in the image corresponds to the section drawing for the grave (right).

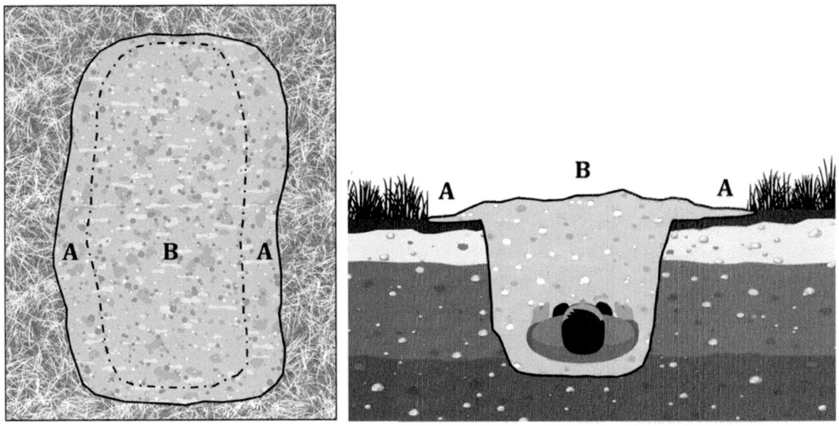

Figure 6.11 Plan view (left) and section view (right) showing changes to soil typically occurring when backfilling a grave: (a) excess sediment is usually scattered around the grave outline; (b) the grave fill becomes intermixed and less compact, and the volume of the body also displaces a portion of the original fill, leaving a small mound of sediment over the top of the grave.

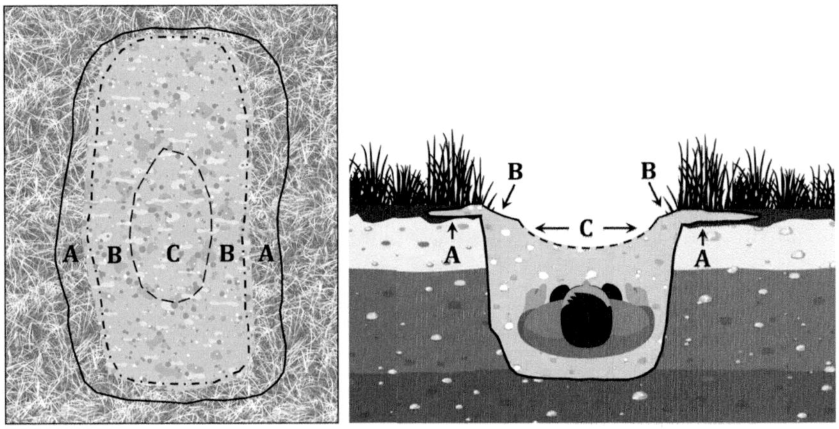

Figure 6.12 Plan view (left) and section view (right) of a grave showing: (a) variations in localized areas of plant growth and topsoil around the grave outline; (b) a primary grave depression resulting from compaction of the loose fill placed over the body and the collapsing thorax and abdominal areas of body during decomposition; and (c) a secondary grave depression resulting from additional sediment compaction and collapse during soft tissue decomposition.

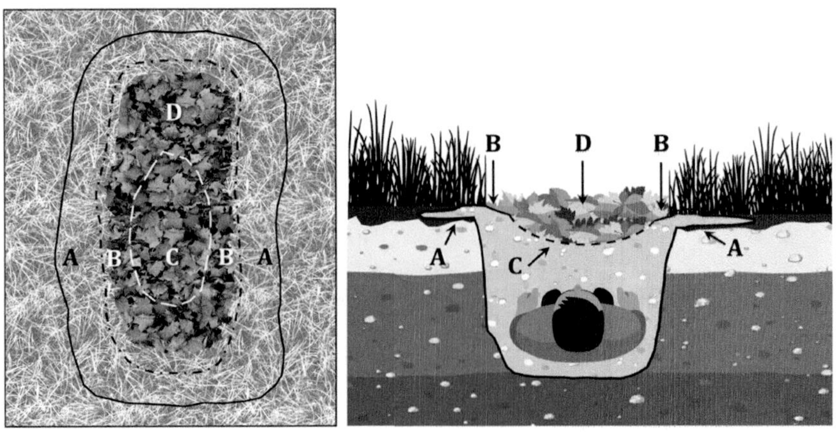

Figure 6.13 Plan view (left) and section view (right) of a grave through seasonal change over time, including: (a) plant growth and heavier topsoil obscuring the grave outline; (b) a primary grave depression; (c) a secondary grave depression; and (d) seasonal leaf litter build-up in primary depression providing surface indications of the grave outline.

In many instances, there are noticeable changes in vegetation over and around the grave because of damage to existing ground cover and disturbance of soil horizons. The intermixing of soil horizons may limit or destroy the high level of organic nutrients commonly found on or near the ground surface (Figures 6.14a and 6.14b). In addition, the mixing of these horizons will affect the number and types of plants that germinate in the disturbed soil. If the soil surface was left bare, plant composition over the grave is initially dominated by "weedy" species that tend to colonize disturbed or bare soil, such as grasses (Figure 6.14c). A typical sequence of plant succession would then follow, such as herbaceous plants, shrubs, and trees. However, if tree seeds are present in the disturbed soil, they will germinate as conditions become suitable, and a concentration of young seedlings will be evident (Figure 6.14d). Germination and growth of tree seedlings also can assist in determining when the burial occurred. For example, if a body was buried in autumn, when most tree seeds are prevalent, the surface of the grave might be populated with tree seedlings the following spring. In addition, localized areas of sparse, new ground cover surrounded by dense, mature ground cover may indicate some kind of recent disturbance to the soil horizons, most likely within at least one or two seasons of growth (Figure 6.15a). Localized variations in plant growth may be due to a number of factors. If a body is buried in soil that lacks nutrients, plants over or around the grave may be lusher and more vibrant green in color than surrounding vegetation (Figure 6.15b). This can be attributed to the aerated soil promoting seed germination and byproduct nutrients being released into the soil during body decomposition. If a whole plant or a portion of one (e.g., stems or a few leaves) is covered with sediment and unable to photosynthesize for a period of time, it can become yellowed, lose vigor, and appear stunted. In addition, if remains are wrapped or covered (e.g., cement blocks, sheet metal, plastic tarps) when placed in a shallow grave, root growth may be limited and result in weak stems and sparse leaf cover (Figure 6.15c).

It also may be possible to locate burial sites by searching for surface indicators of animal scavenging. There is a

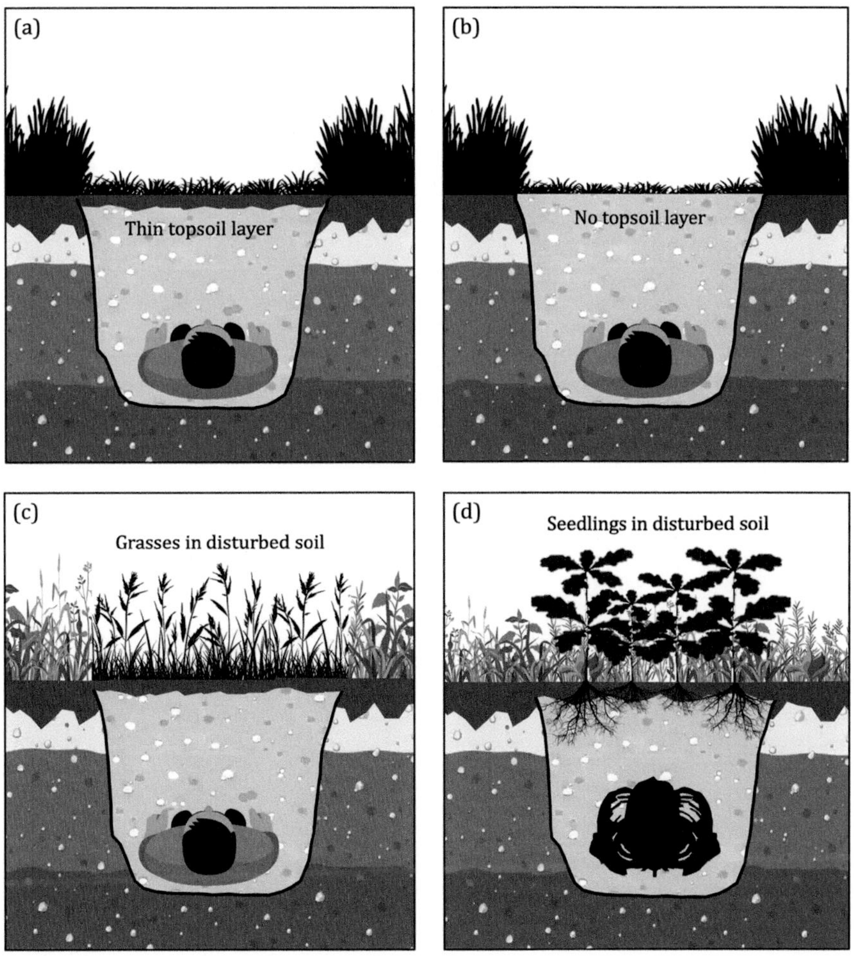

Figure 6.14 Noticeable changes over and around the grave: (a) intermixing of soil resulting in a thin layer of topsoil and limiting organic nutrients; (b) intermixing of soil destroying topsoil layer and organic nutrients; (c) previously bare surface layer initially dominated by grass species that tend to colonize in disturbed or bare soil; and (d) concentration of young tree seedlings that germinated from seeds present in disturbed grave fill.

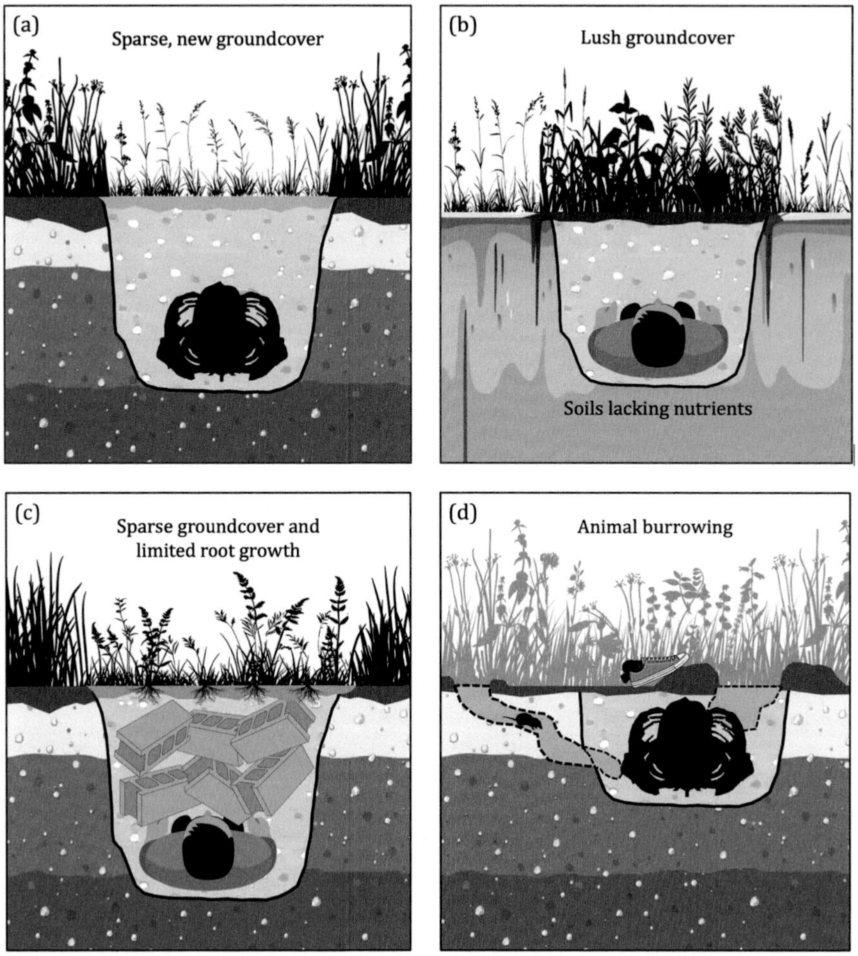

Figure 6.15 Noticeable changes over and around the grave: (a) localized area of sparse, new ground cover in disturbed soil surrounded by dense, mature ground cover; (b) poor quality soil with lusher, more vibrant plants over grave due to aerated soil and byproduct nutrients; (c) plant root growth limited by addition of non-organic materials (i.e., cement blocks) covering body; and (d) localized animal digging and scavenging items from shallow grave.

Table 6.3 Summary of Indicators Used to Locate Buried Bodies

- Skeletal remains and soft tissue brought to the surface
- Clothing or personal effects
- Insect activity
- Animal digging, surface activity, and scavenging
- Abandoned tools or weapons
- Materials used for transporting the body
- Soil or vegetation disturbances (e.g., growth/lack thereof, color changes)
- Depressions, soil disturbances, or unnatural mounding of sediments
- Sediment coloration changes from mixing soil horizons
- Decomposition odor and possible staining
- Decreased soil compaction
- Areas where bushes or tree limbs have been moved or broken to conceal something buried

higher probability that animals will detect and scavenge shallow graves rather than deep ones, as decomposition odors are more evident in surface depositions and shallow graves (Figures 6.10d and 6.15d). Areas of localized animal digging encountered during the search should be examined for skeletal elements or personal possessions (e.g., clothing, jewelry, wallets, backpacks) that were brought to the ground surface by scavenging. In special circumstances, digging tools and/or weapons that may have been discarded or accidentally left behind most likely indicate that a grave is in the vicinity. Table 6.3 provides a list of indicators used to locate buried bodies.

HUMAN REMAINS DETECTION DOGS

Human remains detection (HRD) dogs, also commonly referred to as cadaver dogs, are air scent dogs specially trained to alert to the generic scent of human decomposition from a dead body or tissue and fluid from a decomposed body and assisting in locating human bodies, body parts, and body fluids. They can be invaluable during searches for human remains from a variety of contexts.

It is important to understand the capabilities and limitations of HRD dogs and their handlers when choosing and working with an HRD team during a body search. The purpose of this section is to educate anyone requiring the assistance of an HRD team for a search. This section is not about handling HRD dogs. For information on choosing, training, handling, and understanding HRD dogs, please see *How to Train a Human Remains Detection Dog* by Christy Judah and Tracy Sargent (2015), *Detector Dogs and Scent Movement: How Weather, Terrain, and Vegetation Influence Search Strategies* by Tom Osterkamp (2020), *Cadaver Dog Handbook: Forensic Training and Tactics for the Recovery of Human Remains* by Andrew Rebmann, Edward David, and M.H. Sorg (2000), and *Buzzards and Butterflies: Human Remains Detection Dogs* by J.C. Judah (2008).

What Are HRD Dogs Trained to Do?

HRD dogs are trained to provide their handlers with an alert when they detect odors associated with human decomposition and to ignore other odors, including scents associated with nonhuman animal decomposition (Figure 6.16). HRD dogs can be trained to recognize and alert to a variety of decomposition by-products such as gases, liquids, acids, adipocere, and the musty odor from mummified tissue (Rebmann et al., 2000), and also assist in locating buried bodies, disarticulated remains, bodies submerged in water, or those hidden in vehicles or structures (Lowy and McAlhany, 2000). They will alert to bodies that lack any signs of decomposition detectable by humans (i.e., those with a very short postmortem interval), remains in advanced stages of decomposition, skeletal remains, and even soil and other materials (e.g., carpets and fabrics, truck beds, wood surfaces) containing fluids from human decomposition (Rebmann et al., 2000). In addition, experimental research has shown that HRD dogs detected buried human remains at different depths (1 ft [0.3048 m] and 2 ft [0.6096 m]) and decomposition states with varying success, including some dogs detecting buried skeletal remains (Lasseter et al., 2003). However, an HRD dog may only alert in a localized area where a body is buried and not necessarily the exact spot. This may be due to environmental factors that carry the decomposition odor (i.e., scent molecules) to another location. It is also possible for dogs to be overwhelmed by scent in a given area due to multiple bones in proximity; while the area can be detected, individual bones within it may not be. Because of this possibility, it is always important to search the area surrounding where the dog alerted, using traditional search methods to determine the origin of the decomposition odor.

The scent of a body, especially as it decomposes, is not uniform. It is most intense around the body itself, creating a concentrated area of odor. When scent molecules from decomposing human remains are dispersed into the air, the dogs register a sensory reaction in the brain that categorizes these molecules and recognizes them as a unique 'total odor' effect, allowing for scent-specific work (Rebmann et al., 2000). This sensory reaction also allows the dog to detect the relative concentration of scent in a **scent pool**, which is the concentration of scent either at the point of origin or trapped at a remote

Figure 6.16 Cadaver dog, Ruger, with master canine trainer, Mary Peter. Ruger is searching while on a leash (a), allowing for a more detailed search in particular areas of interest, and (b) searching a defined area without a leash.

Table 6.4 Understanding Presence and Distortion of Decomposition Scent Cones

• Primary scent pools form above and around decomposing remains • Scent cones form as scent molecules are dispersed away from the source by airflow or thermal uplifting • Variable winds can cause uneven dispersal of scent molecules or multiple scent cones around the remains • Water may move the scent away from the source in response to currents, gravity, surface or underground waterways, erosion, or drainage patterns • Scent barriers, such as vegetation or terrain, may form remote secondary scent pools and scent cones • Scent voids near the remains can form in areas where water flow interrupts the absorption of decomposition fluids into the soil or in cases where the body is elevated in relation to the ground surface (e.g., a body hanging from a tree)

Source: Adapted from Rebman et al. (2000)

location. They can also follow it in a **scent cone** as it disperses outward from the source through the environment. Rebmann et al. (2000) discuss the basic principles of scent cone presence and distortion (Table 6.4) that are key in understanding the actions and alerts provided by HRD dogs when conducting searches. The scent molecules shed from decomposing remains form a primary scent pool around and above the body when the air is stagnant (Figure 6.17a). This effect can be intensified with the addition of thermal uplift caused by heat from the sun, at times dispersing the scent well above the ground surface (Figure 6.17b). With wind, a horizontal scent cone forms with the scent becoming more and more dispersed as it is carried away from the body (Figure 6.17c). Conditions with light and variable winds may produce multiple horizontal scent cones, which disperse the scent away from the body in different directions. Many additional factors can alter or distort the position of the scent cone in relation to the position of the body, such as terrain, vegetation, water flow, climate, and seasonal weather. For example, scent molecules of a decomposing body located on the ground surface or buried in a shallow grave can be carried away from the body by flowing ground water and reappear in areas remote from the disposal site (Figure 6.18a). In this example, the HRD dog would most likely indicate the presence of a buried body or surface deposition at a remote location. In addition, HRD dogs can detect bodies submerged in water, because the decomposition odor of the body

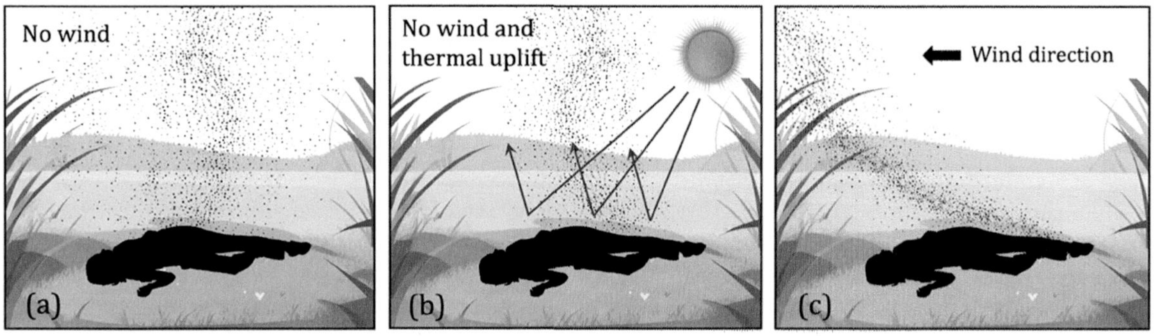

Figure 6.17 Presence of a primary scent pool and distortion of scent cone around decomposing remains in a surface deposition with (a) no wind and molecules from the scent cone spreading and dissipating in the air, (b) no wind and thermal uplift of molecules in scent cone due to radiating heat, and (c) wind from a single direction carrying molecules in scent cone away from the body.

Figure 6.18 Presence of a primary and remote secondary scent pools around decomposing remains: (a) a surface deposition with groundwater runoff transporting scent molecules from the body to a secondary pool downhill, and (b) water currents and thermal uplift in water transporting scent molecules from the primary pool at the body to a secondary pool at a remote surface location.

can be carried to the surface of the water by currents or natural turbulence. However, like wind, water currents can carry the scent of a submerged decomposing body away from the remains, leaving a scent void in the water directly above the body (Figure 6.18b).

Weather and environmental conditions are also a consideration when performing searches for buried remains. According to Osterkamp (2020), optimal environmental conditions for detecting buried remains involve a combination of dry soils and elevated humidity levels, dew, or light rain. These factors enhance ground moisture, facilitating the release of absorbed scents from the soil surface into the atmosphere. At the same time, wind speed is also a consideration for search dogs locating scent sources. For example, when the wind is nearly calm or when it is extremely turbulent, the handler will need to develop strategies to assist the dogs during searches (Osterkamp, 2020).

Limitations of HRD Dogs Searches

A successful search using HRD dogs depends on numerous factors, including the investigation prior to the search, type of search method, the dog handler's skills, weather during the search, terrain of the search area, circumstances leading to death and deposition of the body, and time since death (Rebmann et al., 2000). Table 6.5 provides a few questions that may help in understanding the limitations of HRD dogs and scent detection during body searches. It is important to note that the dog's ability to pinpoint the exact location of a buried body depends on decomposition odor reaching the surface. Decomposition odor from a buried body can be detected by a search dog as a plume on the ground surface if it can move through the pore spaces of the soil while in the gas and liquid phases and then continue through the ground cover and scent boundary layer (Osterkamp, 2020). However, decomposition odor may not reach the ground surface if the body is too deep, if the grave fill is too compacted, or if the body is wrapped in material that will not release the odor (Rebmann et al., 2000). The soil may need to be vented when a HRD dog is not able to locate a suspected grave in a given area or when a dog does not alert to the exact location of a buried body. The search area can be vented with a T-bar probe (refer to Probe Searches section in this chapter) to bring decomposition odor to the ground surface (Figure 6.19). Rebmann et al. (2000) suggest venting every 18 inches (46 cm) utilizing grid lines and offsetting the holes between adjacent lines.

Table 6.5 Understanding Limitations of HRD Dog Scent Detection

- Are the remains actually present within the search area?
- Are the remains creating a scent pool and a scent cone above ground?
- Is there significant air movement between the scent pool and the dog?
- Is the temperature in range for detection? (between 32°F/0°C and 90°F/32°C)
- Does the handler guide the dog to the correct area?
- Does the handler correctly interpret the dog's behavior?

Source: Adapted from Rebman et al., 2000.

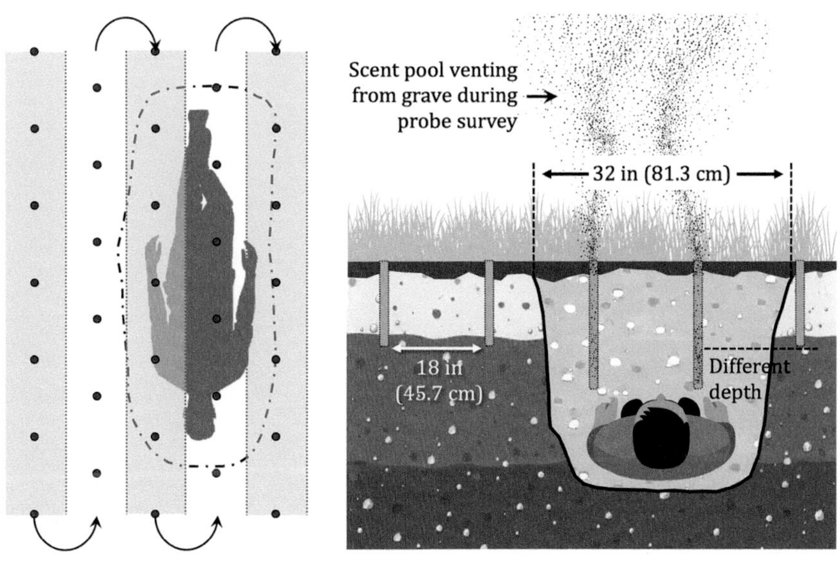

Figure 6.19 Example of a strip line search pattern (left), with 18-inch-wide search lanes used to vent the ground surface of an area containing a suspected grave. Probing vent holes are placed approximately every 18 inches along each search lane. Note the offset of probing holes in the search lanes. Differences in probe depth (right) occur due to differential resistance in grave fill versus surrounding compacted soil horizons, and a scent pool forms from venting the grave during the probe survey.

Locating a HRD Dog Team

Although there is an obvious need for HRD dogs, they have been minimally represented in the law enforcement canine population across the United States, and smaller law enforcement agencies may not have their own dog (Lowy and McAlhany, 2000). The canine HRD specialty has not been given the same attention as dogs that are trained in the explosive and narcotic specialties, since it may not be feasible to include another canine specialty in smaller law enforcement agencies for the occasional search. Smaller agencies can usually request the services of a larger nearby department, thereby justifying not having a HRD dog program. When agencies seek the assistance of an HRD team, it is essential to determine their level of expertise because the experience and abilities of teams vary. It is important to ask questions about team qualifications, including training, certifications, and the number of cases handled (Lowy and McAlhany, 2000). Several national organizations provide HRD dog search certification, such as the National Narcotics Dog Detector Association (NNDDA), the National Association of Search and Rescue (NASAR), and the North American Police Working Dog Association (NAPWDA). To receive an HRD dog search certification, testing of the dog's abilities requires alerting to human bone, fluid, and tissue, while ignoring nonhuman remains. Various county, state, and federal law enforcement agencies may be able to provide you with recommendations for HRD teams throughout your area.

INTRUSIVE SEARCH METHODS

After the nonintrusive search techniques have been exhausted, there are a number of intrusive techniques that can be used to further explore areas of interest. A key concern is that intrusive methods can ultimately destroy the site, so the decision to use them must be made with great care.

Probe Searches

The most common intrusive search method is using a probe to locate a clandestine grave and the outline of the grave itself. Numerous authors have discussed the effectiveness of using probes to locate forensic and archaeological graves (e.g., Boyd, 1979; Imaizumi, 1974; Killam, 2004; Morse et al., 1983; Owsley, 1995; Ruffell, 2005). This method should be used systematically across a search grid and can also be used as a follow-up method after a visual search to further inspect areas of interest.

The most common probe used for forensic investigations is called a **T-bar probe** (refer to Figure 2.2h). Probing is conducted by pushing a pointed metal or fiberglass rod, typically 4 ft (1.2 m) in length and around ½ inch (approximately 1 cm) in diameter with a crossbar handle at the top, into the ground at regular intervals (Figure 6.20). This method is used to determine the qualitative differences in density of subsurface materials, because the grave fill will be less dense than the surrounding undisturbed soil. When using equal amounts of pressure, the probe will penetrate deeper and easier into grave fill than it will into undisturbed soil. Since probing is based on relative and subjective resistance, a single person should operate the probe within each survey grid if time permits. With practice in the given search area, an individual can get a good idea of the amount of pressure needed to probe to a specific depth or through a specific type of soil layer. As individuals systematically progress through the grid, they note areas where the probe easily penetrates the soil for further investigation.

If a T-bar probe is going to be used as a primary search tool, a grid pattern should be used across the search area (Figure 6.19). Grid lines should be placed close enough together so that the buried item in question will not be missed between two adjacent lines. A recommended grid interval is approximately 1 foot (30 cm) or less. There should be one person using the probe and one person taking notes and marking a scaled map of the search area (refer to Chapter 8 for scaled maps). The individual using the probe should indicate to the note taker whether the soil is more or less compacted. Pin flags should be carefully placed in the areas that require further evaluation. Isolated or suspicious areas exhibiting lower pressure measurements can then be probed with smaller transects to narrow down the size of the area of interest. If the size of the area is consistent with the size of a grave, then further invasive testing will be required to discern if the burial site has been located.

Figure 6.20 Author John Schultz demonstrates the use of a T-bar probe to detect differences in soil compaction in a landscape depression.

Another type of probe that can be used in forensic investigations is a **penetrometer**, which is more commonly used for agricultural applications. A penetrometer has a pressure gauge at the junction of the rod and the crossbar (Figure 6.21) that measures soil compactness, or density, by providing a quantitative measurement. A normal T-bar probe also can be modified and used as a penetrometer by attaching a pressure or weight gauge to record pressure measurements (Ruffell, 2005).

The third type of probe is a **soil-coring probe** or **soil corer** (Figure 6.22a). This probe is not used to determine whether the soil compactness has changed but to determine whether soil horizons are mixed. This is undertaken by removing and examining a vertical core of soil. Soil-coring probes are generally 3 ½ ft (1 m) in length, and the end that is inserted into the ground has a hollow

Figure 6.21 Author John Schultz demonstrates the use of a penetrometer probe with a gauge to measure differences in soil compaction.

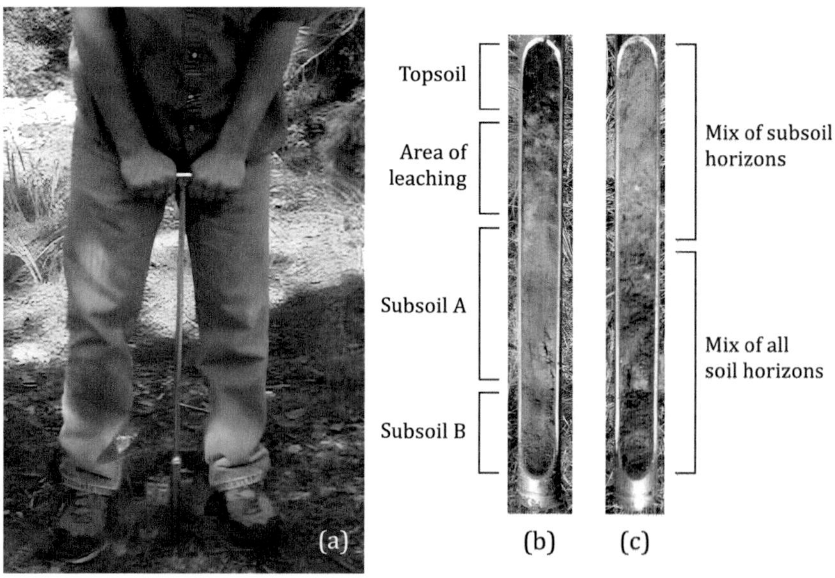

Figure 6.22 Author John Schultz (left) demonstrates the use of a soil-coring probe (a) to detect the presence of disturbed soil. On the right is a comparison of soil cores from (b) undisturbed natural soil horizons and (c) mottled and mixed sediment from grave fill.

soil-coring tube that is ½ to ¾ in (1–2 cm) in diameter and around 10 in (25 cm) in length. One side of the coring tube is open so that the soil horizons can be viewed. Once a core of the undisturbed natural soil is extracted (Figure 6.22b), disturbed soil horizon cores will be easily recognizable with a mottled appearance (Figure 6.22c), resulting from the mixing of the soil horizons. Coring also can be used to assess possible burial sites identified through probing. An advantage of this method over standard probes is that it does not penetrate as deeply, reducing the risk of damaging the body and any associated evidence. It also allows the investigator to see underneath the ground surface without more extensive excavation.

Some inherent difficulties do exist in using soil probe methods. It is not typically used as a systematic search method over large areas because it can be very time-consuming. In addition, this method is invasive and can damage a body or evidence. Soil probes should only be used to locate the disturbed fill of a grave and not the exact location of the body within the grave. For example, when performing a body search with a soil probe, special care must be taken not to push the probe through the body or skeleton. If a probe was used to locate a grave and possibly caused damage to the body or skeleton in the process, the medical examiner or coroner should be informed so that they do not mistake postmortem damage as perimortem trauma. It is important to note that the use of probes may not work in soil comprising homogeneous sands (refer to Chapter 9 for soil types). Since a probe can be easily pushed through undisturbed homogeneous sands, it is generally not possible to discern disturbed areas in this type of soil. Probes will work best in compacted soils, or soils that contain dense layers, where pressure differences from disturbances may persist for many years. Large rocks and tree roots also limit the effectiveness of probing, and densely forested areas may prove too difficult for their consistent, effective use.

Shovel Testing and Shovel Shining

Although invasive testing with a shovel is not a recommended search method, there are cases when this may be the only alternative after other search methods are exhausted or as a follow-up to a visual or probe search. There are two methods for using a shovel when trying to locate or delineate the boundaries of a grave. The first method is **shovel testing** by digging a **test pit** in an attempt to locate buried evidence or a grave outline. In this instance, a small-scale test excavation is dug with a spade shovel (refer to Figure 2.3c), and all removed sediment should be screened so that no potential evidence is missed. However, we caution that this should be used only as a last resort, as it is a highly destructive search method.

If there are possible indicators of burial from either visual or invasive search methods, a sharpened flat-blade transfer shovel (refer to Figures 2.3d and 2.3e) may be used to delineate the grave outline. When removing soil, the proper method is to keep the back of the shovel almost parallel with the ground surface. By applying pressure in a forward skimming motion, also known as **shovel shining**, the sharpened edge of the flat-blade transfer shovel shaves soil in ½ to ¾ inch (1–2 cm) layers from the surface (refer to Box 3). This method does not involve digging; it involves only the removal of small amounts of soil at very slight depths and keeps the surface over the area as level as possible (Figure 6.23). This is to ensure that if the outline of a grave appears, it will not be missed (Figure 6.24).

Figure 6.23 Orange County Sheriff's Office homicide detective Dave Clarke (left) and authors Lana Williams (center) and Sandra Wheeler (right) shovel shining a test excavation while searching for a buried body at a forensic scene.

Heavy Equipment Searches

Most forensic anthropologists have heard the obligatory story of law enforcement using a 'forensic backhoe' to excavate a grave. For obvious reasons, such as extreme damage to skeletal remains or evidence, a **backhoe** is not an ideal piece of equipment to use for a forensic search or excavation. In certain instances, however, a backhoe with a flat-blade bucket (i.e., without teeth, also called a 'clean-up bucket') or an elevated scraper may be a final alternative when all other search methods have been exhausted, or when it may not be possible to use traditional methods in searching for a clandestine grave (Figure 6.25). In some cases, a backhoe may be the only realistic option, such as in landfills, heavily flooded areas, large or deep search areas, and search areas where the soils or groundcover are not suitable for initial geophysical surveying and other less invasive methods. Backhoes and other heavy equipment also can be valuable tools in lifting or removing cement slabs used to conceal the location of a grave (Hawley et al., 1994) or during exhumations.

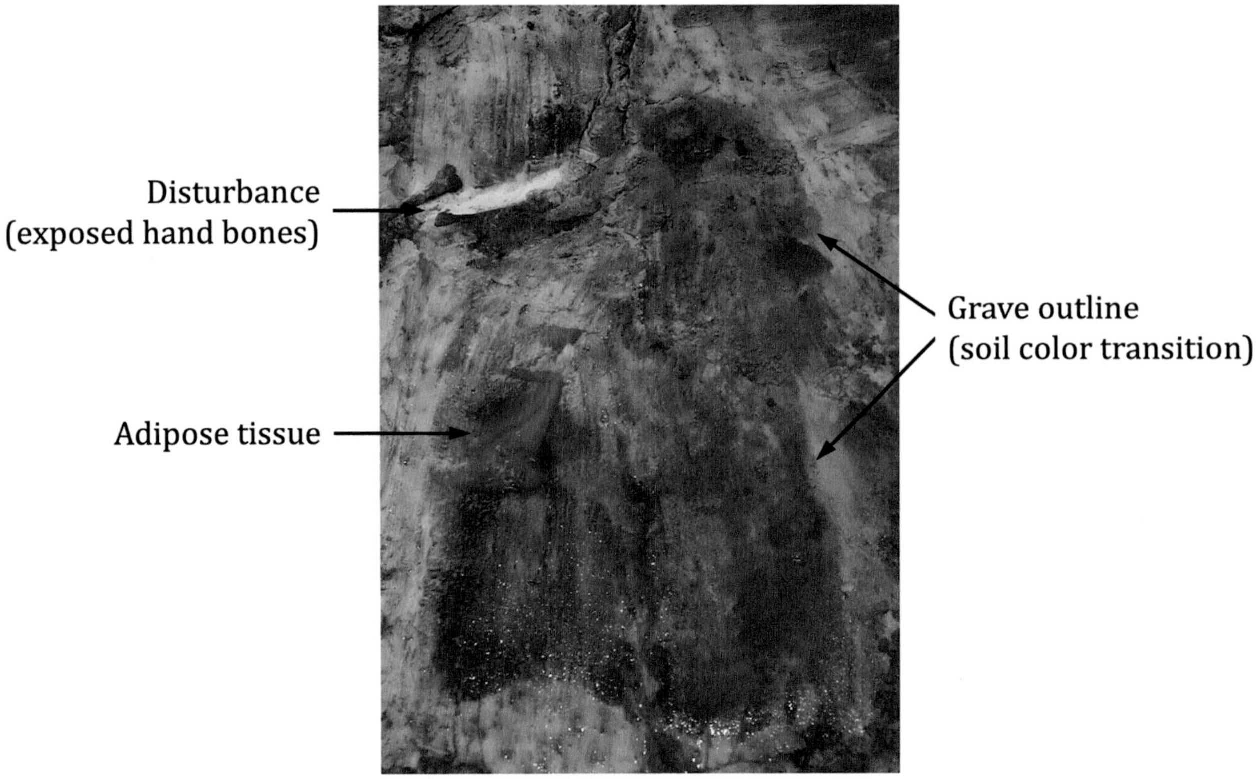

Figure 6.24 Grave outline and associated remains revealed after implementing shovel shining method.

Box #3: How to Shovel Shine

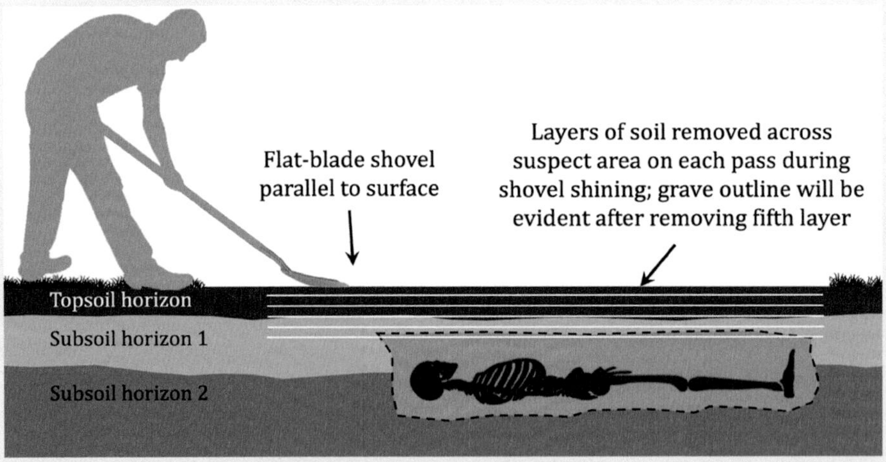

USING A FLAT-BLADE TRANSFER SHOVEL TO SHOVEL SHINE

1. Clear any vegetation by clipping plants and roots at the ground surface. If necessary, use a trowel to remove roots from smaller plants (e.g., grasses or non-woody varieties).
2. Once the ground in the area of interest is exposed, position the shovel blade edge facing up and the pan almost parallel to the ground surface.
3. Apply a slight amount of downward pressure and move the shovel blade forward in a skimming motion to remove soil in a ½ to ¾ inch (1–2 cm) layer from the ground surface.

4. Repeat this action across the entire area of interest, keeping the ground surface as level as possible.
5. Continue removing soil in this same manner, layer by layer, until the outline of a grave appears, evidence is encountered (e.g., previously cut roots, personal items), or the suspect area is cleared as a possible grave site.
6. Photographs and proper notation of soil horizons and elevation should be kept during the process.
7. A designated team member should periodically check suspect areas within the shovel shined ground surface using a trowel for excavation or soil probe to discern differences in soil compaction.

Figure 6.25 Heavy equipment (Caterpillar 320B Trackhoe excavator with extended boom) being used to search a suspected location of a buried car containing two bodies.

The greatest advantage in using a backhoe is that it can remove a considerable amount of soil in a short period of time. However, backhoes also have been used in archaeology to locate graves by carefully scraping sterile topsoil and exposing the outline of cemetery or historic period graves (Bass, 1963; Ubelaker, 1999). Because the use of a backhoe involves extending the bucket over a smaller area of interest, the heavy equipment will not damage material by driving over the search area. An experienced operator can meticulously control the bucket so that the soil is removed a few inches at a time, leaving a relatively smooth surface with a single soil layer exposed at each depth (Figure 6.26).

Bulldozers should not be used in forensic searches, as they can quickly and significantly damage evidence as well as the search area. Bulldozers are designed to push soil around, creating a greater chance of mixing soil horizons and damaging evidence when their metal tracks drive over and compress the soil. Nevertheless, use of a 'forensic bulldozer' can be warranted through the trench-and-shift technique (Christensen et al., 2009). This method involves first digging a trench adjacent to the search area and carefully scraping soil from the side of the trench (refer to Case Study #6), rather than the heavy equipment moving over the top of the search area and possibly damaging a potential grave.

There should always be a forensic archaeologist guiding the backhoe operator and checking the ground as the soil is being scraped to determine whether a grave outline, or soil change, has appeared. Depending on the angle and amount of sunlight, soil changes and early indications of grave outlines may appear differently from various perspectives. Therefore, as the ground is scraped, additional team members should be watching for differences in color changes in relation to the surrounding undisturbed soil and taking notes on elevations for each soil layer. Designated team members should periodically check suspicious areas with trowels as well as soil probes

Figure 6.26 A backhoe (Case 680 loader with Extendahoe) being used to clear an area of interest. Note the smooth, level surface of the cleared area and (a) exposure of a dark, highly organic soil horizon, located below (b) a lighter-colored sand horizon. Information provided by the land owner indicated that the buried darker, organic soil horizon was the original ground surface, while the sand layer was added on top to level the property after an old grove of trees had been removed.

to discern differences in soil compaction. Grave fill is generally a different color from the surrounding layer or may appear mottled due to mixing of the soil layers and decomposition products. If the soil profile consists of multiple discernable soil layers such as a hardpan or clay horizon, the entire layer can be exposed using the backhoe (Figure 6.26a). It may then be possible to locate a clandestine grave by noting the isolated soil changes within the layer, much like the changes seen in the smaller-scale process of shovel shining. During a backhoe search, it is also important to have someone visually checking each bucket of removed soil for any evidence. If possible, it is recommended to have someone experienced with human skeletal remains at the scene assisting with the search. Once anything suspicious is located in the area being scraped, all work with the backhoe must cease, and less destructive methods should then be used to determine whether a grave is present. After all evidence has been cleared, or in cases where no evidence was found, the forensic archaeologist should coordinate with law enforcement investigators and the backhoe operator about backfilling all areas that were investigated.

CASE STUDY #6: TRY AND TRY AGAIN

In May 2005, authors John Schultz and Tosha Dupras were asked to participate in the search for the burial site of a 12-year-old female. Law enforcement officials had received a tip from an informant that the girl had been killed a year and a half before and placed in a grave approximately 6 ft (1.8 m) deep in a residential backyard. Investigators felt that the information was credible also because an HRD dog had alerted in the suspected area. This case utilized several types of search methods prior to using a backhoe to assist in locating the grave. Upon arriving at the scene, a search survey was conducted first using ground-penetrating radar (GPR) (refer to Chapter 7 for GPR equipment and use); however, this technique was inconclusive due to interference from tree roots in the area. Probes were then used in the area, though soil compaction differences were not noted. Flat-edged transfer shovels were then used to shovel shine the search area, and trowels were used for detailed work in clearing the area. Although large networks of undisturbed tree roots were present, we did note that a number of surface roots were previously severed (Figure 6.27), but this had not been a recent occurrence, as several of these roots had developed root balls with smaller roots growing out of them (Figure 6.27b). This was consistent with information concerning one of the children at the residence periodically digging in the backyard for worms being used as fishing bait. None of these search methods yielded evidence of a clandestine grave.

To completely clear the area, the detective in charge requested that we follow up with a backhoe search. We were provided with a city-owned backhoe, but the city was unable to provide one with a flat-blade bucket. Instead, we received a backhoe with a 'rock' bucket (i.e., a toothed bucket) (Figure 6.28). Since it was not possible to scrape the ground surface with this bucket, we decided to improvise using a trench-and shift-technique by first digging a trench outside the search area. This allowed us to view the natural stratigraphy of the soil profile, which consisted of distinct and contrasting soil horizons. Shovel shining was used to check the bottom of the trench before the work continued. The backhoe proceeded to slowly remove soil from the exposed wall of the trench, working toward the main area of interest. Each time the backhoe removed a strip of soil, we would scrape the newly exposed wall and floor surfaces with trowels to discern any soil changes that might indicate a grave outline (Figure 6.29). The entire area was cleared using this method, confirming our previous search results and verifying that no grave was present within the search area.

Figure 6.27 Network of large tree roots present in the area of a suspected grave. This image shows (a) two large uncut roots and (b) a severed root with smaller roots growing from the cut end.

Figure 6.28 Author John Schultz shovel shining the bottom of the trench dug by a backhoe with a rock bucket (circled).

Figure 6.29 Author John Schultz working with the trench-and shift-technique by first digging a trench adjacent to the search area and carefully scraping soil from the wall of the trench with a trowel to discern any disruption of the natural soil horizons.

CASE STUDY #7: THE GOOD, THE BAD, AND THE MUDDY

In September of 2001, authors Tosha Dupras, Lana Williams, and Sandra Wheeler were asked to assist in the search for the remains of a 22-year-old male who had been missing for approximately 15 months. Information from one of the suspects, already incarcerated for another offense, led law enforcement to search an abandoned pig farm. The suspect indicated that the victim had been lured to the area with false hopes of a romantic rendezvous, and upon his arrival four individuals proceeded to beat him to death and then bury him on the property.

The detectives had set a perimeter before we arrived on the scene. The suspect had been brought out to the scene the previous day and had indicated areas of interest. The area marked as searchable by the police was approximately 50 by 75 ft (15 by 23 m) in size and was bordered on the north by a tree line and fire break trench, on the south by a dirt road, and on the east and west by low brush cover. The area to be searched included tall grass, brush, and brambles. Police HRD dogs had been brought in to assist with the search, and they had alerted at two particular spots (Figure 6.30). A walking survey was very difficult, as the surface features were not discernable through the vegetation, so a decision was made to clear the area. A large field mower was brought in to clear low brush and small trees, and a prison detail of ten inmates was brought out to clear the remainder of the ground cover (Figure 6.31). After the ground was cleared, there were two disturbed areas that were investigated in addition to the areas that the dogs alerted on earlier. All of the disturbed areas were first shovel shined to discern any feature outlines and then excavated with trowels to examine any suspected features. These areas revealed only butchered pig bones and turtle shells. Toward the late afternoon, heavy rainfall caused the search to be suspended for the day.

Figure 6.30 Cadaver dog search in the suspected burial site. Note the growth of grasses, low brush, and trees that needed to be cleared before a detailed search could be conducted.

On the second day of the search, the suspect was brought back out to give us further indication of where to search and provide a description of the burial. The suspect had a difficult time indicating where to search, because the environment had been changed dramatically after removal of the foliage. It was decided at this point to use a backhoe so that the entire area could be searched in a timely manner (Figure 6.32). Initially, there were a few minutes of anxious anticipation when the backhoe overturned a turtle shell. With only part of the shell exposed, it looked remarkably like a human skull! Alas, no human bones were uncovered, and, like the day before, a torrential downpour began around 3:00 pm, creating a very muddy area. The search was once again suspended for the day.

Figure 6.31 Area of interest after all vegetation was removed with a large field mower. Note flagging pin marking area of HRD dog alert.

Figure 6.32 View of scene showing backhoe (front center), command vehicles, and the two areas (arrows) dug up by the backhoe on the second day of the search. (*Photograph courtesy of the Orange County Sheriff's Office*)

On the morning of the third day, the HRD dogs were brought back out to search the area. On occasion, a secondary canine search is performed once vegetation is removed or soil is disturbed by a backhoe, as this can potentially cause the release of decomposition molecules to trigger a canine alert. The HRD dogs hit on one area that was further explored.

By this time, our search area had turned into a giant mud bowl. The summer of 2001 had been a particularly bad year for rainfall, and the ground was already saturated with water before we started searching this new area indicated by the canine unit. With the addition of multiple days of heavy rain, the water was unable to drain from the ground surface and pooled in every depression where the backhoe had been used to dig. It is also imperative at this point to emphasize the importance of working with an experienced and skilled backhoe operator who can take directions and properly remove soil in small, level increments. In this particular search, the operator actually contributed to the difficulties in excavation. The operator did not listen to our needs and instead produced large holes and piles of dirt in areas that, when combined with the rain, created unsteady and hazardous working conditions. Because of the condition of the terrain, a special type of backhoe, called a spider backhoe, was brought in by law enforcement to continue excavations. The spider backhoe has extension legs that allow for the stabilization of the machine on uneven terrain. At 2:45 pm on the third day of the search, the bucket of the spider backhoe snagged and exposed what appeared to be a human leg bone. All excavations were suspended until the local medical examiner arrived at the scene to verify that the bone was human and then instructed us to continue with the recovery.

The rain continued, and a temporary shelter was erected over the site where the bone was discovered (Figure 6.33). The large quantities of standing water, however, made excavation very difficult. The sides of the excavation area were unstable and continued to collapse. Water continually ran down the sides of the excavation area and also seeped in from the surrounding walls. Efforts were made to construct drainage trenches around the area so that the water could be diverted. The spider backhoe was used to dig a reservoir pit so that the water would accumulate there instead of the grave. Because of these difficult conditions, we knew we had to work faster than normal to recover the remains.

Flat-blade transfer shovels were used to shovel shine the area, revealing the outline of the grave (Figure 6.34).

Figure 6.33 Temporary shelter erected over the burial site. This image also shows the mess that was made by the backhoe operator and the pooled rainwater.

Because this area was an abandoned pig farm, there was a thick, decomposed organic layer of soil over the sand. When the grave was dug and filled, these two soil horizons were intermixed, making the grave outline very evident. The grave outline, 2.5 ft in width by 4 ft in length (0.76 m by 1.2 m), was clearly defined as a dark area in comparison with the surrounding white sterile sand layer. Traditional excavation techniques, such as setting up a grid, were impossible in this case due to the muddy, unstable conditions and the continual water flow. The site and excavation were primarily documented using photography. Layers of sediment in the feature were removed slowly and carefully with a flat-blade transfer shovel until the skull was located. At this point, trowels and small excavation tools were used to excavate and reveal the entire individual. Although the individual had been interred for 15 months, the burial environment and copious amount of rain led to conditions conducive to the formation of adipocere and, therefore, much of the soft tissue was still present on the postcranial portion of the body. Once the body was completely uncovered, it was removed as a single unit and placed in a body bag. The area under the body was excavated to make sure that none of the smaller bones or any associated evidentiary items were missed.

As a follow-up to this case, the four individuals responsible for this crime were charged and convicted of first degree murder and are all continuing to serve out their sentences.

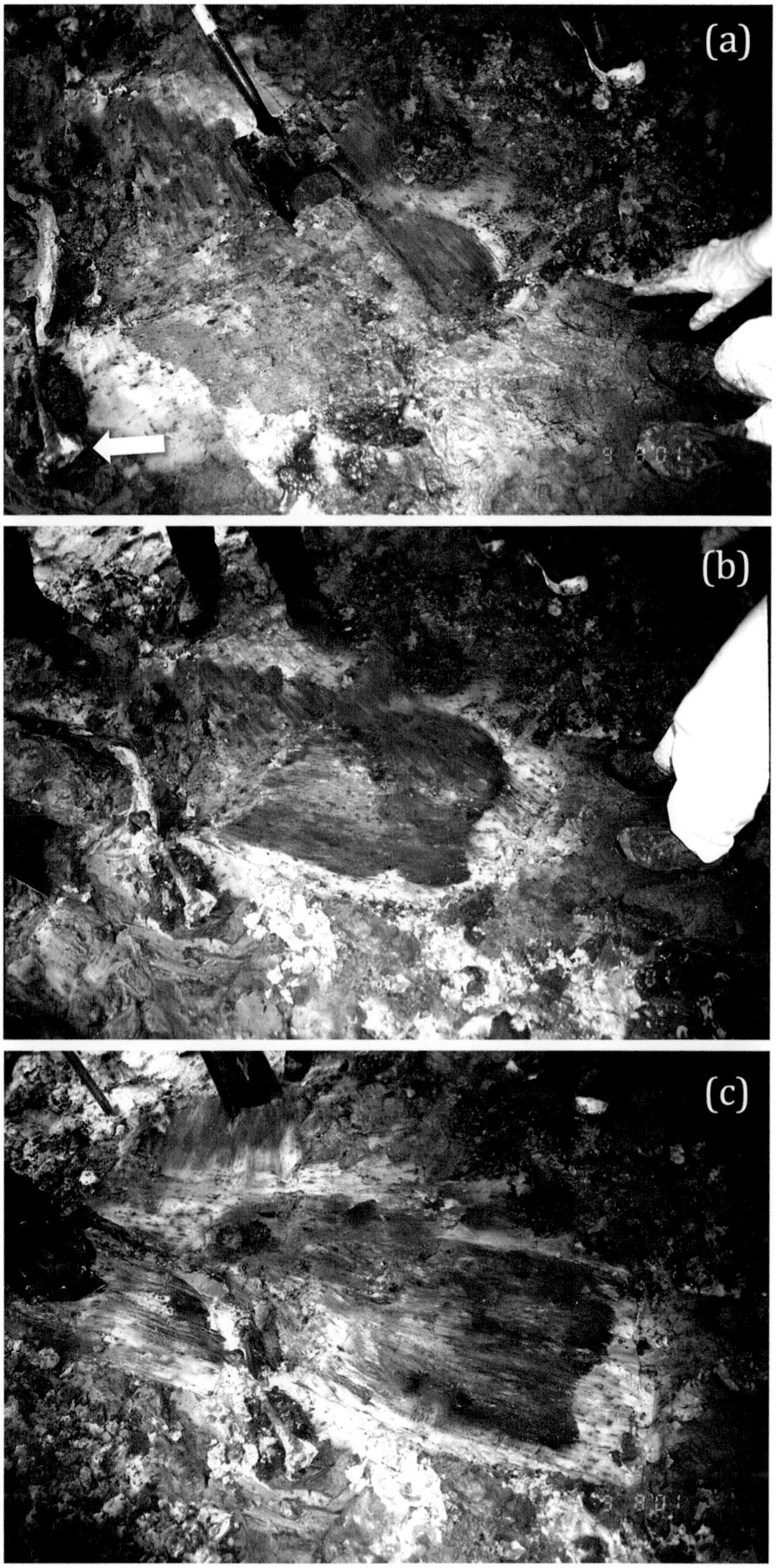

Figure 6.34 Shovel shining process showing the progressive exposure of the grave outline: (a) first portion of the grave exposed. The tibia dislodged by the backhoe is present in the lower left part of the image (arrow); (b) grave outline half exposed; and (c) entire grave outline exposed.

Key Terms

backhoe
bulldozer
burial
burial site
clandestine grave
grave
grave outline
grid pattern
HRD dogs
inside-out pattern
intrusive searches
nonintrusive searches
obstructed areas
open areas
penetrometer
primary grave depression
scent cone
scent pool
search sweep
searching
secondary grave depression
shovel shining
shovel testing
site processing
soil horizons
soil-coring probe
spiral pattern
strip (line) pattern
submerged areas
T-bar probe
test pit
transects
visual surface search
zone search

REVIEW AND DISCUSSION QUESTIONS

1. The local police receive a tip concerning an individual who had gone missing three years ago. The informant stated that the individual was buried in an old apple orchard that is no longer harvested. The general landscape of the orchard is flat with tall grass and trees and covers about one square mile (1.6 km^2). Considering these factors, answer the following:
   - How would you go about searching for the remains? What search pattern would you use?
   - How many people would be needed on the search team? What would the spacing be between individuals?
   - When would you consider using an invasive method in your search? What method(s) would you use and why?
2. A hiker disappeared two years ago in some rocky terrain in a river valley. HRD dogs were used in a recent search for the missing hiker and alerted to an area at the bottom of a 20-ft (6 m) cliff that ran along a closed mountain bike trail. The local police searched the area and along the edge of the river, which was approximately 15 ft (4.5 m) away from the bottom of the cliff. No bones or associated evidence were found in the area indicated by the dogs. Considering these factors, answer the following:
   - What processes would cause the dogs to alert to this area even though no remains were found? Describe the possible scenario of scent pool and scent cone formation.
   - What would you do at this point in the search? Explain your reasoning using the information provided.
   - Is there any additional information that the HRD team could provide that may help explain why the human remains detection dogs alerted to this area?
3. You are assisting in a search that is using a backhoe and have been asked to keep a set of notes for the lead forensic archaeologist. What kinds of information should you be collecting? What other method(s) of data collection might you use to go along with your written notes?
4. Discuss the ground surface and subsurface changes that occur during digging, and over time, in a clandestine grave. What criteria are important for locating a possible clandestine grave and confirming its location?

Suggested Readings

Haglund, W.D. 1997. Scattered skeletal human remains: Search strategy considerations for locating mussing teeth. In: Haglund, W.D., Sorg, M.H., eds. *Forensic Taphonomy: The Postmortem Fate of Human Remains*, pp. 383–394. Boca Raton, FL: CRC Press.

Osterkamp, T. 2020. *Detector Dogs and Scent Movement: How Weather, Terrain, and Vegetation Influence Search Strategies*. Boca Raton, FL: CRC Press.

Owsley, D.W. 2005. Techniques for locating burials. *Journal of Forensic Sciences* 40:735–740. DOI:10.1520/JFS15375J

Pokines, J.T. 2015. A procedure for processing outdoor surface forensic scenes yielding skeletal remains among leaf litter. *Journal of Forensic Identification*. 65(2):161–172.

Pokines, J.T., Baker, J.E. 2022. Effects of recovery methods. In: Pokines, J.T., L'Abbé E.N., Symes, S.A., eds. *Manual of Forensic Taphonomy*, 2nd ed., pp. 605–629. Boca Raton, FL: CRC Press.

Rebmann, A., David, E., Sorg, M.H. 2000. *Cadaver Dog Handbook: Forensic Training and Tactics for the Recovery of Human Remains.* Boca Raton, FL: CRC Press.

References

Bass, W.M. 1963. The use of heavy power equipment in the excavation of human skeletal material. *Plains Anthropologist* 8(20):122–123.

Boyd, R.M. 1979. Buried body cases. *FBI Law Enforcement Bulletin* 48(2): 6–11.

Christensen, A.M., Lowe, W.M., Reinecke, G.W. 2009. The 'forensic bulldozer' as a clandestine grave search tool. *Forensic Science Communications* 11(4). https://www.fbi.gov/hq/lab/fsc/current/technical/2009_10_Technical_Note.html.

France, D.L., Griffin, T.J., Swanburg, J.G., Lindemann, J.W., Davenport, G.C., Tramell, V., Travis, C.T., Kondratieff, R., Nelson, A., Castellano, K., Hopkins, D. 1992. A multidisciplinary approach to the detection of clandestine graves. *Journal of Forensic Sciences* 37:1145–1458. DOI:10.1520/JFS13337J

France, D.L., Griffin, T.J., Swanburg, J.G., Lindemann, J.W., Davenport, G.C., Tramell, V., Travis, C.T., Kondratieff, R., Nelson, A., Castellano, K., Hopkins D., Adair T. 1997. NecroSearch revisited: Further multidisciplinary approaches to the detection of clandestine graves. In: Haglund, W.D., Sorg, M.H., eds. *Forensic Taphonomy: The Postmortem Fate of Human Remains*, pp. 497–510. Boca Raton, FL: CRC Press.

Haglund, W.D. 1997a. Scattered skeletal human remains: Search strategy considerations for locating missing teeth. In: Haglund, W.D., Sorg, M.H., eds. *Forensic Taphonomy: The Postmortem Fate of Human Remains*, pp. 383–394. Boca Raton, FL: CRC Press.

Haglund, W.D. 1997b. Dogs and coyotes: Postmortem involvement with human remains. In: Haglund, W.D., Sorg, M.H., eds. *Forensic Taphonomy: The Postmortem Fate of Human Remains*, pp. 367–382. Boca Raton, FL: CRC Press.

Hawley, D.A., Harruff, R.C., Pless, J.E., Clark, M.A. 1994. Disinterment from paving materials: Use of heavy equipment for exhumation and examination of bodies. *Journal of Forensic Sciences* 39:100–106. DOI:10.1520/JFS13575J

Imaizumi, M. 1974. Locating buried bodies. *FBI Law Enforcement Bulletin* 43(8):2–5.

Judah, J.C. 2008. *Buzzards and Butterflies: Human Remains Detection Dogs*, 2nd ed., Wilmington, NC: Coastal Books.

Judah, J., Sargent, T. 2015. *How to Train a Human Remains Detection Dog.* Scotts Valley, CA: CreateSpace Independent Publishing Platform.

Killam, E.W. 2004. *The Detection of Human Remains*, 2nd ed., Springfield, IL: Charles C Thomas.

Lasseter, A.E., Jacobi, K.P., Farley, R., Hensel, L. 2003. Cadaver dog and handler team capabilities in the recovery of buried human remains in the Southeastern United States. *Journal of Forensic Sciences* 48:617–621. DOI:10.1520/JFS2002296

Lowy, A., McAlhany, P. 2000. Human remains detection: The latest police canine detector specialty. *FDIAI News* April/June: 6–8.

Morse, D., Duncan, J., Stoudamire, J. 1983. *Handbook of Forensic Archaeology and Anthropology.* Tallahassee, FL: Rose Printing.

Osterkamp, T. 2020. *Detector Dogs and Scent Movement: How Weather, Terrain, and Vegetation Influence Search Strategies*. Boca Raton, FL: CRC Press.

Owsley, D.W. 1995. Techniques for locating burials, with emphasis on the probe. *Journal of Forensic Sciences* 40:735–740. DOI:10.1520/JFS15375J

Pokines, J.T. 2015. A procedure for processing outdoor surface forensic scenes yielding skeletal remains among leaf litter. *Journal of Forensic Identification* 65(2):161–172.

Pokines, J.T., Baker, J.E. 2022. Effects of recovery methods. In: Pokines, J.T., L'Abbé E.N., Symes, S.A., eds. *Manual of Forensic Taphonomy*, 2nd ed., pp. 605–629. Boca Raton, FL: CRC Press.

Pokines, J.T., Mammano, K., Studebaker-Reed, M., Mowery, J., Patterson, M., Schneider, C., Trapp, B., Mincher, C. 2018. Success rates of recovering dispersed bones among leaflitter. *Forensic Anthropology* 1(4):189–200. DOI:10.5744/fa.2018.1029

Pokines, J.T., Robinson, S., Mansz, J., Heidel, N., Jasny, K., Gilligan, J., Carmona, A., Kroll, J., Lavigne, S., Calle, S. 2019a. Success rates of forensic surface search for osseous remains in a New England, U.S.A. environment. *Forensic Anthropology* 2(1):9–20.

Pokines, J.T., Udoni, M.M., Sanders Stark, S., Cassidy, S., Atkinson, M.L., Church, E., File, C.L., Green, M.K., Herrera, M.D., Kilroy, G.S., Peace, B.N., Purcell, B.J., Reinman, A.S., Sanchez, A.M., Springman, S.J. 2019b. Success rates of recovering teeth and infant-sized bones dispersed among leaf litter. *Forensic Anthropology* 2(3):168–177. DOI:10.5744/fa.2019.1033

Rebmann, A., David, E., Sorg, M.H. 2000. *Cadaver Dog Handbook: Forensic Training and Tactics for the Recovery of Human Remains.* Boca Raton, FL: CRC Press.

Ruffell, A. 2005. Burial location using cheap and reliable quantitative probe measurements. *Forensic Science International* 151:207–211. DOI:10.1016/j.forsciint.2004.12.036

Ubelaker, D.H. 1999. *Human Skeletal Remains: Excavation, Analysis, Interpretation.* 3rd ed., Washington, DC: Taraxacum.

CHAPTER 7

METHODS OF GEOPHYSICAL SURVEY

Learning Objectives

- Introduce different geophysical tools used in archaeological and forensic contexts.
- Outline geophysical approaches for locating forensic graves and buried metallic evidence and for locating submerged bodies and evidence.
- Provide casework examples that are useful in understanding how to incorporate geophysical methods during a search for forensic graves and buried metallic evidence.

Learning Connections

- Review the types and parameters of scenes that need to be evaluated when considering a geophysical search for a forensic context.
- Establish the interconnectedness of incorporating a geophysical search for a buried body or forensic metallic evidence with traditional search methods.

Conducting a geophysical survey in a forensic context is important for not only locating buried bodies and forensic evidence but also equally as important for clearing suspected areas so law enforcement can direct investigations elsewhere. **Geophysical prospecting** is the study of locating and mapping hidden objects or features that are underground or underwater. In most instances, methods of geophysical prospecting are nonintrusive or nondestructive. Therefore, one advantage of incorporating geophysical methods in forensic and archaeological searches is preservation of the scene or site since the ground is not disturbed. Methods of geophysical prospecting can be used as a follow-up technique after initially searching potential areas using visual search methods or an human remains detection (HRD) dog search, as well as in isolating smaller areas for further investigation (refer to Chapter 6). In addition, geophysical prospecting methods can be effective in search areas where traditional search methods are inadequate, such as over concrete and pavement. For example, a geophysical survey is the only type of search method that can be performed over a house foundation without any initial destruction to the slab during a search for a forensic target (Schultz, 2007, 2012). If there are potential areas under the slab that need further investigation, there will be only minimal destruction, because the exact areas to search will have been highlighted using methods of geophysical prospecting. Case Study #7 in this chapter provides an example of a ground-penetrating radar (GPR) survey over a concrete garage slab during a search.

The purpose of conducting a **geophysical survey** is to systematically detect subsurface anomalies or reflections, which are recognized as localized areas of contrasting physical properties such as a metallic weapon buried in the soil horizons. In this case, the buried metallic weapon may be detected with various geophysical prospecting tools, because it would have different electrical properties (e.g., measures of **electrical conductivity**, how strongly a material conducts electrical current, or **electrical resistivity**, how strongly a material resists electrical current) than the surrounding soil horizon. However, the only way to determine what produces the anomaly is to then use a destructive follow-up method such as probing or excavating. Table 7.1 provides a summary of commonly used tools and their applications in geophysical survey.

Geophysical prospecting methods can be classified into two basic types: active and passive (Reynolds, 1997). **Active geophysical prospecting methods** send an induced signal into the ground by a **transmitter (Tx)** and then measure the returning signal via a **receiver (Rx)**. Conversely, **passive geophysical prospecting methods** only contain a receiver that measures variations within the natural forces of the earth, such as magnetic fields, that are generally produced by buried metallic objects.

The following description of geophysical prospecting tools is not an exhaustive list of those used in forensic and archaeological applications. The purpose of this chapter is to discuss the optimal equipment to use in various terrestrial contexts when searching for buried bodies and metallic forensic evidence and to explain the operation

DOI: 10.4324/9781315201658-7

Table 7.1 Summary of Commonly Used Terrestrial Geophysical Prospecting Tools*

Tool	Primary Applications	Disadvantages
Electromagnetic (EM) induction meters	• Detects larger metallic weapons and other large metallic objects • May detect graves • Can work through snow	• Expensive • Requires expert operator • Shallow depth detection • Not effective in clayey soils
Resistivity meters	• Detects graves • Can be used where GPR is less effective	• Moderately priced • Requires some ground disturbance • Dry soils limit effectiveness
Electrical resistivity tomography (ERT)	• Detects graves • Can be used where GPR is less effective	• Expensive • Requires expert operator • Requires some ground disturbance • Dry soils limit effectiveness
Magnetometers	• Detects ferrous metallic weapons and other metal evidence • Can work through snow	• Expensive • Requires expert operator • Not effective in chalky soils or gravel deposits
Magnetic locators	• Detects ferrous metallic weapons and other metal evidence	• Shallow depth detection, but deeper detection than metal detector
Metal detectors	• Detects metallic weapons and other metal evidence	• Shallow depth detection

* Information regarding the use of ground-penetrating radar can be found in Table 7.3

and use of the equipment in the field. This chapter reviews the more common tools used in forensic and archaeological surveys, such as GPR, electromagnetic (EM) induction meters, electrical resistivity meters and electrical resistivity tomography (ERT), magnetometers, magnetic locators, and metal detectors. These tools provide excellent resolution of many types of archaeological features and can be operated under a wide range of conditions. Of all these, GPR is generally the optimal option when searching for buried remains or clandestine graves. However, if it is not possible to use a GPR system, either due to equipment availability, unsuitable site conditions, or when searching for small metallic evidence, then one of the alternate geophysical prospecting tools described in this chapter could be considered. Additionally, the use of side-scan sonar, remotely operated vehicles (ROVs), and associated search methods, such as dive teams, will be briefly discussed. This combination of search tools is most commonly employed for submersed evidence and body searches.

PLANNING THE GEOPHYSICAL SEARCH

Prior to conducting a geophysical search for a clandestine grave or buried forensic evidence, it is important to undertake a planning phase to increase the chances for a successful search (Schultz, 2012). During the planning phase, the first consideration is whether the scene characteristics are appropriate for operating a GPR or other types of geophysical tools. For example, it would not be appropriate to operate a GPR unit during a clandestine grave search in an area that is fully overgrown with brush and trees. Soil type, topography characteristics, and whether the ground surface is saturated with water are other considerations for the applicability of conducting a geophysical survey. In addition, it is important to ascertain if death investigators have already searched the suspected area and if destructive methods were previously used during the initial search. For example, it is common for law enforcement to conduct clandestine grave searches using search lines and HRD dogs, and investigators sometimes will conduct digging of suspicious areas. At that point, investigators may consider whether GPR is a possible search method. If suspicious areas have already been disturbed through digging, the subsurface has been disturbed, and those disturbed areas should not be surveyed with GPR. Thus, it is ideal when the geophysical tool operator can be involved at the scene during the early search phase prior to conducting any destructive methods.

It is essential to ascertain as much information about the site characteristics and the burial scenario to plan proper search strategies. While a visit to the scene is suggested prior to the geophysical survey, comparing present-day pictures and aerial images with those of past aerial images prior to the forensic target being buried is essential to understand site characteristics at the time of the burial and subsequent changes that have occurred to the site after the burial. Further, it is important to learn about the burial process and if the suspected grave was hand-dug or buried with heavy equipment, since the depth of investigation will differ. At the same time, if other items were added to a grave, such as items placed over the body or used to store or wrap the body prior to burial, these items may increase the likelihood of geophysical detection, particularly if metallic objects were included. In addition, if the survey is conducted in an urban area, it is preferable to determine during the planning phase where buried utility lines, pipes, septic tanks, and other structures may be located so that the ground surface can be marked prior to the survey. Finally, it also important to learn about the soil type, which may dictate the type of geophysical tool that can be used during the search. Table 7.2 provides a list of questions that should be discussed with homicide investigators and other death investigators involved with the case prior to committing to and performing a geophysical survey.

During the planning phase, investigators should determine the feasibility of performing a geophysical survey after learning as much as possible about the parameters involved with the search. The next step is to determine if site conditions are appropriate for a geophysical survey, and if they are, which geophysical survey method(s) will be incorporated into the search protocol. Initial testing of site conditions can be conducted with the geophysical equipment to determine the optimal geophysical tool to use and the proper operational settings.

Table 7.2 Questions to Ask Investigators Prior to Committing to and Performing a Geophysical Survey

- Have previous search methods already been utilized by investigators, including conducting any digging at the site?
- What are the site characteristics, including topography, vegetation growth, soil type, saturation of the soil horizon, etc.?
- When did the suspected burial of the forensic target occur?
- Can current scene and aerial images or satellite images be provided, including images of the site prior to burial and immediately after the suspected burial of the forensic target?
- How deep was the forensic target buried, and was anything added during the burial process, or used to store or wrap forensic target?
- How has the present-day search area changed since the time at which the forensic target was thought to have been buried?
- Are there any buried utility lines, pipes, septic tanks, etc. within the proposed survey area?

Source: Derived from Schultz (2012)

GROUND PENETRATING RADAR (GPR)

Ground pepentrating radar (GPR) has proven to be the optimal geophysical tool to use for grave searches in archaeological, forensic, and controlled contexts. For example, GPR has been used to locate or verify the location of historic or archaeological graves (Bevan, 1991; King et al., 1993; Vaughn, 1986), and it has been used to locate an increasing number of clandestine graves involving bodies interred in varying environments and over various postmortem intervals (Calkin et al., 1995; Davenport, 2001a; Mellett, 1992; Nobes, 2000; Schultz, 2007). At the same time, controlled studies using buried pig cadavers have demonstrated that a GPR system is the most effective geophysical prospecting tool used to delineate graves in forensic contexts (France et al., 1997).

Standard GPR systems consist of four main components: the control unit, the transmitter, the receiver, and the display unit. Systems used in archaeology and forensics typically have **monostatic antennae** where the transmitter and receiver are contained within the same antenna housing. GPR systems can be configured in a number of different configurations for use in the field. The most common configuration is to mount all of the GPR components onto a cart that can be operated by one individual (Figure 7.1). The second option has one individual pulling the antenna and operating a control unit that is attached to the body via a harness (Figure 7.2). The last option is to separate the antenna and control unit, where one individual pulls the antenna across each transect on a grid while another individual monitors the GPR signal on the control unit and directs the antenna operator. If a geophysical survey was performed inside a house or structure, using a separate antenna and control unit may be preferable, because this configuration allows for more detailed work.

Figure 7.1 Author John Schultz demonstrating how the GPR is operated when using a survey cart with the 500-MHz antenna secured to the bottom of the cart.

Figure 7.2 Author John Schultz demonstrating how the GPR is operated when one individual is pulling the 500-MHz antenna with the monitor secured to the body via a shoulder harness.

Operating the GPR system begins with placement of the antenna on, or near, the ground surface and then moving it over the area being surveyed. When the GPR system is active, it emits continuous EM pulses of short duration that propagate from the transmitting unit in the antenna downward into the ground. As the signal penetrates into the subsurface, it will be reflected, refracted, and scattered as it encounters materials of contrasting electrical properties (Figure 7.3). The receiving portion of the antenna records the returning signal and sends it back to the control unit. The control unit amplifies and formats the raw, reflected signal for immediate display on a video monitor. The GPR data files can also be downloaded to an external computer and stored for further viewing and processing (e.g., to increase resolution of the reflection profile) using a variety of software applications offered by GPR manufacturers or standalone programs.

Antennae for GPR systems are manufactured in standard frequencies that are designated by the frequency corresponding to the peak power of the radiated spectrum, or the center frequency. The most common GPR systems available from commercial manufacturers employ pulsed radar energy of one center frequency. Antenna choice is a compromise between depth of penetration and subsurface resolution. Lower frequency antennae (e.g., 300 MHz) are used for much deeper surveys but have a lower resolution of small subsurface targets. In some instances, a higher resolution antenna (e.g., 900 MHz) may yield so much detail or **clutter** (small discontinuities that reflect energy but are not the target of the survey) that the target may not be readily identified (Nobes, 2000; Schultz, 2007). Antennae with frequencies from 400 to 500 MHz are generally appropriate for most forensic and archaeological applications, because they provide an

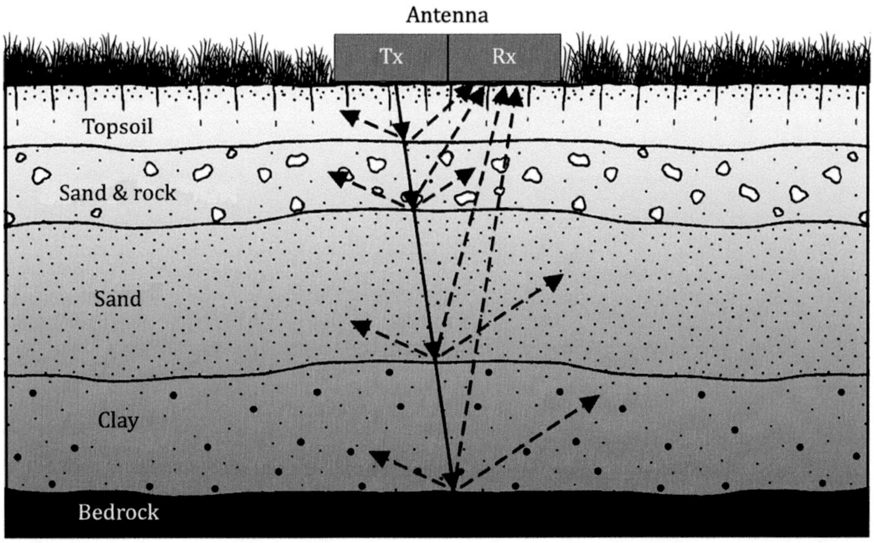

Figure 7.3 Radar waves transmitted (Tx) from the antenna and then received (Rx) after being reflected and scattered as they encounter soil horizon interfaces with differing properties of conductivity and density.

excellent compromise between depth of penetration and resolution of subsurface features (Schultz, 2008; Schultz et al., 2007). Further, controlled research comparing 500 and 250 MHz antennae have demonstrated that a 250 MHz antenna is also an appropriate option for forensic contexts (Schultz and Martin, 2011). In particular, the 500 MHz antenna provides increased detail of the grave compared with the 250 MHz antenna. At times, the less detail of the 250 MHz antenna may be optimal, because the grave may be highlighted as one stark reflection that is easily discernable, rather than a forensic target that may appear as several smaller reflections (Schultz and Martin, 2011). Soil type and subsurface characteristics, however, must also be considered when choosing antenna size. For example, in soils with extensive clutter in the subsurface such as anthropogenic soils (when natural soil profiles change due to human activity) or soils that have been cleared of brush, it may be difficult to discern a forensic target using the 500 MHz antenna, because the antenna will highlight too much subsurface clutter.

Soil type is also a consideration when selecting antenna size because depth of penetration of the EM wave will be reduced in certain soil types, particularly with saturated soils and soils comprising a high clay content. For example, for soils with a high clay content, depth of penetration will be reduced, because the EM wave will be dissipated or attenuated. When soil properties limit the depth of penetration, a lower frequency antenna must be considered, such as a 250 MHz antenna. Pre-survey testing with more than one antenna can be very beneficial in determining the optimal antenna frequency for a particular soil type, or if GPR is an option for a geophysical survey. If GPR is not an option due to soil properties and ground foliage, electrical resistivity should be considered as an option.

It is important to note that an exact picture of the subsurface is not provided with a GPR system. Instead, it produces a two-dimensional GPR **reflection profile** that represents a grid transect line in the search area and is a cross section of the subsurface, providing length and depth. Features are generally detected by GPR systems due to increases in conductivity, changes in density, and voids. Increases in conductivity are primarily due to an increase in water content in certain soils or disruptions of stratigraphic layers such as clay. For example, when soil is disturbed during the digging of a grave, the space between the particles increases and results in greater moisture retention and conductivity in the backfill compared with the surrounding undisturbed soil. Conductivity increases also occur with buried metallic objects and buried electric lines. When a subsurface feature is detected and noted on the two-dimensional GPR reflection profile, as shown in Figure 7.4, it is called a **reflection**, or anomaly, which can be produced from a feature described as either a **point source** or **planar surface** (Conyers and Goodman, 1997). Reflections are non-specific features, and in many instances, limited exploratory probing or excavation may be required to determine the exact item or feature that was detected. Point sources, or small hyperbolic reflections are due to smaller features such as tunnels, voids, pipes, graves, buried remains, small archaeological features, and weapons (Figure 7.4a). Planar surfaces, conversely, can be due to interfaces of stratigraphic layers (e.g., sand, clay, loam), water tables, or large archaeological features, such as floors and foundations (Figure 7.4b). In addition, prominent horizontal bands of antenna noise, known as **ringing** (Figure 7.4c) may appear in the top portion of most GPR reflection profiles (Shih and Doolittle, 1984; Sternberg and McGill, 1995). If the ringing obscures the GPR reflection profile, it can be removed during processing of the data.

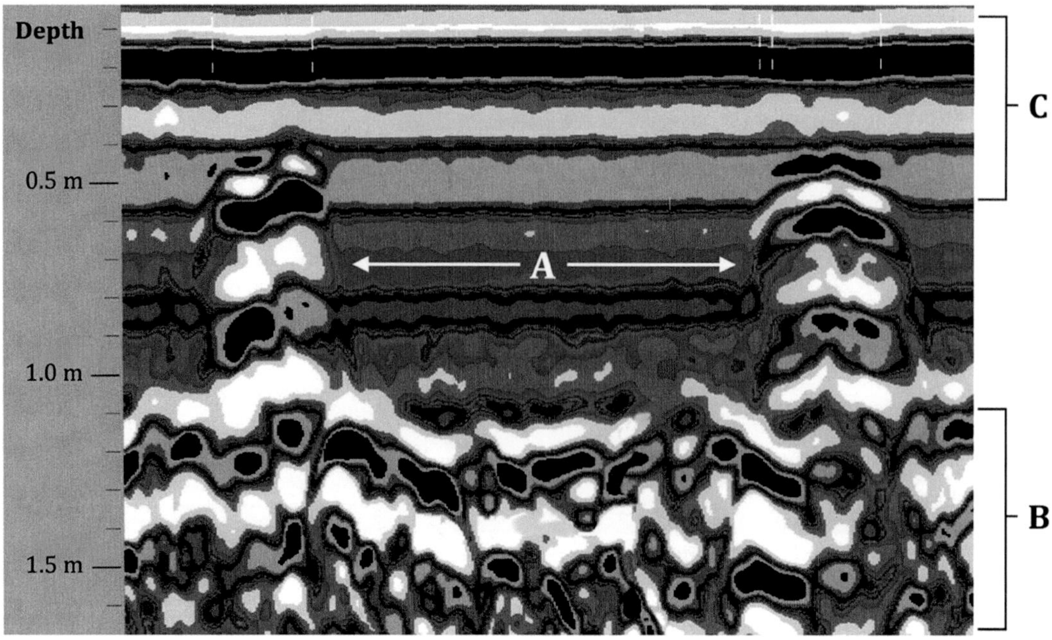

Figure 7.4 Two-dimensional GPR reflection profile of two pig cadavers buried at approximately 60 cm. The reflection profile shows two point sources from the buried pig cadavers (a). A planar surface (b) is demarcated by a clay horizon in the bottom portion of the reflection profile, while ringing (c) is evident in the horizontal banding within the top section of the two-dimensional profile.

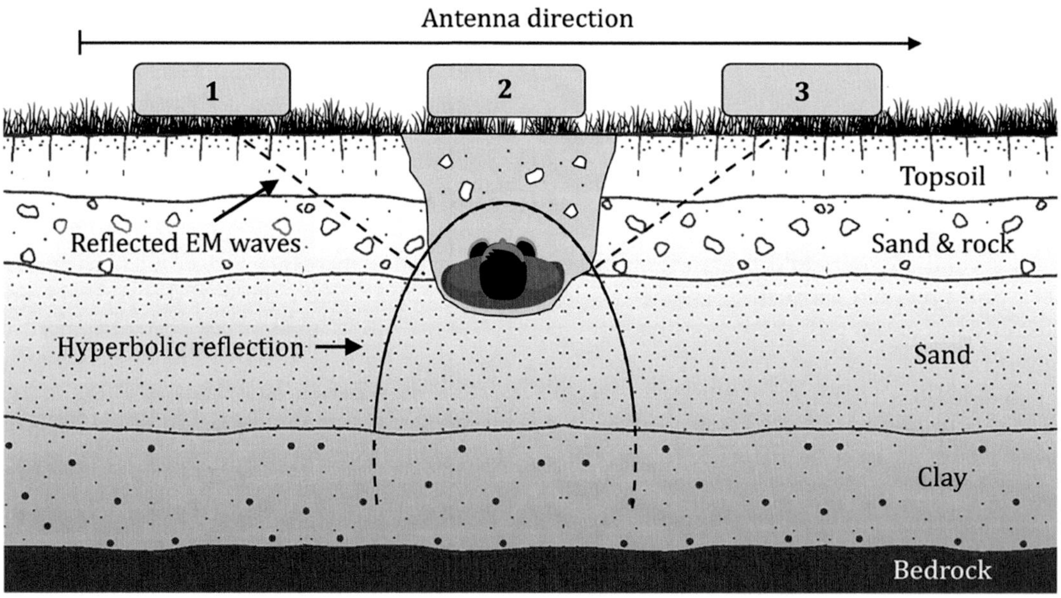

Figure 7.5 Illustration of how a GPR system detects an anomaly such as a buried body. A point source or hyperbolic reflection is generated from one single subsurface feature due to the wide angle of the transmitted radar beam. The hyperbolic characteristics of the reflection are due to the increased travel time of the radar signal before and after the subsurface feature is detected.

Hyperbolic-shaped reflections visible on the GPR profile are produced from the wide angle of the transmitted radar pulse, which is in the shape of an elliptical cone. The long axis of the ellipse is parallel to the direction that the antenna travels, and the radiation pattern on a horizontal plane is directed below the antenna, as well as in front, behind, and to the sides as it travels across the ground surface (Conyers and Goodman, 1997; Schultz, 2007). Therefore, as the antenna is dragged over a subsurface object, it will detect the object prior to arriving directly over it, as well as when it is directly over it, and will continue to detect the subsurface object after passing it (Figure 7.5). When the point source is detected prior to and after the antenna has passed, it is recorded as if the point source is directly beneath the antenna, but the travel time of the radar signal to the object is increased.

The hyperbolic characteristics, or the addition of the tails, are due to the increased travel time of the radar signal before and after the subsurface feature is detected. This shape is important because it allows the GPR operator to note when a feature is located on the GPR profile.

By incorporating GPR profile data into a search grid (refer to Appendix D for GPR grid search log), the operator can also provide horizontal slices, which show a plan view of the data at designated depths. The GPR software interpolates the distance between the grid lines, which are represented by the GPR profiles, to make a cube (Figure 7.6). The software can then 'slice' through the cube to view the subsurface at different depths. The horizontal slice (Figure 7.7) is the most common view and is very popular for archaeology and cemetery work. If horizontal slices are incorporated, it is recommended to evaluate both the horizontal slices and individual two-dimensional GPR profiles for reflections during forensic searches. Additionally, while GPR data is normally assessed in the field during a geophysical survey, the data should be processed back in the lab to determine whether if additional reflections become discernable after completing the survey.

There are many advantages for using a GPR system in forensic contexts. The data are displayed in real-time, and, for forensic surveying, the excellent resolution of subsurface features is only surpassed by side-scan sonar (refer to Section VIII). It is also possible to estimate the depth of forensic targets in the field without having to dig up or ground truth the target by evaluating the GPR data. Geophysical surveys using GPR systems work best in dry, sandy soils with little subsurface debris, but the equipment can also be used in a variety of contexts such as over concrete, pavement, and hard-packed surfaces. In addition, GPR systems can be used to search for large metallic evidence. For example, the contrast of a grave will be increased if a large metallic object, such as a shotgun or rifle, was buried in a grave with a body. Although GPR components can be used in a boat over fresh water to search for submersed bodies, larger metal drums, or vehicles, GPR should only be considered in this manner if side-scan sonar is not available.

There are also a number of disadvantages that will limit or prevent the use of a GPR system as a search tool. First, the equipment is expensive, and it requires an experienced operator to interpret the data. Also, the search area must be fairly level, smooth, and open with few trees, and must have relatively fewer buried large metal objects, as they can produce a reflection similar in size and shape to that of a buried body or a grave. Experienced operators may be able to exclude specific reflections based on their experience and the context of the reflections in relation to specific site features. For example, reflections detected near a large tree are most likely caused by the tree roots. Soil properties significantly affect GPR system performance, as reduced data quality in water-saturated and clayey soils may make it extremely challenging to locate buried bodies or forensic evidence. Additionally, performing a geophysical survey with a GPR system could require a significant amount of time. For example, conducting a detailed GPR survey in an area spanning several acres would not be feasible to complete within a single day. Table 7.3 summarizes advantages and disadvantages of GPR use in forensic contexts.

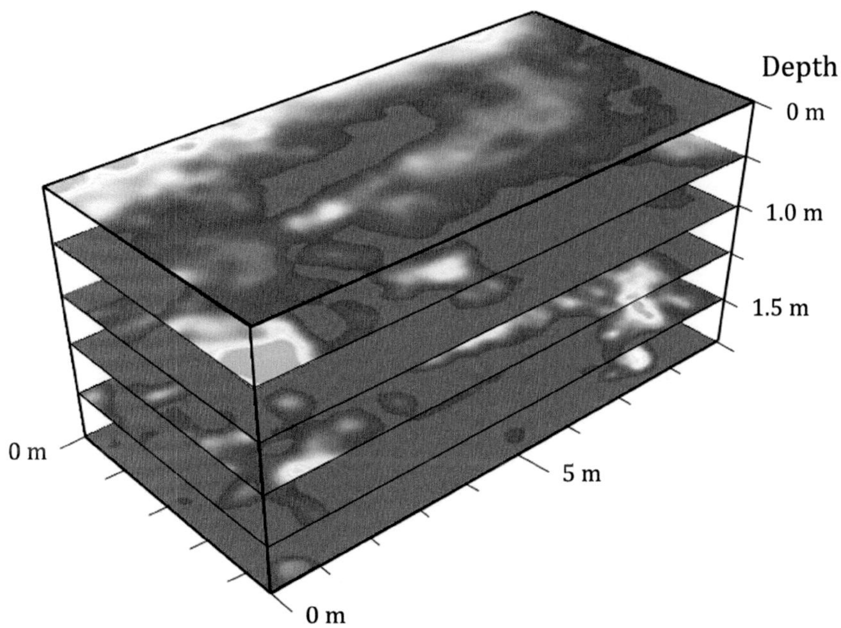

Figure 7.6 Vertical GPR profiles can be processed into a cube and then horizontal slices can be produced to view the subsurface layers. These slices are akin to plan map views, which represent different depths.

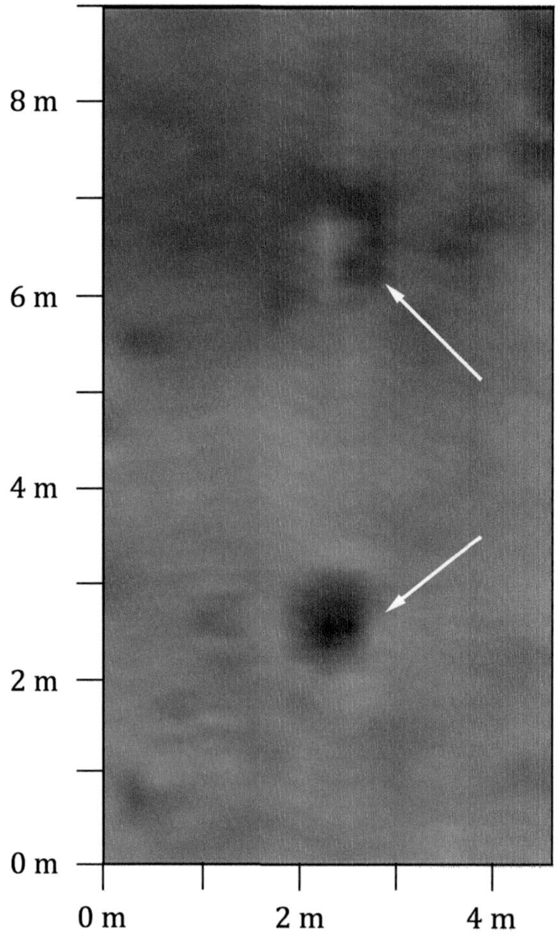

Figure 7.7 Horizontal slice detecting two controlled graves (arrows) containing pig carcasses.

Table 7.3 Advantages and Disadvantages of GPR System Use in Forensic Searches

Advantages	Disadvantages
• Real-time display • Immediate results in the field • Excellent resolution • Detection of graves and metallic objects • Estimation of size and depth of forensic targets • Penetration of concrete and pavement • Penetration through snow	• Expense of equipment • Requires experienced operator • Slow coverage speed • Generally non-specific imagery features • Ground must be relatively level, smooth, and open • Targets can be obscured by clutter in subsurface • Poor penetration in high clay, high saline, and saturated soils • May not detect older graves

ELECTROMAGNETIC (EM) INDUCTION METERS

Electromagnetic (EM) induction meters, more commonly called EM conductivity meters, are active EM instruments that contain a transmitter and a receiver and are used to measure differences in the electrical conductivity of the ground. The transmitter projects a primary low-frequency EM field into the ground that generates a small eddy of current on the surface of conducting (**ferrous** and **non-ferrous**) objects or features. The eddy of current in turn creates a secondary EM field that is measured by the receiver (Figure 7.8). Therefore, the operator must remove all metal items from their person such as car keys, belt buckles, and steel-toed boots before conducting a search using an EM induction meter. Conductivity is measured in millisiemens per meter (mS/m), and measurements should be recorded along a grid with data saved in a data logger. Data can then be downloaded to a mapping program and plotted similar to a surface contour map for interpretation and detection of conductivity anomalies.

The most popular EM induction method for forensic and archaeological contexts is the horizontal loop or slingram method. A typical EM induction meter (e.g., Geonics EM31 model) used in archaeological contexts (Figure 7.9) contains a long antenna rod measuring 4 m (smaller models are available) with transmitting and receiving units mounted on opposite ends. Generally, the further the distance the receiver and transmitter are separated, the deeper the maximum depth of detection. The unit is operated by one person and is carried horizontally above the ground. An EM induction meter

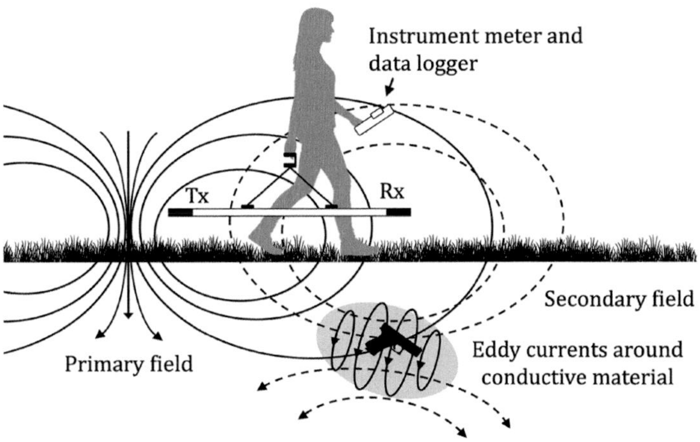

Figure 7.8 A primary electromagnetic field is transmitted into the ground from the transmitting coil (Tx), which generates a small eddy of current on the surface of conducting objects (e.g., handgun). This eddy of current in turn creates a secondary electromagnetic field that is measured by the receiver coil (Rx). The instrument meter provides measures of conductivity, which are then recorded along a grid with data saved in a data logger.

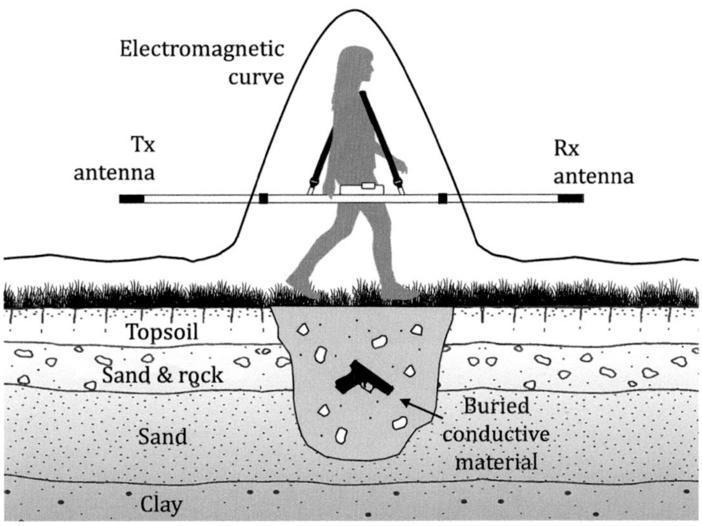

Figure 7.9 The slingram EM induction method shown here consists of a 4-m-long antenna pole with transmitting and receiving antennae mounted at opposite ends of the pole. The unit is operated by one person and should be carried horizontally above the ground.

Figure 7.10 Field assistant William Hawkins demonstrating the use of the more popular small-sized EM induction meter during a forensic search.

of this type averages conductivity measurements to a depth of approximately 6 m with the highest sensitivity for features located in the top meter of soil horizons. Therefore, in a forensic context, this type of EM induction meter is best suited for detecting buried metal objects at shallow depths or large metallic objects at deep depths. More commonly, a smaller EM induction meter (e.g., Geonics EM38 model) is used in forensic geophysical surveys because of its size (approximately 1 m in length), portability, and ease in maneuvering (Figure 7.10). The maximum depth for this kind of meter is limited because the signal strength peaks at 40 cm for the deepest mode with signal strength decreasing as depth increases (Geonics, 2006).

A major advantage of using EM induction methods is that the units do not have to be in contact with the ground surface (Davenport, 2001b; Reynolds, 1997). All EM induction meters will detect metallic objects such as guns, knives, and other metallic evidence, and in certain instances, it might be possible to detect a grave if there is enough contrast between the backfill and undisturbed soil. For example, the commonly used smaller-sized EM induction meter can detect a variety of buried metallic weapons and other metallic forensic targets (Dionne et al., 2011). While targets comprising ferrous metals were detected at the deepest depth, the largest weapons, including shotguns and a rifle were detected at a depth of approximately 75 cm, which is a greater depth than the detection limits of less expensive options, such as a metal detector or magnetic locator (both tools discussed below). Most EM induction meters can be used in wooded areas and over hard ground and concrete. In addition, large open areas can be surveyed in a timely manner using a combination of EM induction and GPR methods. In particular, Nobes (2000) initially used an EM induction meter to survey a large open area during a forensic search. Subsequently, GPR was employed to conduct a more detailed investigation of localized areas of interest in the detection of a buried body. EM induction meters can also be used through snow, but the depth of snow penetration is limited, and the accuracy of the data can be affected by the snowpack thickness, meaning deep snow can significantly dampen the signal and reduce the effectiveness of the measurement (Glaser et al., 2019).

Davenport (2001b) notes a number of limitations using EM induction to measure conductivity. One disadvantage is that the measurements produced by an EM induction meter are only averages of all ground conductivities within the depth range. As a result, a basic conductivity contour map does not provide an accurate depth of forensic targets. Instead, there may only be a depth range based on the unit settings at the time of data collection. Another major disadvantage of using an EM induction method concerns the signal noise or 'clutter' created by metallic objects in the vicinity such as fences, pipes, or power lines. In addition, certain geologic features that have high conductivities, such as clayey soils, may quickly dissipate the EM fields and not permit signal penetration.

ELECTRICAL RESISTIVITY METERS AND ELECTRICAL RESISTIVITY TOMOGRAPHY (ERT)

Electrical resistivity is a measure of how strongly a material opposes the flow of electrical current and is the reciprocal of **electrical conductivity**. **Electrical resistivity surveys** involve sending an electrical current into the ground and then calculating the resistance. Features or changes in the subsurface are detected when they register readings that are more or less conductive than the surrounding subsurface. For example, features that readily allow for the flow of an electrical charge (e.g., graves) have low resistivity, while features that impede the flow (e.g., stone foundations) have high resistivity (Cheetham, 2005). Cheetham (2005) notes that while the type of resistance anomaly is complex, a forensic grave with nothing added normally appears as a low resistance anomaly due to backfill retaining excess water and moisture from the decomposing body. However, over time, after the body is skeletonized and there are dry air cavities, it may appear as a high resistance anomaly. Conversely, the same grave can then appear as a low resistance anomaly after a heavy downpour (Cheetham, 2005).

A resistivity survey focuses on a particular depth range and the equipment involves inserting four electrodes into the ground. The current does not jump in a single direct line between the electrodes, but fans out to form a zone of electrical potential, which is measured by two low-voltage electrodes. (Figure 7.11). While wider spacing of the electrodes will result in deeper depths of propagation of the electric current in the subsurface, the spatial resolution is decreased when the electrode spacing is increased (Wadsworth and Eastaugh, 2021). The pattern of spatial ordering and relative separation of the electrodes define the particular array (Cheetham, 2005). However, two of the electrodes provide the known electric current of the ground, while the other two measure any voltage changes, or resistance in the survey area, measured in ohms (Ω), between the two electrodes. Cheetham (2005) recommends the twin electrode array configuration for forensic applications because it can provide high-resolution surveys needed to detect graves in forensic work. This array configuration involves the movement of two electrodes with 50 cm separation, typically mounted in a rectangular-shaped square frame with a data logger, within the survey area, and the other two fixed at one location outside the survey area to measure the known ground current. It is recommended to collect data every 25 cm along transects spaced 25 cm apart for grave detection (Wadsworth and Eastaugh, 2021) (Figure 7.12).

Electrical resistivity tomography (ERT) is a geophysical technique that uses electrical measurements to construct images of subsurface structures. Resistivity data can be downloaded into specialized software to produce a plotted map of a surveyed area and display resistivity values at a particular depth to help identify features that have higher or lower resistivity values compared with their surroundings (Figure 7.13).

Controlled research has been important in detecting controlled graves using resistivity and ERT in different types of soils. For example, in England (Jervis et al.,

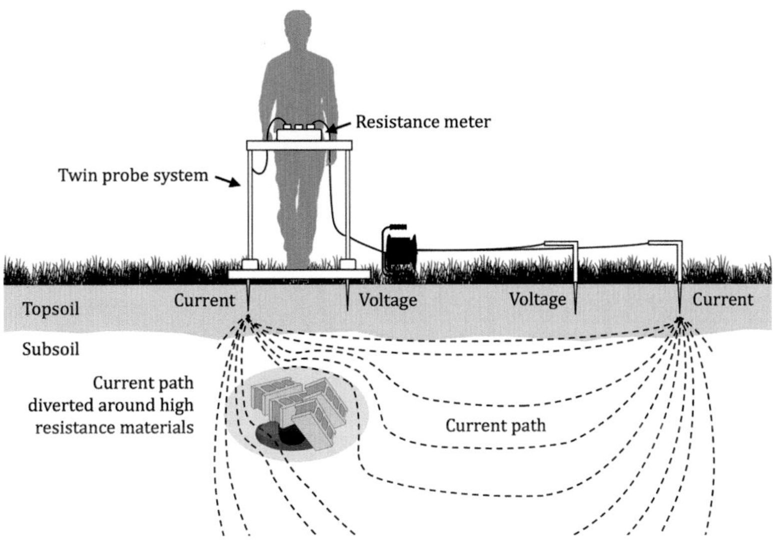

Figure 7.11 Twin probe configuration in a frame-mounted electrical resistivity meter shown here that introduces current into the earth, while voltage probes measure the voltage (electrical potential) of the current as it passes through the ground, indicating localized resistivity anomalies. In this example, cinder blocks are placed over a buried body that impedes movement of an electrical charge, resulting in a high resistivity anomaly.

Figure 7.12 Twin probe configuration of frame-mounted electrical resistivity meter exhibiting 50 cm separation of the two electrodes in the frame and the other two fixed at one location outside the survey area to measure the known ground current. Note that data is ideally collected every 25 cm for forensic applications along transects spaced 25 cm apart for grave detection.

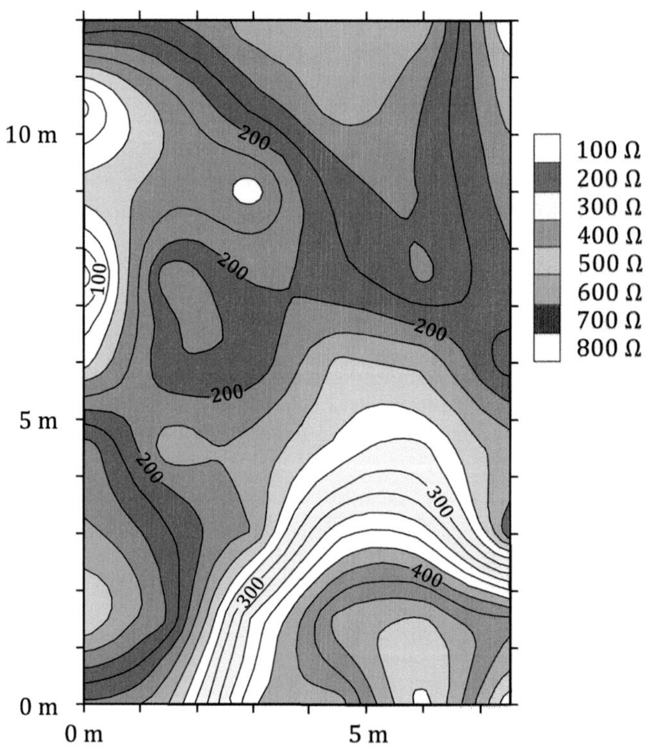

Figure 7.13 Resistivity contour distribution map showing varying levels of soil resistivity across a survey area. The areas of higher resistivity (lower right corner) contained backfill materials that retained more moisture than the surrounding sandy soil horizons.

2009; Pringle et al., 2012, 2016), research has shown that resistivity has successfully detected graves containing pig carcasses over extended time frames, and ERT research in Columbia has also demonstrated success detecting graves that contained animal and human remains over extended time frames (e.g., Molina et al., 2024). In the United States, ERT has been used successfully for detecting controlled individual and mass graves containing human cadavers (Doro et al., 2022). These controlled studies have been important in demonstrating that resistivity can provide a geophysical option in soils that limit the effectiveness of GPR. The ERT method involves inserting electrodes mounted to a cable (e.g., 48 electrodes) in the ground in a line or grid configuration, while the attached computer data and display unit calculates the ground resistance of the area (Wadsworth and Eastaugh, 2021) (Figure 7.14). This is used to construct cross-sectional images of depth resistivity distribution along vertical transects. Multiple

Figure 7.14 Electrical resistivity tomography unit with an electrode cable profile set up for display with 50 cm spacing of electrodes.

parallel lines or transects can be combined using processing software to provide a three-dimensional survey of the subsurface. Although this is a slow method that requires setting up the equipment at each survey location and inserting the electrodes in the ground, detailed subsurface maps and profiles can be constructed (Wadsworth and Eastaugh, 2021).

Resistivity is a reliable method in soil types and environments where GPR is limited such as high clay/saline environments and areas with surface obstructions and vegetation (Wadsworth and Eastaugh, 2021). However, there are a number of disadvantages when using this method for forensic applications (Killam, 2004). Coverage of larger survey areas is slower than using GPR, because ground contact is required. Since there is a minimal amount of surface destruction, this can result in damage to evidence at shallow depths. There can also be interference from metal and electrical sources such as power lines and above ground metal objects. In addition, graves may have such a low resistivity contrast with the surrounding soil that they may not be detected. Also, while GPR may be effective when surveying dry soils, this type of environment is less favorable for resistivity (Wadsworth and Eastaugh, 2021).

MAGNETOMETERS

Magnetometers (MAGs) are passive geophysical tools that measure small variations in the Earth's magnetic field, which are caused by ferrous concentrations (e.g., iron, steel, and nickel), burned soils and clays, and differences in the magnetic susceptibility of soils, stone, or decayed organic matter (Figure 7.15). For example, burning permanently changes the magnetic properties of the surrounding soil by altering the magnetism of minute iron particles. If this soil is moved, either through natural or mechanical processes, the soil magnetism will vary in relation to the general magnetic background of its new location. Magnetometry, however, only works when past activities produce a measurable pattern of magnetic contrast.

Most MAGs do not transmit a signal into the ground and, therefore, do not have a transmitter. Instead, they have a single or paired receiver that detects the magnetic field of buried ferrous objects. MAGs that contain paired receivers, which are usually separated by a distance of 2–3 ft (60–90 cm), are more commonly called gradient magnetometers or gradiometers. There are a variety of commercially available MAGs such as proton precession magnetometers (PPM), fluxgate magnetometers, and cesium vapor magnetometers, and of these, the PPM is most often used in archaeological contexts.

Data are collected in the field along a grid with readings taken every meter or half-meter along grid transects and then downloaded to a computer for processing in special software. Anomalies can be recognized on a contour magnetic intensity map via contrasts between the target and the magnetic background of the surrounding soil horizons. To avoid contaminating data, individuals conducting the survey and those surrounding the survey area must be free of magnetic materials, such as credit cards and metallic jewelry, clothing fasteners, eyeglasses, and shoe eyelets.

Detecting magnetic anomalies is a function of the differences in contrast due to the magnetic properties, size, shape, orientation, and distance between a ferrous object and point of measurement (Davenport, 2001b). In forensic contexts, a MAG survey is most useful in detecting weapons. Magnetometry will not directly detect a grave, as the process of burial usually involves putting the removed soil back into the grave after it is dug out, leaving little to no measurable variation. However, magnetometry may be helpful in locating a grave if ferrous materials are also buried with the remains or if the remains have been cremated. An advantage of a MAG over a metal detector or magnetic locator is that it provides quantitative measurements used to construct a map indicating the strength of different magnetic anomalies. The major disadvantage of a MAG can be interference or noise from cultural features (e.g., fences, pipes, power lines, and metal debris) and geological features in the vicinity. Davenport (2001b) recommends using a gradient magnetometer in forensic contexts because this equipment has a number of advantages over a traditional MAG with a single receiver. For example, the gradiometer's two receivers decrease the noise from surface debris and cultural features, and they provide increased resolution of subsurface features.

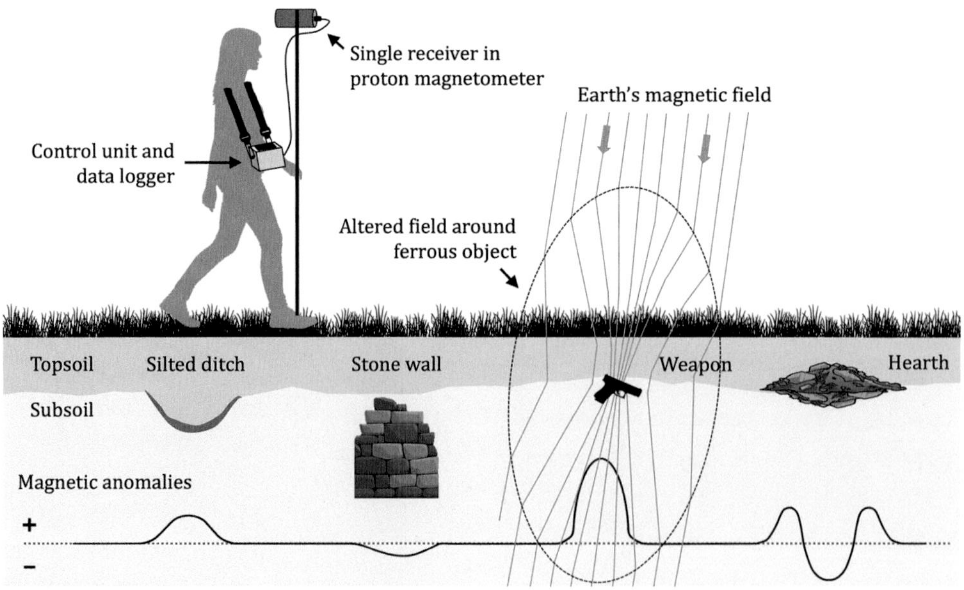

Figure 7.15 A diagram showing the use of a magnetometer (MAG) during a survey for a buried handgun at a shallow depth comprised ferrous metals. The weapon can be detected with this geophysical tool because it provides a high magnetic contrast with the surrounding soil horizons.

MAGNETIC LOCATORS

Figure 7.16 Author John Schultz demonstrating the use of a magnetic locator, which is swept from side to side when searching for buried metal (ferrous) objects.

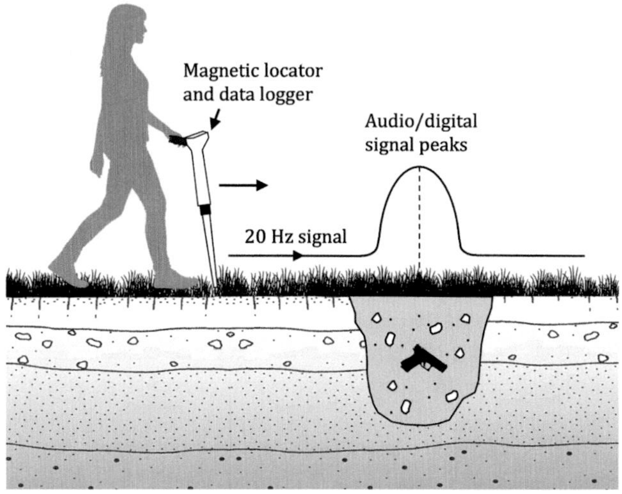

Figure 7.17 When operating a magnetic locator, there will be a pronounced audio signal and an increase in the digital readout when the sensors respond to changes in the magnetic field as it passes over a buried target.

Magnetic locators, also called valve and box locators, are passive instruments that operate on principles similar to a gradient magnetometer. Manufacturers design this equipment as a walking staff, usually 35–42 in (89–106 cm) in length with a small control box at the top end (Figure 7.16). The shaft contains two sensors that respond to changes in magnetic fields surrounding buried ferromagnetic objects, including metallic weapons that are in close proximity to the shaft. The readout and sound operate very similarly to a metal detector (refer to the following section); as you move closer to a metal target, an audible sound or digital readout will become higher in pitch (Figure 7.17). During use, the shaft should be swept from side to side in front of the operator.

In comparison with a MAG, a magnetic locator is a less expensive option and a much easier piece of equipment to operate when locating ferromagnetic objects. A magnetic locator can locate larger objects at deep depths, such as a large steel container drum up to 10 ft (3.05 m) deep and a well casing up to 18 ft (5.49 m) deep (Schonstedt Instrument Company, 2024). Smaller objects can only be detected at shallow depths, and handguns may only be detected at depths of 1.5 ft (45.7 cm) (Schonstedt Instrument Company, 2024). Magnetic locators are effective in snow cover and can be used by thrusting the locator into the snow as deep as necessary to locate a target. They may also be used in flooded areas; however, the electronic unit must be kept above the water surface (Schonstedt Instrument Company, 2024). Controlled research with a commercially available magnetic locator has shown that large handguns can be detected at depths greater than 30 cm, and long guns (e.g., rifle, shotgun) can be detected at depths of 60 cm or greater (Rezos et al., 2011). Before using a magnetic locator for a weapons search, it is important to first determine if the suspected weapon comprises ferromagnetic components. If the suspected weapon was a handgun primarily comprising a nonferromagnetic metal, or the composition is unknown, then an all-metal detector would be a better option to use for this application.

METAL DETECTORS

Metal detectors are the most common geophysical tools because they are relatively inexpensive and easy to use when compared with other equipment. For these reasons, they are very popular with law enforcement (Figure 7.18). Metal detectors operate on the same principle as other EM equipment. The basic metal detector consists of an adjustable stem with a control box near the handle and an antenna, which is pointed toward the ground. The antenna head, or search coil, contains transmitting and receiving coils. A primary EM field is transmitted into the ground from the transmitting (Tx) coil (Figure 7.19). The EM field encounters a conducting object (e.g., a knife) and creates circulating eddy currents across the object's surface. The eddy currents receive their power from the transmitted primary EM field, which results in a detectable power loss (Garrett, 1998). In addition, these eddy currents generate a secondary EM field that flows outward into the surrounding soil horizons and is detected by the receiver (Rx) coil for evaluation.

Metal detectors will detect conductive metals and some minerals, while discrimination of different metals is an option with more expensive models. One popular type is an all-metal detector that electronically balances out or rejects, either manually or automatically, the natural mineral content of the soil or ground surface. The average all-metal detector does not discriminate between ferrous and non-ferrous metallic objects, and therefore, many indicated targets are just shallowly buried trash metals. In contrast, many high-end metal detectors have discriminating capabilities that can accurately indicate the type of metallic target, thereby reducing the number of false positives by ignoring signals from small iron and aluminum trash metals. Furthermore, computerized models can also be helpful in determining the precise location and depth of targets (Garrett, 1998).

One option available with most metal detectors manufactured today is the ability to change the antenna head for specific targets. Large heads, 10–18 in (25–45 cm) in diameter, can penetrate deeper but only locate larger objects. Larger heads do not detect smaller objects, because they are treated as noise. Conversely, smaller heads, (e.g., 5 in or 12 cm in diameter), are better for detecting smaller objects, but only penetrate shallower depths. A general-purpose head is typically 7–9

Figure 7.18 Orange County Sheriff's Office homicide detective Dave Clarke uses a metal detector during a forensic search.

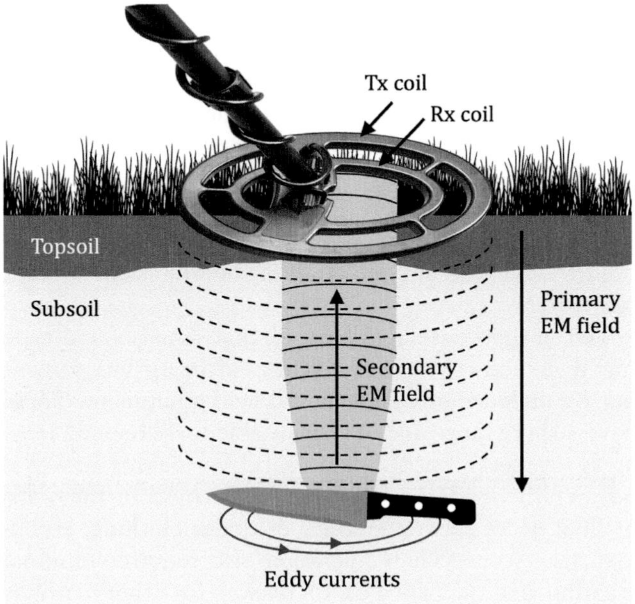

Figure 7.19 On a typical metal detector, an electromagnetic field is transmitted into the ground from the transmitter (Tx) coil. When the field encounters a conducting object, such as the knife shown here, an eddy current is produced. In turn, this generates a secondary electromagnetic field that is detected by the receiver (Rx) coil.

in (18–23 cm) in diameter depending on the manufacturer and type of detector. It should be lightweight, respond to a number of different target sizes, and have good scanning width (Garrett, 1998). Other options may be available to increase detection depth, such as depth multiplier attachments that can easily attach to existing heads. Various manufacturers also offer larger metal detectors called two-box systems that are designed to locate large objects (e.g., buried steel container drums) at much greater depths than a traditional metal detector. A two-box system consists of separate transmitting and receiving coils that are mounted on either end of a pole with the complete unit measuring approximately 50 in (125 cm). Submersible antenna heads are also available and can be useful when searching in a shallow water environment where a gun or knife may have been discarded.

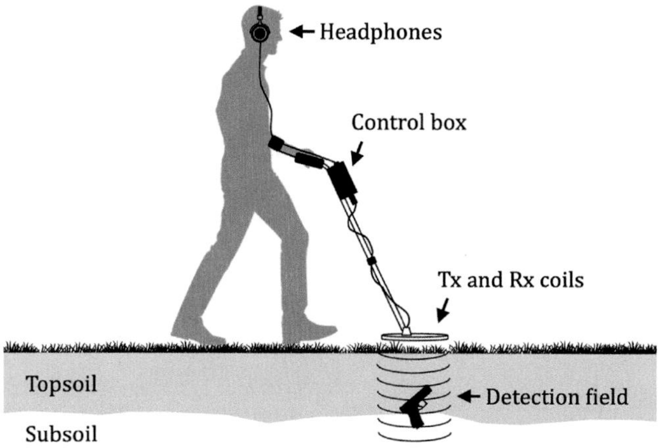

Figure 7.20 When using the metal detector, the head containing the transmitter (Tx) and receiver (Rx) coils should be held in front of the operator, parallel to and as close to the ground as possible for maximum coverage and depth. The audio signal will be loudest, and the digital signal will be strongest when the head is directly over a buried target.

Before using a metal detector, it is important to first calibrate the machine to local soil conditions per manufacturer directions. The use of headphones is also recommended to enhance audio perception while simultaneously masking potential interference in noisy areas (Garrett, 1998). When using the metal detector, the head should be held in front of the operator, parallel and as close to the ground as possible for maximum coverage and depth (Figure 7.20). The head should be moved in sweeping motions with at least one half the diameter of the head overlapping the adjacent search lanes to ensure 100% coverage of the search area (Figure 7.21). When operating a metal detector, there will be a pronounced audio signal and an increase in the analog or digital readout when the head passes over a buried target. The audio signal will be loudest when the head is directly over the target. To pinpoint the exact location of the target, move the search coil across the area from different directions.

Law enforcement should include a high-end metal detector in their tool kit for searches and may also consider including several different-sized antenna heads. This equipment is best suited for detecting small objects that

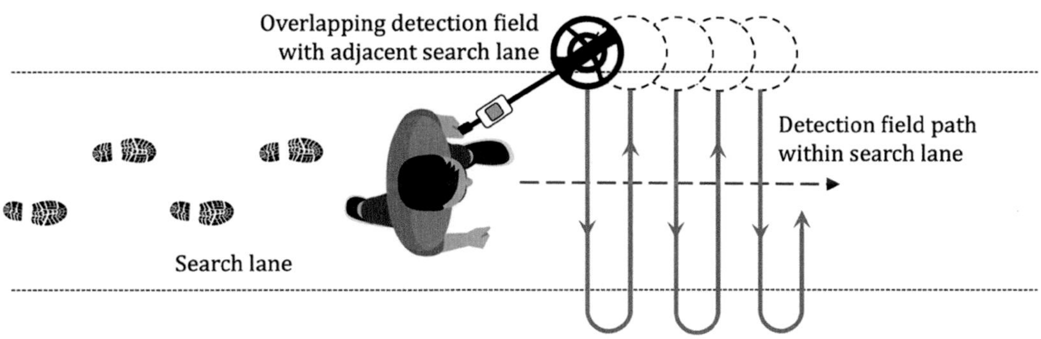

Figure 7.21 The antenna head of a metal detector should be moved in sweeping motions with at least one half the diameter of the head overlapping the adjacent search lanes to ensure 100% coverage of the search area.

are buried at shallow depths. Metal detectors are helpful in locating shallow buried bullets, bullet casings, weapons, and other buried metallic forensic evidence. Also, metal detectors are commonly employed by military Explosive Ordnance Disposal (EOD) technicians when surveying former aircraft crash sites for traces of wreckage. These surveys are conducted both before and during Defense POW/MIA Accounting Agency (DPAA) operations. These missions routinely have an EOD technician as part of the excavation team, and their job duties include the removal of any unexploded ordnance from DPAA scenes.

Controlled research with a commercially available all-metal detector has shown that large handguns can be detected down to 40 cm in depth and long guns (e.g., rifle, shotgun) can be detected down to depths of 45–55 cm (Rezos et al., 2010). In addition, metal detectors can be useful when used in combination with more sophisticated geophysical equipment (Davenport, 2001b). They can be used prior to and after conducting magnetic, EM induction, or GPR geophysical surveys by delineating near surface objects and trash that can produce interference in other equipment. The greatest disadvantage of this method is that metal detectors will not be able to directly detect a grave unless there are metal objects in the grave at a shallow enough depth. In terms of training, a basic all-metal detector generally requires minimal training before use. However, high-end computerized models with discrimination capabilities will require advanced operator training before use in a weapons search.

The authors also recommend that small, wand-type metal detectors, such as those used in airport screening, be included among standard field equipment. These have a short range and are unsuitable for screening large areas for metal, but they are useful for making sure that no metallic evidence has been left behind in the walls or floor of an excavated grave or under clothing, etc. in a surface scene. Their operation also requires minimal training, and they are a useful backup for other methods of evidence detection.

DETECTING SUBMERGED OBJECTS: SIDE-SCAN SONAR AND ROVs

Law enforcement personnel may be involved in water searches for a variety of targets such as planes, boats, vehicles, weapons, contraband, explosives, human bodies, and animal carcasses. While water searches are not the focus of this chapter, this section is included for informational purposes since it is likely that law enforcement personnel and investigators may be involved with cases involving water searches. Similar to terrestrial searches, it is suggested to incorporate multiple search methods for water searches when it is not possible to drain the body of water. These search methods can include using dive teams, deploying underwater cameras on remotely operated vehicles (ROVs), deploying HRD dogs in a boat, and integrating geophysics in search protocols (Armstrong and Erskine, 2010; Parker et al., 2010; Schultz et al., 2013; Teather, 1994). Integrating geophysical tools with water searches can include deploying tools directly from a boat or divers integrating hand-held geophysical tools. Geophysical tools employed by a diver can include hand-held magnetometers (detects ferrous metals) and all-metal detectors (detects ferrous and non-ferrous metals) during searches for evidence with a metallic composition such as weapons. In addition, a hand-held sonar unit can be used during forensic searches by divers when visibility is limited and would be employed during a search by pointing the unit in the last known direction of a forensic target that includes a submerged body (Armstrong and Erskine, 2010). While the purpose of this section is not to provide an overview of the different geophysical tools that can be deployed during water searches, the goal is to focus on the application of side-scan sonar, since it is the most common geophysical tool that is deployed from a boat for water searches involving forensic applications. Additionally, the use of a ROV that is commonly used for water searches and in in conjunction with side-scan sonar will also be discussed.

Side-scan sonar is a marine geophysical tool that uses sound waves to produce a detailed graphic image of the seafloor surface, riverbed, or lake bottom, similar to an aerial image. The system includes a torpedo-shaped **towfish** (Figure 7.22), a data collection control unit or computer, a tow cable, and a power supply. The towfish is typically towed in the water behind a boat at a depth of 10–20 ft (3–6 m) above the seafloor or lakebed. The side-scan sonar towfish contains a transducer with a transmitter and receiver that projects high or low frequency bursts of acoustic energy on both sides (either side can also be selected) of the towfish in thin fan-shaped beams (Figure 7.23a). The sound pulses, or echoes, reflecting off of the relief or objects projecting above the bottom surface, are received by the transducers, amplified, and transmitted up the tow cable to the graphic recorder on the survey vessel. The strength and travel time of reflected pulses are recorded and processed into an image or picture of the bottom surface. The image has several notable features that are influenced by the reflective properties of bottom materials (Figure 7.23b). For example, since rocks and metals have higher reflection coefficients, as well as rougher appearances, these materials will exhibit stronger reflective acoustic returns than a bottom surface such as fine-grained sands (Armstrong and Erskine, 2010; Bowens, 2009; Parker et al., 2010). The contrasting reflection coefficients can facilitate detection of targets on the side-scan-sonar image that includes a raised object with a strong return signal against a flat bottom surface with a weak acoustic reflective surface (Armstrong and Erskine, 2010; Parker et al, 2010). At the same time, another important feature that facilities detection is an **acoustic shadow** appearing on the opposite side of a raised target, such as a body, from the towfish. The acoustic shadow indicates a raised surface and therefore provides a three-dimensional feature to two-dimensional imagery by providing additional information about the shape of a target (Figures 7.23a and 7.23b).

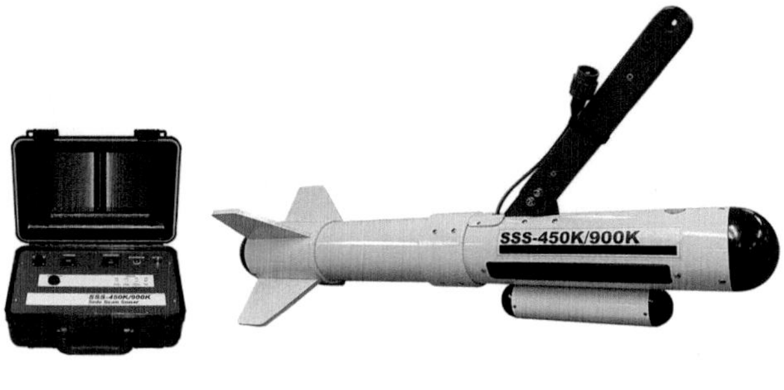

Figure 7.22 Common model of topside data collection and display unit (left) and side-scan sonar towfish (right).

Side-scan sonar has many uses but has become an important tool when conducting underwater searches in archaeological and forensic contexts. For example, side-scan sonar is routinely used to search for old shipwrecks, archaeological sites, downed aircraft, and submersed vehicles. This method has also been used to successfully locate drowned victims laying on the underwater ground surface (Figure 7.24). The major advantages of sonar include the following: it can be deployed in both fresh and saltwater and in deep waters, it is not affected by murky or black water, and it also provides a representative picture of the submersed object. Disadvantages of side-scan sonar include its limited ability to detect objects completely buried beneath the seafloor. Additionally,

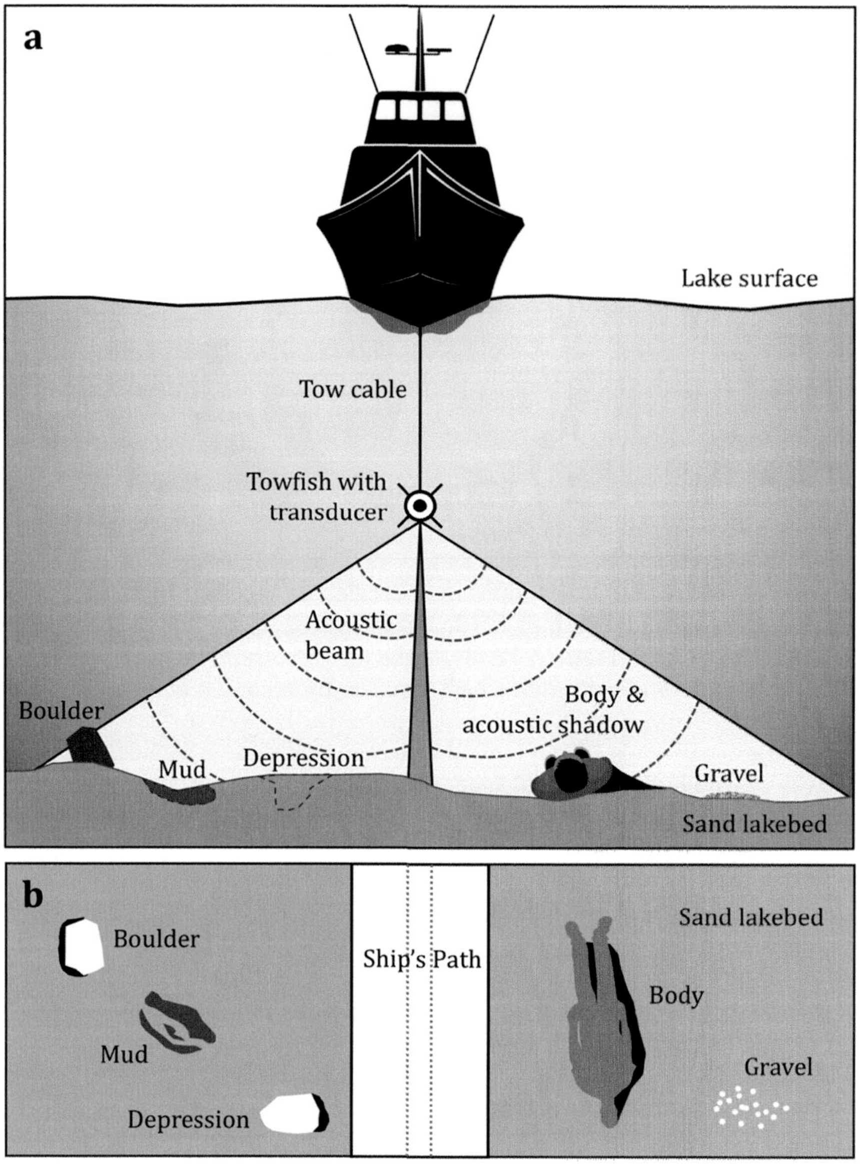

Figure 7.23 A side-scan sonar diagram (a) shows a towfish emitting fan-shaped bursts of acoustic energy on both sides, directed down toward the lakebed at a wide angle perpendicular to the towfish path in the water. Items are detected when the returning intensities of the acoustic reflections record the reflective properties of bottom materials (b), as well as reflections from relief or objects projecting above the bottom surface. Note that bodies or items of forensic interest can be detected on the lakebed in the image based on the recognition of their shape and acoustic shadow.

extremely rocky, grassy, or irregular underwater surfaces can make interpreting sonar returns challenging.

Search and recovery teams involved with water searches for submersed bodies and other targets will also deploy small-sized **remotely operated vehicles (ROVs)** along with other search options based on the underwater conditions of a search area (Schultz et al., 2013) (Figure 7.25). The ROV can be deployed in waters by search and rescue personnel when it is not safe for divers to conduct searches, or they can be deployed in conjunction with other underwater search methods (Christ and Wenerli, 2007; Schultz et al., 2013). The simplest form of an ROV contains a camera housed in a waterproof enclosure that is tethered to the surface through a cable that transmits the video signal back to the boat (Christ and Wenerli, 2007). A pilot on the boat will operate the ROV that can be equipped with lights, camera, video, and a manipulator arm. Depending on the application, additional instruments can be mounted on an ROV.

While an ROV can perform many of the tasks performed by a dive team, there are a number of advantages when using an ROV instead of divers (Armstrong and Erskine, 2010, Bowens, 2009; Zanoli and Conte, 2003). For example, ROVs can be deployed in deeper search areas that are not accessible by divers, and the operation of ROVs is not limited by the duration that divers can spend under pressure. ROVs may be able to be deployed in areas with underwater obstructions that would

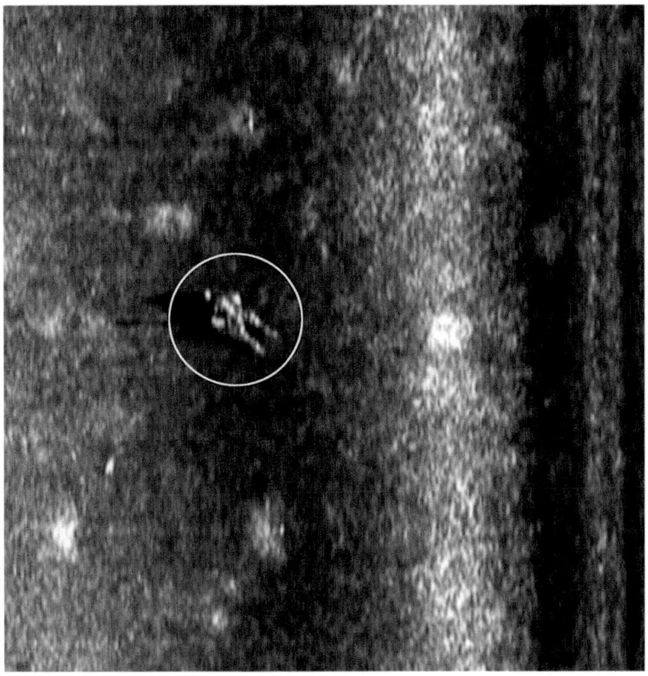

Figure 7.24 Side-scan sonar image of a drowned victim (white circle) exhibiting an acoustic shadow across the bottom of a lake floor. The towfish path can be seen on the right side of the image. *(Photograph courtesy of G. Ralston)*

preclude using divers due to safety issues. At the same time, an ROV equipped with image-intensifiers will provide improved imagery resolution underwater compared with the resolution that the diver can discern (Bowens, 2012). However, it may not be possible to deploy ROVs and divers in murky water when there can be issues visualizing targets, and when potential search targets are within areas containing underwater foliage and obstructions that can lead to entanglement of ROVs and divers (Schultz et al., 2013).

An ROV can be routinely used in conjunction with other geophysical methods such as side-scan sonar

Figure 7.25 Explosive Ordnance Disposal Technician 1st Class Nicholas Wyatt, assigned to Commander, Task Group (CTG) 56.1, retrieves a SeaBotix remotely operated vehicle (ROV) during a mine inspection training operation.

Source: Image by U.S. Navy Mass Communication Specialist 1st Class Peter Lewis is within Public Domain (US Dept of Defense), from https://www.dvidshub.net/image/1001283/seabotix; The appearance of U.S. Department of Defense (DoD) visual information does not imply or constitute DoD endorsement.

(Armstrong and Erskine, 2010; Ralston and Pinksen, 2010; Schultz et al., 2013). For example, side-scan sonar can be used to perform a body search in a large underwater area. After a body, or potential target, is located during a side-scan-sonar search, the water surface is marked with a buoy and an acoustic device is deployed from the boat to mark the location of the target (Atherton, 2011; Ralston and Pinksen, 2010). The buoy line can be used as a search guide for the ROV operator by following it to the bottom surface and then using the acoustic device to guide the ROV to the body or potential target. During this type of scenario, the body can then be recovered from the bottom surface by grasping it with the ROV arm if the depth is too deep for divers to retrieve the body.

LOCATING A GEOPHYSICAL SURVEY CONSULTANT

It is important to note that surveys using geophysical tools must be performed and interpreted by experienced operators. Unfortunately, the high cost of a number of geophysical tools, particularly GPR systems, means that it is not feasible for most law enforcement agencies to own their own equipment and that they must bring in an outside consultant to perform a geophysical survey. In most instances, GPR systems will be the best tool to use for body searches if site conditions are favorable. Law enforcement agencies can search for a geophysical specialist or GPR operator by inquiring at local universities, environmental or archaeological firms, or by performing an internet search. The most limiting factor when using geophysical tools for forensic applications is the operator's experience. When selecting a consultant for a geophysical survey, it is important to make inquiries about the consultant's experience and how they will conduct the geophysical survey. Preference should be given to operators who have experience searching for small subsurface objects buried at shallow depths, such as bodies and archaeological features. Conducting a GPR survey to detect subsurface objects commonly encountered in forensic and archaeological contexts requires specialized training, not only in interpreting the results but also in setting up grid transects and executing the survey. A consultant experienced in searching for large geologic features may lack training in archaeological search methods or familiarity with the parameters used in forensic searches.

CONDUCTING A GEOPHYSICAL SURVEY

A geophysical survey should be conducted in concert with traditional search methods (refer to Chapter 6) as another step in the search protocol. Traditional search methods are normally used to narrow a larger search area so a more time intensive geophysical search can be conducted over smaller areas. For example, a geophysical survey is commonly conducted to locate a clandestine grave after other search methods (e.g., pedestrian surveys, HRD dog surveys) have located suspicious areas (e.g., disturbed and/or depressed area or an alert by an HRD dog) that need further testing before invasive testing is performed. In this scenario, a small grid would be constructed and a geophysical survey, typically using GPR, could be conducted to ascertain if there is an indication of a grave (detection of body and/or disturbed soil horizons from burial). At the same time, initial search surveys may not narrow down a smaller area for conducting limited geophysical surveys. It is up to the GPR operator to then determine how large of a survey is possible based on time and site conditions.

All geophysical surveys should be conducted with a grid survey. A **grid survey** is used to provide investigators with spatial information about the location of follow-up areas within the entire search area. The grid is needed to ensure that the entire search area has been adequately searched, and areas between grid lines have not been missed. Spacing between grid lines is a consideration when constructing a grid, because the tighter the spacing, the longer it takes to perform the survey. Geophysical grids for forensic contexts are normally conducted with 25- or 50-cm spacing. According to Conyers (2006), a 50 × 50-m grid should take one day to perform a survey in traditional archaeology. While it will take twice as long to complete a survey with 25-cm spacing compared to 50-cm spacing, the likelihood of detecting smaller targets (e.g., metallic weapons) increases with narrower grid spacing (Figure 7.26), and size information of larger targets (e.g., graves) is possible to determine with narrower spacing when targets are detected along multiple grid lines (Schultz, 2012). Additionally, the detection of forensic targets can vary depending on the survey orientation with metallic objects (Richardson and Cheetham, 2013) and the position of the forensic target in the ground such as a grave (Schultz and Martin, 2011). Therefore, narrow 25-cm spacing should be used when conducting a survey for a forensic target since the likelihood of missing the target is reduced, particularly when searching for smaller-sized targets such as weapons and child-sized graves.

When conducting the survey, the data are collected in real-time when using several geophysical tools such as a metal detector, magnetic locator, or GPR. As a result, in-field assessments can be made during the survey. Team members can use nonmetallic pin flags on the grid to mark suspect areas indicated by a geophysical tool. In addition, a paper map of the grid can be updated with the location of smaller follow-up areas during the survey. Once the survey is completed, the next step is investigation of the detected areas. While additional geophysical testing could be performed that is limited to all potential areas indicated during the survey, some type of ground truthing or digging will eventually need to be undertaken,

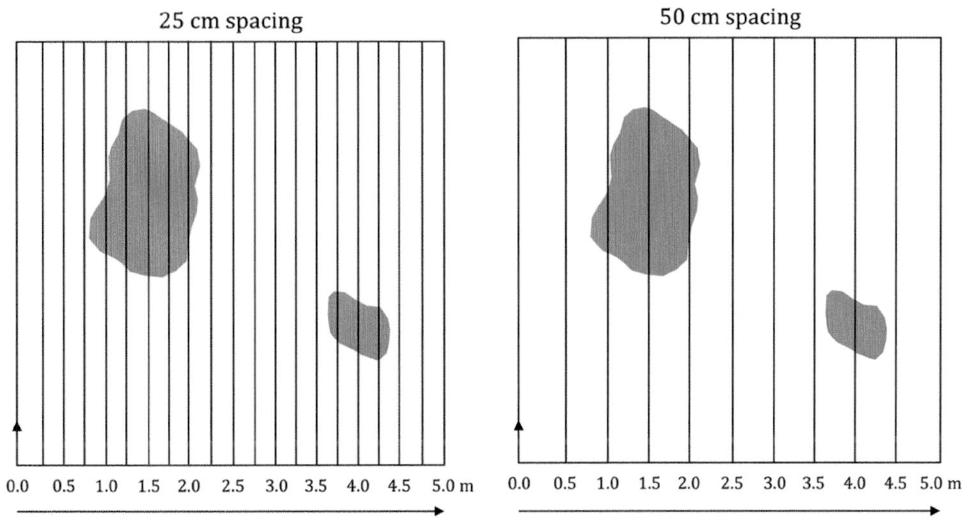

Figure 7.26 Note that transect interval spacing is a consideration based on target size. Detection of a target on multiple GPR transects can provide size and shape information. In the diagram, transect interval spacing is shown for two hypothetical grid searches with 25- and 50-cm spacing (left and right, respectively). The larger grave feature would be detected during both surveys, while the smaller child-sized grave feature may be missed during a 50-cm survey, as it may only be detected during one GPR transect. *(Diagram adapted from Schultz, 2012)*

including soil coring as a first step. If the survey involves the use of a metal detector to locate a discarded or intentionally buried metallic weapon, all areas indicating the presence of metallic material must be investigated with digging until the weapon is recovered or all detected areas are cleared as a weapon target.

Since the objective of the survey is to locate a clandestine grave or clear a suspected area, all potential targets must be thoroughly evaluated to ensure confidence that the area has been cleared. It is also important to note that geophysical detection of graves may change over time. Consequently, it may not be possible to fully guarantee that an area is cleared solely through a geophysical survey combined with limited invasive testing. For example, when using GPR to monitor controlled graves, the response from the grave was shown to decrease over time, particularly during drier times of the year, resulting in difficulty detecting the location even of known graves (Schultz, 2008; Schultz and Martin, 2012; Schultz et al, 2006, 2016). As a result, a grave may go undetected during a geophysical survey if its geophysical response has diminished over time.

CASE STUDY #8: CONCRETE COVER-UP

In December of 2003, author John Schultz was requested by the Orange County Sheriff's office (OCSO) to perform a GPR search at a residential home. The case involved a son who was accused of killing his father 15 years earlier and more recently killing his mother. Homicide detectives had received a number of tips that lead them to believe that one body, the father's, had been buried under the concrete slab in the garage. One informant, a neighbor, had noticed that the cement floor in the garage had been repaired and was told by the son that a leaking water pipe had been repaired. This was suspicious, because water pipes did not run under the concrete slab in this area of the house. In addition, the son had contracted with a stone specialist to surface the entire garage floor with Chattahoochee stone, which is a common patio surface for in-ground pools and not garage floors. Furthermore, the stone specialist reported that half of the garage floor, the right side, was lined with 4 × 8-ft (1.2 × 2.4 m) sheets of diamond-plated steel. The son preferred that the steel plates remain in place and be concealed beneath the Chattahoochee stone surface, rather than removed prior to surfacing the floor.

Homicide detectives also believed that the mother, who had been missing for approximately three months, was buried in the backyard of the residence. When detectives and crime scene personnel conducted a preliminary search, it was noted that two recently poured concrete slabs were present in the backyard. It was decided to first perform a GPR survey of the smaller of the two slabs in the backyard. Results of the survey indicated that a grave was not present under the first slab and therefore eliminated this area from further searching. While preparing to survey the second slab in the backyard, law enforcement received a tip that the second body was located at a second residential home, which was confirmed later that evening.

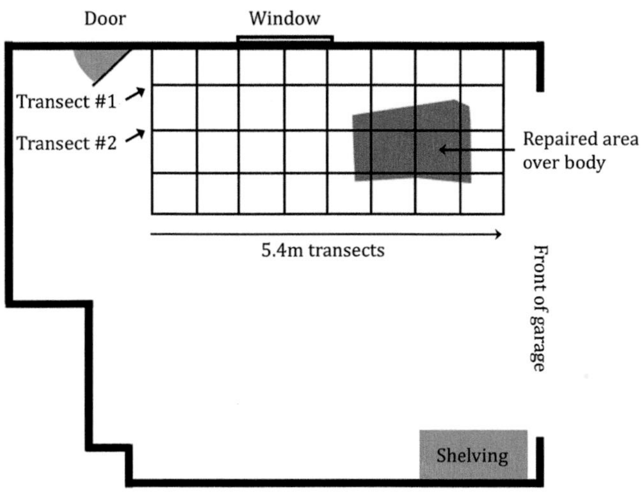

Figure 7.27 Garage plan showing transect grid over the area of interest that included the floor repair concealed by diamond-plated steel sheets and Chattahoochee stone. GPR signal profiles for Transects #1 and #2 are shown in Figure 7.28.

Prior to performing the GPR survey in the garage, an HRD dog had alerted on the floor in an area where the concrete slab had been repaired. The Chattahoochee stone and diamond-plated steel sheets lining one side of the garage were removed, exposing a repaired section of the cement floor. Multiple GPR transects were laid out and data were collected on this side of the garage (Figure 7.27). The GPR results from the area beneath the repaired section revealed a disturbance significant enough to suggest the presence of a buried body (Figure 7.28). After the positive results from the GPR survey, OCSO personnel were comfortable with the decision to break the cement floor and excavate the area of interest. Careful excavation of the area revealed a skeleton that was later positively identified as the father. The son eventually pled no contest to killing both his parents.

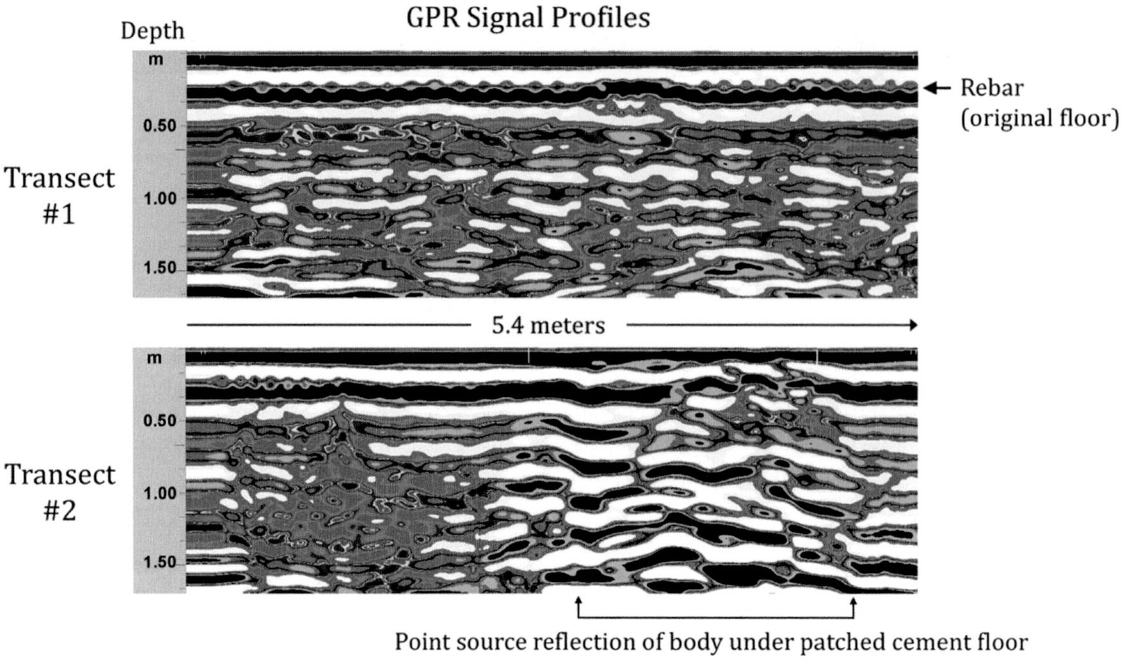

Figure 7.28 Two-dimensional GPR reflection profiles of garage floor, with Transect #1 showing the rebar embedded in the original concrete slab flooring and no indications of a buried body. Transect #2 shows the point source reflection of the buried body directly under the area where the floor had been repaired. Note the lack of rebar in the repaired area over the body.

CASE STUDY #9: TRASH, NOT TREASURE

Author John Schultz was requested by the Orange County Sheriff's Office to assist with a search for two weapons, a long-gun and a handgun, thought to be buried in a residential backyard. No information was provided as to the specific make or model or to the metallic composition of the weapons. Due to the unknown composition of the weapons, author Schultz used an all-metal detector for the search. A controlled survey of the backyard was performed using 1-m wide (approximately 3 ½ ft) survey lanes set up with flagging tape. This spacing allowed for overlapping of adjacent search lanes when sweeping the metal detector antenna head during the search. In addition, crime scene personnel assisted Schultz by placing nonmetallic flags at the locations of all detector hits (Figure 7.29). Once a lane was completed, additional personnel intrusively checked all flagged locations. Due to the use of an all-metal detector, numerous shallowly buried metallic debris were identified. However, no firearms or other weapons were discovered, and the area was subsequently cleared from further searches.

Figure 7.29 Author John Schultz conducting a survey for weapons using an all-metal detector. Note the use of nonmetallic flags for marking detector hits during survey.

Key Terms

acoustic shadow
active geophysical prospecting method
clutter
electrical conductivity
electrical resistivity
electrical resistivity surveys
electrical resistivity tomography (ERT)
electromagnetic (EM) induction meter
ferrous/non-ferrous materials
geophysical prospecting
geophysical survey
grid survey
ground-penetrating radar (GPR)
magnetic locator
magnetometer (MAG)
metal detector
monostatic antenna
passive geophysical prospecting method
planar surface
point source
receiver (Rx)
reflection
reflection profile
remotely operated vehicle (ROV)
ringing
side-scan sonar
towfish
transmitter (Tx)

REVIEW AND DISCUSSION QUESTIONS

1. You have been asked to perform a GPR survey to locate a clandestine grave of a homicide victim. What information must you ask the homicide detective to determine if you can perform a survey in this area?
2. If you needed to secure the services of a GPR consultant, where would you find a consultant and what types of information must you determine prior to securing their services and performing the search?
3. You have been asked to search for a buried firearm in a remote wooded area. The search area is approximately 1 acre (63 m^2) in size. Law enforcement officers learned through an informant tip that the firearm is a small revolver and that it is buried at a depth of approximately 1 ft (30 cm). However, the informant was unsure of the metallic properties of the weapon. Answer the following based on this information:
   - What geophysical tool should you use for the search and why?
   - What are the recommendations you would provide to law enforcement personnel to ensure that a controlled geophysical survey is undertaken?
4. You are searching for a submerged body in a lake using side-scan sonar. How would you recognize a submerged body on a lake floor? How does the data imagery for this method differ when compared with the other geophysical survey methods discussed in this chapter?
5. You are searching for a body buried at a wooded location and the potential area consists of a clay soil. Explain which geophysical tool is the best option for the search based on site characteristics.
6. You have been informed that a body has been buried in a residential backyard and that the homeowner built a concrete patio over the grave. The lead homicide detective would like to confirm that a body is under the patio prior to actually breaking up a section of the concrete slab. You suggest to the detective that a GPR system is the best tool for this application. However, the detective asks if you will be able to discern a picture of the skeleton. What will you explain to the detective about GPR imagery of a grave and how a trained operator can ultimately discern what is buried underground?

Suggested Readings

Cheetham, P. 2005. Forensic geophysical survey. In: Hunter, J., Cox, M., eds. *Forensic Archaeology: Advances in Theory and Practice*, pp. 62–95. New York: Routledge.

Davenport, C.G. 2001a. Remote sensing applications in forensic investigations. *Historical Archaeology* 35:87–100.

Rezos, M.M., Schultz, J.J., Murdock, R.A., Smith, S.A. 2010. Controlled research utilizing a basic all-metal detector in the search for buried firearms and miscellaneous weapons. *Forensic Science International* 195:121–127. DOI:10.1016/j.forsciint.2009.12.003

Schultz, J.J. 2007. Using ground-penetrating radar to locate clandestine graves of homicide victims: Forming forensic archaeology partnerships with law enforcement. *Homicide Studies* 11:15–29. DOI:10.1177/1088767906296234

Schultz, J.J. 2012. The application of GPR for forensic grave detection. In: Dirkmaat, D.C. ed. *A Companion to Forensic Anthropology*, pp. 85–100. Hoboken, NJ: Blackwell Publishing Company.

Schultz, J.J., Healy, C.A., Parker, K.G., Lowers. B. 2013. Detecting submerged objects: The application of side scan sonar to forensic contexts. *Forensic Science International* 231:306–316. DOI:10.1016/j.forsciint.2013.05.032

Wadsworth, T.D., Eastaugh, E. 2021. Resistivity survey: Recommended data collection procedures for locating unmarked graves. Canadian Archaeological Association, Version 1.0, December 13. https://canadianarchaeology.com/caa/sites/default/files/page/resistivity_survey_dec_13.pdf. Accessed 2024, September 30.

References

Atherton, M. 2011. *Echoes and Images, the Encyclopedia of Side-Scan and Scanning Sonar Operations*. Vancouver, BC: Oysterlink Publications.

Armstrong, E.J., Erskine, K.L., 2010. *Water-related Death Investigation: Practical Methods and Forensic Applications*. Boca Raton: FL CRC Press.

Bevan, B.W. 1991. The search for graves. *Geophysics* 56:1310–319. DOI:10.1190/1.1443152

Bowens, A. Underwater Archaeology: 2009. *The NAS Guide to Principals and Practice*. West Sussex: Wiley-Blackwell.

Calkin, S.F., Allen, R.P., Harriman, M.P. 1995. Buried in the basement - Geophysics role in forensic investigation. *Proceedings of the Symposium on the Application of Geophysics to Engineering and Environmental Problems (SAGEEP)*, pp. 397–403. European Association of Geoscientists and Engineers.

Cheetham, P. 2005. Forensic geophysical survey. In: Hunter, J., Cox, M., eds. *Forensic Archaeology: Advances in Theory and Practice*, pp. 62–95. New York: Routledge.

Christ, R.D., Wenerli, L.W., Sr. 2007. *The ROV Manual: A User Guide for Observation Class Remotely Operated Vehicles*. Oxford: Butterworth-Heinemann.

Conyers, L.B. 2006. Ground-penetrating radar techniques to discover and map historic graves. *Historical Archaeology* 40:64–73.

Conyers, L.B., Goodman, D. 1997. *Ground-Penetrating Radar: An Introduction for Archaeologists*. Walnut Creek, CA: AltaMira Press.

Davenport, C.G. 2001a. Remote sensing applications in forensic investigations. *Historical Archaeology* 35:87–100.

Davenport, C.G. 2001b. *Where Is It? Searching for Buried Bodies and Hidden Evidence*. Church Hill, MD: Sportwork.

Dionne, C.A., Schultz, J.J., Murdock, R.A., Smith, S.A. 2011. Detecting buried metallic weapons in a controlled setting using a conductivity meter. *Forensic Science International* 208:18–24. DOI:10.1016/j.forsciint.2020.10.019

Doro, K.O., Emmanuel, E.D., Adebayo, M.B., Bank C.G., Wescott, D.J., Mickleburgh, H.L. 2022. Time-lapse electrical resistivity tomography imaging of buried human remains in simulated mass and individual graves. *Frontiers in Environmental Science* 10:882496. DOI:10.3389/fenvs.2022.882496

France, D.L., Griffin, T.J., Swanburg, J.G., Lindemann, J.W., Davenport, G.C., Tramell, V., Travis, C.T., Kondratieff, R., Nelson, A., Castellano, K., Hopkins, D., Adair, T. 1997. NecroSearch revisited: Further multidisciplinary approaches to the detection of clandestine graves. In: Haglund, W. D., Sorg, M. H., eds. *Forensic Taphonomy: The Postmortem Fate of Human Remains*, pp. 497–510. Boca Raton, FL: CRC Press.

Garrett, C.L. 1998. *Modern Metal Detectors*. Dallas, TX: Ram Publishing Company.

Geonics Limited. 2006. *EM38 Ground Conductivity Meter Operating Manual*. Mississauga, ON: Geonics Limited.

Glaser, D.R., Wagner, A.M. 2019. Dynamic cold regions terrain effects on time-domain electromagnetic induction data. *Cold Regions Science and Technology* 158:52–61. DOI:10.1016/j.coldregions.2018.11.008

Jervis, J.R., Pringle, J.K., Tuckwell, G.W. 2009. Time-lapse resistivity over simulated clandestine graves. *Forensic Science International* 192:7–13. DOI:10.1016/j.forsciint.2009.07.001

Killam, E.W. 2004. *The Detection of Human Remains*, 2nd ed., Springfield, IL: Charles C. Thomas.

King, J.A., Bevan, B.W., Hurry, R.J. 1993. The reliability of geophysical surveys at historic-period cemeteries: An example from the Plains Cemetery, Mechanicsville, Maryland. *Historical Archaeology* 27:4–16.

Mellet, J.S. 1992. Location of human remains with ground-penetrating radar. *Geological Survey of Finland* 16:359–365.

Molina, C.M., Wisniewski, K.D., Salamanca, A., Saumett, M., Rojas, C., Gómez, H., Baena, A., Pringle, J.K. 2024. Monitoring of simulated clandestine graves of victims using UAVs, GPR, electrical tomography and conductivity over 4–8 years post-burial to aid forensic search investigators in Colombia, South America. *Forensic Science International* 355:111919. DOI:10.1016/j.forsciint.2023.111919

Nobes, D.C. 2000. The search for 'Yvonne': A case example of the delineation of a grave using near-surface geophysical methods. *Journal of Forensic Sciences* 45:715–721. DOI:10.1520/JFS14756J

Parker, R., Ruffell, A., Hughes, D. Pringle, J. 2010. Geophysics and the search of freshwater bodies: A review. *Science & Justice* 50:141–149. DOI:10.1016/j.scijus.2009.09.001

Pringle, J.K., Jervis, J.R., Hansen, J.D., Cassidy, N.J., Jones, G.M., Cassella, J.P. 2012. Geophysical monitoring of simulated clandestine graves using electrical and ground penetrating radar methods: 0–3 years. *Journal of Forensic Sciences* 57:1467–1486. DOI:10.1111/j.1556–4029.2012.02151.x

Pringle, J.K., Jervis, J.R., Roberts, D., Dick, H.C., Wisniewski, K.D., Cassidy, N.J., Cassella, J.P. 2016. Geophysical monitoring of simulated clandestine graves using electrical and ground penetrating radar methods: 4–6 years. *Journal of Forensic Sciences* 61:309–321. DOI:10.1111/1556–4029.13009

Ralston, G., Pinksen, J. 2010. Underwater technology used to bring closure to families of drowning victims. *Journal of Ocean Technology* 5:20–25.

Reynolds, J.M. 1997. *An Introduction to Applied and Environmental Geophysics*. New York: Wiley and Sons.

Rezos, M.M., Schultz, J.J., Murdock, R.A., Smith, S.A. 2010. Controlled research utilizing a basic all-metal detector in the search for buried firearms and miscellaneous weapons. *Forensic Science International* 195:121–127. DOI:10.1016/j.forsciint.2009.12.003

Rezos, M.M., Schultz, J.J., Murdock, R.A., Smith, S.A. 2011. Utilizing a magnetic locator to search for buried firearms and miscellaneous weapons at a controlled research site. *Journal of Forensic Sciences* 56:1289–1295. DOI:10.1111/j.1556–4029.2011.01802.x

Richardson, T., Cheetham, P.N. 2013. The effectiveness of geophysical techniques in detecting a range of buried metallic weapons at various depths and orientations. In: Pirrie, D., Ruffell, A., Dawson, L. A., eds. *Environmental and Criminal Geoforensics*, pp. 253–266. Geological Society, London: Special Publications 384.

Schonstedt Instrument Company. 2024. *Instruction Manual: Model GA-52Cx*. Kearneysville, WV: Schonstedt Instrument Company.

Schultz, J.J. 2007. Using ground-penetrating radar to locate clandestine graves of homicide victims: Forming forensic archaeology partnerships with law enforcement. *Homicide Studies* 11:15–29. DOI:10.1177/1088767906296234

Schultz, J.J. 2008. Sequential monitoring of burials containing small pig cadavers using ground-penetrating radar. *Journal of Forensic Sciences* 53:279–287. DOI:10.1111/j.1556–4029.2008.00665.x

Schultz, J.J. 2012. The application of GPR for forensic grave detection. In: Dirkmaat, D. C. ed. *A Companion to Forensic Anthropology*, pp. 85–100. Hoboken, NJ: Blackwell Publishing Company.

Schultz, J.J., Collins, M.E., Falsetti, A.B. 2006. Sequential monitoring of burials containing large pig cadavers using ground-penetrating radar. *Journal of Forensic Sciences* 51:607–616. DOI:10.1111/j.1556–4029.2006.00129.x

Schultz, J.J., Healy, C.A., Parker, K.G., Lowers, B. 2013. Detecting submerged objects: The application of side scan sonar to forensic contexts. *Forensic Science International* 231:306–316. DOI:10.1016/j.forsciint.2013.05.032

Schultz, J.J., Martin, M.M. 2011. Controlled GPR grave research: Comparison of reflection profiles between 500 and 250 MHz antennae. *Forensic Science International* 209:64–69. DOI:10.1016/j.forsciint.2010.12.012

Schultz, J.J., Martin, M.M. 2012. Monitoring controlled graves representing common burial scenarios with ground penetrating radar. *Journal of Applied Geophysics* 83:74–89. DOI:10.1016/j.jappgeo.2012.05.006

Schultz, J.J., Walter, B.S., Healy, C. 2016. Long-term sequential monitoring of controlled graves representing common burial scenarios with ground penetrating radar: Years 2 and 3. *Journal of Applied Geophysics* 132:60–74. DOI:10.1016/j.jappgeo.2016.06.015

Shih, D.G., Doolittle, J.A. 1984. Using radar to investigate organic soil thickness in the Florida Everglades. *Soil Science Society of America Journal* 48:651–656. DOI:10.2136/sssaj1984.03615995004800030036x

Sternberg, B.K., McGill, J.W. 1995. Archaeology studies in southern Arizona using ground-penetrating radar. *Journal of Applied Geophysics* 33:209–225. DOI:10.1016/0926-9851(95)90042-X

Teather, R.G. 1994. *Encyclopedia of Underwater Investigation*. Flagstaff, AZ: Best Publishing.

Vaughn, C.J. 1986. Ground-penetrating radar surveys used in archaeological investigations. *Geophysics* 51:595–604. DOI:10.1190/1.1442114

Wadsworth, T.D., Eastaugh, E. 2021. Resistivity survey: Recommended data collection procedures for locating unmarked graves. Canadian Archaeological Association, Version 1.0, December 13. https://canadianarchaeology.com/caa/sites/default/files/page/resistivity_survey_dec_13.pdf. Accessed 2024, September 30.

Zanoli, S.M., Conte, G. 2003. Remotely operated vehicle depth control. *Control Engineering Practice* 11:453–459. DOI:10.1016/S0967-0661(02)00013-8

CHAPTER 8

SURVEYING AND MAPPING METHODS

Learning Objectives

- Understand the general units of measure and terminology used in map construction and interpretation.
- Introduce different survey and mapping techniques.
- Outline the stages involved in constructing scaled drawings of a scene or specific features.
- Utilize survey and mapping techniques with alternate low-technology systems that can be easily adapted to any situation.

Learning Connections

- An understanding of maps and various survey and mapping techniques is crucial in constructing accurate scaled drawings of a scene or specific feature during the search, discovery, and excavation phases.
- Practical mapping skills play a vital role in documenting scene information, ensuring that the scene context is accurately recorded and preserved.

During a forensic investigation, one of the most important principles to remember is that once an item is moved, it can never be put back in its exact position or orientation. For this reason, practical skills in various survey and mapping techniques will allow investigators to maintain a quality record of where every item of evidence was found within a defined area, and if necessary, will also assist the investigator in recreating the order of events surrounding the items being recorded.

The end result of all surveying and mapping, in archaeology as well as in forensic contexts, is an accurate scale map of the scene. Many investigators incorrectly believe that survey and mapping skills to be beyond their ability. However, an overview of the techniques involved and some practice in the field can turn the fledgling into a specialist very quickly. In fact, if an investigator is working without these skills, they should not attempt recovery of any remains, whether working with a surface deposit or a burial in a forensic context. The authors would also like to note that there is an enormous amount of technology used today in recording forensic scenes, from laptops and digital cameras to global positioning systems (GPS) and high-resolution laser surveys – all of which have an amazing capacity to fail at the most critical moment in the most remote location. At times, there is no better backup than the traditional scaled drawings and simple compass and tape measure survey. This chapter is intended to aid forensic investigators in achieving a respectable level of survey and mapping skills with a minimum of technical explanation and to have multiple backups on hand.

DOI: 10.4324/9781315201658-8

UNITS OF MEASURE

In surveying and mapping, there are two different kinds of quantity that are measured, distances and angles. Most people are familiar with measures of length and distance, in either feet (ft) and meters (m), or miles (mi) and kilometers (km). An additional measure of distance is **elevation**, or how far an object is above (i.e., **height**) or below (i.e., **depth**) a fixed reference point. Elevation is mainly used when referring to points on a landscape and is depicted using **contour lines**, which join points of equal elevation on a map to show valleys, hills, and steepness of slopes. When used in this manner, the fixed reference point is usually mean sea level (MSL), or the average height of the ocean's surface. In archaeological survey, an **elevation plane** is an imaginary horizontal flat surface that extends outward in all directions from a surveyor-designated fixed point of reference, known as a **datum**. The datum is used for all elevation and angle measurements made during mapping and excavation. In measures of distance, metric units should always be used in forensic investigations, making it easier to record and convert measurements of larger areas and smaller features to scaled preprinted graph paper. For this reason, all measurements in this chapter are provided using the International System of Units (SI), which is more commonly known as the metric system. Please refer to a standard metric conversion chart or calculator for equivalent units in the U.S. Customary System.

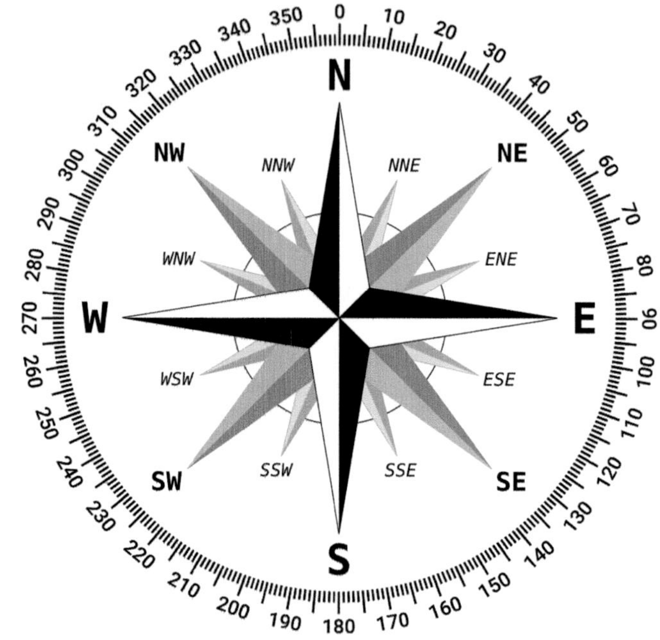

Figure 8.1 Cardinal directions routinely associated with mapping and their corresponding azimuths (horizonal angles measured in degrees of a circle progressing from 0° to 360° in a clockwise fashion).

When discussing angles, the measure of reference may not be as well understood. A complete circle contains 360° with the degrees progressing from 0° to 360° in a clockwise fashion. By dividing a circle into quadrants, a coordinate system can be imposed onto the degree marks with north at 0°/360°, east at 90°, south at 180°, and west at 270° (Figure 8.1). When using this coordinate system, the projected angle from the center of the circle to a direction of interest is called the **azimuth**. Most tend to think of angle measurements as only being measured in terms of degrees. However, there are other common systems of angle measurement. For example, the U.S. military favors the use of the angular mil, where a circle is divided into 6,400 equal units. This system is used for artillery range finding and is based on the simple relationship that an angle of 1 mil subtends a distance of approximately 1 m at a range of 1 km. When selecting field equipment, such as a compass, it is important to check the instrument gradations, because many commercially available prismatic compasses (refer to section on compass survey methods) are designed for military use and may be marked in radians (i.e., angular mils) rather than degrees.

USING MAPS

Maps are a way of transforming three-dimensional points on the Earth's surface into a flat, two-dimensional plane of reference. One spatial reference system that many are familiar with is the **Geographic Coordinate System (GCS)**, which uses latitude and longitude coordinates for communicating positions on Earth's surface. **Latitude** specifies the north-south position of a point, measured in degrees from the equator (0°) to 90° north or 90° south, while **longitude** specifies the east-west position, measured in degrees from the Prime Meridian (0°) to 180° east or 180° west. Points recorded using GCS can easily be converted to other coordinate systems.

It is important to note the specific system used to generate any map that you are using as a reference in archaeology and forensic investigations, as the same grid reference used in a different system will not refer to the same location. For example, the Universal Transverse Mercator (UTM) Grid system is a widely used metric coordinate system that divides the Earth into 60 equal zones from west to east and is used to map locations two-dimensionally in latitude and longitude (Howard, 2007). The UTM, which is commonly used in military applications, provides a more accurate representation of distances and areas within each zone compared to using latitude/longitude for smaller areas. The World Geodetic System (WGS84) is a standard reference system used for cartography, geopositioning, and navigation (Howard, 2007), and it is the reference system used by the satellite-based navigation system known as the **Global Positioning System (GPS)**. The WGS84 defines position in degrees of geodetic latitude and longitude on a 3D ellipsoid model of Earth's surface, meaning the ground distance represented by a degree of longitude varies significantly with latitude, while the UTM defines position using a constant distance relationship within its zones, using planar (km/mi) measurements projected onto a flat, grid system. If you are referencing points taken with a GPS using the WGS84 system on a UTM system map, the plotted points will need to be corrected as the units and positioning references do not align. The National Geodetic Survey provides an online converter for coordinate systems (https://www.ngs.noaa.gov/NCAT/).

In archaeological and forensic contexts, there are several different types of maps that you may encounter when searching for remains. One of the most widely used of all maps is a **topographic map**, which portrays natural and built surface features and contour lines for a detailed representation of the shape and elevation of the landscape (U.S. Geological Survey, 2024). The wide range of information provided by topographic maps make them extremely useful in professional settings, and the **U.S. Geological Survey (USGS)** provides large-scale topographic maps that cover in detail the entire area of the 48 contiguous states, Alaska and Hawaii. An **orthophoto map**, also known as an orthoimage, is constructed using a process called **photogrammetry**, which involves analyzing multiple overlapping images of the same area to assemble a highly accurate map. Digital orthophoto maps are built by combining a satellite and aerial image that has been geometrically corrected. These maps often combine the visual characteristics of a photograph with the geometric qualities and spatial accuracy of a topographic map (U.S. Geological Survey, 2022). Unlike an aerial photograph, an orthophoto has a uniform scale across the entire image, allowing for direct measurement of distances and areas. It can be used as a base map for various applications because it accurately represents the geographic location of features. They are widely used in **Geographic Information Systems (GIS)**, urban planning, environmental monitoring, and other fields where accurate spatial information is crucial, making them very useful in a forensic search. An orthoimage is included as an optional layer for USGS digital topographic maps published after 2009. Prior to this date, their coverage was often restricted to major urban areas and their immediate environs. Topographic maps and orthophoto maps can be accessed through the USGS National Map Downloader (https://apps.nationalmap.gov/downloader/). Other types of maps often encountered in archaeology are **geological maps** depicting rock formations, geological zones, and soil types, and **maritime charts** depicting underwater formations and the depth of the sea floor. Geological maps for the United States can be accessed through the USGS National Geologic Map Database (https://ngmdb.usgs.gov/), and maritime charts for U.S. coastal areas are available through the National Oceanic and Atmospheric Administration (NOAA) chart locator (https://www.charts.noaa.gov/). Many of the maps provided through USGS and NOAA are digitally accessed and downloadable free of charge. Additional government agencies that provide this type of service include the U.S. Public Land Survey System (PLSS), the U.S. Environmental Protection Agency (EPA), and the Land Boundary Information System (LABIS). The maps and photographs available from the EPA are exceptionally helpful when lakes, rivers, canals, and shorelines are the primary focus in a forensic search. The PLSS and LABIS are excellent sources for detailed country area, railroad, side road, or logging area maps.

Each map should contain a directional indicator, usually a north arrow, a scale, and a legend to explain the mapping conventions used to indicate features or objects. Most maps are oriented with the north at the top, south at the bottom, and east and west to the right and left, respectively. There are various navigational terms used to identify how the orientation of north is defined and depicted in mapping systems. **True north**, also known as geographic north, is the direction along the surface of the Earth that ends in the location of the North Pole, which is one end in the axis of the Earth's rotation. Lines of longitude can also be used as true north reference lines, as they converge at the true north and south poles. The vertical edges of many maps are defined by a meridian of longitude and can be used as a true north reference. **Magnetic north** is aligned with the Earth's magnetic field. A free-floating magnetic needle in a compass will align itself with the magnetic field and therefore points to the magnetic poles. Very importantly, the magnetic pole of the Earth is not located at the geographic north pole. **Declination** is the angular difference between true north and magnetic north for a given location, and is measured in degrees, minutes, and seconds (e.g., –7° 53' 26" indicates the location is approximately 7.89° west of true north). Declination changes depending on your position relative to the two poles, and it also changes over time, because the locations of the magnetic poles change with time. Most GPS receivers will calculate the declination for their current position. This is often referred to as "automatic" north reference. Another source of current declination at a given location is the National Geophysical Data Center's declination calculator (https://www.ngdc.noaa.gov/geomag/calculators/magcalc.shtml#declination). **Grid north** refers to the northward direction indicated by the north-south grid lines on a map. Grid north is a convenient reference point for navigation, especially when using maps with grid systems like the UTM grid system. Unlike true north and magnetic north, grid north is aligned with the map's grid lines and is constant for a given map projection. It is typically within 2° east or west of true north and varies with your position within a UTM Grid zone. When minimal accuracy is all that is required, it is common to treat grid north lines as true north lines without accounting for the small difference. Some maps, such as those published by the USGS, use a **declination diagram** to show the angular relationship of the three north references (Figure 8.2). Typically, there will be an arrow that points to the top of the map and is parallel to the edges of the map. This is the "top of the map" north reference that was used when the map was printed. Commonly, it will be either true north (designated with a star or the letters TN) or grid north (designated with the letters GN). The angles between the three north references will be printed on the diagram along with the date that the angle between true north and magnetic north was determined.

Scale refers to the relationship between distance on a map and the corresponding distance on the ground.

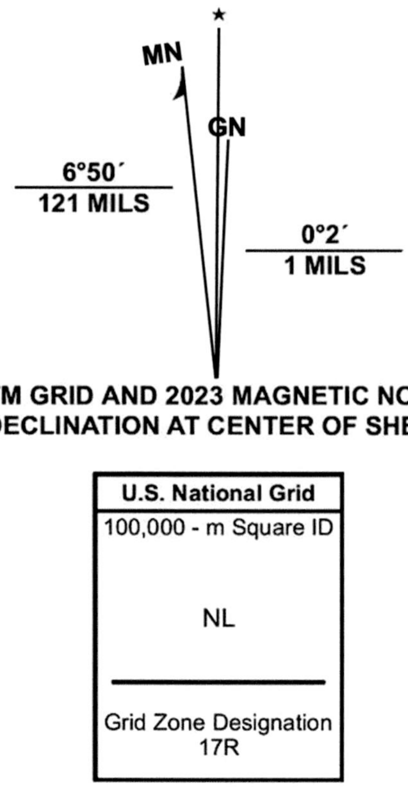

Figure 8.2 Example of a declination diagram indicating true north (designated by a star), magnetic north (designated by 'MN'), and grid north (designated by 'GN'), and the angles between the three north references. Note the year (2023) in which the angles were measured and the location for declination (17R grid zone of the U.S. National Grid) in the UTM grid system.

This is most often expressed as a ratio (or representative fraction) of the size of a feature or object as it is drawn on the map to its actual size, such as 1:100, meaning that one unit of measurement on the map is equal to 100 units of the same measurement on the ground. Maps come in a standard range of scales (Figure 8.3), although not all scales are available for each area. For example, most USGS topographic maps are produced using the WGS84 reference system at a scale of 1:24,000 (where 1 in represents 2,000 ft). These maps are commonly known as 7.5-minute quadrangle maps, because each map covers a four-sided area of 7.5 minutes of latitude and 7.5 minutes of longitude, which covers nearly 50 mi^2 (80 km^2). USGS orthophoto maps, also produced using the WGS84 reference system, are typically in a 1:6,000 scale covering approximately 3 km^2 (1.2 mi^2). In forensic contexts, the most widely used topographic maps are based on PLSS where the maps refer to a surveyed township unit of land that is approximately 6 mi^2 (9.7 km^2) in size and are further divided into 36 sections, each approximately 1 mi^2 (1.6 km^2) in size.

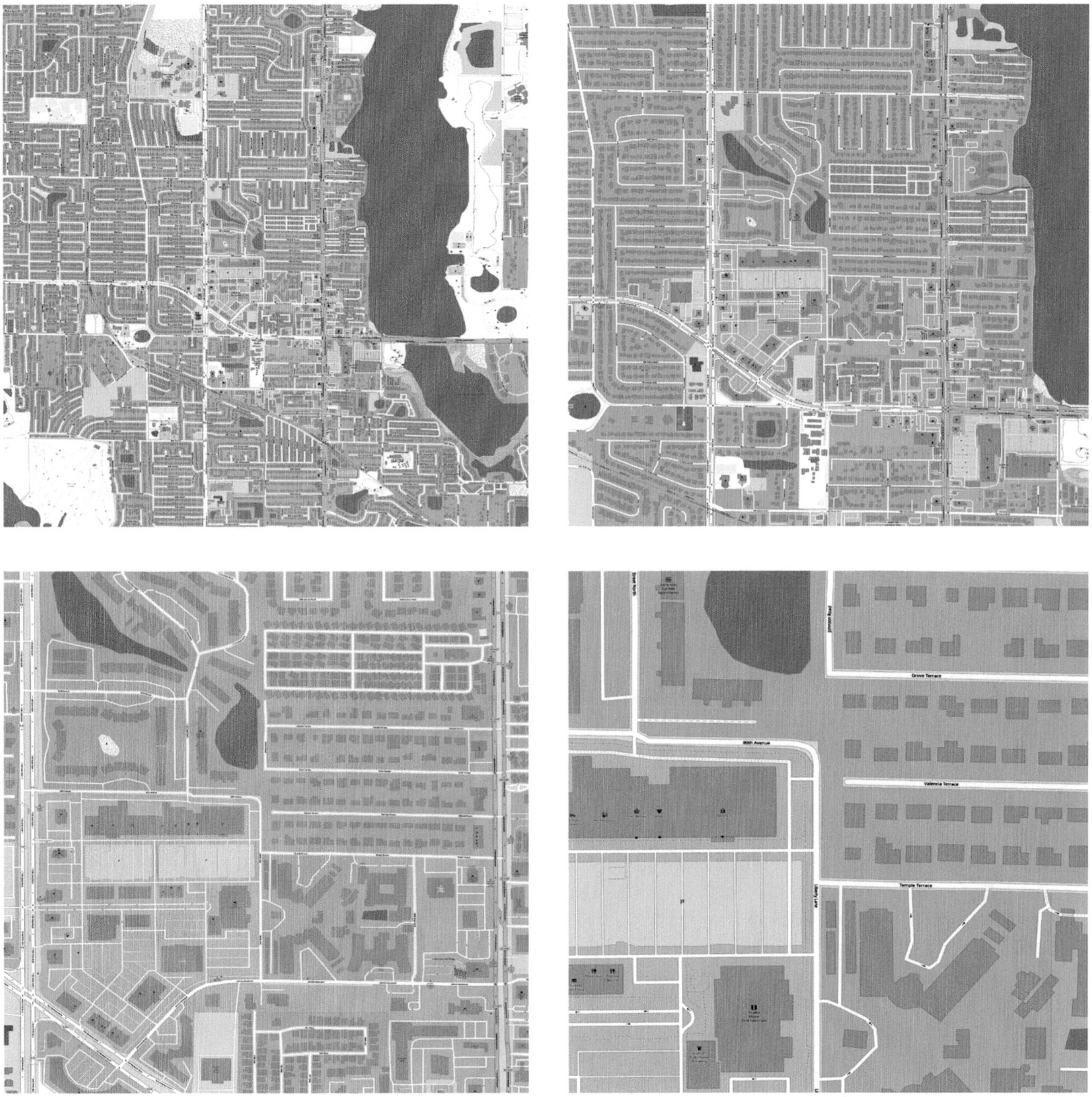

Figure 8.3 Examples of different scaled maps illustrating differences in detail: top left scale 1:10,000; top right scale 1:5,000; bottom left scale 1:2,500; and bottom right scale 1:1,000. (*Map data from OpenStreetMap.*)

Source: Figure 8.3 Map data from OpenStreetMap (https://www.openstreetmap.org/copyright); licensed under the Open Data Commons Open Database License (ODbL; http://opendatacommons.org/licenses/odbl/1.0/) by the OpenStreetMap Foundation (OSMF; https://osmfoundation.org/).

USING THE GLOBAL POSITIONING SYSTEM

The Global Positioning System (GPS) was developed in 1973 by the U.S. Department of Defense. It is currently made up of a linked system of 31 operational satellites and provides critical positioning capabilities to military, civil, and commercial users around the world (Federal Aviation Administration, 2024). Each of the 31 satellites emits signals that enable electronic receivers, through a combination of signals from at least four satellites, to compute latitude, longitude, altitude, and time. This allows users to determine their exact positions and time, 24 hours a day, from any place on or near the surface of Earth, and in any weather conditions.

Because of the great demand for GPS use in the public sector, many of the newer lightweight, waterproof, and shock-resistant recreational GPS models (i.e., those not used for professional survey) provide users with approximately 3-m horizontal and 5-m vertical accuracy, 95% of the time. However, with recreational models, various environmental factors may affect the accuracy and the receiver's capabilities. For example, the length of time allowed for the device to settle before recording a point can degrade accuracy up to 5 m, and, when working under tree cover, accuracy can degrade up to 10 m or even further (Schaefer and Woodyer, 2015). Currently, real-time submeter GPS units are commercially available for professional survey, but this equipment is expensive and requires an experienced surveyor and operator to process the data. These types of units have an average of 50-cm horizontal and 85-cm vertical real-time accuracy. Accuracy can be as high as 2 cm horizontal and 5 cm vertical with 20 minutes of satellite tracking time and postprocessing with specialized software (Trimble Navigation Limited, 2022).

If you are using a GPS unit in a forensic investigation, you should always include the make and model of the receiver in your notes, as the degree of accuracy varies among different brands, as well as the number of satellites tracked and the error range for that particular reading. A GPS receiver can be a valuable mapping tool for recording site locations, delineating site boundaries, mapping in isolated finds away from dense areas of a site that were mapped more precisely and recording the position of skeletal deposits or grouped evidence within a site. Coordinates obtained using a GPS receiver can also be used to relocate sites that were recorded in the past. One major advantage of using GPS coordinates for site mapping is that the data can be downloaded and used in GIS software that integrates your coordinates into preexisting maps. The major disadvantage of using the less expensive recreational GPS receivers is that they are not accurate enough to provide the level of precision required in scaled mapping of a grave and its contents or individualized pieces of evidence contained in surface deposits.

When you first turn on a GPS receiver, it should uplink to all available satellites, provided that the receiver has a clear and uninterrupted signal path. In addition, most satellites orbit the equator, so when using a GPS in the northern hemisphere, you should hold the unit facing south so that your body does not interfere with the satellite signal. It is recommended that you leave the GPS unit on for a few minutes prior to collecting any data, as sometimes initial readings can be misleading because of delays in satellite signal reception, which may result from atmospheric conditions, accessibility, or signal reflection. You should always set the GPS grid reference system to match the reference system on any published maps used for plotting coordinates; since GPS error rates are variable from unit to unit, and it is a good practice to confirm coordinates using an official published map or a total station while working in the field. Any commercially available GPS receiver will store several mapping systems, and the user must be aware of which settings control this aspect.

USING AERIAL IMAGERY

Aerial imagery refers to photographs or digital images of the Earth's surface taken from airborne platforms like airplanes, drones, or satellites. Aerial images of a region of landscape are taken either at low or high altitudes. High-altitude aerial imagery (Figure 8.4) typically shows details of the types of terrain as well as any built structures or urban development in the area. This type of imagery is an excellent resource to use when developing a strategy for searching a larger area. However, because of the average level of resolution, it is difficult, if not impossible, to detect smaller disturbances, such as graves or surface deposits, using high-altitude images. Low-altitude aerial images (Figure 8.5) are commonly used in forensic search and recovery. These usually include a smaller region of the landscape and have a better resolution for detecting smaller disturbances or features. In fact, recent low-altitude images can be easily compared with those from an earlier date to determine how much of the terrain has changed or if there are any newly placed features, such as a swimming pool, patio, or barbeque pit.

A few quality sources for high- and low-altitude digital aerial imagery obtained from satellites include 360 Earthview (https://360earthview.com/aerial-maps/) and USGS Earth Explorer (https://earthexplorer.usgs.gov/). Additionally, Maxar Open Data Program (https://www.maxar.com/open-data) and OpenAerialMap (https://openaerialmap.org/) provide access to commons of openly licensed satellite and drone imagery and map layer services. Google Maps (http://maps.google.com) is a quick resource for aerial imagery that includes the names of streets and roadways as well as GPS and geo-tags that identify many built structures and landscape features; however, keep in mind that coordinates listed in Google Maps default to the WGS84 latitude-longitude positioning references, which may need to be converted if comparing these to locations positioned on a UTM system map. Local and regional sources for current and historical low-altitude imagery obtained from drones and aerial photography include county planning commissions, local and government civil engineering agencies, and local and government water management services.

Figure 8.4 High-altitude aerial image of a neighborhood; image used during investigation to identify houses with separate garage units.

Source: Figure 8.4 Bristol Berry Drive -10/27/2023 by Vlad Puchek is licensed under CC BY-4.0 International (https://creativecommons.org/licenses/by/4.0/ deed.en); enlarged and cropped for use.

Figure 8.5 Low-altitude aerial image of an industrial storage lot and adjacent empty lot; image used during an investigation regarding a tip about large pit (center left) recently dug on property to conceal evidence.

Source: Figure 8.5 Kaaiweg -4/7/2025 by Ben Bousché is licensed under CC BY-4.0 International (https://creativecommons.org/licenses/by/4.0/ deed.en); enlarged and cropped for use.

CONSTRUCTING SKETCH MAPS

The first type of map constructed during any search or investigation is a simple, rough plan of the scene known as a **sketch map**, or 'mud map' as it is called in archaeology. Sketch maps are not drawn to scale, but they do include overall measurements of the surroundings and the location of evidence recovery areas in relation to landscape features or built structures (Figure 8.6). They are primarily used to provide an overview of the most significant information needed during the planning of a recovery. For example, the entrance and exit routes to the scene can be quickly evaluated and marked using the information provided by a sketch map. It is recommended that you never rely on a sketch map as your primary form of mapping a scene; instead, it should only be used as a tool in the staging of the recovery process or as a preliminary form of data collection before creating a more detailed, scaled-distance reference map.

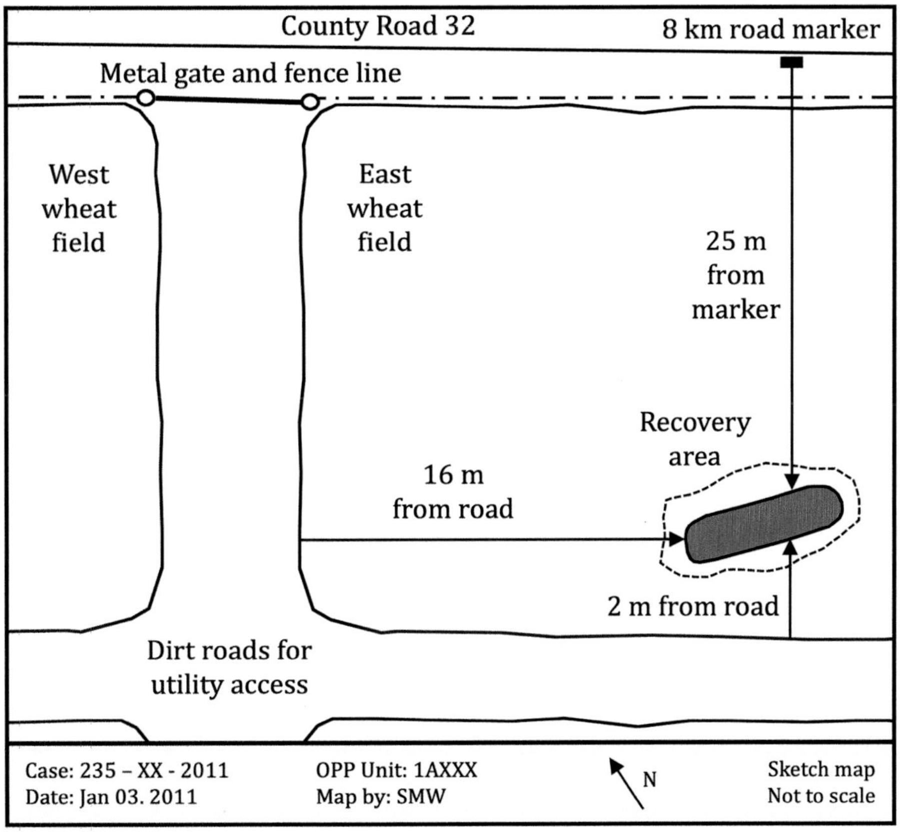

Figure 8.6 Example of a sketch map used in planning scene entrances and exits during recovery of surface remains in a wheat field near utility access roads.

CONSTRUCTING A SITE PLAN

A **site plan** is a detailed, scaled drawing that represents the horizontal layout of a site, including natural features, built structures, and limits of recovery areas and excavations, in relation to a fixed reference point. It is essentially a 'bird's eye view' of the site. While a sketch map and a site plan may seem similar, they serve two different purposes. A sketch map is visual representation of an area and is commonly used for navigational and planning purposes or to understand the topography of an area, while a site plan is a drawing with technical details of a specific place to scale and is used to illustrate the current conditions of a site.

The site plan is an essential part of any forensic investigation. It is crucial for recording and analyzing spatial relationships between the elements of the site, aiding in understanding past activities and site development. Site plans are usually constructed using methods of survey, which involve the use of specialized equipment or something as simple as a protractor compass. An effective rule of thumb in constructing a site plan is to map from the whole to the part. In other words, begin by mapping the established site limits and then incorporate detailed, scaled representations of built structures and features. This rule should also be applied to any additional scaled drawings that illustrate the particular details of recovery areas and excavations.

The choice of method used to construct a site plan will come down to time and resources. If you are mapping a site that may be destroyed, either through construction work, removal of built structures (e.g., concrete slabs, fence lines) or during the process of excavation, then you would want to be cautious and take reasonable care in recording each feature, as this may be the final record of the site as it exists at the time of recovery. On the other hand, if you are producing a site plan illustrating a grave or surface remains in relation to the main physical features of a site that would not be damaged during recovery or any other immediate means, then the greatest amount of time and detail will be in the construction of scaled drawings of the recovery area and the evidence being recovered.

Digital Photography Documentation

Forensic photography, also known as crime scene photography, is used to document carefully and thoroughly and visually preserve an accurate representation of the contextual relationships of evidence related to criminal investigations, legal proceedings, and scientific analysis (Robinson, 2024). Investigators and technicians often have access to high-quality cameras and specialized photography equipment to document accurately various aspects of the scene and site plan. Nevertheless, it is always sound practice for the forensic archaeologist to be familiar with the basics of digital photography when producing a site plan and in documenting the scene and details of a surface recovery or excavation (refer to Figure 2.7 for equipment used in site photography).

Digital images that accompany a site plan, scene description, or final report are not evidence in and of themselves but instead are a form of documentation that may be used in later analysis or possibly as future courtroom exhibits. If the scene is not thoroughly and accurately documented, it could be detrimental to the investigation and hinder later analysis and reconstruction of events. The advent of digital photography has helped to make some aspects of recording details of each photograph simpler and more verifiable (e.g., date/time, exposure settings, and GPS location automatically embedded within each digital image file); however, a basic photograph log (Appendix B) should be kept and include relevant details, including the image frame number, type of image view, and description of image that includes direction and distance from the main boundary, location, or object depicted (Vecellio and Byrant, 2025).

Photography at any scene should not just focus on the obvious. There are four main guidelines recognized in photographing forensic scenes: objectivity, authenticity, relationships, and relevancy (Robinson, 2024). All images should impartially and faithfully represent the scene, and a knowledgeable person must be able to verify the image's accuracy of what is being represented. All images should be free of distortion and clearly show what is there, identify where it is within the scene, and how it is contextually situated, whether it is obviously connected to events or not. Finally, all images should enhance the investigative evaluation of whether an event did or did not occur.

To ensure that all details, distances, and spatial relationships have been fully captured in photographically documenting the scene, three types of image views are commonly used: overviews, midrange views, and close-ups (Figure 8.7). **Overviews** capture the complete scene, showing layout and orientations, including major landmarks (e.g., landscape features, buildings, doors, trees and ground cover, grave) (Vecellio and Byrant, 2025). These images are typically taken in an overlapping fashion from the outside boundaries looking in, and from the center of the scene looking out. Their purpose is to show exactly where the scene was, to the exclusion of any other location, and to show all the boundaries of the scene. While spatial relationships among various types of evidence may be visible, they are not the main subject of the overviews. Instead, overviews serve to establish the context of the scene before any evidence is moved or disturbed during investigation. **Midrange views** focus on the relationships among specific features or items of evidence

Figure 8.7 Examples of the three types of image views commonly used in forensic photography: overview (left), midrange view (center), and close-up view (right).

and their surroundings, allowing investigators to firmly link objects depicted in close-up views to their environment depicted in overviews (Vecellio and Byrant, 2025). They demonstrate how evidence is situated within the scene and its connection to other elements. Typically, this is done by depicting a single object or feature in relation to a fixed object in the scene to show precise position, proper context, perspective, and scale. **Close-up views** depict individual items or feature details to the exclusion of anything else, clearly showing any markings, defects, or other identifying features from all sides (Vecellio and Byrant, 2025).

Using a tripod and aligning the camera's image sensor parallel to the surface being photographed is a best practice for producing sharp, rectilinear images. It stabilizes the camera and eliminates keystoning, a common form of perspective distortion. The item being photographed should fill the frame so maximum detail can be captured *in situ* (exactly as it was first found), and shadows must be eliminated unless they are intentional (e.g., oblique lighting to highlight texture, impression details, or compressions in soil). It is a common practice for close-up views to be taken twice: first with a scale and then without. The scale should be placed at the same level and on the same plane as the item or feature detail.

Many agencies have specific procedures outlining the process for storing and working with digital images, and the forensic archaeologist should familiarize themselves with any requirements. After completing photography at the scene, promptly save all images (uncompressed files, such as TIFF or RAW, are best) in a secure location (Vecellio and Byrant, 2025). Once the images are saved, copies can be made to disseminate to investigators if required. Refrain from editing, enhancing, or otherwise altering any of the original images. If any enhancements or alterations to images are necessary for reproduction in a final report, a copy of the original image should be used, and a log of any changes should be kept as documentation to avoid any suggestion that the original images were altered. While a full description of various exposure settings, lighting options, and composition used in forensic photography is beyond the scope of this section, there are books written by forensic photographers that provide a more in-depth understanding of best practices in documenting scenes and physical evidence, such as the *Pocket Guide to Crime Scene Photography* by Mark Vecellio and Erick Bryant (2025) and *Advanced Crime Scene Photography* by Christopher Duncan (2023).

Datum Points, Baselines, and Offsets

To maintain consistency and accuracy in all measurements when mapping a burial site or surface remains, a ground control point should be used. A **datum** is a fixed point of reference for all elevation and angle measurements made during survey mapping and excavation. The **primary datum** should be permanent, since all measurements within the boundaries of the site are taken from this point, and it may be used in any future work at the site as well. Building corners, utility poles, or datum points that you have added to the scene tend to be the most permanent and reliable points for use, while trees, fence posts, and other seemingly permanent features should not be used as a primary datum, because they can easily be removed. If there are no permanent and reliable points for use, a ten-inch galvanized landscaping spike or a length of steel rod or pipe can serve as an excellent primary datum point. After being partially driven into the ground, the metal should be etched with a file at the ground level and again at the point where the elevation line is attached. When the site is cleared, the spike or rod serving as the primary datum can be driven completely into the ground or close to the surface, and then easily located later using a metal detector. At any time, it can be reset to its proper height at ground level and a new elevation line can be added using the previously etched markings. At times, a **secondary datum** may be needed to map a portion of the site not visible from the primary datum. When mapping excavations, a **temporary datum** may also prove useful, but it must be mapped in relation to the primary datum prior to its removal.

Figure 8.8 Example of a USGS benchmark (left) and a county engineering survey marker (right). Both are permanent disks used to mark a point as an elevation reference.

All USGS and county survey maps provide the locations of precisely determined elevation points called **benchmarks** or survey marks (Figure 8.8). These marks are established in the field by licensed surveyors and are made of stamped brass disks affixed to rock outcrops, bridges, buildings, sidewalks, or other prominent features. Multiple points can be measured along a distance from a benchmark to obtain an accurate elevation for a datum or to record the exact location of a burial scene in reference to an officially recorded point if needed. This is referred to as 'tying in' your datum to official elevations or survey markers. When tying in your site datum to a benchmark, it is best to use a transit survey system (if available) or the compass survey method outlined in this section.

The site datum is often related to an arbitrary line established for the purpose of mapping a larger area. This arbitrary line is called the **baseline**. Any horizontal measurement taken at a right angle (90°) from this baseline is referred to as an **offset**. The placement of your baseline will depend on the size and shape of the site. If your site is particularly large and spread out, as is often the case when recovering surface remains, you may need to establish multiple baselines, using a different one when recording each heavily localized area of evidence. If you are using a grid overlay for recording the location of evidence in a grave or when recovering primary surface remains, one of the outermost lines of the grid often serves as a baseline. It is always good practice to tie in all baselines to the site datum so that each separate plan view drawing can be combined, showing their relationship to each other in an overall site plan if necessary.

Electronic Survey Systems

In surveying, a **traverse line** is a sequence of connected lines, measured in azimuth and distance, which defines a path or establishes the location of points and features. When using survey systems for mapping, the instrument operator records the distance, azimuth, and change in elevation between a known reference point and a desired survey point, 'traversing' the survey area. An **electronic transit theodolite** is a specialized optical instrument equipped with a precision telescope that measures both horizontal and vertical angles. Inside the telescope are vertical and horizontal target cross hairs. This assembly rotates horizontally in reference to a circular lower plate scaled from 0° to 360° and vertically from 0° to 90°. The instrument assembly is mounted onto a tripod and is always leveled before obtaining vertical and horizontal measurements. The importance of electronic transit theodolites has been decreasing since more compact and highly accurate **electronic distance measurement (EDM)** systems have become widespread tools, but electronic transit theodolites still find use as lightweight, precision tools in archaeology because they are relatively inexpensive, easy to use, and require minimal training.

After an electronic transit theodolite is set up and leveled, it is often used in combination with a self-reading **stadia rod**, which is marked with known measures, so elevations can be measured along with distance and azimuth relative to the instrument (Figure 8.9). Azimuth

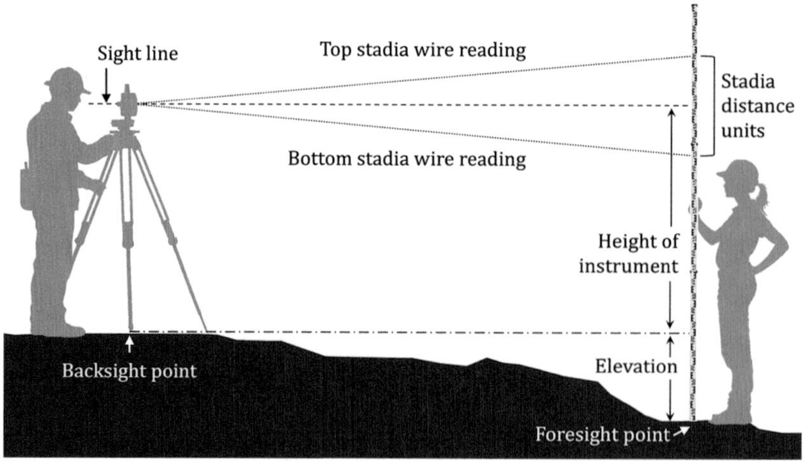

Figure 8.9 Basic schematic of measuring distance, azimuth, and elevation of a foresight point using an electronic transit theodolite and stadia rod.

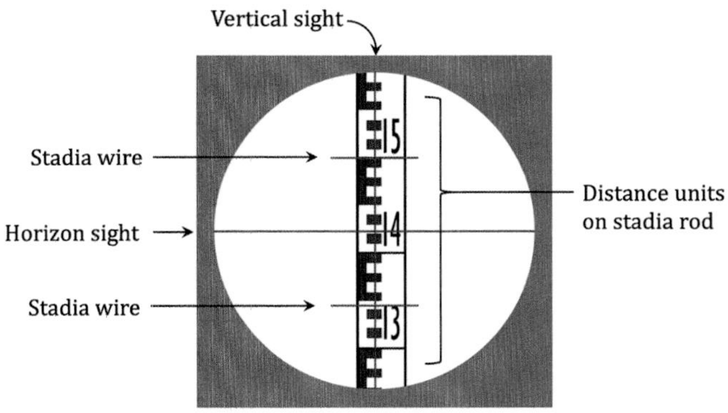

Figure 8.10 Example of crosshairs seen through a transit theodolite telescopic sight superimposed onto a metric stadia rod held at a distant point. The crosshairs indicate a horizon level reading of 1.422 m, interpolated between the 1.420 m and 1.430 m marks. The top stadia wire is at 1.500 m and the lower is at 1.345 m. The difference between the rod readings is 0.155 m, yielding a distance to the rod of 15.5 m (with stadia interval factor constant of 100).

Figure 8.11 Example of a total station with data logger (left). Research assistant Jeff Brzezinski (right) using a total station. (*Photo courtesy of S.B. Barber.*)

measures are the horizontal angle from the instrument to the stadia rod. Distance and elevation measures are based on fine crosshairs that are mounted horizontally inside the telescopic sight. When the operator looks through the sight, the crosshair wires are optically superimposed on the stadia rod marks (Figure 8.10). The operator observes the number of stadia rod marks visible between the crosshairs and can equate that to the distance between the transit and the stadia rod using a stadia interval factor (a mathematical constant, usually an interval multiplier of 100 for most modern instruments), as well as determine any elevation changes between the transit point and rod point (base of the stadia rod).

Reduced to the basics, a **backsight** is the initial rod reading taken on a point of known elevation, often a benchmark, datum, or a known intermediate traverse point from a previous survey. The purpose of this initial reading is to establish the **height of instrument** by adding the backsight reading to the known elevation point. A **foresight** is any rod reading taken to establish the elevation of a new, unknown point. By subtracting the foresight reading from the established height of the instrument, the elevation of the new point is determined. To survey more points, move the instrument to a new location and set it up to take a backsight on the **turning point**, or the elevation point that was just measured. This new backsight is used to calculate the new height of instrument, and continued foresight and backsight readings extend the traverse line until all necessary points are surveyed.

Today, total station surveying instruments have replaced most electronic transit theodolites. A **total station** is an advanced surveying instrument that integrates an electronic transit theodolite, an EDM system, and a data collector and microprocessor (Figure 8.11). The transit theodolite is used to precisely target a specific point, while the EDM emits a laser beam toward a reflector positioned at the target. By calculating the time for the laser to travel to the reflector and back, the system accurately determines the distance to the target. The unit also calculates the horizontal angle of reflection, vertical angle changes, and any other programmed functions from the total station's position in relation to the reflector positioned at the target. The onboard computer then processes the computation of coordinates, distances, and elevations for the user, to deliver precise measurements essential for mapping. Many total stations also have the capability to store data through a separate data logger, allowing for easy transfer to a computer or other device for further analysis. Some total stations can also be controlled remotely, allowing the user to take measurements from a safe distance.

Total stations have become increasingly popular in forensic investigations, as they are a very efficient means of mapping forensic scenes and allow for greater detail and accuracy in measurement, and the data can be analyzed in various ways depending on the software applications being used. Figures 8.12 and 8.13 are examples of site plans produced by a total station during a forensic investigation. If a total station is used in the field, it is highly recommended that the information be recorded in field notes as a backup just in case any problems occur when downloading data. The total station is, however, considered to be the primary data source if any conflicts occur between the written and electronic records.

High-resolution laser scanning has been in use for some time in archaeology to record the surfaces of features such as gravestones or rock art (Howard, 2007). In the last few years, this non-invasive technology has been used in combination with ground penetrating radar (GPR) and targeted photogrammetry to allow for integration of sub-surface features and standing architecture

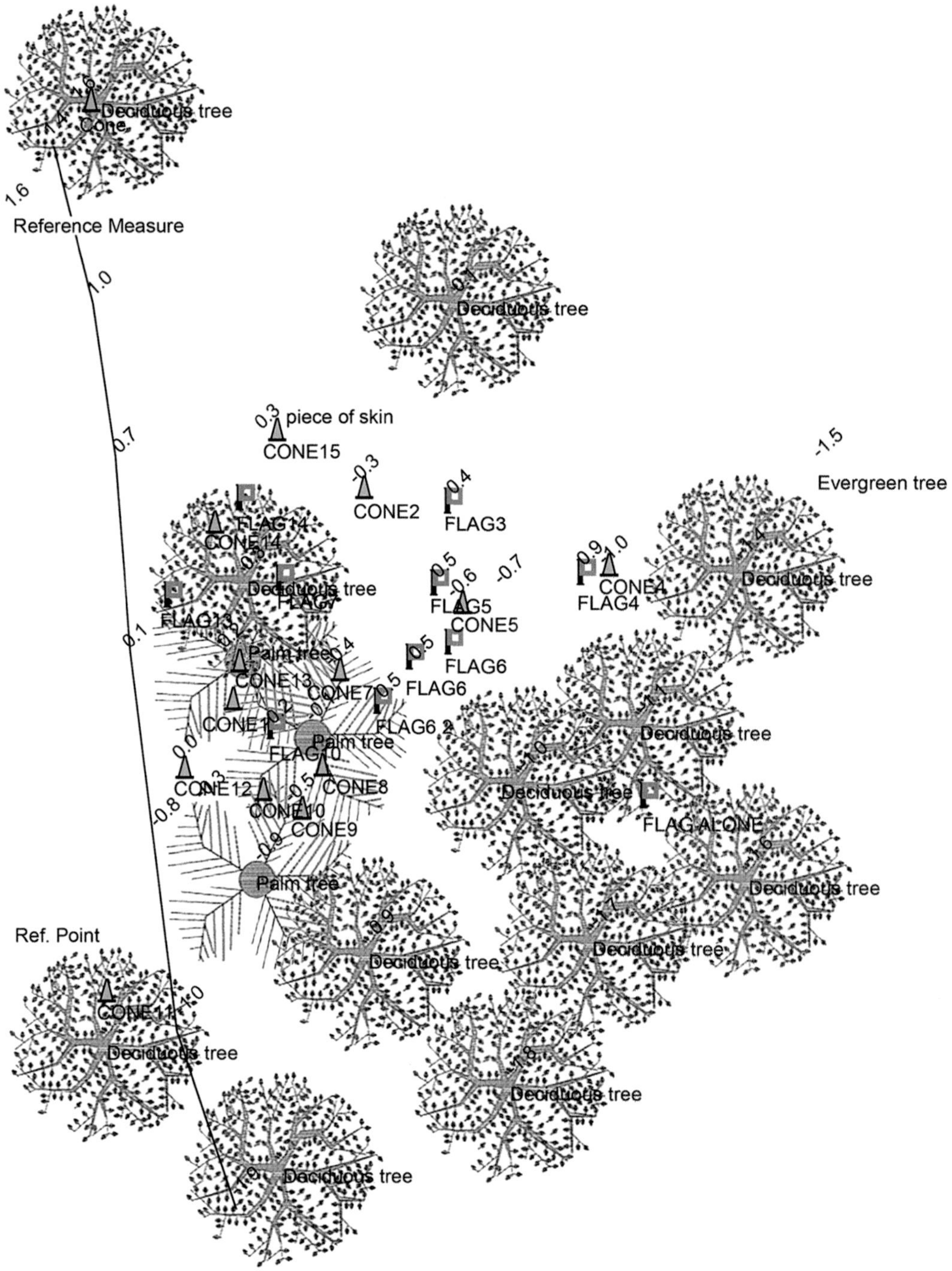

Figure 8.12 Site plan produced using a total station for mapping during the recovery of scattered remains from a surface deposit. This plan shows the large trees and the placement of evidence markers within the crime scene. (*Site map courtesy of Orange County Sheriff's Office, Florida.*)

(Figure 8.14) (Cooper et al., 2023). This same laser scanning technology has extended to indoor crime scene investigations. The scanner is set up on a tripod in the same way as a total station and can be set to automatically record the three-dimensional position of a series of points to define the surface of objects. The resulting point cloud is dense enough to create surfaces between the points. When viewed on a computer screen, details of the target surfaces are clearly visible.

Compass Survey Method

If particular survey equipment is not available, compass surveying will also allow you to obtain the direction of an object from an established or known point. For example, a field compass used in conjunction with a 50-m field tape can provide azimuth and distance measurements that can be used at a later date to relocate a datum from a known point. This method is especially helpful when

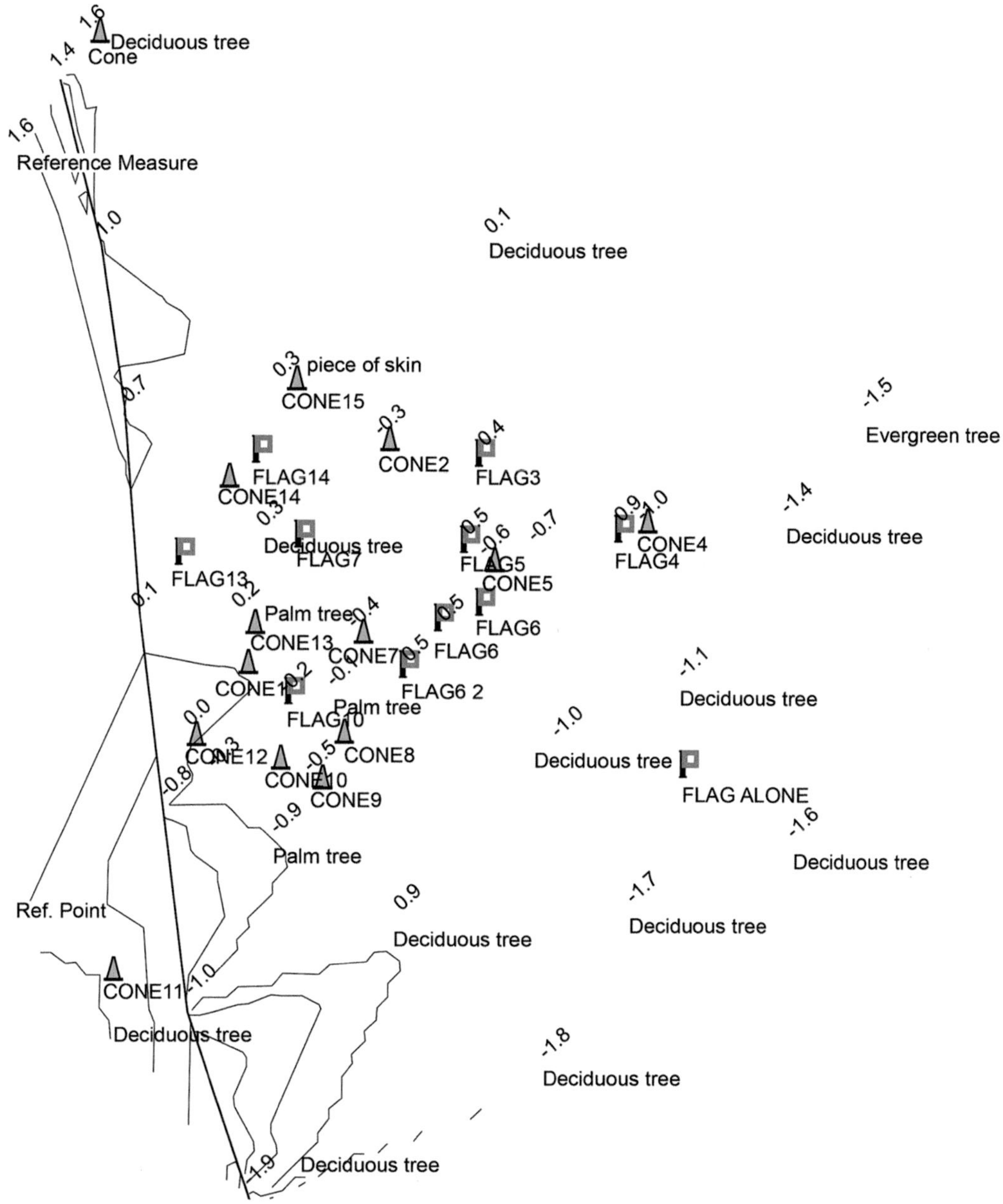

Figure 8.13 Site plan produced using a total station for mapping during the recovery of scattered remains from a surface deposit (same plan shown in Figure 8.12). This plan shows elevation contour lines and the placement of evidence markers within the crime scene. (*Site map courtesy of Orange County Sheriff's Office, Florida.*)

working in an area where the terrain has heavy ground cover or in cases where the use of flagging tape may draw unwanted attention to the area of investigation.

All forensic archaeologists and others recording evidence from a site, must be proficient in how compasses function, their error limits, and how to use them in mapping, at the very least to orient the scene in mapping and indicate in which direction photographs have been taken. When using a compass, you should always remember that the pointer will pull toward ferrous objects. Compasses cannot be used accurately if you are standing next to a car, beside power lines, near fencing wire, or too close to a total station and its magnetic field. In some instances, personal belongings, cellular phones, metallic medical implants, or holding the compass too close to a chaining pin can also affect the accuracy of compass readings.

A compass uses a magnetized pointer that aligns itself with the north and south poles of Earth's natural magnetic field, making it fairly easy to determine accurately the basic directions of north, south, east and west. To align a compass to north, you simply turn the degree dial or compass body so that 0°/360°, or 'N,' on the dial matches the direction of the north end of the magnetic arrow pointer. The simplest professionally used type, an **orienteering compass**, or baseplate compass (Figure 8.15a), consists of a rotating magnetic pointer,

Figure 8.14 Example of a high-resolution laser scanning point cloud representing the standing architectures of a church interior integrated with the location of sub-surface tombs recorded by GPR survey.

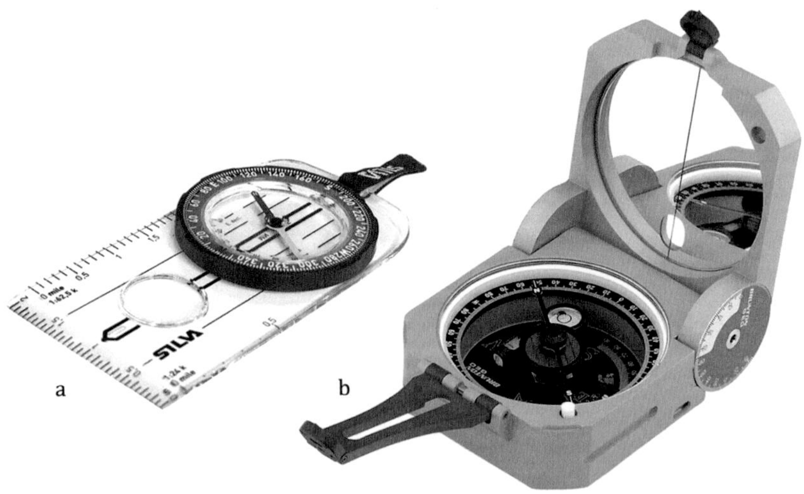

Figure 8.15 Example of an orienteering, or baseplate, compass (a), which has a rotating dial with degree marks, and a prismatic, or transit, compass (b). Note the reverse degree dial, or counterclockwise numbering, in the prismatic compass designed for the direct read of a bearing.

with one end marked for north, and a rotating degree dial, both supported by a handheld base plate with a sightline and directional markings (Figure 8.16). This type of compass typically has a clear plastic base that is overlaid on a map to read the features underneath. They are commonly used for orienteering on a map during outdoor activities such as hiking but can also be used for simple mapping if a more accurate compass is not available. The degree dial on most orienteering compasses is laid out clockwise from 0° to 360°. For use, the compass

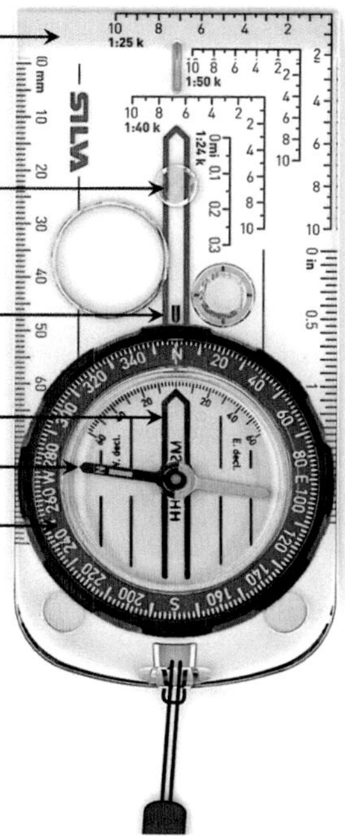

Figure 8.16 Parts of a baseplate orienteering compass used in obtaining a bearing to a desired location or distant object.

sight line parallel to the rectangular base plate is aimed at the desired location or object, then the degree dial is rotated until the orienting arrow lines up with the magnetic north pointer. The **bearing** (compass direction) to the distant location or object is then read at the index line at the top of the degree dial. If the compass degree dial does not rotate, the degree mark lining up with the magnetic needle is subtracted from 360° to get the bearing. For example, if an object is lining up at the 340° mark on the dial, the object's true compass bearing is at 20°.

The preferred type of field compass for forensic mapping is a **prismatic compass**, or transit compass (Figure 8.15b). Most prismatic compasses have some sort of forward sighting mark, often incorporated into a hinged lid. The rear sight usually swings up into position and lines up with the forward sight. The user lines up both sights with the target object and the prism or mirror then reflects the point where an index line passes through the compass dial, providing the bearing (to the object). The user may also line up the sights on a specific sight line so a distant object can be placed in relation to the point of origin, such as the placement of a chaining pin in a baseline used for mapping. An additional design feature in some prismatic compasses (e.g., Brunton) is a **reverse degree dial**; instead of the degrees running from 0° to 360° clockwise, they are labeled counterclockwise. This means that no subtraction is necessary when determining a bearing. The user aims the compass at the object requiring a bearing and reads the degree of bearing directly from the compass. Some of the more expensive prismatic compasses are also designed for survey purposes and can be mounted onto a leveling staff for elevation and distance measurement. When measuring bearings, most prismatic compasses are accurate to about half a degree.

Many reputable orienteering instrument brands (e.g., Suunto) also produce hand-held high-precision compasses. These are optical sighting compasses that allow you to simultaneously look at a distant object through the viewfinder and read the magnetic bearing. While these provide extremely accurate readings compared with standard compasses, especially for distant targets, they are designed for professional use, often by surveyors, foresters, and geologists.

Setting Traverse Lines

In the compass survey method, setting traverse lines involves establishing a series of connected survey points and measuring the distances and bearings between them to construct an accurate and reliable map of a site. Key steps include taking foresight readings, which provide the forward bearing of a new traverse line, and backsight readings in the opposite direction of the foresight to determine a back bearing, which serve as an accuracy check on foresight bearings.

Use the following steps to determine bearing and distance of traverse lines when constructing a compass survey site plan:

1. Using a wooden stake or metal rod (or other metal marker such as a pipe or 25 cm galvanized nail), establish your primary datum from which you are going to map the bearing and distance for objects and features within the site. Record its position using overview and midrange photographs and a detailed description in your field notes.
2. Run a meter tape from your datum toward a distant point that you want to record. Mark this point with a chaining pin and record the distance measurement in your field notes.
3. Leaving the meter tape in place, return to your datum and align the sight line of your compass with the eye of the chaining pin marking the distant point. Your compass sight line should follow the line of the meter tape.
4. Keeping the compass sight line fixed on the eye of the chaining pin, rotate the compass degree dial so the 0°/360° is aligned with the north end of the compass magnetic north pointer.
5. The foresight, or traverse line bearing from the datum to the distant point, can now be read at the degree mark where the compass index mark crosses the degree dial. Record the foresight bearing in your field notes.
6. Using the same methods, determine the backsight, or traverse line bearing from the distant point to the datum. Check your foresight bearing accuracy by calculating the difference of the two readings, which should always equal 180° (angle

representing a straight line that bisects a circle into two equal halves), although an error of ± 2° is often unavoidable. For example, if your foresight bearing from the datum to the distant point is 60° and the backsight bearing from the distant point to the datum is 239°, the difference would be 179°, a difference within the acceptable ± 2° error range.

7. Repeat these same steps, starting from either the newly set survey point or the primary datum, until the traverse line bearings for all relevant objects, features, or intermediate survey points are recorded in the site plan.

Measuring Relative Elevations

If relative elevations are to be included in your site plan, these measures can be obtained using the following steps when using the compass survey method:

1. Construct a **datum line** by tying a length of mason's line to the datum to ensure a consistent and level elevation reference; the datum line should be long enough to reach the furthest point to be surveyed for your site plan. If you are using a wooden stake as the datum, drive a nail in the end of the stake to hold the datum line in place. If you are using a metal rod, pipe, or galvanized nail, use electrical tape to secure the position of the datum line.
2. Mark the ground surface onto the datum and record the height of the datum line above the ground surface in your field notes.
3. Attach a line level to the datum line and extend it out over the distant point to be measured for elevation.
4. Place the zero-end of a stick tape vertically on the ground next to the distant point. Keeping the datum line level, move the stick tape so it is at a 90° (right angle) to the datum line.
5. Read the measure where the datum line intersects with the stick tape and record the measure in your field notes. To calculate the relative elevation of the point above or below the datum, you will need to subtract the height of the datum line from the reading. For example, if the measure where the datum line intersects with the stick tape is 35 cm, and the height of the datum line is 15 cm, then the relative elevation of the survey point is 20 cm above the datum. However, if the measure where the datum line intersects with the stick tape is 7 cm, then the relative elevation of the survey point is 8 cm below the datum.
6. Repeat these same steps to obtain necessary elevations for any objects, features, or intermediate survey points within the compass survey site plan.

Tying into a Datum

Tying into a datum allows archaeologists to link the precise location of objects, features, and excavations with other well-established points at local and regional scales. When a transit survey system is not available, the compass survey method is commonly used to link a secondary datum to the primary datum. This method can be used to link the site's primary datum to a more permanent, well-established datum or reference point, such as a benchmark or other survey marker. In an urban forensic setting, tying into a benchmark allows investigators to return to the same location and measurements can then be repeated consistently if needed. In addition, it links the site to accurate and detailed spatial positioning, which can be crucial in legal proceedings. Referencing established benchmarks can enhance the credibility of a survey site plan in a legal context, as it demonstrates adherence to recognized surveying standards. This practice also places the forensic findings within a larger geospatial context, producing data that can be entered into broader systems of incident reporting (e.g., GIS mapping). Figure 8.17 is an example of a forensic site map where the datum from a recovery scene was tied into a surveyor's benchmark using the compass survey method.

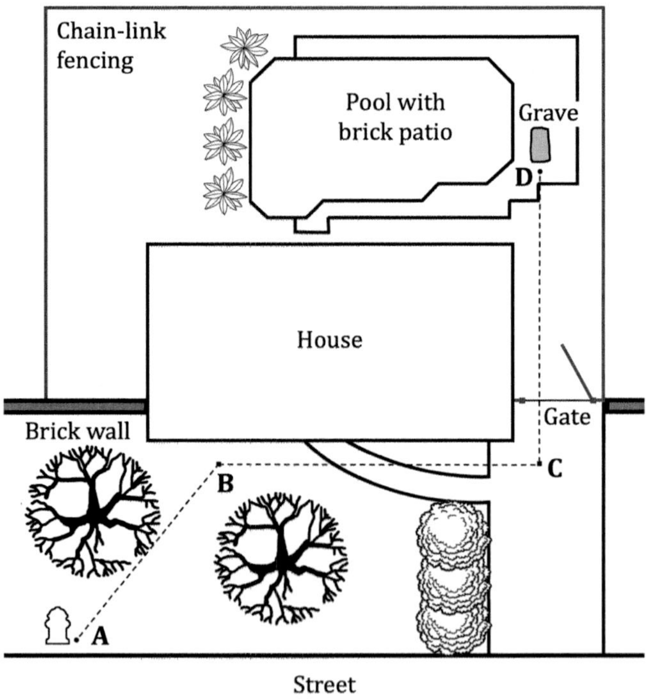

Figure 8.17 A site plan showing the use of the compass survey method to tie a site datum (Point D) into a survey benchmark (Point A). Starting at Point A, backsights and foresights were used to determine the bearing of each midpoint in the traverse line leading to the site datum. Meter tapes were used to determine distance between points, and chaining pins, a stick tape, and a mason's line with line level were used to calculate any changes in elevation.

CONSTRUCTING SCALED DRAWINGS

When first faced with the responsibility of constructing scaled drawings of a specific feature, most beginners are at a loss as to how to start. The secret is to mark the scene limits, determine the types of drawings and scale required to best relate the information in an illustrated form, choose a framework for constructing the drawings that would best fit the kinds of evidence being recorded, and then record the details of the evidence using the appropriate steps for your chosen method.

Within a forensic context, there are two forms of detailed drawings that are common; the **plan drawing**, which is the two-dimensional 'bird's eye' view with which most people are familiar, as it is the view used in most maps, and the **section drawing**, or the 'cross-section' view one would have if an imaginary vertical plane cut through a feature to show the relationship between different layers of stratigraphy or details in object placement. A section drawing is often confused with an archaeological profile drawing, which also shows the vertical relationship between different layers of stratigraphy. Profiles are drawings of the walls of an excavation, while sections are imaginary vertical cuts through an excavation. Another form of drawing, called an orthographic projection, or multi-view drawing, shows two sides of a feature from an angle. Although these are often used in field archaeology to depict architectural features or show complex relationships among artifacts, they are rarely needed in a forensic context.

It is important to consider carefully the 'grid-to-ground' scale of your plan or section drawing prior to recording any information, since this is the one factor that will determine how accurately the measurements should be read during the mapping process. A ratio of 1:10 (i.e., 1 cm on the drawing is equal to 10 cm on the ground) is the standard for most grave excavation plan drawings, heavily localized areas of evidence within surface scatters, or any other detailed relationship of evidence. If the primary site is quite large (e.g., containing multiple graves or a very large burial pit), it may be more beneficial to use a scale of 1:20. Drawings of widely scattered evidence are typically recorded in a ratio of 1:50 or 1:100 and usually consist of labeled points within the full limits of the site rather than a more detailed representation of evidence. It is also recommended practice to use the same standard size graph paper (e.g., 10 sq/cm) as, over time, this creates a familiarity with scale when recording data. Table 8.1 provides a simple reference for the relationship between scales commonly used in plan and section drawings and real ground distance. Scale will also make a difference in how accurate you will need to be in measurement and how much detail you will be able to plot on your plan or section drawing. There is no point in taking the time and trouble to measure distance with exceptional accuracy if it is impossible to plot the work onto the plan with a corresponding degree of accuracy. For example, it might be possible to measure the length of a femur to the nearest millimeter (mm), but on a 1:10 or 1:20 scaled plan drawing, 1 mm will not be discernable. Always be sure that your measurements reflect what you can actually record in the drawing, keeping in mind that more accurate measures, if needed, can be included in field notes.

Table 8.1 Relationship between Scales Commonly Used in Plan and Section Drawings and Real Ground Distance

Scale of Drawing	Scaled Measurement	Real Ground Distance
1:10 (1 cm on drawing = 10 cm on the ground)	5 cm on drawing	50 cm on ground
	10 cm on drawing	1 m on ground
	20 cm on drawing	2 m on ground
	30 cm on drawing	3 m on ground
	50 cm on drawing	5 m on ground
	100 cm on drawing	10 m on ground
1:20 (1 cm on drawing = 20 cm on the ground)	2.5 cm on drawing	50 cm on ground
	5 cm on drawing	1 m on ground
	10 cm on drawing	2 m on ground
	15 cm on drawing	3 m on ground
	25 cm on drawing	5 m on ground
	50 cm on drawing	10 m on ground
1:50 (1 cm on drawing = 50 cm on the ground)	1 cm on drawing	50 cm on ground
	2 cm on drawing	1 m on ground
	4 cm on drawing	2 m on ground
	6 cm on drawing	3 m on ground
	10 cm on drawing	5 m on ground
	20 cm on drawing	10 m on ground
1:100 (1 cm on drawing = 100 cm on the ground)	0.5 cm on drawing	50 cm on ground
	1 cm on drawing	1 m on ground
	2 cm on drawing	2 m on ground
	3 cm on drawing	3 m on ground
	5 cm on drawing	5 m on ground
	10 cm on drawing	10 m on ground

It is also important to maintain a sense of neatness in maps, drawings, and corresponding field notes. Notes should be understandable and legible, not only to the person recording the information but to other people. Messy maps, incomplete drawings, poor field notes, and the process of copying work into neater formats at a later time typically generate errors that can easily be avoided with a little care. Always check your work, and whenever possible, do your error check using an alternate method of measurement or calculation. An easy and reliable way to ensure accurate positioning in a plan drawing is through a simple line-of-sight method, where various objects and features that align on a drawing can be checked by creating an imaginary reference line-of-sight between the physical objects and the observer's eye to determine if the objects do in fact align with each other in the same pattern.

Establishing Limits and the Datum

The first concern is marking the limits of the scene surrounding the evidence being mapped and drawn to scale. A rectangle or square is typically constructed using wooden corner stakes and brightly colored mason's line to mark the limits (Figure 8.18). Thinner metal rods can also be used, including chaining pins or less expensive alternatives. It is advisable to include an interior 'buffer zone' (e.g., 50 cm) on each side when setting limits to prevent disturbing or damaging any potential evidence. This buffer also makes it easier to add to your drawing any newly discovered evidence that extends beyond the main area of interest. It is also recommended that you orient your limits in either a north-south or east-west direction to simplify reporting directional and angled relationships between objects or feature details when mapping and drawing to scale.

When constructing rectangular or square limits, trilateration is used to ensure that 90° angles are formed in each corner. Many people confuse trilateration with triangulation. **Triangulation** involves the measure of the angles of a triangle, while **trilateration** involves the measure of the sides of a triangle. Trilateration is based on the calculation of the hypotenuse length (c^2) of a triangle when the length of the base (a^2) and one side (b^2) are known ($a^2 + b^2 = c^2$). Whole-meter measures are recommended to make your trilateration calculations easier in setting the corners of your limits. A very easy one to remember that is useful for many small scenes is the 3–4–5 triangle: a triangle with the proportions 3, 4, and 5 (in any units, as long as they are consistent) will form a right angle (90°) where the sides that are 3 and 4 units in length meet. ($3^2 + 4^2 = 5^2$, or 9 units + 16 units = 25 units). Common lengths of baselines, side limits, and the associated hypotenuse lengths can be found in Table 8.2.

Figure 8.18 Author Sandra Wheeler (left) assists a student in setting up a baseline using a compass and meter tape.

To construct limits around areas to be mapped and drawn to scale (e.g., surface scatters or excavation areas), use the following steps:

1. Determine the extent of the area to be mapped, including an interior 'buffer zone' on each side. Using your compass, determine the overall central orientation (north-south or east-west) of the distribution of evidence in relation to magnetic north.
2. Place the first corner stake in the ground at one corner of the extent of your area. Secure and extend a meter tape (Tape A) out from this point across the length of the area to be mapped. Using your compass, orient the meter tape in a north-south or east-west line, whichever best fits the distribution of evidence.
3. Leaving Tape A in place, locate the first whole-meter mark along this line (e.g., 5 m) that extends well beyond the area containing evidence. Place the second corner stake in the ground at this point. This first side of your limit forms the baseline.
4. Using Tape A and your compass, extend the meter tape out at a 90° angle from the newly established baseline to form the side of the limit. Locate the nearest marked whole-meter point on this line that it is beyond the area containing evidence (e.g., 4 m). This is the length of your side limit.
5. Using the length of your baseline and length of your side limit, find the length of your hypotenuse using trilateration. For example, if the length of your baseline is 5 m and the length of your side limit is 4 m, then your hypotenuse length (found in Table 8.2) is 6.4 m.
6. Secure an additional meter tape (Tape B) to the second corner stake and extend it out at an angle toward the side limit mark on Tape A.
7. Holding Tape A in one hand and Tape B in the other, bring them together as level as possible, keeping Tape A at a 90° angle to the baseline. Align the mark on Tape B indicating the hypotenuse length (e.g., 6.4 m) with the side length mark on Tape A (e.g., 4 m). The point where these two

Table 8.2 Common Baseline Lengths and Associated Hypotenuse Measures for Constructing Scene Limits or Grids for Mapping

Side length	1	2	3	4*	5	6	7	8	9	10
1	1.41	2.24	3.16	4.12	5.10	6.08	7.07	8.06	9.06	10.05
2		2.83	3.61	4.47	5.39	6.32	7.28	8.25	9.22	10.20
3			4.24	**5.00**	5.83	6.71	7.62	8.54	9.49	10.44
4				5.66	6.40	7.21	8.06	8.94	9.85	10.77
5					7.07	7.81	8.60	9.43	10.30	11.18
6						8.49	9.22	**10.00**	10.82	11.66
7							9.90	10.63	11.40	12.21
8								11.31	12.04	12.81
9									12.73	13.45
10										14.14

* Note the simple math of the 3-4-5 unit triangle shown in bold.

measures intersect is the point of position for the third corner of your limit.

8. Move to the second corner stake, leaving both meter tapes secured to the first and second corner stakes. At the second corner stake, Tape B now becomes Tape A and Tape A becomes Tape B, reversing their purpose and use in the process. Repeat Steps 3–7 to determine the position of the fourth corner of your limit. As a check for accuracy, the distance between the third and fourth corner stakes should match the baseline distance between the first and second corner stakes.
9. Note that all of the above movements can be accomplished with a single measuring tape, but the operator must remember to add the sides of the triangle linearly to know at which point to place the corner stakes.

Figures 8.19 and 8.20 provide examples of the trilateration process when constructing limits prior to mapping and constructing a scaled drawing of a grave.

After scene limits have been set, a primary datum can be established if one was not already set during site

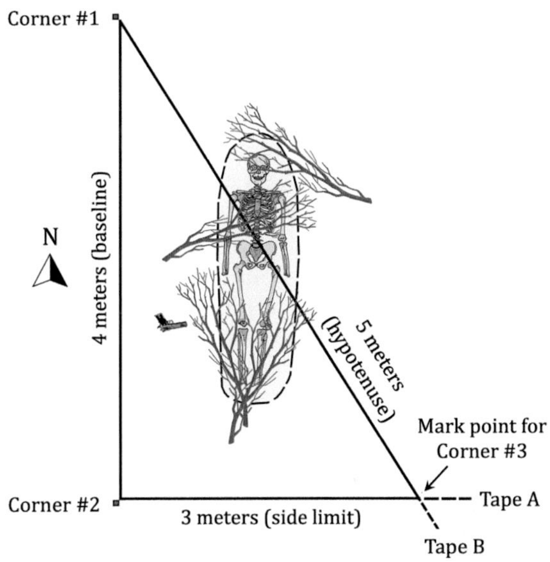

Figure 8.19 An example of trilateration using a 3-4-5 unit triangle in constructing limits for mapping and scale drawing of a grave and associated evidence.

Figure 8.20 Author Sandra Wheeler (right) assisting students in setting up the meter tapes for the trilateration measure of the hypotenuse when setting the final corner in the scene limits.

plan survey mapping. The datum used for scale drawings should be in a location clear of all obstructions in relation to the evidence and be positioned above any elevation changes in the ground surface. If a previously set primary datum is too distant or obstructed from the feature or surface scatter being drawn, a secondary datum can be established and later tied into the primary datum. In many cases, the first corner stake set in the baseline is used as a secondary datum.

Frameworks for Drawing to Scale

There are two primary frameworks in archaeological methods of drawing to scale that are commonly used in forensic contexts. These frameworks are designed to facilitate the construction of scaled plans or section drawings that accurately depict the sequence of events and findings at the scene. The first framework, **control-point mapping**, is concerned with determining the position of an object or feature in relation to a known point. When using this framework, investigators locate evidence and make the best possible record of it. Control-point mapping typically involves survey equipment or simple mapping tools when evidence is spaced out across a larger area, such as surface scatters or in areas surrounding a grave. There are two approaches to control-point mapping: one involves the use of azimuths and a centralized datum as the control point, while the other uses right angles (90°) and the baseline of your limit as the control point.

The second framework, **grid-system mapping**, is concerned with laying out grid squares over the scene to control the work area and record evidence in great detail. Grid-system mapping is usually best applied over a grave or heavily localized areas of evidence in a surface deposit as the level of detail is much greater than the level of detail recorded using control-point mapping. However, the same basic principles for scale drawing are used in both frameworks.

Azimuth Control-Point Method

Azimuth control-point method, also known as polar coordinate mapping, is a simple and accurate approach to recording scattered surface remains or other scattered types of evidence when a total station is not available. It is also very conducive to working in smaller, confined spaces (e.g., indoors) or in areas with a constructed ground surface (e.g., cement pad) (Hochrein, 2002). Unlike Cartesian coordinate systems that use horizontal and vertical distance for data point locations, azimuth control-point mapping uses direct distance and angle from a fixed point, or axis of the plane, for data point locations. This method uses a meter tape, chaining pin, mason's line with a line level, and an azimuth board to determine the distance, azimuth, and elevation of feature details or each piece of evidence from a fixed center point. You will also need a protractor, a centimeter ruler, and graph paper for constructing the map.

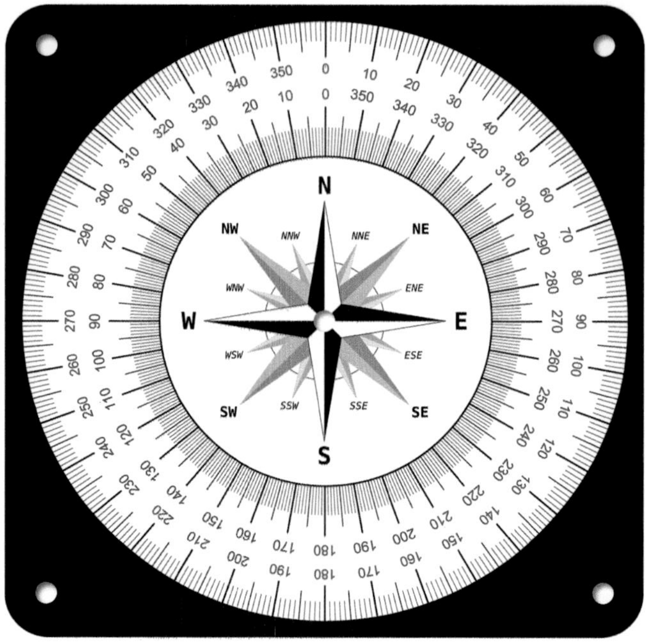

Figure 8.21 A fixed dial azimuth board used in azimuth control-point mapping. There are holes at each corner of the board for stakes or suction cups, which hold the board in place during use, and a hole at the center point of the azimuth dial, which holds a chaining pin that is used as a secondary datum. Note that this degree dial includes both clockwise and counterclockwise 360° protracted scales.

A typical azimuth board (Figure 8.21) has either a fixed or rotating 360° dial that can be locked into place on a base and includes small stakes or suction cups to keep the board in place during use. Some azimuth boards include clockwise and counterclockwise 360° protracted scales; always record which directional scale is being used if this is the case. Although this method is primarily used with the azimuth board placed at the center of the area being mapped, the center point of the azimuth board can also be placed at the center point of a baseline if there is no clearly defined space free of evidence in the area being mapped. In this instance, only 180° (half of the degree dial) of the azimuth board would be used, but the steps taken to record the evidence would be much the same.

When using this method, it is best to have one person determine angles and record data at the azimuth board and another to call out distances and elevations across the area being mapped. Mapping should start with evidence closest to the azimuth board and then moving further away in stages to avoid damaging or displacing any evidence with meter tapes and elevation lines during the mapping process.

To construct a 360° azimuth control-point scale drawing of scattered surface remains, use the following steps:

1. Determine the extent of the area to be mapped, including a 'buffer zone' extending beyond the visible surface scatter. Using your compass, determine the overall central orientation (north-south

or east-west) of the distribution of evidence in relation to magnetic north.

2. Establish and construct the limits around the area to be mapped and drawn to scale. Using a scale (e.g., 1:10, 1:20) that best suits the detail needed for the area, draw the limits on your graph paper.
3. Locate the center point of the limit area on your graph paper and on the ground. Ensure the center point is free of evidence prior to placing the azimuth board on the ground. If there is evidence at the center point that would be displaced or damaged, place the azimuth board at the center of the established baseline. If the center is clear of evidence, position the center of the azimuth board over the center point of the area to be mapped. Determine magnetic north using your compass and set the 0°/360° mark on the azimuth board degree dial to match the direction shown on your compass.
4. Place the pointed end of a chaining pin through the metal D-ring at the start of the meter tape and carefully push the chaining pin though the center of the azimuth board into the ground. The chaining pin will serve as the axis of the plane and as a centralized primary or secondary datum depending on circumstances of the scene. Tie a length of mason's line (long enough to reach the most distant point of your limit) to the top of the chaining pin to construct a datum line. Attach a line level and extend it out to measure the height of the datum line above the ground surface at the edge of azimuth board (equivalent to determining HI in transit survey when calculating elevation). If you are working on a hard, smooth surface where a chaining pin cannot be used (e.g., cement pad), a long, galvanized nail with a large head can be inserted through the underside to hold the meter tape D-ring in place. The mason's line can be tied onto the nail and held in place with electrical tape. The placement of the line can also be etched onto the nail using a permanent marker.
5. Starting with evidence that is closest to the azimuth board, extend the meter tape out to the object being mapped to determine the distance of the object from the central datum. While the meter tape is in place, determine the azimuth of the object by reading the degree mark where the meter tape crosses the azimuth degree dial. Record the distance and azimuth in your field notes, then map the information on your graph paper using a protractor for the azimuth and a centimeter ruler for scaled distance.
6. After distance and azimuth are recorded, take the elevation measure by placing the zero-end of a stick tape vertically on the ground next to the object or feature detail. Keeping the datum line level, move the stick tape so it is at a 90° (right angle) to the datum line. Read the measure where the datum line intersects with the stick tape and record the measure in your field notes. Remember that any elevations taken during the mapping process should be adjusted to reflect the height of the secondary datum above the ground surface. Record the object's description and any corresponding legend identifier assigned to that object in your field notes.
7. Moving across the limit area and further away from the azimuth board in a clockwise or counterclockwise manner, repeat Steps 4–5 until all objects and/or feature details have been recorded. It is good practice to always record measurements in the same order (e.g., azimuth, distance, elevation, description) to avoid any confusion and resulting errors. Figure 8.22 shows an example of azimuth control-point mapping used to record a scattered surface deposit.

Baseline Control-Point Method

When surface scatter remains are found with a large degree of dispersal, the **baseline control-point method** is the most efficient approach to recording and mapping this kind of evidence. In some cases, scenes can be quite extensive, and setting a defined limit would serve no real purpose in the mapping process. Instead, large sections of ground surface can be mapped quickly by establishing a **central axis baseline**, bisecting the area into two halves, or an outer limit baseline, working from only one side of the area, and measuring offsets (horizontal distances of objects at a 90° angle from the baseline). This method works very efficiently

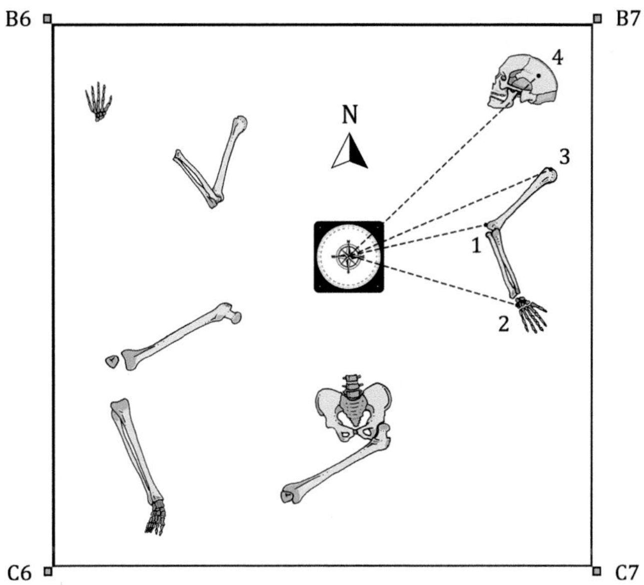

Figure 8.22 Example of azimuth control-point mapping used to record scattered remains. The surface scatter was contained within a 2 × 2 m grid space in the search area (corner stakes are labeled with grid references). Coordinates were recorded starting with the skeletal element closest to the azimuth board and then moving in a counterclockwise direction until all skeletal elements were mapped.

with two people: one person working along the baseline and recording the data, and another to call out offset distances and elevations across the area being mapped. An individual could effectively use this method, but it would be a bit more time-consuming and cumbersome.

To construct a baseline control-point scale drawing of scattered surface remains, use the following steps:

1. Determine the extent of the area to be mapped, including a 'buffer zone' extending beyond the visible surface scatter. Using your compass, determine the overall central orientation (north-south or east-west) of the distribution of evidence in relation to magnetic north. Determine if a central axis or an outer limit baseline would be most effective in recording and mapping the surface remains.
2. Establish the baseline by placing an end stake in the ground at one extent of your area. Extend a meter tape out from this point across the length of the area to be mapped. Using your compass, orient the meter tape in a north-south or east-west line, whichever best fits the distribution of evidence, and place the other end stake in the ground at the opposite extent of the area to be mapped.
3. Secure a meter tape to the ground surface along the baseline. Large 1-in lumber staples or small, hooked tent anchors can be easily pushed into the ground to hold the tape in place at the ends and along its length without damaging it. If the ground surface is too hard to insert staples or tent anchors, place rocks or heavier tools on top of the tape to hold it in place.
4. Set a datum line at one end of the baseline. If the length of the baseline is quite extensive, you may need to set an additional temporary datum at the center point of the baseline, but it should be tied into the secondary datum prior to its use to ensure accuracy in elevation measures. Record the height of the datum line above the ground surface in your field notes.
5. Using a scale (e.g., 1:10, 1:20) that best suits the detail needed for the area, draw the baseline and mark the datum on your graph paper. If you are using an outer limit baseline, it will be drawn lengthwise along one edge of your graph paper. If you are using a central axis baseline, it will be drawn lengthwise in the center of your graph paper, essentially dividing it into two halves.
6. Starting at the zero mark of the baseline meter tape, follow the baseline until you are on a direct line-of-sight with an object that needs to be mapped.
7. At the point where a line-of-sight with an object intersects with the baseline, run an additional meter tape out to the object being mapped. Maintain a 90° angle between the baseline and the distance tape using a compass or large, right-angle protractor. Determine the object's offset by reading the distance of the object from the baseline. Record the baseline mark and the offset in your field notes.
8. Using the datum line, determine the elevation of the object and record it in your field notes. Remember that any elevation taken during the mapping process should be adjusted to reflect the height of the secondary datum above the ground surface. Record the object's description and any corresponding legend identifier assigned to that object in your field notes.
9. Continue along the baseline in the same manner described in Steps 7–8 until all objects and/or feature detail have been recorded. It is good practice to always record measurements in the same order (e.g., baseline mark, offset, elevation, description) to avoid any confusion and resulting errors. Figure 8.23 shows the fundamental aspects of determining offsets from a central axis baseline when mapping scattered evidence using the baseline control-point method. The same fundamentals also apply to an outer limit baseline approach.

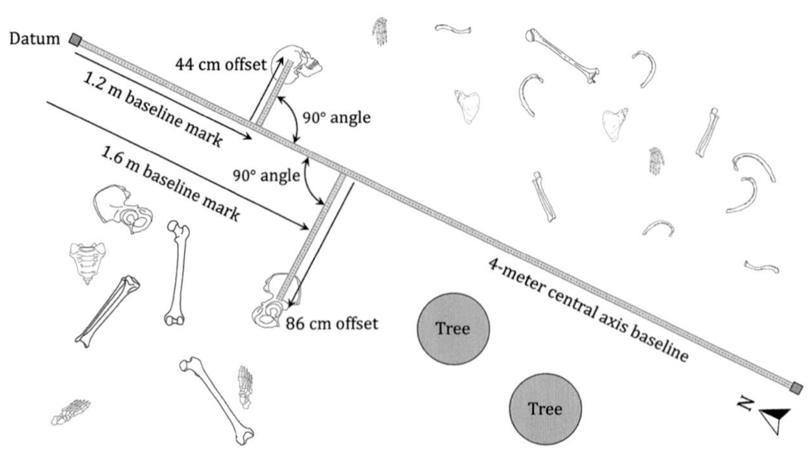

Figure 8.23 Example of baseline control-point method in mapping for scale drawing. This approach used a central axis baseline running through the center of the surface scatter. The same fundamentals in obtaining baseline measures and offsets would apply when using an outer limit baseline approach.

Grid-System Method

The grid-system method of mapping and constructing a scale drawing of a grave or other highly localized areas of evidence is a much more time-consuming process in relation to the previous methods. However, this method allows for a much more refined recording of detail for each object and its relationship to all other objects within a specific area. With better control over the work area, specific regions within the grid can be mapped with an even higher resolution of detail (e.g., 1:5 scale drawing) if necessary. In most instances, a 3 × 4 m limit should be large enough to accommodate a grave thought to contain a single individual and any evidence immediately surrounding the grave. The established limits of this size area may also be used as a closed-security area in which to work within a larger site area.

Prior to setting up the grid system, ensure that all photographs and related field notes have been completed for the scene in general. Setting up a grid system involves extensive walking over the ground surface, and extreme care should be taken to not damage or displace any evidence. This method works best with two people: one to measure within the grid system and another to record the data.

To set up a grid system and construct a plan drawing using this method, follow these steps:

1. Determine the extent of the area to be mapped, including a 'buffer zone' extending beyond the visible surface scatter. Using your compass, determine the overall central orientation (north-south or east-west) of the distribution of evidence in relation to the magnetic north.
2. Establish and construct the limits around the area to be mapped and drawn to scale. Using a scale (e.g., 1:10, 1:20) that best suits the detail needed for the area, draw the limits and label your datum on your graph paper.
3. Set your datum line and record its height above the ground surface in your field notes.
4. Along the north-south and east-west sides of the limit, position a wood stake or chaining pin at 1-m intervals. Tie brightly colored mason's line onto a 1-m interval stake and string it across the limit to the equivalent stake on the opposite side of the limit. Using a compass or large, right-angle protractor, verify that you are maintaining a 90° angle between the grid line and limits. The mason's line should be tied far enough off the ground surface so it does not interfere with any surface features or evidence within the limit.
5. Continue stringing mason's line to each pair of stakes in both directions, forming a pattern of 1-m grid squares within the limit.
6. Starting at the datum, label the grid squares along the baseline with capitalized letters. Along the datum side that is at a 90° angle to the baseline, label the grid squares with numbers. This is called the reference number line. The datum line for the grid is now located at the A1 grid mark. Add the baseline and reference number line grid labels on your graph paper.
7. When evidence is encountered within a grid square, its exact position can be determined by measuring from the corner of the square that is closest to the datum along the square's two grid lines running parallel to the baseline and the reference number line. Using a pair of stick tapes, hold one along the gridline parallel to the baseline with the zero point at the corner closest to the datum. Then place the other so that it intersects at a 90° angle with the first stick tape and the point on the object being mapped. The first measure is the baseline measure and the second measure is the reference number measure within the grid square.
8. Locate the corresponding grid square on your graph paper. Using the proper scale, plot the point just measured within that grid square using your baseline and reference number measures.
9. Repeat Steps 7–8 for each point on the object that needs to be mapped. For example, if you are mapping the position of a femur within a grid square at 1:10 scale, you would want to measure enough points on the femur (e.g., the proximal and distal ends and the midpoint of the diaphysis) to accurately represent its position at that scale.
10. Once the object has been mapped, its elevation should be recorded using the datum line. Remember to also record the object's description and any corresponding legend identifier assigned to that object in your field notes.
11. Proceed throughout the grid continuing in the same manner described above until all objects and/or feature details have been recorded. It is good practice to always record measurements in the same order (e.g., baseline measure, reference number line measure, elevation, description) to avoid any confusion and resulting errors.

An example of a grid positioned over a slightly eroded and disturbed grave is shown in Figure 8.24.

When continuing with a scaled plan drawing of a grave during excavation, we recommend using a series of **overlay sheets** in plan drawings (Figure 8.25) so all data are recorded in a clear and legible manner at different depths.

To produce an overlay for your scaled plan drawing, follow these steps:

1. After all surface evidence and features are mapped and drawn to scale, place an overlay sheet of tracing paper over your graph paper. Hold it in place with drafting tape or large bulldog clips.
2. The graph paper and designated labels for the grid squares should show through the overlay sheet. Mark a set of crosshairs at each corner of your limit and label the datum. The crosshairs

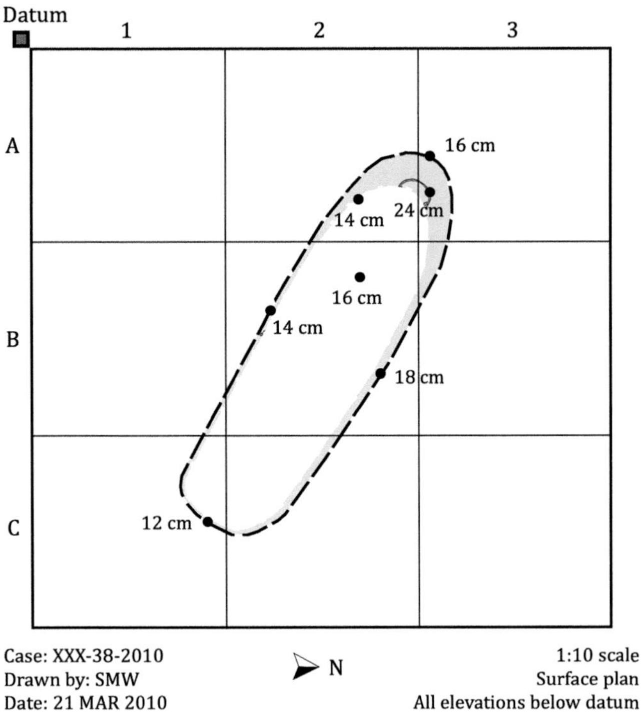

Figure 8.24 Example of a 1:10 scale surface plan drawing of a slightly eroded and disturbed grave using grid-system mapping.

on your overlay are used to realign this data with the original drawing. Label this overlay as 'Overlay #1.'

3. Map the next layer of data on your overlay sheet. Your previously recorded data on the original drawing will still be visible and you can retain the necessary level of detail in scale drawing without cluttering the map.
4. Remove each overlay and add a new one following Steps 1–3 as necessary throughout the mapping and excavation process until all evidence has been recorded. Remember to trace the crosshairs from the original graph paper onto each overlay and label each overlay in consecutive order.
5. You can add details, such as grid lines, labels, and outer limits to your overlays at a later date by aligning your cross hairs with the original drawing and tracing this information onto the overlay sheet.

As mentioned earlier, densely localized areas of evidence can be recorded in higher resolution of detail by using an archaeological **planning frame** placed over the evidence. Planning frames are typically 1-m^2 metal frames that have been subdivided into 10-cm sub-squares using lines attached to the frame at (Figure 8.26). When a planning frame is used, the sub-squares are labeled first with the grid square identifier followed by letters and numbers corresponding to the same system as the larger grid system; however, the letters used for the sub-squares are in lowercase instead of uppercase. For example, if a planning grid is placed over grid square B6 to map a heavily localized area of skeletal remains, a recorded skeletal element may be labeled as 'B6/d2/–21 cm.' This means that the item was located in grid square B6, located in sub-square d2, at an elevation of 21 cm below datum.

Section Drawings from Mapped Data

Section, or cross-section, drawings are used to depict elevation relationships among surface contours, objects, and soil layers. These drawings can be easily constructed from the elevation measurements taken during survey mapping, excavation, or surface recovery, and the distance measurements from plan drawings.

To construct a scaled section drawing from previously recorded elevation and distance measurements, use the following steps:

1. On graph paper, mark the position of the primary datum. If you are constructing a section drawing that represents depth in elevation, the datum would be placed at the top of the graph paper. If you are recording height in elevation, it will be placed at the bottom of the graph paper.
2. From the datum, draw a baseline that represents the width of the section plane that you want to construct. Mark the height or depth elevations of surface contours found along this baseline and connect the data points to represent the surface horizon line. Follow the same procedure when constructing lines of stratigraphic change in-depth elevations.
3. Below the horizon line, mark the depth elevations of all mapped objects and soil or sediment layers. For height elevation maps, all mapped objects would be above the horizon line. Be sure to label each data point (or set of data points depending on scale) and any layers with the corresponding legend identifiers to avoid any confusion or errors when reviewing your work.

Figure 8.27 provides an example of how depth measurements are taken from a datum line for use in sections drawings. Figure 8.28 is an example of a section drawing using depth elevation measurements taken during excavation.

Mapping on a Slope

All of the previously discussed techniques assume that your scene has a flat or gently sloping surface. However, forensic investigators are likely to come up against ravines, rock falls, forested hollows, and human-constructed embankments that will call for a certain amount of ingenuity when recording evidence. When measuring on steep slopes, the most important consideration is to exercise extreme caution when traversing the slope. It is sometimes difficult to keep measuring tapes level, and you may find yourself paying more attention to the positioning of the meter tape rather than where you are placing your feet.

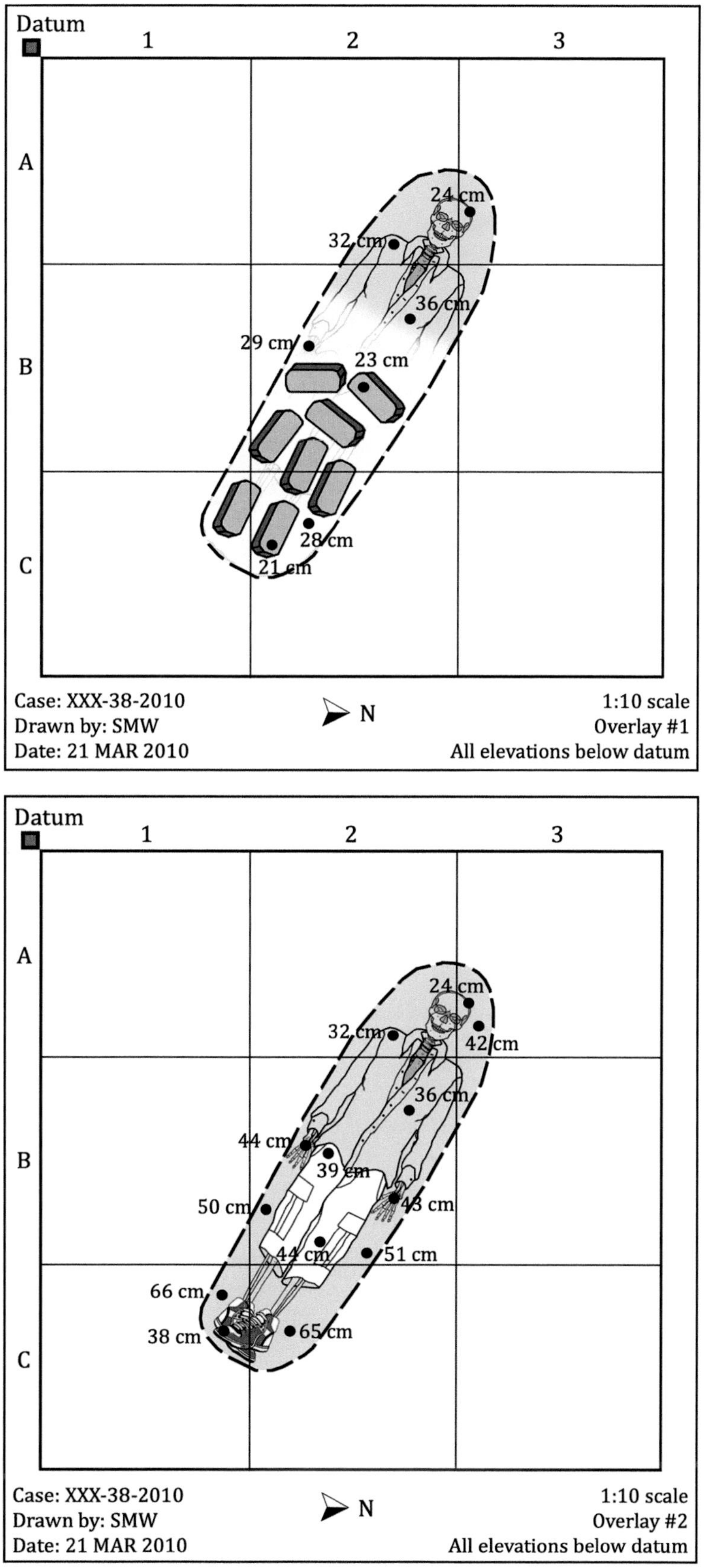

Figure 8.25 After the surface evidence of this grave was recorded in the scale plan drawing (Figure 8.24), a layer of soil was removed, and the grid was used to construct a plan drawing overlay (top; Overlay #1) to show the positions of brick debris and the position of the remains. After the remains were completely exposed, another overlay (bottom; Overlay #2) was produced, providing mapped data on the full extended position of the remains and preserved clothing.

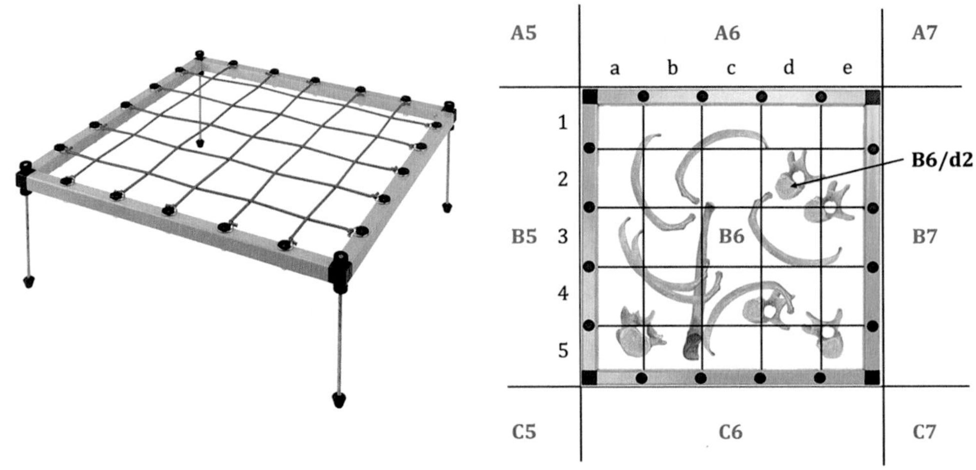

Figure 8.26 Example of a collapsible archaeological planning frame (left) used in mapping densely localized evidence. The frame is placed over the evidence within a 1 × 1 m grid space (right), with sub-squares labeled by letters and numbers corresponding to the same system as the larger grid system but with lowercase letters instead of uppercase.

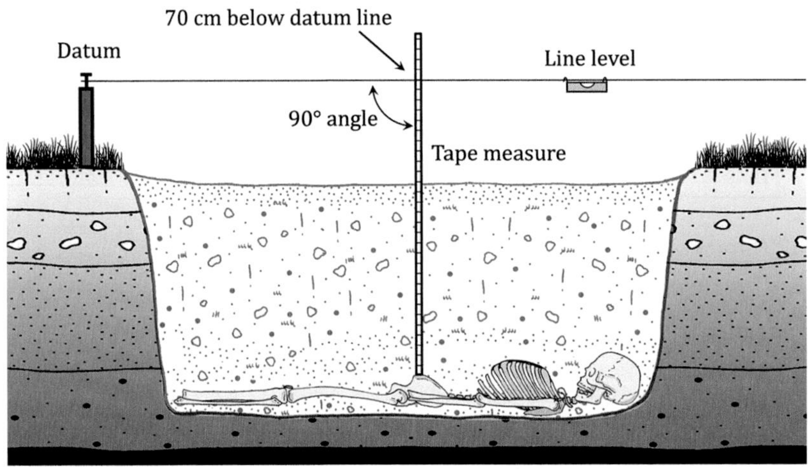

Figure 8.27 Example of using a datum line to measure the elevation of an object for use in constructing a section drawing.

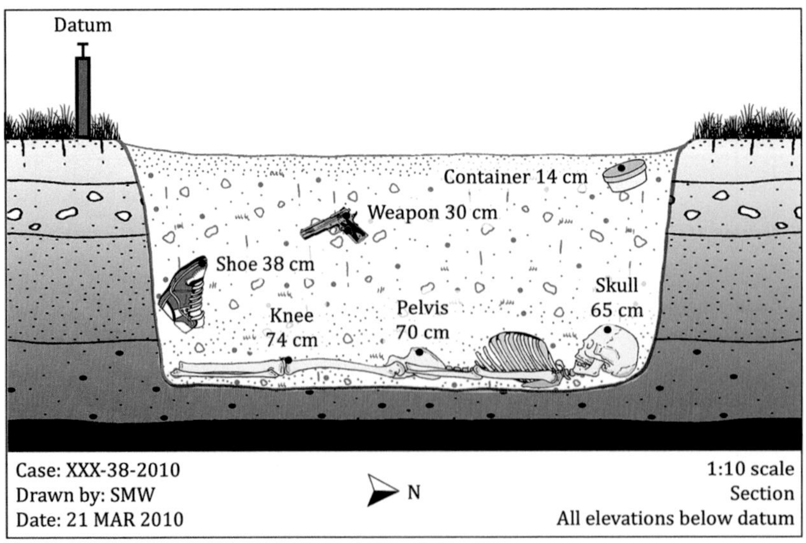

Figure 8.28 An example of a section drawing using depth measurements taken during excavation. This portrays the relative position of the skeletal remains, associated evidence within the grave, and the soil or sediment layers encountered during excavation.

It is recommended that an electronic transit theodolite or total station is used when recording skeletal remains located on a slope; however, if one is not available, the remains can be accurately recorded by setting a series of stepped baselines and using the control-point framework for mapping across the face of the slope. This method requires at least two individuals: one working along the baseline and recording data, and one working upslope from the baseline. Mapping should always proceed from the base of the slope upward to avoid displacing any rock scree or other debris that may slide downhill and damage or shift the location of evidence along the slope.

If an electronic transit theodolite or total station is not available, evidence located on a slope can be mapped using the following steps:

1. Using the steps described earlier, establish a baseline at the bottom of the slope, keeping it as level as possible across the ground surface. The baseline should extend across the length of the recovery area being mapped.
2. Secure a meter tape to the ground surface along the baseline. Large 1-in lumber staples, hooked tent anchors, or chaining pins can be easily pushed into the ground over the tape, securing it in place without damaging it. If the ground surface is too hard to insert staples or tent anchors, place rocks or heavier tools on top of the tape to keep it from moving. The zero-mark end of the meter tape also serves as a 'zero' elevation secondary datum when mapping the slope.
3. Starting at the zero-mark end of the baseline meter tape, follow the baseline until you are on a direct line-of-sight with an object to be mapped. Place the zero-mark end of a stick tape vertically at a 90° angle to the baseline at the point where the line-of-sight intersects with the baseline and the object being mapped.
4. Run a length of mason's line with an attached line level out horizontally along the line-of-sight from the object being mapped to the stick tape positioned on the baseline, keeping it level with the elevation of the object being mapped. Read and record the elevation of the object at the point where the mason's line crosses the stick tape at a 90° angle.
5. Replace the mason's line with a second meter tape, running horizontally from the object being mapped out to the previously recorded elevation mark on the stick tape. Keeping a 90° angle between the stick tape and the second meter tape, read and record the distance from the object to the stick tape.
6. Proceed across the baseline in the same manner until all evidence within a safe upslope distance has been recorded. Remember to also record an object's description and any corresponding legend identifier assigned to that object in your field notes. It is good practice to always record measurements in the same order (e.g., baseline point, elevation, distance, description) to avoid any confusion and possible errors.
7. To proceed over extended sloped areas or safely on very steep slopes, additional intermediate baselines can be established upslope using the methods described in Steps 1–6 until all evidence has been recorded. When establishing an intermediate baseline, it will need to be laid out parallel to the primary baseline. In other words, you would measure a rectangle or square on the slope and use the side parallel with the original baseline as your new intermediate baseline for measurement. Also, remember to measure the elevation from your primary baseline to your intermediate baseline and add this to all elevation measures taken from the intermediate baseline. For example, if your intermediate baseline is 3 m above your primary baseline, and an object's elevation from your intermediate baseline was 50 cm, then the actual elevation of that object would be 3.5 m above the primary baseline.

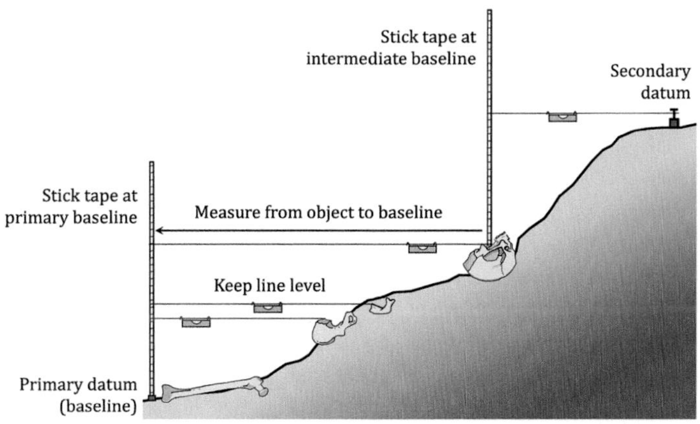

Figure 8.29 Example of using intermediate baselines when mapping remains found on a slope. The stick tape on the left is positioned over the primary baseline with skeletal elements in the first step being mapped off of this line. An intermediate baseline is set at the position of the stick tape in the center of the slope and again further up at a secondary datum to safely and accurately map any remaining skeletal elements positioned upslope.

An example of the stepped baseline method for mapping on a slope is shown in Figure 8.29. Once all of the data has been collected from the slope, a plan and section drawing (refer to Figure 1.2) can be scaled onto graph paper using the recorded elevations and distances to provide details of the distribution of remains across the slope.

Box #4: How to Construct a Map Using a Spreadsheet Application

Producing a two-dimensional (2D) forensic archaeology map does not require a great deal of artistic or graphic design skill. Simple, competent map can be done using a spreadsheet application (e.g., Microsoft Excel, Google Sheets, Numbers, Airtable), and present forensic scenes clearly in reports and courtroom settings. The overall goal of accurately depicting the spatial arrangement of the mapped objects is far more important than drawing ability. On a larger-scale map, many objects can only be represented by small dots, making it impossible to include fine detail in certain cases. However, the following procedure is straightforward to initiate independently and will improve with practice and effort over time.

1. Mapped points are obtained from manual methods (e.g., baseline, etc.) or total station download. The data files from a total station are small and can be copied into a spreadsheet; the data from manual methods can be entered directly. Position the East (X-axis) data column directly before the North (Y-axis) column to streamline the subsequent steps. Each entry also should include the objects' identifier and designation. Since the relative height or depth (Z-axis) will not be depicted in the 2D map, these data are not used (however, these data should be retained in case it is needed at a later date for inclusion in any kind of three-dimensional (3D) mapping or to determined burial depth, slope, etc.).
2. Select all of the East and North data and insert a scatter plot (with only markers, no lines). This diagram will form the basis of your site map.
3. Formatting of the scatter plot will have to be performed, including removing any unneeded legends or titles, adding major grid lines if not present in both directions, and reducing the number of decimal places of the numbers on the axes. At this stage, it is essential to adjust the scatter plot's aspect ratio by stretching it in whichever direction is needed such that each unit forms a perfect square: the diagram initially produced by the spreadsheet application will likely have rectangles for units. If this situation is not corrected, then the units will be longer in one direction than the other (e.g., a 1 m^2 from the site will appear as 2.0 cm in one direction and 2.4 cm in the other direction on the map). Such distortion will make the map unusable.
4. Individual mapped items can then be drawn over the scatter lot using the Insert Shapes menu. This can be done directly within the spreadsheet, or by first copying the scatter plot into a slideshow design application (e.g., Power Point, Google Slides, Keynote, Impress) and then adding the shapes. If it is difficult to identify which markers on the scatter plot correspond to which mapped points, printing out the scatter plot at this stage and drawing some items by hand on paper first can be helpful. Alternatively, one can temporarily delete data for individual mapped points from the East and North columns, and the points on the scatter plot corresponding to these will disappear. By successively un-deleting and re-deleting the data entries on the scatter plot, the corresponding markers can be made to "blink," helping you locate the correct positions more easily within a dense cluster. Finding the correct points for drawing objects among a swarm of points is therefore much easier. As a final step, restore any points that were temporarily deleted to ensure completeness of the dataset.
5. If preferred, the markers for the mapped items produced by the scatter plot can be deleted as the final step in creating the map, as these tend to peek out behind the items drawn on top of them. They can be reintroduced for storing the spreadsheet file.
6. Larger-scale maps including all mapped objects spread out at a scene at some distance can be constructed in this manner, with an additional smaller-scale map zooming in on skeletal concentration(s). To expedite this process, save all of the mapping data on a different spreadsheet page, then delete unneeded points (e.g., distant bones and objects, fence lines, trees, and usually the datum point) for the smaller-scale map. One can achieve the same effect without deleting any data points by limiting at which value the X and Y axes terminate. It may be easier to draw the smaller-scale map first, then group and copy drawn objects onto the larger-scale map and shrink them down to the appropriate size. For complicated maps, legends designating certain item types (e.g., isolated vertebrae, ribs, etc.) can be added to reduce overall visual clutter.

CASE STUDY #10: A BEND IN THE TRUTH

Authors Sandra Wheeler and Lana Williams were involved in the search for and recovery of a missing individual who had been deposited in a wheat field. The information leading to the location of the individual came from a hiker who stumbled across the remains while cutting across the field. The area immediately surrounding the remains was mucky, hard to walk in, and would not have supported a grid system that could be used with any accuracy. The depression holding the remains was filled with water and decomposition fluids, which was host to a large number of insect larvae as the remains were in an advanced state of decomposition. Because of the working conditions, the scene was photographed using overviews and midrange views, and a detailed control-point framework was selected for mapping, setting a baseline lengthwise across the center axis of the remains. A scale of 1:10 was used for the plan drawings. A primary datum was established, and all surface contours, objects, and remains encountered during recovery were mapped and recorded with depths and descriptions.

During the initial stages of mapping the remains, it was noted that bent wheat stalks extending out from under the individual's remains appeared to all point in one direction, while the wheat stalks in the area immediately to the south of the body were bent in various directions that centered on one point. The individual was in an extended, prone position with the arms pinned under the front of the body. In addition, the back of the shirt the individual was wearing was pulled up across the shoulders and the individual's boxer shorts were extending out of the beltline of the pants. The individual was wearing a pair of shoes, one of which was partially off the right foot. All of these details were included in the plan drawing (Figure 8.30). After recovery, all remains and evidence were taken to the Coroner's Office for analysis. There was no identification present on the individual or found at the scene.

Initially during recovery, it was believed that the individual's hands may have been bound at one time because of the positioning of the arms and hands; however, during questioning, the suspect denied that this was the case and also stated that the victim had been left in the field face up rather than face down, the latter of which was the position of the body at the time of recovery. Investigators reviewed the photographs and scaled drawing in recovery files and also noticed the direction of the wheat stalks and positioning of the clothing as well as the arms did not fit the information provided by the suspect, who later confessed to placing the body in the field. At that point, they decided to also question the hiker who initially found the remains.

Shortly into the questioning, the hiker admitted to turning the body over by grabbing the underside edge of the individual's shirt, which slipped up to the shoulders and also displaced the boxer shorts at the beltline of the pants. This action further caused the arms to become pinned under the body and the wheat stalks to be bent in a single direction away from the remains. When the body was initially placed in the wheat field, the stalks of wheat were bent in various directions from one center point because the victim was tossed on top of the wheat rather than rolled into the field. The hiker also admitted to stealing the victim's wallet from the back pocket of the pants and waiting approximately two weeks before calling the police to report the location of the remains. In this case, photography using overviews and midrange views and careful mapping and recording of all surrounding evidence explained the differences between information provided in the suspect's confession and the state of the remains at the time of recovery.

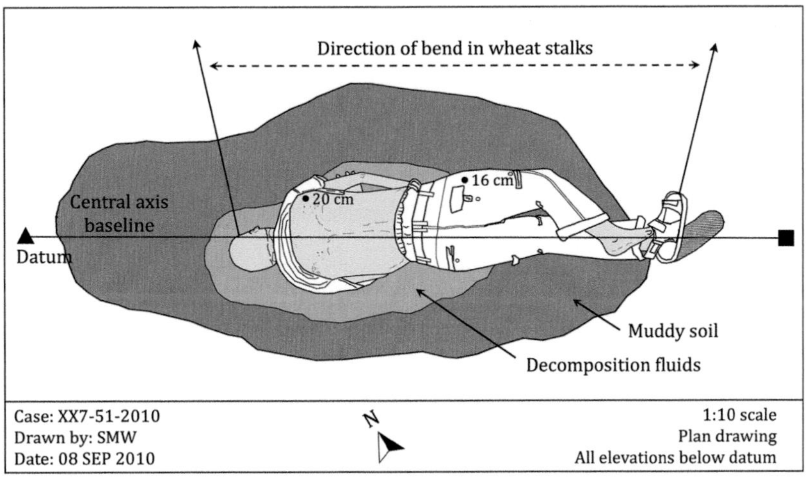

Figure 8.30 Surface plan drawing constructed using detailed control-point mapping framework from an established baseline that ran through the center axis of the remains. This flexible approach was used because of the working conditions surrounding the remains.

CASE STUDY #11: ASHES TO ASHES, TO ... ZIPPER TEETH?

Authors Sandra Wheeler and Lana Williams assisted in the recovery of evidence from a large open fire pit outside the residence where a crime had occurred. The goal of investigating the fire pit was to discern the number and order of burn events and whether or not the items contained within the topmost layers were related to the crime being investigated. The fire pit was roughly circular, approximately 4 m in diameter, and approximately 40 cm at its highest point from the surrounding ground surface. Four separate concentrations of burned material were identified at the surface of the fire pit. The remains of a large, upholstered piece of furniture, mainly the frame and springs, overlaid one of the concentrations of burned material, and overall, there was a strong odor of accelerant associated with the concentrated burn areas. Several additional items, situated outside of the four concentrations, were recognized as being in association with the most recent burn event due to their similarity in nature to the items in the concentrated burn areas and their position on top of, rather than embedded within, the upper layers of the fire pit. After photographing the scene using overviews and midrange views and recording the scene context in the field notes, a primary datum was set, and a quadrant grid was constructed over the fire pit for mapping the outer limits and all evidence on the surface of the fire pit. As each item was mapped and photographed in close-up view, it was cataloged and bagged by the evidence officer. After all surface evidence was recorded and removed, the ash from the surface layer was carefully collected and screened, and any evidence recovered during screening was bagged and cataloged separately by grid quadrant.

To understand the sequences of burn events that took place in the fire pit, a section of one quadrant was cut from the center of the pit to the outer edge. From this profile, at least seven major burn events could be identified (Figure 8.31). The lower layers contained general debris and household trash. These items were deeply embedded in the fire pit layers and were not a part of the most recent burn event. The uppermost layer contained the residue of the most recent burn event in the fire pit and ranged between 1 and 8 cm in thickness. From this top layer, over 338 items of evidence were mapped, recovered, and identified on a plan drawing (Figure 8.32), including steel toes from a pair of boots, the remains of cell phones, eyeglasses, and a multitude of small metal fragments representing all that remained of various clothing items, such as zipper teeth, snaps, buttons, and shoe eyelets. Later investigation determined that the four individuals who committed the crime had placed their clothing and personal items, as well as personal items from the victims into garbage bags prior to burning them, which is what led to the four

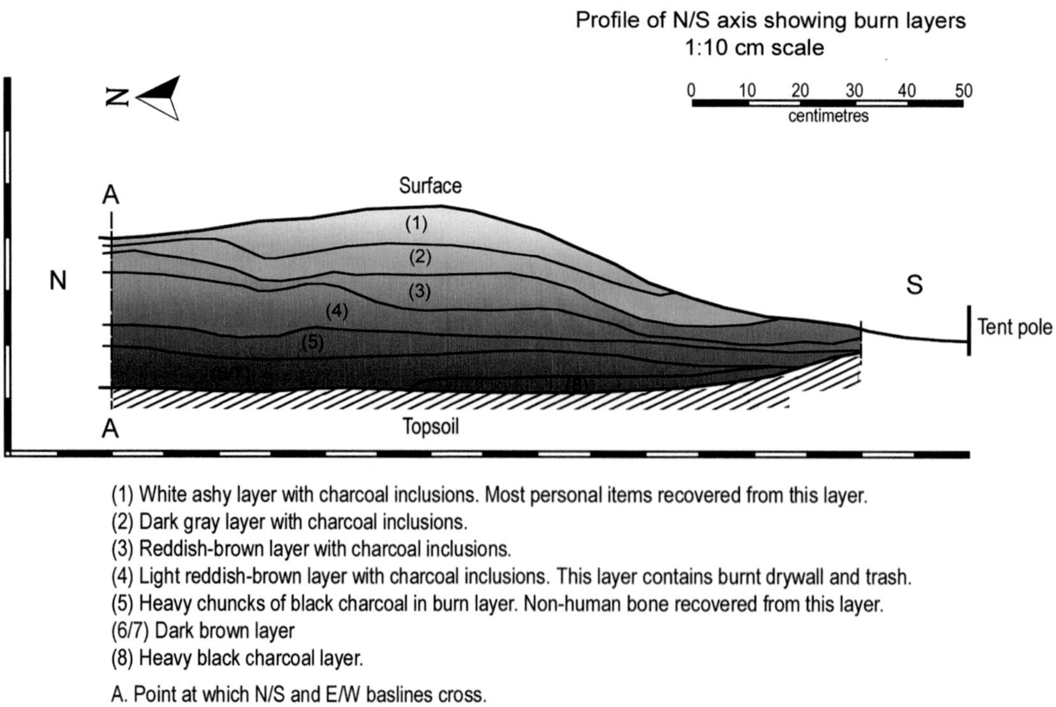

Figure 8.31 Profile drawing of a section cut into a fire pit. Note that color change in the ash layers was used to identify the various burn events that took place in the fire pit.

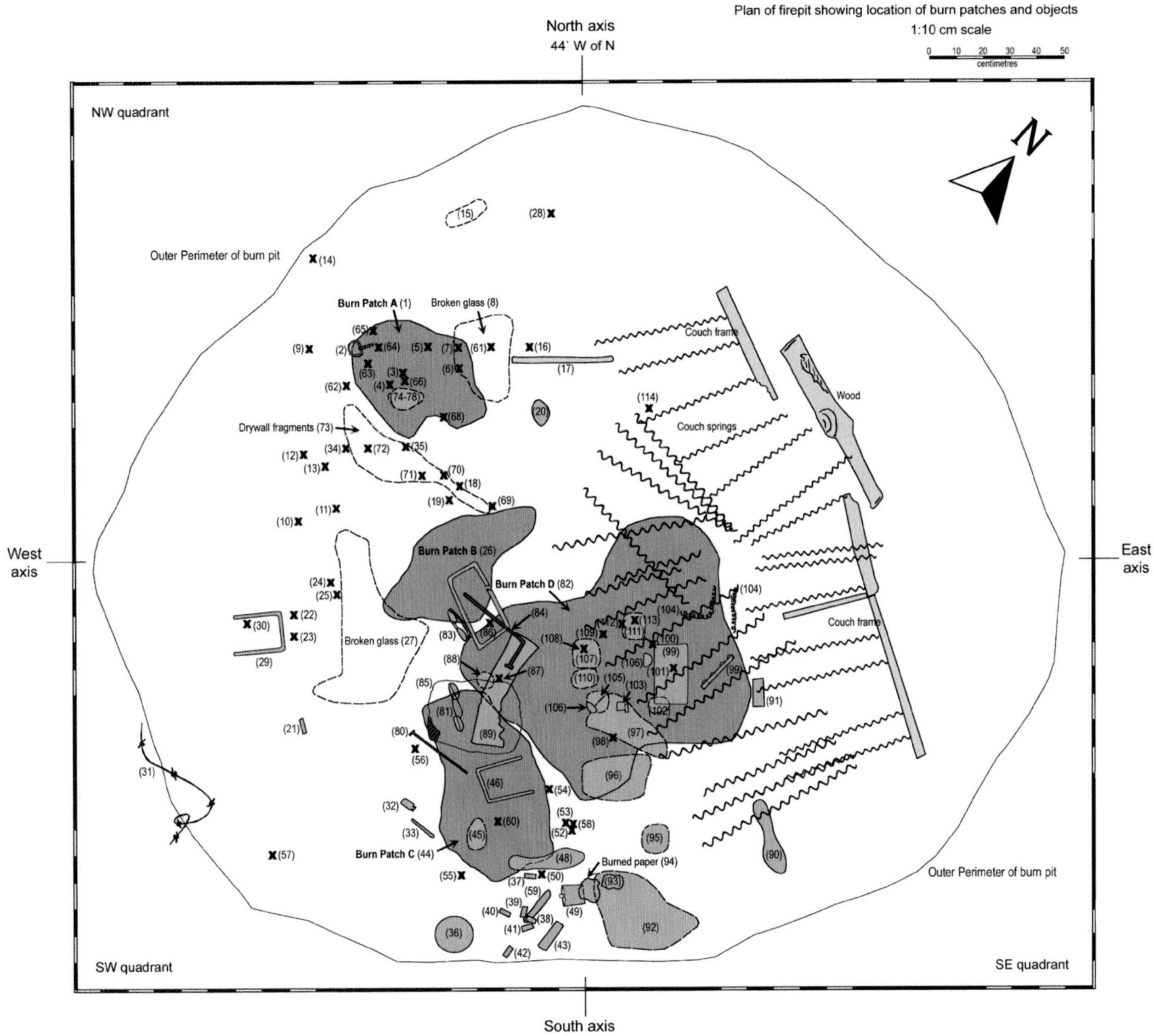

Figure 8.32 Plan drawing of a fire pit. All evidence recovered from the fire pit was recorded with a legend identifier. This legend was cross-referenced with identifiers assigned by the evidence officer at the scene.

distinct concentrations of burning in the uppermost layer. Therefore, the recovered items represented the personal belongings from the individuals involved in the crime and the victims, with almost all the recovered items later being directly linked to each of the individuals. Without using this accurate mapping method, the defined areas within the most recent burn event and the exact locations of evidence would not have been identified, possibly hindering the use of this information in linking personal items directly to the individuals involved.

Key Terms

- aerial imagery
- azimuth
- azimuth control-point method
- backsight
- baseline
- baseline control-point method
- bearing
- benchmark
- close-up views
- contour lines
- control-point mapping
- datum
- datum line
- declination
- declination diagram
- electronic distance measurement (EDM)

electronic transit theodolite
elevation (height/depth)
elevation plane
forensic photography
foresight
Geographic Coordinate System (GCS)
Geographic Information Systems (GIS)
geological maps
Global Positioning System (GPS)
grid north
grid-system mapping
height of instrument
latitude/longitude
magnetic north
maritime charts
midrange views
offset
orienteering compass
orthophoto map
overlay sheet
overviews
photogrammetry
plan drawing
planning frame
primary/secondary datum
prismatic compass
reverse degree dial
scale
section drawing
site plan
sketch map
stadia rod
topographic maps
total station
traverse line
triangulation
trilateration
true north
turning point
U.S. Geological Survey (USGS)

REVIEW AND DISCUSSION QUESTIONS

1. Explain the difference between topographic maps, orthophoto maps, and aerial imagery.
2. Describe how the alignment of true north, magnetic north, and grid north differ.
3. Describe the types of information displayed on a sketch plan, a site plan, and a scaled plan drawing. How does the amount of detail differ among these records?
4. Explain the purpose of an overview, midrange view, and close-up view in forensic photography.
5. When using an orienteering compass, what would the true bearing be for the following degree dial readings:
   - 180°
   - 235°
   - 72°
   - 160°
6. Figure 8.17 shows the location of a grave in the backyard of a residence. A datum was set during excavation and tied into the surveyor's benchmark located next to the fireplug. Is there a more direct route (i.e., using fewer transverse lines) that could be used when tying the scene datum into the benchmark? Explain the steps you would use in your simplified path using compass survey.
7. A primary surface scatter of skeletal remains, approximately 3 × 3 m in area, and two secondary surface scatters, both approximately 2 × 2 m in area, were discovered during a search. One secondary scatter is approximately 5 m north of the primary scatter, while the other is 2 m south of the primary scatter. How would you go about selecting a framework for mapping these surface deposits? What additional kinds of information would help you in making this decision?
8. You are using a control-point mapping framework with a baseline to construct a scaled plan drawing of a surface scatter. While recording this evidence, you discover an area of densely localized burned bone fragments and a few empty shotgun shell casings, all within a 1 × 1 m area extending slightly beyond the expected limits. What method should you use to map this area with the greatest amount of detail? How would you tie the 1 × 1 m area being mapped into your existing framework of mapping?
9. You are conducting a search with a first-responder team in an emergency setting when you discover dispersed human skeletal remains and associated artifacts in a flat, lightly forested area. You have been notified that flood waters from an adjacent river are rising and will cover the area in about four hours, washing away most of the locally dispersed evidence, so there is no time to acquire typical mapping equipment. All that you have is a pen, a note pad, a long spool of string, and the rocks and sticks found in the forested area. What steps would you take to map the scene in the time available?

Suggested Readings

Hawker, J.M. 2001. *A Manual of Archaeological Field Drawing*. Hertford: RESCUE – The British Archaeological Trust.

Hochrein, M.J. 2002. Polar coordinate mapping and forensic archaeology within confined spaces. *Journal of Forensic Identification* 52:733–749.

Jasiak, C. C., Schultz, J. J., Ferrell, M.J. (2023). Documenting outdoor simulated scenes with photogrammetry: Methods for improving harsh natural lighting conditions. *Forensic Anthropology* 6(3):123–137. DOI:10.5744/fa.2022.0020

Kipfer, B.A. 2023. *The Archaeologist's Fieldwork Guide, 2nd ed.*, Hoboken, NJ: Wiley-Blackwell.

Vecellio, M.E., Bryant, E.P. 2025. *Pocket Guide to Crime Scene Photography*. Boca Raton, FL: CRC Press.

Walter, B. S., Schultz, J.J. 2013. Mapping simulated scenes with skeletal remains using differential GPS in open environments: An assessment of accuracy and practicality. *Forensic Science International* 228(1–3):e33–e46. DOI:10.1016/j.forsciint.2013.02.027

References

Cooper, D., Kay, S., Pomar, E. 2023. Reassessing Italian Renaissance church interiors through non-invasive survey. In *Advances in On-and Offshore Archaeo logical Prospection: Proceedings of the 15th International Conference on Archaeological Prospection*, Held in Kiel, Germany, pp. 155–158. DOI:10.38072/978-3-928794-83-1/p29

Duncan, C.D. 2023. *Advanced Crime Scene Photography*. Boca Raton, FL: CRC Press.

Federal Aviation Administration. 2024. Satellite Navigation – Global Positioning System (GPS). https://www.faa.gov/about/office_org/headquarters_offices/ato/service_units/techops/navservices/gnss/gps. Accessed 2025, April 20.

Hochrein, M.J. 2002. Polar coordinate mapping and forensic archaeology within confined spaces. *Journal of Forensic Identification* 52:733–749.

Howard, P. 2007. *Archaeological Survey and Mapping*. New York: Routledge.

Robinson, E.M. 2024. *Crime scene photography*, 3rd ed., New York: Academic Press.

Schaefer, M., Woodyer, T. 2015. Assessing absolute and relative accuracy of recreation-grade and mobile phone GNSS devices: A method for informing device choice. *Area* 47(2):185–196.

Trimble Navigation Limited. 2022. *Datasheet: Trimble R2 GNSS Receiver*. Westminster, CO: Trimble Navigation.
U.S. Geological Survey. 2022. USGS EROS Archive – Aerial Photography – High-Resolution Orthoimagery. https://www.usgs.gov/centers/eros/science/usgs-eros-archive-aerial-photography-high-resolution-orthoimagery-hro?qt-science_center_objects=0#qt-science_center_objects. Accessed 2025, April 18.
U.S. Geological Survey. 2024. Topographic Mapping. https://www.usgs.gov/educational-resources/topographic-mapping. Accessed 2025, April 18.
Vecellio, M.E., Bryant, E.P. 2025. *Pocket Guide to Crime Scene Photography*. Boca Raton, FL: CRC Press.

COLLECTING BOTANICAL AND ENTOMOLOGICAL EVIDENCE

Learning Objectives

- Define forensic botany and introduce examples of different types of botanical evidence that can be collected at a scene
- Define forensic entomology and describe the relevant insect species that can be collected at a scene
- Outline the steps for recording, collecting, and preserving botanical and entomological material.

Learning Connections

- Introduce guidelines for collecting botanical and entomological evidence while processing a forensic archaeology scene
- Establish how botanical and entomological evidence collection is incorporated into field search and archaeological recovery of remains in forensic contexts

Forensic botanists and entomologists are playing an increasingly pivotal role in criminal and medico-legal investigations across the United States and globally. Their expertise is being sought with growing frequency as investigators recognize the critical insights that plant and insect evidence can offer. When properly collected, preserved, and analyzed by trained professionals, botanical and entomological evidence found on or near human remains can yield some of the most revealing clues about a victim's death. These biological markers can reveal attempts to conceal human remains, link suspects or objects to forensic scenes or victims, and offer critical insights into the manner and location of death, as well as the postmortem interval (PMI).

Experts in botanical and entomological forensics are not always readily available to assist during investigations. Consequently, the primary objective of this chapter is to acquaint readers with the types of botanical and entomological evidence that may arise in forensic contexts. To support proper handling, we have outlined recommended collection procedures designed for subsequent examination and interpretation by qualified specialists. It is critical that species identification and PMI estimations be conducted by certified forensic botanists, forensic entomologists, or trained plant and insect taxonomists. For additional guidance on field documentation and evidence collection, we have included the following references authored by experts in each respective discipline: *Forensic Botany: Principles and Applications to Criminal Casework* (2nd edition) edited by Heather Miller Coyle (2024a), *Forensic Botany: A Practical Guide* edited by David Hall and Jason Byrd (2012), *Forensic Entomology: An Introduction* (2nd edition) by Dorothy Gennard (2012), *Forensic Entomology: The Utility of Arthropods in Legal Investigations* (3rd edition) edited by Jason Byrd and Jeffery Tomberlin (2019), and *The Science of Forensic Entomology* (2nd edition) by David Rivers and Gregory Dahlem (2022).

DOI: 10.4324/9781315201658-9

FORENSIC BOTANY

Forensic botany is a specialized field of study focusing on the examination of algae, fungi, and plants in relation to forensic investigations (Coyle, 2024b; Hall, 2012a; Hardy and Wallace, 2012: Sanford et al., 2019). Efforts to use scientific botanical evidence in the courts of France were already undertaken by the end of the 19th century, most notably by Edmond Locard, who is credited with the idea that "every contact leaves a trace" (modern forensic scientists refer to this as Locard's exchange principle) (Gibson, 2022). One of the first highly publicized cases in which botanical evidence was presented in a North American courtroom involved the analysis of wood from the ladder used in the kidnapping of Charles Lindbergh Jr., ultimately contributing to the 1935 conviction of Bruno Hauptmann (Gardner, 2004).

Historically, the term ***plant*** has primarily referred to organisms that cannot move voluntarily, have no sensory organs, and generally produce their own nutrients through photosynthesis (Merriam-Webster.com, 2025). However, its usage has also extended more broadly to encompass a diverse array of life forms, fungi, blue-green protists, red, green, and brown algae, diatoms, and certain bacteria (Norris and Bock, 2024). Today, forensic botany encompasses a wide range of plant science subdisciplines, including dendrochronology, limnology, mycology, phycology, palynology, and molecular biology (Coyle, 2024b). Botanical evidence can be encountered at various types of crime scenes, and knowledge of plant locality, seasonality, and life cycles can be instrumental in reconstructing key aspects of a scene or in corroborating, or challenging, a suspect's alibi (Ladd et al., 2024). This field also plays a vital role in clarifying the circumstances of a homicide and identifying those involved (Lane et al., 1990). For example, plant material adhered to clothing or pollen granules found in the respiratory tract may help trace a victim's final movements. If such botanical remains are non-native to the area where a body is discovered, they may suggest the victim's region of origin (Agashe and Caulton, 2010). Determining the PMI is another critical application of forensic botany. Tree root growth through or around remains can indicate how long a body has been in a particular environment (Pokines, 2018; Willey and Heilman, 1987), while the presence of specific seed types may reveal whether, and when, a body was relocated (Gunn, 2019).

Common Sources of Botanical Evidence

The relevance and utility of botanical evidence in forensic investigations largely depend on the nature of the crime and the specific characteristics of the crime scene. Certain types of botanical evidence are relatively straightforward to identify, such as leaves that have been torn or removed during a burial, or broken branches used to conceal a body. In contrast, other forms, like non-native plant materials introduced to the scene or displaced seeds and pollen from nearby vegetation, are more subtle and may require specialized analysis to detect and interpret accurately.

In most cases involving botanical evidence, the plant material is visible to the naked eye and typically does not require magnification for analysis. Such evidence is classified as **macrobotanical** remains. In many instances, human remains lack immediately visible botanical evidence. However, advancements in forensic investigative techniques have led to an increased emphasis on the collection and analysis of **microbotanical** remains. These microscopic plant materials, which are not discernible to the naked eye, require magnification for proper examination (Figure 9.1). While microbotanicals are most commonly recovered during autopsies or in laboratory settings rather than at the scene, it is crucial for investigators to recognize their diverse sources and the valuable information they can yield. Table 9.1 provides a summary of common botanical evidence and its forensic relevance within surface and buried scenes.

Woody Plants

Woody plants have hard, fibrous cells beneath the outer bark layer, and are usually referred to as trees or shrubs (Hall, 2012b). Typically perennial, these plants can live anywhere from a few years to several centuries. Woody plants exhibit a distinctive feature known as **annual secondary growth**, which manifests as **growth rings** within their tissues (Figure 9.2). These rings form due to the gradual reduction in the size of xylem cells as the growing season transitions into dormancy (Willey and Heilman, 1987). At the end of the dormant period, a sudden shift occurs, xylem cells increase in size, creating a visible boundary between growth cycles. This pattern allows the plant to continue increasing in girth, even if its height or length remains unchanged. The number of growth rings reveals the plant's age, while variations in ring width reflect environmental conditions during each year of growth. The scientific study of these patterns is called **dendrochronology**, which involves more than simply counting rings. It also includes comparing ring sequences across different trees or wood samples to draw conclusions about age, origin, and historical climate conditions. As discussed earlier in this chapter, a notable application of dendrochronology occurred during the investigation of the Charles Lindbergh Jr. kidnapping case. Investigators matched the growth ring pattern in the wood used to build a ladder with that of a shortened floorboard found in Bruno Hauptmann's attic, providing critical forensic evidence (Gardner, 2004).

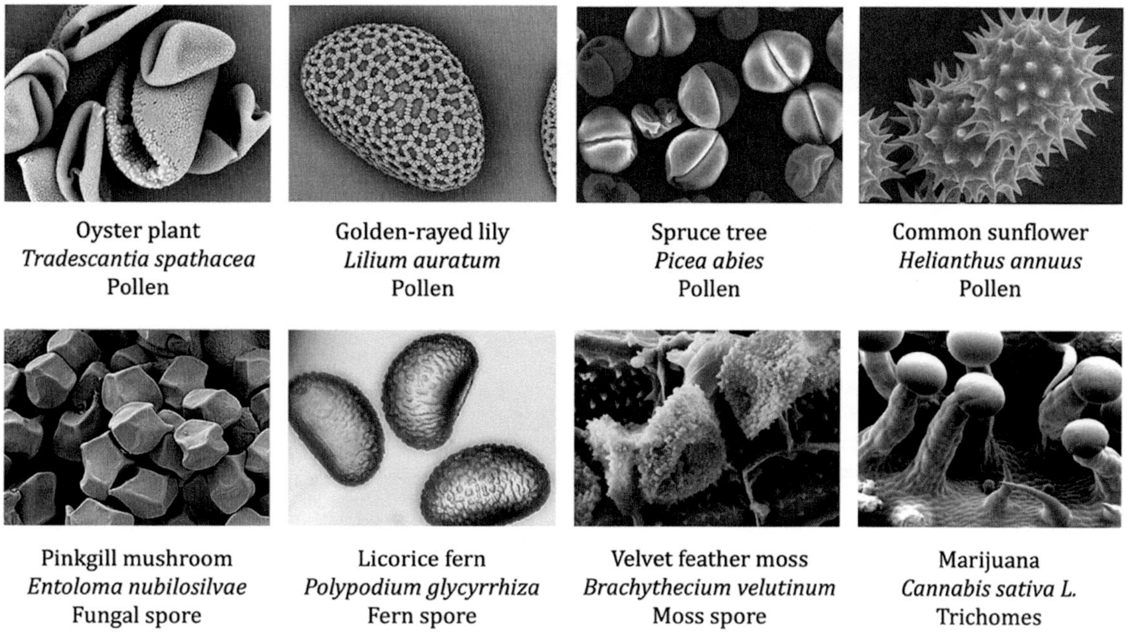

Figure 9.1 Examples of magnified microbotanical remains that are not discernable to the naked eye and are more commonly recovered during autopsies or in a laboratory setting.

Source: Figure 9.1 (top left) https://commons.wikimedia.org/wiki/File:SEM_Tradescantia_spathacea_pollen_0009.jpg;https://creativecommons.org/publicdomain/zero/1.0/

9.1 (top left center) https://en.m.wikipedia.org/wiki/File:Lilium_auratum_-_pollen.jpg;https://creativecommons.org/publicdomain/zero/1.0/

Figure 9.1 (top right center) "Spruce (Picea abies) pollen grains (source: the Biodiversity Unit of the University of Turku, Kari Kaunisto)" by Stephanie Bohlmann et al. (doi.org/10.5194/acp-19–14559-2019) is licensed under CC BY-4.0 International (https://creativecommons.org/licenses/by/4.0/deed.en); cropped for use.

Figure 9.1 (bottom left) "Basidiospores as seen by SEM of Entoloma nubilosilvae (KaiR465, holotype)" by Kai Reschke et al. (doi.org/10.1007/s11557-021-01752-2) is licensed under CC BY-4.0 International (https://creativecommons.org/licenses/by/4.0/deed.en); cropped for use.

Figure 9.1 (bottom left center) "Spores of Polypodium glycyrrhiza (Licorice Fern) under microscope" by Vlisch is licensed under CC BY-4.0 International (https://creativecommons.org/licenses/by/4.0/deed.en); cropped for use.

Figure 9.1 (bottom right center) "Brachythecium velutinum" by Armand Turpel is licensed under CC BY-2.0 Generic (https://creativecommons.org/licenses/by/2.0/deed.en); cropped for use.

Figure 9.1 (bottom right) "Mature stalked-capitate trichomes formed in large numbers" by Zamir Punja, Darren Sutton, and Tommy Kim (doi.org/10.1186/s42238-023-00178-9) is licensed under CC BY-4.0 International (https://creativecommons.org/licenses/by/4.0/deed.en); cropped for use.

Table 9.1 Summary of Botanical Evidence* and Its Forensic Relevance within Surface and Burial Sites

Evidence Source	Forensic Relevance
Whole plant	• Geographical location • Ecological conditions, characteristics, and season • Damage and impressions from tread on shoes or tires • Damage caused by use in concealment of remains or burial • Damage caused by movement (e.g., dragging) of body • Time since damage (level of healing) • Timing of burial or surface placement (e.g., subsequent growth at grave site or through skeletal elements)
Plant leaves	• Geographic location • Ecological conditions, characteristics, and season • Diet and final meal (e.g., digested fragments in gut or feces) • Illegal drug and species trade
Plant roots	• Ecological conditions, characteristics, and season • Timing of burial or surface placement (e.g., damage and subsequent growth around body or through skeletal elements; count of annual growth rings)

(Continued)

Table 9.1 (*Continued*) Summary of Botanical Evidence* and Its Forensic Relevance within Surface and Burial Sites

Evidence Source	Forensic Relevance
Seeds	• Geographic location • Ecological conditions, characteristics, and season • Diet and final meal (e.g., digested fragments in gut or feces) • Cause of death (e.g., poisoning) • Illegal drug and species trade
Pollen	• Geographic location • Ecological conditions, characteristics, and season • Cause of death (e.g., poisoning, allergic reaction)
Wood	• Ecological conditions and characteristics • Time since damage (level of healing) • Tool marks left on stems • Splintering in wounds
Algae and diatoms	• Geographic location • Ecological conditions, characteristics, and season • Cause of death (e.g., drowning, poisoning, allergic reaction)
Mosses and spores	• Geographic location • Ecological conditions, characteristics, and season
Fungi and spores *	• Geographic location • Ecological conditions, characteristics, and season • Cause of death (e.g., poisoning, allergic reaction)
Lichen *	• Geographic location • Ecological conditions, characteristics, and season

Sources: Adapted from Coyle (2024b), Gunn, (2019), and Hall and Byrd (2012)
* Non-plant groups commonly studied by botanists

Figure 9.2 Tree logs exhibiting growth rings on cut ends, which are used in dendrochronology to evaluate age, origin, and historical climate conditions of woody plants and wood materials.

Roots from woody plants can also exhibit growth rings, which may be used to estimate PMI (Willey and Heilman, 1987). When a grave is excavated, surrounding plant roots may be disturbed or damaged but continue to grow. This disturbance often leaves a permanent scar, and the growth rings formed after the scar can indicate the number of growing seasons that have passed since the damage occurred (Quatrehomme et al., 1997). Roots found in direct contact with human remains or personal items can be cross-sectioned at the point of contact to count the growth rings, thereby establishing a minimum PMI. For this method to be valid, the roots must have grown over or penetrated the clothing, bones, or other evidence (Willey and Heilman, 1987). For instance, if a root grew through the nasal opening of a skull (refer to Figure 5.11) and a cross-section revealed five growth rings, the PMI estimate would be at least five annual secondary growth periods. However, the actual PMI could be longer, as it is impossible to determine how much time elapsed before the root began growing into the remains. Another approach involves measuring the annual longitudinal growth of the root, from its point of contact with the remains to its origin in the plant's root system (Quatrehomme et al., 1997. This method requires expert analysis by a forensic botanist familiar with the specific plant species and the geographic region where the remains were found.

Plant Stems and Leaves, Fruits, Flowers, and Seeds

A plant **stem** serves as the main structural axis, supporting leaves, flowers, and fruits while transporting water, nutrients, and sugars between the roots and the rest of the plant (Hall, 2012b). Stems can be herbaceous (soft) or woody and grow through a process called primary growth at their tips. Underground stems may grow upright or parallel to the surface and often contain storage structures known as tubers, such as those found in potato plants. **Leaves** are flattened, green organs specialized for photosynthesis, the process by which plants produce food using sunlight. Their green color comes from a high concentration of chloroplasts, although some leaves are modified into structures like spines or needles. Leaves attach to stems and branches at nodes. If a plant is covered and deprived of sunlight, it will eventually die due to lack of photosynthesis. The emergence of new shoots at the plant's base can indicate a secondary growth phase.

Studies across various species have established typical timelines for new shoot initiation following the removal of stems and leaves. Additionally, the length of these new shoots can define a tertiary time frame. Forensic botanists use these growth stages to estimate PMI by determining minimum time frames for each phase (Norris and Bock, 2024). Genetic analysis techniques, such as DNA barcoding of stems and leaves, can accurately identify plant species, subspecies, or even individual clones, providing a high degree of certainty (Bever et al., 2024).

Many plants flower only once a year, producing fruits and seeds within a limited time frame, which can provide valuable temporal clues when found alongside human remains (Hall, 2012b). **Flowers** typically fall close to their parent plant, and dried or decayed flower fragments can easily adhere to clothing, shoes, or tools. **Fruits** and **seeds** are generally larger, often produced in abundance, and also tend to drop near the parent plant. Many fruits and seeds have protective casings with hooked spines called burs, which cling to passing individuals or animals. When recovering human remains, it is crucial to examine the cuffs of clothing and the seams or welds of shoes carefully, as any attached plant material may carry evidence from a different location. For instance, if remains are found with a shirt bearing numerous small goosegrass (*Galium aparine*) burs on the cuffs and back, but in a location without goosegrass, it suggests the individual was recently in an area where goosegrass was seeding or that the body was moved from elsewhere.

Some fruits and seeds may vanish through animal consumption or germination, yet their casings often remain visible. For instance, Conker, or horse-chestnut trees (*Aesculus hippocastanum*), produce seeds enclosed in a soft, spiky outer casing that easily detaches and falls away (Figure 9.3). If a body is discovered beneath a Conker tree with empty mature casings scattered above, it indicates that the body was present before autumn, the typical season when these seeds drop. Considering the state of the remains, whether decomposing soft tissue or skeletonized, it is possible that casings from multiple years have accumulated. Moreover, if some seeds have germinated over the remains, the growth of the seedlings can help estimate PMI.

Figure 9.3 Seeds (left) from a Conker, or horse-chestnut, tree (*Aesculus hippocastanum*); seedling plants (right) growing on a modern clandestine grave located near a Conker tree in a historic cemetery.

In some cases, a plant's reproductive success relies on its fruit being eaten by animals, with seeds dispersed through their feces. While most fruits are easily digested, the cellulose in leaves or seed casings, such as kaffir lime (*Citrus hystrix*) leaves and watermelon (*Citrullus lanatus*) seeds, is more resistant to gastric breakdown, allowing these parts to pass through the digestive system largely unchanged (Gunn, 2019). When recovering human remains, fecal matter should be meticulously collected, as it may contain undigested remnants of recently consumed foods, which can provide clues about specific cuisines or seasonal dietary habits (Ladd et al., 2024; Norris and Bock, 2024).

Mosses (Bryophytes)

Mosses are non-vascular plants, meaning they lack a specialized system to transport nutrients (Hall, 2012b). With around 12,000 species identified, they form dense, green mats in moist, shady environments across the globe (Gunn, 2019). Mosses have adapted to survive dry periods by entering a dormant state, then rehydrating and resuming growth when moisture returns. Their small, leaf-like structures, called **phyllids**, absorb water directly. Instead of true roots, mosses anchor themselves with thread-like rhizoids. Unlike most plants, mosses do not produce flowers or seeds; they reproduce through spores and clonal reproduction, where fragments can regenerate into new plants. Bryophyte fragments easily cling to clothing, especially shoes, and can remain attached even after hours of walking. Remarkably, bryophyte DNA remains intact over time, enabling DNA profiling long after detachment from the original plant (Merkel et al., 2025).

Pollens

Forensic palynology, a specialized branch of forensic botany, employs **pollen** and **spores** as crucial evidence in legal investigations (Agashe and Caulton, 2009; Milne et al., 2024). Despite its significant potential, forensic palynology is often underutilized or overlooked. Nevertheless, it offers valuable associative evidence that can confirm or refute connections between individuals, locations, and objects (Horrocks et al., 1998; Milne et al., 2024). In addition, it aids in tracing the origins of drugs, food, and merchandise, as well as identifying the use of gardening tools (Agashe and Caulton, 2009; Milne et al., 2024).

Pollen grains are microscopic particles that differ in shape, structure, color, and surface patterns (refer to Figure 9.1). The amount of pollen a plant releases depends on its pollination method. Self-pollinating plants, such as **autogamous** species, produce very few pollen grains and are seldom found in forensic investigations due to their limited quantity (Milne et al., 2024). In contrast, wind-pollinated, or **anemophilous**, plants can release tens of thousands of pollen grains per flower, some equipped with air sacs to aid dispersal (Milne et al., 2024). This abundance creates a "pollen rain" that affects any object in the vicinity. Such pollen is often inhaled and can be detected in the respiratory system during autopsies (Agashe and Caulton, 2009). Cannabis plants (*Cannabis sativa*) are examples of anemophilous species. When cultivated, their pollen spreads across all surfaces and onto the clothing of anyone entering the space (Agashe and Caulton, 2009; Milne et al., 2024) (refer to Case Study #13). Even after removal of the cannabis plants from indoor cultivation sites, their presence can be identified easily by pollen residues found in digital devices, air filters, cracks, crevices, and door hinges (Milne et al., 2024).

Zoogamous, or animal-pollinated, plants release significantly more pollen than autogamous plants, but considerably less than anemophilous plants (Milne et al., 2004). Zoogamous pollen is especially valuable in forensic investigations because its transfer requires direct contact between the plant, an object, a person of interest, or a pollinator. Therefore, a substantial amount of zoogamous pollen found in a forensic sample is unlikely to be due to environmental contamination and can help pinpoint a specific location (Milne et al., 2024). For instance, although dandelions (*Taraxacum* spp.) and foxglove (*Digitalis purpurea*) are morphologically adapted for insect pollination, their pollen typically remains close to the parent plants (Agashe and Caulton, 2009; Wiltshire, 2006). If pollen from both species is detected on a person's clothing, it indicates direct contact with the plants or the surrounding soil. This specificity often allows forensic experts to determine precise locations based on the combination of pollen types found in a sample. Moreover, since many pollens are produced seasonally and can be accurately identified, they hold significant forensic potential. However, forensic palynology has limitations. Identifying some pollen to the species level can be challenging without pollen DNA barcoding (Milne et al., 2024). In addition, some plant species require years to mature and produce pollen, so a pollen profile may not fully represent all plant species present in a suspected area of activity (Milne et al., 2024).

Algae and Diatoms

Algae constitute a vast and diverse group of simple organisms, with over 50,000 known species ranging from single-celled to multicellular forms (Guiry, 2012). The scientific study of algae is **phycology**. While algae are widespread across terrestrial and aquatic ecosystems, a notable subgroup of unicellular algae called **diatoms** is frequently utilized as forensic evidence. Diatoms possess uniquely patterned silica-based cell walls known as frustules. With around 20,000 known species (Guiry, 2012), each diatom species features a distinct frustule design that aids forensic botanists in identification. Diatoms inhabit nearly every water-containing environment, including oceans, seas, lakes, streams, and moist soils. Most thrive in open water, though some form surface films at water-sediment interfaces, such as tidal pools or lakebeds. Their abundance and species composition vary according to factors like temperature, salinity, pH, and nutrient availability.

The presence of individual species or combinations of diatoms or algal growth in forensic samples, whether collected from water sources, soils, or associated clothing, can provide investigators with valuable insights about specific habitats or localities at particular times of the year. This information can shed light on the manner of death, PMI, and potentially link a suspect to a victim or crime scene. For instance, the relative densities of diatoms found in a victim's lungs, stomach, major organs, and bone marrow have been used to suggest drowning as the cause of death (Hürlimann et al., 2000). By comparing diatoms discovered in the victim's tissues during autopsy with those sampled from a suspected water source or recovery site, investigators may obtain corroborative evidence regarding the drowning location (Ludes et al., 1999). For example, finding freshwater diatoms in remains recovered from a marine environment would indicate the victim likely died elsewhere. However, diatoms can also enter tissues due to decomposition during prolonged submersion (Krstic et al., 2002). In addition, diatoms are present in many manufactured products such as insect repellents, foodstuffs, and construction materials. Consequently, diatoms may be inhaled or ingested from these sources and appear in tissues of individuals who died from causes other than drowning (Yen and Jayaprakash, 2007). Even in such cases, information about exposure to specific contaminants or foodstuffs during life can aid investigations. Diatom compositions found in mud and lake soils on clothing, footwear, or vehicles have been used to associate or dissociate suspects with crime scenes (Siver et al., 1994). Moreover, algal growth rates have been proposed as a method to estimate how long remains or related objects have been submerged (Haefner et al., 2004). The presence and density of blue-green algae, or cyanobacteria, have also been studied to estimate the duration bones have been exposed to natural environments (Haglund et al., 1988).

Fungi and Lichens

Fungi constitute a kingdom of vastly diverse organisms, with over 1.5 million species identified worldwide (Stephenson, 2010). Lacking chlorophyll, fungi can thrive in both dry and moist environments and reproduce through microscopic spores that are commonly dispersed by the wind. The scientific discipline dedicated to the study of fungi is known as **mycology**. Most fungi, including mushrooms, toadstools, molds, rusts, and smuts, are multicellular and composed of long, thread-like structures called hyphae. In contrast, yeasts are unicellular fungi characterized by elongated, thin buds known as pseudohyphae (Hall, 2012b).

Most fungi are **saprophytes**, meaning they feed on dead organic matter. They are involved in all stages of human decomposition, from immediately after death to skeletonized or mummified remains (Said al Na'imi, 2008). Some fungal species have been proposed as indicators for locating clandestine graves and estimating PMI (Hitosugi et al., 2006). Although fungal growth on decomposing human remains in outdoor environments has shown promise for PMI estimation, there is ongoing debate about which fungal species should be considered relevant, as factors like geographic location and environmental conditions play a crucial role (Hitosugi et al., 2006; Menezes et al., 2008; Said al Na'imi, 2008). Fungal spores, which are produced in large numbers like pollen, have morphological traits that allow species identification by a forensic botanist (refer to Figure 9.1). Some fungi have very restricted habitats and ecological requirements, dictating the production of spores during certain seasons of the year. The presence of these types of spores may be useful in associating a person with a specific location or crime scene. However, it is important to remember that certain types of blowflies (e.g., *Calliphora*), which often contribute important entomological evidence to PMI estimates, can also distribute fungal spores and, in some instances, may be fungal breeders (Gunn, 2019).

Lichens are unique composite organisms formed through a symbiotic partnership between a fungus and a photosynthetic partner, typically a green alga or cyanobacterium. The fungus constructs the main body of the lichen, offering protection from environmental elements and providing a stable structure. It absorbs water and minerals from rain and the atmosphere. Meanwhile, the alga or cyanobacterium synthesizes nutrients for the fungus via photosynthesis, benefiting from a protected and hydrated habitat in return. This mutually beneficial, self-sustaining relationship enables lichens to thrive in extreme environments where neither organism could survive independently. Although not classified as plants, lichens encompass over 18,000 known species worldwide, exhibiting diverse colors and forms (Gunn, 2019). They reproduce primarily through clonal propagation or spores. Notably, several species have been documented growing on skeletal remains, even in harsh environments like Antarctica (de Albuquerque et al., 2018; Merkel et al., 2025). For instance, *Caloplaca s.l.* and *Lecanora s.l.* frequently colonize bones and hold potential forensic applications, such as estimating PMI through growth-rate analysis (de Albuquerque et al., 2018).

Locating a Forensic Botanist

Locating a forensic botanist can be more challenging than finding professionals in other forensic disciplines, such as archaeology, anthropology, or entomology, each of which typically has a recognized certification board. Forensic botany, by contrast, lacks a standardized credentialing system, making careful selection essential. When selecting a forensic botanist, prioritize candidates with a Ph.D. and substantial expertise in botanical taxonomy and plant identification. Equally important is regional familiarity; a specialist who understands the local flora will be far more effective in forensic investigations tied to specific geographic areas. Most forensic botanists are affiliated with university biology or botany departments. Reaching out to nearby academic institutions is a practical starting point. In addition, archaeology departments may offer referrals to experts who collaborate with cultural resource management firms in your region. Beyond academic institutions, professional botanists may be found through county extension offices, local and state park services, horticulture and forestry companies, and various government agencies. Many specialists also promote their services online. While an Internet search can be helpful, it's crucial to verify credentials and experience, just as you would for any professional.

RECORDING, COLLECTING, AND PRESERVING BOTANICAL EVIDENCE

Although it is ideal for a forensic botanist to oversee the recording, collection, and preservation of botanical evidence, circumstances may not always permit their direct involvement. In such cases, all botanical materials gathered at the scene should be promptly transferred to a qualified expert for identification and analysis to ensure the integrity and usefulness of the evidence.

Comprehensive guidelines for the recording, collection, and preservation of botanical evidence are available in several authoritative sources, including Coyle (2024a) and Hall and Byrd (2012). The procedures outlined in this section are adapted from these sources; however, these references should be consulted for additional procedural detail as needed.

Recording the Scene and Habitat

During the initial site walk-through, it is essential to document general environmental conditions, including wind, humidity, temperature, cloud cover, and precipitation, as well as any other relevant scene-specific observations (refer to Appendix B). At this stage, all vegetation present should be carefully assessed for signs of disturbance that may indicate entry to or exit from the area. This assessment should include detailed notes on any broken branches, flattened grasses, or vegetation that appears displaced. Such damage may result from walking, vehicle movement, or the dragging or carrying of a body, and can help delineate pathways leading to surface deposits or burial sites. Recognizing and interpreting these indicators can expand the defined site boundaries and yield critical insights for investigators. Overview and mid-range view photographs should be taken to capture the broader landscape and any visible disturbances (Figure 9.4). Prior to collecting other types of physical evidence, samples of affected plant material should be gathered from both the approach and exit routes, as well as from the perimeter of the scene.

Next, closely examine vegetation in areas showing signs of disturbed soil or potential burial activity. It is important to understand that plant materials do not need to be **green** and actively growing to be useful. The process of digging a grave inevitably disrupts the surrounding plant life – roots may be severed, stems broken, and foliage displaced. These disturbances can help delineate the boundaries of a grave. As soil is shoveled back to conceal remains, fragmented plant material is often unintentionally mixed in, further altering the natural composition. In addition, efforts to smooth or restore the ground surface, such as raking or scraping, can inflict further damage on nearby plants. All visible signs of plant disruption should be carefully photographed and thoroughly documented for analysis.

Figure 9.4 Mid-range photograph of corn stalks pushed to the side by an individual dragging a body during the process of concealing it in the cornfield.

Before collecting any botanical evidence, its location and condition must be meticulously documented. This should include a concise description of the evidence's placement, physical state, and prevalence at the site. Additional contextual details, such as proximity to flowering plants or shrubs, presence of broken branches, signs of trampling, and nearby vegetation bearing seeds or fruit, should also be noted. Photographs of both the surrounding landscape and the botanical evidence itself must be taken prior to collection. Close-up photographs should be taken during collection of any smaller forms of botanical evidence. For standardized recording, refer to the sample site botanical recording form in Appendix C.

Collecting Botanical Evidence

During sample collection, it is essential to minimize the risk of contamination. All equipment, such as soil corers, screens, sample vials, and collection nets, must be thoroughly cleaned prior to use to ensure the integrity of the specimens. Many microbotanical materials discussed earlier in this chapter are often recovered during autopsy or subsequent laboratory analysis (refer to Case Study #13). Examples include seeds, spines, thorns, pollen, spores, and fine plant hairs, which can easily become embedded in or attached to personal items like jewelry, smartphones and their cases, as well as clothing features such as pockets, cuffs, embroidery, seams, shoelaces, and eyelets. In addition, plant resins and saps from damaged vegetation can cause botanical materials to adhere to garments and footwear. To prevent cross-contamination, it is strongly advised that all personal items, clothing, and footwear belonging to the victim be handled with utmost care during recovery. These items should be immediately bagged and sealed to preserve potential botanical evidence.

Whole Plants, Trees, and Woody Stems

When collecting a tree, branch, or woody stem to document evidence of damage or growth, begin by photographing the specimen in situ to capture its original context. For smaller trees, branches, or stems, take close-up photographs of any damaged ends, fractures, visible sap, or wilted leaf tips to ensure detailed visual records. Whenever feasible, cut branches and woody stems at least 15 cm (6 in) below the point of damage or breakage to preserve the integrity of the sample. For larger trees that cannot be collected in their entirety, remove a section of the trunk with a minimum of 15 cm (6 in) above and below the affected area. This segment should be preserved using the same protocols applied to other large plant samples. In addition, collect representative samples of leaves, fruits, or flowers to aid in species identification. These should be labeled with the same item number as the corresponding trunk or stem section but stored separately to maintain sample clarity and prevent cross-contamination.

Plant Leaves, Mosses, Fruits, Flowers, Seeds, and Roots

Fresh plant materials, including mosses, often contain high amounts of moisture and sugars, which promote the growth of bacteria and fungi, increasing the degradation rates of samples. Under conditions of high heat, complete decomposition of fresh plant remains can occur within two to three days if not packaged properly. Fresh leaves or other smaller-sized samples of vegetation should be placed into individual paper bags that are labeled with the date, time of collection, coordinates of the location, and the case number or investigator's name, and then refrigerated as soon as possible. If plant samples are wet or soaked with decomposition fluids, they should be collected in plastic bags and refrigerated until they can be properly dried using a **botanical field press** (refer to Figure 2.13).

Flowers and seeds can be collected in small paper bags; however, small seeds should first be placed into small paper envelopes that can be sealed to avoid loss or cross-contamination with other collected samples. Fruits are commonly excessively wet samples and will stick to paper or carboard containers. They should be wrapped in waxed paper, which controls leakage of liquids and still allows for drying placed around them, before placing them in paper packaging.

When a root is cut, it may heal over or branch out at the damaged area and continue to grow after it is reburied. Roots with cuts, damage, or regrowth should be traced back to their source plant when possible, as many plants are difficult to identify from roots alone. A sample of the source plant should be collected, and the root should be pruned at a reasonable distance from the damaged or cut area to preserve internal structure. Smaller roots can be placed into paper bags, and if larger, in a carboard box.

Algae and Diatoms

Many algae and diatom species grow in seasonal blooms, which can be short-lived. Therefore, it may be necessary to take sequential seasonal samples from the suspected water source to attempt matching species composition recovered from the remains to a specific locality. In rivers and streams, samples should be taken both above and below the site at which the remains were found as there may be differences in the algal flora and water currents may have moved the remains away from the original site of deposition. In open water sites, such as lakes, samples should be taken from the surface, the shoreline closest to the remains, and near the water bed. Blanks, or sample vials of distilled water, should be prepared in the field and processed to test whether samples collected as evidence are free of contamination and carry over.

Fungi and Lichens

Larger forms of fungi, such as mushrooms or toadstools, located around the grave or surface remains should also be collected in paper bags and transported to a forensic botanist for identification as soon as possible, as the specimen will decay very quickly once removed from their natural environment, especially if they are damp. Smaller fungi, such as molds and rusts, should only be collected from remains by the medical examiner or forensic pathologist. Lichens should not be removed from their substrate, such as skeletal remains or clothing, and instead are collected along with those forms of evidence but also noted as botanical evidence in scene documentation. Fungi and lichen specimens are typically identified microscopically and may need to be cultured, and in some instances, they may also be identified using methods of molecular taxonomy.

Preservation and Storage of Botanical Evidence

Refrigeration during and after field collection can slow the deterioration and decomposition of fresh vegetation samples, but it cannot completely halt these processes. Therefore, all samples should be examined as soon as possible. If samples must be stored for an extended period before examination by a forensic botanist, plant evidence should be kept in a cool, dry area, with each sample separated until fully dry. The drying process is most effective when plants are pressed flat in a botanical field press, with paper layers changed regularly. Most fungi and larger plant remains will dry naturally in cardboard boxes if humidity is low. After drying, individually labeled and bagged samples may be stored in larger cardboard boxes. A few mothballs or a small roll of newsprint can be added to absorb humidity in the larger box. Using mothballs and no-pest strips during drying and storage also helps repel insects that might consume the dried plants.

FORENSIC ENTOMOLOGY

Forensic entomology is the scientific study of insects and their application in forensic investigations. While the term primarily refers to insects, it is occasionally broadened to include other arthropods such as spiders, centipedes, and scorpions (Byrd and Tomberlin, 2019b; Gennard, 2012; Gunn, 2019). The use of entomological evidence in forensic contexts dates back to centuries. The earliest known case originates from 10th-century China (Greenberg and Kunich, 2002). By the 13th century, the significance of insects in death investigations was well established, as evidenced by their inclusion in *Washing Away Wrongs*, a pioneering forensic manual authored by Sung Tz'u (translated by McKnight, 1981). A major leap in forensic entomology occurred in the late 19th century with the publication of *La Faune des Cadavres: Application de l'Entomologie à la Médicine Légale* by Mégnin (1894). This work highlighted the relationship between human decomposition and the predictable succession of insect colonization on corpses, an insight that remains foundational to the field.

Today, a wide range of insect and other arthropod species contribute critical evidence in forensic investigations. These include determining time and season of death, geographic location of death, movement or concealment of remains, physical sites of trauma and sexual violence, and toxicological and DNA analyses (Byrd and Tomberlin, 2019a; Gennard, 2012; Gunn, 2019; de Lourdes Cháves-Briones et al., 2013; Peruch et al., 2024). Forensic entomological analysis is grounded in two principal approaches:

- Insect life-cycle analysis – focusing on developmental stages, which are influenced by environmental factors such as temperature and humidity.
- Successional colonization patterns – focusing on how insects colonize decomposing remains in a generally predictable sequence.

Insect Life Cycle

Accurately identifying and collecting the developmental stages of insects, particularly flies and beetles, plays a crucial role in estimating the number of generations that have occurred, thereby enabling a more precise determination of PMI. Insects undergo metamorphosis, progressing from egg to adult, with each stage marked by distinct physical changes and varying durations. These developmental timelines differ not only between species but also in response to environmental conditions. For instance, elevated temperatures can significantly accelerate early growth stages, shortening the time between transitions. As a result, weather data collection is an essential component of forensic entomology. Controlled laboratory experiments and field studies have established baseline developmental rates across a range of temperatures and environmental settings (e.g., Hwang and Turner, 2005), providing critical reference points for PMI estimation.

Flies (Order Diptera)

Flies undergo a complete metamorphosis during their life cycle (Figure 9.5), progressing through four distinct stages: egg, larva, pupa, and adult. The cycle begins when an adult female deposits clusters of 150–200 **eggs** in moist, sheltered environments near a food source. Over her lifetime, a single female may lay several thousand eggs. These eggs are typically shiny white and measure between 1 and 1.5 mm (0.04 and 0.06 in.) in length (Gennard, 2012). On human remains, eggs are most commonly laid in areas that offer protection and access to nutrients. These include natural orifices such as the nostrils, mouth corners, and eyes; open wounds; folds of clothing near the face or injuries; hair in contact with the ground; and crevices formed where the body meets the ground (Rivers and Dahlem, 2022). These sites often experience accelerated decomposition due to early insect colonization. Within hours of being laid, the eggs hatch into the first of three larval stages, known as **instars**, but more commonly referred to overall as **maggots** (Figure 9.6). Larval size varies with food availability and quality. Typically, first instar **larvae** are under 2 mm (0.08 in) long, second instar larvae range from 2 to 9 mm (0.08 to 0.35 in), and third instar larvae can reach up to 22 mm (0.9 in) in length (Green et al., 2003). During the third instar stage, mature larvae cease feeding and begin migrating away from the remains in search of cooler, darker environments. In outdoor settings, they

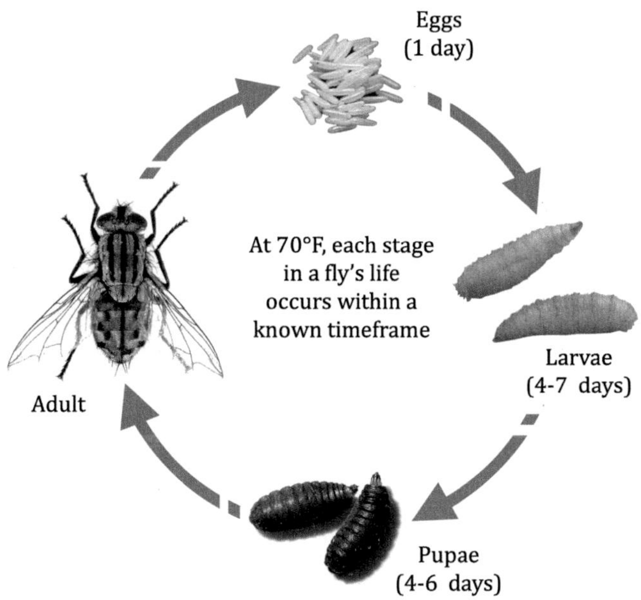

Figure 9.5 Average life cycle of a fly (*Diptera*) in optimum environmental conditions.

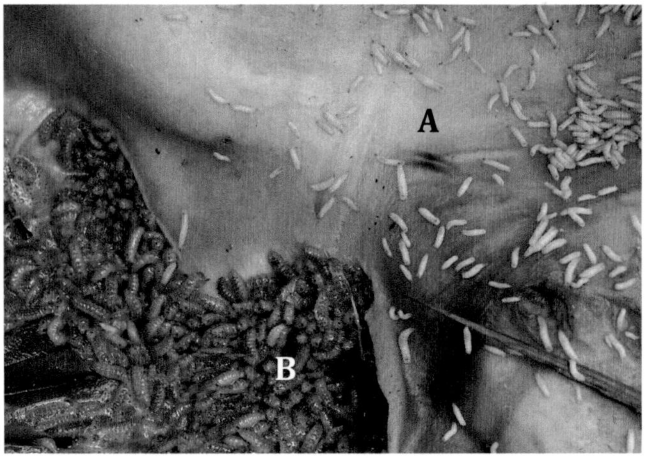

Figure 9.6 Fly larvae (maggots) developing on a decomposing pig cadaver. Different instar stages of development are present: (a) younger larvae, and (b) older larvae.

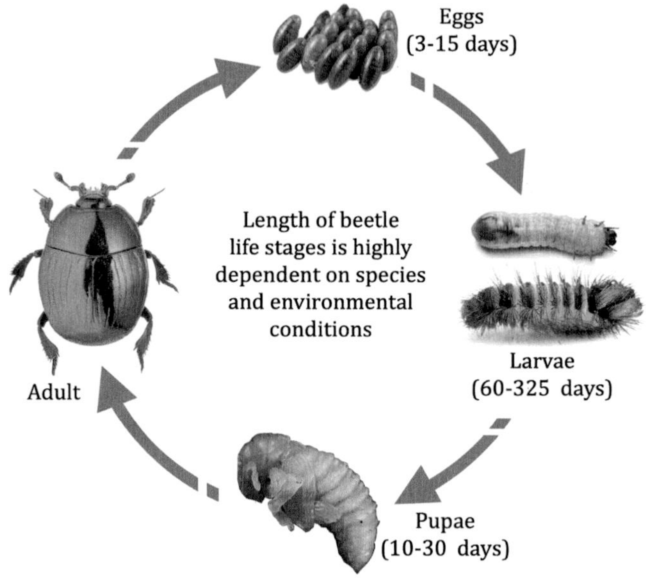

Figure 9.7 Average life cycle of a beetle (*Coleoptera*) in optimum environmental conditions.

may travel as far as 6 m (Gennard, 2012). Once they find a suitable location, such as soil, clothing folds, or beneath floor coverings, they burrow in and enter the pupal stage. Here, their larval exoskeleton hardens into a protective casing called the **puparium**, which gradually shrinks and darkens from brown to reddish brown to nearly black. After several days of development, the **adult** fly emerges from the puparium, often pushing up through the soil and leaving behind the empty case. The cycle then begins anew, as newly emerged females mate and lay eggs on decomposing remains. Under optimal environmental conditions, the entire transformation from egg to adult can occur in just seven to ten days. Adult flies typically live from a few weeks to several months (Gennard, 2012; Gunn, 2019).

Figure 9.8 Fly larva (top) and beetle larva (bottom) are different in many ways. In particular, beetle larvae have pairs of legs and readily visible chewing or pinching mouthparts.

Beetles (Order Coleoptera)

Beetles undergo complete metamorphosis, progressing through four distinct stages: egg, multiple larval instars (which vary by species and environmental conditions), pupa, and adult (Figure 9.7). Their eggs are typically oval or spherical and are often laid in concealed, protected locations to safeguard them from predators and environmental stressors. Beetle larvae, often referred to as **grubs**, are generally hidden from view, commonly residing underground or beneath decomposing organic matter saturated with decomposition fluids. They can be identified by their small legs and a hardened, often darkened head equipped with pincher-like mandibles (Figure 9.8). Larval behavior varies across species: for example, rove beetle larvae are highly mobile and independently forage for food, whereas carrion beetle larvae rely on adult care until they reach maturity (Brundage, 2019; Gennard, 2012). When ready to pupate, beetle larvae burrow into the soil or seek out sheltered areas. Their puparial casings transition from a pale yellowish hue to a darker brown as they develop. Most beetle species reproduce annually, though their life cycles differ significantly. Some, like rove beetles, complete development from egg to adult in just seven to ten days, while others, such as dung beetles, may take up to a year to mature and live an additional two to three years as adults (Brundage, 2019; Gennard, 2012). A notable forensic detail is beetle **frass**, or dry, crumbly, brownish strands of adult beetle feces and masticated materials, which can aid experts in estimating PMI in forensic investigations (Rivers and Dahlem, 2022).

Insects Attracted to Decaying Remains

Numerous insect species are drawn to human remains, where they serve distinct ecological roles: feeding on decomposing tissues, preying on other insects and their larvae, and consuming fecal matter from the body, larger scavengers, or frass produced by the insect colony. Table 9.2 summarizes the insect taxa and additional invertebrates commonly associated with human decomposition and outlines their generally predictable patterns of colonization. While many insects are directly involved in the decay process, others may be incidentally present,

Table 9.2 Summary of Common Insects and Additional Invertebrates Attracted to Human Remains

Common Name	Stage(s) of Decay	Activity
Blow fly	• Fresh through advanced decay	• Lay eggs in early stages • Larvae feed early through advanced
Flesh fly	• Fresh through dry decay	• Lay eggs early through late stages • Larvae feed early through dry
House flies and latrine flies	• Early through advanced decay	• Lay eggs early in wounds or feces • Larvae feed early through advanced
Scuttle fly	• Early through dry decay	• Lay eggs early through late stages • Larvae feed early through dry • Can colonize buried remains
Skipper fly	• Active through dry decay	• Lay eggs active through dry stages • Larvae feed active through dry
Soldier fly	• Advanced through dry decay	• Lay eggs advanced through dry stages • Larvae feed through dry • Can colonize buried remains
Carrion beetle	• Early through active decay	• Lay eggs in early stages • Adults and larvae feed on remains and other insect larvae
Clown beetle	• Early through advanced decay	• Lay eggs early through late stages • Adults feed on other insect larvae and larvae feed on remains and other insect larvae
Rove beetle	• Early through advanced decay	• Lay eggs early through late stages • Adults and larvae feed on remains and other insect larvae
Hide beetles and skin beetles	• Dry decay	• Lay eggs in dry stage • Adults and larvae feed on remains
Wasps	• Fresh through dry decay	• Lay eggs in fly larvae and pupae • Feed on other insects and remains
Ants	• Fresh through dry decay	• Adults feed on remains, other insects and their larvae
Moths	• Dry decay	• Lay eggs in dry stage • Larvae feed through dry
Cockroaches	• Fresh through dry decay	• Adults feed on remains, other insects and their larvae
Termites	• Dry decay and skeletonization	• Adults feed on dry bone tissue
Mites	• Fresh decay	• Adults feed on remains, other insects and their larvae
Snails and slugs	• Fresh through active decay	• Adults feed on remains and larvae of other insects

Note: Insects and other invertebrates may arrive or depart earlier or later depending on individual circumstances of decomposition process.
Source: Adapted from Gunn (2012), Gennard (2012), and Rivers and Dahlem (2022).

trapped in clothing, wrappings, or containers surrounding the body. Some species exhibit limited geographic ranges, are tied to specific habitats, or are active only during certain seasons. These characteristics can provide valuable clues about the location and timing of death. In addition, insects may have antemortem associations with the deceased, particularly in cases involving poor hygiene or unsanitary living conditions. To ensure comprehensive evidence collection and preservation, readers are encouraged to familiarize themselves with the types of insects that colonize human remains and to recognize the various stages of their life cycles. Unless otherwise indicated, the following descriptions are informed by the foundational work of Byrd and Tomberlin (2010b), Gennard (2012), and Rivers and Dahlem (2022).

Detritivores

Detritivores are organisms that derive nutrients by feeding on decomposing organic material. Among them, certain insect species play a crucial role in the breakdown of human remains, which offer a readily accessible food source. These insects swiftly consume soft tissues that degrade easily, thriving in the early stages of decomposition. However, as the nutrient-rich material diminishes, the environment can no longer sustain their rapid reproduction and short life cycles. Below are concise profiles of several common detritivorous insects frequently found in association with human remains. Figure 9.9 illustrates a selection of these taxa.

Blow Fly (Family Calliphoridae)

Blow flies (family Calliphoridae) comprise over 1,900 species distributed globally (Rivers and Dahlem, 2022). They are commonly found near refuse and decaying organic matter, particularly during warmer months. Drawn to decomposing tissues, blow flies are typically the first insects to arrive at a corpse, often within minutes of exposure. Their rapid colonization of fresh or early-stage remains makes them invaluable for estimating PMI. Adult blow flies range from 6 to 14 mm (0.2 to 0.5 in) in length,

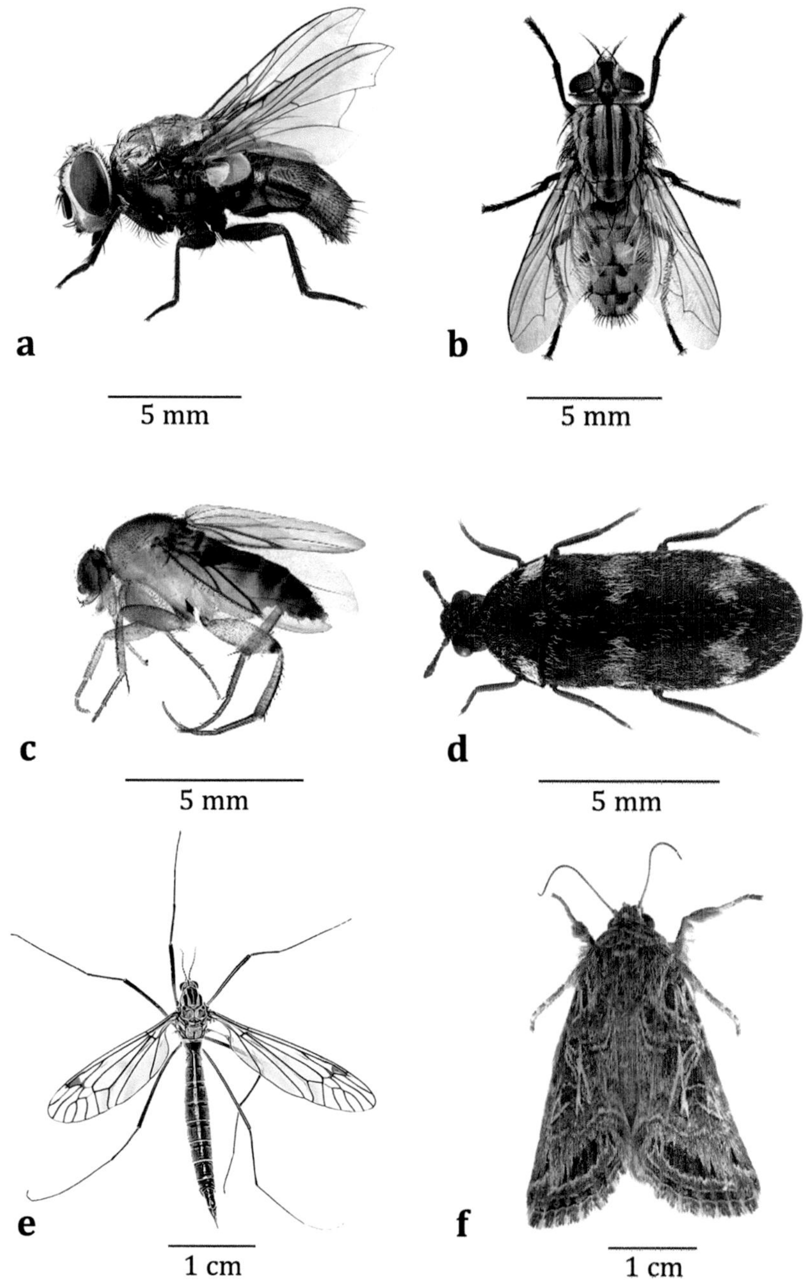

Figure 9.9 Detritivorous insects commonly associated with human remains: (a) green bottle (blow) fly (*Lucilla sericata*), (b) flesh fly (*Sarcophaga* sp.), (c) scuttle fly (*Megaselia scalaris*), (d) zebra carpet beetle (*Megatoma undata*), (e) crane fly (*Trichocera annulata*), and (f) clothes moth (*Tinea pellionella*).

with size influenced by species and nutritional availability during larval development. Most exhibit a striking metallic sheen, typically blue or green, earning them the common names "blue bottle" and "green bottle" flies (Figure 9.9a). Their bristly bodies and prominent reddish eyes are characteristic, though some species may display metallic bronze or glossy black coloration. Females preferentially deposit eggs in natural body openings or sites of trauma, contributing to uneven tissue degradation during decomposition. While adults may feed on desiccated remains, egg-laying requires moist conditions. Notably, some blow fly larvae exhibit predatory or cannibalistic behavior toward other maggots. Mature larvae measure between 8 and 23 mm (0.3 and 0.9 in) with coloration ranging from white or cream to darker grayish-brown. They may also possess distinctive fleshy protrusions along their bodies.

Flesh Fly (Family Sarcophagidae)

Over 3,000 species of flesh flies (family Sarcophagidae) are distributed globally, with the majority inhabiting tropical and temperate regions (Rivers and Dahlem, 2022). Unlike blowflies, flesh flies remain active during wet weather, making them among the earliest insects to colonize human remains. They are frequently observed on decomposing tissue throughout both the initial and advanced stages of decomposition and are commonly found on remains located indoors. Adult flesh flies are medium-sized, measuring between 5 and 18 mm (0.2 and 0.7) in length (Figure 9.9b). They are characterized by their grayish coloration, often marked with dark longitudinal stripes or a distinctive checkerboard pattern on the abdomen, and possess strikingly bright red eyes. A key reproductive distinction from other fly species is that flesh flies are ovoviviparous, meaning they do not lay eggs. Instead, their eggs develop internally and are deposited as first instar larvae directly onto decomposing material. These larvae typically range from white to pale yellow and measure between 3 and 19 mm (0.1 and 0.7 in) in length.

Scuttle Fly (Family Phoridae)

Scuttle flies (family Phoridae) comprise over 4,200 known species worldwide (Rivers and Dahlem, 2022). These small insects range from just 0.5 to 6 mm (0.02 to 0.2 in) in length, allowing them to infiltrate containers and enclosed spaces that typically exclude larger flies such as blowflies. Their distinctive behavior, darting erratically across surfaces when disturbed rather than taking flight, has earned them the common name "scuttle flies." Adult phorid flies exhibit a range of colors, including grayish-brown, blue, and yellow, and are easily identified by their characteristic humpbacked thorax (Figure 9.9c), which also gives rise to the alternate name "humpback flies" (Gennard, 2012). Their larvae are notably flattened and feature a pair of anterior horns.

While some species are predatory or parasitic, the majority thrive in decomposing organic matter, whether of human, animal, or plant origin. Among them, several are colloquially known as "coffin flies," a reference to their association with decaying flesh, including human remains. One particularly remarkable species, *Conicera tibialis*, is capable of burrowing up to two meters into the soil to reach buried corpses (Byrd and Tomberlin, 2019b). These flies can complete multiple generations entirely underground and are often observed congregating on the surface of graves, making them a valuable forensic indicator in locating clandestine burials (Byrd and Tomberlin, 2019b).

Skipper Fly (Family Piophilidae)

Skipper flies (family Piophilidae) are a relatively rare group, with fewer than 100 known species documented worldwide (Rivers and Dahlem, 2022). These insects are typically encountered in forensic contexts during the final stages of active decay, when human remains begin to desiccate. Adult skipper flies measure between 2.5 and 4.5 mm (0.1 and 0.2 in) in length and exhibit a glossy black coloration, which can appear metallic blue or green under certain lighting conditions. Their larvae, reaching up to 10 mm (0.4 in) long, are notably slender compared with the more robust blowfly larvae.

A subset of these species is commonly known as "cheese skippers," named for the remarkable behavior of their mature larvae. These larvae can arch their bodies backward, grasp their posterior with specialized mouth hooks, and then release suddenly, catapulting themselves up to 15 cm (6 in) into the air and nearly double that distance horizontally (Gennard, 2012). This leaping ability is both distinctive and fascinating, making cheese skippers a memorable presence when collecting forensic samples.

Soldier Fly (Family Stratiomyidae)

More than 2,700 species of soldier flies (family Stratiomyidae) have been identified across the globe, with adult specimens typically measuring between 5 and 20 mm (0.2 and 0.8 in) in length (Byrd and Tomberlin, 2019b; Gennard, 2012). These flies are most commonly observed during the late drier stages of decomposition, often colonizing remains after blow fly activity has subsided. Adult soldier flies are strikingly colored and feature prominent dorsal spines, earning them the nickname "wasp flies" due to their resemblance in both appearance and behavior. Soldier fly larvae exhibit considerable variation in size, ranging from 4 to 40 mm (0.2 to 1.5 in). They possess a flattened, segmented body covered in coarse hairs, and their habitat preferences span both aquatic and terrestrial environments, depending on the species. As they mature, the larvae develop a tough, leathery exterior and shift in coloration from gray to brown. These advanced-stage larvae are frequently found on buried remains or within the soil beneath surface deposits (Lord et al., 1994).

Hide, Skin, Carpet, and Larder Beetles (Family Dermestidae)

Dermestid beetles (family Dermestidae), comprising over 1,500 species worldwide (Rivers and Dahlem, 2022), play a notable role in forensic and archaeological contexts due to their ability to cause minor bone modifications in certain cases (Backwell et al., 2022). These beetles are relatively small, measuring between 2 and 12 mm (0.1 and 0.5 in) in length, and typically exhibit an elongated, oval-shaped body. Some adult specimens display striking, colorful patterns across their exoskeleton (Figure 9.9d). Their development is highly sensitive to environmental conditions, with larvae sometimes undergoing more than six instar stages. Known colloquially as "woolly bears," dermestid larvae range from 5 to 15 mm in length and are covered in dense tufts of hair of varying lengths. Their coloration spans shades of brown to black (Gennard, 2012).

Dermestids, such as the hide and skin beetle, are particularly efficient at skeletonizing remains that have begun to desiccate. Larvae are most commonly found during the dry and skeletal stages of decomposition, typically seeking shelter in cavities or recesses away from light. Adults exhibit cannibalistic behavior, consuming their own eggs and larvae as well as those of other species, making it essential to isolate individuals when collecting specimens. A telltale sign of prolonged dermestid activity is the presence of sawdust-like frass, which indicates sustained feeding on tissue. This material is frequently observed on desiccated remains recovered from indoor environments (Byrd and Tomberlin, 2019b; Gennard, 2012).

Winter Crane Fly and Winter Gnat (Family Trichoceroidae)

Approximately 160 species of these cold-adapted insects, commonly referred to as "daddy long leg flies," are distributed across the globe (Rivers and Dahlem, 2022). Winter crane flies and gnats are typically found in damp or frigid environments and are most active during the colder months, including winter. Adult males are often observed swarming in dense clouds over open landscapes, particularly in the late afternoon sunlight. Due to their delicate appearance, they are frequently mistaken for mosquitoes. These adults possess slender bodies measuring up to 12 mm (0.5 in) in length, supported by fine, spider-like legs and adorned with long, translucent wings (Figure 9.9e). Their reproductive cycle begins in decaying organic material, where females deposit their eggs. Remarkably, some species have been documented colonizing human remains in conditions too cold for other insects to remain active (Erzinçlioğlu, 1980). The larvae are elongated and thread-like, distinguished by their well-developed heads and ability to thrive in low-temperature environments.

Meal and Clothes Moths (Family Pyralidae and Tineidae)

Adult meal (e.g., *Aglossa caprealis*) and clothes (e.g., *Tinea pellionella*; Figure 9.9f) moths and their larvae are occasionally found in association with fully desiccated or skeletonized human remains (Rivers and Dahlem, 2022). These insects feed primarily on keratin-rich materials such as hair and nails, as well as any residual dried tissue still clinging to bone. Under certain environmental conditions, the larval stage may persist for up to four years. Upon reaching maturity, the larvae typically construct a protective silken cocoon in which they undergo pupation.

Cockroaches and Termites (Order Blattodea)

Cockroaches are social insects, typically measuring between 10 and 90 mm (0.4 and 3.5 inches) in length and possessing a distinctive flattened body shape. Upon hatching, the nymph closely resembles the adult form but lacks wings. It undergoes several molts before reaching maturity, at which point it develops fully functional wings. These insects are predominantly tropical and nocturnal, emerging at night to scavenge for food. Most species are omnivorous and will consume nearly any organic material that doesn't escape quickly enough, including other cockroaches and insect larvae. They are known to begin feeding on dead organisms almost immediately after death. In forensic contexts, cockroach activity can complicate wound analysis. Postmortem feeding may leave marks that are initially invisible but become apparent as the skin dries. Lesions on the face, neck, and hands can resemble injuries sustained before death, potentially leading to misinterpretation during examinations.

Termites are predominantly tropical insects, though some species have adapted to temperate climates, including parts of southern Europe. Typically small in size, they range from 4 to 15 mm (0.1 to 0.6 in) in length. Despite being commonly referred to as "white ants" because they are pale or translucent, termites are not closely related to ants and belong to the same distinct order as cockroaches. These social insects thrive in dark, humid environments, which provide ideal conditions for colony formation and nesting. While termites are best known for their wood-feeding habits, all species consume a variety of plant materials, including paper and fungi. Their diet also extends to other insects, such as ants, and even deceased members of their own colony, allowing them to recycle nitrogen and other essential nutrients. Remarkably, termites exhibit **osteophagic** behavior, meaning they consume bones. This trait is relatively common and not confined to any particular taxonomic group (Huchet et al., 2011). Evidence of termite activity often includes characteristic "mud trail" tunnels, constructed from a mixture of chewed material, saliva, and fecal matter. Damage to bones is typically marked by small, star-shaped indentations and holes on the cortical surface, which lead into tunnels carved through the nutrient-rich cancellous bone. In tropical regions, where decomposition and skeletonization occur rapidly, termites can significantly alter skeletal remains. Their impact is observed in both contemporary forensic investigations and ancient archaeological contexts (Queiroz et al., 2016).

Coprophiles

Coprophiles are organisms that consume fecal matter, either their own or that of other species. Among insects, dung beetles are notable for relying primarily on feces as a food source. However, most coprophilous insects also utilize other forms of decomposing organic material in their diet. These insects typically colonize human remains when clothing is soiled at the time of death or when internal contents are exposed due to trauma or advanced decomposition. Figure 9.10 illustrates two coprophilous species frequently found in association with human remains.

House and Latrine Flies (Family Muscidae and Fanniidae)

Over 5,400 species within these families of flies are distributed globally and exhibit a strong affinity for human environments (Rivers and Dahlem, 2022). These flies

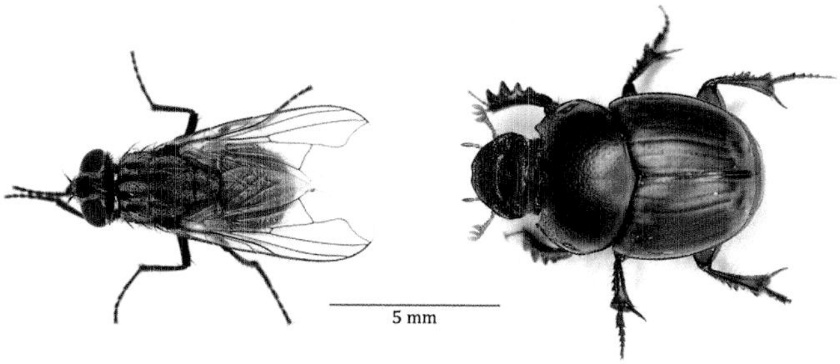

Figure 9.10 Coprophagous insects commonly found in association with human remains: common house fly (*Musca domestica*) (left), and gazelle dung beetle (*Digitonthophagus gazella*) (right).

are opportunistic feeders, consuming decaying plant and animal matter, feces, and blood. They are frequently encountered near garbage, sewage, and other unsanitary conditions, and are particularly attracted to human remains, especially when clothing is soiled with urine or feces, or when internal organs are exposed.

Adult house and latrine flies are typically small, measuring between 3 and 10 mm (0.1 to 0.4 in) in length (Figure 9.10). They are dull gray in color, often marked with darker longitudinal stripes along the thorax. Their development is temperature-dependent, and under optimal warm conditions, they can complete their entire life cycle, from egg to adult, in as little as six to eight days. The larvae are pale in color, ranging from white to cream or yellow, and grow to lengths of 5–12 mm (0.2–0.5 in). They possess flattened bodies with small projections that aid in floating through semiliquid substrates. As they mature, the larvae migrate to drier areas to pupate, often burrowing into fluid-saturated soil beneath or around decomposing remains. Notably, some larval species exhibit predatory behavior, feeding on the eggs and larvae of other insects.

Dung Fly (Family Scathophagidae)

Over 400 species of dung flies (family Scathophagidae) have been identified, with the vast majority inhabiting the Northern Hemisphere (Rivers and Dahlem, 2022). These flies are drawn to ammonia, which is present in urine and feces on soiled clothing and is also released during the decomposition of organic remains. Adult dung flies measure approximately 7–10 mm (0.3–0.4 in) in length and are typically reddish or yellowish in color, distinguished by their hairy bodies. When laying eggs, female dung flies tend to avoid depressions, instead favoring elevated surfaces. The eggs hatch into predatory larvae that consume both dung and the larvae of other insects. As they mature, these larvae burrow into dung, decaying matter, or soil to pupate. Adult dung flies continue their predatory behavior, feeding on other fly species.

Scavenger Fly (Family Sepsidae and Scatopsidae)

Scavenger flies, commonly known as "waggle flies," comprise over 630 species distributed across the globe (Rivers and Dahlem, 2022). These small insects measure just 3.5–5 mm (0.1–0.2 in) in length and exhibit a glossy appearance in shades of black, purple, or red. Their resemblance to flying ants often leads to misidentification, especially as they characteristically wave their wings outward while walking, a behavior that inspired their colloquial name. Drawn to dung and decomposing organic matter, scavenger flies frequently appear in large numbers during the active stages of decomposition. Their larvae, equally small at 3–6 mm (0.1–0.2 in) long, thrive in these nutrient-rich environments, contributing to the breakdown and recycling of organic material.

Dung Beetle (Family Scarabaeidae and Geotrupidae)

Dung beetles, also known as scarab beetles or *tumblebugs*, comprise over 8,000 species distributed across the globe (Cooter and Barclay, 2006; Rivers and Dahlem, 2022). These insects are renowned for their distinctive behavior of shaping dung or decaying organic matter into compact spheres. These balls serve dual purposes: as nourishment for adults and as brood chambers for developing larvae.

Species commonly found in association with human and animal remains (e.g., *Onthophagus hecate*) typically exhibit a dull black coloration and possess a robust, rounded body form, measuring approximately 1–2.5 cm (0.4–1.0 in) in length (Figure 9.10). Although less frequently encountered, some iridescent green species have also been documented in such contexts (Byrd and Tomberlin, 2019b). Male beetles of certain species may feature prominent anterior horns in addition to strong pincers. Females deposit their eggs within a prepared dung ball, providing a secure environment for the larvae. These larvae are plump, white-bodied with brown heads, and characteristically curled into a C-shape. Pupation typically occurs within the dried dung or other desiccated organic material, completing the beetle's life cycle.

Scavengers and Parasitoids

As decomposition progresses, early colonizers like detritivores and coprophiles are gradually replaced by **scavenger** insect species with longer life spans and lower reproductive rates. These later-stage invaders excel at scavenging, frequently consuming the larvae of other insects along with any residual human tissue. In contrast, **parasitoid** insects follow a more specialized strategy: they deposit their eggs within the bodies or pupae of other insects, allowing their larvae to consume the host from within as a nutrient source. Figure 9.11 illustrates several scavengers and parasitoids commonly associated with the insect succession on decomposing human remains. Given the sensitive and biologically active nature of their feeding behavior, this group of insects should be carefully isolated during live field collection to preserve the integrity of samples for forensic analysis.

Rove Beetle (Family Staphylinidae)

With over 63,000 known species, rove beetles (family Staphylinidae) represent one of the largest beetle families in the world (Rivers and Dahlem, 2022). Commonly referred to as "devil's coach horses," these beetles are frequently drawn to human remains during active decomposition, where they feed on fly larvae. Interestingly, while adult beetles thrive in moist environments, their larvae tend to prefer drier conditions. Adults range in size from 1 to 35 mm (0.04 to 1.4 in), though most measure between 2 and 8 mm (0.08 and 0.3 in), and are characterized by their slender, elongated bodies (Figure 9.11c). Their coloration varies widely, typically spanning yellow, reddish brown, and black. Agile and fast-moving, they are also capable fliers. When threatened, some species arch their abdomens over their backs in a display that mimics a scorpion's posture, giving them an intimidating appearance (Gennard, 2012). In addition, they can release a pungent, unpleasant odor as a defense mechanism. The larvae are similarly slender and pale, with darkened heads, and are known to be predatory, often feeding on the larvae of other insects.

Carrion Beetle (Family Silphidae)

Carrion beetles, comprising over 210 species globally, possess an extraordinary ability to detect dead organisms from considerable distances (Rivers and Dahlem, 2022). They are among the earliest insects to arrive at human remains, often appearing within 24 hours of death (Byrd and Tomberlin, 2019b). Most carrion beetles are typically large and robust, most often measuring between 10 and 35 mm (0.4 and 1.4 in), and are distinguished by their flattened bodies adorned with vivid yellow, orange, or red markings, though some species are entirely black (Figure 9.11d and e). Also referred to as "burying beetles" (e.g., *Nicrophorus marginatus*), adults exhibit a unique behavior: they chew and bury fragments of decomposing tissue, creating a nutrient-rich site where females lay their eggs. In some cases, females carve shallow depressions directly into the tissue to house their eggs and the developing larvae. Remarkably, adult beetles provide parental care, guarding and nurturing their offspring through the early larval stages. Larvae, which grow to lengths of 15–30 mmm (0.6–1.2 in), feed exclusively on decaying organic matter. Adult carrion beetles, however, are more opportunistic. They consume both decomposing remains and larvae, including those of blowflies. This predation can significantly impact blowfly populations, altering larval abundance and instar distribution (Gennard, 2012).

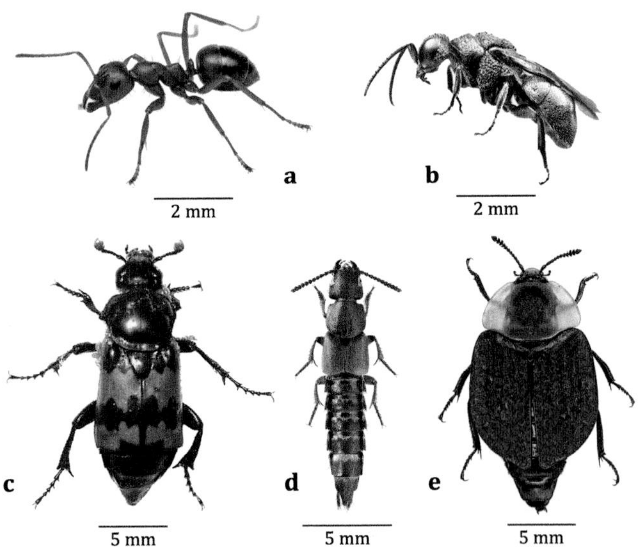

Figure 9.11 Scavenger and parasitoid insects commonly found in association with insect colonization of human remains: (a) red imported fire ant (*Solenopsis invicta*), (b) parasitoid wasp (*Colotrechnus* sp.), (c) rove beetle (*Platydracus latebricola*), (d) common burying beetle (*Nicrophorus marginatus*), and (e) American carrion beetle (*Necrophilia americana*).

Clown Beetle (Family Histeridae)

Clown beetles, with over 4,100 known species distributed across the globe, are remarkably adaptable and can thrive in nearly any environment (Rivers and Dahlem, 2022). These beetles are typically small and rounded, measuring just 10 mm (0.4 in) in length, and exhibit a glossy black or metallic green sheen. They are frequently encountered on actively decomposing remains, often arriving several days after blowflies have colonized the site. Both adult clown beetles and their larvae are nocturnal, commonly sheltering beneath remains during daylight hours. When threatened or disturbed, many species exhibit thanatosis (feigning death as a defensive behavior). Notably, clown beetles are voracious predators and exhibit cannibalistic tendencies. Adults primarily consume other beetles and fly larvae, while the larvae target fly maggots and puparia as their main food sources.

Wasps and Ants (Order Hymenoptera)

Adult social wasps (family Vespidae) are known to scavenge tissue from human remains and actively prey on the eggs and larvae of other insects (Rivers and Dahlem, 2022). Their own larvae are carnivorous, nourished with prey items collected and delivered to the nest by adult foragers. Adult parasitoid wasps (family Pteromalidae), such as *Colotrechnus* sp. (Figure 9.11b) and *Nasonia vitripennis*, exhibit a specialized reproductive strategy: females deposit their eggs by penetrating the puparia of blowflies (Grassberger and Frank, 2003). Upon hatching, the wasp larvae consume the developing fly pupa, complete their own pupation within the host's puparium, and eventually emerge as adults. Notably, *N. vitripennis* targets blowfly pupae that are precisely 24–30 hours old, making its developmental timeline a potentially valuable indicator for estimating PMI in forensic investigations (Grassberger and Frank, 2003).

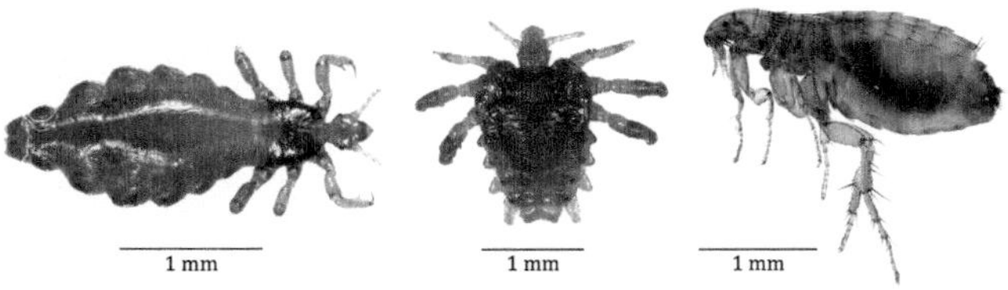

Figure 9.12 Ectoparasites, such as a human head louse (*Pediculus humanus capitis*), a human pubic louse (*Pthirus pubis*) (center), and a human flea (*Pulex irritans*) (right) may be associated with human remains or encountered at various sites in a forensic context.

Source: Figure 9.12 (left and center) "Pediculus humanus capitis, Pthirus pubis" by Yi-Tan Fu et al. (doi.org/10.1186/s40249-022-00986-w) is licensed under CC BY-4.0 International (https://creativecommons.org/licenses/by/4.0/deed.en); cropped for use.

Ants (family Formicidae), comprising over 12,000 described species, inhabit nearly every terrestrial ecosystem on Earth, with the notable exception of Antarctica (Rivers and Dahlem, 2022). In tropical regions, fire ants (Figure 9.11a) and acrobat ants frequently dominate the insect fauna found on human remains across all stages of decomposition. Their presence can significantly delay blowfly colonization, typically by three to four days, due to their active predation on fly eggs and early instar larvae (Wells and Greenberg, 1994). Paradoxically, while these ants suppress blowfly activity, they may simultaneously accelerate decomposition by consuming soft tissues directly. However, this effect is species-dependent; not all ants are carnivorous or interact with remains in a way that influences decomposition. Accurate species identification is therefore essential in forensic contexts. Interestingly, certain scuttle flies (family Phoridae), which are natural predators of fire ants, may be drawn to decomposing remains specifically because of ant activity, adding another layer of ecological complexity to the decomposition process (Rivers and Dahlem, 2022).

Ectoparasites

Ectoparasites, or external parasites that inhabit and feed on the surface of their host, are frequently encountered in forensic investigations (Gunn, 2019). Among the most common are fleas and lice (Figure 9.12). Humans may carry a small number of fleas, typically acquired from domestic animals such as dogs and cats (e.g., *Ctenocephalides canis* and *C. felis*). However, significant infestations are generally indicative of neglect or poor hygiene. Body and head lice (*Pediculus humanus*) are more prevalent and often associated with close physical contact, including sexual activity. Notably, fleas and lice tend to abandon a host shortly after death, as the body cools. Therefore, the presence of live ectoparasites in a decedent's hair or clothing strongly suggests a brief PMI. It is also important to recognize the potential of these parasites to serve as vectors for disease, which warrants caution during collection and examination.

Additional Invertebrates as Forensic Indicators

Additional invertebrates not typically involved in the decomposition process may become associated with a body. When such invertebrates often possess limited geographic ranges, are tied to specific habitats, or are active only during certain seasons, their presence can offer valuable clues about the individual's location and the time of death. They also carry significant potential to mislead interpretations of insect colonization patterns and complicate the assessment of perimortem trauma in victims.

Gastropods

Gastropods, such as snails and slugs, have been documented consuming and altering the tissue of freshly deceased or decomposing corpses (Figure 9.13) (Baumjohann and Beneke, 2022). Notably, the decollate snail (*Rumina decollata*) is a predatory, omnivorous species that actively hunts and consumes other snails, yet it also scavenges carrion. Marine-dwelling *Nassarius* snails (e.g., *Nassarius consensus*) inhabit sandy soils and feed on decomposing organic material such as carrion and decaying food remnants. Among terrestrial slugs, the leopard slug (*Limax maximus*) and various red and black slugs (genus *Arion*) are particularly known for consuming dead animal tissue and even other slugs.

These gastropods introduce a potential variable in PMI estimations based on the size and developmental stage of blowfly eggs and larvae as they also consume insect eggs and larvae. They feed by scraping soft tissue with their radula, initially creating small abrasions. However, as feeding continues, the repeated rasping action, combined with the mechanical properties of the decomposing

Figure 9.13 Slugs colonizing, consuming, and altering the tissues of a decomposing pig. Note the mass of fly eggs located across the pig's snout and face, which are also being disturbed by the slugs' activity.

Source: Figure 9.13 "Preference for cadaver tissue by snail" by Kristina Baumjohann and Mark Benecke (doi.org/10.3390/forensicsci2040054) is licensed under CC BY-4.0 International (https://creativecommons.org/licenses/by/4.0/deed.en); cropped for use.

tissue, can enlarge these defects, sometimes resulting in distinct holes. The morphology of these feeding marks is highly variable and can easily be misinterpreted as signs of trauma. In particular, abrasions and holes caused by snail or slug activity may resemble injuries from physical assault, especially in regions such as the head and neck where scratch-like patterns are common.

Terrestrial Earthworms (Family Lumbricidae)

Earthworms are a remarkably diverse group of terrestrial detritivore invertebrates. Over 3,000 species have been identified worldwide, yet taxonomic family groups often possess very limited geographic ranges (Gunn, 2019). Although earthworms may appear similar at first glance, they occupy distinct ecological niches and are classified into three functional groups:

- Epigeic species (e.g., *Eisenia fetida*) live in surface layers such as leaf litter and manure, thriving in environments rich in organic matter. They do not burrow into the soil.
- Endogeic species (e.g., *Octolasion cyaneum*) tunnel horizontally through the soil, feeding on its organic content. These worms do not create permanent burrows.
- Anecic species (e.g., *Lumbricus terrestris*) construct deep, vertical burrows and emerge at night to pull surface debris into their tunnels for nourishment.

Earthworms, particularly epigeic and endogeic species, are known to feed on decomposing animal remains, frequently ingesting insect larvae in the process (Curry and Schmidt, 2007). Like gastropods, the presence of terrestrial earthworms among decomposing remains can introduce an additional variable that complicates PMI estimations. However, earthworms are highly sensitive to changes in soil chemistry, particularly pH, and tend to avoid areas contaminated by acidic runoff.

Mites

Mites (superorder Acariformes) are not insects, but rather tiny **arachnids** (eight-legged arthropods) closely related to spiders and ticks. Typically, mites possess a rounded body and short legs. During their larval stage, they have three pairs of legs, while adults develop four pairs. Although this pattern is common, exceptions do exist. Unlike insects, mites lack wings, and their minute size restricts their ability to travel independently over long distances. They are frequently found in large numbers on decomposing bodies. This widespread presence is largely due to their phoretic behavior: many mite species hitch rides on other organisms, particularly flies, to reach new food sources. Once their host arrives at a suitable site, the mites disembark to feed and reproduce.

Mites colonize corpses throughout all stages of decomposition, from the fresh phase to the final skeletal remains. Their ecological roles vary: some species consume the decaying tissue itself, others prey on detritivores, and some feed on fungi and microbes that flourish on the body. As decomposition progresses, the composition of mite colonies shifts, with different species dominating at different stages. This dynamic succession makes mites valuable indicators of the decay timeline. Because mite development is influenced by environmental conditions, researchers can estimate their time of arrival on a body, which in turn helps determine PMI. Mites are particularly useful in forensic investigations involving buried remains, where insect activity may be limited due to soil depth and conditions. In such cases, mites can provide critical clues about the timing and progression of decomposition (Rai et al., 2021).

Locating a Forensic Entomologist

If a forensic entomologist is unavailable during the recovery of remains, it is critical to locate one for subsequent analysis of collected entomological evidence. The selected expert should hold a Ph.D. and possess substantial experience in the taxonomic identification of insects and arthropods relevant to forensic investigations. Regional expertise is also essential, as familiarity with local species enhances accuracy. Ideally, the entomologist should be academically active, a member of the American Academy of Forensic Sciences, affiliated with the Entomological Society of America (ESA), and certified by the **American Board of Forensic Entomology (ABFE)**. There are currently 18 board-certified forensic entomologists in North America. A complete list of diplomates and members, including contact details, is available on the ABFE website (https://forensicentomologist.org/#members). To locate a forensic entomologist practicing outside of North America or who is familiar with the entomology of various geographic regions of the world, the website of the European Association for Forensic Entomology (EAFE; https://eafe.online/) has a list of regular members working throughout Europe and many associate members working throughout the world.

RECORDING, COLLECTING, AND PRESERVING ENTOMOLOGICAL EVIDENCE

The collection of entomological evidence must adhere to standardized procedures across all death scenes, regardless of environmental variability. Upon receiving authorization from the lead investigator, the remains should be examined systematically, ensuring that all evidence is gathered in coordination with the crime scene unit or designated evidence officer. Comprehensive guidelines for the collection and preservation of entomological evidence are available in several authoritative sources, including Gennard (2012), Sanford et al. (2019), and Rivers and Dahlem (2022). These references should be consulted for additional procedural details as needed. The procedures outlined in this section are adapted from Amendt et al. (2015) and Sanford et al. (2019).

The documentation and collection process typically follows eight systematic steps (Figure 9.14), which are applicable across a wide range of geographic regions and habitats:

1. Record the scene and habitat by documenting key environmental features such as vegetation, water sources, soil composition, and landscape characteristics.
2. Assess insect colonization by observing and recording insect activity on the remains and in the immediate vicinity.
3. Gather environmental information by collecting relevant site-specific climate data including temperature, humidity, and other ecological variables.
4. Sample adult insects by collecting adult flies, beetles, and other relevant species found on or near the remains.
5. Sample insects in immature stages by retrieving eggs, larvae, and pupae directly from the remains for analysis.
6. Assess surrounding insect migration by retrieving larvae and pupae found on or near the remains.
7. After the remains are removed, gather additional insect specimens and soil samples from the site.
8. Package all collected specimens appropriately for delivery to a forensic entomologist.

When working with buried remains, it is important to recognize that the process allows for a degree of flexibility. To ensure thorough documentation, refer to the recording forms provided in Appendix C, which are designed to capture scene details, environmental conditions, and specimen data. This form should be completed progressively, aligning with each step of the recovery and sampling process.

In addition to the recording forms, prepare a set of pre-printed paper and self-adhesive labels to accompany

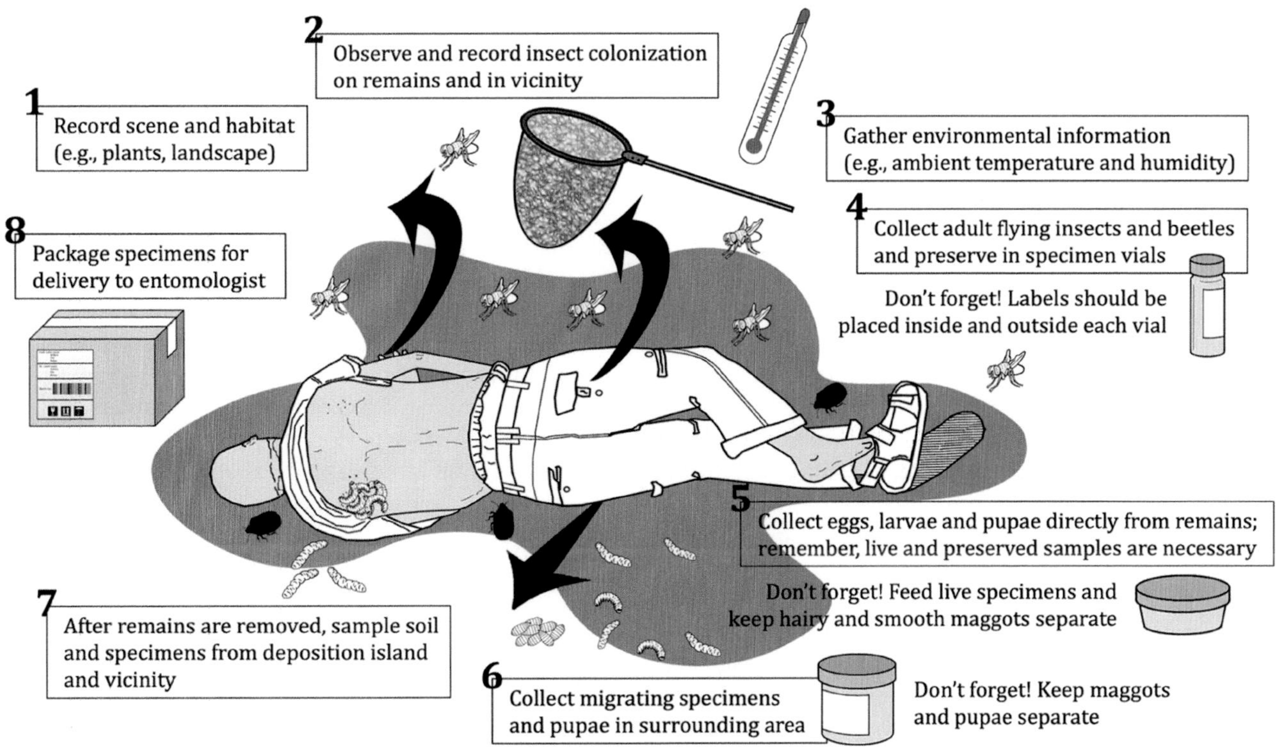

Figure 9.14 Illustration of the basic steps required in documenting and collecting entomological evidence.

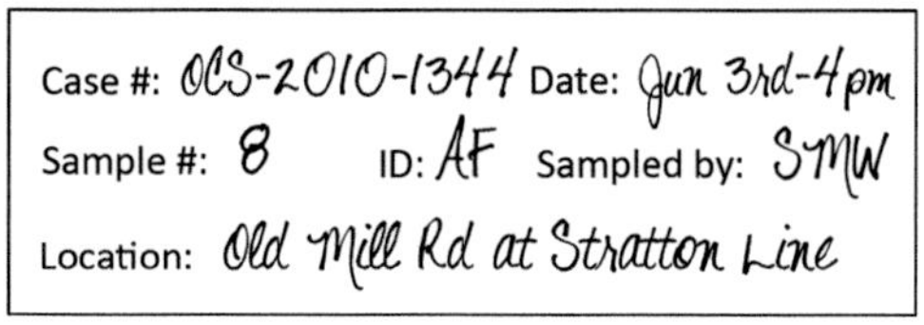
Case #: OCS-2010-1344 Date: Jun 3rd-4pm
Sample #: 8 ID: AF Sampled by: SMW
Location: Old Mill Rd at Stratton Line

Figure 9.15 Example of a pre-printed label used to identify each collected entomology sample.

every sample collected. Each label must clearly display the sample number and identifier, date and time of collection, scene location, case number, and the name of the individual responsible for collecting the sample (Figure 9.15). Adopt a double-labeling protocol as standard practice. Place one label inside the sample container (e.g., jar, vial, plastic container, or cardboard box) alongside the specimen, and affix the second, self-adhesive label to the exterior of the container or sample bag. This redundancy ensures that critical information remains intact even if the outer label is damaged or lost. To maintain legibility, all labels should be completed using pencil, as ink is prone to smearing or dissolving when exposed to the chemical solutions commonly used for killing and preserving entomological specimens.

Recording the Scene and Habitat

The first step in forensic entomological analysis involves a thorough visual survey of the scene and detailed documentation of the habitat where the remains are found. This foundational information is critical – it enables the forensic entomologist to assess which insect species should naturally occur in the environment, identify any unusual or unexpected species, and evaluate whether local vegetation might inhibit insect activity or development. Key elements of habitat documentation include:

- A general description of the site
- Presence of nearby water sources
- Types and density of vegetation
- Slope and composition of the groundcover
- Whether the remains are wrapped, buried, or otherwise concealed.

Current weather conditions (e.g., sunlight, shade, rain, or snow) must also be recorded, as these factors influence insect behavior and colonization patterns. Overview photographs should be taken in a full 360° sweep around the remains, beginning from the north compass reading to ensure consistent orientation. Overhead mid-range photographs of the remains are also used to document exposure to direct sunlight. However, these should be taken later in the process (i.e., immediately prior to collection) to minimize disruption to the insect colony. Scene personnel must take care not to cast shadows over the remains, as abrupt changes in lighting can startle insects and cause them to scatter, potentially compromising the integrity of the entomological evidence.

Assessing Insect Colonization

Once the overall scene has been thoroughly documented, attention should shift to the extent and distribution of insect activity. Initial documentation should be conducted from a distance, adhering to the previously outlined safety protocols. When approaching the remains, plastic stepping plates, if available, should be used to minimize contamination and preserve the integrity of the site.

Written records should detail the types of insects observed and their relative abundance. These notes must be supported by close-up and mid-range photographs, taken with a photographic scale to aid forensic entomologists in accurately identifying and sizing the specimens. While video may seem useful, Sanford et al. (2019) caution against relying on it as the primary visual record due to its typically low resolution. Instead, digital still photography is preferred for its ability to capture fine detail and close-up imagery, which is essential for evaluating entomological evidence.

Collecting Climate Data

Accurate climate data are crucial when estimating PMI using entomological evidence. Environmental factors such as temperature and humidity significantly influence the developmental timeline of insect species commonly found at death scenes. While current climate conditions at the scene provide a baseline, it is equally important to collect additional ambient air and ground temperature and humidity data from the recovery site over the three to five days following the body's discovery. After establishing a PMI estimate, investigators should also obtain historical climate records, specifically from one to two weeks prior to the estimated time of death, by downloading data from the nearest National Weather Service station (NWS; http://www.weather.gov).

The following environmental measurements should be systematically recorded to support forensic analysis of entomological evidence:

- Ambient air temperature and humidity is measured using a hand-held digital temperature and humidity meter at two heights near the remains: 30 cm (1 ft) and 1.3 m (4 ft).
- Ground surface temperature is measured by placing a digital bimetal probe thermometer directly on the surface ground cover.
- Body-ground interface temperature is measured by carefully sliding a digital bimetal probe thermometer between the underside of the remains and the ground surface.
- Body temperature is measured by placing a digital bimetal probe thermometer directly on the remains, preferably at the upper thoracic, pelvic, and knee regions.

- If visible, larval mass temperature is measured by inserting a digital bimetal probe thermometer into the center of each larval mass to capture internal temperature.
- After remains are removed, soil temperature is measured directly beneath the body at a depth of approximately 5 cm (2 in) and at a distance of 1–2 m (3–6 ft) from the location of recovery, at a depth of 10 cm (4 in).
- If the remains are recovered from or near a body of water, use an alcohol thermometer to measure water temperature 10 cm (4 in) below the surface.

To ensure accurate temperature readings, always shield the thermometer from direct sunlight. As you collect data throughout the process, remain mindful of best practices to minimize insect dispersal and avoid disturbing their natural behavior.

Sampling Adult Flying and Crawling Insects

The initial insect samples to be collected should include adult flying insects (e.g., flies) and crawling insects (e.g., beetles). Flying insects are typically sampled using aerial netting. This involves rapidly sweeping a net back and forth above the body or through surrounding vegetation. After each pass, the net opening should be rotated 180° to prevent captured insects from escaping. An alternative technique involves approaching flying insects with a downward swatting motion, keeping the net's opening angled upward. This method exploits the insects' natural tendency to fly upward into the net. To ensure a representative sample, aerial netting should be conducted three to four times directly above the remains. In addition, at least two complete 360° sweeps of vegetation located 1.5–3 m (5–10 ft) from the remains are recommended.

Once the insects are collected, insert the end of the net into a wide-mouthed kill jar and promptly cap the jar to prevent escape. The **kill jar** should contain either several cotton balls or a block of plaster (gypsum cement) at the bottom, freshly soaked with **ethyl acetate** (more commonly known as nail polish remover) or **Kahle's solution** (refer to Table 9.4). Allow the insects to remain in the jar for approximately two to five minutes, which is typically sufficient to immobilize them. Using light-tension (**feather touch**) forceps, carefully transfer the adult insects into a glass vial with Kahle's solution, which is a **fixative and preservative**, or a glass vial filled with **80% ethanol (ETOH)**, which is a preservative most often used for long-term storage.

Another method for collecting flying insects in forensic investigations involves the use of sticky traps. These traps typically consist of cardboard coated with a strong adhesive and are either suspended above the scene or placed on the ground near the remains. While various commercial adhesive insect traps are available, they are generally insufficient for forensic purposes. Instead, cardboard-based rodent glue traps are recommended for effective entomological collection (Sanford et al., 2019). In the field, open the trap and fold it into a V-shape with the adhesive surface facing outward. Attach a clothespin to each corner to serve as legs, elevating the trap slightly above the surface. After all other specimens have been collected and the remains cleared, remove the clothespins and invert and roll the trap into a cylinder with the sticky side on the inside (do not overlap the edges). Fasten the cylinder in place with a rubber band or bulldog clips. Once fastened, place the trap in a large polyethylene specimen bag and store it in a freezer until it can be transported to a forensic entomologist.

To collect adult crawling insects, use medium or fine-point dissecting forceps or gloved fingers. Be aware that many of these insects are highly agile and quick to flee any disturbance. For initial collection efforts, it may be helpful to have multiple people involved, as the insects tend to retreat into soil or nearby groundcover at the slightest disturbance. Once collected, adult beetles should be placed directly into a glass vial containing 80% ethanol (ETOH) for preservation. Keep in mind that many adult beetle species are predatory and may consume newly emerged flies or even other beetles. To prevent such interactions, promptly separate and preserve each specimen after collection.

Sampling Insects on Remains

Sampling insects from human remains is a delicate process that requires meticulous care to avoid introducing postmortem artifacts or compromising other evidence. Begin collecting at the head, proceeding through the thoracic region, arms, and hands, and concluding with the legs and feet. After thoroughly examining the upper surface of the body and ensuring all relevant personnel have documented the body's position, carefully inspect the underside of the remains. Document any visible wounds and record them on the evidence collection form. If authorized by the lead investigator, briefly examine pockets and folds in the clothing (or other materials used to conceal the body) at the scene. Additional entomological evidence may be collected by the medical examiner during the autopsy, including samples from both the clothing and the body.

Insect sampling directly from remains typically includes the collection of eggs and larvae. To ensure a representative sample, it is essential to gather larvae of varying sizes, not only average-sized individuals, but also the largest and smallest, to document the full range of size variation. Samples should be taken from multiple colonization sites and preserved separately, with temperature readings recorded at each location. Following the preservation of specimens, an equivalent live sample should be collected from the same site whenever feasible.

Eggs

Adult female flies typically deposit their eggs in clusters, which may resemble mold or sawdust to the untrained eye. These eggs are commonly located in dark, moist regions of the body, including the eyes, nostrils, ears, scalp, joint creases, genitalia, anus, and areas of trauma. In addition, eggs may be found on clothing saturated with decomposition fluids. In contrast, beetles generally lay their eggs individually, making them more difficult to detect. They are often concealed within folds, crevices, and body cavities.

The standard sample size for fly eggs ranges from 50 to 100 eggs, typically forming a clump approximately the size of a pencil eraser. Samples should be collected from multiple locations on the remains using a wooden tongue depressor or a moistened camelhair brush. Each clump should be divided into two subsamples:

- One portion should be preserved in a glass vial containing 80% ethanol (ETOH).
- The second portion should be placed in a separate glass vial with a moistened (preferably sterile) paper towel to prevent desiccation.

Beetle eggs should be collected and preserved using the same protocol. Live specimens will be reared to adulthood by a forensic entomologist to assist in estimating PMI.

Larvae

Larvae regulate their microenvironment by forming large aggregates, known as larval masses, which generate heat and help maintain optimal temperatures for development. Typically, larvae are collected alongside eggs and are often located in the same regions of the body. In some cases, they may also form substantial internal maggot masses. First instar larvae are the smallest and most delicate; they should be collected using light-tension forceps or a small, moistened camelhair brush. As larvae progress to the second and third instar stages, they tend to cluster and can produce significant heat. Each larval mass should be documented prior to sampling, noting its location, approximate size, and internal temperature. To measure the temperature, gently insert a digital bimetal probe thermometer into the center of the mass and record the highest reading observed.

Do not place live larvae directly into any preserving solution (e.g., 80% ethanol), as this can lead to darkening and shrinkage due to putrefaction. Such changes may obscure key morphological features and introduce errors in PMI estimation. The following method is recommended for collecting and preserving live larvae:

- Collect live larvae samples in batches of 50–100 using a clean plastic spoon or large spooned silicone spatula.
- Immediately immerse the larvae in very hot distilled water (≥90°C/194°F) for approximately 30–60 seconds. This blanching process ensures optimal preservation of soft-bodied samples.
- After blanching, pour off the water into a designated waste container. Rinse the larvae briefly with clean distilled water to remove any residual debris.
- If DNA analysis of the sample is a possibility, the use of a fixative (e.g., KAA or Kahle's solution) is not recommended. Instead, the sample should be stored in either 80% ethanol (ETOH) or **99% propylene glycol**.
- If DNA analysis is not a concern, transfer the rinsed larvae into a collection jar containing Kahle's solution for fixation. Once fixation is complete, larvae may be transferred to a clean collection jar containing either ETOH or fresh Kahle's solution for long-term storage.

To ensure the safe transport of live insect larvae for forensic analysis, the following steps are recommended:

- Prepare a maggot-rearing container by selecting a 16-ounce plastic container with a tight-fitting, sealable lid. Add a 2.5 cm (1 in) layer of vermiculite to the bottom of the container. Vermiculite helps maintain moisture and provides a substrate for the larvae. Use a metal dissecting probe to carefully pierce several small air holes in the lid to allow for ventilation.
- Collect 30–50 live larvae for transport using a clean plastic spoon or large spooned silicone spatula.
- Separate fly larvae (smooth-bodied) from beetle larvae (hairy with visible legs), as some beetle larvae are predatory and may consume fly larvae during transport.
- Construct a feeding pouch by cutting a piece of aluminum foil measuring 15 × 18 cm (6 × 7 in). Fold the foil into thirds horizontally, then into thirds vertically to form a compact 5 × 7 cm (2 × 3 in) rectangle. Unfold the foil and crimp the corners together to create an open-topped, three-dimensional pouch.
- Place a small ball of lean ground pork (90–50 gm/3–5 oz) inside the pouch and then add the larvae. This will serve as a food source to sustain the larvae for up to 24 hours during transport. If transporting beetle larvae, you may use fly larvae as their food source, since beetle larvae typically feed on them.
- Crimp the remaining edge of the pouch to seal the larvae and food inside. Place the pouch into the prepared container with vermiculite.

You may also use polyethylene specimen bags instead of plastic containers if none are available. Include both the feeding pouch and vermiculite inside the bag, ensure the bag is properly sealed, and pierce small pinholes in the plastic to allow for adequate ventilation.

Sampling Insects Migrating from Remains

After sampling insects directly from the body, the surrounding area should be thoroughly investigated for additional specimens. A significant number of insects may remain on the ground surface, concealed beneath debris, or burrowed into the soil. Migrating larvae and pupae are typically found within a 6 m (20 ft) radius of the remains, at depths ranging from 2.5 to 5 cm (1 to 2 in). However, these distances and depths can vary depending on terrain and soil compaction. Larvae often congregate in dense vegetation, around tree trunks, and beneath rocks or fallen limbs. Always use gloves and appropriate protective gear during sampling to ensure safety and prevent contamination. To sample these insects:

- Carefully remove surface debris using a hand trowel or similar tool.
- Sift through the debris to locate mature larvae or pupae.
- Collect topsoil samples and sift them to recover burrowed insects or fragments.
- Use labeled containers to store specimens and avoid cross-contamination.

Document the compass direction and distance from the remains for each sample. This spatial data are critical for reconstructing insect migration patterns and estimating PMIs. For photographic documentation, capture images of migrating insects and pupae in situ if possible. Include scale markers and note environmental conditions (e.g., lighting, temperature).

A representative sample of mature larvae should be preserved using the method described above. In addition, a second group of similarly mature larvae should be collected alive for rearing purposes. Pupae may be housed in the same type of plastic containers used for larvae; however, a feeding pouch is unnecessary, as pupae do not feed during this stage. Any residual materials, such as pupal skins, empty puparia, or beetle frass, should be stored in polyethylene specimen bags or glass vials, each containing a piece of dry paper towel to absorb excess moisture.

Sampling Insects after Removing Remains

In cases of extensive insect colonization, adult beetles (e.g., carrion and rove beetles), larvae, and pupae may be recovered from the soil beneath the body. Any surface litter found under the remains should be collected for forensic entomological examination and placed in a labeled cardboard box. A generous layer of vermiculite should be added to the bottom of the box to absorb residual fluids, and the box should be sealed to prevent further insect migration.

Soil samples taken directly beneath the head, torso, and extremities, as well as areas adjacent to the body and up to 1 m (3 ft) from the remains, can yield various species and stages of pupae. These samples are also valuable for biochemical analysis of decomposition fluids. Each sample should measure approximately 10 cm^2 (4 in^2), be placed in plastic containers or paper evidence bags, and labeled consistently with other entomological evidence. Precise documentation of each sample's location is essential, and these are often mapped on the site plan.

Packing Collected Specimens

After collection and documentation, all samples should be placed in a cooling bag or box for transport. During warmer months, include a small reusable ice pack to help maintain a stable temperature. When possible, retain both preserved and live specimens from each body site in pairs. Because larvae are highly mobile, ensure live sample containers are fully and securely sealed – preferably with painter's tape around the lid edges.

To maintain chain of custody and sample integrity, all items accepted by the crime scene unit or evidence officer must be properly sealed. Live specimens should be transferred to a forensic entomologist for rearing within 24 hours. If shipping is required, consult the entomologist for appropriate packaging guidelines. Typically, samples can be placed in smaller cardboard boxes and then packed into a larger shipping container. Take care not to obstruct ventilation holes with packing materials or other sample boxes.

Basic Entomology Collection Kit

Table 9.3 outlines the essential equipment and supplies required for the proper documentation and collection of entomological evidence at a recovery site, ensuring accurate delivery to a forensic entomologist. These items are available as pre-assembled kits from various biological and scientific supply companies (see Table 2.1) or can be customized to meet specific needs. Collection and preservation solutions may be purchased separately from the same suppliers or prepared in advance. Table 9.4 provides component lists and proportions for commonly used kill, fixative, and preservative solutions.

Table 9.3 Example Checklist of Equipment Used in Entomology Collection

Items	Number	Items	Number
Equipment			
Large plastic equipment case	1	Plastic step plates (15x15 in)	4
Insect identification cards	1	Plastic clothes pins	10
Plastic hand trowel	2	Magnifying lens	1
Large silicone spooned spatula	2	Nitrile gloves	20+
Plastic spoons	10+	Featherweight tweezers	2
Large paper glue traps/boards	10	Metal dissecting probe	2
Sifting screen (8 × 10 in #7 mesh)	2	Fine curved dissecting forceps	2
Artist camel hair brush (#2 size)	2	Disposable scalpel	5
Painter's tape (0.5 in roll)	1	Disposable eye dropper pipettes	5
Aluminum foil (roll)	1	Disposable tongue depressors	50
Vermiculite (8 qt bag/bucket)	1	4-oz plastic collection jars	10+
Paper towels (roll)	1	16-oz plastic food container (+lid)	15+
Cotton balls (bag)	1	32-oz plastic food container (+lid)	15+
Small plastic funnel	1	6 x 9 in polyethylene bags	20+
Plastic bottle for waste (64 oz)	1	Interior paper labels	50+
Dark graphite (#2) pencils	3	Exterior adhesive labels	50+
Photo scale and white card	2	Specimen collection forms	20+
12-in collapsizble entomology net with handle extension			1
12-in digital bimetal probe thermometer and 10-in alcohol thermometer			1
Digital temperature and humidity meter (hand held)			1
Glass collecting vials with screw tops (4 dram size)			30
4-oz and 8-oz wide-mouth glass kill jar with screw tops and plaster block			2
Cardboard boxes (shoebox size)			5
Chemicals			
Ethyl acetate (common nail polish remover, 4 oz)			2
80% ethanol preservative solution (8 oz)			1
Kahle's (or KAA) fixative solution (12 oz)			1
Distilled water (32 oz)			1
99% propylene glycol (8 oz)			1
Time-Sensitive Items to Prepare			
Thermos of boiling (≥90°C/194°F) distilled water (32 oz)			
Larval food source (e.g., 9 oz lean ground pork or beef, ambient temperature)			
Cooler bag or box with reusable ice packs used for transport of live samples)			

Table 9.4 Common Entomology Fixative and Preservation Solutions

ETOH (80% ethanol)

- Commonly known as ethyl alcohol
- Best used in:
  - Killing and preserving adult specimens
  - Preserving eggs
  - Preserving soft-bodied larvae after blanching with hot water or fixation

Kahle's Solution (Fungal Control Agent and Fixative)

- To prepare 250 ml (8.4 fl oz), use the following method in a fume hood or well-ventilated area and when wearing appropriate personal protective equipment (PPE). Components should be added to ethanol in order to avoid adverse reactions when mixing:
  - 70 ml (2.4 fl oz) of 95% ethanol
  - 25 ml (0.8 fl oz) of formaldehyde
  - 150 ml (5.1 fl oz) of distilled water
  - 5 ml (0.2 fl oz) of glacial acetic acid
- Best used in:
  - Killing and preserving adult specimens
  - Preserving larvae

(Continued)

Table 9.4 (*Continued*) Common Entomology Fixative and Preservation Solutions

DNA Preservation Solution

- For preservation and long-term storage of hard and soft-bodied samples that may be used for DNA characterization, ETOH or 99% propylene glycol (less volatile and evaporates much slower than ethanol) is recommended

KAA Fixative

- To prepare 250 ml (8.4 fl oz), use the following method in a fume hood or well-ventilated area and when wearing appropriate personal protective equipment (PPE). Components should be added to ethanol in order to avoid adverse reactions when mixing:
  - 208 ml (7.0 fl oz) of 95% ethanol
  - 42 ml (1.4 fl oz) of glacial acetic acid
  - 21 ml (0.7 fl oz) of kerosene
- Best used in:
  - Killing larval specimens
  - Preserving eggs
- If DNA characterization is a possibility, use of this fixative is not recommended
- Specimens should be transferred to ETOH solution immediately after death for long-term storage

Source: Adapted from Byrd and Tomerlin (2019)

CASE STUDY #12: BARKING UP THE WRONG TREE

Authors Sandra Wheeler and Lana Williams assisted in the recovery of the remains of an unclothed individual found shortly after a winter thaw in a small clearing of a wooded area. A number of various-sized deadfall branches and a layer of leaf litter covered the body. One of the first steps in the recovery was to record the landscape and plant growth surrounding the surface deposit. While recording this information, authors Wheeler and Williams noticed that the concentration of branches over the body was considerably greater than any other location at the site. At this point, there was an agreement among investigators that branches and leaf litter were most likely used to conceal the body and should be recorded as evidence (Figure 9.16).

After the deadfall branches were mapped and photographed in situ, they were removed in reverse order from which they were placed. In addition to deadfall branches and leaf litter, the entire top half of a sizable tree sapling had been placed directly over the head and chest of the body. The trunk end of the sapling had an odd appearance when compared with the deadfall branches. Approximately 20 cm (8 in) of wood and bark was stripped away along the length of the trunk, and the remaining wood was frayed at the end, making it obvious that the sapling had been 'green' (i.e., living) when broken and stripped. In addition, exposed growth rings in the wood indicated the sapling was at the end of a growing season when it was used in this manner. The lower portion of the sapling was soon found still in the ground not far from the body (Figure 9.17). The top portion of the sapling was matched to this lower portion and both parts of the sapling were collected as evidence.

Remaining leaf litter was then removed, and a substantial amount of animal activity in the gut, upper thigh area, and feet was noted. Tufts of animal hair were still attached to the margins of the gut and thigh area damaged by carnivore activity, and all toes were missing, also the result of carnivore activity. After the remains were recovered, areas around and under the body were searched with a metal detector and excavated with hand trowels to recover any additional items or associated evidence; however, nothing further was found. Based on the botanical evidence as well as the level and type of animal activity, it was determined that the body was concealed late in the fall season before the first snow, perhaps when the sapling still had its leaves, providing greater concealment of the body at that time.

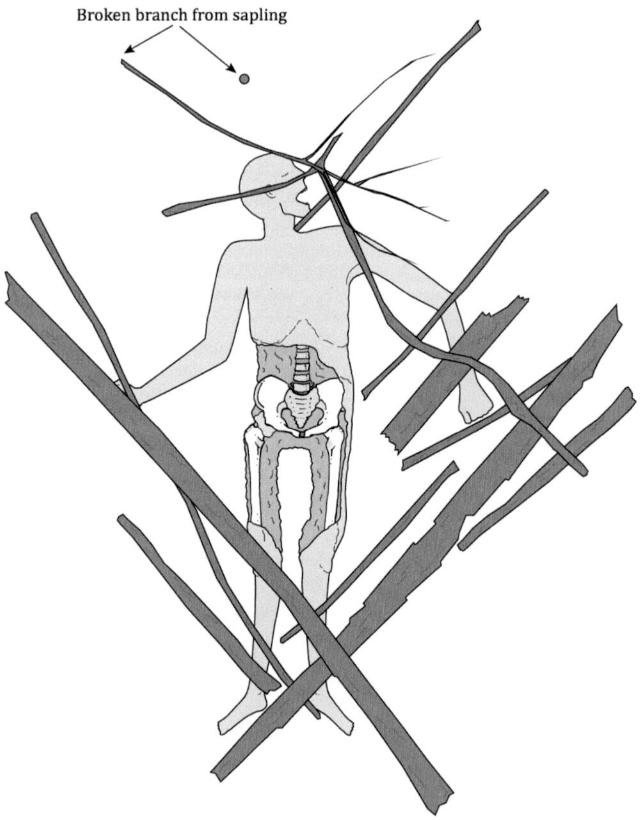

Figure 9.16 Illustration showing the purposeful placement of deadfall branches and a broken sapling over remains in a surface deposit. Note the proximity of the sapling trunk to the body.

Figure 9.17 The remaining trunk of a sapling used to conceal remains in a surface deposit. Note the frayed wood and length of stripped wood and bark that resulted from breaking the living wood of the sapling.

CASE STUDY #13: TENDING A STICKY ICKY GARDEN

During early spring, authors Sandra Wheeler and Lana Williams assisted in the recovery of human remains and associated items discovered near a camping tent in a restricted-access forest in Ontario. The tent had been pitched in a densely wooded area approximately 500 m (0.3 mi) from a nearby stream. The remains were found midway between the tent and the water's edge. Although the body was in an advanced state of decomposition, it had not yet reached skeletonization and showed minimal signs of animal disturbance. Investigators recovered the remains along with the tent, clothing, and a small number of personal belongings found inside. An autopsy was conducted the following day. No signs of trauma were observed. However, forensic examiners collected several samples of a pale yellow, sticky, dust-like substance resembling cornmeal from the victim's flannel shirt, pants, and boots and forwarded to a forensic botanist. In addition, a soft, slimy, yellowish-brown mass was preserved in the stomach and was also sampled for toxicological analysis along with other tissue samples.

Laboratory analyses identified the dust-like residue on the victim's clothing as pollen from *Cannabis indica*, specifically the strain known as Northern Lights Kush. Meanwhile, the stomach contents revealed fungal spores from *Amanita phalloides*, commonly referred to as the Death Cap mushroom. Male *Cannabis indica* plants typically release pollen during their flowering phase, which spans late summer to early fall, peaking in September and October under hot, dry conditions (Duvall, 1999). The *Amanita phalloides* mushroom is notoriously lethal, accounting for approximately 90% of fatal mushroom poisonings worldwide (Moor-Smith et al., 2019). Its appearance can easily be confused with that of psychedelic mushrooms, posing a significant risk to inexperienced foragers. These mushrooms fruit in late summer and autumn, and their toxins remain potent despite cooking, drying, or soaking. Ingestion of just half a cap may contain enough toxins to be fatal to an adult (Moor-Smith et al., 2019).

Following the discovery of a significant concentration of *Cannabis indica* pollen, local investigators revisited the scene and conducted a systematic search using a large grid pattern extending over a kilometer from the original campsite. During the sweep, they discovered a grow patch containing remnants of more than 80 mature *Cannabis indica* plants. Evidence suggests that the victim had been residing in the tent and actively cultivating the crop throughout the growing season. It is believed that during this period, the individual inadvertently consumed a Death Cap mushroom, leading to fatal poisoning.

CASE STUDY #14: SUNSHINE AND STICKY TRAPS

Authors Sandra Wheeler and Lana Williams assisted in the recovery of a partially clothed individual deposited on the side of an embankment between an All-Terrain Vehicle (ATV) trail and a canal. The area that the ATV trail ran through was mostly swampy and covered with reeds about 2 m (6.5 ft) in height. The body was lying halfway down the side of the canal embankment in a slight depression. A wall of reeds separated the body from the canal, suggesting the body had been rolled down the embankment from the ATV trail. The depression had prevented the body from rolling further down into the canal. The body was largely intact but in an advanced state of decomposition with the skin of the limbs and torso partially mummified. The skull, however, was skeletonized. The cranium had separated and rolled a bit further down slope of the body. There was no evidence of animal scavenging anywhere on the body other than insect activity.

At the scene, the body had been largely shaded from the sun because of the density and height of the surrounding reeds. Maggots were still visible, and there were major breaches in the skin where we could see further evidence of prior insect activity (Figure 9.18), but there were very few flying insects. After initial observations were recorded and photography of the site and remains were complete, a decision was made to cut back the reeds immediately surrounding the body to clear a working space for mapping and examining the remains. Almost immediately after cutting back the reeds and exposing the remains to full sunlight, the insect activity increased dramatically, including the presence of flying insects. Sticky traps were set up in the immediate proximity of the remains and all work ceased for a period of time to minimize disturbance. During this break in disturbance, the ambient temperature and the temperature of the remains also increased, stimulating the remaining maggot masses and causing many larvae to seek out more beneficial environmental conditions away from the remains (Figure 9.19). After a significant number of flying insects were collected on the sticky traps, they were inverted and rolled into a cylinder with the sticky side on the inside, fastened, labeled, and stored in a polyethylene bag in a cooler. Both live and preserved entomological samples, including maggots, beetles, and various larvae, were collected from exposed interior regions of the body and around the remains, packaged, and stored for transport.

When entomological sampling was finished and all records of the scene were reviewed, the cranium was collected and packaged separately for transport, and the body was carefully transferred to a body bag with a backing board to preserve positioning of the limbs as much as possible. After the remains were removed from the ground surface, the soil immediately under the body was sampled for pupae. Additional soil samples were collected outside of the decomposition island when areas of pupal migration were detected. The areas around and under the body were searched with a metal detector and excavated with hand trowels to recover any additional items or associated evidence; however, nothing further was found. All of the entomological samples were packaged by the crime scene personnel for transport to a local forensic entomologist for analysis. The results of the entomological analysis later confirmed the PMI estimate based on information obtained from an informant.

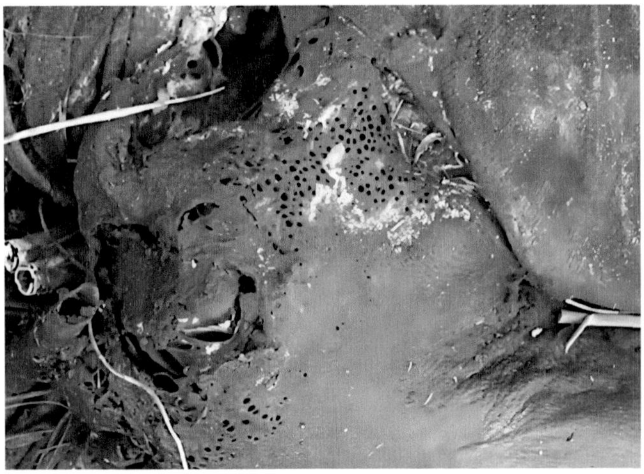

Figure 9.18 Area of skin across the shoulders and back of an individual who had become partially mummified during decomposition. The small holes indicate previous cycles of activity, where insects have bored through the skin during larval stages.

Figure 9.19 Area of increased insect activity after the temperature increase from exposure to full sun. Prior to sun exposure, no maggots were visible in this area of the leg; however, soon after exposure, the remaining maggot mass became active and was sampled to determine postmortem interval. The smaller holes surrounding the larger opening indicate previous cycles of insect activity.

Key Terms

80% ethanol (ETOH)
99% propylene glycol
ABFE
algae
anemophilous plants
annual secondary growth
autogamous plants
blow flies
botanical field press
carrion beetles
coprophiles
dendrochronology
detritivores
diatoms
ectoparasites
eggs
ethyl acetate
fixative/preservative
flowers/fruits/seeds
forensic botany
forensic entomology
forensic palynology
frass
fungi
gastropods
growth rings
Kahle's solution
kill jar
larvae (maggot, grub)/instars
lichens
macrobotanicals
microbotanicals
mites
mosses
mycology
osteophagic
parasitoids
phycology
phyllids
plant
pollen
puparium/adult
roots/stems/leaves
saprophytes
scavengers
spores
woody plants
zoogamous plants

REVIEW AND DISCUSSION QUESTIONS

1. What are three examples of how root growth might be used to estimate PMI for remains recovered from a grave?
2. In late autumn, a body in an advanced state of decomposition is found near a lake surrounded by ragweed, oak trees, and goosegrass. Pants and shoes are still associated with the remains, but no other personal possessions are recovered. In this case, what kinds of botanical and entomological evidence should you look for and consider for collection? Explain the forensic significance of each type of evidence you could potentially collect.
3. What are the main concerns in packaging and storing botanical remains collected as possible evidence?
4. Why is correct species identification so important in forensic botany and forensic entomology?
5. Why is important to determine if DNA analysis will be used for insect species identification prior to collecting any entomological samples?
6. Describe the differences between fly and beetle larvae. Why is it important to know these differences when collecting live samples?
7. When collecting maggots from human remains, why should you always attempt to include the largest maggots present?
8. Why should maggot length be calculated before the specimens are placed in preserving solution?
9. Why is it important to also sample soil in the vicinity of the remains and sediments from below the remains?

Suggested Readings

Aquila, I., Gratteri, S., Sacco, M.A., Ricci, P., 2018. The role of forensic botany in solving a case: scientific evidence on the falsification of a crime scene. *Journal of Forensic Sciences* 63(3):961–964. DOI:10.1111/1556–4029.13639

Caccianiga, M., Caccia, G., Mazzarelli, D., Salsarola, D., Poppa, P., Gaudio, D., Cappella, A., Franceschetti, L., Tambuzzi, S., Maggioni, L., Cattaneo, C., 2021. Common and much less common scenarios in which botany is crucial for forensic pathologist and anthropologists: a series of eight case studies. *International Journal of Legal Medicine* 135(3):1067–1077. DOI:10.1007/s00414-020-02456-0

Castner, J.L., Byrd, J.H. 2000. *Forensic Insect Field Identification Cards*. Gainesville, FL: Feline Press.

Gibson, D. 2022. *Planting Clues: How Plants Solve Crimes.* Oxford: Oxford University Press.

Erzinçlioğlu, Z. 2002. *Maggots, Murder, and Men: Memories and Reflections of a Forensic Entomologist.* New York: Thomas Dunne Books.

Kasprzyk, I. 2023. Forensic botany: who?, how?, where?, when?. *Science & Justice* 63(2):258–275. DOI:10.1016/j.scijus.2023.01.002

Lindgren, N.K., Sisson, M.S., Archambeault, A.D., Rahlwes, B.C., Willett, J.R., Bucheli, S.R., 2015. Four forensic entomology case studies: records and behavioral observations on seldom reported cadaver fauna with notes on relevant previous occurrences and ecology. *Journal of Medical Entomology* 52(2):143–150. DOI:10.1093/jme/tju023

Margiotta, G., Bacaro, G., Carnevali, E., Severini, S., Bacci, M., Gabbrielli, M., 2015. Forensic botany as a useful tool in the crime scene: report of a case. *Journal of Forensic and Legal Medicine* 34: 24–28. DOI:10.1016/j.jflm.2015.05.003

Schroeder, H., Klotzbach, H., Püschel, K. 2003. Insects' colonization of human corpses in warm and cold season. *Legal Medicine* 5:S372–S374. DOI:10.1016/S1344–6223(02)00135-9

References

Agashe, S.N., Caulton, E. 2009. *Pollen and Spores: Applications with Special Emphasis on Aerobiology and Allergy.* Enfield, NH: Science Publishers.

de Albuquerque, M.P., Putzke, J., Schünemann, A.L., Vieira, F.C.B., de Carvalho Victoria, F., Pereira, A.B. 2018. Colonisation of stranded whale bones by lichens and mosses at Hennequin Point, King George Island, Antarctica. *Polar Record* 54(1):29–35. DOI:10.1017/S0032247418000062

Amendt, J., Anderson, G., Campobasso, C.P., Dadour, I., Gaudry, E., Mjr, H., de Carvalho Moretti, T., Sukontason, K.L., Villet, M.H. 2015. Standard practices. In: Tomberlin, J.K., Benbow, M.E., eds. *Forensic Entomology: International Dimensions and Frontiers*, pp. 381–398. Boca Raton, FL: CRC Press/Taylor and Francis Group.

Backwell, l., Huchet, J.B., du Guesclin Harrison, J., D'Errico, F. 2022. Invertebrate modification of bone. In: Pokines, J.T., L'Abbé, E.N., Symes, S.A., eds. *Manual of Forensic Taphonomy*, 2nd ed., pp. 631–666. Boca Raton, FL: CRC Press.

Baumjohann, K., Benecke, M., 2022. Mind your decompositional assumptions. *Forensic Sciences*, 2: 725–740. DOI: 10.3390/forensicsci2040054

Bever, R.A., Sanger, M., Linacre, A., Hsieh, H.M., Lee, J.C.I. 2024. Plant identification by DNA. In: Coyle, H.M., ed. *Forensic Botany: Principles and Applications to Criminal Casework*, pp. 235–250. Boca Raton, FL: CRC Press.

Brundage, A. 2019. General entomology and basic arthropod biology. In: Byrd, J.H, Tomberlin, J.K., eds. *Forensic Entomology: The Utility of Arthropods in Legal Investigations*, 3rd ed., pp. 1–14. Boca Raton, FL: CRC Press.

Byrd, J.H., Tomberlin, J.K. (eds). 2019a. *Forensic Entomology: The Utility of Arthropods in Legal Investigations*, 3rd ed., Boca Raton, FL: CRC Press.

Byrd, J.H, Tomberlin, J.K. 2019b. Insects of forensic importance. In: Byrd, J.H., Tomberlin, J.K., eds. *Forensic Entomology: The Utility of Arthropods in Legal Investigations*, 3rd ed., pp. 15–62. Boca Raton, FL: CRC Press.

Cooter, J., Barclay, M.V.L. 2006. *A Coleopterist's Handbook*, 4th ed., Kent: Amateur Entomologists' Society.

Coyle, H.M. 2024a. *Forensic Botany: Principles and Applications to Criminal Casework*, 2nd ed., Boca Raton, FL: CRC Press.

Coyle, H.M. 2024b. Introduction to forensic botany. In: Coyle, H.M., ed. *Forensic Botany: Principles and Applications to Criminal Casework*, 2nd ed., pp. 1–6. Boca Raton, FL: CRC Press.

Curry, J.P., Schmidt, O. 2007. The feeding ecology of earthworms–a review. *Pedobiologia* 50(6):463–477.

Duvall, C. 1999. *Cannabis*. London: Reaktion Books.

Erzinçlioğlu, Y.Z. 1980. On the role of Trichoceridae larvae (Diptera: Trichoceridae) in decomposing carrion in winter. *Naturalist* 105:133–134.

Gardner, L. 2004. *The Case That Never Dies: The Lindberg Kidnapping*. Piscataway, NJ: Rutgers University Press.

Gennard, D. 2012. *Forensic Entomology: An Introduction*, 2nd ed., Wiley. West Sussex: Wiley.

Grassberger, M., Frank, C. 2003. Temperature-related development of the parasitoid wasp Nasonia vitripennis as a forensic indicator. *Medical and Veterinary Entomology* 17:257–262. DOI:10.1046/j.1365–2915.2003.00439.x

Green, P.W.C., Simmonds, S.J., Blaney, W.M. 2003. Diet nutriment and rearing density affect the growth of the black blowfly larvae, *Phormia regina* (Diptera: Calliphoridae). *European Journal of Entomology* 100:39–42.

Greenberg, B., Kunich, J.C. 2002. *Entomology and the Law*. Cambridge: Cambridge University Press.

Guiry, M.D. 2012. How many species of algae are there? *Journal of Phycology* 48(5):1057–1063. DOI:10.1111/j.1529–8817.2012.01222.x

Gunn, A. 2019. *Essentials of Forensic Biology*, 3rd ed., Hoboken, NJ: Wiley-Blackwell.

Haefner, J.N., Wallace, J.R., Merritt, R.W. 2004. Pig decomposition in lotic aquatic systems: The potential use of algal growth in establishing a postmortem submersion interval (PMSI). *Journal of Forensic Sciences* 49:1–7.

Haglund, W.D., Reay, D.T., Swindler, D.R. 1988. Tooth mark artifacts and survival of bones in animal scavenged human skeletons. *Journal of Forensic Sciences* 33:985–997.

Hall, D.W., Byrd, J.H. 2012. *Forensic Botany: A Practical Guide*. Hoboken, NJ: Wiley-Blackwell.

Hall, D.W. 2012a. Introduction to forensic botany. In: Hall, D.W., Byrd, J.H., eds. *Forensic Botany: A Practical Guide*, pp. 1–11. Hoboken, NJ: Wiley-Blackwell.

Hall, D.W. 2012b. Plants as evidence. In: Hall, D.W., Byrd, J.H., eds. *Forensic Botany: A Practical Guide*, pp. 12–41. Hoboken, NJ: Wiley-Blackwell.

Hardy, C.R., Wallace, J.R. 2012. Algae in forensic investigations. In: *Forensic Botany: A Practical Guide*, pp. 145–174. Oxford: Wiley.

Hitosugi, M., Ishii, K., Yaguchi, T., Chigusa, Y., Kurosu, A., Kido, M., Nagai, T., Tokudome, S. 2006. Fungi can be a useful forensic tool. *Legal Medicine* 8:240–242.

Horrocks, M., Coulson, S.A., Walsh, K.A.J. 1998. Forensic palynology: Variation in the pollen content of soil surface samples. *Journal of Forensic Sciences* 43:320–323.

Huchet, J.B., Deverly, D., Gutierrez, B., Chauchat, C. 2011. Taphonomic evidence of a human skeleton gnawed by termites in a Moche-civilisation grave at Huaca de la Luna, Peru. *International Journal of Osteoarchaeology* 21(1):92–102.

Hürlimann, J., Feer, P., Elber, K., Niederberger, K., Dirnhofer, R., Wyler, D. 2000. Diatom detection in the diagnosis of death by drowning. *International Journal of Legal Medicine* 114:6–14.

Hwang, C., Turner, B.D. 2005. Spatial and temporal variability of necrophagous Diptera from urban and rural areas. *Medical and Veterinary Entomology* 19:379–391.

Krstic, S., Duma, A., Janevska, B., Levkov, Z., Nikolova, K., Noveska, M. 2002. Diatoms in forensic expertise of drowning – a Macedonian experience. *Forensic Science International* 127:198–203.

Ladd, C., Schierenbeck, K., Lee, H. 2024. The use of biological and botanical evidence in criminal investigations. In: Coyle, H.M., ed. *Forensic Botany: Principles and Applications to Criminal Casework*, 2nd ed., pp. 63–75. Boca Raton, FL: CRC Press.

Lane, M.A., Anderson, L.C., Barkley, T.M., Bock, J.H., Gifford, E.M., Hall, D.W., Norris, D.O., Rost, T.L., Stern, W.L. 1990. Forensic botany: Plants, perpetrators, pests, poisons and pot. *Bioscience* 40:34–39.

Lord, W.D., Goff, M.L., Adkins, T.R., Haskell, N.H. 1994. The black soldier fly Hermetia illucens (Diptera: Stratiomyidae) as a potential measure of post-mortem interval: Observations and case histories. *Journal of Forensic Sciences* 39:215–222.

de Lourdes Chávez-Briones, M., Hernández-Cortés, R., Díaz-Torres, P., Niderhauser-García, A., Ancer-Rodríguez, J., Jaramillo-Rangel, G., Ortega-Martínez, M. 2013. Identification of human remains by DNA analysis of the gastrointestinal contents of fly larvae. *Journal of Forensic Sciences* 58(1):248–250. DOI:10.1111/j.1556–4029.2012.02279.x

Ludes, B., Coste, M., North, N., Doray, S., Tracqui, A., Kintz, P. 1999. Diatom analysis in victim's tissues as an indicator of the site of drowning. *International Journal of Legal Medicine* 112:163–166.

Mégnin, P. 1894. *La Faune des Cadavres. Encyclopédie Scientifiques des Aide Memoire*. Paris: Villars et Fils, Masson et Gauthier.

Menezes, R.G., Kanchan, T., Lobo, S.W., Jain, A., Bhat, N.B., Rao, N.G. 2008. Cadaveric fungi: Not yet an established forensic tool. *Journal of Forensic and Legal Medicine* 15:124–125.

Merkel, J., Konrat, M., Stark, L., Laurence, A., Briscoe, L., Collings, B., Carrington, P., Kreider, D., Larraín, J., Lichamer, A., Merrill, G., 2025. Green clues: Unveiling the role of bryophytes in forensic science. *Forensic Sciences Research* owaf026. DOI:10.1016/j.forsciint.2006.11.012.

Milne, L.A., Bryant, V.M. Jr., Mildenhall, D.C. 2024. Forensic palynology. In: Coyle, H.M., ed. *Forensic Botany: Principles and Applications to Criminal Casework*, 2nd ed., pp. 112–146. Boca Raton, FL: CRC Press.

Moor-Smith, M., Li, R., Ahmad, O. 2019. The world's most poisonous mushroom, Amanita phalloides, is growing in BC. *British Columbia Medical Journal* 61(1).

Norris, D.O., Bock, J.H. 2024. Uses of plant anatomy, taxonomy, and ecology in forensic investigations. In: Coyle, H.M., ed. *Forensic Botany: Principles and Applications to Criminal Casework*, 2nd ed., pp. 76–95. Boca Raton, FL: CRC Press.

Peruch, M., Buffon, M., Jakovski, Z., Spiliopoulou, C., Addobbati, R., Franzin, M., Magni, P.A., D'Errico, S. 2024. Comparative toxicological analyses of traditional matrices and blow fly larvae in four cases of highly decomposed human cadavers. *Insects* 15(7):500.

"plant." Merriam-Webster.com, Merriam-Webster 2025. https://www.merriam-webster.com/dictionary/plant#dictionary-entry-2. Accessed 2025, July 18.

Pokines, J.T. 2018. Two cases of dendrochronology used to corroborate a forensic postmortem interval. *Journal of Forensic Identification* 68(4):457–465.

Quatrehomme, G., Lacoste, A., Bailet, P., Grevin, G., Ollier, A. 1997. Contribution of microscopic plant anatomy to postmortem bone dating. *Journal of Forensic Sciences* 42:140–143.

Queiroz, R.A., Soriano, E.P., Carvalho, M.V.D., Caldas-Junior, A.F., Souza, E.H.A., Coelho-Junior, L.G.T.M., Campello, R.I.C., Almeida, A.C., Farias, R.C.A.P., Vasconcellos, A. 2016. First forensic records of termite activity on non-fossilized human bones in Brazil. *Brazilian Journal of Biology* 77:127–131.

Rai, J.K., Pickles, B.J., Perotti, M.A. 2021. Assemblages of Acari in shallow burials: Mites as markers of the burial environment, of the stage of decay and of body-cadaver regions. *Experimental and Applied Acarology* 85(2):247–276.

Rivers, D.B., Dahlem, G.A. 2022. *The Science of Forensic Entomology*, 2nd ed., Hoboken, NJ: Wiley Blackwell.

Said al Na'imi, K. 2008. Basics of forensic fungi. In: Coyle, H.M., ed. *Nonhuman DNA Typing: Theory and Casework Applications*, pp. 135–166. Boca Raton, FL: CRC Press.

Sanford, M.R., Byrd, J.H., Tomberlin, J.K., Wallace, J.R. 2019. Entomological evidence collections methods: American Board of Forensic Entomology approved protocols. In: Byrd, J.H., Tomberlin, J.K., eds. *Forensic Entomology: The Utility of Arthropods in Legal Investigations*, 3rd ed., pp. 63–85. Boca Raton, FL: CRC Press.

Siver, P.A., Lord, W.D., McCarthy, D.J. 1994. Forensic limnology: The use of freshwater algal community ecology to link suspects to an aquatic crime scene in southern New England. *Journal of Forensic Sciences* 39:847–853.

Stephenson, S.L. 2010. *The Kingdom Fungi*. Portland, OR: Timber Press.

Tz'u, S. 1981. *The Washing Away of Wrongs* (B. McKnight, trans.) Ann Arbor: University of Michigan Press.

Wells, J.D., Greenberg, B. 1994. Effect of the red imported fire ant (Hymenoptera: Formicidae) and carcass type on the daily occurrence of postfeeding carrion-fly larvae (Diptera: Calliphoridae, Sarcophagidae). *Journal of Medical Entomology* 31:171–174.

Willey, P., Heilman, A. 1987. Estimating time since death using plant roots and stems. *Journal of Forensic Sciences* 32:1264–1270.

Wiltshire, P.E.J. 2006. Consideration of some taphonomic variables of relevance to forensic palynological investigation in the United Kingdom. *Forensic Science International* 163:173–182.

Yen, L.Y., Jayaprakash, P.T. 2007. Prevalence of diatom frustules in non-vegetarian foodstuffs and its implications in interpreting identification of diatom frustules in drowning cases. *Forensic Science International* 170:1–7.

APPLYING ARCHAEOLOGICAL METHODS IN A FORENSIC CONTEXT

Learning Objectives

- Understand general principles of archaeology and their role in site formation.
- Identify and describe characteristics of soils, stratigraphic layers, and sediments.
- Outline stages in archaeological recovery and tools used in the process.
- Assess context and apply archaeological approaches to recovering human remains.

Learning Connections

- Incorporate information from prior field search, discovery, and mapping of the site with the process of excavation and/or surface recovery of human remains and associated evidence.
- Explain planning, excavation process, and recovery of remains and associated evidence using proper terminology, skill criteria, and best practices guidelines when writing a final report.

Historically, the analytical expertise of forensic investigators and archaeologists has been combined on numerous occasions. Both emerged as scientific disciplines in the 19th century, sharing a common focus on accurately identifying and recording materials encountered in the course of investigation (Davis, 1992; Renfrew and Bahn, 2018). There is a theme common to the work of archaeologists and forensic investigators; they attempt to understand the nature, sequence, and underlying reasons for certain events in the past. The final goals may differ, but the philosophy is much the same. Both disciplines use and present evidence to prove their cases.

Clyde Snow, a noted forensic anthropologist, stated, "… systematic recovery of the materials from burial and surface sites is best accomplished by suitably modifying methods long employed by archaeologists to solve similar problems" (1982:118). Archaeology and forensic investigation are both based on highly detailed modes of data collection, documentation, data processing, and analysis. In terms of contemporary evidence gathering, it could be said that archaeologists work on some of the coldest cases in existence. It is understood that

> each [type of investigation] gathers data in the hope of reconstructing events to solve a problem. Each looks for the agents responsible for the physical evidence. Each should operate through the cooperation of many disciplines working together to provide a complete response to the available data.
>
> *(Davis, 1992:152)*

Therefore, successful investigations in both fields are similarly oriented in reconstructing what happened at the scene based on physical evidence. In archaeology, artifacts, which are portable objects made, used, or modified by humans, serve as evidence to understand the behavior of human populations and their relationships with one another and their environment. In forensic investigation, this same type of evidence is used to reconstruct events or to relate an object or a person from one place to another.

The purpose of this chapter is to introduce the general principles and terminology used in archaeology and to provide the basic steps for the most effective and efficient excavation and recovery of remains in a forensic context. In many instances, forensic investigators rarely supervise the recovery of buried remains and are generally not experienced in processing this type of scene. Many times, the common tactic is to recover the remains as quickly as possible, which can lead to the destruction and loss of valuable evidence. Most experienced archaeologists will have excavated numerous assemblages of human remains during their careers, under different conditions and in different soil environments. Archaeologists are trained in how to locate, excavate, and record a human skeleton in order to maximize the information collected during recovery. This information may help in determining its date, the manner of its deposition, or the relationship of any associated objects or surviving elements – all before it is removed from the ground for analysis. An archaeologist who has worked in a forensic setting has the added benefit of fully understanding crime scene protocols and

DOI: 10.4324/9781315201658-10

the evidentiary requirements of additional agencies that may be involved in the scene.

Forensic archaeology is the application of standard archaeological principles and methods to locate and recover human remains and associated evidence within the context of a forensic investigation. The chief concern of both the forensic archaeologist and the forensic investigator is controlled, legal acquisition of evidence that can be used to establish connections among a suspect, victim, and crime and its potential use in future legal proceedings. The application of archaeological techniques within a forensic context can greatly assist the investigator in accurately and thoroughly documenting and recovering all potential evidence, aid in reconstructing events surrounding an individual's death, and if applicable, substantiate or disprove informant statements concerning the crime. By using methods familiar to both parties, shared resources and cooperation can lead to more effective and efficient results. Table 10.1 provides a summary of advantages for investigators working with a forensic archaeologist in recovering human remains and other kinds of physical evidence. Appendices A, D, E, and F contain sample forms typically used by a forensic archaeologist during the surface recovery and excavation of remains.

Table 10.1 Advantages for Investigators Working with a Forensic Archaeologist

- Knowledge of and familiarity with:
  - Site formation processes
  - Events surrounding and subsequent to burial process
  - Post-burial site disturbances and their causes.
- Using systematic and controlled approach easily adapted to any constraints
- Providing increased accuracy and precision in collecting and recording skeletal remains and associated evidence
- Preventing damage to skeletal remains and associated evidence during recovery
- Recording and collecting environmental data that can be used by other specialists (e.g., geologists, botanists, entomologists, DNA analysts)
- Processing the scene in a professional manner with the shared goal of diligence and care in thoroughly recording and recovering all potential evidence

Source: Modified from Dirkmaat and Adovasio, 1997.

GENERAL PRINCIPLES OF ARCHAEOLOGY

The goal of any archaeological **excavation** is to try to understand what may have happened at a site by carefully excavating the material remains that represent past behavior. **Field archaeology** examines changes in societies over long periods, rather than the much shorter time scales of forensic archaeology. However, in both instances, excavation requires great care and patience as each layer is slowly stripped away in succession to reveal material evidence. The most basic principle of any excavation is to proceed horizontally first and vertically second, by removing a single layer in its entirety before proceeding on to the next, as if moving through a layer cake one layer at a time. In addition, much of the evidence recovered in forensic archaeology is not instantly recognizable in a three-dimensional form. For example, subtle changes in soil color may indicate the outline of a grave or the remnants of decomposition fluids from a body. This evidence can be easily lost if proper care is not taken during the excavation process. An understanding of the basic principles of excavation and key terminology used in archaeology will be helpful when applying the following archaeological techniques to the forensic recovery of human remains.

Provenience, Association, and Context

When something is buried, the object is surrounded by **matrix**, usually some sort of sediment, such as gravel, sand, silt, or clay. An object that has not been moved from its original place of deposition is said to be in situ (Renfrew and Bahn, 2018). **Provenience** is the precise position of an object within the matrix. In archaeology, a three-dimensional grid system is used to record provenience, by measuring in meters (m) or centimeters (cm) the horizontal (x- and y-coordinates) and vertical position (z-coordinate, or depth/height elevation) of an object in relation to a datum (Renfrew and Bahn, 2018). Provenience is often confused with the art history term **provenance**, or the detailed history of an object's ownership, from the time of its creation to the present, which is crucial for establishing the object's authenticity, significance, value, and ethical acquisition (Stokstad and Cothren, 2017).

Association is an object's relationship to other objects or features found within the same archaeological level or general location (Renfrew and Bahn, 2018). The primary factor in association is the context in which objects are found (refer to section Principles of Deposition). Objects found together in a way suggesting they were deposited at the same time, like in a grave, are considered to be in **closed association**. **Open associations**, such as a knife found near a grave, are those where simultaneous deposition is only assumed and not proven.

Context, one of the most important terms in archaeology, is an object's exact place in time and space and its association and relationship with other items – that is, where it is, when it arrived, and how it got there (Renfrew and Bahn, 2018). Context is the most easily lost form of information among all potentially recoverable information. Removing an object from its archaeological context without proper documentation significantly diminishes its potential to aid in reconstructing the behavior that led to its placement. For instance, when associated objects are moved without their context being recorded, they may no longer be interpreted as having played a direct role in past events, but rather only a circumstantial one.

Context is equally as important in forensic investigations as it bears a legal importance in developing the reconstruction of events at a crime scene. Evidence loses most of its value if the provenience and/or association in which it is found is lost. This is extremely important considering that associated relationships between objects found at a crime scene are not always immediately apparent. In many cases, remains are removed quickly with brief notations on placement within the crime scene, resulting in the loss of the primary depositional context and incomplete scene reconstruction (Dirkmaat and Adovasio, 1997). Compromising the context of evidence can occur as easily as an untrained individual picking up, examining, or removing skeletal elements in an attempt to identify whether they are human. Once an object is moved, it is almost impossible to return it to its exact position and orientation. In some instances, the context of the scene may not always correspond to the evidence (refer to Case Study #10).

Features

In field archaeology, artifacts are portable objects used, modified, or made by humans. But, unlike artifacts, which can be removed for later analysis, features have to be fully documented where they are found. **Features** are non-portable elements of a site that cannot be removed without altering or destroying their form (Renfrew and Bahn, 2018). A few examples include an animal burrow, posthole, ditch, trash pit, or built structure. Although archaeologists cannot remove a posthole from a site, they can learn much about the structure of the site and human behavior by documenting such features.

A grave is an example of a common feature found in a forensic context. It is part of the site that cannot be removed, but if excavated properly, valuable information regarding the tools used in grave digging, depositional characteristics, and natural or human-induced alterations can be preserved.

Figure 10.1 Major horizons commonly described during archaeological excavations.

Source: Figure 10.1 is adapted from A Detailed Cross Section of Soil Layers with Growing Grass on Top Free PNG (https://www.vecteezy.com/png/59939396-a-detailed-cross-section-of-soil-layers-with-growing-grass-on-top) and Cross-section of soil layers with lush green grass on top showing different layers of earth Free PNG (https://www.vecteezy.com/png/59939371-crosssection-of-soil-layers-with-lush-green-grass-on-top-showing-different-layers-of-earth) by sm wizard hosted by Vecteezy.com (https://www.vecteezy.com/free-png/png-file); composite overlay 3D diagram using elements from both images

Stratigraphy, Soil, and Sediments

Archaeological sites often have layers of soil, sediment, and debris accumulating over time. For an archaeologist, these layers, or **strata**, provide a record of past events. They are the primary basis for understanding buried materials and provide the most direct information on how objects came to be buried. **Stratigraphy** is the analysis of layered deposits to understand the chronological sequence of events and how they relate to human activity, environment, and site formation (Renfrew and Bahn, 2018). The strata can be viewed as the pages in a book, while the stratigraphy is the story that is being told (Dirkmaat and Adovasio, 1997).

Soil Horizons

Soil is the layer of generally loose mineral and/or organic materials that occurs in the land surface and usually hold liquid, gases, and biota (Soil Survey Staff, 2022). Soil is affected by physical, chemical, and or biological processes and is characterized by layers that are distinguishable from the underlying parent material. Soils differ from **sediments**, which are transported or deposited particles or aggregates derived from rocks, soils, or biological material (Soil Survey Staff, 2022). Sediments may be transported by natural forces (e.g., wind, water, ice) or mechanical processes (e.g., digging, tillage). The terms *soil* and *sediment* cannot be used interchangeably: sediments are primary constituents in soil, but soils take a long time to develop their physical, chemical, and biological properties and characteristics (Soil Survey Staff, 2022).

Soil may also be characterized by **soil horizons**, or distinct layers with unique physical, chemical, and biological characteristics resulting from soil-forming processes (Figure 10.1). The arrangement of these horizons is known as a **soil profile**. Most soil conforms to a similar general pattern of horizons in profile (Soil Survey Staff, 2022):

- Organic (O horizon): uppermost layer rich in loose organic matter, like decaying leaves and other plant debris.
- Topsoil: (A horizon): mixture of mineral and organic matter, often with a granular structure and friable consistency and where most biological activity occurs.
- Eluviated (E horizon): lighter-colored layer where minerals and organic matter have been leached out by water, leaving behind mainly sand and silt.
- Subsoil (B horizon): zone of accumulation where materials leached from above horizons are deposited.
- Substratum (C horizon): partially weathered layer of unconsolidated parent rock material from which soils develop.
- Bedrock (R horizon): underlying consolidated bedrock layer.

In forensic archaeology, **sterile soil** refers to any soil horizon in an excavation or within a burial site that does not contain evidence or data relevant to the specific incident under investigation.

Soil Characteristics

The mineral particles that make up soil are categorized into three groups by size: sand, silt, and clay. Sand particles are the largest and clay particles are the smallest (Figure 10.2) (Soil Survey Staff, 2022). Most soil is a

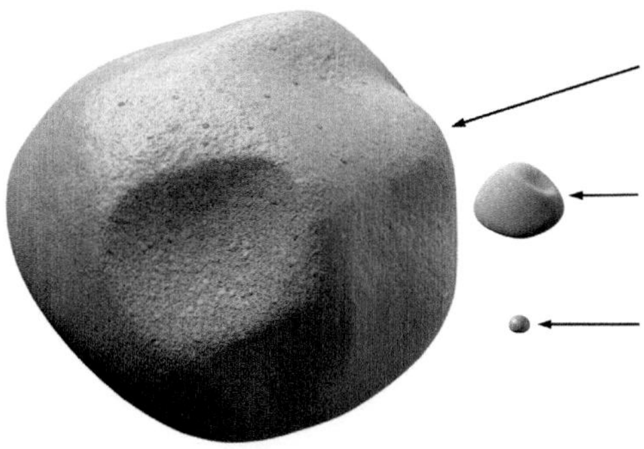

Figure 10.2 Relative size comparison of sand, silt, and clay particles.

Table 10.2 Main Types of Soil and Their Natural Characteristics

Sandy
• Formed from larger, coarse particles that do not adhere or stick to one another, and grate against each other when rubbed together
• Nutrient-poor, loose density, quick drainage, and often highly acidic
• Well aerated; decomposition often occurs more quickly in this burial environment*
Silty
• Formed from medium-sized particles that are smooth in texture
• Nutrient-rich, medium density, moderate drainage, and slightly acidic to slightly alkaline
Clayey
• Formed from small, tightly packed particles that are sticky and plastic when wet
• Nutrient-rich, high density, poor drainage, and alkaline
• Poorly aerated; decomposition often occurs more slowly in this burial environment*
Loamy
• Balanced mixture of sand and silt, and a smaller proportion of clay, with added organic material
• Nutrient-rich, medium density, good drainage, and often slightly acidic
Peaty
• Formed from partially decayed organic matter in oxygen-deficient conditions
• Nutrient-rich, low density, waterlogged, and acidic
Chalky
• Formed from small, tightly packed particles with a high proportion of calcium-rich minerals
• Nutrient-poor, medium density, moderate drainage, and alkaline

Source: Information derived from USDA Natural Resources Conservation Service, U.S. Department of Agriculture at https://www.nrcs.usda.gov/resources/guides-and-instructions/soil-classification

* Denotes information from authors and not attributed to USDA NRCC source

combination of the three. Table 10.2 provides a description of the main categories of soil recognized in field archaeology. Soil is commonly described using a standard method, developed by the U.S. Department of Agriculture's Natural Resources Conservation Service (NRCS), that distinguishes differences in texture, color, consistency, composition, and chemistry.

Soil texture refers to the relative proportions of sand, silt, and clay in a given amount of soil (Soil Survey Staff, 2022). When recording soil texture during excavation, it is more efficient to use a general measure of the soil texture. Most archaeologists use the following rule after lightly moistening the soil being described: clay coheres, silt adheres, and sand does neither (refer to Appendix E for flowchart of the process). In other words, clayey soils are sticky and plastic, silty soils are smooth, and sandy soils are gritty. There are a variety of soil texture guides that may be used to easily identify particle size as well as the texture class (refer to Figure 2.11). A soil texture triangle is also used to help identify the 12 basic **soil texture classes** (Figure 10.3). A clay loam, for example, contains nearly equal parts of sand, silt, and clay, while a sandy loam contains around twice the amount of sand as silt and clay.

In archaeology, the color of soil is evaluated using commercially available color reference systems. The most common system, the **Munsell soil color book** (refer to Figure 2.11), uses a set of color chips that are matched

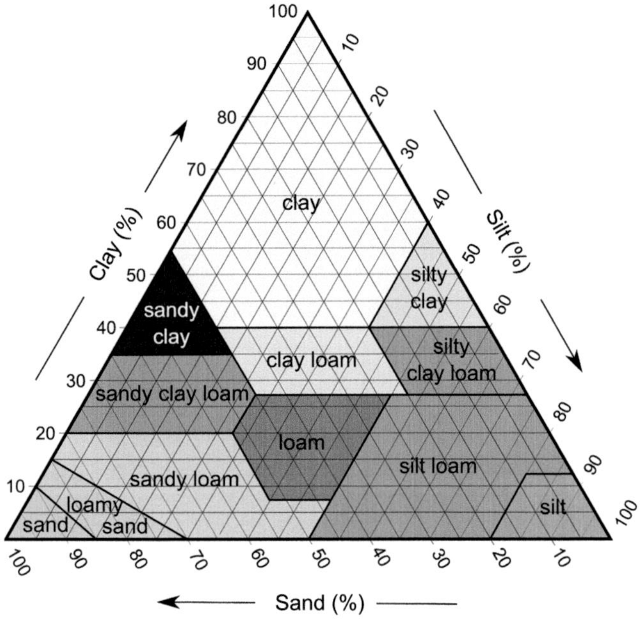

Figure 10.3 Soil texture triangle showing the percentages of clay, silt, and sand in the 12 basic texture classes recognized by the United States Department of Agriculture.

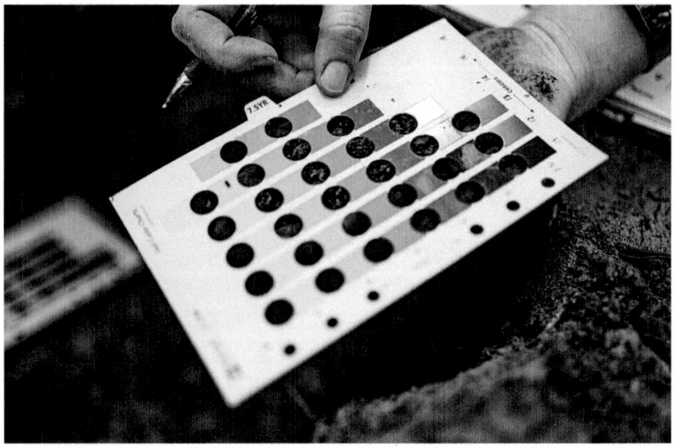

Figure 10.4 Dr. Audrey Scott, a scientific recovery expert with Defense POW/MIA Accounting Agency, uses a Munsell Soil Color Chart during an investigative recovery mission in Sekong Province, Laos Democratic People's Republic, November 17, 2019.

Source: is a Photograph by U.S. Navy Mass Communication Specialist 1st Class Tyler Thompson who is within Public Domain (Defense POW/MIA Accounting Agency (DPAA)), adapted from https://www.dvidshub.net/image/5965716/us-team-investigates-sites-laos-remains-missing-service-members; the appearance of U.S. Department of Defense (DoD) visual information does not imply or constitute DoD endorsement.

with soil, and an alphanumeric notation for the soil color hue (color family), value (lightness or darkness), and chroma (intensity) is identified (Figure 10.4). Soil color hue is influenced primarily by mineral content. For example, soil containing iron is typically yellowish or reddish in color, while soil containing calcite or quartz tends to be whitish gray or very pale brown in color (Soil Survey Staff, 2022). The value of soil color is often the result of its carbon content, as with the darker values commonly seen in topsoil. Soil color value and chroma changes with the amount of moisture it contains; therefore, an estimate of the level of moisture in the soil (e.g., wet, moist, dry) at the time the color is referenced should be noted (Soil Survey Staff, 2022).

Soil consistency is the degree to which soil particles stick together and resist deformation or rupture (Soil Survey Staff, 2022). At different moisture levels, soil can exhibit varying consistencies, and is often measured for wet, moist, and dry soil samples. Table 10.3 provides a list of descriptors that are easy to use in the field when describing consistency of a moistened cube of soil when pressed between thumb and forefinger or by squeezing in the palm of the hand.

Soil composition refers to the proportions of different components that make up soil. These components include mineral particles, organic matter, water, and air, as well as living organisms (Soil Survey Staff, 2022). **Soil chemistry** analyzes the types and amounts of chemical elements and compounds present in the soil (Soil Survey Staff, 2022). This includes properties like soil pH, oxidation potential, and the capacity to store and supply essential nutrients. For archaeological purposes, soil chemistry is important in understanding how chemical processes interact with human remains and other evidence that may be found in contact with soils or buried in them. For example, **soil pH**, which is the measure of acidity or alkalinity, significantly affects the preservation of materials. Acidic sediments tend to produce conditions for poor preservation of soft tissues and bone, while alkaline sediments tend to produce conditions for good preservation of bone but poor preservation of soft tissues. Soil sample tins or soil sample bags (refer to Figure 2.11) are used to collect soil and sediments for composition and chemical analysis.

Table 10.3 Simple Field Assessment of Soil Consistency

Consistency	Structure of Moistened Cube of Soil
Loose	Cannot be formed into a cube (i.e., non-coherent single grain structure)
Weak	Falls apart easily with very slight force
Friable	Crushes easily with little resistance under slight force
Firm	Crushes with noticeable resistance under moderate force
Hard	Crushes with moderate resistance under strong force
Cemented	Cannot be crushed, or breaks apart only under extreme force

Source: Information derived from USDA Natural Resources Conservation Service, U.S. Department of Agriculture at https://www.nrcs.usda.gov/resources/guides-and-instructions/soil-classification

During excavation, each soil horizon and its characteristics should be described in your field notes (refer to Appendix E for sample recording form). This information aids in identifying any stratigraphic disturbances and reconstructing the events that may have caused them. Official soil descriptions for each county in the United States are listed on the United States Department of Agriculture (USDA) Natural Resources Conservation Services (NRCS) website (http://soils.usda.gov/survey/printed_surveys). By selecting your state from the list, you will be forwarded to a list of county soil publications (e.g., maps, local soil taxonomy) that are available for download free of charge.

Principles of Deposition

Soil horizons, sediments, and depositions of debris that form strata will vary due to topography, climatic and environmental changes, as well as biological factors (e.g., plants, animals, microorganisms) and human interventions (e.g., building a road, digging a hole), and these variations can occur over long or short periods of time. In archaeology, it is assumed that the order in which the different strata are deposited will reflect the sequence of events that occurred at the site. Figure 10.5 shows an example of stratigraphy encountered during excavation at a forensic scene and the documented reconstruction. The stratigraphy includes differing soil horizons and sediment layers as well as features, such as an old barn foundation (c), a cement floor (f), and a pit containing human remains (h). It is impossible to dig a hole and fill it exactly as it was without leaving evidence of disturbance within the strata. From a forensic perspective, digging a grave disturbs the strata, inevitably making the gravesite detectable either to the trained eye of the forensic archaeologist (refer to Chapter 6) or by using specialized equipment, such as ground-penetrating radar (refer to Chapter 7). In most situations, when a perpetrator fills in a grave, the sediment used to **backfill** the hole will consist of a mix of the strata removed during digging, and in some cases, additional materials from the surrounding surface area. A grave is typically identified by a characteristic known as a **burial cut**, which is the line of definition between the backfill sediment and the strata through which the grave has been dug. In Figure 10.5, the burial cut is indicated by disturbances in the sandy clay soil layer (d), the cement floor (f), the construction debris layer (g), and the mixed fill from removal during burial and then used to cover the remains (j). All stratigraphic reconstruction in archaeology is based on four basic principles of deposition: superposition, association, reversal, and intrusion.

Superposition

The principle of **superposition** simply presumes that more recent sediment layers are laid down on top of older ones and that the strata are found in a position like that of their original deposition (Harris, 1989; Renfrew and Bahn, 2018). Archaeologists use the principle of superposition to establish a relative chronology of strata and the artifacts and features they contain. For example, an object found in a layer closer to the surface will typically be considered a more recent deposit than the objects deposited in layers beneath it. This information can help reconstruct the events that occurred at the site; however, it is important to note that superposition places objects in analytical order based on their sequence of deposition, not on the exact chronological age of the objects themselves.

Superposition can easily be applied to forensic recovery, particularly in cases involving multiple individuals and associated evidence. When excavating these types of graves, bodies and objects that are closer to the surface of the grave can be interpreted as being placed last, while those found at the bottom of the grave would have been placed first. The relative dating information acquired through careful excavation of the remains and

Figure 10.5 Example of a section drawing of the stratigraphy associated with a burial (in order of deposition): (a) consolidated rock layer, (b) sterile silty clay soil layer, (c) barn foundation, (d) sandy clay soil layer, (e) barn wall, (f) cement floor, (g) construction debris layer, (h) human remains, (i) chemical layer added to speed decomposition, (j) mixed fill removed during burial and used to cover remains, (k) bricks used to fill hole in cement floor, (l) remaining mixed fill used to conceal hole in cement floor, and (m) topsoil layer and surface vegetation.

the sediment layers can supply invaluable information to investigators. For instance, a bullet casing deposited on the surface of a grave must have been placed there after the burial process was finished, but not before or during the process. Objects found in a layer above, beneath, or with the remains must have been deposited before, after, or at the time of burial respectively. Objects found in any strata of a grave may yield physical evidence that should be interpreted relative to the layer from which it was recovered. When excavating, it is important to keep in mind that new strata, such as a layer of lime or various chemicals, may have been added in an attempt to conceal or aid in decomposition of the remains.

Referring to Figure 10.5, we can develop a sequence in the burial of a body under the cement floor by using superposition. After digging through a layer of construction debris (g), a cement floor (f) was broken, and grave was then dug for the body (h). After placing the body in the grave, a chemical substance (i) was dumped on top of the body and the grave was then backfilled using the sediment from the disturbed strata, which is now a mix (j) of sandy clay and construction debris. Bricks (k) were placed in the break of the cement floor and then covered with the remaining mixed fill (l). We know from superposition that the body was placed in the pit before the added chemical substance, and the bricks were placed in the burial pit before being covered with a layer of remaining mixed fill. We can also determine that the surface layer (m) was deposited after the burial took place, as it lies on top of the construction debris layer (g) and the burial cut.

Association

The principle of **association** presumes that objects found together within the same layer or feature were deposited at approximately the same time (Renfrew and Bahn, 2018). As discussed earlier, it's crucial to understand the context in which objects are found. This includes not just the stratum, but also the specific feature and the spatial relationship between objects. However, this principle must be used with caution, as some objects are held for a very long time before they are discarded (e.g., family heirlooms, tools, coins), making them chronologically much older than the other objects with which they may be associated. For example, coins are typically in circulation over a lengthy period of time, and most individuals do not throw coins away; still, they seem to work their way into sediment layers through various means. If coins are found in association with human remains recovered in a forensic context, the dates on the coins can provide some information concerning the time of deposition, but not the actual date. The individual would have been buried after the most recent date on the coins, not necessarily during the year that the coin was minted. This same principle applies to other objects that contain dates of copyright, patent, production, and shelf life.

While the principle of association is a powerful tool in reconstructing events, it is not foolproof. Investigators should be aware that natural processes and human activities can disturb layers and cause objects to be redeposited in different contexts.

Reversal

In rare cases, objects or materials may have been moved from one location and deposited in another in reverse order. In archaeology, this is principle is called **reversal** (Hester et al., 2009). Natural causes of reverse stratigraphy include rockslides, tree throws, banked wall collapse, or soil erosion. **Erosion** is the wearing-away of soil horizons by natural forces such as wind, ice, or water flow (Soil Survey Staff, 2022). As an example, a body placed in a depression might be covered with surface debris, and the surrounding soil from higher ground may erode and eventually cover the body as well as the surface debris. This can result in a reversal of layers over the remains and surface debris.

Human activity also plays a huge role in reverse stratigraphy – construction, excavation, and general digging all disrupt soil horizons and deposit material in reverse order. For example, when digging a grave, the existing strata are disturbed as material is removed and placed next to the hole. In undisturbed soil, topsoil is dug first and throw onto the ground surface. Then, lower horizons are dug and thrown onto that, and so on, until the required depth for the grave is reached.

Intrusion

Intrusions are disturbances that cut into previous deposits and introduce materials from a different context or time sequence (Hester et al., 2009). This principle recognizes that any intrusion must be more recent than the deposit through which it cuts. In forensic contexts, animal burrows, tree root displacement, and mechanical disturbance during construction, farming, or gardening cause most intrusions. During the excavation of remains, it is important to determine whether or not the initial burial cut has been disturbed and identify the cause of any intrusions within the backfill strata. In forensic investigations, it is fairly common to encounter intrusions caused by later removal or alteration of the contents of a grave (refer to Case Study #15 as an example).

Specific Forms of Perturbation

Archaeologists recognize specific natural and cultural processes that are a part of site formation; however, they also alter and affect a site's features and subsurface environment. **Perturbation** refers to any event, natural or human-induced, that disrupts the normal structure of in situ soils and sediments. These processes often include bioturbation, erosion and sedimentation, frost heaving, compaction and depression, and compression caused by human activities such as movement across the site and tool use. In a forensic context, the focus on changes from these types of processes center on the grave and the immediate surrounding environment in efforts to recognize the exact source of any disturbances as well as possibly identify the initial method of digging.

Bioturbation

Bioturbation is the process where living organisms disturb, mix, and rework soils and sediments. This includes animal activities such as movement, burrowing, and ingestion and defecation of sediment particles. It also includes plant root growth, decomposition, and secretion. The taxa responsible include earthworms, termites, rodents, and rabbits (Fowler et al., 2004; Pelletier et al., 2017).

Bioturbation can disrupt a grave by displacing sediments, affecting soil composition, and even influencing how a body decomposes. For example, scavenging animals tend to displace evidence when digging and will often carry skeletal elements back to their burrows or through their tunnels for consumption or gnawing purposes (refer to Chapter 5). The burrowing activity tends to move buried objects downward as tunnels collapse underneath them (Morin, 2006), although rodents are capable of transporting bones through a tunnel network, especially where these are a nutrient source or object for gnawing. Tunneling activity also could deposit small bones on the surface along with removed sediments. Traces of tunnels and skeletons of small mammals that died in their burrows (and may be highly complete) are important indicators that some movement of human remains within a grave may have occurred. It is sometimes necessary to follow these tunnels or dig into a nearby animal burrow to recover smaller skeletal elements. Changes in nutrient levels due to bioturbation affect the type of microbes involved in decomposition (Overturf, 2022), and the redistribution of organic matter during decomposition may draw in insects and scavenging animals (Haługzko et al., 2022).

Seasonal information from plant growth as well as animal and insect activity can often assist with determinations of postmortem interval (PMI). Root networks from plants can either hold together or displace burial evidence; therefore, the rate of root growth could be an important factor in understanding changes in the remains and the surrounding environment. In addition, slice or cut marks in roots that were caused by digging tools during the burial process are often overlooked. The amount of regrowth or decomposition in plant roots can also aid in seasonal or yearly determination of PMI (Bock and Norris, 1997; Willey and Heilman, 1987).

Sedimentation

Sedimentation is the process by which particles settle out of fluid and accumulate on a surface. This includes the deposition of rock fragments, finer-grained minerals, organic matter, and dissolved materials that have been transported by water, wind, or ice during erosion. For example, water flowing over or through a grave may result in the sedimentation of eroded silts or the formation of fissures. The formation of fissures from water flows can cause skeletal elements or objects to become embedded in soil horizons beneath the grave. When fissures are encountered in a grave, they should be carefully excavated in an attempt to recover any missing skeletal elements. Careful excavation can also help determine the number of rain events that led to the buildup of silt layers. This information may be matched with local weather records to estimate the PMI. Evaporation of moisture from silty or clayey soils may result in cracking patterns that change during wet and dry phases. These patterns can be affected over time by soil and remains settling within the grave, and, on occasion, the patterns may be used to locate edges of a burial cut (Hochrein, 2002).

Frost Heave

Frost heave occurs when water in the soil freezes and expands, causing the upward or outward movement of the ground surface or objects within the ground. This is particularly noticeable in cold regions with frost-susceptible soils and higher water tables. In regions with consistent freezing and thawing, frost heaving can affect cemeteries, causing tombstones, coffins, and burial vaults to shift and crack. This process can also significantly impact the positioning of remains through upward lifting and displacement of skeletal elements and other evidence within a grave.

Compaction and Depression

In archaeology, **compaction** refers to the reduction in volume or density of soil or sediments due to applied force. Compactions are familiar elements in most forensic scenes and include impressions from such things as a suspect's shoes, tires, and hands and knees, as well as the backs of shovel blades, which are commonly used to pack and flatten the fill on top of a grave. In addition, areas of extreme compaction may retain cloth impressions, particularly those from denim, wool, or other types of heavy, coarse-weave fabrics. All compaction marks should be photographed or cast to preserve their details so that they may be later used as evidence in identifying a suspect.

When working with graves, depressions are changes in the surface contours of the soil that usually result from decomposition and settling of the remains. They are typically described as being either primary or secondary formations. A **primary grave depression** forms as a result of natural compaction of the loose sediment that was placed over the body and settling after the release of gases and the collapse of the abdominal region during decomposition (refer to Figure 6.10). A **secondary grave depression** may form within the primary depression due to additional sediment compaction and soft tissue decomposition (refer to Figure 6.12). Eroded holes made by scavenging animals over the burial are commonly mistaken for a secondary depression.

Compression Marks

Compression marks are produced when an object is pressed against another object or material with sufficient force to leave an impression, usually as a negative contour variation of the object's surface. Compression marks left by tools or footwear used during burial are routinely overlooked even though they may be well preserved on or beneath the ground surface (Evis et al., 2016; Stephens et al., 2020). Understanding how the grave was dug and what tools were used may offer insight into the amount of planning and forethought that went into preparing the grave. Some soils, such as clays and silts, readily retain tool marks; however, sandy soils and gravels are too coarse and dry to retain these kinds of details. Often soil and sediments adhere to digging tools and may be matched to a specific soil horizon associated with the burial cut.

If there is a possibility that tool mark evidence may be preserved, every effort should be made to avoid **contamination** or destruction of existing tool marks by tools used during excavation and recovery. To prevent this from happening, the forensic archaeologist should clearly define the outline of the burial cut, and excavations should begin inside of this line with small hand tools. When the excavation level is below the areas possibly containing tool marks, small hand tools and brushes can be used to expose the marks for close-up photography and casting. Castings of tool marks are typically made using dental gypsum and a mason's board to form a negative image of the tool mark. These casts often show notches and striae that have formed along the edges of the digging tool, which can be matched with the exact tool or, at the very least, with the class of tool used. In addition, paint chips from the surface of a tool, not evident to the naked eye, may also be recovered in the casting process. It is important to keep in mind that while compression marks can indicate the type and dimensions of the tool used, they may not always be unique enough to identify a specific tool.

ARCHAEOLOGICAL APPROACHES TO RECOVERING HUMAN REMAINS

As most forensic archaeologists can attest, every recovery scene involving human remains is different, and as such, the archaeological techniques used to excavate a site must be adapted to each particular scene. While each scene is different, the general methodology of excavation and recovery of remains is similar. Forensic archaeology makes use of systematic and controlled approaches that can be effectively applied no matter the condition or context of the recovery scene, but flexibility is key when evaluating the environment and working conditions encountered during the recovery process.

Recovering Surface Site Remains and Associated Evidence

Human remains that are left on the surface are likely to be disturbed in some manner prior to recovery (Killam, 2004). In these instances, every effort must be made to recover as much evidence as possible, especially in locations where the terrain is difficult and scattering may be extensive. Accurate recording and mapping of **primary** and **secondary surface sites** are also important in these instances so investigators can better understand and reconstruct the events that took place during the PMI (refer to Chapter 8). At the start, both the forensic archaeologist and crime scene personnel should keep duplicate records of all scene personnel involved in the recovery, all photographs, and all evidentiary materials, as well as the chain of custody for any materials recovered by the forensic archaeologist and removed from the scene (refer to Appendix B and Appendix F for sample recording forms).

Stage 1: Examining and Recording the Scene and Recovery Area

Typically, a forensic investigator will determine the perimeter of the scene, and crime scene personnel will carry out all initial documentation of evidence. However, in some instances, the forensic archaeologist will assist in this process.

It is recommended that in either situation, the forensic archaeologist should take the following steps to examine and record the scene and recovery area prior to any recovery actions:

1. Record the context of the scene and recovery area (refer to Appendix B for sample recording forms) and appraise any constraints on recovery (e.g., landscape, weather, time limits, labor, and equipment availability).
2. Plan any adaptations to archaeological methods for recovery.
3. Determine the extent of the primary surface site associated with the remains and designate the perimeter of the recovery area. If possible, determine if there are associated secondary surface sites.
4. Establish whether or not restricted routes of access to and from the primary surface site, as well as in and out of the recovery area, have been set by the crime scene personnel.
5. Complete detailed descriptions and a general overall sketch of the scene and recovery area. It is also recommended that the recovery area and its immediate surroundings be photographed.

Stage 2: Establishing Spatial Controls and Recording Surface Sites

Provenience and context are equally important in surface and burial recovery. Establishing spatial controls early in the process of surface recovery will help ensure that, from the start, all data are recorded properly, and that the entire scene can be reconstructed with as much accuracy as possible.

This is most often accomplished using the following steps:

1. Construct a baseline and set a primary datum for mapping surface levels and evidence in the recovery area (refer to Chapter 8). In some instances, you may need to construct multiple baselines or reference grids within the site when recording various concentrations of evidence.
2. Record and map any specific perturbations and any material evidence found on the surface of the recovery area, avoiding the primary surface site at this time. Move from the perimeter inward in a 1-m interval spiral pattern to avoid disturbing or damaging any secondary surface sites in the area (refer to Chapter 6 for additional surface search patterns that may be useful).
3. Remove or trim any surface vegetation to expose the remains for photography, recording, and mapping.
4. Record and map all secondary surface sites and any additional associated evidence, starting with secondary sites that might be disturbed when working to record and recover the primary surface site.
5. After any secondary surface sites or additional associated evidence within the recovery area have been mapped and recorded, determine the method of mapping that will be used to record the primary surface site.

6. Construct a baseline or reference grid for exposing and recovering the primary surface site and set a secondary datum (if the primary datum for the recovery area is still within workable distance for mapping the primary surface site, a secondary datum is not necessary). If time and space permits, it is recommended that a reference grid is used in recovery and mapping of the primary surface site to ensure all evidence is recorded with the greatest amount of accuracy possible.

During the recording and mapping of evidence within the recovery area, it is recommended that a metal detector be used (refer to Chapter 7) to locate any bullets, casings, or additional metal-based evidence (e.g., jewelry, coins, medical devices) prior to removing and screening any surface materials (refer to Chapter 6). The screening process can easily abrade metal objects and, especially in the case of bullets and casings, this can damage fine striations that may be used in comparative evidence analysis.

Stage 3: Exposing, Recording, and Removing a Secondary Surface Site

After the forensic archaeologist and the crime scene personnel review all evidence records and maps associated with secondary surface sites in the recovery area, the remains may be removed and recorded. Use a separate surface site recovery form (refer to Appendix D for sample form) for each feature encountered in surface site recovery.

Keeping flexibility in mind, the following steps should be used based on the context of each secondary surface site:

1. Remove any loose debris (e.g., leaves, sticks, trash) surrounding the remains in the secondary surface site. Screen or sort through the loose debris. If working in a large area, keep materials separate based on mapping references used to record position of remains.
2. Record and map any newly exposed elements or associated evidence.
3. If the skeletal remains overlap each other, treat the remains as if they were in layers, recording and mapping each layer prior to its removal. If any remains are partially embedded in the ground surface, be sure that each element is carefully loosened from the surrounding sediment with small excavation tools before attempting removal. Never pull any evidence out of the ground, as this can cause unnecessary damage to the remains.
4. If the forensic archaeologist is trained in human osteology, the skeletal elements may be inventoried during recovery. Otherwise, the visual summary of elements recovered and condition of the remains should be recorded (refer to Appendix A for sample inventory forms).
5. During removal, any entomological or botanical samples that are related to the remains should be collected and recorded (refer to Chapter 9, and Appendix C for sample forms).
6. All remains should be handled and packaged following proper collection guidelines (refer to Chapter 11).
7. Once all of the evidence has been removed from the secondary surface site, the ground surface should be examined with a metal detector, if available.

Stage 4: Exposing and Recording the Primary Surface Site

Extreme care should be used when clearing and exposing the ground surface of the primary surface site, as small bones, teeth, and hair tend to be swept up in leaf litter or debris. If these materials are swept up, these items should be recovered during proper screening and sorting of the material and their associated baseline transect or reference grid location recorded (refer to Chapter 8).

Using the following steps:

1. Remove any loose debris (e.g., leaves, sticks, trash) from the surface of a baseline transect area or reference grid area one square at a time by hand or with a hand trowel keeping materials from each baseline transect or reference grid square separate.
2. Remove or trim any surface vegetation to expose the remains for recording and mapping. Take care to record any in situ debris or vegetation that may have been purposefully placed over the remains. Screen or sort through surface vegetation, keeping material from each baseline transect or reference grid square separate.
3. Record and map all exposed elements and associated evidence.

Any piles of debris around the remains, whether natural (e.g., tree limbs or leaves, rocks or gravel) or cultural (e.g., trash heap, construction materials) in origin, should be carefully examined and treated and recorded as possible evidence of concealment. For example, when searching through any twigs or larger branches, examine them for signs of 'greenstick' breaks and stripped bark (refer to Chapter 9). These typically occur when breaking and removing branches from living trees, and they may indicate intentional concealment of the body.

Stage 5: Removing Remains at a Primary Surface Site

Like the secondary surface site process, the forensic archaeologist and the crime scene personnel should review all evidence records and maps associated with primary surface site prior to removal of any remains. Any possible errors in recording or labeling can be detected before the primary site is disturbed.

Again, keeping flexibility in mind, the following steps should be used:

1. When encountering skeletonized remains, if they are clearly disarticulated, remove skeletal elements starting at the outermost edges and work toward the greatest concentration. If the skeletonized

remains appear to be in anatomical position or only slightly disarticulated, start removal at the feet (or most distal elements present) and work toward the skull. If the remains are partially decomposed and still retain soft tissues, it may be necessary to clear an area adjacent to the remains so they can be carefully lifted or rolled, preserving their integrity as much as possible, and placed into a body bag.

2. If the skeletal remains overlap each other or if it is suspected that more than one individual may be present, treat the remains as if they were in layers, recording and mapping each layer prior to its removal. If any remains are partially embedded in the ground, be sure that each element is carefully loosened from the surrounding sediment with small excavation tools before attempting removal. Never pull any evidence out of the ground as this can cause unnecessary damage to the remains and disturb the context of any evidence hidden beneath the surface.
3. If the forensic archaeologist is trained in human osteology, the skeletal elements may be inventoried during recovery. Otherwise, the visual summary of elements recovered and condition of the remains should be recorded (refer to Appendix A for sample inventory forms).
4. During removal, any entomological or botanical samples that are related to the remains should be collected and recorded (Appendix C; refer to Chapter 9).
5. All remains should be handled and packaged following proper collection guidelines (refer to Chapter 11).
6. Once all of the evidence has been removed from the baseline or grid area, a sediment sample should be collected from the area thought to be directly below the abdominal region of the remains and the ground surface should be examined with a metal detector, if available.

Stage 6: Examining Soil Horizon Beneath Surface Sites

In many instances, smaller elements from a surface site may settle into the soil over time and become covered with eroded sediments or buried during animal scavenging. In addition, some insects associated with the decomposition of human remains tend to dig into the soil horizon beneath the remains during certain stages of their life cycle.

For these reasons, it is recommended that the soil horizon beneath any surface site is thoroughly examined using the following steps:

1. Using a hand trowel, the ground should be carefully scraped down to sterile soil. All of the removed sediment should be screened. In a primary surface site, sediment recovered from each grid square should be kept separate.
2. A final sweep using a metal detector should be completed after sterile soil has been exposed to ensure that all metallic evidence has been collected.

After the sterile soil beneath all surface sites has been cleared in a final sweep, the recovery area should be double-checked by the forensic archaeologist and crime scene personnel for any remaining details. Any secondary datum set during recovery should be tied in to the primary datum for the recovery area. All evidentiary materials, tools, and equipment should be removed from the scene, except for the datum. Final overview and midrange photography should be completed at each primary and secondary surface site, the recovery area, and the overall scene after everything has been cleared and removed.

Recovering Buried Remains and Associated Evidence

When excavated properly, graves have many of their own characteristics that can provide vital information to the investigation. Table 10.4 provides a list of questions that a forensic archaeologist usually keeps in mind throughout the recovery process. Recognizing the various types of evidence depends on systematic and careful removal of the grave fill from the original walls and floor of the burial cut. Extreme care should be taken at each step of the process to ensure proper recording and mapping of evidence with nothing being moved or removed without first noting its position and marking it for later identification on scale drawings. Photographs should be used as a backup to the written record and not as the principal source of information.

There are two distinct methods for approaching and performing a grave excavation. **Pedestal excavation** involves carefully exposing remains while leaving them supported by a column or 'pedestal' of the surrounding sediment. While this approach allows the forensic archaeologist to investigate the remains in their original position and context, and also gather information

Table 10.4 Common Questions Forensic Archaeologists Should Consider during Excavation of Graves

- How was the grave originally dug? What tools were used?
- Was the grave dug quickly, or was it carefully prepared?
- Was the grave left open for a span of time prior to burial?
- Can a sequence of events be determined for construction of the grave?
- Is there consistent evidence throughout that can be used to estimate postmortem interval?
- Is the burial deliberate or due to natural processes (e.g., soil reversal during erosion)?
- Is there evidence connecting the grave, the individual buried, and the gravedigger?
- Is there anything in the sediments that is foreign to the original soil layers (e.g., lime or quicklime)?
- Is there evidence that could indicate manner of death?

from the surrounding layers, it presents a greater risk of damaging or destroying associated evidence or skeletal elements not in an expected anatomical position or elevation within the grave. It is recommended that this approach be used only by expert excavators in cases with highly complex contexts of recovery. **Platform excavation** refers to the process of cutting into the horizontal area adjacent to the primary feature being excavated, after the area it has been fully documented, and creating a platform from which to work safely. This is often used when working in soils that easily collapse (e.g., sandy or muddy contexts), and if the excavation is deep enough where there is a risk of dropping equipment or tools on remains when handing them off between the excavator and any crime scene personnel. In many instances, it is helpful to combine platform excavation with pedestal excavation when densely packed concentrations of evidence are encountered. The excavation of human remains generally follows a series of stages, which are presented here.

Stage 1: Examining and Recording the Recovery Area

This stage follows a process similar to the initial steps of surface site recovery. Any precautions mentioned in the recovery of surface remains should also be observed when working with buried remains.

Using the following steps:

1. Record the context of the site and recovery area (refer to Appendix B for sample forms) and appraise any constraints on recovery (e.g., landscape, weather, time limits, manpower, and equipment availability).
2. Plan any adaptations to archaeological methods that may be necessary for recovery.
3. Determine the extent of the scene associated with the grave and designate the perimeter of the recovery area. If the grave appears to be disturbed, determine if there are any secondary surface sites that may be associated with the grave.
4. Establish whether or not restricted routes of access to and from the scene associated with the grave, as well as in and out of the recovery area, have been set by the crime scene personnel.
5. Complete detailed descriptions and a general overall sketch of the site and recovery area. It is also recommended that the recovery area and its immediate surroundings be photographed.

Stage 2: Establishing Spatial Controls

This stage is the most important aspect to the excavating and recording processes involved in the recovery of buried remains. Without proper spatial control, provenience and associations among recovered evidence and the potential for reconstructing events surrounding the burial process may be lost. When screening materials from an excavation, the screening area should be set up on flat ground not too far from the excavation but carefully selected so as not to interfere with the reference grid if, for various reasons, it should need to be enlarged.

Using the following steps:

1. Construct a baseline and set a primary datum for mapping surface levels and evidence in the recovery area (refer to Chapter 8). In some instances, you may need to construct an additional baseline or reference grid in any area with a heavy concentration of evidence located away from the primary area of recovery.
2. Record and map any specific natural or cultural alterations and any material evidence on the surface of the recovery area, avoiding the immediate area surrounding the grave at this time. Move from the perimeter of the recovery area inward in a 1-m interval spiral pattern to avoid disturbing or damaging any surface deposits in the area that may be related to the grave (refer to Chapter 6 for additional surface search patterns that may be useful).
3. Using methods in the recovery of surface remains described previously, record and remove surface evidence from the recovery area, avoiding the immediate area surrounding the grave. The ground surface of the recovery area should be examined with a metal detector, if available, to identify any metallic evidence.
4. After the surface evidence from the recovery area has been removed, record and map any surface evidence immediately surrounding the grave that might be disturbed during the construction of a reference grid.
5. Construct a reference grid over the grave (Figure 10.6) and establish a secondary datum within the reference grid for use during excavation (refer to Chapter 8).

Stage 3: Identifying and Recording the Burial Cut

The second most important aspect in the recovery of buried remains is the identification of the burial cut. In some cases, skeletal elements may sustain damage when clearing the ground surface or when shovel shining is used in an attempt to identify the outline of a grave (refer to Chapter 6). Extreme care should be used when clearing and exposing the ground surface as sediment may have eroded to the extent that the remains or associated evidence may be slightly exposed or just below the surface. As a general rule when excavating, whenever you encounter a noticeable change in sediment (e.g., texture, color, consistency, composition), stop and assess the situation before you proceed. Stratigraphy recording forms (Appendix E) and a grave excavation recovery form (Appendix D) should be used for recording during all stages of the excavation.

Figure 10.6 Students constructing a grid over a suspected grave at a simulated crime scene.

Using the following steps:

1. Remove any loose debris (e.g., leaves, sticks, trash) and surface vegetation from the reference grid area one square at a time by hand or with a hand trowel, keeping materials from each reference grid square separate. Any piles of debris around the remains, whether natural (e.g., tree limbs or leaves, rocks or gravel) or cultural (e.g., trash heap, construction materials) in origin, should be carefully examined and treated and recorded as possible evidence of concealment. Screen and sort through all materials removed from the surface of the burial site.
2. Scrape surface soil, no deeper than 1 cm at a time, into dustpans and buckets for screening. Keep materials from different grid squares separate during screening so that any evidence recovered during this process can be placed in association with other items and properly referenced.
3. Continue removing the uppermost soil in 1-cm layers until you can identify the burial cut by changes in soil color or other characteristics such as cracks, depressions, or tool marks (refer to inset 'How to Shovel Shine' in Chapter 6 if this method would be applicable). Figure 10.7 illustrates an example of an exposed burial cut shown in a reference grid plan and section drawing.
4. Once the burial cut has been identified, clear the entire grid area to the same level and map the surface contours, burial cut of the grave, and any exposed remains or associated evidence. In certain geographical locations, soil and sediments may homogenize after a length of time has passed, and the burial cut may not be defined. If this is the case, map any surface contours, changes in soil characteristics, and any exposed remains or associated evidence before moving on to the next stage of recovery.

Stage 4: Excavating and Recording the Grave Feature

At this stage, there are two options in proceeding with excavation, depending on whether the burial cut can be identified.

If the burial cut is not clearly defined by color differences in the soil or other characteristics, proceed in the following manner:

1. Working from a corner and then across the grid, excavate soil in 5-cm layers one square at a time using a hand trowel, keeping all grid squares at the same depth. If a stratigraphic change is encountered, adjust excavation depth to an arbitrary level following the stratigraphic change across all grid squares.
2. Screen all sediment from each layer removed from the grid area, keeping materials separate during screening. Record the elevation of the sediment from each grid square so any objects recovered during screening can be placed in association with other items in reference to the datum.
3. Record and map any objects encountered before moving on to remove the next soil layer.
4. If a burial cut is encountered, proceed with the excavation as outlined in the following set of steps; if remains, containers, wrappings, or other items used for concealment or as grave fill are encountered, move to Stage 5 to expose and record the remains and/or objects.

If the burial cut is evident, it is recommended that investigators excavate the grave feature, meaning that

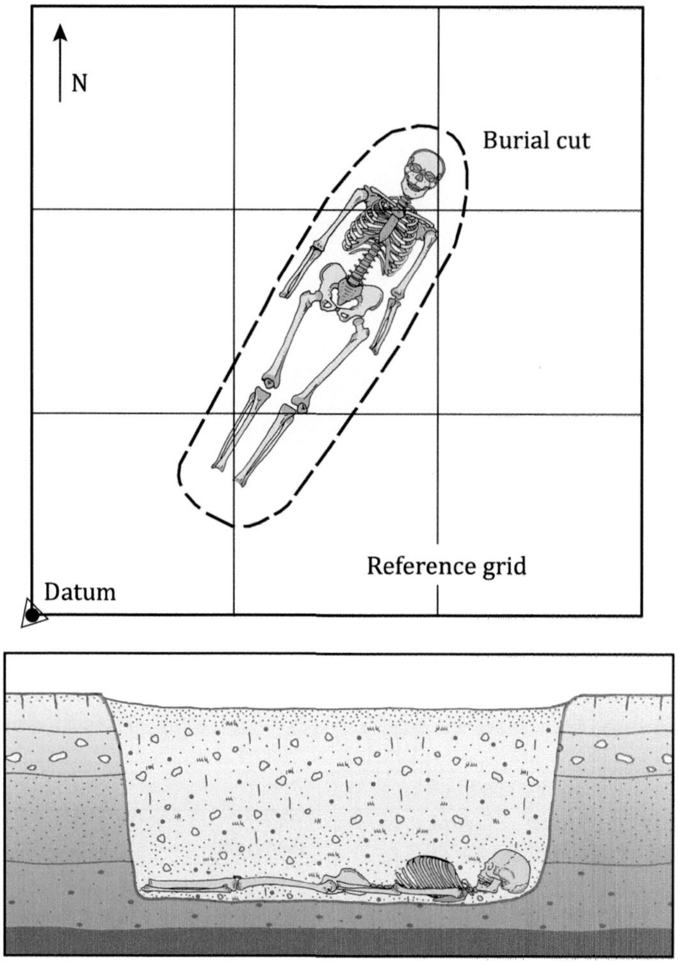

Figure 10.7 Example of an exposed burial cut shown in a reference grid plan (top) and complete profile drawing (bottom).

the removal of grave fill will primarily occur in stages within the defined burial cut (Connor and Scott, 2001) (Figure10.8). If the burial cut is ignored as a defining limit during the recovery process, there is every probability that materials from surrounding soil horizons can contaminate the burial and be mistakenly introduced as evidence.

Excavation of a grave feature with a defined burial cut should proceed as follows:

1. Initially, only one half of the grave should be excavated until remains or any containers or wrappings are encountered. This reveals a profile of the position and orientation of the body within the grave that can be clearly shown in drawings and photographs (Figure 10.9). Once the profile has been recorded, the other half of the grave may be excavated in the same manner.
2. Excavation should begin in the grid square over the center of the grave and move out toward the burial cut, leaving a 3–5-cm margin of grave fill along the outline. This preserves the walls of the burial cut, increasing the possibility of recovering evidence from any compression tool marks.

Figure 10.8 Author Sandra Wheeler (right) demonstrates the proper procedures for excavating a burial feature.

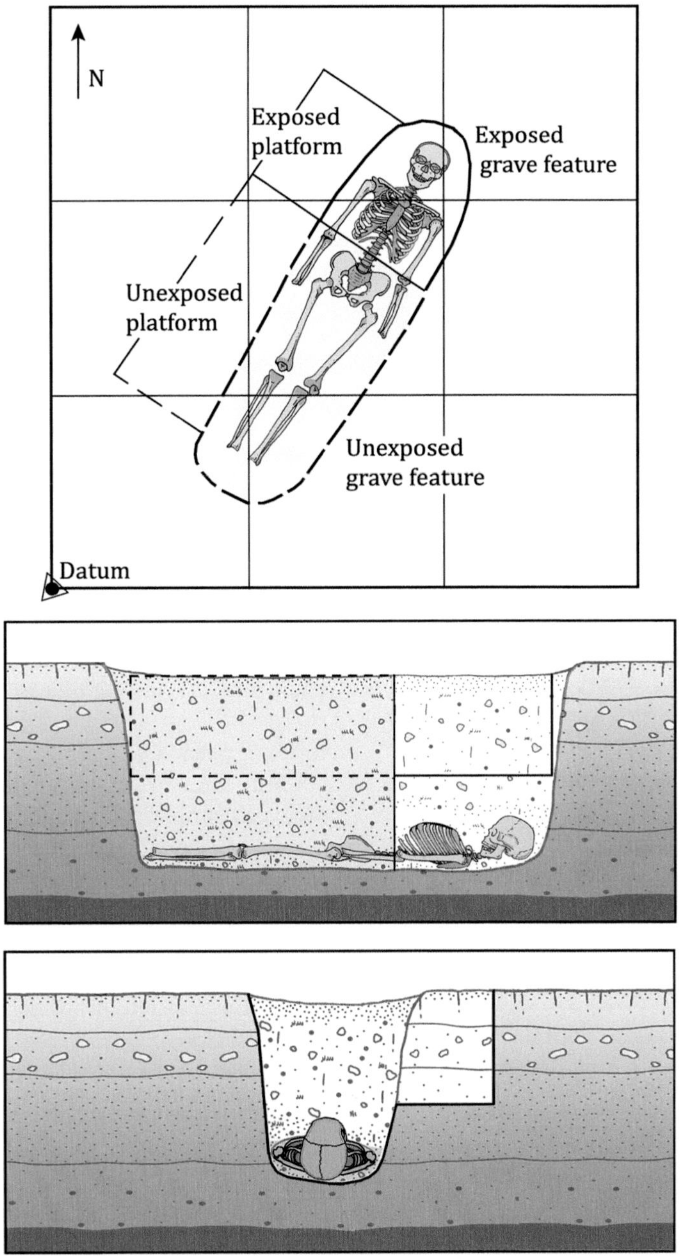

Figure 10.9 An example of a reference grid (top), profile (center), and section (bottom) drawing with a portion of the grave feature exposed. In this instance, a working platform was constructed after the wall of the burial cut was examined for tool mark evidence.

3. Continue removing grave fill in 3–5-cm layers across the grave feature, again leaving a 3–5-cm margin of grave fill along the outline. If the remains are thought to be in an extended position, use extreme care when removing fill from the ends of the grave, as one end will contain the skull and the other, the feet, both of which can easily be disturbed or damaged if the depth of the grave is unknown.
4. Screen all fill from each layer removed from the grave feature, keeping materials from each grid square separate during screening. Record the depth of the soil being screened so any associated evidence recovered in this process can be placed in association with other items and properly referenced.
5. After the first 20–25 cm of fill has been removed from within the grave feature, extreme care should be taken when excavating the remaining fill along the walls of the burial cut, using only small hand tools and brushes to avoid damaging any tool marks that may be present.
6. Depending on soil and safety conditions (e.g., sandy soil collapse, water table depth), it may be beneficial to construct a working platform (Figure 10.9) along the length of one wall of the

Figure 10.10 Orange County homicide detective Dave Clarke (right) uses a datum line to record depth measurements for exposed clothing and skeletal elements at a simulated crime scene.

burial cut after the wall has been fully examined and recorded. This provides not only a working area closer in depth to any encountered remains, but also a platform that facilitates better photographic angles when documenting the excavation, remains, and associated evidence.

7. Record and map any objects encountered before moving on to remove the next layer (Figure 10.10). Note any differences in stratigraphy by placing markers in one excavation wall to assist in recording and constructing a scaled section drawing. It is also good practice to take a midrange-view photograph of these markers as well.
8. Once remains, containers, wrappings, or other items used for concealment or as grave fill are encountered, move to Stage 5 to expose and record the remains.

Stage 5: Exposing and Recording the Remains *In Situ*

During this stage, all residual grave fill surrounding the remains should be excavated. The process of gradually uncovering remains *in situ* is designed to preserve the position of the body and the relationship of any associated evidence, such as wrappings around the remains, containers, or any materials added with the remains, or discarded prior to filling the grave.

If containers (e.g., storage bins, coolers, luggage, shipping boxes), wrappings (e.g., carpets, blankets, tarps), or other items used for concealment or as grave fill are encountered, these should be treated as any other layer within the grave and excavated with care as additional evidence may be collected from the folds or surfaces of the materials. The forensic archaeologist should work in tandem with the lead investigator to determine the degree to which remains held in containers or wrappings will be excavated. Depending on preservation and context, an evaluation of whether the container or wrappings with remains will be removed as a single unit or if remains will be recovered from the container or wrappings at this stage of excavation.

Extreme care should be taken when exposing the remains as many important items may be overlooked if not considered during recovery. Such things as contact lenses, pacemakers, prosthetic implants, and items associated with surgical procedures (refer to Chapter 4) are quite common in modern populations, and most can play a role in the identification of an individual. Any unidentified objects found in association with the individual should be kept as evidence until a medical examiner or forensic pathologist can review the materials.

From this point onward, everyone involved in the recovery should follow health safety protocols for crime scene personnel who come in contact with human remains. Although wearing gloves when handling human remains is a common precaution against viral or bacterial infections, another reason for this practice is that certain materials may have been added during burial to accelerate decomposition or applied to the body to preserve the remains. For example, many embalming fluids contain high levels of formaldehyde, and in some environments, this chemical may oxidize into formic acid, which, upon contact with skin, can cause a reaction equivalent to that of bee stings or fire ant bites (International Agency for Research on Cancer, 2006). In addition, many corrosive household cleaners contain lye (sodium hydroxide or potassium hydroxide), a very strong caustic substance, which can cause severe chemical burns when coming into contact with skin, as well as the fumes causing extreme irritation in the eyes, nose, and mouth (NIOSH Pocket Guide to Chemical Hazards, 2019). Wearing gloves also reduces the chances of DNA contamination of the remains.

Table 10.5 provides a list of small hand tools (refer to Figures 2.9 and 2.10) used to minimize damage to remains and evidence during excavation.

Table 10.5 Use of Small Hand Tools to Minimize Damage to Remains and Evidence during Excavation

Bypass Pruning Shears

- Cut roots as they are exposed (without pulling)

Leaf and Square Trowel

- Gently remove very thin layers of sediment located in tight spaces between remains or evidence by inserting tool between sediment and object (but not in contact with objects)
- Use square or leaf end to produce very precise edges in excavation unit or in sediment around remains or evidence prior to photography

Leaf and Point Dental Tools

- Gently remove sediment located in very tight spaces between remains or evidence by inserting tool between sediment and object (but not in contact with objects)

Plastic Sculpting Tools and Bamboo Paddle Skewers

- Gently remove sediment located in very tight spaces between remains or evidence when contact with the surface is necessary

Kitchen Utility Scoop or Plastic Hand Scoop

- Remove loose sediment around remains or evidence in grave feature by brushing it into hand scoop and transfer to dustpan or bucket

Coffee Scoop or Spoon

- Gently remove loose sediment in tight spaces around remains or evidence after clearing the sediment with leaf and square trowel and dental or sculpting tools

Short Handle Angled Sash Paint Brush

- Gently brush loose sediment to expose remains or evidence while excavating
- Brush loose sediment into hand scoop for transfer to dustpan or bucket
- Clean-up surface areas prior to photography

Round Trim Paint Brush or Toothbrush

- Gently brush loose sediment to expose remains or evidence
- Clean-up area close to remains or evidence prior to photography

Cosmetic Powder Brush

- Delicately brush loose sediment to expose fragile or friable bone and evidence
- Clean-up delicate surface areas on bone or evidence prior to photography

Small Bulb Syringe

- Clean-up delicate surface areas on bone or evidence prior to photography

Box #5: How to Use an Archaeological Hand Trowel

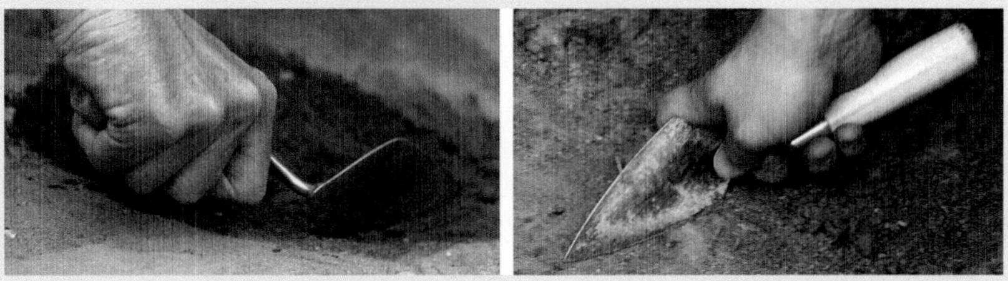

TO USE AN ARCHAEOLOGICAL TROWEL

1. Hold the trowel with four fingers wrapped around the handle and the thumb pressed down toward the blade.
2. Place the longer, bottom edge of the trowel on the soil surface, with the top edge angled away. The angle of the trowel may vary depending on the specific context. For general cleaning purposes, a shallow angle is typically most effective for slicing thin layers from the surface, resulting in a clean and precise cut. For removing thicker layers of soil or cleaning around rocks or roots, a steeper angle may be needed.

3. Using your arm (not your wrist), scrape away a thin layer of soil by moving the blade toward yourself in a smooth motion for a clean, even surface. Avoid digging into the soil with the point or corners of the blade.
4. Always trowel in the same direction to maintain a consistent surface and avoid creating holes or patterns that might be mistaken for features.
5. Pull the sediments scraped from the surface toward you and then away from the excavation area into a dustpan for removal.

TROWEL EXCAVATION TIPS

- Troweling is a skill that improves with practice. Experiment with different grips to find the one that provides the best balance and control for the task at hand.
- While the trowel can be used to remove soil, it is not intended for extensive digging. Use other tools like shovels or spades when digging is necessary.
- Never use the tip of the trowel for detailed cleaning, such as defining edges of bones or other evidence found in a forensic context. A variety of small detailing tools (refer to Figure 2.10) are discussed in Chapter 2.

To gradually uncover remains *in situ*, carefully proceed with the following steps:

1. As a general rule, when exposing remains, hand trowels should only be used in areas two-to-three times the size of the blade and never near bone or other evidence. Working carefully with small hand tools, expose all remains within the grave feature (Figure 10.11). Always work laterally from exposed areas toward unexposed areas, keeping the excavation surface level as much as possible. Use a leaf and blade trowel to carefully loosen sediment near remains or evidence, avoiding surface contact with any objects. Use a small slant-edge or round sash paintbrush to move any loose sediment into a hand scoop or kitchen utility scoop, then deposit it into a dustpan or bucket.
2. When working in tight spaces where tools may come into contact with remains or evidence or when clearing grave fill from surfaces of remains or evidence, always use plastic sculpting tools or bamboo paddle skewers to loosen sediment (Figure 10.12). Use a round sash paintbrush or cosmetic brush to move any loose sediment from surfaces or tight spaces into a spoon, coffee scoop, plastic beach shovel, or kitchen utility scoop, then deposit it into a dustpan or bucket. Avoid using paintbrushes on any fabrics, as this can damage or destroy fiber evidence. If the remains or evidence appear to be fragile or friable, a cosmetic brush and small bulb syringe may be the best option when carefully exposing surfaces for recording and photography.

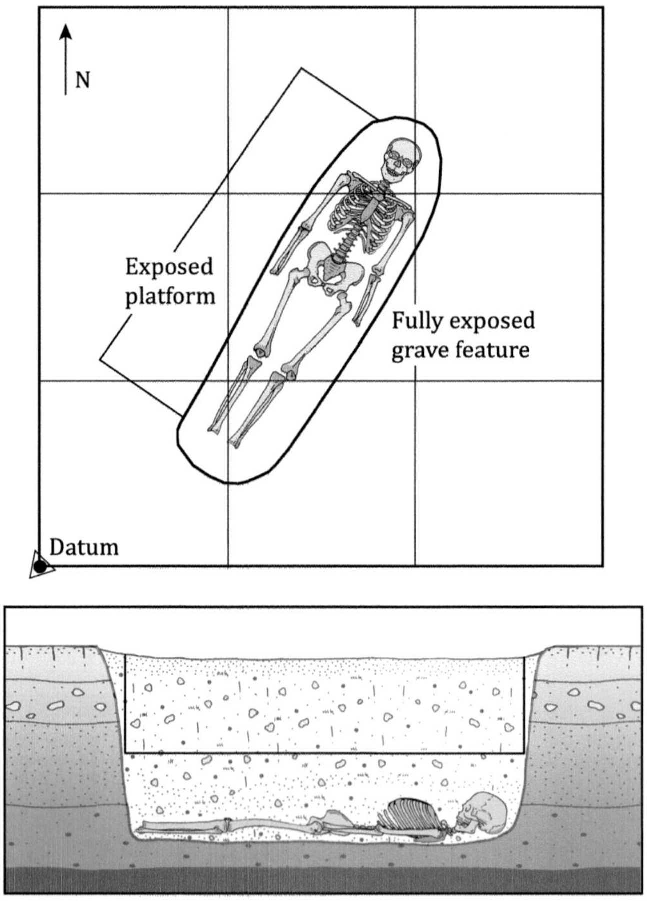

Figure 10.11 Example of a reference grid (top) and a profile (bottom) drawing of a grave feature with the remains fully exposed. After examining each section of the burial cut wall for tool marks, a platform area was excavated along the full length of the burial cut to provide a safe working environment during excavation.

Figure 10.12 Author Sandra Wheeler (front right) and students expose and clean the skeleton for mapping and photography at a simulated crime scene.

3. All excavation notes should contain details of any damage that may occur during recovery to avoid any confusion about tool marks on the remains at a later date.
4. As remains or associated evidence are exposed in the excavation, they should be recorded and mapped. With the exception of any mapped and fully recorded smaller items that may impede excavation, nothing should be removed from the excavation at this stage.
5. When excavating in areas around the abdominal and pelvic regions, extreme caution should be used, as fetal remains may be present in females. These are very fragile and expert handling is recommended (refer to Chapter 11 for collecting and packaging juvenile remains).
6. Grave fill in the thoracic and abdominal cavity areas tends to contain insects and other chemical evidence not easily detected in the field. Entomological samples (refer to Chapter 9) and sediment samples (refer to Appendix E) should be taken prior to fully exposing the area around the pelvis and lumbar vertebrae. Plastic sculpting tools and bamboo paddle skewers should be used when excavating these areas to gently loosen and sift through the sediment prior to screening.
7. If the remains are held in a container or wrapping, the following points should be mapped with elevations recorded using the datum line:
   - Any corners, handles, or closures on the container
   - Any edges or folds that are significant in concealing the remains.

   If the remains are not held in a container or wrapping, the following points, at a minimum, should be mapped with elevations recorded using the datum line (Figure 10.13):
   - Skull
   - Thoracic region
   - Pelvic bones
   - Knees, elbows, shoulders, hands, and feet
   - Any objects associated with the remains.
8. All remains and associated evidence should be fully recorded and mapped. All documentation from the excavation should be reviewed. A summary of the condition of the remains (D) should be completed before moving to Stage 6 of the process.

Figure 10.13 Author Sandra Wheeler (front left) and students record depths for points on a skeleton using a datum line at a simulated crime scene.

Stage 6: Removing the Remains

The following process largely refers to skeletal remains in a supine position (i.e., horizontal body position with the face and torso facing up) but can be adapted to remains found in various stages of decomposition. If the skeletal remains are not in a supine position, the sequence and direction of removal may vary considerably. In cases such as this, skeletal elements that overlap one another should be removed and recorded in layers using the following suggested order when possible. All skeletal elements should be inventoried as they are removed. Visual skeletal inventory forms are provided in Appendix A. All remains should be handled and packaged following proper collection guidelines (refer to Chapter 11).

Remains held in partial articulation by preserved clothing, such as shirts, pants, shoes, or socks, should be removed as a unit and investigated under more controlled conditions. Any skeletal elements not contained within clothing should be removed and packaged separately from those contained in preserved clothing. If remains still retain a large percentage of soft tissue, every effort should be made to avoid damage to the existing tissues. As skeletal elements are removed, be sure to check for any jewelry, such as necklaces, earrings, rings, or bracelets, which may have slipped into the surrounding grave fill or soil horizon.

If there is a possibility of skeletal elements disintegrating upon removal in a waterlogged environment, a fiberglass metric tailor's tape (refer to Figure 2.4) can be used to obtain in situ length measures of all long bones and recorded in the field notes.

To minimize disturbance and damage to an individual:

1. First remove the left and right patellae and lower legs.
2. The feet should be removed next, keeping the bones from the left and right feet separate. Take extreme care to recover any toenails that may be found near the ends of toes.
3. To remove a femur, carefully lift the distal end and gently move it toward the opposite side of the body. This will loosen the proximal portion of the bone from the pelvis. Repeat this for the other side.
4. If the hands are positioned at the sides or placed across the abdomen, they should be removed next, keeping the bones of the left and right hands and wrists separate. If they are placed underneath any other part of the skeleton, remove them after the other skeletal elements have been recovered. Take extreme care to recover any fingernails that may be found near the ends of fingers.
5. The pelvis is removed next. It may be necessary to further detail and loosen soil around the edges and underside of the innominates (os coxae) or sacrum before lifting. After the innominates (os coxae) have been loosened from the grave fill, gently rotate them toward the center line of the body to loosen the articular surface shared with the sacrum. This also allows access for further loosening of soil below the sacrum before removal. Check for possible soft tissue preservation or clothing between these bones and the underlying soil.
6. Next, remove the lower arm by carefully lifting the distal ends of the radius and ulna upward, loosening the proximal portions of the bones from the humerus. Repeat this for the other side.
7. To remove a humerus, carefully lift the distal end and gently move it toward the opposite side of the body. This will loosen the proximal portion of the bone from the scapula. Repeat this for the other side.
8. Next, remove the clavicles, and then remove the ribs, starting with rib #1 and working down toward rib #12, keeping the left and right sides separate and, if possible, in correct order. Taking great care, loosen each rib individually before removal and avoid pulling.
9. To remove the left and right scapula, loosen soil around the edges and undersides starting with the distal end and working toward the proximal end. Gently lift each scapula from the lateral edge for removal. Check for possible soft tissue preservation or clothing between these bones and the underlying soil.
10. Vertebrae should now be removed in order from the lowest lumbar vertebra through to the top cervical vertebra.
11. The hyoid and mandible are removed next, taking great care so the lower dentition remains in the mandibular sockets.
12. Finally, after ensuring the grave fill around the cranium is loosened enough for lifting, gently cradle it in both hands with equal pressure on the fingertips and palms of your hands. It may be necessary to gently move the cranium side to side while holding it to check for invasive roots before fully lifting and removing it. Never lift the cranium up by the eye orbits or any other opening, as the bones in these areas are very fragile and will easily break. Check for possible soft tissue preservation or clothing between cranium and the underlying soil. Also be aware that scalp and facial hair may have slipped from position and may be preserved under the cranium or around the lower facial region.
13. If the forensic archaeologist is trained in human osteology, the skeletal inventory (Appendix A) should be reviewed at this time to account for any possible missing elements.

Stage 7: Recording and Excavating the Grave Feature Floor

The grave feature floor is often mistakenly thought to be the point at which the evidence stops, but at times, it can contain some of the most important evidence within the burial context. Many items or materials may have penetrated the floor in a visually unrecognizable manner (e.g., bullets fired through a victim, permeating toxic chemicals added to accelerate decomposition, teeth, and small hand and foot bones) and at times, further entomological evidence may be recovered from these sediment layers (refer to Chapter 9).

The following process will complete the recording of the grave and aid in the detection of any remaining evidence associated with the grave feature:

1. Record soil types and elevations of each stratigraphic layer (Appendix E) using the markers placed in the wall of the grave when stratigraphic changes were encountered. These data can be used in constructing a scaled section or profile drawing. It is also good practice to take a midrange-view photograph of these markers after all remains have been removed.
2. Collect and record a sediment sample from the floor of the feature (Appendix E) and another sample from at least 5 cm beneath the grave floor. A metal detector should also be used over the floor at this time, if available.
3. Using a hand trowel, carefully scrape all surfaces of the grave feature and screen for evidence that may have been embedded in the walls or under the body. If any missing skeletal elements or embedded evidence is encountered, change to small hand tools to avoid damage during their recovery.
4. Scrape the floor of the feature using a hand trowel until sterile soil is detected across the entire area. Follow any fissures caused by erosion, cracks, or animal burrows to recover displaced remains or associated evidence.
5. Record and map any additional evidence recovered in relation to the grave feature.
6. Once everything has been recorded and collected, the lead investigator and forensic archaeologist should determine whether the grave should be backfilled at this time. If the grave is to be backfilled, the removed sediment should be used and then leveled with the surrounding surface.
7. After the recovery area has been double-checked for any remaining details, all materials should be removed from the scene except for the datum. If a secondary datum was set during excavation and recovery, it should be tied in to the primary site datum. Final overview and midrange photography should be completed.

CASE STUDY #14: ONE PERSONA AT A TIME, PLEASE

Authors Sandra Wheeler and Lana Williams assisted in the recovery of human remains discovered in a supposedly empty cemetery plot. Using heavy equipment, gravediggers discovered that the plot reserved for a recently deceased individual was already occupied. The operator of the backhoe noticed some bones in the soil that had been removed from the plot and immediately stopped digging. The cemetery manager notified local law enforcement of the situation. Upon our arrival at the scene, law enforcement personnel had set up a tent with a portable heater over the disturbed grave, as it was winter with a layer of snow on the ground. Our first task was to investigate the fill removed from the plot as well as the sediment in the backhoe bucket. This task was somewhat challenging as groundwater from the snow melt was flowing through the fill and had turned it into a pile of mud. A few loose teeth, three cervical vertebrae, and a pair of glasses were found.

After clearing the fill and backhoe bucket of any remains, a ladder was placed in the grave so the rest of the remains could be recovered (Figure 10.14). This also proved challenging, as a small, ice-cold spring of groundwater was running through the floor of the grave, waterlogging the soil, the remains, and the excavators. Once the mud fill surrounding the body had been cleared away, we could see that the cranium had been dislodged by the backhoe, but the rest of the remains were largely undisturbed. The individual appeared to be dressed in a suit, shirt with a tie, and shoes and socks. Large fragments of pressboard and coffin handles were recovered along the walls of the excavation.

The remains were placed in a body bag as a single unit within the excavation and then lifted out of the grave. The associated evidence and the previously discovered skeletal elements were packaged separately, and all the remains were taken to the Coroner's Office for analysis. The area around and beneath where the body was positioned was investigated further, but no other evidence was recovered. Subsequent investigation of the remains indicated that this individual had been autopsied prior to burial. This treatment and evidence of a coffin suggested that this case was not of forensic significance, but rather was the result of a clerical error on the part of the cemetery, perhaps accidentally burying someone in the wrong plot.

Figure 10.14 Author Lana Williams excavating remains discovered in a cemetery plot that should have been empty. Note the water pump hose to the left of the grave and the condition of the soil. A square section of plywood was used as a platform to keep investigators from sinking down into the mud while excavating.

CASE STUDY #15: THE INTRUSIVE INMATE

Figure 10.15 The wooded lot identified by Smith as the spot where he buried Lisa Brighton.

Figure 10.16 After completing the search, work areas were sectioned by survey tape, and investigators cleared the surface debris in each section. Note the survey flags marking the areas where the metal detector alerted to a target.

Fourteen-year-old Lisa Brighton was last seen on May 25, 1987, walking near a convenience store with Wayne Smith. At this time, Smith was already under investigation for the rape of another woman. Formal charges were brought against Smith for this rape, and he was sentenced to three years in jail. While Smith was serving his sentence, investigators were building a case against him for the suspected murder of Lisa.

In 1991, Smith was released from prison. Since investigators suspected him in the disappearance and murder of Lisa, they assigned officers to tail Smith in the hope that he would return to Lisa's burial site. One afternoon, Smith escaped the scrutiny of his observers, and during this time, he did return to Lisa's grave, dug up her remains, and removed certain skeletal elements. Smith had conducted research while in prison as to which skeletal elements were typically used for identifying an individual. If Lisa's remains were ever discovered, Smith wanted to ensure that investigators could not identify her. Of course, this was prior to DNA being used as a reliable method for forensic identification. Although they never discovered the location of Lisa's remains, investigators were able to amass enough information to arrest and charge Smith with Lisa's murder six years after her disappearance. Prosecutors convinced a jury of Smith's guilt, without the discovery of Lisa's remains, and he was sentenced to death.

In September of 2001, 14 years after Lisa's disappearance, a rare and highly unusual plea deal was arranged in which Smith agreed to confess to Lisa's murder and reveal the location of her remains. For his cooperation, Smith's death sentence would be converted to a life sentence without parole. At this time, Smith revealed the details of Lisa's murder and also told investigators about revisiting Lisa's grave in 1991 and removing certain skeletal elements. Under heavy security, Smith identified a wooded lot and the general area in which Lisa was buried (Figure 10.15). Although Smith could not pinpoint the exact location of the grave, as the vegetation had changed dramatically over 14 years, he revealed pertinent details that assisted investigators in their search plan. Smith indicated that he had buried Lisa in a shallow natural depression, with her head beside the root of a large tree. At the time of Lisa's burial, the area around the wooded lot was under heavy construction, and Smith said he took large strips of metal from the construction site and placed them over her body. He then used a metal bucket to scoop dirt and cover the body. When Smith returned to the burial site in 1991, he said that he lifted several of the metal pieces and removed Lisa's skull and her right leg in an effort to mask her identity. Smith's rationale for removing these skeletal elements was that Lisa's teeth could be used to make a dental identification, and he knew when Lisa was younger, she had been in a serious car accident that required surgical reconstruction of her right leg, leaving behind signs of trauma and an orthopedic screw plate that might be used to identify her.

The investigating team, including authors Tosha Dupras, Sandra Wheeler, and Lana Williams, proceeded to search the area using multiple techniques. First, the area was searched using a strip or line search method. During this time, investigators looked for any signs of a grave depression, and also for the descriptors that Smith had mentioned. After the visual search was conducted, a metal detector was used to scan the area for the strips of metal Smith reported using to cover Lisa's body. Survey flags were used to mark any metal detector alerts. The last search technique used was a cadaver dog, alerting

Figure 10.17 Author Lana Williams (left) and a crime scene investigator screening all surface debris in buckets identified by surface section.

Figure 10.19 Excavation using hand trowels and bypass pruning shears revealed several large pieces of metal.

to an area associated with the metal detector alerts. The combination of all these search techniques indicated a particular area within the wooded lot. The perimeter of the area was marked with flagging tape, and the ground surface was cleared of debris (Figure 10.16). All the removed debris was then screened, so that no possible evidence would be overlooked (Figure 10.17).

After clearing the surface, a grid was set up over the area (Figure 10.18) and excavation proceeded. It was not long before several strips of metal were revealed (Figure 10.19). At each stage, the scene was documented with photographs, and evidence was mapped on plan (Figure 10.20) and section drawings. After the metal strips were documented and removed, excavations continued, and within the next few centimeters of fill, the skeletal remains were revealed. One particularly important piece of evidence, a tooth, was discovered in the thoracic region (Figure 10.21). If improper excavation techniques had been employed, this tooth may not have been collected. Although Smith had made every effort to remove all dental evidence, the tooth must have fallen out of the skull as he removed it, and due to its similarity

Figure 10.18 After clearing the surface, a grid was established over the area. Letters were placed along the baseline and numbers were placed along the reference lines to identify each grid square.

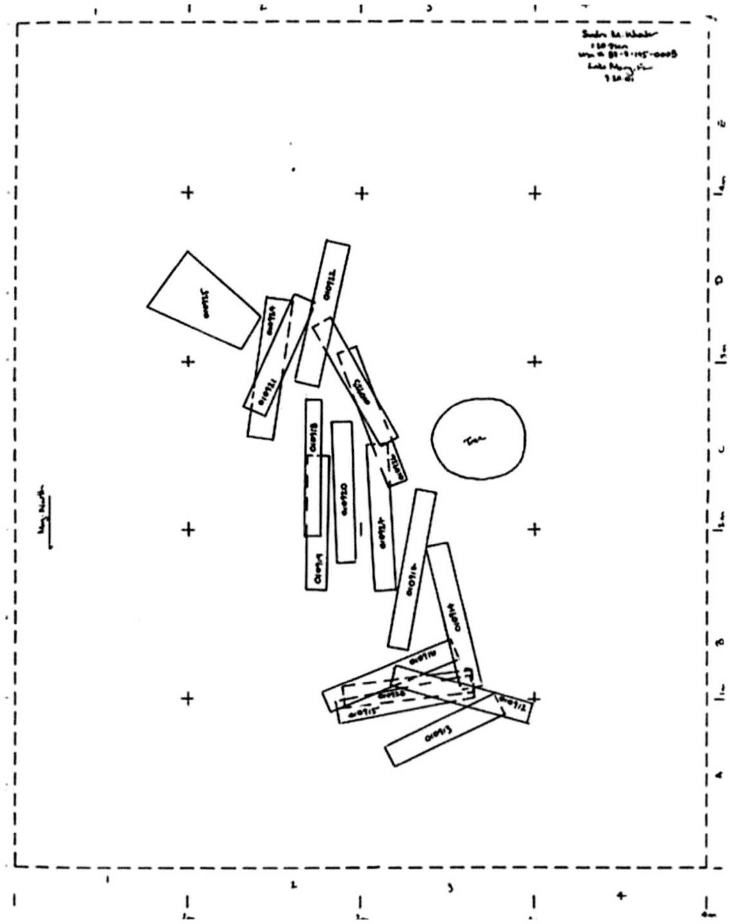

Figure 10.20 Scaled field plan drawing showing the placement of the metal strips in relation to the large tree. Note each metal strip is labeled with a corresponding number from an evidence collection list maintained by the crime scene technician.

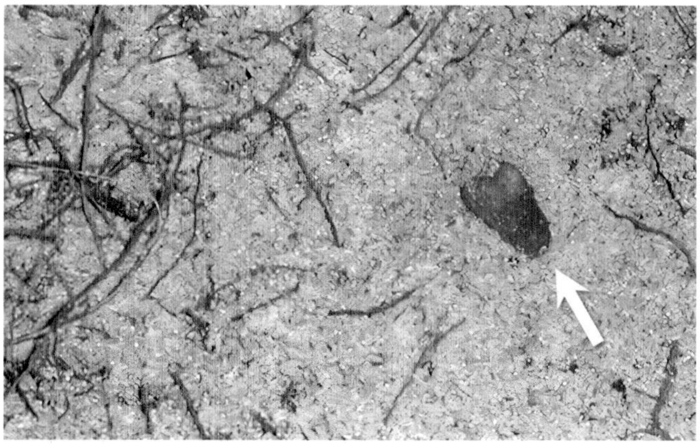

Figure 10.21 Single tooth (arrow) recovered from Lisa Brighton's grave.

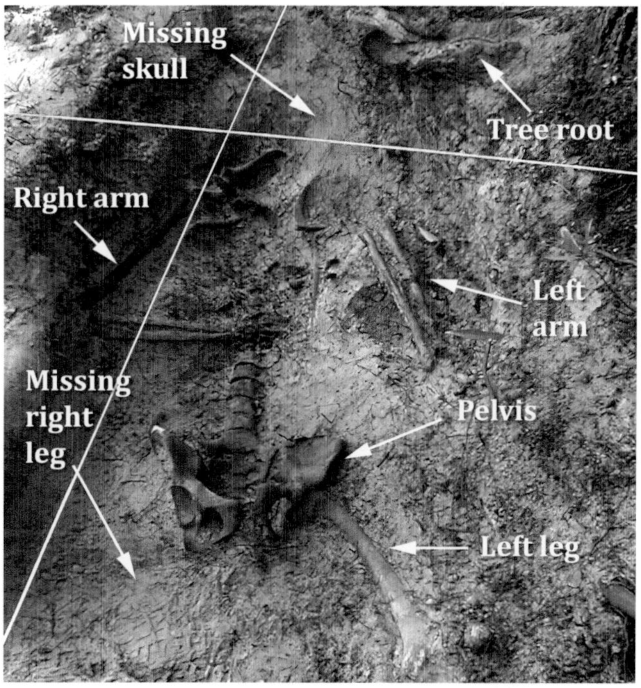

Figure 10.22 Exposed remains of Lisa Brighton. Note the missing skull and right leg.

in color to the surrounding grave fill, it went unnoticed. While it was insufficient for dental identification, this tooth was later used for DNA analysis and contributed to the positive identification of Lisa's remains.

Excavations proceeded until the entire skeleton was exposed (Figure 10.22). Once the skeleton was completely uncovered, some of the details of Smith's description were confirmed. For example, the position of the skeleton was such that the skull would have been beside or slightly under a large tree root. In addition, both the skull and the right leg were missing. Detailed plan and section drawings were constructed before the skeleton was removed (Figures 10.23 and 10.24). After removal, the skeleton was brought to the local Medical Examiner's Office for further analysis. Lisa's remains were positively identified and then returned to her family. Smith's original death sentence was reduced to a life sentence.

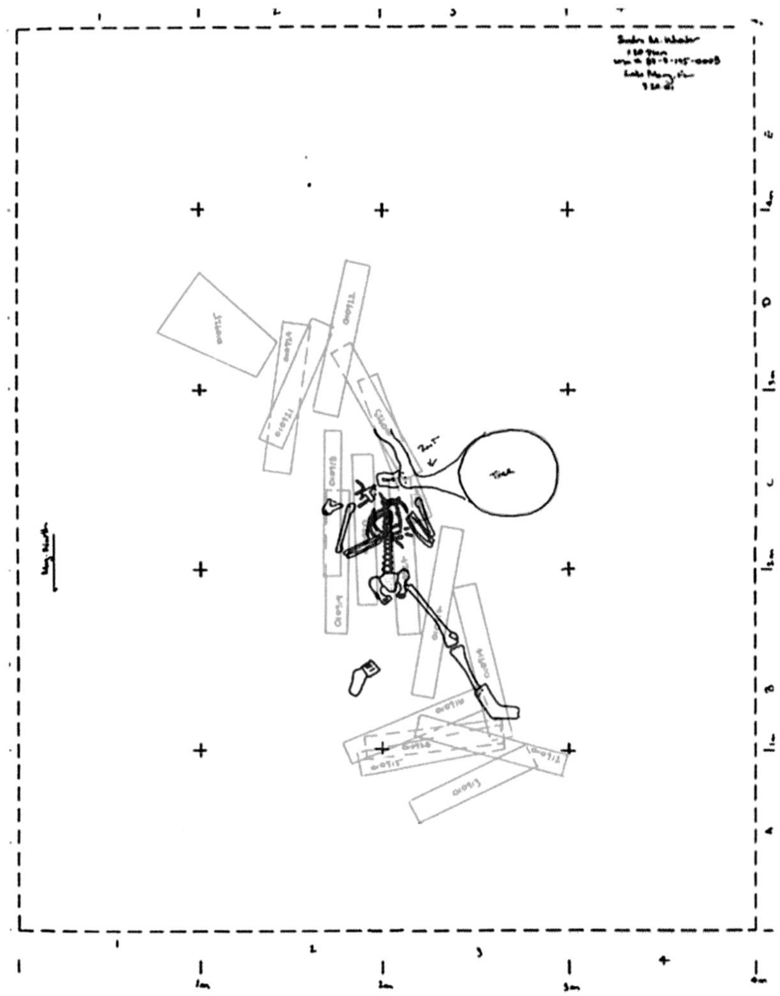

Figure 10.23 Scaled field plan drawing showing the position of Lisa Brighton's remains and preserved clothing in relation to the tree and metal strips used to conceal the body.

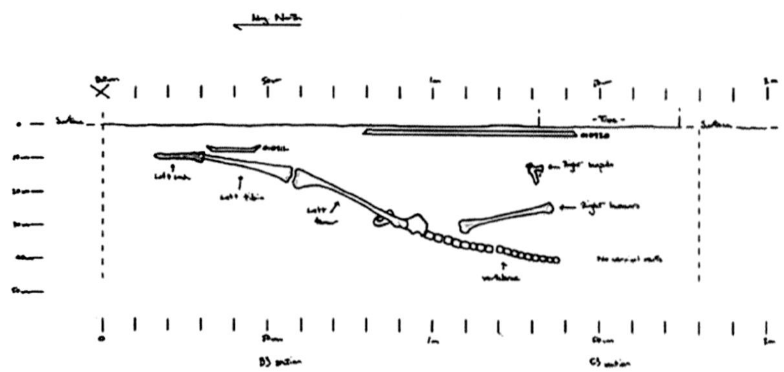

Figure 10.24 Scaled field section drawing showing the position of Lisa Brighton's remains in the surface depression used for burial and in relation to the metal strips used to conceal the body.

Key Terms

association
backfill
bioturbation
burial cut
compaction
compression marks
contamination
context
excavation
feature
field archaeology
forensic archaeology
frost heave
in situ
intrusions
matrix
Munsell soil color book
open/closed association
pedestal excavation
perturbation
platform excavation
primary/secondary grave depression
primary/secondary surface site
principle of association
principle of reversal
principle of superposition
provenience
sedimentation
sediments
silty/sandy/clayey/loamy soils
soil chemistry
soil composition
soil consistency
soil horizons
soil pH
soil profile
soil texture
soil texture classes
soils
sterile soil
strata (stratum)
stratigraphy

REVIEW AND DISCUSSION QUESTIONS

1. Explain how you would identify clayey, silty, and sandy soils. How would you determine their consistency? Why is this important to record in your excavation notes?
2. During the recovery of a surface deposit located in a ravine, an investigator sat down nearby on a large boulder to have lunch. While seated, he reached down and pulled at a root that was sticking out of the ground and a bone that appeared to be a human ulna popped out of the silty surface soil. What events should occur (after lunch, of course) surrounding the recording and recovery of this newly discovered evidence?
3. Based on information obtained from a suspect, a reference grid was established over an area thought to contain a grave. The soil within the reference grid and across the recovery area is weak, very moist, and has a high percentage of clay content. While clearing away surface debris, you discover a bullet. In the suspect's statement, there was mention of at least seven bullets being fired at the scene. What events should occur to record and recover this evidence and any additional evidence of this type? What precautions should be put in place to avoid damaging this type of evidence?
4. During the recording of a skeleton that was exposed during excavation, you discover that there is a second skeleton located directly beneath the first individual. How would you proceed with the excavation of the first individual? What events should occur concerning the second individual?
5. You are assisting with the removal of a skeletonized individual that is in a grave over 80 cm (2.5 ft) deep. What steps can you take to recover the remains safely and continue with the excavation after their recovery? What evidence should be recorded before these steps are taken?

Suggested Readings

Evis, L.H., Hanson, I., Cheetham, P.N. 2016. An experimental study of two grave excavation methods: Arbitrary level excavation and stratigraphic excavation. *STAR: Science & Technology of Archaeological Research* 2(2):177–191. DOI:10.1080/20548923.2016.1229916

Harris, E.C. 1989. *Principles of Archaeological Stratigraphy*, 2nd ed., London: Academic Press.

Kipfer, B.A. 2023. *Archaeologist's Fieldwork Guide*. 2nd ed., Hoboken, NJ: John Wiley & Sons.

Ruffell, A., Donnelly, C., Carver, N., Murphy, E., Murray, E., McCambridge, J. 2009. Suspect burial excavation procedure: A cautionary tale. *Forensic Science International* 183:e11–e16. DOI:10.1016/j.forsciint.2008.10.013

References

Bock, J.H., Norris, D.O. 1997. Forensic botany: An underutilized resource. *Journal of Forensic Sciences* 42:364–367. DOI:10.1520/JFS14130J

Connor, M., Scott, D.D. 2001. Paradigms and perpetrators. *Historical Archaeology* 35(1):1–6. DOI:10.1007/BF03374522

Davis, J. 1992. Forensic archaeology. *Archaeology Review from Cambridge* 11:151–156.

Dirkmaat, D.C., Adovasio, J.M. 1997. The role of archaeology in the recovery and interpretation of human remains from an outdoor forensic setting. In: Haglund, W.D., Sorg, M.H., eds. *Forensic Taphonomy: The Postmortem Fate of Human Remains*, pp. 39–64. Boca Raton, FL: CRC Press.

Evis, L.H., Hanson, I., Cheetham, P.N. 2016. An experimental study of two grave excavation methods: Arbitrary level excavation and stratigraphic excavation. STAR*: Science & Technology of Archaeological Research* 2(2):177–191. DOI:10.1080/20548923.2016.1229916

Fowler, K.D., Greenfield, H.J., van Schalkwyk, L.O. 2004. The effects of burrowing activity on archaeological sites: Ndondondwane, South Africa. *Geoarchaeology* 19(5):441–470.

Haługzko, A., Kadej, M., Gmyrek, G., Guziński, M. 2022. Let's make a mess, maybe no one will notice. The impact of bioturbation activity on the urn fill condition. *PLoS One* 17(9):e0274068. DOI:10.1371/journal.pone.0274068

Harris, E.C. 1989. *Principles of Archaeological Stratigraphy*, 2nd ed., London: Academic Press.

Hester, T.J., Shafer, H., Feder, K. 2009. *Field Methods in Archaeology*, 7th ed., Walnut Creek, CA: Left Coast Press.

Hochrein, M.J. 2002. Autopsy of the grave: Recognizing, collecting, and preserving forensic geotaphonomic evidence. In: Haglund, W.D., Sorg, M.H., eds. *Advances in Forensic Taphonomy: Method, Theory, and Archaeological Perspectives*, pp. 45–70. Boca Raton, FL: CRC Press.

International Agency for Research on Cancer. 2006. Formaldehyde, 2-Butoxyethanol and 1-tert-Butoxypropan-2-ol. In: *IARC Monographs on the Evaluation of Carcinogenic Risks to Humans* 88, pp. 39–325. Lyon, France: International Agency for Research on Cancer.

Killam, E.W. 2004. *The Detection of Human Remains*, 2nd ed., Springfield, IL: Charles C Thomas.

Morin, E. 2006. Beyond stratigraphic noise: Unraveling the evolution of stratified assemblages in faunal turbated sites. *Geoarchaeology* 21(6):541–565.

NIOSH Pocket Guide to Chemical Hazards. 2019. Cincinnati, OH: U.S. Department of Health and Human Services, Centers for Disease Control and Prevention, National Institute for Occupational Safety and Health. https://www.cdc.gov/niosh/npg/npgd0565.html

Overturf, I. 2022. *Spatial Geochemical Changes in Central and East Texas Soils over Time Resulting from Human Decomposition*. CMC Senior Theses. 3003. https://scholarship.claremont.edu/cmc_theses/3003

Pelletier, M., Royer, A., Holliday, T.W., Discamps, E., Madelaine, S., Maureille, B. 2017. Rabbits in the grave! Consequences of bioturbation on the Neandertal "burial" at Regourdou (Montignac-sur-Vezere, Dordogne). *Journal of Human Evolution* 110:1–17. DOI:10.1016/j.hevol.2017.04.001

Renfrew, C., Bahn, P.G. 2018. *Archaeology Essentials: Theories, Methods, Practice,* 4th ed., London: Thames & Hudson.

Snow, C.C. 1982. Forensic anthropology. *Annual Reviews in Anthropology* 11:97–131. DOI:10.1146/annurev.an.11.100182.000525

Soil Survey Staff. 2022. *Keys to Soil Taxonomy,* 13th ed., Washington, DC: USDA-Natural Resources Conservation Service.

Stephens, M., Errickson, D., Giles, S.B., Ringrose, T.J., 2020. Assessing the quality of footwear marks recovered from simulated graves. *Science & Justice* 60(6):512–521. DOI:10.1016/j.scijus.2020.07.005

Stokstad, M., Cothren, M.W. 2017. *Art History,* Volume 1, 6th ed., Prentice Hall and Harry Abrams.

Willey, P., Heilman, A. 1987. Estimating time since death using plant roots and stems. *Journal of Forensic Sciences* 32(5):1264–1270. DOI:10.1520/JFS11177J

CHAPTER 11

COLLECTING SKELETAL REMAINS

Learning Objectives

- Describe the sequential steps involved in the recovery of human remains and associated evidence, from initial discovery to final collection.
- Explain the risks of postmortem damage during, collection, transport, and storage of remains and provide strategies to mitigate damage to bones, especially for fragmentary remains.
- Apply distinguishing criteria to differentiate and classify common nonhuman remains from human skeletal material, including examples of nonhuman remains and other materials frequently misidentified as fragmentary human remains.

Learning Connections

- Connects to broader forensic and archaeological concepts and reinforces the role of evidence collection integrity at forensic scenes and chain of custody in legal investigations.
- Integrates field skills, guidelines, and proper procedures in recovery with the processing, and curation of human skeletal remains and associated evidence.

After the discovery of human remains, searching for additional scattered remains will occur if needed, followed by excavating the remains and processing the scene for surveying and mapping. The final step is collection of the remains and associated evidence (Figure 11.1). Skeletal remains should be treated like any other evidence recovered from a scene. Remains must be collected, packaged, and recorded properly to avoid any potential problems concerning chain of custody and to avoid postmortem damage to the remains during transport, particularly when they are fragmentary due to subaerial weathering. This chapter discusses proper handling, packaging, and storage of all remains, including cremains and those with preserved soft tissue.

In this chapter, we discuss both human (refer to Chapter 3 for a detailed description of the human skeleton) and nonhuman skeletal remains. The purpose of including a section on nonhuman skeletal remains is twofold – first, it is included to demonstrate that nonhuman skeletal material can easily be mistaken for human remains, reinforcing the necessity of an experienced osteologist making the final determination; and second, it is included to introduce

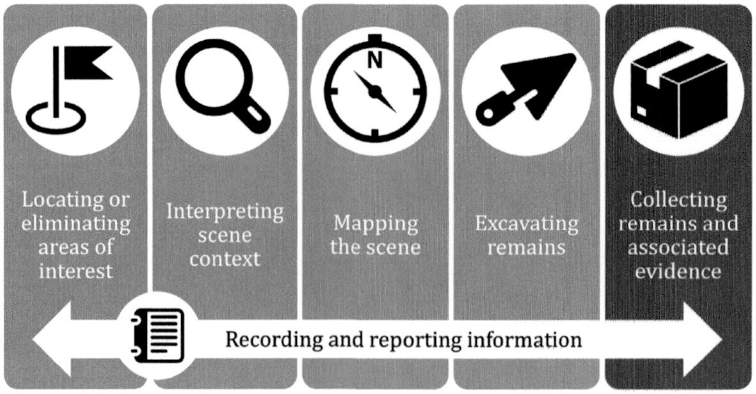

Figure 11.1 Collection of remains and associated evidence as the final step in the five primary responsibilities directly associated with the forensic archaeologist during a forensic investigation.

DOI: 10.4324/9781315201658-11

forensic archaeology students to various examples of nonhuman bones that can easily be confused with human bones. It is important to note that even personnel with human osteology proficiency may have difficulty identifying bone fragments with limited diagnostic features and fragments that have undergone taphonomic modifications (refer to Chapter 5). During these instances, identification of bone fragments may only occur after consulting with comparative nonhuman skeletal material and nonhuman skeletal atlases or books in the laboratory.

HUMAN REMAINS

Proper collection methods are vital not only to protect the remains from postmortem damage and degradation, but also to maintain chain of custody. While established collection procedures for adult human skeletal remains should be standardized, death investigation personnel may have to modify those methods when recovering and collecting juvenile, fleshed, fragmentary, or burnt remains.

Collecting Adult Skeletal Remains

At the time of collection, all remains must be properly recorded with pertinent case information and packaged to avoid damage and maintain chain of custody. While one of the primary goals of the forensic archaeologist during search and recovery is to avoid any postmortem damage to the remains, in certain circumstances, it may be unavoidable. For example, authors Sandra Wheeler and Lana Williams were assisting in the recovery of human remains previously discovered by inexperienced personnel using an edge spade to investigate ground disturbances during a search. Unfortunately, the spade shovel struck the buried remains, causing severe postmortem damage to a long bone (Figure 11.2). If this occurs, either through the actions of inexperienced personnel or the forensic archaeologist, all damage, no matter how slight, should be recorded, and the information should be included with the damaged material during packaging. Even though forensic anthropologists may have experience distinguishing postmortem damage from perimortem trauma, the goal should be to avoid any postmortem damage during the search, recovery, packaging, shipping, analysis, and storage phases. In addition, field personnel involved with the recovery may not have experience distinguishing bone from non-bone materials or human bones from nonhuman bones. In these instances, all suspected bone-like materials and associated items must be collected and properly documented so experienced personnel can sort out the human bone and possible associated evidence.

Packaging Skeletal Remains

Identifying marks should never be placed directly on any bone. Each bone should be identified inside and outside of its package, noting its corresponding precise location or coordinates from the scaled mapping system used at the scene (refer to Chapter 8). Any evidence numbering system used by the forensic investigation team should be duplicated in the mapping and excavation notes and on the tags for each bag or container to prevent any confusion about identification at a later date.

Field personnel should avoid placing all disarticulated bones in a loose and haphazard fashion directly in a body bag or container. Buried remains are inevitably going to retain some moisture, and packaging in plastic bags or aluminum foil does not allow for moisture to evaporate, promoting the growth of fungus and mold. In addition, the moisture may accelerate the degradation of skeletal material (Skinner and Lazenby, 1983). Therefore, paper bags are key in maintaining the integrity of the remains once they have been recovered from the scene.

Packaging guidelines for skeletal human remains free of soft tissue are simple: everything should be placed in labeled paper bags before being placed in a larger container or bag for transport, including a body bag of appropriate size. "Everything" includes personnel effects (i.e., clothing, jewelry, wallet, purse, etc.) along with associated bones and body parts that include bones still connected via desiccated connective tissue. Each agency may also have its own mandate for preserving evidence and chain of custody. If this is the case, then the required agency guidelines should be followed. It should be noted that some items, including firearms and cell phones, may be retained by law enforcement and will not accompany remains, but the presence at a scene and the final

Figure 11.2 Evidence of postmortem damage to bone that occurred during recovery. Note the color change (arrows) where the damaged surface of the cortical bone is much lighter in color than the outer surface, which is stained by the burial environment.

disposition of all evidence should still be recorded. Medical examiners also need to examine clothing for signs of trauma (e.g., bullet holes), and these are often examined as a part of autopsy procedures.

A tag (refer to Appendix F) should be added to each individual bag with the pertinent information about the bone or other evidence inside the paper bag before sealing it. The opening of each paper bag should be folded over at least twice and then stapled or sealed with tape across the fold and at the ends to prevent bones and evidence from falling out during transport. At a minimum, each bag should be clearly labeled on the outside with information regarding the contents, location, case information, date, and investigator's name. Small bags can be placed inside large ones, which in turn can be loaded and sealed into clean cardboard boxes or body bags. Padding, such as crumpled paper or bubble wrap should be used between packages to prevent breakage, and care should be taken in stacking packages on top of one another when placing them in boxes. Tamper-proof evidence tape with the investigator's or evidence technician's signature should be placed across the seal of any bag, box, or container for purposes of chain of custody.

The skull should be packaged separately from the other remains to prevent any damage and to retain any soil or other deposits located inside the cranium. This will also prevent the teeth from becoming fractured, broken, dislodged from the tooth sockets, or lost during transport. Pelvic bones should also be packaged separately from other elements, taking special precautions with the pubic symphyseal surfaces. It is common to recover fingernails and jewelry in association with wrist, hand, and finger bones from their respective sides. When possible, each hand should be packaged separately based on their respective sides. Ankle, foot, and toe bones, including toenails, should also be packaged separately based on their respective sides. If wrist, hand, and finger bones are recovered in a glove, or ankle, foot, and toe bones are recovered in a sock or shoe, they should be packaged in their entirety and not removed from the respective clothing items. If the vertebrae no longer have any connective soft tissue in place, they should be bagged together either in cervical, thoracic, and lumbar packages or bagged in packages containing only four or five vertebrae to reduce possible damage during transport.

Storage of Skeletal Remains

If skeletal remains are to be packaged for shipping or long-term storage, special care must be taken. If bones need to be shipped for analysis, large bones should be wrapped individually first in acid-free tissue paper and then in large unsealed padded envelopes or bubble wrap prior to placement in a shipping container. Smaller bones should be wrapped in acid-free tissue paper and then placed in unsealed padded envelopes or ventilated boxes or containers before placement in the shipping container. Each package should include an accompanying identification tag or label. It is recommended that the shipping container is lined with a clear plastic bag that can be tied closed after packing and that any accompanying forms or shipping paperwork are placed in a separate sealable bag. This is to avoid any possible leakage or staining from the bones during shipment, some of which may still retain fluids, bone marrow, or adhered tissues that could be affected by the transport environment.

Unidentified remains typically need to be packaged for long-term storage, which generally occurs at the medical examiner or coroner offices, or a forensic anthropology laboratory. Prior to storage, bones should be cleaned following laboratory protocols and depending on the system used, individual bones may be labeled with the case number. Bones should then be placed neatly in an acid-free cardboard box with the case number on the outside of the box. Additional acid-free packing materials can be used for stabilization during storage. It is important to note that the top of the storage box should allow for ventilation to avoid mold or mildew formation. All skeletal remains in long-term storage should be kept in a fairly stable temperature- and humidity-controlled environment (e.g., 60–68° F [16–20° C] with humidity at 45% +/–5%).

Collecting Juvenile Skeletal Remains

The challenges involved in locating and excavating juvenile remains are much greater than those typically encountered when dealing with adult remains. Juvenile bones are not only considerably smaller than adult bones, but there are also numerous unfused skeletal elements that allow for bone growth, which results in accounting for and identifying greater numbers of bones (refer to Chapter 3). For example, the diaphyses of long bones are not fused to the epiphyses during growth (refer to Figure 3.21). The number of bones present can be misleading, as elements often appear fragmentary and nonhuman in nature. These small skeletal elements are also extremely fragile and do not have the rigidity and hardness often associated with adult bone. Depending on an individual's developmental age, juvenile bones will be less mineralized than those of an adult, possibly resulting in increased degradation and differential preservation of skeletal elements under certain taphonomic conditions. The environment and scavenging animals may also easily displace or consume small juvenile remains, especially those of infants. In addition, infant and fetal remains could easily be misidentified as items typically found in a recovery area, such as twigs, pebbles, small animal skeletons, or the trash remnants of a chicken dinner.

Great care must be taken when processing any recovery site that might involve a juvenile. As a result of the challenges in the recovery and collection process, many juvenile skeletal elements will likely be missed unless all materials are properly collected. When confronted with the morphology of the juvenile skeleton, the number of individual unfused skeletal elements, and the level of possible differential preservation, identification of juvenile remains can even prove difficult for osteologists having extensive experience working with adult skeletal remains. It is highly recommended that investigators work with an osteologist well versed in juvenile osteology, ensuring the proper collection, preservation, documentation, and analysis of this type of evidence.

Collecting Partially Decomposed Remains

There are instances when the degree of human decomposition is such that a different type of approach may be necessary; however, partially decomposed remains should be excavated using the same systematic and controlled approaches as described previously in Chapter 10. Modification of the recovery process usually occurs when the remains are exposed, and minor adjustments may be necessary to preserve as much of the original burial environment as possible when removing the remains for investigation under more controlled conditions.

When the majority of a body is exposed, there is a tendency to want to pull it free from the grave fill. There is a danger that weakened articulations, especially the neck, elbows, wrists, knees, or ankles, may separate, leaving disarticulated portions in the grave fill. This presents the potential for losing important pieces of soft tissue evidence, such as fingernails, fingerprints, and defensive wounds or ligature marks. The best method for removal is to expose the remains completely, work around and loosen the areas where the remains are in contact with the floor of the grave, then lift the remains as a whole, preferably with a mortuary transfer board for support or with many individuals positioned at the legs, head, and torso and lifting at the same time. Once the body is removed, excavations can continue with investigation of the grave floor and any additional associated evidence.

Forensic personnel involved in the recovery of bodies and body parts in various stages of decomposition can be exposed to a variety of biological hazards (Galloway and Snodgrass, 1998). All crime scene personnel and forensic investigators should take appropriate precautions when working in an environment where they can be exposed to a variety of molds, fungi, or infectious diseases, as well as corrosive chemicals. All personnel should maintain current vaccinations and consistently wear appropriate personal protective equipment (PPE) (Galloway and Snodgrass, 1998). Safety protection during the recovery of decomposing remains, including exhumations, includes disposable protective clothing (e.g., Tyvek chemical resistant suits), examination gloves, masks, eyewear, and face shields if needed (refer to Chapter 2).

Remains in an advanced state of decomposition with wet soft tissue still present should be packaged so fluids do not leak during transport. The most efficient method is to wrap the body parts in a sterile cotton sheet or other sterile disposable lint-free material and then place them into a zippered body bag. Do not fully seal any plastic bag with tissues inside unless the odor is extreme, and even then, only during the time required for transport. Any associated clothing, wrappings, or containers from the burial should accompany the remains for further investigation and should also be packaged accordingly.

Collecting Burnt Remains

The nature of burnt remains differs greatly from other skeletal remains. The temperature of the fire and the length of time that a body is exposed to the fire will determine the appearance of the remains. Bone will change color, crack, warp, and crumble when exposed to high temperatures. Recent research with cremains has shown them to have greater potential for molecular and chemical analysis than previously thought, specifically with the use of isotopic and infrared analyses to determine body positioning, presence of clothing items, geographic mobility during life, and methods used in burning the body (e.g., temperatures, fuel type) (Salesse et al., 2021; Snoeck, 2023; Snoeck et al., 2025). In addition, DNA may still be recovered from cremains in some instances (Latham et al., 2022; Redsicker and O'Connor, 1996; Smith and Sweet, 2010; Zapico and Stone-Gordon, 2023).

Cremated or burnt remains are found in all sorts of contexts, but most are encountered in surface and shallow burials or in containers (Fairgrieve and Molto, 1994; Murad, 1998; Ubelaker et al., 2023). Burnt bones are extremely fragile and must be disturbed as little as possible during recovery. A common methodology in fire investigation is to rake through the coals to recover as much as possible as quickly as possible, thus disturbing any relationship that existed between the remains and any other associated evidence. It is crucial that a forensic archaeologist and forensic anthropologist who is familiar with fire recovery techniques and bone identification be used to recover evidence of this type (refer to Case Study #11) (Friedlander et al., 2024; Milligan et al., 2023). A forensic archaeologist and forensic anthropologist specializing in burnt remains could potentially determine a substantial amount of information from an in situ assessment of burnt human remains (Correia and Beattie, 2002; Dirkmaat, 2002; Friedlander et al., 2024; King and King, 1989; Klales et al., 2023; Milligan et al., 2023):

- Identify human versus nonhuman remains.
- Establish whether the remains were burned at the scene or burned elsewhere and then redeposited at the scene.
- Establish the number of individuals recovered from the fire debris and their locations and orientations during the fire.

- Increase the accuracy and precision in the collection of evidence and minimize the damage to bone fragments and associated evidence.
- Aid in establishing body position and why certain body elements are missing or more altered.
- Aid in scene reconstruction with details on fire intensity, duration, and patterns of body and tissue alteration or destruction due to fire exposure.

Special care is required when collecting and packaging burnt remains due to the friable nature of the material. Many forensic anthropologists have analyzed burnt remains where crime scene personnel have placed all of the body parts into one body bag during recovery. This collection method results in not only excessive commingling of the remains, but also extreme fragmentation, as the brittle, porcelain-like structure of the bones are not stabilized for transport. To preserve continuity and prevent further fragmenting when collecting burnt remains with soft tissues still present, hands, feet, elbow and knee regions, the skull, and pelvic bones must be stabilized using plastic wrap or heavy-duty aluminum foil and placed separately in a container or secured to a hard surface for transport. When fully skeletonized burnt remains are encountered, individual bones should be wrapped and packaged separately using a variety of materials such as paper towels, tissue paper, plastic wrap, or heavy-duty aluminum foil and then placed into a container or carboard box. When encountering remains that are nearly cremated or highly fragmentary, all remains and associated fire debris should be collected and packaged for later sorting under more ideal conditions. Large plastic pails or containers with sealable lids should be used for transporting ash or fire debris to a laboratory for sorting (Klales et al., 2023). Small sterile plastic vials or boxes with cotton layering should be used for small fragile items such as dental remains (Fairgrieve, 2008).

Since chemical laboratory testing of bone samples packaged and stored in aluminum foil for a six-week period demonstrated no significant change in detected levels of aluminum, it is recommended to continue to use aluminum foil as a packing medium (Lewis and Christensen, 2015). However, if there is any possibility that chemical testing (e.g., trace elements) will be performed on the remains at a later date, it is recommended that burnt bones should only be stabilized with aluminum foil during transport and not during curation. Further, if aluminum foil or plastic wrap are used to provide stability during transport, the foil or wrap must be unsealed and left open shortly after arriving at the laboratory to allow moisture to evaporate.

Collecting Evidence of Surgical or Dental Modifications

Among the most important items for positive identification of remains includes evidence of surgical implants and dental work. While larger items, such as joint replacements, plates and screws to reduce and stabilize broken bones, and dental orthopedics are more easily recognized (refer to Figures 4.8 and 4.9), there are numerous smaller items that may be unrecognizable to most death investigators as surgical or dental implants if the items are not found attached to bones and teeth. Several surgical items added to the body that are never attached to bone include breast implants, **portacaths** (injection ports), heart valves and repair rings, and small metallic and non-ferrous vascular clips (Figure 11.3), all of which may become disassociated from the skeleton after decomposition. Furthermore, during instances of bone fragmentation, bone erosion, and burnt remains, these forensically important items may be separated from skeletal remains and altered due to taphonomic processes. Most death investigators will be unfamiliar with the range of surgical and dental orthopedics encountered with decomposing bodies and skeletal material. Therefore, we recommend that all unrecognizable 'trash' debris and loose material should be collected at the scene, particularly in cases involving burnt remains, and be examined by knowledgeable personnel.

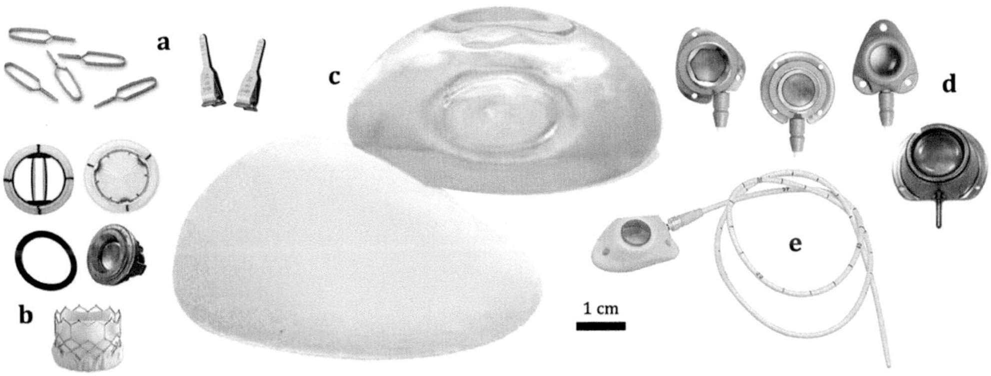

Figure 11.3 Additional materials that may be missed or regarded as refuse during recovery of human remains: (a) metallic and non-ferrous vascular clips; (b) mechanical and tissue heart valves and repair rings; (c) saline and silicone breast implant; (d) plastic and stainless steel portacath (injection port) bodies; and (e) portacath body with catheter tube.

Sampling for Genetic Testing

More often than not, sampling for genetic testing is conducted in the laboratory during analysis of the remains. This usually entails a sample taken from the diaphysis of the tibia or femur, and/or healthy dental tissue. Field recovery of genetic samples, including remains temporarily exhumed for sampling, requires meticulous adherence to strict forensic protocols to prevent contamination and degradation, ensuring the integrity of evidence for analysis. The process involves specialized equipment, careful collection techniques, proper packaging, and an unbroken chain of custody.

If a decision is made to take samples in the field for genetic testing for identification purposes, sampling should be conducted once all field records and notes have been completed, unless exceptional circumstances warrant otherwise (e.g., imminent degradation, time-sensitive opportunity, logistical constraints). This ensures the integrity of the collected DNA evidence and its associated contextual information.

At a minimum, the following steps should be undertaken in the field:

- *In situ* photography of samples with a scale and case-identifying tag.
- Proper personal protection equipment (e.g., face mask, double gloving, shoe, and hair covers) and sterile, disposable forceps are used when recovering samples.
- Dry- or wet-swabbing kits may be used to recover body fluids or on non-porous surfaces for trace DNA analysis (Kuffel et al., 2024).
- If the condition of the remains allows teeth to no longer be retained in the mandible or maxilla, the proximal phalanx of the first (large) toe, the first cervical vertebra, hair with roots attached, and/or fecal materials are often used as intact field samples (Hofreiter et al., 2021).
- Appropriate vials, containers, envelopes, and packaging for each sample should be supplied by crime scene personnel.
- All personnel having contact with the remains should be listed on appropriate forms and delivered along with the sample to the genetic laboratory where the testing will be performed.

NONHUMAN SKELETAL REMAINS

Distinguishing between human and nonhuman skeletal remains is a task that should only be undertaken by a forensic anthropologist or other professionally trained individuals experienced in human osteology. In the field, an experienced forensic archaeologist or forensic anthropologist should be able to address one of the most primary concerns: Is the suspect material actually bone? For example, rocks can appear in shapes that mimic some adult skeletal elements (e.g., carpals, tarsals) as well as many elements from juvenile remains (e.g., epiphyses). However, in most cases, rock is heavier than bone. Many small, irregular or rounded skeletal elements tend to have a greater concentration of cancellous bone in relation to cortical bone, making them significantly lighter than rocks. Many other materials can appear to be bone, including burnt drywall fragments, which can calcinate in high heat, burnt plastics, which often forms a bubbled texture that can mimic cancellous bone, and fire-resistant silicone rubber, especially when the objects have become soil-stained or weathered (Figure 11.4). Plant materials also can mimic bone, including bamboo and coconut shell (Figure 11.5). An experienced forensic anthropologist should be able to easily distinguish bone from other kinds of materials.

More commonly, a forensic anthropologist will be asked to determine whether skeletal remains are human

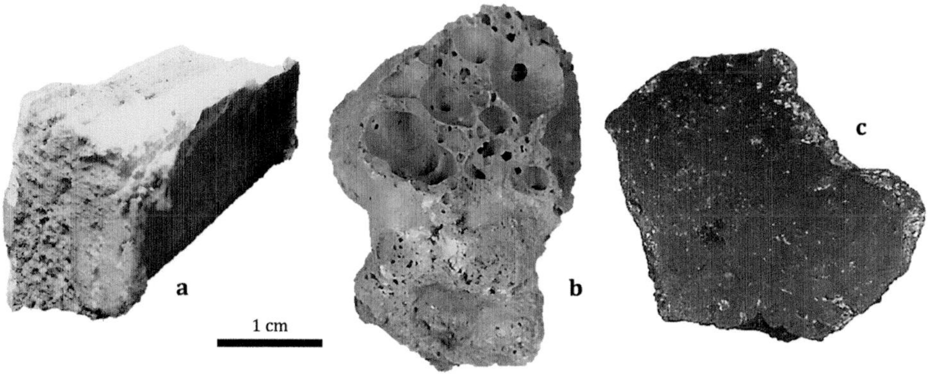

Figure 11.4 Common materials that mimic bone when burnt: (a) drywall fragments; (b) plastic; and (c) fire-resistant silicone rubber.

Figure 11.5 Plant materials that mimic bone when weathered and fragmented include bamboo (top right inset) and coconut shell.

or nonhuman. In many cases, differentiation of human remains from faunal material enables investigators to eliminate cases initially considered forensic in nature, although in rarer instances, faunal remains may be forensically relevant. The forensic anthropologist should strive to determine species or class of animal as a minimum, as well as the bone type. The caseload for a forensic anthropologist can include a substantial number of cases involving nonhuman remains, and the total percentage of nonhuman cases identified by forensic anthropologists will differ. The more common nonhuman species identified by most forensic anthropologists during their casework include medium and large-sized mammal species, larger size birds, and on occasion bones from a more exotic species that do not have a home range in the local jurisdiction, where the bone was recovered or confiscated. For example, the caseload for William Bass, a noted forensic anthropologist formerly at the University of Tennessee, noted an increase to 29.2% of cases involving nonhuman bones over the period 1990–1993 compared with five-year averages from 1970 to 1989 that ranged from 17.8% to 23.7% (Marks, 1995). It was noted that nonhuman bones are commonly discovered during the cooler months when hikers and hunters are more active in rural areas (Marks, 1995). It was also noted that deer, dog, pig, and cow bones were the most common species identified and outnumbered the remainder of nonhuman cases (Marks, 1995). Conversely, Pokines (2015) reported a much higher number of nonhuman cases during a three-year period (2012–2014) that covered all jurisdictions for the commonwealth of Massachusetts. For example, there was an average of 90.1% nonhuman, 9.0% human, and 0.9% cases involved human and nonhuman bones. In that environment, there was also a peak in cases (including human) during late spring, possibly because more people were outdoors and snow cover had dissipated, but significant plant growth had not obscured the ground surface yet.

While the number of nonhuman cases that forensic anthropologists identify will vary each year and geographically, the diversity of species that they identify also will vary. For example, during November 2011 through September 2025, author J.T. Pokines examined updated case totals, including 1,703 nonhuman and non-osseous cases representing a more diverse number of species than most forensic anthropologists identify. The nonhuman taxa compiled do not include those from ritual cases, where a high degree of biodiverse taxa (including mollusks, corals, bats, scorpions, reptiles) can accompany human remains (Schultz et al., 2020). Overall, deer, cattle, pig, and large bird were the most common taxa identified (Table 11.1), and these four taxa are normally the most frequently analyzed species that author J.J. Schultz identified in Central Florida. At the same time, author J.T. Pokines surprisingly identified a high number of seal bones, and some dolphin and sea turtle bones (Figure 11.6a–c) due to the eastern coast of Massachusetts bordering the Atlantic Ocean.

Table 11.1 Total Number of Nonhuman Species and Non-osseous Remains Identified During Forensic Casework*

Common Name	Taxon	*n*
White-tailed deer	*Odocoileus virginianus*	432
Cattle	*Bos taurus*	428
Pig	*Sus scrofa*	318
Bird, large		126
Seals	Phocidae	84
Sheep/goats	*Ovis/Capra*	55
Unknown large mammal		51
Dog	*Canis familiaris*	40
Horse	*Equus caballus*	25
Chicken	*Gallus gallus*	22
Fish		16
Cat	*Felis catus*	14
Non-osseous		12
Black bear	Ursus americanus	12
Unknown small mammal		10
Beaver	*Castor canadensis*	6
Moose	*Alces alces*	5
Canada goose	*Branta canadensis*	4
Dolphins	Delphinidae	4
Turkey	*Meleagris gallopavo*	4
Raccoon	*Procyon lotor*	4
Canada goose	Sea turtle Chelonioidea	4
Unknown mammal		4
Bird, small		3
Gulls	Laridae	3
Ducks	Anserinae	2
Mute swan	*Cygnus olor*	2
Rats	*Rattus*	2
Ostrich	*Struthio camelus*	2
Coyote	*Canis latrans*	1
Leatherback turtle	*Dermochelys coriacea*	1
Rabbits/hares	Leporidae	1
Bobcat	*Lynx rufus*	1
Groundhog	*Marmota monax*	1
Woodland vole	*Microtus pinetorum*	1
Oysters	Ostreidae	1
Eastern gray squirrel	*Sciurus carolinensis*	1
Fox squirrel	*Sciurus niger*	1
Total		1,703

* Casework conducted for the Commonwealth of Massachusetts, Office of the Chief Medical Examiner by coauthor J.T. Pokines from November 2011 through September 2025.

There also were two cases of ostrich bone (Figure 11.6d), the presence of which became much more explicable in one case when law enforcement confirmed after the identification that there was a former ostrich farm nearby. The other ostrich case consisted of a bone sold commercially as a dog treat.

Thus, basic knowledge of the human and nonhuman skeleton can help save time when determining the forensic significance of whole or fragmentary skeletal remains.

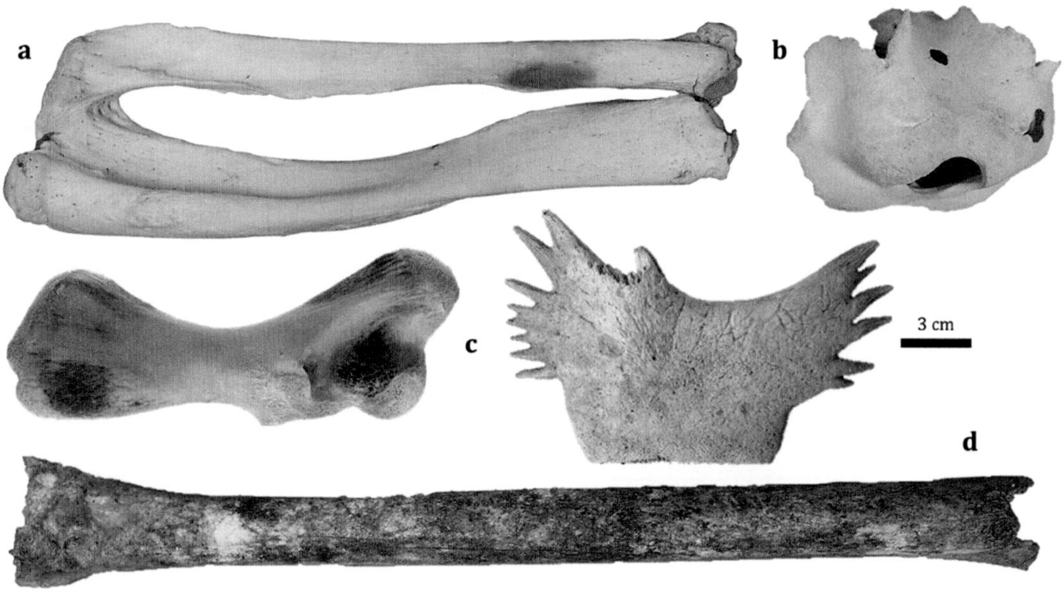

Figure 11.6 Unusual nonhuman bones identified in relation to forensic searches: (a) seal (Phocidae sp.) tibiofibula; (b) dolphin (Delphinidae sp.) occipital; (c) loggerhead turtle (*Caretta caretta*) femur and hypoplastron; and (d) ostrich (*Struthio camelus*) tibotarsus.

Nevertheless, a forensic anthropologist should still examine all bones recovered from a scene to confirm whether the remains are human or nonhuman. In particular, when bones are highly weathered, eroded, and fragmented, identification may only be possible by a forensic anthropologist. If a forensic anthropologist is not at the scene or readily available, digital photographs of the remains should be emailed to a forensic anthropologist for identification. The remains should be photographed using a scale and *in situ* if possible, to avoid damaging or destroying any contextual information. Many forensic anthropologists have reviewed photographs via email to assist in the identification of human versus nonhuman bones. This can save a tremendous amount of time and resources for everyone involved.

It is important for professionally trained osteologists to be familiar with fauna located in their geographical region when considering the various species that might be confused with human skeletal remains. Osteologists can become familiar with nonhuman skeletal material by constructing a comparative skeletal collection of local known fauna. This collection can then be used to help identify questionable skeletal material. Further, a free web tool (OsteoID; https://boneidentification.com/) is now available to assist with nonhuman identifications (Garvin et al., 2022). The user selects the type of bone from a set of images, and, following the input of a few basic measurements, the tool returns high-quality color photographs of potential species for visual comparison and identification. Users may also build their own virtual comparative collections using three-dimensional (3D) scans or print the 3D models.

In addition to comparative collections, or in cases where a comparative collection is not available, there are various books and atlases that can be consulted for more in-depth comparative analysis of nonhuman skeletal biology. The most informative and popular guides for **zooarchaeology**, forensic archaeology, and forensic anthropology are listed below for bird, fish, mammals, and reptiles, in addition to comparative human and nonhuman osteology texts.

The recommended texts that focus on comparative human and nonhuman osteology provide a nonhuman component that primarily consists of mammal and include: *Comparative Osteology: A Laboratory and Field Guide of Common North American Animals* by B.J. Adams and P. Crabtree (2011); *Human and Nonhuman Bone Identification: A Color Atlas* by D.L. France (2009); *Human and Nonhuman Bone Identification: A Concise Field Guide* by D.L. France (2011). Also, there are several comprehensive comparative texts that compare human adult and subadult examples with mammal, bird, and reptile (e.g., alligator and turtle) and include: *Comparative Bone Identification: Human Subadult to Nonhuman* by D.L. France (2016); and *Comparative Bone Identification: Human Subadult and Nonhuman – A Field Guide* by D.L. France (2021). In addition, *Animal Skulls: A Guide to North American Species* by M. Elbroch (2006) includes mammals and birds.

There are a number of recommended texts that focus solely on mammalian osteology, and include: *Mammalian Osteology* by B.M. Gilbert (2003); *Mammal Remains from Archaeological Sites: Southeastern and Southwestern United States* by S.J. Olsen (2004a); *Mammal Bones and Teeth: An Introductory Guide to Methods of Identification* by S. Hillson (1992); *Field Guide to Skulls and Bones of Mammals of the Northeastern United States (Vol. 1: Skulls and Mandibles)* by R. Wolniewicz (2001a); and *Field Guide to Skulls and Bones of Mammals of the Northeastern*

United States (Vol. 2: The Long Bones) by R. Wolniewicz (2001b).

Also, recommended texts that also focus on different classes of animals such as bird, fish, and reptiles include: *Fish, Amphibian and Reptile Remains from Archaeological Sites: and Southeastern and Southwestern United States* by S.J. Olsen (2004b); and *Avian Osteology* by B.M. Gilbert, H.G. Savage, and L.D. Martin (1996).

Nonhuman Mammal Skeleton

Large mammal bones such as cattle, bear, deer, large dogs, and pigs are most often confused with adult human bones, while remains of smaller animals may be confused with juvenile or fetal bones. From an anatomical perspective, because humans are **mammals**, they possess many of the same skeletal characteristics and can be very similar in their skeletal components as nonhuman mammals. For example, bone structure of most nonhuman mammalian long bones includes a diaphysis composed of thick cortical bone and metaphyses and epiphyses composed of cancellous bone, which is very similar to that of humans (refer to Figure 3.3). However, if it was not possible to visually identify a small bone fragment without morphological indicators, there are several laboratory methods for identifying whether it is human or nonhuman, including histological examination, protein radioimmunoassay, or DNA analysis (Cattaneo et al., 1999; Mulhern and Ubelaker, 2012; Ubelaker et al., 2004).

Upon gross examination, there are two main characteristics of bones that are normally used to easily distinguish between human and nonhuman: maturity and morphology. Maturity aids in differentiating small nonhuman fauna that, even after reaching adulthood, have bones similar in size to those of juvenile humans. As discussed in Chapter 3, depending on the level of developmental maturity, juvenile human long bones may have separate epiphyses or may not possess any at all (refer to Figure 3.21). The proximal and distal ends of juvenile human long bones will have a roughened appearance where the epiphyses will eventually fuse to the metaphyses. Conversely, long bones of small adult fauna will have fused epiphyses. As a result, small adult faunal bones can be easily differentiated from those of juvenile humans by examining the degree of bone maturity (Figure 11.7).

The second characteristic of bone that aids in the distinction between human and nonhuman mammalian bone is morphology, or the shape of the bone. As mentioned previously, humans and other mammals share many of the same skeletal components and we also share the same basic architecture (e.g., two femora, two humeri, two scapulae) required by our soft tissue structures. However, because humans are bipedal and walk upright, we have a distinct skeletal morphology that distinguishes us from quadrupeds, which are adapted for four-legged locomotion. Figure 11.8 presents two examples of the generalized mammalian skeleton, to illustrate several of the skeletal features that are related to quadrupedal locomotion in a domesticated cat and horse.

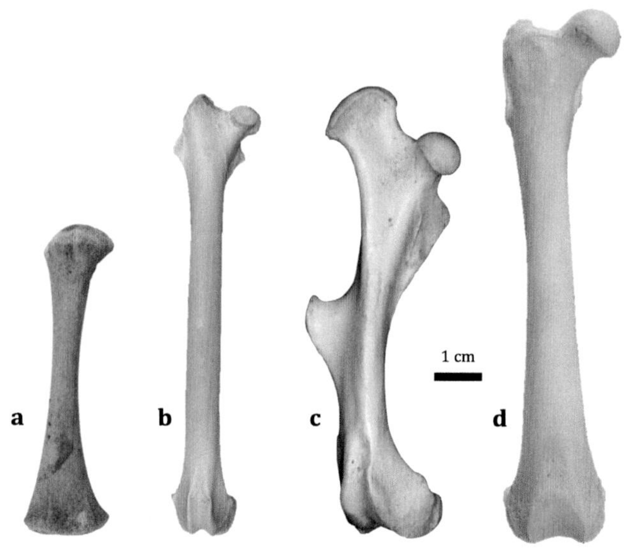

Figure 11.7 Comparison of epiphyseal maturity in the femur of a human infant (a) with femora of small mammals: (b) rabbit (*Sylvilagus* sp.); (c) armadillo (*Dasypus* sp.); and (d) raccoon (*Procyon lotor*).

When comparing humans with other mammals, the dissimilarity in the shape of long bones (Figures 11.9 and 11.10) and other bones of the body such as the scapula (Figure 11.11) can be very distinct and can quickly lead to a positive identification of human or nonhuman remains. Mammals belonging to the order Artiodactyla (i.e., hoofed mammals that have two or four toes on each foot) can be easily distinguished from humans by the presence of a **metapodial**. In these animals (e.g., deer, sheep, goat, moose, caribou, elk), the third and fourth metacarpals and third and fourth metatarsals fuse together into one structure early in development. These fused structures (collectively referred to as metapodials) are easily recognized by a number of morphological indicators: the shafts are long, thin, and straight, and they still retain a clear groove down the shaft where they have fused. The proximal end is flat, while the distal end is unique with double rounded articular surfaces (Figure 11.12). Metapodials are long in certain species and therefore could be mistaken for human long bones.

Morphologically, small nonhuman fauna may have a noticeable curvature in the diaphyses of some long bones or appear to be completely flat. In contrast, long bone diaphyses in a healthy juvenile human should have a slight curvature toward the anterior (Figure 11.13). In addition, in a number of small nonhuman fauna, the fibula is reduced in size and is fused to the shaft of the tibia (i.e., **fused tibia-fibula**) (Figure 11.14). Some larger mammal species (e.g., pig, sheep, and deer) have a curved and fused radius and ulna (Figure 11.15). In humans, neither the radius and ulna nor the fibula and tibia fuse together, unless there is a pathological

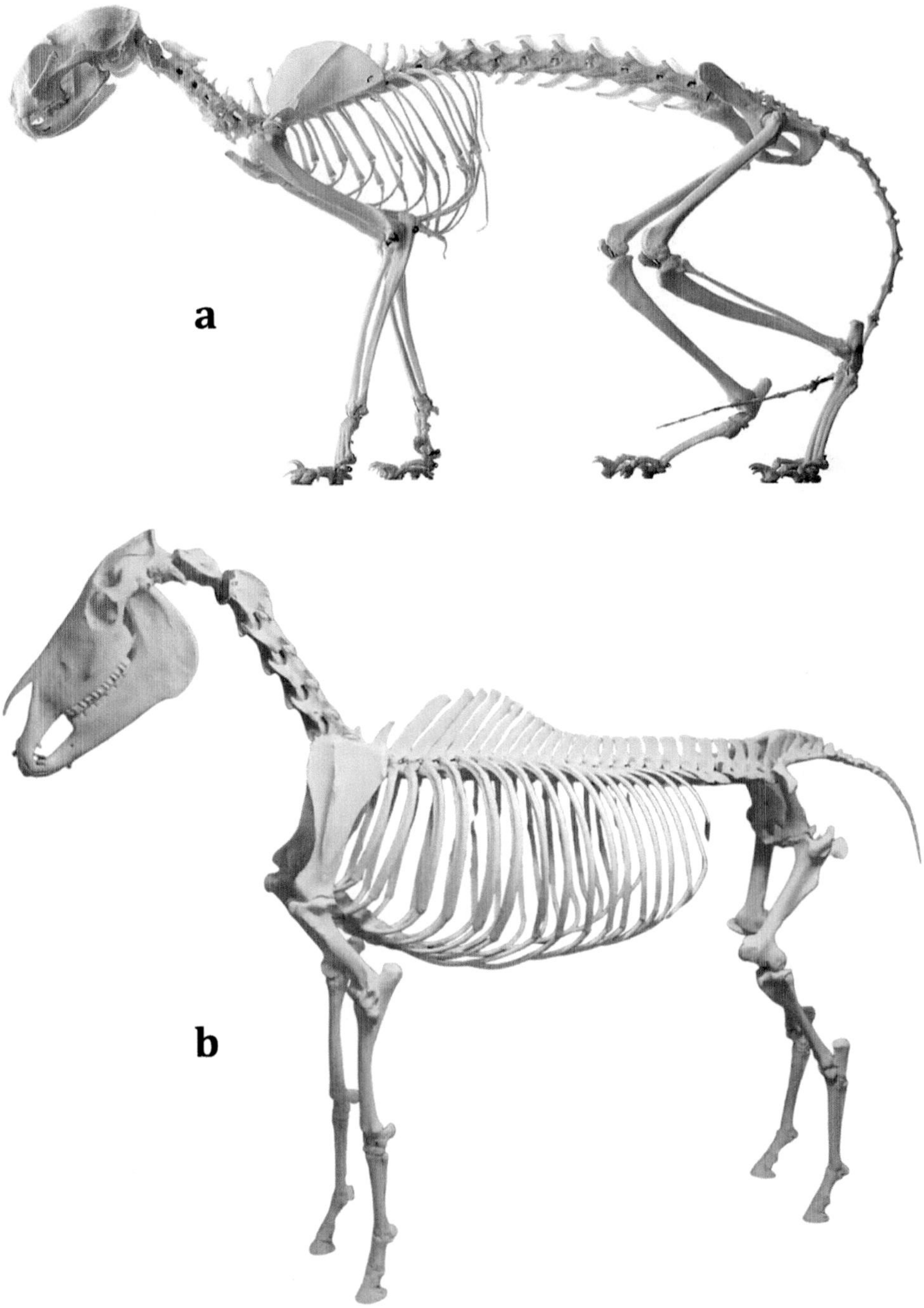

Figure 11.8 Examples of quadrupedal mammal skeletons: (a) domesticated cat (*Felis catus*) and (b) horse (*Equus ferus callabus*). (Images not to scale)

condition such as ossification of ligaments that serve to keep both bones articulated. The pelvis is another skeletal structure of small nonhuman fauna that could possibly be confused with juvenile human remains. If a small pelvis is fused into one unit (i.e., two innominates and a sacrum), it will be faunal, as a comparably sized pelvis in a juvenile human would contain multiple elements that would not be fused (Figure 11.16). In addition, the innominates of the adult human pelvis do not normally fuse to the sacrum, unless there is a pathological condition that affects the sacroiliac joints or the pubic symphysis. The human cranium is quite distinct from most other mammals (excluding apes), because humans have a large, rounded braincase and flat, or orthognathic, face when viewed in profile. Since human crania are so distinct from other mammals, and misdiagnosis is unlikely, further differentiation will not be discussed. The reporting of nonhuman crania to

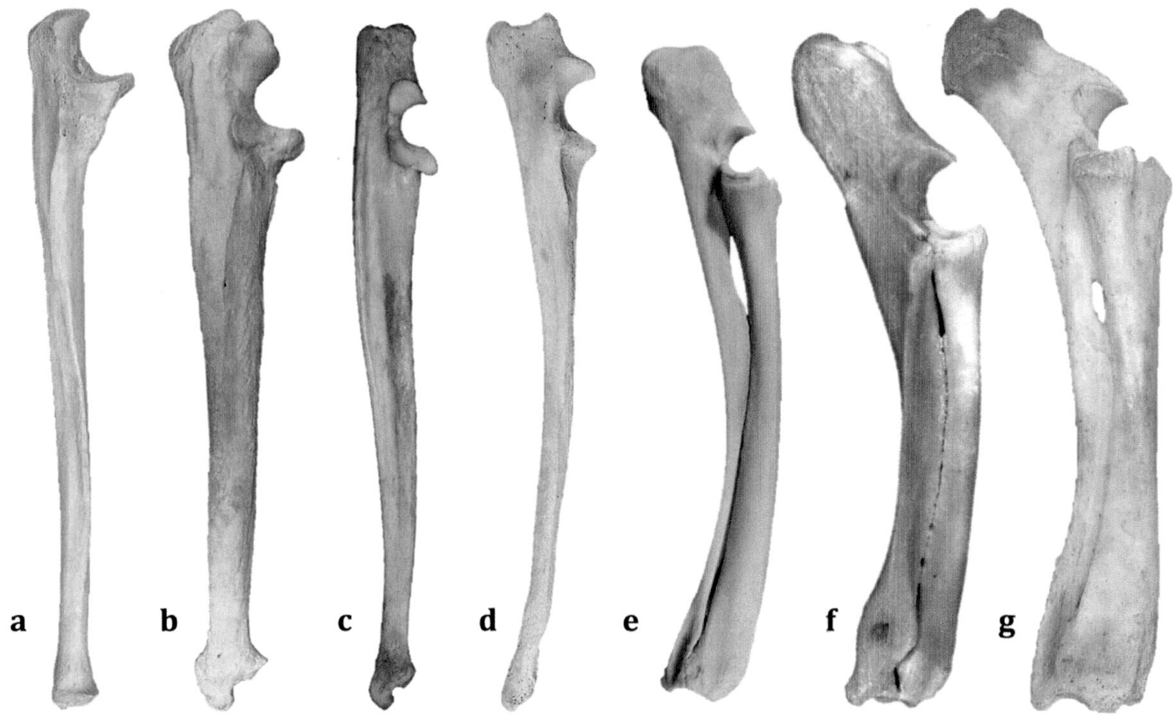

Figure 11.9 Morphological comparison in lateral view of adult human ulna (a) with ulnae in large mammals: (b) bear (*Ursus americanus*); (c) bobcat (*Lynx rufus*); (d) wolf (*Canis lupus*); (e) white-tailed deer, fused with radius (*Odocoileus virginianus*); and (f) domestic pig (*Sus scrofa*), fused with radius; and (g) domestic cow (*Bos taurus*), fused with radius. (Images not to scale)

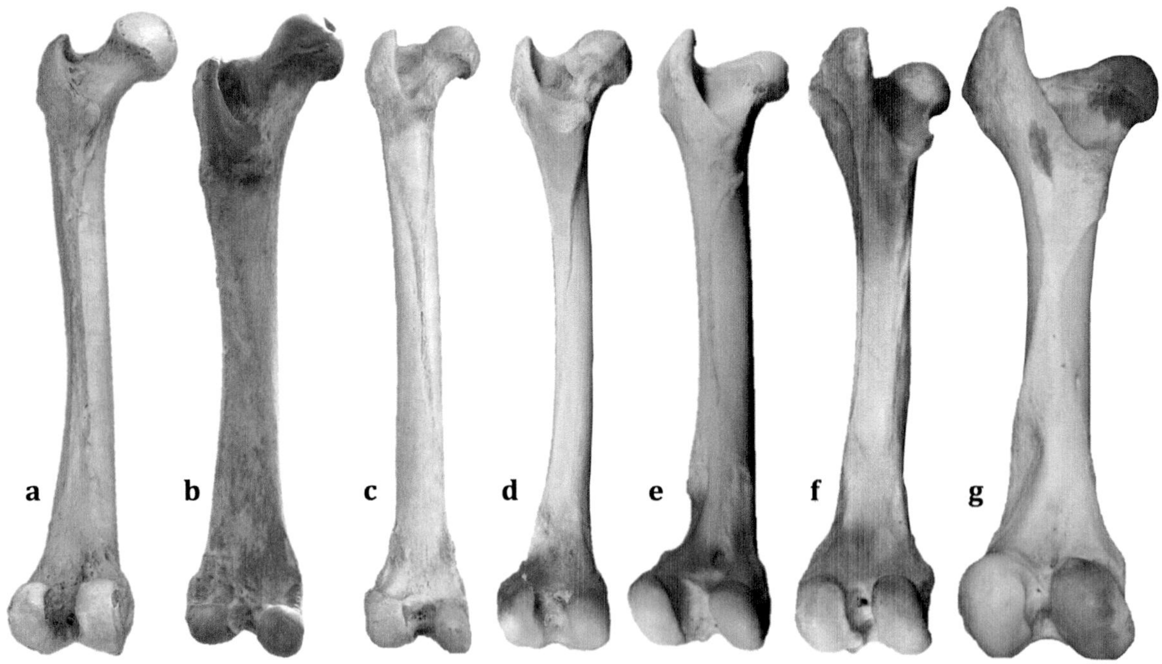

Figure 11.10 Morphological comparison in posterior view of adult human femur (a) with femora in large mammals: (b) bear (*Ursus americanus*); (c) bobcat (*Lynx rufus*); (d) wolf (*Canis lupus*); (e) white-tailed deer, fused with radius (*Odocoileus virginianus*); and (f) domestic pig (*Sus scrofa*), fused with radius; and (g) domestic cow (*Bos taurus*). (Images not to scale)

law enforcement is also relatively rare, as most people can recognize these as nonhuman. The skulls, however, often get collected by one person, and a subsequent person finding any associated postcranial remains may then be more likely to report them as possible human bones (Pokines, 2015).

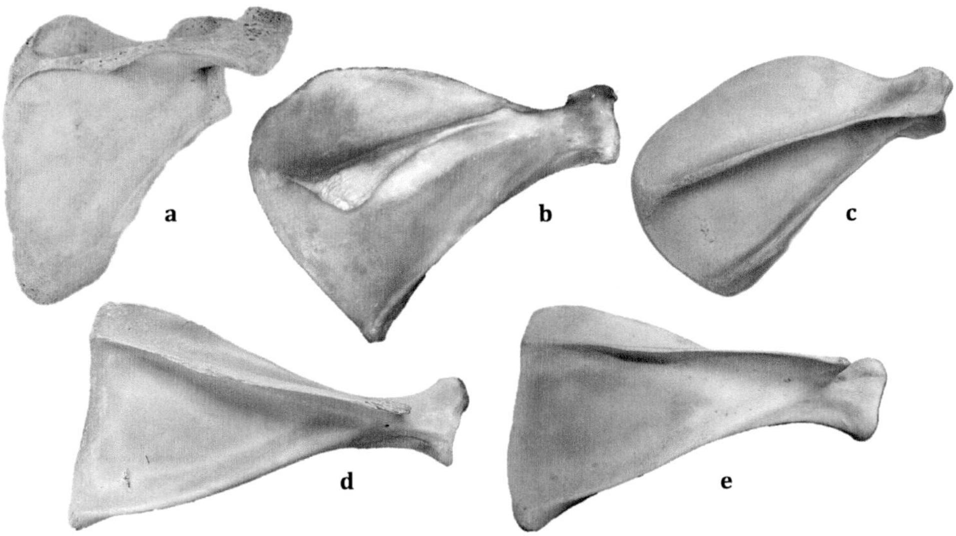

Figure 11.11 Morphological comparison in posterior view of adult human scapula (a) with scapulae in large mammals: (b) domestic pig (*Sus scrofa*); (c) wolf (*Canis lupus*); (d) domestic sheep (*Ovis aries*); and (d) white-tailed deer (*Odocoileus virginianus*). (Images not to scale)

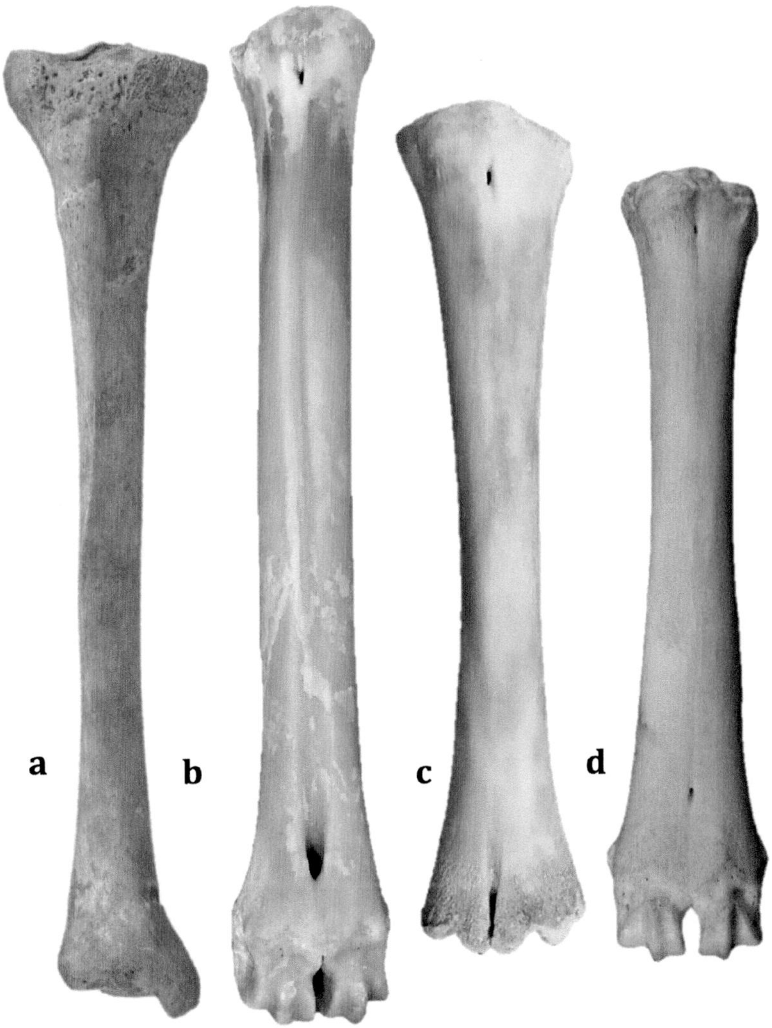

Figure 11.12 Morphological comparison in anterior view of adult human tibia (a) with metapodials in large mammals: (b) adult elk (*Cervus canadensis*); (c) juvenile elk (*Cervus canadensis*), without epiphyseal ends; and (d) domestic sheep (*Ovis aries*). (Images not to scale)

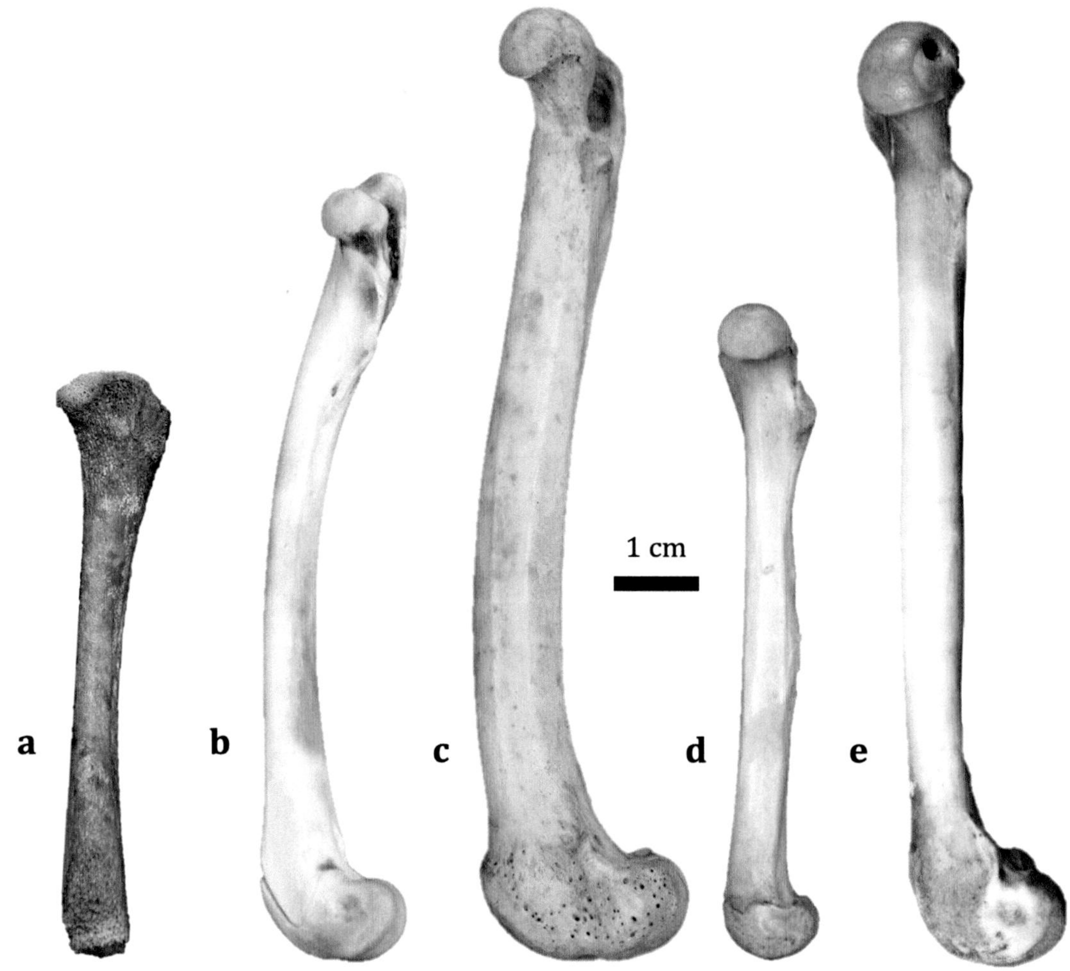

Figure 11.13 Morphological comparison of curvature in medial view of infant human femur (a) with femora of small mammals: (b) rabbit (*Sylvilagus* sp.); (c) small dog (*Canus familiaris*); (d) opossum (*Didelphis virginiana*) and (d) raccoon (*Procyon lotor*).

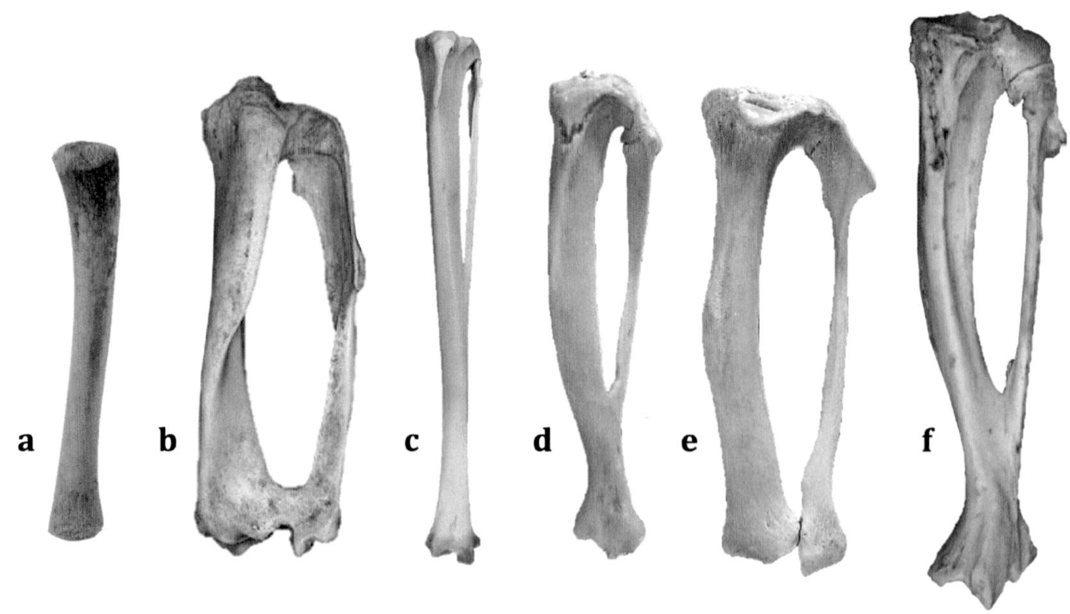

Figure 11.14 Morphological comparison in anterior view of infant human tibia (a) with fused tibiae-fibulae in small mammals: (b) armadillo (*Dasypus* sp.); (c) rabbit (*Sylvilagus* sp.); (d) Norway rat (*Rattus norvegicus*); (e) porcupine (Erethizon dorsatum); and (f) beaver (*Castor canadensis*). (Images not to scale)

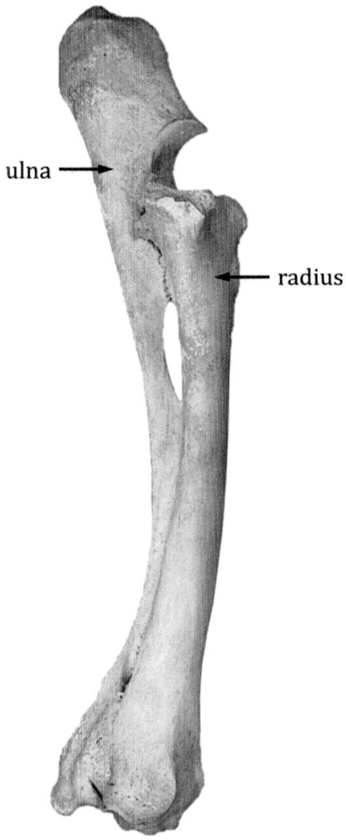

Figure 11.15 Example of curved diaphyses and fusion of the ulna and radius in a domestic sheep (*Ovis aries*).

Avian Skeleton

There are several differences between an **avian**, or bird, skeleton (Figure 11.17) and a human skeleton. Of course, birds have a very distinctive cranium, and the presence of a beak is a feature that provides a means of quick identification. Overall, birds tend to have fewer individual bones than mammals due to the presence of fused bone segments and the evolutionary loss of some, and almost all bird skeletons are light in weight, because they are adapted for flight. Such adaptations include the presence of the **furcula** (e.g., the wishbone), and the **synsacrum**, which is the large number of fused vertebrae that form a solid skeletal connection between the axial skeleton, the remaining vertebrae and the pelvic girdle. Another distinct feature is that the bodies of the vertebrae are saddle-shaped. On most birds, the sternum has a feature called the carina, a keel-like structure to which the muscles for flight are attached. Since the forelimb of a bone is adapted for flight, there are a number of skeletal modifications in the shoulder and forelimb. In particular, the most recognized bone is the **carpometacarpus** that is formed by the fusion of three homologous bones of the mammalian metacarpals and part of the carpal bones. In addition, the lower limb of the bird skeleton is also unique because it is comprises three long bone segments. While the femur is the proximal segment, the **tibiotarsus** is the middle segment, and it consists of the homologous mammalian tibia and several fused tarsal bones at the distal end. The distal bone of the bird hind limb is the **tarsometatarsus**, which is a fused segment homologous to the mammalian ankle and foot bones.

The long bones of large birds, particularly the tibiotarsus and the tarsometatarsus, may be confused with human skeletal elements due to their long length; however, the unique morphology of bird long bones should preclude them from being misidentified. Bird long bones can be easily differentiated from human long bones, because they have an outer surface that is generally smooth except for

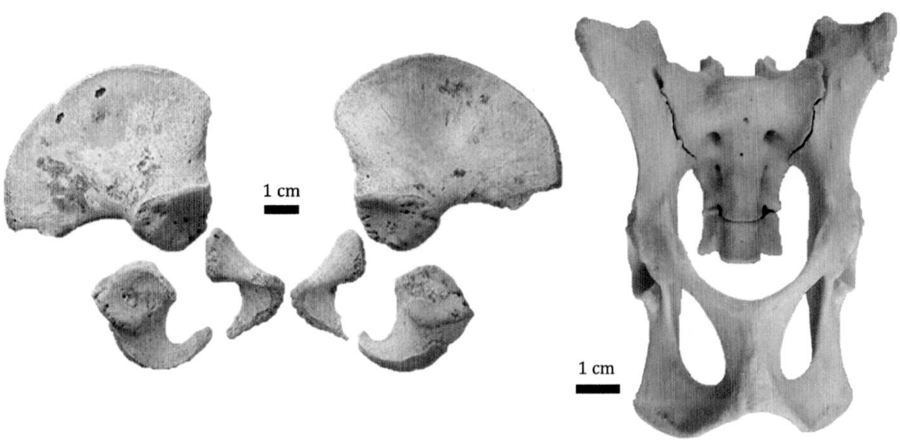

Figure 11.16 Morphological comparison of maturity in a human infant pelvis (left) and an adult raccoon (*Procyon lotor*) (right). Although roughly the same size, the human pelvic elements remain unfused in young children along with separate sacral vertebral skeletal elements, which are not depicted.

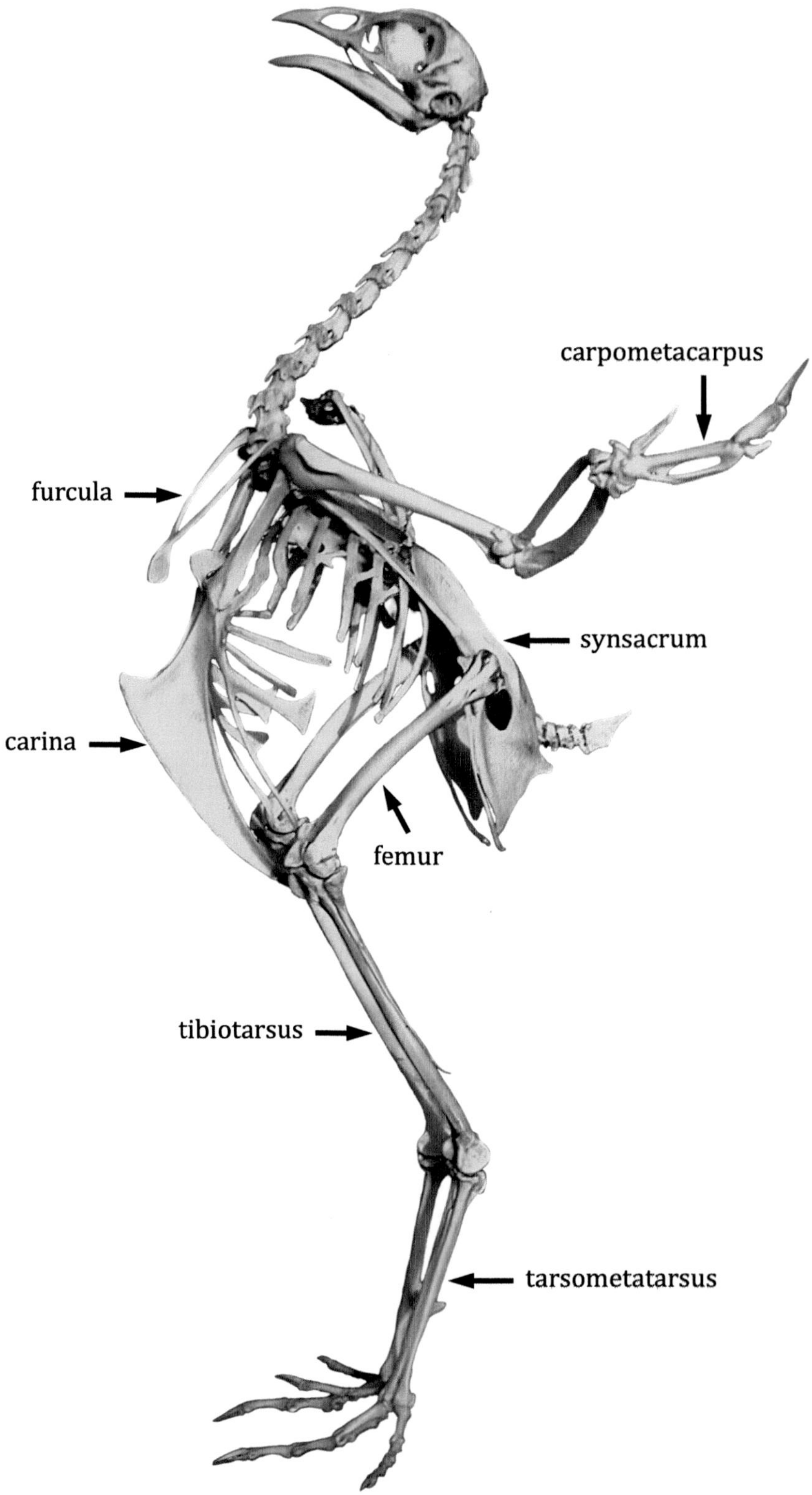

Figure 11.17 Example of an avian skeleton represented by a domestic chicken (*Gallus gallus domesticus*). Distinct fused bone segments adapted for flight are identified.

the ends, which contain irregular articular surfaces and small, roughened muscle attachment sites (Figure 11.18, left). Another differentiating feature is the actual structure of a bird long bone, which is what makes a bird skeleton light. Bird long bones have very thin cortical bone (Figure 11.18, right) and are mostly hollow with small struts of bone, called spicules, that cross the medullary cavity and provide structural support like that of an airplane wing. This feature is unique to birds and is not found in any other animal.

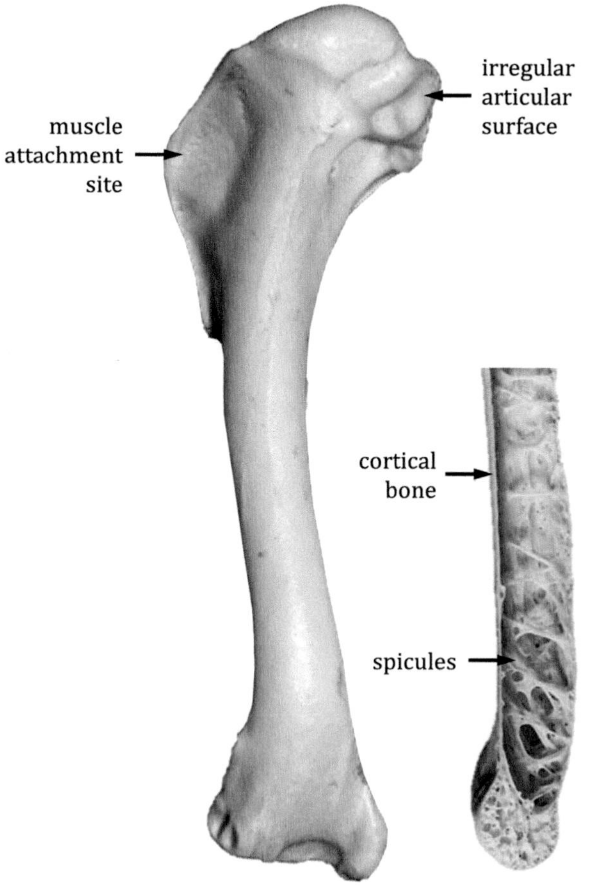

Figure 11.18 A peregrine falcon (*Falco peregrinus*) humerus (left) with a very smooth cortical surface, small, roughened muscle attachment sites, and irregular articular surfaces. A cross-section the humerus (right) shows the thin, lightweight cortical bone and the medullary spicule formations that provide structural support.

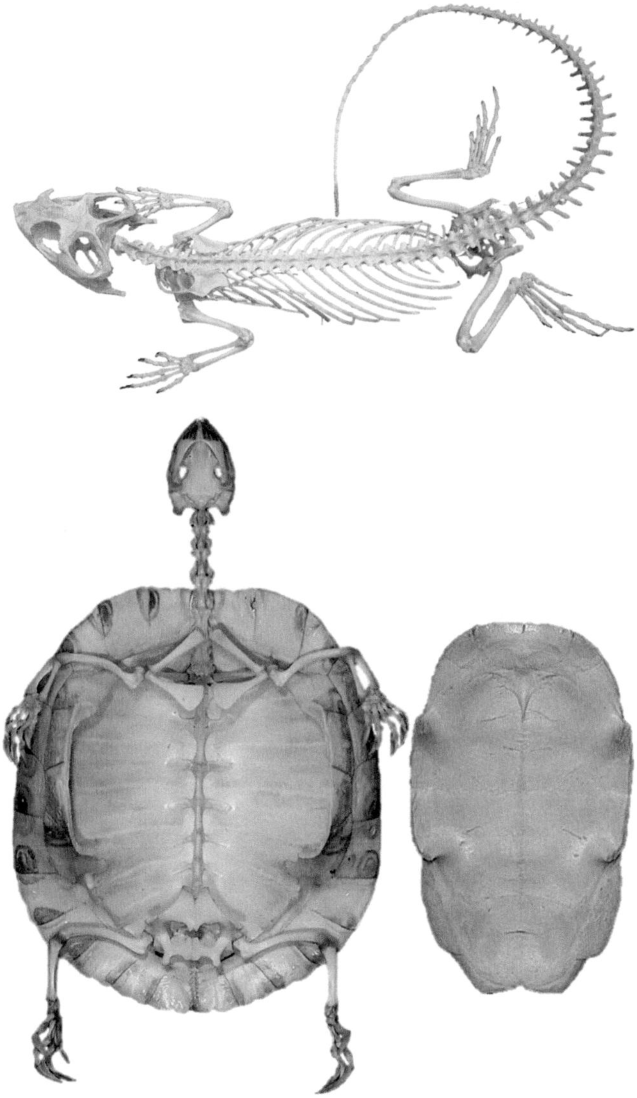

Figure 11.19 Examples of reptilian skeletons: (top) a bearded dragon lizard (*Pongona vitticeps*) and (b) slider turtle (*Trachemys* sp.) (bottom with intact plastron plate. (Images not to scale)

Reptile Skeleton

Reptiles include animals such as turtles, lizards, snakes, and alligators. Reptiles have many unique skeletal characteristics that make them readily identifiable (Figure 11.19). Reptiles possess a type of joint articulation known as **ball-socket vertebrae**, with the cranial side of the vertebra being concave, and the caudal side being convex (Figure 11.20). Unlike the mandible found in adult mammals, the lower jaw of a reptile consists of several skeletal elements. In addition, reptile jaws have conical peg-like teeth that are all the same type, referred to as a **homodont dentition** (Figure 11.21). This dentition is related to their feeding habits, as reptiles do not chew their food; instead, they bite, tear, and swallow it. Some reptiles, such as alligators (*Alligator mississippiensis*) and geckos (Gekkonidae) also have **polyphydont dentition**, meaning their teeth are continuously replaced throughout life.

Reptile long bones should be easily differentiated from human long bones. However, eroded and fragmented alligator long bones could cause some confusion in comparison with humans, as alligator bone fragments can be quite large in size. Overall, reptile long bones are moderately heavy with thick cortical bone, a very small medullary cavity, and no epiphyses. In addition, reptile long bones, such as those from an alligator, do not have the roughened and prominent muscle attachment sites commonly seen on human bones (Figure 11.22). It has been suggested that the proximal pedal phalanges of American alligators (*Alligator mississippiensis*) closely resemble the proximal and intermediate hand phalanges of adult humans (Ferraro and Binetti, 2014). However, this is only an issue when confronted with isolated hand phalanges, which would be a rare occurrence and geographically restricted.

Amphibian Skeleton

Amphibians include animals such as frogs, toads, and salamanders. Their skeletal elements are very light and few in number (Figure 11.23). There is great diversity among

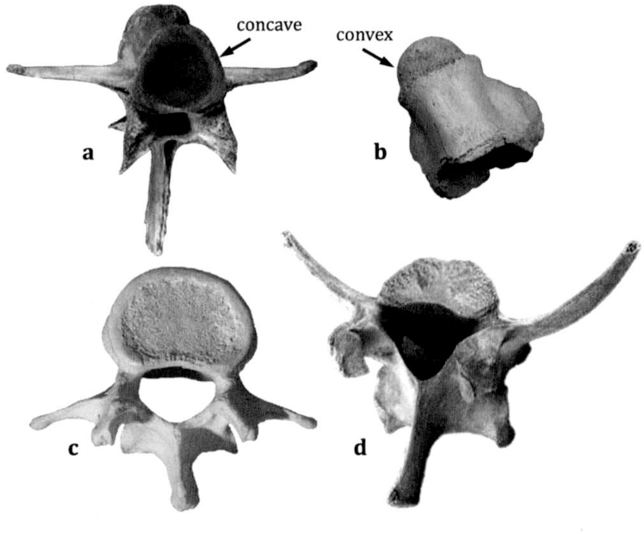

Figure 11.20 Alligator (*Alligator mississippiensis*) vertebrae (a–b) can be confused with vertebrae from large mammals such as (c) adult human and (d) white-tailed deer (*Odocoileus virginianus*). However, alligator vertebrae can be identified by the concave and convex surfaces (arrows) on the vertebral bodies. (Images not to scale)

Figure 11.21 An example of homodont reptilian dentition from an alligator (*Alligator mississippiensis*) (top) with close up view (bottom). Alligators are also polyphyodonts, meaning their teeth are continuously replaced throughout life.

amphibious species in thickness of the cortical bone and the presence of medullary cavities in the long bones. One consistent feature is that amphibian long bones do not have epiphyses. Some species have cartilaginous ends to their long bones, and once decomposed, the bones become hollow tubes. For the most part, there should not

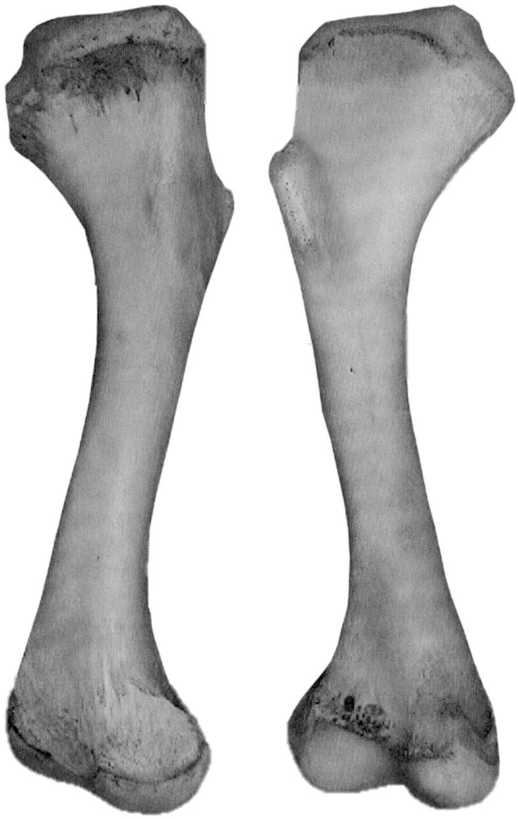

Figure 11.22 Anterior (left) and posterior (right) views of an alligator (*Alligator mississippiensis*) humerus showing the smooth cortical surface, lack of prominent muscle attachments, and lack of defined epiphyses.

be any confusion between amphibian and human skeletal elements as amphibians are usually small and possess very unique skeletal morphology.

Fish Skeleton

There should be no confusion when identifying skeletal elements from **fish**, because their morphology is very different from any other animal. In comparison with the mammalian skeleton, fish have fewer skeletal elements (Figure 11.24), and, as they are adapted to an aquatic environment, all of the bones reflect an adaptation for swimming, such as the absence of cancellous bone and medullary cavities. Like amphibians, fish bones do not have epiphyses. Fish bones are commonly described as being **translucent** or semitranslucent, and they often emit a fishy odor, which is an uncommon trait in most other animals.

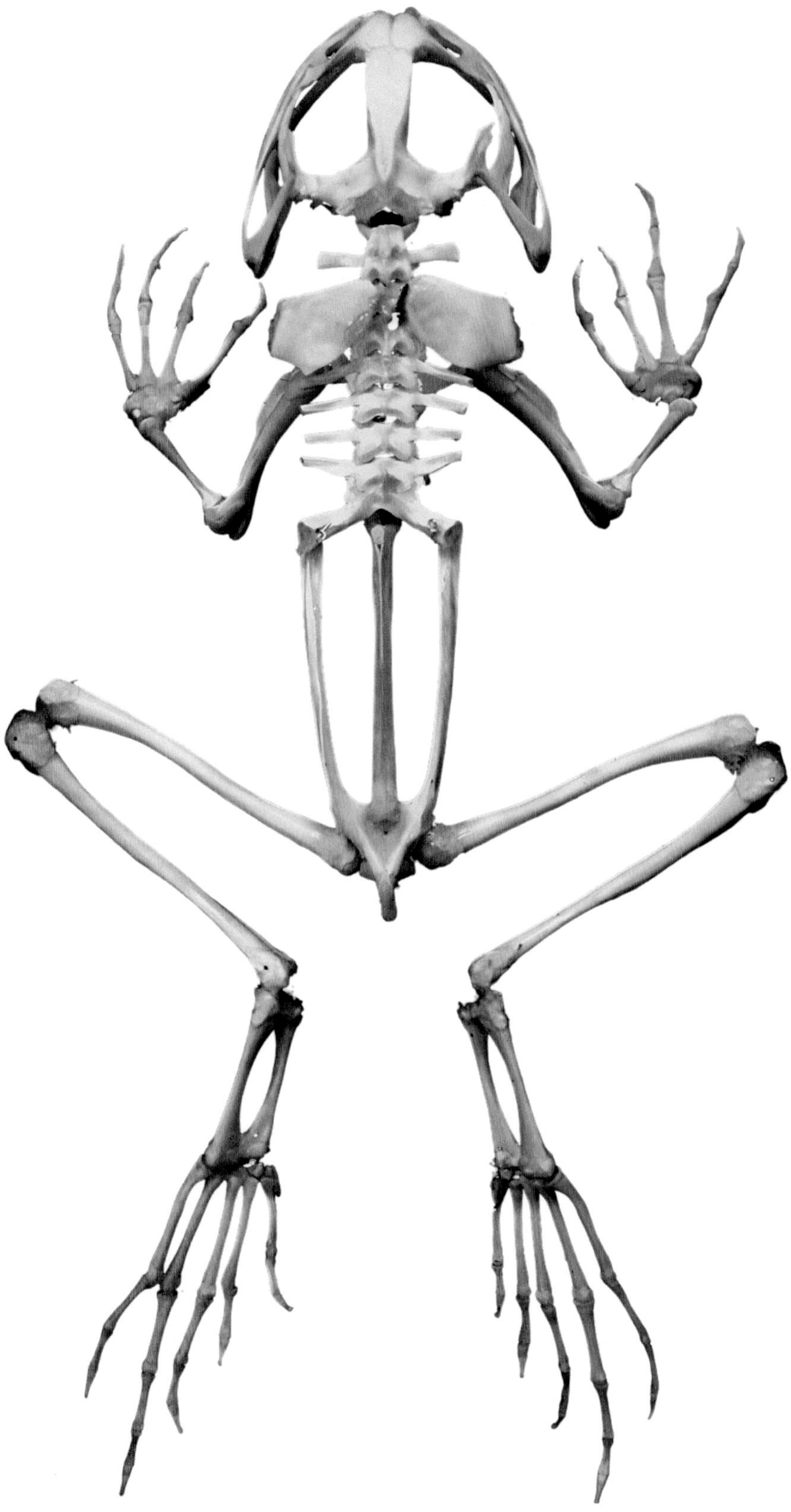

Figure 11.23 Example of an amphibian skeleton represented by a bullfrog (*Rana* sp.).

Figure 11.24 Example of a fish skeleton represented by a red snapper (*Lutjanus campechanus*).

COMMON MISIDENTIFICATIONS OF HUMAN AND NONHUMAN BONE

There are several nonhuman animals that have bone structures or features that appear similar to human skeletal material. Table 11.2 presents a summary of basic skeletal features that may be used to distinguish the different classes of animals. There are several skeletal elements, however, that are commonly misidentified, such as the bones of a bear paw, pig teeth, the knee of a pig, turtle shell bone, and large avian furcula. Disarticulated bear paws are commonly confused with human hands and feet (Figure 11.25). After a hunted bear has been killed, the claws are usually removed as a trophy, and the paws are sometimes discarded after they are skinned. There is a striking resemblance between a bear paw and a human hand and foot after decomposition of the soft tissue has started. However, a bear paw can be easily differentiated from a human hand or foot by examining the individual bones, and this can be accomplished without cleaning the soft tissue from the bone. A radiograph will clearly show the differences in morphology between bones in a bear paw and those in a human hand or foot.

Table 11.2 Morphological Characteristics Used to Differentiate Human from Nonhuman Bones

Skeletal Characteristic	Human	Nonhuman
Cranium shape and position of foramen magnum	Large, bulbous shape with inferior position	Small, often elongated shape with posterior position
Cranial vault muscle markings	Relatively smooth	Pronounced with sagittal crest
Eye orbit position	Anterior position above nasal aperture	Lateral position and posterior to nasal aperture
Mandible shape	U-shaped and fused	V-shaped and separates at midline
Dentition type	Omnivore dentition with four tooth types; 2:1:2:3 dental formula	Varies in number of tooth types and dental formula
General vertebra shape	Vertebral bodies with flat superior and inferior surfaces; short spinous processes	Vertebral bodies with convex and concave superior and inferior surfaces; long spinous processes
Sacrum shape	Generally, five fused segments with short and broad, triangular shape	Three or four fused segments with long and narrow shape
Pelvis shape	Broad and short with bowl shape	Long and narrow with tube or blade shape
Radius and ulna fusion	Separate bones	Fused bones
Femur shape	Longest bone	Similar length to other limb bones
Tibia and fibula fusion	Separate bones	Fused bones

Source: Adapted from Watson and McClelland, 2018

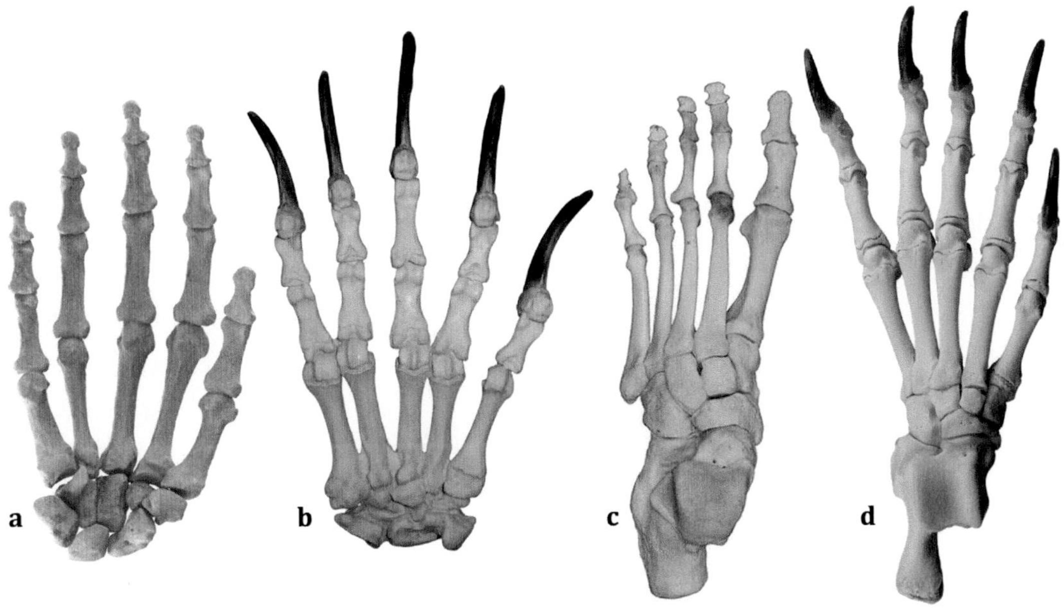

Figure 11.25 Morphological similarity of bones in an adult human hand (a) and foot (c) compared with those in a front (b) and rear (d) paw of a bear (*Ursus americanus*).

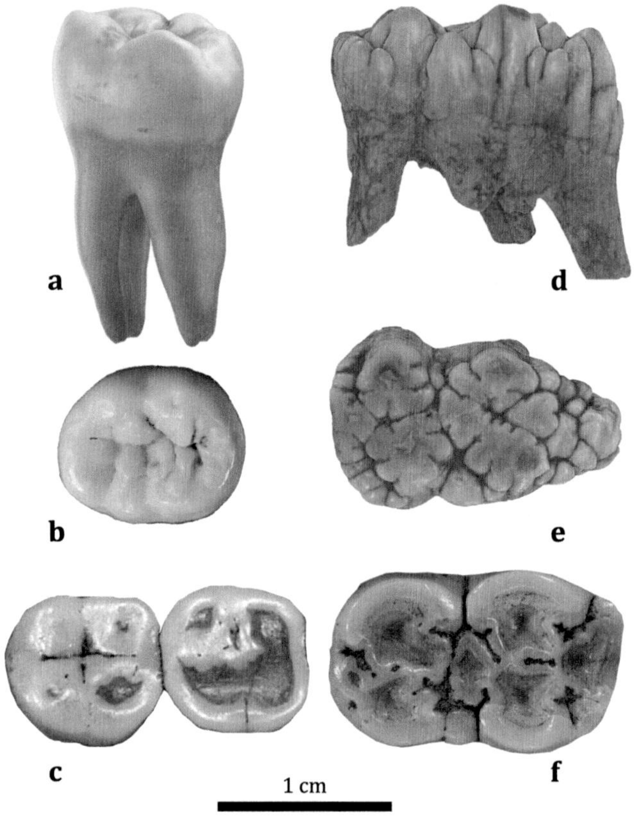

Figure 11.26 Morphological characteristics of an adult human molar tooth (a–b) compared with a domesticated pig (*Sus scrofa*) molar tooth (d–e). Note the similarities between worn human molars (c) and a worn pig molar (f).

Worn pig molars also show a striking resemblance to human molars, because pigs, like humans, are omnivorous, and their teeth are designed for a generalized diet (Figure 11.26). However, pig molars are larger than human molars and have pointier cusps. The proximal part of the pig tibia, called the tibial plateau, can be easily misidentified as a human tibial plateau by an inexperienced osteologist as they share a similar morphology (Figure 11.27) (Pokines, 2015). The tibial plateau of a butchered pig knee or an unfused proximal tibial epiphysis may be easily identified when a portion of the proximal pig fibula is also available for examination. However, if only the top section of the tibial plateau (proximal aspect of bone) is available without the shaft of the tibia, it can be very difficult to differentiate from a human tibia. Conversely, the tibial plateau of the deer is easily differentiated from the human knee because of the strikingly different morphology (Figure 11.27c).

The top portion of a turtle shell is called the **carapace**, while the bottom portion is called the **plastron**. Each portion of the shell is made up of fused bone plates, or **hypoplastrons**, which are covered by an outer layer of keratinized pieces called **scutes**. When the scutes separate from the shell, the underlying hypoplastron bone may resemble the top of a human skull (Figure 11.28). This is particularly true if only a portion of the bone layer is visible through the soil and has been bleached from sun exposure. Fragments of either the carapace or plastron can be easily mistaken for fragments of human cranial bone, because the flat shape and thickness is similar in form to human cranial vault fragments (Figure 11.29). At the same time, weathered and soil-stained fragments may be difficult to differentiate from weathered and soil-stained human cranial vault fragments. If there are no diagnostic characteristics on the surfaces of the shell fragment, then the cross-sectional morphology of the shell fragment can be used to differentiate it from the unique cross section of human cranial bones.

A furcula from a large avian species can sometimes reach size proportions equivalent to the human mandible, especially furcula from swans, geese, storks, and herons. The confusion between a human mandible and a large avian furcula occurs in instances where the lower dentition in a human mandible has been removed or lost and the tooth sockets have been resorbed into the mandible, leaving a smooth, curved surface (Figure 11.30). This likeness in whole bone is quite similar; however, in fragmentary remains, it becomes fairly obvious to a

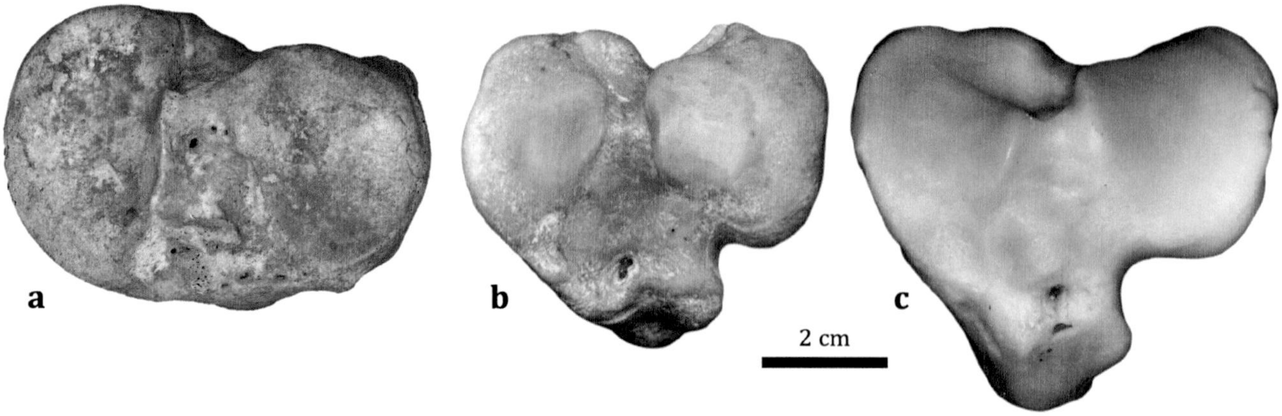

Figure 11.27 Morphological comparison in superior view of adult human tibial plateau (a) with tibial plateau of: (b) domesticated pig (*Sus scrofa*); and (d) white-tailed deer (*Odocoileus virginianus*).

trained osteologist whether the fragments are human or avian when the bone structure is exposed. In the furcula, the cortical bone is very thin, and the cancellous bone reflects adaptations for flight (refer to Figure 11.18), while in the human mandible, there is fairly thick cortical bone and dense cancellous bone.

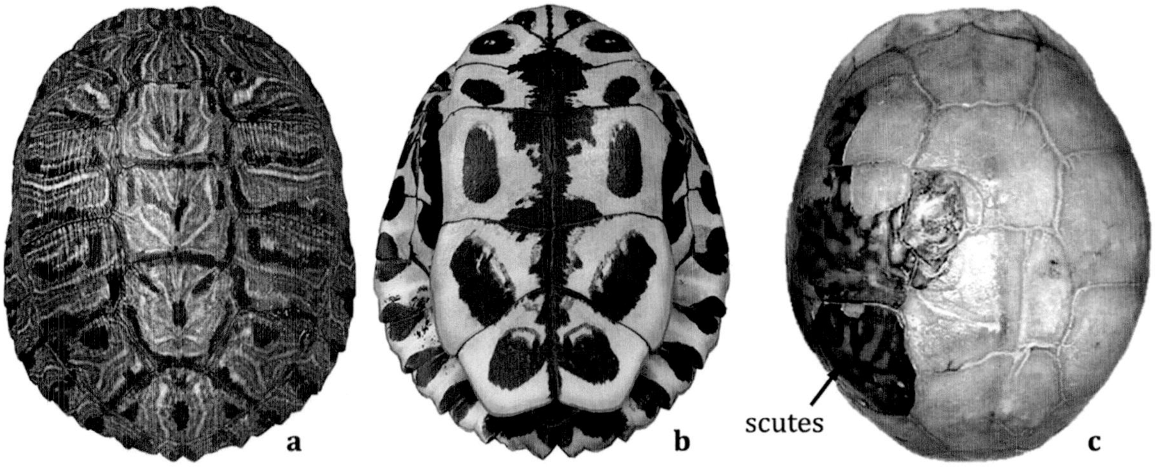

Figure 11.28 Slider turtle (*Trachemys* sp.) carapace (a) and intact plastron plate attached to carapace (b). Note the presence of scutes still attached to bone carapace (c) in a Florida box turtle (*Terrapene carolina bauri*).

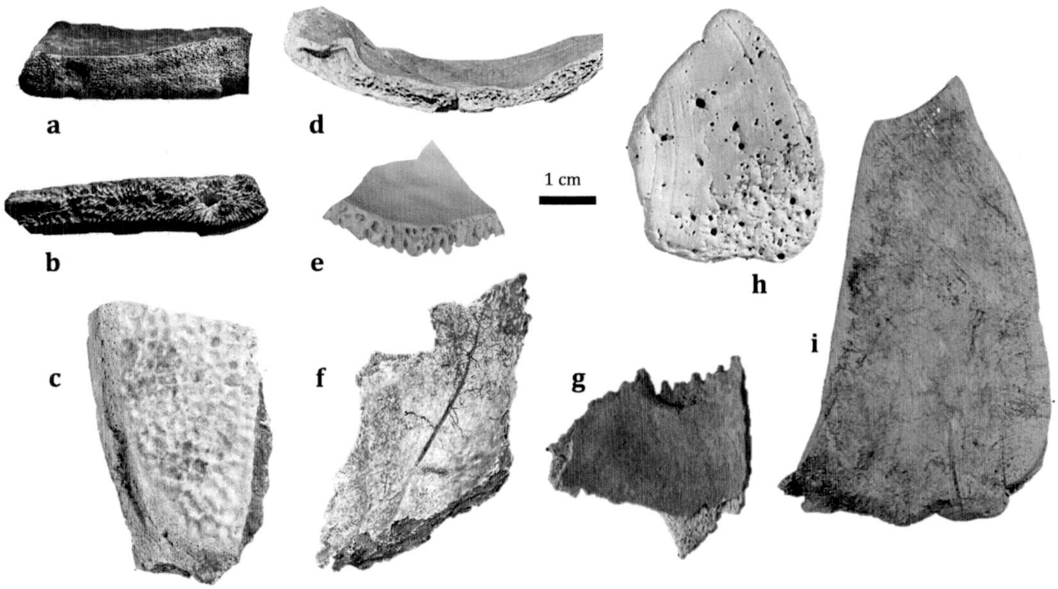

Figure 11.29 Comparison of materials easily confused in a forensic or archaeological context: (a–c) turtle shell fragments and human skull fragments (d–f); (g) weathered marine shell fragment (h) archaeological human cranial vault fragment; and (i) weathered PVC pipe fragment.

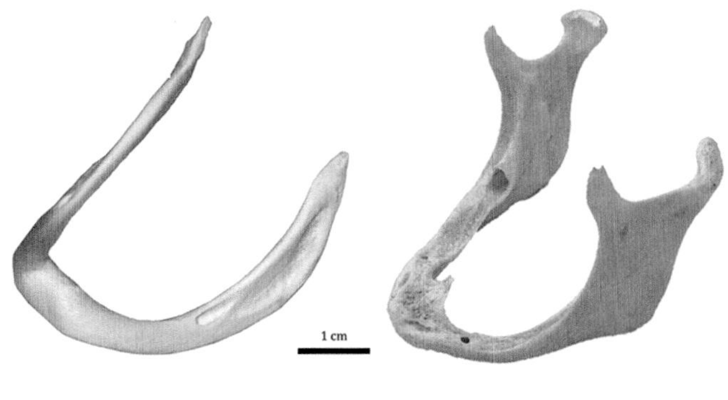

Figure 11.30 Morphological comparison of a mute swan (*Cygnus olor*) furcula (left) in inferolateral view with an adult human edentulous (toothless) mandible (right) in anterolateral view (b).

CASE STUDY #17: THE HOG HESITATION

Authors John Schultz and Tosha Dupras were asked to investigate remains located at a downtown construction site. Heavy equipment was being used to clear multiple large tree stumps when bones were discovered in the disturbed soil (Figure 11.31). The heavy equipment activities ceased, and the scene was secured by local law enforcement until they could arrive to distinguish if the remains were human or nonhuman. After examining the scene and the remains, it was noted that there were a number of diagnostic bone fragments present, including an innominate, proximal ulna, and second cervical vertebra. The overall morphology of these bones was clearly different than that of a human, such as structural adaptations to quadrupedal locomotion. It was determined that all of the fragmented skeletal materials were from a juvenile pig (*Sus scrofa*) (Figure 11.32). At that point, the scene was cleared, and construction activities resumed.

It is fairly common in forensic settings to distinguish nonhuman remains from potential human remains. Many cases involving questionable human or nonhuman skeletal remains result in bones and fragments being removed and transported to the medical examiner's office, where they are then examined outside of their original context. This case was somewhat unique in that the construction was stopped and the bones were left in situ so they could be examined in their original context after discovery. After it was determined on scene that the bones were nonhuman, the bones were collected to avoid any identification issues in the future, which is the standard procedure for nonhuman bone field identification.

Figure 11.31 Secured construction site where bones were discovered during the removal of tree stumps.

Figure 11.32 Fragmented skeletal remains identified as pig (*Sus scrofa*) bones (trowel for scale).

CASE STUDY #18: A NONHUMAN HUMAN

During a death investigation, crime scene personnel were unsure if they had discovered possible human skull fragments eroding from the ground surface. To be certain, author John Schultz was requested to identify the remains in situ. Upon arriving at the scene, it was noted that none of the bone fragments had been moved and crime scene personnel had placed flags in the ground to mark the extent of the discovered remains. The fragments consisted of numerous sun-bleached skeletal elements that were small, square, and flat (Figure 11.33). Many of the fragments were adhered to the ground surface by small fibrous roots. The bone fragments were immediately recognized as parts of a turtle carapace and plastron.

Given that land and water turtles are very prevalent in Florida, forensic anthropologists frequently identify this type of material for law enforcement and medical examiners. While a forensic anthropologist is not needed to identify a complete turtle shell, a trained osteologist should always be consulted when identifying turtle shell fragments lacking scutes. In this case, the small fragments were the individual parts of the turtle shell that became disarticulated after the shell dried. Since the fragments were flat, particularly the plastron portion of the shell, they were easily confused with human cranial fragments by someone not familiar with this material. After the bone fragments were identified as nonhuman, the material was collected to avoid any misidentification in the future.

Figure 11.33 Flagged remains of a turtle with shell fragments scattered across the ground surface.

Key Terms

amphibian
avian
ball-socket vertebrae
carapace/plastron
carpometacarpus
fish
furcula
fused tibia-fibula
homodont dentition
hypoplastrons
mammal
metapodial
polyphydont dentition
portacath (injection port)
reptile
scutes
synsacrum
tarsometatarsus
tibiotarsus
translucent bone
zooarchaeology

REVIEW AND DISCUSSION QUESTIONS

1. You have been asked to assist in collecting and packaging burnt skeletal remains found in a residential house fire that was just extinguished by firefighters and cleared for investigation. What materials will you need for collection and packaging of these remains? What special concerns should be considered when collecting and packaging the remains?
2. What are some of the major concerns for the forensic archaeologist when collecting and packaging fleshed remains?
3. Which bones of the human skeleton could be mistaken for a metapodial?
4. Why is it important for the forensic anthropologist to become familiar with the nonhuman species for a local geographic area?
5. A construction crew worker found a fragment of a mandible during the installation of some new playground equipment. The fragment has three pointy teeth remaining in the tooth sockets and you are not sure if it is human. What methods can be incorporated to confirm the species of the fragment?
6. A bone, approximately 6 cm in length with what appears to be eroded ends, was found during a search for the remains of a missing adult woman in a remote wooded area. The bone was found in association with a concentration of small rocks, some twigs, and a patch of something that resembles hair or fur. What factors should be considered in identifying, collecting, and packaging these materials?

Suggested Readings

Adams, B.J., Crabtree, P.J., Santucci, G. 2008. *Comparative Skeletal Anatomy: A Photographic Atlas for Medical Examiners, Coroners, Forensic Anthropologists, and Archaeologists*. Totowa, NJ: Humana Press.

Elbroch, M. 2006. *Animal Skulls: A Guide to North American Species*. Mechanicsburg, PA Stackpole Books.

Ellingham, S., Adserias-Garriga, J., Zapico, S., Ubelaker, D. 2023. *Burnt Human Remains: Recovery, Analysis, and Interpretation*. New York: John Wiley and Sons.

France, D.L. 2008. *Human and Nonhuman Bone Identification: A Color Atlas*. Boca Raton, FL: CRC Press.

France, D.L. 2021. *Comparative Bone Identification: Human Subadult and Nonhuman – A Field Guide*. Boca Raton, FL: CRC Press.

Galloway, A., Snodgrass, J.J. 1998. Biological and chemical hazards of forensic skeletal analysis. *Journal of Forensic Sciences* 43:940–948. DOI:10.1520/JFS12338J

Garvin, H.M., Dunn, R., Sholts, S.B., Litten, M.S., Mohamed, M., Kuttickat, N., Skantz, N. 2022. Forensic tools for species identification of skeletal remains: Metrics, statistics, and OsteoID. *Biology* 11(1):25.

Gilbert, B.M., Savage, H.G., Martin, L.D. 1996. *Avian Osteology*. Columbia, MO: Missouri Archaeological Society.

Milligan, C., Galloway, A., Kendall, A., Zephro, L, Willey, P., Bartelink, E. 2023. Recovery and identification of fatal fire victims from the 2018 Northern California camp fire disaster. In: Ellingham, S., Adserias-Garriga, J. Zapico, S., Ubelaker, D., eds. *Burnt Human Remains: Recovery, Analysis, and Interpretation*, pp. 371–382. New York: John Wiley and Sons.

Olsen, S.J. 2004. *Fish, Amphibian and Reptile Remains from Archaeological Sites: Southeastern and Southwestern United States* (No. 2). Cambridge, MA: The Peabody Museum Press.

References

Adams, B.J., Crabtree, P.J. 2011. *Comparative Osteology: A Laboratory and Field Guide of Common North American Animals*. Cambridge, MA: Academic Press.

Cattaneo, C., DiMartina, S., Scali, S., Craig., O.E., Grandi, M., Sokol, R.J. 1999. Determining the human origin of burnt bone: A comparative study of histological, immunological and DNA techniques. Forensic Science International 102:181–191. DOI:10.1016/S0379–0738(99)00059-6

Correia, P.M., Beattie, O. 2002. A critical look at methods for recovering, evaluating, and interpreting cremated human remains. In: Haglund, W.D., Sorg, M.H., eds. *Advances in Forensic Taphonomy: Method, Theory, and Archaeological Perspectives*, pp. 435–450. Boca Raton, FL: CRC Press.

Dirkmaat, D.C. 2002. Recovery and interpretation of the fatal fire victim: the role of forensic anthropology. In: Haglund, W.D., Sorg, M.H., eds. *Advances in Forensic Taphonomy: Method, Theory, and Archaeological Perspectives*, pp. 451–472. Boca Raton, FL: CRC Press.

Elbroch, M. 2006. *Animal Skulls: A Guide to North American Species*. Mechanicsburg, PA Stackpole Books.

Fairgrieve, S.I. 2008. *Forensic Cremation: Recovery and Analysis*. Boca Raton, FL: CRC Press.

Fairgrieve, S.I., Molto, J.E. 1994. Burning point: Canadian case studies of intentionally cremated human remains. In: Herring, A., Chan, L., eds. *Strength in Diversity: A Reader in Physical Anthropology*, pp. 385–402. Toronto: Canadian Scholar's Press.

Ferraro J.V., Binetti, K.M. 2014. American alligator proximal pedal phalanges resemble human finger bones: Diagnostic criteria for forensic investigators. *Forensic Science International* 240:151.e1–151.e7. DOI:10.1016/j.forsciint.2014.04.011

France, D.L. 2009. *Human and Nonhuman Bone Identification: A Color Atlas*. Boca Raton, FL: CRC Press.

France, D.L. 2011. *Human and Nonhuman Bone Identification: A Concise Field Guide*. Boca Raton, FL: CRC Press.

France, D.L. 2017. *Comparative Bone Identification: Human Subadult to Nonhuman*. Boca Raton, FL: CRC Press.

France, D.L. 2021. *Comparative Bone Identification: Human Subadult and Nonhuman – A Field Guide*. Boca Raton, FL: CRC Press.

Friedlander, H., Kim, J., Allen, J. 2024. Development of human remains investigations at fatal fire scenes: Bridging anthropology and fire sciences in the United States. *Wiley Interdisciplinary Reviews: Forensic Science* 6(6):e1527. DOI:10.1002/wfs2.1527

Galloway, A., Snodgrass, J.J. 1998. Biological and chemical hazards of forensic skeletal analysis. *Journal of Forensic Sciences* 43:940–948. DOI:10.1520/JFS12338J

Garvin, H.M., Dunn, R., Sholts, S.B., Litten, M.S., Mohamed, M. Kuttickat, N., Skantz, N. 2022. Forensic tools for species identification of skeletal remains: Metrics, statistics, and OsteoID. *Biology* 11(1):25. DOI:10.3390/biology11010025

Gilbert, B.M. 2003. *Mammalian Osteology*. Columbia, MO: Missouri Archaeological Society.

Gilbert, B.M., Savage, H.G., Martin, L.D. 1996. *Avian Osteology*. Columbia, MO: Missouri Archaeological Society.

Hillson, S. 1992. *Mammal Bones and Teeth: An Introductory Guide to Methods of Identification*. London: University College London Institute of Archaeology.

Hofreiter, M., Sneberger, J., Pospisek, M., Vanek, D. 2021. Progress in forensic bone DNA analysis: Lessons learned from ancient DNA. *Forensic Science International: Genetics* 54:102538. DOI:10.1016/j.fsigen.2021.102538

King, C.G., King, S. 1989. The archaeology of fire investigation. *Fire Engineering* 142(6):70–74.

Klales, A., Nesbitt, A., Dirkmaat, D., Cabo, L. 2023. Recovery and interpretation of human remains from fatal fire scenes. In: Ellingham, S., Adserias-Garriga, J. Zapico, S., Ubelaker, D., eds. *Burnt Human Remains: Recovery, Analysis, and Interpretation*, pp. 37–57. New York: John Wiley and Sons.

Kuffel, A., Nic Daeid N., Gray, A. 2024. Comparison of swabbing and cutting-out DNA collection methods from cotton, paper, and cardboard surfaces. *Forensic Science International: Synergy* 8:100453. DOI:10.1016/fsisyn.2023.100453.

Latham, K.E., Madonna, M.E., Hipp, J.L. 2022. DNA survivability in skeletal remains. In: Pokines, J.T., L'Abbé, E.N., Symes, S.A., eds. *Manual of Forensic Taphonomy*, 2nd ed., pp. 555–579. Boca Raton, FL: CRC Press.

Lewis, L., Christensen, A.M. 2015. Effects of aluminum foil packaging on elemental analysis of bone. *Journal of Forensic Sciences* 61(2):1534–1531. DOI:10.1111/1556-4029.12994

Marks, M.K. 1995. William M. Bass and the development of forensic anthropology in Tennessee. *Journal of Forensic Sciences* 40(5):741–750. DOI:10/1520/JFS15376J

Milligan, C., Galloway, A., Kendall, A., Zephro, L, Willey, P., Bartelink, E. 2023. Recovery and identification of fatal fire victims from the 2018 Northern California camp fire disaster. In: Ellingham, S., Adserias-Garriga, J. Zapico, S., Ubelaker, D., eds. *Burnt Human Remains: Recovery, Analysis, and Interpretation*, pp. 371–382. New York: John Wiley and Sons.

Mulhern, D.M., Ubelaker, D.H., 2012. Differentiating human from non-human bone microstructure. In: Crowder, C., Stout, S., eds. Bone Histology: *An Anthropological Perspective*, pp. 109–134. CRC Press: Boca Raton.

Murad, T.A. 1998. The growing popularity of cremation versus inhumation: some forensic implications. In: Reichs, K., ed. *Forensic Osteology: Advances in the Identification of Human Remains*, 2nd ed., pp. 86–106. Springfield, IL: Charles C Thomas.

Olsen, S.J. 2004a. *Mammal Remains from Archaeological Sites: Southeastern and Southwestern United States*. Cambridge, MA: Peabody Museum Press.

Olsen, S.J. 2004b. *Fish, Amphibian and Reptile Remains from Archaeological Sites: Southeastern and Southwestern United States* (No. 2). Cambridge, MA: The Peabody Museum Press.

Pokines, J.T. 2015. Identification of nonhuman remains received in a medical examiner setting. *Journal of Forensic Identification* 65(3):223–246.

Redsicker, D.R., O'Connor, J.J. 1996. *Practical Fire and Arson Investigation*, 2nd ed., Boca Raton, FL: CRC Press.

Salesse, K., Stamataki, E., Kontopoulos, I., Verly, G, Annaert, R., Boudin, M., Capuzzo, G., Claeys, P., Dalle, S., Hlad, M., De Mulder, G. 2021. These boots are made for burnin': Inferring the position of the corpse and the presence of leather footwears during cremation through isotope ($\delta^{13}C$, $\delta^{18}O$) and infrared (FTIR) analyses of experimentally burnt skeletal remains. *PLoS One* 16(10):e0257199. DOI:10.1371/journal.pone.

Schultz, J.J., Green, A., Murdock II, R.A., Hansen, M.H., Stephany, J.D., Garavaglia, J.C. 2020. The use of human skeletal remains in Palo rituals in Orange County, Florida. In: Garvin, H., Langley, N., eds. *Case Studies in Forensic Anthropology: Bonified Skeletons*, pp. 255–268. Boca Raton, FL: CRC Press.

Skinner, M., Lazenby, R.A. 1983. *Found! Human Remains: A Field Manual for the Recovery of the Recent Human Skeleton*. Burnaby, BC: Archaeology Press Simon Fraser University.

Smith, B.C., David Sweet, O.C. 2010. DNA and DNA evidence. In: Senn, D.R., Stimson, P.G., eds. *Forensic Dentistry*, 2nd ed., pp. 103–136. Boca Raton, FL: CRC Press

Snoeck, C. 2023. Isotope analysis from cremated remains. IIn: Ellingham, S., Adserias-Garriga, J. Zapico, S., Ubelaker, D., eds. *Burnt Human Remains: Recovery, Analysis, and Interpretation*, pp. 273–289. New York: John Wiley and Sons.

Snoeck, C., Beasley, M., Wolfe Steadman, D. 2025. Understanding intra-individual variability in modern cremated human remains for forensic and archaeological studies. *PLoS One* 20(4):e0320396. DOI:10.1371/journal.pone.0320396

Ubelaker, D.H., DeGaglia, C.M., Khrosrowshahi, H. 2023. Analysis of burnt human remains: Statistical perspectives from casework in forensic anthropology. In: Ellingham, S., Adserias-Garriga, J. Zapico, S., Ubelaker, D., eds. *Burnt Human Remains: Recovery, Analysis, and Interpretation*, pp. 336–344. New York: John Wiley and Sons.

Ubelaker, D.H., Lowenstein, J.M., Hood, D.G. 2004. Use of solid-phase double-antibody radioimmunoassay to identify species from small skeletal fragments. *Journal of Forensic Sciences* 49:924–929. DOI:10.1520/JFS2003399

Watson, J.T., McClelland, J., 2018. *Distinguishing human from non-human animal bone*. Arizona State Museum, University of Arizona, Tucson.

Wolniewicz, R. 2001a. *Field Guide to Skulls and Bones of Mammals of the Northeastern United States* (Vol. 1: Skulls and Mandibles). Magnolia, Mass: Richard Wolniewicz.

Wolniewicz, R. 2001b. *Field Guide to Skulls and Bones of Mammals of the Northeastern United States* (Vol. 2: The Long Bones). Magnolia, Mass: Richard Wolniewicz.

Zapico, S.C., Stone-Gordon, R. 2023. DNA profiling from burnt remains. In: Ellingham, S., Adserias-Garriga, J. Zapico, S., Ubelaker, D., eds. *Burnt Human Remains: Recovery, Analysis, and Interpretation*, pp. 213–238. New York: John Wiley and Sons.

CHAPTER 12

WRITING THE FINAL REPORT

Learning Objectives

- Introduce the sections and appendices that are included in a forensic archaeology report.
- Understand how to write a forensic archaeology report with the appropriate information and appendices.

Learning Connections

- Establish how the collection and documentation procedures outlined in this book are intended to preserve context and can then be incorporated in a final archaeology report.
- Reinforces that the forensic archaeology report will be one of several reports resulting from an investigation of a death scene following proper archaeological methods.

During the documentation and note-taking process, it is essential to operate under the assumption that a final report will be required at the end of the investigation. While some cases may ultimately be deemed as non-forensic and may not require a final report, it is best to treat every scene as if a comprehensive final report will be necessary. In fact, even when a case is determined to be non-forensic, a report may still be needed to justify that determination clearly, much like the rationale provided in skeletal reports (Pokines, 2020).

In most instances, the forensic archaeology report forms part of a broader set of documents prepared by the lead investigator, medical examiner, or coroner. When drafting the report, it is essential to consider the intended audience, as this will determine the language used and content required. The writing should be clear, concise, and free of typographic, grammatical, or spelling errors. A minor typographical error, such as confusing meters (m) with millimeters (mm), can easily lead to a significant misinterpretation of the findings. Although technical terminology may be necessary at times, it should be used sparingly and always accompanied by clear explanations to ensure the report remains accessible to all law enforcement professionals, attorneys, judges, and other nonscientific specialists. Overly complex language can hinder effective communication and reduce the report's utility. However, the report must be detailed and precise enough to enable other forensic archaeologists to grasp fully the significance of the findings. It is also important to remember that the report may be presented in a court of law. Therefore, a straightforward and objective style is recommended to support legal proceedings. Some laboratories, employ multi-tiered systems of peer and managerial review as part of their reporting protocols. These systems often include formal training in report writing, helping ensure consistency, accuracy, and professionalism throughout the documentation process.

Upon completion of work at the scene, the forensic archaeologist should provide the investigative team with an estimated delivery date for the final report. This estimate should take into consideration the complexity of the case and the scope of the report required. While it is a best practice to submit the report as promptly as possible, the forensic archaeologist must also be prepared to deliver an interim report if requested. In the event of any delays in producing the report, the investigative team must be promptly informed, along with a clear explanation of the reasons for the delay.

DOI: 10.4324/9781315201658-12

REPORT CONTENTS

Thorough documentation in the field is essential. All relevant observations, measurements, and findings should be recorded diligently in field notes. Appendices A through G provide sample forms that can assist in documenting this information systematically. These records serve as the foundation for the final report. It is a critical responsibility of the forensic archaeologist to demonstrate clearly the preservation and protection of all data that justify their actions and decisions made at the scene. Forensic archaeologists must store all records in a secure location to safeguard sensitive information. Electronic records should be housed in a protected directory (i.e., secured by password authentication or restricted user access) and supported by a routine backup protocol to prevent data loss.

While each case may present unique circumstances, certain core components should remain consistent across reports. The following outline offers a general framework for structuring your report, with adjustments made as necessary to suit the specific nature of the case. Visual elements such as photographs, maps, and diagrams can enhance clarity and should be incorporated into relevant sections where appropriate. Additional supporting materials may be included in the appendices to ensure comprehensive documentation.

When the report is complete, the forensic archaeologist should conduct a thorough review of all sections to ensure internal consistency, that all findings are well-supported by the data presented, and that the report stands as a complete, self-contained document.

Case Records Identification

Every report must begin with a comprehensive listing of all relevant case numbers. These may include identifiers from various law enforcement agencies (e.g., Sheriff's Office, Medical Examiner's Office) and, when applicable, individualized case numbers assigned by forensic archaeologists. Including all associated case numbers ensures accurate cross-referencing and prevents discrepancies across documentation. The introductory section of the report should also clearly state the following:

- Location of the case
- Date(s) of investigation or report preparation
- Report author information, including their full name, contact details, and pertinent qualifications (e.g., degree, related professional certifications and/or position)
- Recipient information, including the full name and contact details of the individual or agency to whom the report is being submitted

This standardized format promotes consistency, clarity, and accountability across all case documentation.

Case Summary

The report should begin with a clear and concise summary of the case, enabling readers to grasp quickly the key events and findings without navigating the entire document. This overview must detail:

- Initiation of the investigation—specify who contacted the forensic archaeologist (and/or other search and recovery specialists), the date of contact, and their role in the case.
- Briefing—summarize information provided at the briefing stage of the investigation (although considered hearsay evidence, its inclusion is deemed acceptable, provided that the source of the information is clearly identified).
- Scene involvement—indicate the date the forensic archaeologist arrived at the scene.
- Search and/or excavation methods—describe the techniques and procedures employed during the investigation.
- Findings—summarize any significant discoveries resulting from the search and excavation.
- Evidence disposition—outline how collected evidence was handled, including its current status or location.

This structured summary ensures clarity, promotes accessibility, and sets the stage for the detailed report that follows.

Participants

All individuals present at the scene must be documented (refer to Appendix B). This includes any relevant senior police officers, crime scene examiners, and other attending forensic specialists. Along with their names, it is essential to gather additional details such as organizational affiliation and contact information. In fast-paced or high-pressure environments, identifying every participant can be challenging; however, attending officers typically maintain a roster of personnel on site. To streamline the information-gathering process across multiple agencies, field teams should always carry business cards as part of their standard equipment. These can be quickly exchanged to ensure accurate and efficient recordkeeping.

Scene Information

If relevant to the search, reporting on the land-use history of a scene, such as what happened there before the remains were introduced, can be included in the report. This history can include if the area was fenced (restricting scavengers), former agricultural land now returned to forest (thus affecting the soil horizons encountered during excavation), previous disposal of trash items on the surface that could be mistaken for relevant evidence, or naturally prone to flooding (also affecting sediments).

Upon arrival, essential details about the scene should be documented (refer to Appendix B). This includes noting whether the location is indoors or outdoors, describing the topography (e.g., flat terrain, hills, water features) and identifying plant or ground cover (e.g., wooded areas, grass, gravel, pavement, tree canopy, understory vegetation, leaf litter). Architectural features and general exposure to weather conditions, such as sun or shade, should also be recorded, along with any notable elements (e.g., remains found inside a vehicle or container). Scene access must be clearly described. If field maps or aerial imagery were used to locate the scene or guide search efforts, these resources should be listed and included as an appendix to the report. Any evidence of taphonomic disturbance, whether caused by human activity or animal interference, should be carefully noted and described. Recommended visual documentation for this section includes aerial photographs, satellite images (e.g., Google Earth Pro), orthographic maps with the scene highlighted, and overview photographs of the complete scene, showing layout, orientations, and major landmarks.

Search Summary

Depending on the circumstances of the case, a search may be necessary. All search methods, whether adopted or excluded, should be clearly documented, along with a rationale for each decision. This includes both non-intrusive methods (e.g., visual foot surveys, cadaver dog deployment, or geophysical scanning) and intrusive methods (e.g., probing, coring, or shovel or pit testing). Any modifications to the originally proposed methodology that arose during the course of the work must also be described, including the reasons prompting these changes. All individuals involved in the search should be identified, with particular attention given to any specialists (e.g., geophysical equipment operators or forensic experts). Where applicable, mid-range photographs of the search process, especially those showing grid layouts or key areas, should be included to support the documentation and provide visual context.

Surface Scatter Summary

In some instances, human remains may be encountered as a surface scatter, either during an organized search (refer to Appendix D) or through accidental discovery by individuals who subsequently report the find. The mode of discovery should be documented first, specifying whether it was accidental, part of a formal search, or reported by a witness. When remains are found exposed on the surface, it is essential to determine and record whether the surface scatter is a primary surface scene (in situ) or secondary surface scene (i.e., displaced from the primary). In addition, note whether the remains are fully exposed or only partially visible. For partially visible remains, the surrounding context, such as plant material, detritus, or evidence of erosion, must be described in detail. Recovery methods should be thoroughly documented, including any screening or sifting techniques employed. This section must also include overview and mid-range photographs that accurately depict the surface scene and spatial distribution of the remains.

Excavation Summary

Whenever excavations are undertaken, meticulous documentation is essential. It must be understood that excavation, like any intrusive search technique, irreversibly alters or destroys the original context of the scene. Therefore, the notes recorded during this process, along with the final report derived from them, may serve as the only means of reconstructing the scene and understanding what transpired. Just as with search methods, all excavation techniques, whether adopted or rejected, should be thoroughly documented, with clear justification provided for each decision. Any modifications to the original methodology that arise during the course of the work must also be recorded, along with a rationale explaining why these adjustments were necessary. If any portion of the archaeological work was conducted by others or with their assistance, those individuals must be identified, and their specific contributions clearly described. In addition, it should be explicitly stated which elements of their work were performed under the direction or supervision of the forensic archaeologist.

This section should be as comprehensive and detailed as possible (refer to Appendixes D and E). Begin by specifying the size and precise location of the excavated area, including the method by which it was identified (e.g., witness testimony, systematic search). Follow with a clear description of the excavation techniques employed. This should include:

- Type of equipment used (e.g., heavy machinery, hand tools)
- Gridding procedures
- Excavation methods (e.g., stratigraphic, arbitrary levels)
- Mapping procedures (e.g., total station with data logger, tape measure and line level)
- Screening techniques, including mesh size and wet or dry.

Clarify whether the excavation focused on a specific feature or grid, or if a pedestal method was utilized. All mapping procedures must be thoroughly described, including the use of instruments such as total stations, data loggers, GPS units, or compasses. Explain how datum points and grids were established and maintained throughout the process. In addition, provide a detailed account of the grave and surrounding soil. Mid-range photographs documenting each stage of the excavation should be included to visually support the written record.

Relevant Findings

This section should present a clear listing and interpretation of all relevant findings, grounded in the factual evidence that supports those conclusions. All findings should be presented clearly and logically, ensuring they are easy to understand. Explanations must be fair, impartial, and well-supported, without favoring any particular side. When findings allow for multiple explanations, the forensic archaeologist must clearly justify the rationale for favoring one explanation over others. Based on the forensic archaeologist's findings, it should be possible to reconstruct the sequence of events associated with the surface scene or archaeological feature and its contents.

Recovered Remains

When human remains are discovered, it is essential to document their context, location, and physical characteristics in a clear and easily accessible manner (refer to Appendices D and E). The forensic archaeologist's role is strictly objective and observational. It is essential to recognize that forensic archaeologists are not responsible for analyzing human remains at the scene. Such analyses fall outside their scope and must never be included in a forensic archaeology report under any circumstances. Key observational details to record include:

- Mode of deposition – whether the remains are located on the surface, buried, submerged, or in another setting.
- Condition and completeness – noting any signs of preservation, damage, or fragmentation.
- Orientation and position – describing how the body is situated in relation to its surroundings.
- Scattered – if describing a scavenged grave or dispersed surface deposit, describe how the remains have been dispersed.
- Seasonality – if bones on the ground surface were resting on top or underneath a layer of leaves, this can indicate deposition before or after the autumn season.
- Associated materials – identifying any clothing, personal effects, or other items found with the remains.

This documentation should be factual and descriptive, avoiding hearsay, speculation, or conclusions about biological profile, cause of death, identity, or PMI.

Surface or Archaeological Contexts

The reliability of each conclusion based on context should be carefully assessed. Alternative explanations must be considered and, where discounted, the rationale for doing so should be clearly articulated. If certain findings are deemed irrelevant, the forensic archaeologist must provide a reasoned explanation for their exclusion. When reporting findings from surface recovery, remains should not be dismissed as non-forensic based solely on isolated characteristics such as bone color, mass, or degree of preservation. This caution is particularly vital in cases involving surface discoveries or remains retrieved from aquatic or waterlogged environments, where preservation conditions can vary widely and may obscure forensic relevance. Archaeological explanations must be substantiated by appropriate and verifiable data. The dating and characterization of finds or features should be determined using relative methods (such as stratigraphy and contextual analysis) and/or absolute techniques (including scientific testing), as appropriate to the context.

Associated Evidence and Collected Samples

All evidence removed from the scene must be thoroughly documented, as outlined in Appendix F. This includes any items collected during the search for or recovery of human remains. Each piece of evidence should be recorded in the order it was discovered and must include a detailed description, the name of the individual who logged it, and a unique evidence number. In cases where evidence is transferred, a completed chain of custody form must accompany the item to ensure traceability throughout the investigative process (refer to Appendix F).

Collection of samples for future analysis may occur during search and recovery operations. The report must clearly specify all materials submitted for further analysis by the forensic archaeologist. These may include, but are not limited to, botanical, soil, and entomological specimens. Each sample should be documented with its corresponding context and identification number using a separate collection form (refer to Appendices C and E) to ensure accurate tracking. Close-up view photographs of all collected samples should be included in this section to provide visual reference and support.

Additional supplementary analysis may involve the examination of retained sediments associated with the skeletal remains or containing preserved human tissue. If this responsibility is assigned to the forensic archaeologist, it is imperative that the process be carried out under strictly controlled conditions to preserve the integrity of the evidence. The forensic archaeologist must also adhere to all relevant legislation and established professional standards related to retention of human remains.

The forensic archaeologist may also offer critical insight into complementary analytical methods, such as osteological or isotopic analysis, that may significantly advance the investigation. Upon consultation and request by the investigative team, they should be prepared to coordinate and/or facilitate these procedures.

Appendices

Supplementary materials such as aerial photographs, topographical maps, case maps, and other relevant visuals not included in the main body of the report should be placed in the appendix.

Photography and Video Records

Law enforcement agencies typically conduct their own photographic and video documentation of the scene, including search, excavation, and recovery procedures. In addition, it is strongly recommended that the forensic archaeologist independently photograph all stages of the investigation. Photography of the scene should occur before, during, and after the scene is processed. During an excavation or recovery, photography should include mid-range and close-up photographs of all stages of the excavation process and recovery of remains and associated evidence. A detailed photographic log (refer to Appendix F) should accompany this documentation, noting the camera model, memory card type (for digital cameras), photograph number, and a brief description of each image. All photographs should be formatted, compiled, and submitted on a CD/DVD or other accepted media storage as part of the final report.

To enhance the report's clarity and evidentiary value, selected photographs may be embedded within the main body or included in the appendices, depending on relevance to specific sections. In terms of imagery to include in a report or appendices, an overall aerial image with the site location, burial location, and areas searched is a typical image in a report. This can be followed by relevant images documenting the area prior to being excavated, or if surface remains, prior to the recovery. In addition, images of the collection procedures can be included, particularly when they depict the body or skeletal position, and associated evidence that is collected. At the same time, it is vital to include imagery that documents specific aspects of scene context in the final report (e.g., jewelry or wallet in association with the remains). It is important to remember that all images captured during search and recovery are admissible in court. Therefore, ensure that each photograph is appropriate, relevant, and accurately reflects the context of the case. At the same time, at least one map of the scene should be included in the report – refer to previous chapters for examples of field maps based on the type of recovery.

Field Drawings and Maps

Field drawings and maps play a crucial role in forensic reporting. While photographs capture visual details, maps provide spatial context, illustrating the precise location of remains and their relationship to potential evidence. They also offer a level of documentation that other methods often cannot achieve. For instance, cross-sectional plans/diagrams can reveal how remains are distributed across varying depths, situated on slopes, or aligned with evidence at different stratigraphic levels. While field drawings and maps may be discussed in a separate dedicated section, they are more often referenced throughout the report, making it vital to include them in the appendices for clarity. Refer to the previous chapters for the different types of maps and diagrams that can be included in a report or the appendices based on the type of recovery. At a minimum, a site plan map should be included for scattered remains and a scale plan drawing for a burial.

References

References may need to be included in the report, particularly when published methods are employed during the investigation. If these methods are too complex or lengthy to describe in full, citing the original source allows the report to remain concise while still providing access to essential details. The source of imagery, including Google Earth Pro and the version utilized, also may be included.

Signatures and Dates

A designated space for original signatures and the report completion date should be included at the end of the main body. This section typically precedes the references and appendices, depending on whether those elements are part of the report.

EXAMPLE OF FINAL REPORT

This section presents an example of final report. Since a forensic anthropologist is not always present at a scene during the recovery, the example report is written from the perspective of a forensic archaeologist. To safeguard the identities of those concerned, certain names, dates, locations, and details have been altered to preserve confidentiality.

The forensic archaeology report typically does not include information about the skeletal analysis. If a forensic anthropologist recovers the remains, they may submit one report that includes both the skeletal analysis and field recovery. While this report example does not contain images or appendices, the example suggests where these supplementary materials should be incorporated in the final field report.

Forensic Clandestine Grave Report: Search, Excavation, and Analysis

OCSO Case ID: 25–00134-H
ME Case ID: District 9 03–00681-25
UCF Forensic Case ID: UCF-2025/3-003
Location: 980 S County Road 419 (Parcel #21–24–32–5CG-0400-0000)
Date(s) of Recovery: March 23–24, 2025
Date of Report: April 01, 2025

PREPARED FOR

Detective Justin Case, CID-Homicide
Orange County Sherriff's Office, 555 Court Drive, Orlando, FL 32555
Dr. Sunny Day, Chief Medical Examiner
D9 Medical Examiner's Office, 555 Carver Lane, Orlando, FL 328555

PREPARED BY

Dr. Roxanne Bownes, PhD, Lead Forensic Archaeologist
Department of Anthropology, University of Central Florida, Orlando, FL 32816
Ms. Penny Graves, Graduate Geosciences Research Assistant
Department of Anthropology, University of Central Florida, Orlando, FL 32816

CASE SUMMARY

This report details the systematic search, forensic recovery, and analysis of unidentified human remains (confirmed by the Medical Examiner, Dr. Sunny Day) found within a clandestine burial site discovered on March 23, 2025, in a wooded area at 970 S County Road 419. The surface GPR and HRD dog searches identified the possible grave location, as confirmed by excavation. No identifying personal effects other than remnants of clothing and shoes were found in association with the remains. The context of the burial site included the grave's irregular construction (i.e., not uniform in size and shape) and the presence of two projectiles recovered after the removal of the remains. The findings have been documented and presented to the investigative team. The remains and associated evidence were transported to the District 9 Medical Examiner laboratory for osteological analysis, while the two projectiles were retained by the District Sherrif's Office Crime Forensic Unit.

CASE BACKGROUND

The investigation was initiated based on a tip received by local law enforcement regarding a potential clandestine burial site. At the request of the Orange County Sheriff's Office on March 23, 2025, a forensic team was deployed to a rural, wooded property in Orange County, FL, to investigate a suspected clandestine grave. The purpose of this investigation was to locate and forensically excavate the grave, recover any human remains and associated evidence. The area was secured, and a ground search team that included a human remains detection

(HRD) dog identified an area of interest. Ground-penetrating radar (GPR) confirmed soil anomalies consistent with a disturbed area in the location where the HRD dog alerted. The forensic team was then tasked with the archaeological excavation of the site and the recovery of any human remains and associated evidence.

PARTICIPANTS

The following participants were involved at the scene (refer to Appendix A for contact details) and were present throughout the investigation. For logs of exact dates and times, refer to OCSO Report #2025–000458.

1. Dr. Roxanne Bownes, UCF Associate Professor, Forensic Archaeologist
2. Penny Graves, UCF Graduate Geosciences Research Assistant
3. Justin Case, Detective, Orange County Sheriff's Office
4. Jack Sparrow, Detective, Orange County Sheriff's Office
5. Martin Finder, Detective, Orange County Sheriff's Office
6. John Dutie, Deputy, Orange County Sheriff's Office
7. Stacy Hounder, Sergeant, Orange County Sheriff's Office, Canine Unit
8. Victor Spatter, Crime Scene Investigator, Orange County Sheriff's Office
9. Dee Comper, Death Investigator, District 9 Medical Examiner Office
10. Cecil Cuffs, Officer, Orange County Corrections
11. Elmer Smiter, Inmate (Defendant), Orange County Corrections
12. Rocky Onlooker, Inmate (Witness), Orange County Corrections
13. Vick Carrier, Inmate (Witness), Orange County Corrections

SCENE DESCRIPTION

The scene was located on the left side of County Road 419 heading south and entered via County Rural Route #5 dirt road access. A tree line and a fire trench bordered the northern side of the site. The western side was bordered by low bush cover along a dirt road (CRR #5). The eastern and southern sides were sparsely wooded with low bush understory. The burial scene is located in a flat area among young pine trees with mostly open canopy exposure to sunlight and covered by dense grass and low understory.

Aerial photographs, site overview photographs, and a site plan indicating major landmarks and orientation are provided in Appendix A. (All digital photographs supplied in this report were taken using a Nikon D7500 DSLR and stored on a 128 GB SD card.)

SEARCH SUMMARY

Search of the area was initiated at approximately 8:30 am on March 23, 2025. In attendance was OCSO detectives Justin Case, Jack Sparrow, and Martin Finder. An OCSO deputy, John Dutie, was present to secure the scene, and a member of the Orange County Sheriff's Office Canine Unit, Sergeant Stacy Hounder, was present with her HRD dog.

An initial walk-through of the area was conducted based on information from one of the suspects who had been escorted on the scene the previous day. The area marked by police as "searchable" measured approximately 25 m by 17 m and a site datum was added to the southwest corner of this area. Scene tape was added around this searchable area, and security of the scene was maintained by an OSCO deputy and the Entry/Exit Log Station entrance maintained by the deputy was on Country Rd. 19.

The area was sparsely covered in young pine trees, with grass and low brush ground cover. Three areas containing features (disturbed ground surface) from the surrounding area were identified through a visual search of the grid as possible areas to explore based on disturbed soils and or depressions. Sergeant Stacy Hounder led the HRD dog search in each area, and the dog alerted at one of the areas of interest. The suspected burial scene was delineated using a total station and data logger, and all grid coordinates were established for mapping. The site grid was aligned to magnetic north using a Brunton compass with the site datum. The site datum was then tied to two telephone poles on Country Road 19 (OCF-DU-123456 and OCF-DU-123457) using triangulation.

Further visual inspection was performed of the searchable area of identified disturbed soil, a possible primary grave depression, with variation in vegetation growth from the surrounding area. These indicators were documented and photographed. At approximately 11:00 am, a 5 m by 5 m grid was set up with the location of the purported grave positioned in the center and the geophysical grid tied to the site datum. A cart mounted GPR with 250 MHz antenna was used to survey the grid using 50 cm transects in both north to south and west to east directions by Research Assistant Penny Graves. Results of the geophysical survey confirmed the location and approximate dimensions of the subsurface disturbance that were consistent with an adult-sized clandestine grave.

Before any excavation was undertaken, mid-range photographs that were taken of the search process and suspected burial scene and grave, and a scaled plan of the suspected burial scene are provided in Appendix B.

EXCAVATION SUMMARY

March 23, 2025

At approximately 1:30 pm, Dr. Roxanne Bownes and Penny Graves cleared the surface area using hand trowels within a 3 × 3 m grid area centered over the suspected grave. All loose surface debris and vegetation was cleared by grid square, sorted, and dry-screened (¼ in/6.35 mm mesh) over a tarp placed outside of the excavation area.

Excavation was performed with hand trowels and detail hand tools in 5-cm arbitrary layers within the grave fill, with sediments removed using dust pans and then screened to locate any small items of associated evidence or small skeletal elements. After the first 5-cm layer was removed, a dark discoloration in the sediment was evident and delineated the oval burial cut of the grave, which measured 2.10 m in length and 0.83 m in width at the top. The burial cut was documented and photographed. Excavation proceeded in 5 cm layers, within the grave feature. Three distinct layers of grave fill were identified at depths of 12 cm, 18 cm, and 27 cm below surface, which were documented. Each of these layers revealed distinct mixed soil textures and colors due to disturbance during digging of the grave and burial of the body. The fill at 12–18 cm depth was loosely compacted loam and included pine needles. The fill at 18–27 cm depth was a moderately compacted mix of loam and sand and included small root growth from nearby vegetation. The fill below 27 cm was predominantly heavily compacted sand with small root growth infiltrating from nearby vegetation.

At approximately 4:30 pm, a light rain began to fall, and it was decided to stop excavation for the day prior to uncovering any skeletal remains. A tarp was placed over the excavation site to prevent weather-related damage and mid-range photographs were used to document the closing of the excavation. An OCSO deputy was called to secure the scene overnight.

March 24, 2025

Excavation resumed at approximately 8:00 am, with the same excavation team. At a depth of 65 cm, the toe cap of a shoe was identified in the grave. Once it was confirmed that the shoe was in association with skeletal remains, all work stopped so that Detective Justin Case could send two digital photographs to the medical examiner, Dr. Sunny Day, to confirm them as human remains. At approximately 1:00 pm, the medical examiner, Dr. Sunny Day, confirmed the presence of human remains and instructed the investigation lead detective, Justin Case, to continue with the excavation of the grave. Dee Comper, Death Investigator from the District 9 Medical Examiner's office arrived on scene at 1:33 pm. The decision was also made by Dr. Roxanne Bownes to continue the excavation by cutting a working platform along the side of the grave for safety and access. The walls of the grave were examined for any tool mark evidence prior to creating the platform; however, no marks were identified.

Skeletal remains and any associated evidence were pedestaled (i.e., left raised on a column of sediment) within the grave and mapped three-dimensionally in a scaled plan and section view using the total station and data logger.

Recovery of Remains

The skeletal remains were found in a loosely flexed supine (lying on back, face upward) position. Remnants of clothing material and athletic shoes were recovered, suggesting that the individual was probably fully clothed at the time of burial. No evidence of a coffin, container, or wrapping was found. Adhered roots were visible on the left humerus (upper arm) and left side of skull, indicating interaction with nearby plant life.

With the assistance of CSI Victor Spatter, all skeletal remains and clothing remnants were removed and packaged according to standard practices and chain of custody procedures. All packaged remains were combined and secured in a body bag for transport by Dee Comper to the District 9 Medical Examiner laboratory for osteological analysis. In addition, the two projectiles were retained by Victor Spatter, CSI, OCSO.

Closing Excavation and Scene

After removal of the remains, additional loose sediments were excavated to the floor of the grave, which still retained an oval shape and measured 2.0 m in maximum length and 0.68 m in maximum width, indicating an overall irregular size and shape for the grave. A metal detector was used on the floor of the grave, which was at a depth of 1.02 m below the adjacent ground surface. The metal detector indicated that there was an anomaly below the grave floor. Further excavation uncovered two projectiles 8 cm below the grave floor in the general area where the upper torso of the body was located in the grave. These were also mapped three-dimensionally in the scaled plan and section view of the grave. CSI Victor Spatter packaged the bullets according to standard practices and chain of custody procedures. Excavation and burial scene closure occurred at approximately 5:30 pm after all records were reviewed.

Mid-range and close-up photographs of all stages of the excavation process and recovery of remains and associated evidence, and a scaled plan and section drawing of the grave and remains are provided in Appendix C. The skeletal inventory chart and list of associated evidence completed during the recovery process is provided in Appendix D.

LIST OF APPENDICES

Appendix A: Site overview photographs and total station map of site
Appendix B: Burial scene photographs and scaled plan
Appendix C: Excavation photographs and scaled plan and section drawings
Appendix D: Skeletal inventory chart and list of associated evidence

SIGNATURE OF FORENSIC ARCHAEOLOGY TEAM LEAD

____

Dr. Roxanne Bownes, PhD
Lead Forensic Archaeologist
Department of Anthropology
University of Central Florida
Orlando, FL 32816

REVIEW AND DISCUSSION QUESTIONS

1. What are the typical sections that are included in a forensic archaeology report?
2. What information is provided in the case summary?
3. Provide examples of associated evidence that can be documented by the forensic archaeologist and that can be important for a death investigation.
4. What types of imagery and maps are appropriate for a typical forensic archaeology report?

Reference

Pokines, J.T. 2020. The case of the… cases: The flow of the ordinary into a medical examiner's office. In: Garvin, H., Langley, N., eds. *Case Studies in Forensic Anthropology: Bonified Skeletons*, pp. 291–302. Boca Raton, FL: CRC Press.

CHAPTER 13

FORENSIC ARCHAEOLOGY RESEARCH AND TRAINING

Learning Objectives

- Describe examples of forensic archaeology research.
- Summarize how forensic archaeology research has improved the geophysical detection of burials.
- Explain how forensic archaeology research has improved methods for the recovery of human remains on the ground surface.
- Build on examples of classroom exercises and mock forensic archaeology training scenarios.

Learning Connections

- Establish how forensic archaeology research utilizing field methods presented in this chapter continues to improve forensic archaeology practices discussed in this book.
- Understand how different types of classroom exercises and mock forensic archaeology scenarios will improve proficiency in field methods presented throughout this book.

The field of forensic archaeology has evolved and improved by incorporating and adapting archaeological methods when processing crime scenes with decomposing and skeletonized remains. While there are numerous differences between a traditional archaeological site and a forensic scene, archaeological methods are generally adapted for forensic scenes based on the site parameters, legal considerations, and time constraints. Determining how to continually improve forensic archaeology methods requires continued research also to improve forensic archaeology guidelines and best practices. The purpose of this chapter is to highlight how controlled research by two of the authors (John J. Schultz and James T. Pokines) has improved forensic archaeology search and recovery methods for detecting burials and dispersed remains on the ground surface, while improving forensic archaeology practices. At the same time, learning updated forensic archaeology methods is also imperative. A secondary goal of this chapter is to provide examples of forensic archaeology activities through suggested classroom exercises and mock training scenarios that can be implemented for training students and professionals so they can learn how to incorporate proper field methods when involved with recoveries of forensic cases.

DOI: 10.4324/9781315201658-13

RESEARCH ON GEOPHYSICAL DETECTION OF CLANDESTINE GRAVES: PRACTICES AND RESULTS

Research has led to methodological advancements in forensic archaeology, particularly in the methods and protocols used to detect clandestine graves. The research design for grave detection often involves simulating a research site with mock graves that can be monitored over time to document changes within the grave and ground surface. The initial studies by NecroSearch International (France et al., 1992, 1997), an interdisciplinary Colorado-based forensic organization, constructed mock burials using pig (*Sus scrofa*) carcasses as proxies for human bodies and then monitored the burials over time using various methods. In particular, a number of geophysical tools that had been used for detecting archaeology sites and burials were used to monitor the graves. This initial research by NecroSearch (France et al., 1992, 1997) concluded that ground-penetrating radar (GPR) was the most favorable geophysical tool for grave detection, and this research was the impetus for other GPR projects monitoring graves in different areas of the United States and worldwide. Pig carcasses are the primary fleshed body used for this type of geophysical research when simulating human graves. At the same time, a recent study validated the use of pig carcasses as proxies for human bodies when conducting geophysical research. For example, Berezowski and colleagues (2024) concluded that similar geophysical responses were produced when comparing clothed and unclothed graves with pig carcasses and human donor cadavers using GPR and electrical resistivity tomography (ERT).

The primary purpose of these types of geophysically controlled studies is to determine if a buried body can be detected over time using one or several types of geophysical methods (refer to Chapter 7). In addition, several variables have been tested such as soil type, depth of burial, forensic scenario, body size, and data collection parameters. When monitoring a mock burial over time, it is essential that it undergoes the identical types of taphonomic processes that would be encountered in a forensic burial (Schultz, 2016). For example, to replicate the taphonomic environment that a forensic grave would undergo, a body must proceed through stages of decomposition while the backfill of the ground compacts and vegetation changes occur on the ground surface. While a pig carcass can replicate this environment, burying a plastic skeleton cannot replicate the proper taphonomic environment of a real clandestine burial (Schultz, 2012). At the same time, grid data collection must also include a blank control grave that consists of digging an identical-sized grave hole as the pig graves and only returning the displaced dirt (backfill) into the empty grave without adding any other items in the grave. The purpose of the control grave is to determine which component of the grave response is solely due to the disturbed backfill sediment. This is important when comparing the imagery of the control grave to that of a grave with a decomposing pig carcass to differentiate the geophysical response of the decomposing body in the grave.

One of the earliest and largest GPR-monitoring studies (24 graves with carcasses) occurred in Central Florida and tested several variables such as soil composition (sand vs. clay), body size (small and large), grave depth (shallow vs. deep), and length of interment (Schultz, 2008; Schultz et al., 2006). In addition, half of the burials were excavated at 12 months to correlate the decomposition state with the GPR imagery characteristics and were no longer monitored, and the other half were excavated at 21 to 21.5 months. Several important conclusions were gleaned from this research. Overall, this study demonstrated that it became difficult to detect the smaller-sized cadavers buried in sand soon after skeletonization, because the area surrounding the body no longer provided a strong enough contrast compared with that of the surrounding undisturbed sterile soil (Schultz, 2008). Further, shallow buried and larger carcasses in sand were easily detected over 21–21.5 months of monitoring and during advanced stages of decomposition (Schultz et al., 2006). However, large carcasses buried in proximity to a clay horizon became increasingly difficult to image after the first year of interment, including when there was extensive preservation of soft tissue structures. Further, when evaluating small carcasses, depth of burial affected grave detection, because the deeper buried carcasses were detected over a longer PMI due to reduced decomposition rates and preservation of soft tissues (Schultz, 2008). Overall, empty control graves were very important in demonstrating that the detected remains were primarily the result of the decomposing bodies or skeletons buried in sand and not the disturbed backfill sediment (Schultz, 2008; Schultz et al., 2006).

The next phase of geophysical research needed to address how individual grave contents characteristics affected their detection. Schultz and Martin (2012) and Schultz et al. (2016) evaluated the applicability of GPR for detecting controlled graves in a spodosol, a common Florida soil, over three years with six burial scenarios representing common grave scenarios: deep and shallow naked pig carcasses, a deep clothed pig carcass, a deep carcass wrapped in a tarpaulin, a deep carcass wrapped in a blanket, a deep carcass covered with a layer of rocks, and a deep carcass covered with a layer of lime. Overall, several grave scenarios (carcasses wrapped in the tarpaulin and carcasses covered with a layer of gravel) produced more distinctive responses with clearer target reflections compared with imagery from the naked carcasses. One surprising result was difficulty imaging a few scenarios by year 1 (Schultz and Martin, 2016). There was increased detection during the wetter months, and then, during the third year of monitoring, several grave scenarios that were detected were then imaged after increased seasonal rainfall (Schultz et al., 2016). While a simulated grave may be difficult to detect over time, detection of a grave in a spodosol over time may be possible if the disturbed spodic horizon is detected. The spodic horizon contains an accumulation of humus intermixed with iron- and aluminum-bearing minerals that is below a bleached sandy horizon. Overall, this research was important in demonstrating that it may be difficult to detect forensic graves over longer periods, and detection within a spodosol may occur due to the soil disturbance if a disturbed spodic horizon is detected. Further, detection of older graves with a reduced geophysical response may occur when the disturbed ground and items in the grave with the remains are detected due to the retention of increased moisture in the grave compared with the surrounding area.

Controlled research has demonstrated the applicability of selecting the proper antenna size when conducting a forensic GPR survey. As previously mentioned in Chapter 7, selecting antenna size is a compromise between depth of penetration and subsurface resolution of the soil. Lower-frequency antennae (e.g., 300 MHz) provide deeper depth penetration but have a lower resolution of small subsurface targets. Conversely, higher-resolution antennae (e.g., 900 MHz) may image too much subsurface detail or clutter and result in difficulty discerning the target (Nobes, 2000; Schultz, 2003). Antennae with frequencies from 400 to 500 MHz are most used in forensic and archaeological applications, because they provide adequate depth penetration and resolution of subsurface features (Schultz et al., 2006; Schultz, 2008). However, following the initial reporting when the 250 MHz antenna was used for forensic cases (Nobes, 2000; Ruffell, 2005), there was a lack of research reporting direct comparisons between the commonly used 500 MHz antenna option with that of the newly introduced 250 MHz antenna. As a result, it was not reported if the decreased resolution of the 250 MHz antenna would increase or decrease the detection of targets.

The first direct antenna comparison involving the 250 MHz was reported by Schultz and Martin (2011), where a small research grid was constructed that contained one pig carcass grave with an approximate 1-m depth at the grave floor surface. In addition, an empty control grave was also constructed in the grid. The results were surprising when evaluating the GPR imagery. In particular, the 500 MHz antenna provided increased detail of the decomposing pig carcass in the grave compared with the 250 MHz antenna. However, the less detail provided by the 250 MHz antenna that was displayed on the 2D reflection profiles was more advantageous when discerning detection, because the grave was highlighted as one stark reflection, rather than a forensic target that appeared as several smaller reflections due to the increased detail of the 500 MHz antenna (Schultz and Martin, 2011). As a result of this research, the 250 MHz antenna became the primary antenna used by author John J. Schultz for subsequent research and casework. Further, longer-term grave-monitoring studies in the United Kingdom (e.g., Pringle et al., 2016) and Florida (Schultz and Martin, 2012; Schultz et al., 2016) have also concluded that the lower-frequency antennae (225 and 250 MHz) provide optimal imagery compared with other antenna frequencies.

Forensic archaeologists should continually strive to improve grave detection through research. At the same time, conducting geophysical research is not only important when testing variables, it also provides experience to participants. For example, additional research is needed in soil types that have not been evaluated, and studies should continually evaluate monitoring for graves for extended periods. At the same time, newer geophysical GPR research should be making direct comparisons between GPR and ERT (e.g., Pringle et al., 2016), since ERT is the primary option to use when soil conditions are not appropriate for GPR. Further, the primary consideration when conducting forensic GPR research is having access to the geophysical equipment that is expensive and requires training. If possible, forensic practitioners should consider forming partnerships with academic departments (anthropology, archaeology, geology, and soil science) for access to the equipment and training so personnel can conduct research and perform casework (Schultz, 2007). A grid easily can be constructed with several graves (deep and shallow naked carcasses) with one or two control graves and monitored over time or used solely for training death investigation personnel.

RESEARCH ON SURFACE SEARCH: PRACTICES AND RESULTS

In addition to grave detection research, surface remains research should be carried out in multiple environments and situations. As noted above and in the preceding chapters, while graves may be difficult to detect, they generally contain the remains effectively. Excavation can then proceed using the methods outlined in this volume. Exceptions may occur where the skeletal remains have broken down in acidic soil, or some dispersal has occurred from accidental impact by heavy machinery or digging by scavengers. These buried but also dispersed cases present their own problems, including the need for both excavation and surface search. The burial location, however, is likely already known, and the recovery strategy can proceed using this information. Surface-only sites are common (refer to Chapter 4 for data from Massachusetts), and the methods of locating them only partially overlap with detecting graves. Research into the best methods to search for and subsequently recover surface sites therefore is also required.

One of the authors (Pokines, 2015) advocates, where practical for the surface scene in question, an "inside-out" search method. Surface scenes are often encountered through the accidental discovery by a pedestrian of a concentration of possible human remains (Christensen and Pokines, 2020; Pokines et al., 2017). The concentration is often partially obscured by an accumulation of leaf litter and forest understory, making searching it directly at this initial stage prone to stepping on unseen objects. The concentration can be approached from a distance while all the leaf litter and understory are denuded and transported off scene, with the searchers converging on the center. The search direction can then be reversed, and the scene expanded in all directions from the initial perimeter. Other concentrations of dispersed remains (such as partial limbs or the skull) also can be searched around in this manner. The goal is to provide as complete as possible a recovery of all remains and associated artifacts without causing any damage through trampling. This method enables the anthropologist to identify missing bones early in the process, allowing searchers to know what to look for among the remaining skeletal elements. The taphonomic state of the remains also can be assessed with such information, as heavy amounts of carnivore gnawing are relevant to subsequent search efforts. Beyond this core area, a human remains detection (HRD) dog team can search for more highly dispersed remains. In addition, some surface scenes are more highly dispersed and do not present any specific concentration of remains, so the inside-out method would not be applicable.

Forensic archaeological surface search methods such as those described above, also are amendable to research and experimentation. Practitioners need to know the effectiveness of their scene detection methods (i.e., area searches looking for a scene) and their scene processing methods (i.e., recovery rates of remains and associated artifacts once that scene has been located). If a skeleton is recovered incomplete, one cannot necessarily know if (1) the missing bones were not possible to recover, since they were destroyed by carnivore consumption, etc., (2) the bones were still present in the searched environment but were not recovered due to a lack of being seen; some tiny elements, as with unfused adult hyoids or most fetal bones, may be difficult to spot even from a short distance, or (3) the bones still existed but had been previously transported by scavengers, water, etc. beyond the searched area (refer to Chapter 5 for the taphonomic effects of scavenging, including dispersal distances affecting how far search radii should proceed from the main concentration of remains). As indicated above, burials present their own recovery issues, but containment by a grave generally increases the relative amount of remains present to be recovered (Pokines and Mainville, 2025). Recovery rates can also be increased by proper screening of all sediments (Pokines and De La Paz, 2016).

For such surface detection and recovery research, natural nonhuman bone that has undergone taphonomic staining (Pokines, 2016; Pokines and Spiegel, 2022; Pollock et al., 2018; Schultz and Dupras, 2022) may be the best option. The types of staining can include variable shades of brown from soft tissue decomposition, leaf-litter decomposition, and topsoil contact; diffuse green staining from algae growth or more concentrated green staining from adhering moss; variable color staining from lichen growth; and yellow staining from the bone's own grease content leaching. Sun bleaching is also common and may make the bones more visible in some settings (McCallister et al., 2026). Species with a size overlap with humans, such as white-tailed deer (*Odocoileus virginianus*) may be obtainable from the same environment and will thus have undergone similar taphonomic effects to human remains. Pig (*Sus scrofa*) may be used in some situations, although their long bones are much shorter than those of adult humans. Nonhuman crania, however, generally look very little like human ones. Human bone typically could not be used, as any incomplete recovery would in effect be creating a forensic scene, which is certainly not a goal of the research. In addition, unless it came from an actual outdoor forensic scene, human bone would lack natural taphonomic staining. For this reason, plastic replicas of human bones are an inadequate substitute for this purpose; however, they are highly suitable for training in mapping when locating them is not the main concern.

The process of setting up a surface recovery experiment faces a series of systemic problems: (1) devising a way to lay out the objects to be searched for, while (2) doing so quickly so that multiple trials can be run, and (3) putting them out in such a manner that the retrieval of any objects not located by the search teams also can proceed quickly. One system is to stake out a search grid using 10-m units. To lay out the objects to be searched for, pre-establish which objects are going where using some system of random number generation to indicate into which 10-m unit the object is going and its location within that unit (i.e., east *X* m and north *Y* m). The latter numbers are also generated randomly. A separate portion of the experimental team lays out the objects, and the searchers mark all found objects with pin flags. The personnel who laid out the objects also retrieve the ones not located by the searchers, and the locations of the objects if following this procedure are recorded to the nearest meter within a known grid unit (Pokines et al., 2019a). Other possible methods for searching experiments include using nonhuman remains that are more expendable, such that the nonrecovery of some is acceptable (Pokines et al., 2018, 2019b).

An example of surface search research is McCallister et al. (2026), who performed an experiment using nonhuman bones (white-tailed deer postcranial elements and pig crania) that had three color states: natural (minimum decomposition staining), stained (heavy decomposition/soil staining), and sun-bleached. The bone categories were crania, long bones, scapulae/pelves, and vertebrae, and these were distributed over one 30 x 50 m search area divided into 15 10 x 10 m units. The plant cover was primarily mature deciduous trees with little understory. Searches were conducted by personnel from the Massachusetts State Police Special Emergency Response Team (SERT), who are trained in outdoor surface searches for all types of evidence. The grid was searched twice each time, lengthwise then perpendicular to this, and five searchers were spaced at 2-m intervals. Each bone was recorded as found on the first pass, second pass, or not at all. In addition, the distance from the searcher who spotted the bone first to the bone was measured each time. The results indicated in this environment an effect by taphonomic color changes upon the rate and distance at which bones were located. For each sample (n = 60 bones), 70.0% of soil-stained, 100% of sun-bleached, and 96.7% of control bones were recovered after two passes. The mean distance at which bones were spotted also varied by color group, with soil-stained at 4.1 ± 2.8 m, sun-bleached at 8.8 ± 7.8 m, and control bones at 6.7 ± 5.4 m. Overall, sun bleaching made the bones easier and dark staining made them harder to spot than the control bones, and both of these color changes may accrue over time upon exposed bones.

Similar research (Pokines et al., 2019a), in the same field research location as McCallister et al. (2026), also found that element type affected recovery rates, with an overall success rate after two search passes of 90.0% using a search team composed of forensic anthropology graduate students. While all pig skulls used in that research were located, the overall recovery rates for white-tailed deer postcranial remains ranged from 98.3% recovery for the scapulae/pelves, long bones (metapodials) at 96.7%, ribs at 93.3%, and vertebrae at only 70.0%. These bones had variable amounts of color change but were not extremely bleached or stained, and searcher spacing took place at 2-m or 1-m intervals. Surface searches modeled by this research are designed to locate remains, therefore these areas would be searched more closely around bone clusters and isolated bones at real scenes.

Experimentation regarding the bone recovery rates for scene processing includes two projects utilizing naturally stained pig bones in the same forest leaf-litter environment, searching for larger (Pokines et al., 2018) and infant-sized (Pokines et al., 2019b) remains. In each case, a series of ten 10 x 10 m units had a sample of bones placed within the leaf litter, then the unit was searched using a slow, hands and knees crawl while searching through and then removing all living and dead plant matter. To assess the effects of double-searching the same area, the infant-sized remains were first recovered as indicated, then all plant matter was dumped onto a tarp and searched again. Recovery rates from primary infant-sized bone search ranged from 62.4% to 74.7% during the ten trials with an overall rate of 68.8% (Pokines et al., 2019b), which was significantly lower than the overall recovery rate of 76.7% for the research utilizing older juvenile pig bones (Pokines et al., 2018). Secondary search for the infant-sized remains using tarps, however, recovered an additional 17.9% of bones, leading to an overall recovery rate of 86.7%. Isolated pig teeth were recovered through primary search at an overall rate of 38.0%, with an additional 12.0% recovered through secondary search (Pokines et al., 2019b). These experiments indicated that complete recovery of remains, even when a concentration has been located, cannot be assumed. Some problems may be due to element recognition, as the small ribs used in these experiments may be spotted by searchers but mistaken for twigs and discarded. Real forensic scenes, however, often include some articulated remains that are sometimes still encased in clothing, thus likely increasing recovery rates.

Future research in field search methods should continue, and many of these projects are suitable for master's thesis research (Pokines, 2023). Additional research in different environments or with searchers with different backgrounds and training levels could proceed using methods like those of Pokines et al. (2018, 2019a, 2019b). Other possible thesis projects are related to searching and would explore how detectable individual bones are during search. Annually accumulating leaf litter slowly builds up on top of bones and makes them less visible to surface search, as the leaf litter breaks down into the topmost humus horizon of the soil; the rate at which this occurs in multiple forest environments (deciduous, evergreen, and mixed) could be examined in a forensic context. This project would take multiple years and could be initiated by various forensic programs so different micro-environments and ecological conditions are evaluated. Additional research on the effects that natural color changes to bone have upon detection rates during searches is needed, using different environments, seasons, backgrounds, and skill levels (McCallister et al., 2026). The color changes can include sun bleaching from subaerial weathering, green algae staining, moss growth, soil, and decomposition staining (Schultz and Dupras, 2022). Another project could measure and compare the "bone rain" in multiple environments, i.e., the amount of naturally occurring bones that are deposited over time, as background data for what is encountered during deliberate forensic searches in specific environments. This research requires hiking multiple kilometers of transects (see Miller, 2011) and nonhuman bone identification skills to identify the normal density of bone and from which taxa in given environments, including coastal margins, deserts, grasslands, wetlands, and forest types.

TRAINING IN FORENSIC ARCHAEOLOGY

Forensic archaeology training is often provided through classwork in anthropology, archaeology, and forensic departments, as well as through short courses provided to students and forensic personnel (refer to Chapter 1). Training normally consists of classroom discussion, skill development, and mock field scenarios that teach search, recovery, and documentation methods (refer to Box #6). This section provides examples of classroom and field exercises that can be implemented for practical skill development during training and are easily adaptable to needs in variable session schedules.

ACTIVITY #1: SCENE DOCUMENTING SKILL BUILDER

Essential Questions

- How well can others fully understand the information provided in your scene documentation?
- What level of detail is required for accurate replication of scene mapping and reconstruction of processes conducted at the scene?

Learning Objectives

- Assess the clarity of documentation to ensure others that can fully understand and apply the information without confusion.
- Determine the appropriate level of detail required for accurate replication or reconstruction of processes.
- Critique and enhance documentation practices by identifying gaps, redundancies, or ambiguities, and proposing improvements for greater effectiveness.

Time for Activity: approximately 60 minutes

Supplies, Equipment, or Resources Needed

- Approximately 15 small plastic building blocks of different colors and shapes for each pair of participants
- Tray or other object to block view between pairs of participants
- Method for notetaking in documenting the scene

Set Interest (Estimated Time: 5–10 Minutes)

Instructor-led introduction: Imagine you are tasked with gathering the details of a scene and documenting them for a forensic report. Let us try a quick exercise:

- Instructor shows participants a single image containing two objects for one minute.
- Participants are expected to take two minutes to write two or three sentences about the objects in the image.
- Have three or four participants share their work with the group.
- Instructor once again shows image to the group: Which details stood out in the descriptions? Which details were missed? Which details were described clearly?

Learning Activity 1 (Estimated Time: 20 Minutes)

While blocked from view, Participant 1 will build a tower using the 15 different blocks in a random pattern. If possible, take a digital photograph of the tower. Once the tower is complete, they will then deconstruct it while documenting the process in writing.

When Participant 1 is finished, Participant 2 will attempt to reconstruct the tower based entirely on Participant 1's notes. If the documentation of the process is adequate, the reconstructed tower should be identical to the first.

Learning Activity 2 (Estimated Time: 20 Minutes)

Repeat the same process as in Activity 1 but have participants switch tasks.

Reflection Summary (Estimated Time: 5–10 Minutes)

Participants will reflect on learning by answering the following in written format (three or four sentences for each response):

- Was there a difference in the level of detail provided the first time versus the second time when documenting the process?
- What gaps, redundancies, or ambiguities did you identify in your documentation of the scene?
- How might you enhance your practices and improve overall effectiveness in documentation?

ACTIVITY #2: PRACTICING VISUAL SURFACE SEARCHES

Essential Questions

- Which methods are used in visual surface searches to locate human remains and associated evidence?
- What factors must you consider when selecting a visual surface search pattern?
- What are the advantages and disadvantages in effectiveness in evidence discovery for each visual search pattern?

Learning Objectives

- Examine mock search areas by locating and marking evidence using outlined practices for various visual surface search patterns.
- Assess effectiveness and disadvantages in the discovery of evidence for each visual search pattern used.

Time for Activity: approximately 60–90 minutes (variable based on training schedule)

Supplies, Equipment, or Resources Needed

- A few small unessential and expendable personal items (e.g., old keys, wallet, sunglasses, shoes) that are common in forensic scenes
- A few disposable items that seem unimportant to the scene (e.g., business card, eggshells, wadded printed paper, empty drink cup with straw, bungie cord, small screwdriver)
- 50 metal staff marking flags
- Four scene description and search notes sheets
- Four inventory recording sheets (prepared by the instructor)
- Paper lunch bags, mock evidence tags (optional for practicing recovery and packaging at end of search).

Instructor Activity Set-Up (Estimated Time: 45–60 Minutes)

Prepare two larger search areas by seeding each with 20–25 items of evidence for discovery. This may be based on a scenario developed in advance and used in the 'pre-planning' stage prior to the activity.

1. Make an inventory of materials being seeded across search area.
2. Set boundaries for the search area using marker flags or stakes with survey flagging tape.
3. Seed the area with materials for discovery. It is recommended that there are at least two areas of concentration with other materials spread out in a linear or circular pattern from the concentration centers. If time allows, a few mock 'indicators' of a clandestine grave may be constructed in each area.
4. Create a rough sketch map of locations of any features and seeded materials for post-search evaluation.

Set Interest (Estimated Time: 10 Minutes)

Instructor presents materials for the planning stage of the search as the lead investigator. This may include:

- A rough sketch or Google Earth annotated image of the search area
- Brief discussion with lead investigator using questions derived from Table 6.1
- Divide participants into Search Team 1 and Search Team 2. Assign a search area and roles for each team member in the groups. Provide 25 marking flags to each group
- Search Team 1 will use a grid search pattern for discovery and processing, while Search Team 2 will use a strip pattern for initial discovery followed by an inside-out pattern for processing.

Learning Activity 1 (Estimated Time: 20–30 Minutes)

In this activity, search teams will record notes about the scene, use their assigned search pattern within their scene, flag discovered materials, complete an inventory, and record notes on search process.

Once all documentation is confirmed, the search team will carefully remove their marking flags from their search area.

Learning Activity 2 (Estimated Time: 20–30 Minutes)

Repeat the same process as in Activity 1 but have the search teams switch scenes and search patterns.

If the participants will be practicing recovery and packaging at end of search, this can be carried out at the end of the search process, or participants can assist with clean-up and clearing the search areas.

Reflection Summary (Estimated Time: 15–20 Minutes)

Participants will reflect on learning by answering the following in written format (three or four sentences for each response):

- Compare and describe the effectiveness in evidence discovery between the pattern(s) used in Search Area 1 and Search Area 2.
- What were the advantages and disadvantages encountered in each process?
- Was there evidence that was overlooked in the process? How might you enhance your practices and improve overall effectiveness in searching these scenes?

ACTIVITY #3: MAPPING A SURFACE SCATTER

Essential Questions

- If an electronic survey system is not available, what other methods can be used in mapping a surface scatter?
- What factors should you consider in selecting a low-technology method in mapping a surface scatter?

Learning Objectives

- Demonstrate ability to map using a low-technology method that can be easily adapted to a surface scatter site context.
- Assess advantages and disadvantages for each mapping method used.

Time for Activity: approximately 60–90 minutes (variable based on training schedule)

Supplies, Equipment, or Resources Needed

- Approximately 20–30 bones from a non-articulated plastic skeleton (if available) or an equivalent random assortment of unessential and expendable items (e.g., old clothing, wallet, sunglasses, shoes, bungee cords, costume jewelry)
- Wooden stake and mason's line for site datum construction
- Two large 10-inch nails and mason's line for temporary datum construction
- Eight chaining pins and survey flagging tape or mason's line for constructing limits
- Two plastic landscaping stakes or tent anchors
- Two 8-m steel measuring tapes
- 50-m reel measuring tape
- Right-angle protractor
- Azimuth board (or equivalent large 360° laminated wheel) and chaining pin
- Multiple sheets of 1:10 cm graph paper (10 sq/cm)
- Recording sheets for field notes
- Straight edge rulers
- Pencils and erasers
- Paper lunch bags, mock evidence tags, and evidence inventory form (optional for practicing recovery and packaging at end of mapping).

Instructor Activity Set-Up (Estimated Time: 30–45 Minutes)

Prepare two mapping areas fairly close together by seeding 10–15 items for mapping, one intended for a baseline control-point method and the other for an azimuth control-point method. It is recommended that limits in each area are set ahead of time using chaining pins and survey flagging tape or mason's line. However, if time allows, participants may practice this skill with the supplied materials.

Set a site datum between the two areas and construct a datum line reaching into each area being mapped. This will be used by participants to 'tie in' their mapped area to the site datum.

Set Interest (Estimated Time: 5–10 Minutes)

Instructor-led introduction: Imagine you are tasked with mapping a secondary surface scatter within a scene. You are in a remote area with no access to any electronic survey systems. The only available equipment is what is laid out here (equipment, measuring tools, and drawing materials from list). Let us try a quick exercise to review what we have learned about methods of mapping to scale:

- What factors should you consider when deciding between baseline or azimuth control-point mapping methods? What difficulties might you encounter when using these methods?
- Participants are expected to discuss factors, use of equipment, and possible difficulties they might encounter in using these methods.

Learning Activity 1 (Estimated Time: 20–35 Minutes)

In this activity, the instructor divides the participants into Map Team 1 and Map Team 2. Map Team 1 will set up the baseline control-point mapping area and Map Team 2 will set up the azimuth control-point mapping area. Each team will map the evidence in their area, then tie their mapped surface scatter into the site datum.

Once all documentation is confirmed, each mapping team will remove their baseline or azimuth mapping set-up from the scene.

Learning Activity 2 (Estimated Time: 20–35 Minutes)

Repeat the same process as in Activity 1 but have the Map Teams switch scenes, set up the alternate mapping method, map the surface scatter, and tie into the site datum.

If the participants will be practicing recovery and packaging, this can be carried out at the end of the mapping process, or participants can assist with clean-up and clearing the mapping areas.

Reflection Summary (Estimated Time: 5–10 Minutes)

Participants will reflect on learning by answering the following in written format (three or four sentences for each response):

- What were key factors at the scene that impacted the method used and the mapping process?
- Compare the advantages and disadvantages in setting up and mapping with the baseline and azimuth control-point methods.

ACTIVITY #4: INTRODUCTORY GRIDDING AND TROWELING

Essential Questions

- How is a reference grid constructed over a surface area being prepared for excavation and mapping?
- How is a margin trowel used when clearing the surface and during excavation?

Learning Objectives

- Demonstrate ability to set up a spatial control grid using trilateration.
- Building skill level in using a margin trowel when exposing the soil surface and in excavation.

Time for Activity: approximately 1½–2 hours (variable based on training schedule)

Supplies, Equipment, or Resources Needed

- Eight wood stakes for constructing two 3 × 3 m grids
- 16 chaining pins and mason's line for grid construction
- Rubber mallet and multitool
- Wood stake and mason's line for site datum construction
- Four 8-m tapes
- Baseline and hypotenuse table (provided in Table 8.2)
- Two baseplate compasses
- Two right-angle protractors
- Margin trowels
- Brushes
- Dust pans
- Buckets
- Box screen
- Root clippers
- Line level
- Recording sheets for field notes.

Instructor Activity Set-Up (Estimated Time: 10 Minutes)

Select two 3 × 3 m areas somewhat close together where the ground surface can be cleared and excavated to approximately 10 cm in depth. The areas will be backfilled at the end of the exercise but approval and/or permitting should be obtained if necessary.

Set Interest (Estimated Time: 5–10 Minutes)

Instructor-led introduction: Imagine you are tasked with setting up a reference grid over an area thought to contain a grave. Let us try a quick exercise to review what we have learned about setting up a grid and preparing the surface for excavation:

- What are the basic steps in setting up a reference grid?
- Why are margin trowels effective tools in clearing the surface and in excavation? How do we hold the trowel? What edge do we use?
- Participants are expected to describe basic steps in constructing a reference grid (outlined in Chapter 8) and refer to best practices in using a margin trowel (refer to Box 5 in Chapter 10).

Learning Activity 1 (Estimated Time: 90 Minutes)

In this activity, the instructor divides the participants into two excavation teams. Each team will construct a 3 × 3 m reference grid over a set area. Once the grid is assembled, each team member will have an opportunity to clear the surface in a 1 × 1 m grid square, sort and screen recovered materials and excavate their grid square to at least a 5-cm depth below the surface using a margin trowel.

Each member of the team should record field notes on their grid square excavation, including elevations and descriptions of any changes in soil or sediments.

Learning Activity 2 (Estimated Time: 20–30 Minutes)

Once all documentation is complete, participants should remove the reference grid, backfill their excavations, and clean all excavation tools (outlined in Chapter 2).

Reflection Summary (Estimated Time: 5–10 Minutes)

Participants will reflect on learning by answering the following in written format (three or four sentences for each response):

- What was most challenging in constructing the reference grid?
- What was most challenging in learning to use a margin trowel for excavation?
- Why is it important to use the reference grid as a method of control when sorting and screening materials recovered from clearing the surface and excavation?

ACTIVITY #5: MINI 'BODY FARM' ENTOMOLOGY

Essential Questions

- How quickly are insects attracted to decomposing remains?
- What kinds of insects are typically attracted to decomposing remains?
- What environmental conditions affect contributions of insects to decomposition?

Learning Objectives

- Create a mini 'body farm' to attract insects to a 'corpse' (i.e., pieces of meat)
- Observe the number and types of insects that arrive at the 'corpse' over a set period
- Explore how crime scene conditions affect the decomposition of a corpse.

Time for Activity: 2–6 days (variable based on training schedule)

Supplies, Equipment, or Resources Needed

- Six small pieces (approximately 2-in square) of chicken liver
- Six 8 oz. clear plastic cups
- Plastic or metal tweezers
- Permanent marker
- Crushed, dried leaf litter
- 6 oz. of potting soil
- Two small plastic baskets with solid bottom (e.g., storage, organizing, or laundry)
- Two bricks or paving blocks
- Hand magnifying glass
- Nitrile gloves
- Face mask or odor inhibitor (if monitoring experiment over 2+ days)
- Fly life-cycle chart (refer to Figure 9.5)
- Common insect species identification chart (provided by instructor or published identification cards if available)
- Data and Observation Sheet (prepared by instructor).

Safety Note

Raw meat can pose a health risk. Be sure to wash hands before and after the experiment, and wear nitrile gloves when assembling the body farm and inspecting the cups.

As the days proceed, the 'body farm' will smell like decomposing remains; breathing through your mouth instead of your nose is recommended, but also the use of a face mask or odor inhibitor will help as well.

Set Interest (Estimated Time: 5–10 Minutes)

Instructor-led introduction and discussion: Imagine that you enter an open, shady area with a surface scatter of remains. You see some flies, their larvae (maggots), and a few beetles on and around decomposing remains.

- What information would be helpful to know about these insects?
- How might observations and data from these insects help us better understand the scene and decomposition process?

Activity Set-Up (Estimated Time: 30 Minutes)

1. Decide where your 'body farm' will be set up. If possible, select a sunny area and a shady area protected from regular activity (e.g., in a shady hedge, under a large bush, or in a sunny area marked off to pedestrians).
2. Mark two plastic cups as 'Sun Control' and 'Shade Control', two cups as 'Sun 1' and 'Sun 2,' and two cups as 'Shade 1' and 'Shade 2.'
3. Using the tweezers, place a piece of liver in the bottom of each cup.
4. Prepare the 'Sun' and 'Shade' cups using the following scenarios:
   - Sun 1: Remains found in a field, covered with a layer of leaves. The area is sunny, with no trees to provide shade. Cover the piece of liver in the Sun 1 cup with a thin layer (approximately 1 cm) of crushed, dried leaf litter.
   - Sun 2: Remains found in an open field, with a light layer of soil concealing the body. The area is sunny, with no trees to provide shade. Cover the piece of liver in the Sun 2 cup with a thin layer (approximately 1 cm) of potting soil.

- Shade 1: Remains found in the woods, covered with a layer of leaves. The area is shady and not exposed to the sun. Cover the piece of liver in the Shade 1 cup with a thin layer (approximately 1 cm) of crushed, dried leaf litter.
- Shade 2: Remains found in the woods, covered with a light layer of soil concealing the body. The area is shady and not exposed to the sun. Cover the piece of liver in the Shade 2 cup with a thin layer (approximately 1 cm) of potting soil.
    1. In your selected sunny area, place the three 'Sun' cups together under an upside-down laundry basket to protect the cups from scavengers. Place a brick or paving stone on top to keep it in place. Repeat this in the selected area for the three 'Shade' cups.

Activity Monitoring (Estimated Time: 2–6 Days)

Based on length of time in monitoring the activity, return to each location to make observations and collect data twice on the first day and at least once per day over the remaining period. When collecting data, it is okay to move gently any plant material or soil using plastic tweezers to check the surface of the meat and then return the covering.

Data and Observations Sheet (prepared by the instructor): includes question predicting differences between control and scenario cups for each location, and a table to record data on the number and types of insects (e.g., visible eggs, maggots, adult flies, ants, beetles, other) found in the cups at each location over a six-day period (variable based on length of monitoring in activity).

Disposal: After activity ends, cups, meat, all soil and leaf litter, and plastic tweezers should be placed in an outdoor trash receptacle secured from scavengers. Metal tweezers should be cleaned with 80% ethyl alcohol (ETOH) prior to storage.

Reflection Summary (Estimated Time: 25–30 Minutes)

Participants will reflect on learning by answering the following in written format (two or three sentences for each response):

- How quickly were insects attracted to the 'body farm'? Which insects were first to arrive?
- How did the number and type of insects found in the control and scenario cups vary over time?
- After comparing all the scenario and control cups, which conditions attracted more insects? Which conditions attracted fewer?
- Did the maggots in some cups appear to grow faster than maggots in other cups? If so, why do you think that is?
- What patterns do you notice about the different crime scene conditions studied?
- How could the patterns you observed be useful in a real analysis of decomposing remains?

ACTIVITY #6: DETERMINING SOIL TEXTURE

Essential Questions

- How might different soil textures affect preservation and excavation?
- Why is it important to be able to determine soil texture?

Learning Objectives

- Identify the major components of soil.
- Examine how different proportions affect soil texture.
- Describe the concept of soil texture and its importance.
- Determine soil texture by using Feel Method.

Time for Activity: approximately 60 minutes

Supplies, Equipment, or Resources Needed

- A few different soil samples (e.g., from a garden, open field, roadside, lake or stream bed, beach area; amount based on number of participants in activity)
- Spray bottles of water
- Trays (and any clean-up supplies)
- Feel Method Flowchart (provided in Appendix F)
- Soil Texture Triangle worksheet (prepared by instructor)
- Soil Sample Data worksheet (prepared by instructor)
- Soil Texture Guides (if available).

Set Interest (Estimated Time: 3–5 Minutes)

Instructor-led introduction:

Imagine you are beach walking along the shore. Take a minute to visualize and feel the environment around you. Now imagine you are walking barefoot in a yard with small patches of grass in soil, again take a minute to visualize and think about how this environment feels.

- What did the environment at the beach feel like? Could you feel the sand between your toes? How was it different from what you visualized and felt in the yard?

Learning Activity 1 (Estimated Time: 12–15 Minutes)

In this activity, participants will:

- Follow a short lecture presentation by the instructor, which introduces vocabulary used in identifying soil types and textures and addresses essential questions.
- Walk through how to read and use the soil texture triangle and soil texture guide (if available), and work through 1–2 examples before practicing by completing the soil Texture Triangle Worksheet.

Soil Texture Triangle Worksheet (prepared by the instructor): includes the soil texture triangle diagram, a couple vocabulary-based questions, and two sets of soil texture data to plot on the soil texture triangle diagram and associate with the soil texture guide.

Learning Activity 2 (Estimated Time: 20–25 Minutes)

In this activity, participants will:

- Practice determining soil texture with the Feel Method flowchart and soil texture guide.

Prepare active learning stations for 1–2 participants. Include a tray with:

- Two different soil samples and location of collection
- Spray bottle of water
- Feel Method flowchart
- Soil texture guide if available)
- Soil data worksheet.

Steps in activity:

1. Instructor demonstrates how to move through Feel Method flowchart with a soil sample.
2. Participants will then use materials at their station for determining soil texture for each sample provided.
3. Participants will complete the soil sample data worksheet.
4. When participants finish, they should clean their stations and return materials to their proper storage location.

Soil Sample Data Worksheet (prepared by the instructor): example would include vocabulary-based questions, multiple choice questions or chart entry for data obtained during Feel Method analysis, and questions that associate their findings with the soil texture guide (if available).

Reflection Summary (Estimated Time: 7–10 Minutes)

Participants will reflect on learning by answering the following in written format (two or three sentences for each response):

- How noticeable was the difference between each soil sample? What did you notice about their differences? How were they similar to each other?
- If you were recovering remains from a clandestine grave, which of these soil types would you prefer for excavation? Why?
- Why might it be important to know the soil texture when planning an excavation and the potential for preservation of remains and associated evidence?

Box #6: Teaching Forensic Archaeology

Author James T. Pokines teaches a full semester course at Boston University Chobanian and Avedisian School of Medicine on field methods in forensic archaeology, within the Forensic Anthropology Program. This course is taught in the Spring so that classroom instruction can begin before moving on to outdoor activities as the weather improves. Lecture topics include mapping systems and map reading, the Global Positioning System (GPS), soil formation and documentation, detection of surface and buried remains, excavation methods, aircraft crashes, mass burials and human rights, and mass disasters and cremains. The indoor laboratory training covers compasses, mapping and diagramming, determining soil pH, Munsell color charts, excavation equipment, screening mesh sizes, report writing, and multiple weeks of total station and data logger training. Training then shifts outdoors to the program's Outdoor Research Facility (ORF) in Holliston, MA. The ORF has mixed forest cover and wetlands, and much taphonomic research is carried out there (McCallister et al., 2026; Pokines et al., 2018, 2019a, 2019b; Pollock et al., 2018). The outdoor training includes multiple methods of mapping: baseline with measuring tapes, radial with measuring tapes and an azimuth board or compass, setting up a grid using a 3–4–5 triangle, and total station, with notetaking and report writing throughout all mock scenes. Initial training also includes profile drawing of soil exposures, soil probing and soil coring, GPS use, and diagramming. Training then shifts to surface recoveries, including denuding a scene of understory and leaf litter while marking all remains and other evidence and mapping them. Burial training comes last and includes establishing an excavation grid, recording location either by three-dimensional total station mapping or by unit, quadrant, and depth for objects located by screening, and profile drawing. Typically, for the burials, pig remains are used and normally obtained as leftovers from taphonomy and trauma projects at the ORF. These remains are buried years in advance so that the burial fill can undergo normal compaction and root growth, and the bones can take on natural staining and other taphonomic effects. Artifacts are also included in the burials, such as keys, coins, plastic identification cards, ligatures, and glasses. One of the more difficult things to learn when excavating a clandestine burial is where the margins of the burial feature terminate and archaeologically sterile soil is present. This skill is difficult to develop using burials that have only been in place for days or weeks. The burials are excavated in teams, with each student producing a separate set of notes and final report.

REVIEW AND DISCUSSION QUESTIONS

1. Why is forensic archaeology research important to the field of forensic archaeology?
2. How has forensic GPR research improved geophysical grave detection methods?
3. In what ways can training best simulate real-life scenarios?
4. In what ways is taphonomy (refer to Chapter 5) relevant to field recovery planning, execution, mapping, and scene reconstruction?

Suggested Readings

Kolpan, K.E., Passalaqua, N.V. 2023. Forensic archaeology as a high-impact practice. *Journal of Forensic Science* 68:233–241. DOI:10.1111/1556-4029.15184

Pokines, J.T. 2023. Thesis projects in forensic taphonomy. *Forensic Anthropology* 6(2):99–116. DOI: 10.5744/fa.2022.0021

Schultz, J.J. 2007. Using ground-penetrating radar to locate clandestine graves of homicide victims: Forming forensic archaeology partnerships with law enforcement. *Homicide Studies* 11:15–29. DOI:10.1177/1088767906296234

Spurlock, L., Whitman, L., York, H. 2017. The pig dig: A mock crime scene exercise for a forensic archaeology field school. *Practicing Anthropology* 39:36–39.

References

Berezowski, V., Moffat, I., Seckiner, D., Crebert, I., Ellis, J., Mallett, X. 2024. The suitability of using domestic pigs (Sus spp.) as human proxies in the geophysical detection of clandestine graves. *Journal of Forensic Sciences* 69:316–328. DOI:10.1111/1556-4029.15419

Christensen, A.M., Pokines, J.T. 2020. Discovery context of skeletal remains received at the Federal Bureau of Investigation (FBI) Laboratory. *Forensic Anthropology* 3(1):1–5. DOI: 10.5744/fa.2020.1007

France, D.L., Griffin, T.J., Swanburg, J.G., Lindemann, J.W., Davenport, G.C., Trammell, V. 1992. A multidisciplinary approach to the detection of clandestine graves. *Journal of Forensic Sciences* 37:1445–1458. DOI:10.1520/JFS13337J

France, D.L., Griffin, T.J., Swanburg, J.G., Lindemann, J.W., Davenport, G.C., Tramell, V., Travis, C.T., Kondratieff, R., Nelson, A., Castellano, K., Hopkins D., Adair, T. 1997. NecroSearch revisited: Further multidisciplinary approaches to the detection of clandestine graves. In: Haglund, W.D., Sorg, M.H., eds. Forensic Taphonomy: The Postmortem Fate of Human Remains, pp. 497–510. Boca Raton, FL: CRC Press.

McCallister, D., Moore, T.L., Pokines, J.T. 2026. The effects of taphonomic color alteration upon skeletal recovery rates during surface search. *Journal of Forensic Sciences*. DOI:10.1111/1556-4029.70201

Miller, J.H. 2011. Ghosts of Yellowstone: Multi-decadal histories of wildlife populations captured by bones on a modern landscape. *PLoS ONE* 6(3):e18057. DOI:10.1371/journal.pone.0018057.

Nobes, D.C. 2000. The search for 'Yvonne': A case example of the delineation of a grave using near-surface geophysical methods. *Journal of Forensic Sciences* 45:715–721. DOI: 10.1520/JFS14756J

Pokines, J.T. 2015. A procedure for processing outdoor surface forensic scenes yielding skeletal remains among leaf litter. *Journal of Forensic Identification* 65(2):161–172.

Pokines, J.T. 2016. Taphonomic alterations to terrestrial surface-deposited human osseous remains in a New England environment. *Journal of Forensic Identification* 66(1):59–78.

Pokines, J.T. 2023. Thesis projects in forensic taphonomy. *Forensic Anthropology* 6(2):99–116. DOI:10/5744/fa.2022.0021

Pokines, J.T., De La Paz, J. 2016. Recovery rates of human fetal skeletal remains using varying mesh sizes. *Journal of Forensic Sciences* 61(S1):S184–S189. DOI:10.1111/1556-4029.12922

Pokines, J.T., Eck, C.J., Sharpe, M.E. 2017. Sources of skeletal remains at a chief medical examiner's office: Who finds the bones? *Journal of Forensic Identification* 67(2):278–299.

Pokines, J.T., Mammano, K., Studebaker-Reed, M., Mowery, J., Patterson, M., Schneider, C., Trapp, B., Mincher, C. 2018. Success rates of recovering dispersed bones among leaf litter. *Forensic Anthropology* 1(4):189–200. DOI:10.5744/fa.2018.0021

Pokines, J.T., Mainville, A. 2025. Skeletal recovery rates in a New England environment. *Journal of Forensic Sciences* 70(2):669–683. DOI: 10.1111/1556-4029.15706

Pokines, J.T., Robinson, S., Mansz, J., Heidel, N., Jasny, K., Gilligan, J., Carmona, A., Kroll, J., Lavigne, S., Calle, S. 2019a. Success rates of forensic surface search for osseous remains in a New England, U.S.A. environment. *Forensic Anthropology* 2(1):9–20. DOI:10.5744/fa.2018.1029

Pokines, J.T., Spiegel, C. 2022. Subaerial weathering and other terrestrial surface taphonomic processes. In: Pokines, J.T., L'Abbé, E.N., Symes, S.A., eds. Manual of Forensic Taphonomy, 2nd ed., pp. 403–441. Boca Raton, FL: CRC Press.

Pokines, J.T., Udoni, M.M., Sanders Stark, S., Cassidy, S., Atkinson, M.L., Church, E., File, C.L., Green, M.K., Herrera, M.D., Kilroy, G.S., Peace, B.N., Purcell, B.J., Reinman, A.S., Sanchez, A.M., Springman, S.J. 2019b. Success rates of recovering teeth and infant-sized bones dispersed among leaf litter. *Forensic Anthropology* 2(3):168–177. DOI:10.5744/fa.2019.1033

Pollock, C., Pokines, J.T., Bethard, J. 2018. Organic staining on bone from exposure to wood and other plant materials. *Forensic Science International* 283:200–210. DOI:10.1016/j.forsciint.2017.12.021

Pringle, J.K., Jervis, J.R., Roberts, D., Dick, H.C., Wisniewski, K.D., Cassidy, N.J., Cassella, J.P. 2016. Geophysical monitoring of simulated clandestine graves using electrical and ground penetrating radar methods: 4–6 years. *Journal of Forensic Sciences* 61:309–321. DOI:10.1111/1556-4029.13009

Ruffell, A. 2005. Searching for the IRA "disappeared": Ground-penetrating radar investigation of a churchyard burial site, Northern Ireland. *Journal of Forensic Sciences* 50:1430–1435. DOI:10.1520/JFS2004156

Schultz, J.J. 2003. *Detecting Buried Remains Using Ground-Penetrating Radar*. Ph.D. Dissertation. Gainesville, FL: University of Florida.

Schultz, J.J. 2007. Using ground-penetrating radar to locate clandestine graves of homicide victims: forming forensic archaeology partnerships with law enforcement. *Homicide Studies* 11:15–29. DOI:10.1177/1088767906296234

Schultz, J.J. 2008. Sequential monitoring of burials containing small pig cadavers using ground-penetrating radar. *Journal of Forensic Sciences* 53:279–287. DOI:10.1111/j.1556-4029.2008.00665.x

Schultz, J.J. 2012. The application of GPR for forensic grave detection. In: Dirkmaat, D. C., ed. A Companion to Forensic Anthropology, pp. 85–100. Hoboken, NJ: Blackwell Publishing Company.

Schultz, J.J., Collins, M.E., Falsetti, A.B. 2006. Sequential monitoring of burials containing large pig cadavers using ground-penetrating radar. *Journal of Forensic Sciences* 51:607–616. DOI:10.1111/j.1556-4029.2006.00129.x

Schultz, J.J., Dupras, T.L. 2022. Identifying the origin of taphonomic bone staining and color changes in forensic contexts. In: Pokines, J.T., L'Abbé, E.N., Symes, S.A., eds. Manual of Forensic Taphonomy, 2nd ed., pp. 443–472. Boca Raton, FL: CRC Press.

Schultz, J.J., Martin, M.M. 2011. Controlled GPR grave research: Comparison of reflection profiles between 500 and 250 MHz antennae. *Forensic Science International* 209:64–69. DOI:10.1016/j.forscint.2010.12.012

Schultz, J.J., Martin, M.M. 2012. Monitoring controlled graves representing common burial scenarios with ground penetrating radar. *Journal of Applied Geophysics* 83:74–89. DOI:10.1016/j.jappgeo.2012.05.006

Schultz, J.J., Walter, B.S., Healy, C. 2016. Long-term sequential monitoring of controlled graves representing common burial scenarios with ground penetrating radar: Years 2 and 3. *Journal of Applied Geophysics* 132:60–74. DOI:10.1016/j.jappgeo.2016.06.015

Skeletal Inventory Forms

Visual skeletal identification forms allow investigators constrained by time to record essential osteological inventory information efficiently and effectively. The following examples of individual visual inventory forms represent disarticulated bones of the full articulated skeleton and correspond to four age categories:

- adult (ca. 17+ years)
- adolescent child (ca. 7–17 years; mixed dentition and all epiphyses present but unfused)
- young child (ca. 1–7 years; mixed dentition and some epiphyses present but unfused)
- perinate-infant (ca. 7 months in utero development to 1 year after birth; cranium unfused).

The skeletal elements are drawn close to anatomical reality to provide an effective means of quick identification and siding of the bones. Some bones are presented in anatomical position, while others are presented in viewing planes more suitable for identification and siding. Only the cranium is represented in different planes to provide the most accurate inventory. The legend may be used to provide additional qualitative information:

- complete shaded with gray or black fill
- fragmentary shaded with diagonal slashes
- side unknown shaded with yellow highlighter
- found isolated circled in red.

Text boxes also enable the recording of numbers of elements or fragments in cases of imprecise identification in vertebrae and phalanges. For the youngest two age categories, ribs and vertebrae are not drawn on the form, and instead, the investigator records the number of elements present in the provided tables.

The example visual skeletal identification forms were adapted from Bocquentin and Anton (2021:8) open-source files under the conditions of "be[ing] regularly reworked and improved, according to the needs of each anthropologist to meet the needs of each anthropologist and for the use of the greatest number of users." The example forms are not intended for direct distribution or commercialization but rather the sharing of information to support best practices in an educational and professional setting. It is recommended that each user access the adaptive open-source file download and construct forms meeting their individual needs.

Electronic Reference for Adaptive Open-Source File Download

F. Bocquentin and M. Anton, "Visual inventories and field note templates for contextualized recording of human remains", *Bulletins et Mémoires de la Société d'Anthropologie de Paris* [Online], 33 (2) | 2021, Online since 28 September 2021. DOI: 10.4000/bmsap.7750

Example Adult Visual Skeletal Inventory Form

Case #:	Field Recovery #:
Agency:	Location:
Date(s) of Recovery:	

Complete   Fragmentary   Side unknown (yellow)   Found isolated (red)

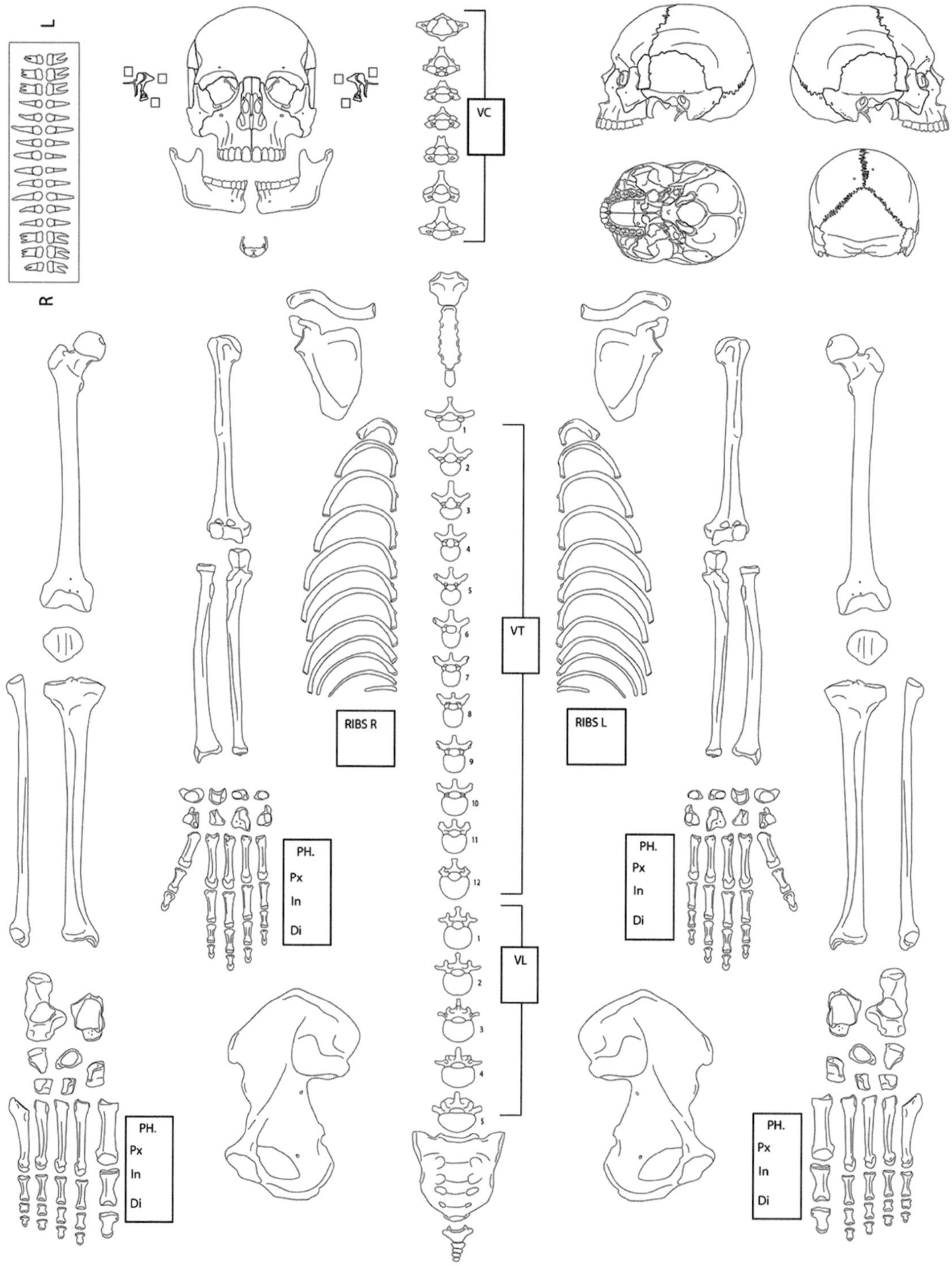

Open Source: Bocquentin and Anton, BMSAP 2021

Example Adolescent Child Visual Skeletal Inventory Form

Case #:	Field Recovery #:
Agency:	Location:
Date(s) of Recovery:	

Complete   Fragmentary   Side unknown (yellow)   Found isolated (red)

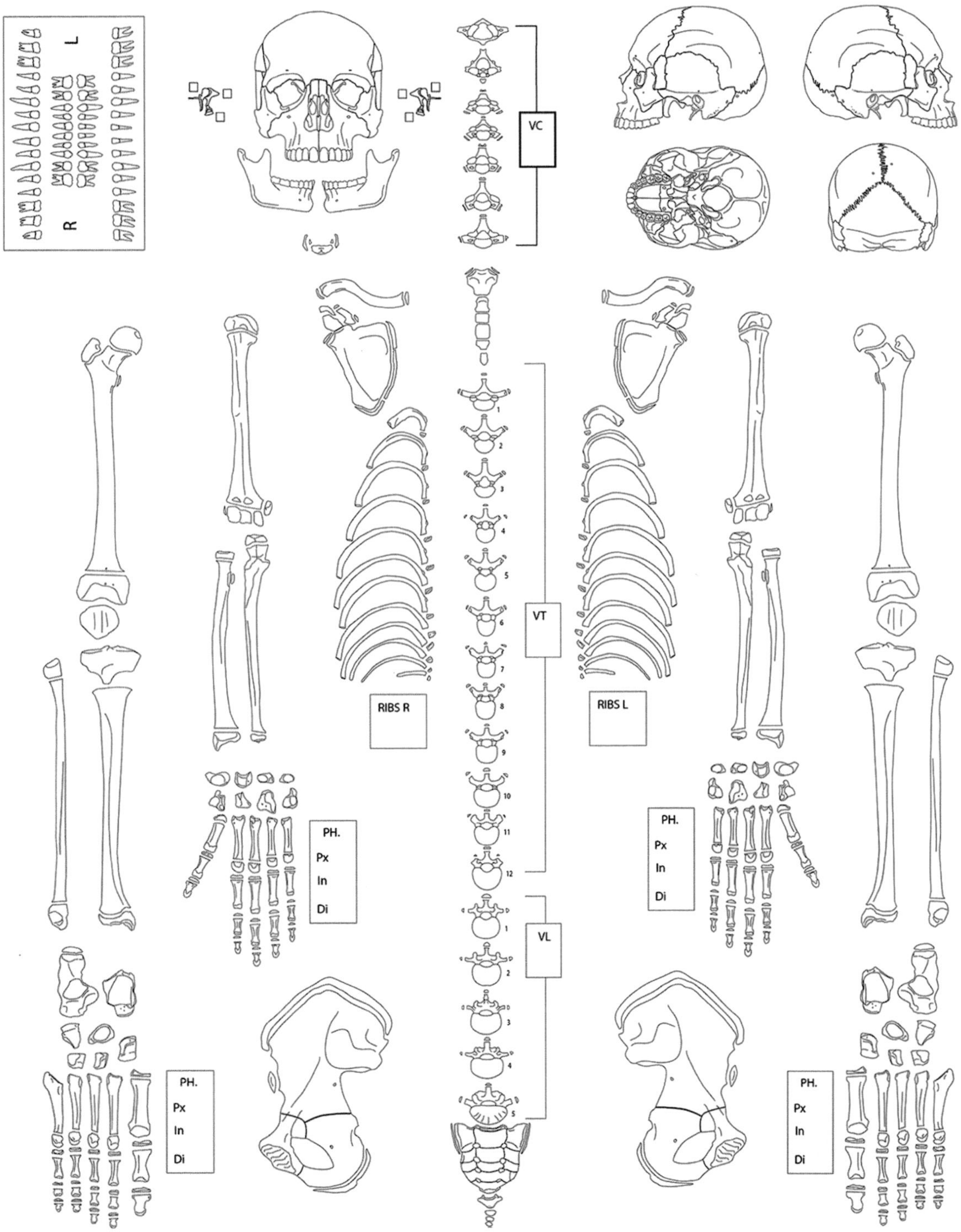

Open Source: Bocquentin and Anton. BMSAP 2021

Example Young Child Visual Skeletal Inventory Form

Case #:	Field Recovery #:
Agency:	Location:
Date(s) of Recovery:	

Complete — Fragmentary — Side unknown (yellow) — Found isolated (red)

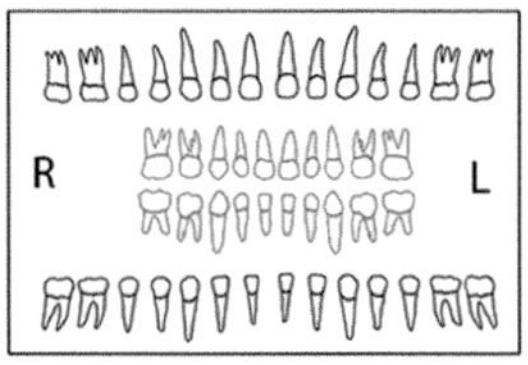

	VERTEBRAE	Neural arch	Centrum
CERVICAL	C1		
	C2		
	C3		
	C4		
	C5		
	C6		
	C7		
	Rey unknown		
THORACIC	T1		
	T2		
	T3		
	T4		
	T5		
	T6		
	T7		
	T8		
	T9		
	T10		
	T11		
	T12		
	Rey unknown		
LUMBAR	L1		
	L2		
	L3		
	L4		
	L5		
	Rey unknown		

RIBS	Right	Left
T1		
T2		
T3		
T4		
T5		
T6		
T7		
T8		
T9		
T10		
T11		
T12		
Rey unknown		
Side unknown		

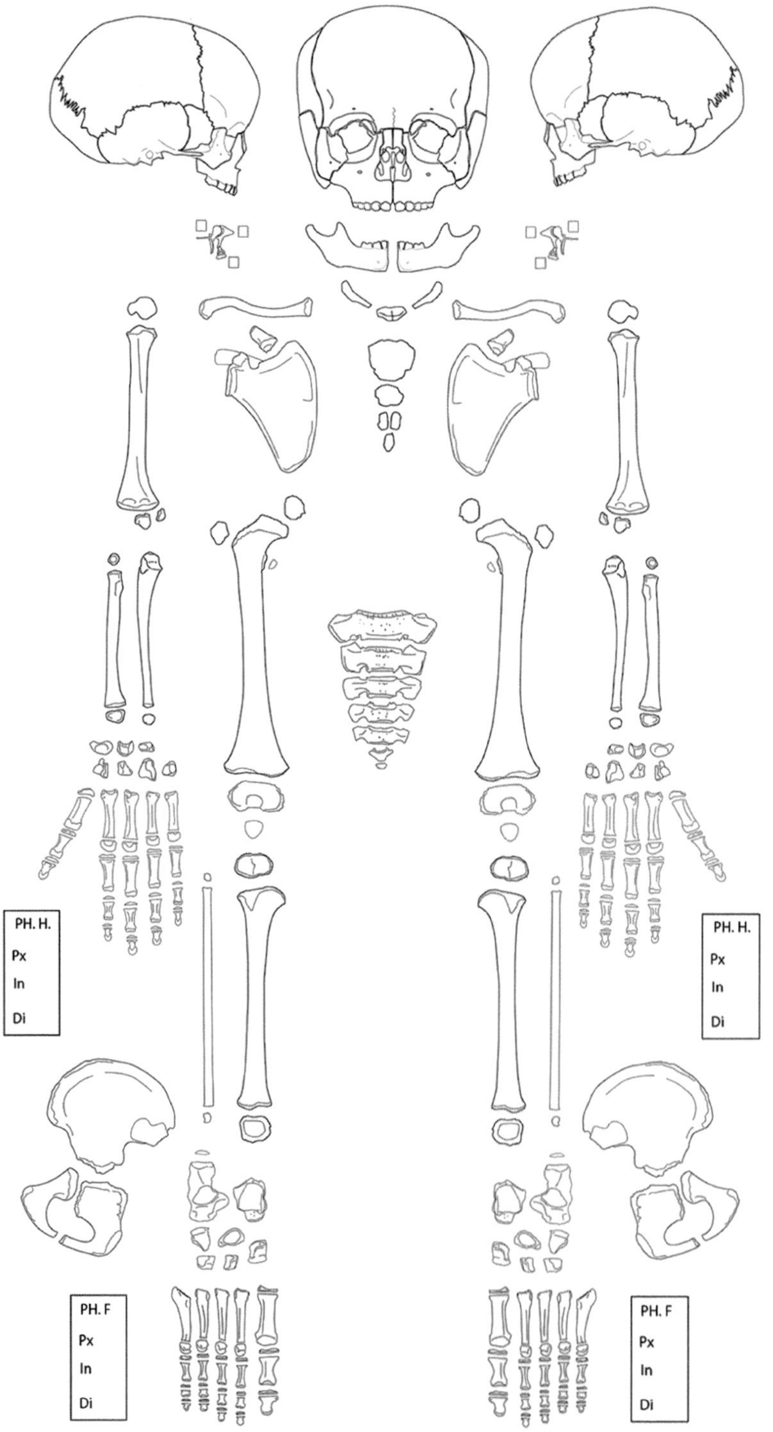

Open Source: Bocquentin and Anton, BMSAP 2021

Example Perinate/Infant Visual Skeletal Inventory Form

Case #:	Field Recovery #:
Agency:	Location:
Date(s) of Recovery:	

Complete | Fragmentary | Side unknown (yellow) | Found isolated (red)

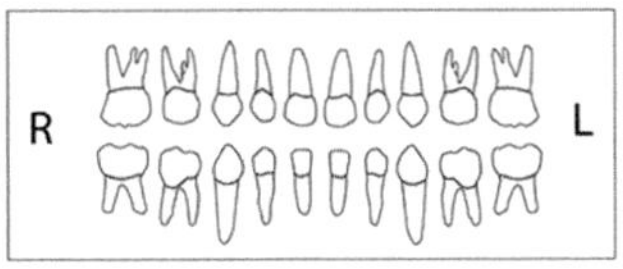

	VERTEBRAE	R neural arch	Centrum	L neural arch
CERVICAL	C1			
	C2			
	C3			
	C4			
	C5			
	C6			
	C7			
	Rey unknown			
THORACIC	T1			
	T2			
	T3			
	T4			
	T5			
	T6			
	T7			
	T8			
	T9			
	T10			
	T11			
	T12			
	Rey unknown			
LUMBAR	L1			
	L2			
	L3			
	L4			
	L5			
	Rey unknown			

		R lateral element	R neural arch	Centrum	L neural arch	L lateral element
SACRUM	S1					
	S2					
	S3					
	S4					
	S5					
	Rey unknown					

RIBS	Right	Left
T1		
T2		
T3		
T4		
T5		
T6		
T7		
T8		
T9		
T10		
T11		
T12		
Rey unknown		
Side unknown		

STERNUM	
manubrium	
sternebrae	

PH. hand rey and side indet.
Px
In
Di

PH. foot rey and side indet.
Px
In
Di

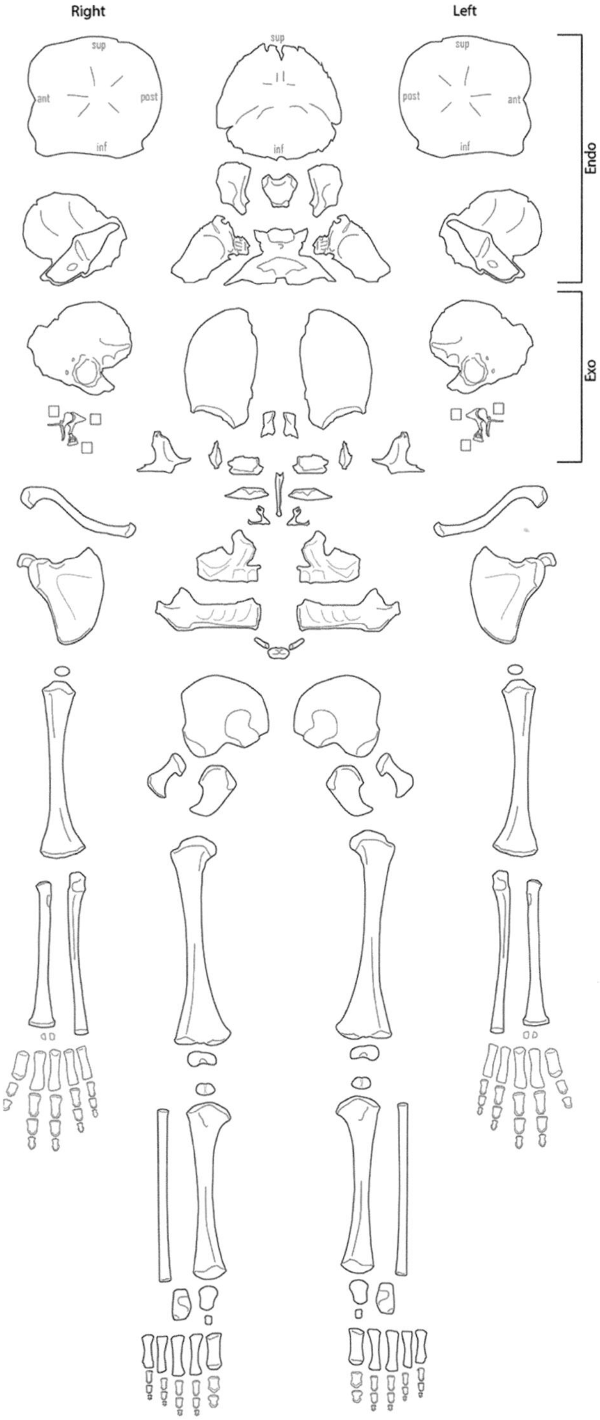

Open Source: Bocquentin and Anton, BMSAP 2021

Personnel and Scene Documentation Forms

Field experts, such as forensic archaeologists, often arrive on scene after the lead investigator or other law enforcements team members. It is crucial to obtain names, roles, and contact information at the scene for those directly involved with searches, recoveries, and evidence control and custody. It is also crucial to record basic information as a scene summary, such as weather conditions, landscape features, and methods and points of access to the scene. The following form is easy to complete at the start of each field search and/or recovery:

- Personnel and Scene Summary Form

A digital photography log will help in organizing the depictions of the overall scene and evidence details if the forensic archaeologist or other investigators need to later review the images. Since digital image files contain camera settings, there is no need to spend time documenting this type of data. The following form is simple and not burdensome to complete:

- Digital Photography Log

Example Personnel and Scene Summary Form

Case #:	Field Recovery #:
Agency:	Location:
Date(s) of Recovery:	

Scene Lead Personnel

Lead Investigator: *Contact information:*	**Recovery Team Lead:** *Contact information:*

Additional Team Personnel

Name	Role	Contact information
1.		
2.		
3.		
4.		
5.		
6.		
7.		

Scene Summary

Weather conditions: *Landscape features (aquatic, wooded, ground cover, structures, etc.):* *Method/point of access:*

Example Digital Photography Log

Case #:	Field Recovery #:
Agency:	Location:
Investigator:	
Photographer:	Date/Time:
Camera Make/Model:	Media Card #:

Digital Photography Log

Image #	View Type	Depiction (include direction/distance)

Botanical and Entomological Evidence Forms

For botanical and entomological materials to be valuable as evidence, it is critical to record several types of information as the scene is processed. To assist with organizing and documenting collected botanical and entomological specimens, the following example evidence forms are provided:

- Botanical Field Data/Collection Form
- Entomological Field Data/Collection Form.

Biological habitat and microenvironmental conditions, including basic weather conditions, are often overlooked and not fully recorded while simultaneously documenting the scene. These features are included in these forms. Where it is feasible, check boxes are used to simplify collection of data followed by areas for additional remarks if needed.

Example Botanical Field Data/Collection Form

Case #:	Agency:
Collected by:	Location:
Date/time of collection:	

Scene Biological Conditions

Types of trees, shrubbery, ground cover and frequency at scene (e.g, common, infrequent, rare, etc.):

Habitat Assessment

Path, trails, or roadway to/through scene:

Obvious broken, bent, or severed branches:

Other obvious habitat disturbance(s):

Visible Botanical Evidence

Plant materials covering body or other objects:

Plant materials visible on body or other objects:

Plant materials in grave or under body or other objects:

Page 1 of 2

Botanical Evidence Collection Record

Use the following to record description, location, and storage.

BX = Paper box **B** = Plastic bag **E** = Paper envelope **WX** = Wax paper

P = Paper bag **XP** = Field press **V** = Vial **S** = Sticky trap (pollen)

Sample Log

Sample #	Description (type, size, color, etc.)	Location	Storage

Page 2 of 2

Example Entomological Field Data/Collection Form

Case #:	Agency:
Collected by:	Location:
Date/time of collection:	

Microenvironment / Condition of Remains

☐ Ground surface ☐ Forest/wood area
☐ Suspended ☐ Field or pasture
☐ Buried ☐ Grass/ground cover
☐ Aquatic ☐ Leaf litter
☐ Indoor ☐ Exposed soil/gravel
☐ Shade ☐ Pavement
☐ Sun exposure ☐ Snow/ice

Concealment: ☐ None ☐ Container ☐ Other
Clothing: ☐ Fully ☐ Partially ☐ Nude
Scavenging: ☐ Yes ☐ No ☐ Unknown
Penetrating trauma: ☐ Yes ☐ No ☐ Unknown
Remains: ☐ Intact ☐ Partial ☐ Scattered
Decomposition stage: ☐ Fresh ☐ Discoloration ☐ Bloat ☐ Skeletonization ☐ Skeletal decay

Additional remarks on conditions:

Insect Stages Present

☐ Adult flies ☐ Adult beetles ☐ Larvae ☐ Eggs ☐ Pupae ☐ Pupal casings

Climate Data

Ambient temp/humidity
Above ground surface (30 cm): ___________
Above ground surface (1.3 m): ___________
Ambient temp
Ground surface: ___________
Body/ground interface: ___________

Soil temp
Below body (5 cm depth): ___________
Away from body (10 cm depth): ___________
Water temp
Below surface (10 cm depth): ___________

Sample Temperatures

Body temperature
Cranial surface: ___________
Thoracic surface: ___________
Pelvic surface: ___________
Knees surface: ___________

Larval mass temperature
Larval mass #1: ___________
Larval mass #2: ___________
Larval mass #3: ___________
Larval mass #4: ___________

Additional remarks:

Page 1 of 3

Entomological Sample Location Record

Use the following anterior and posterior views to record conditions and sample location.

- Visible scavenging (yellow)
- Visible penetrating trauma (red)
- Clothing
- Wrapping
- Larval mass (LM1, LM2, . . .)
- X Sample location (S1, S2, . . .)

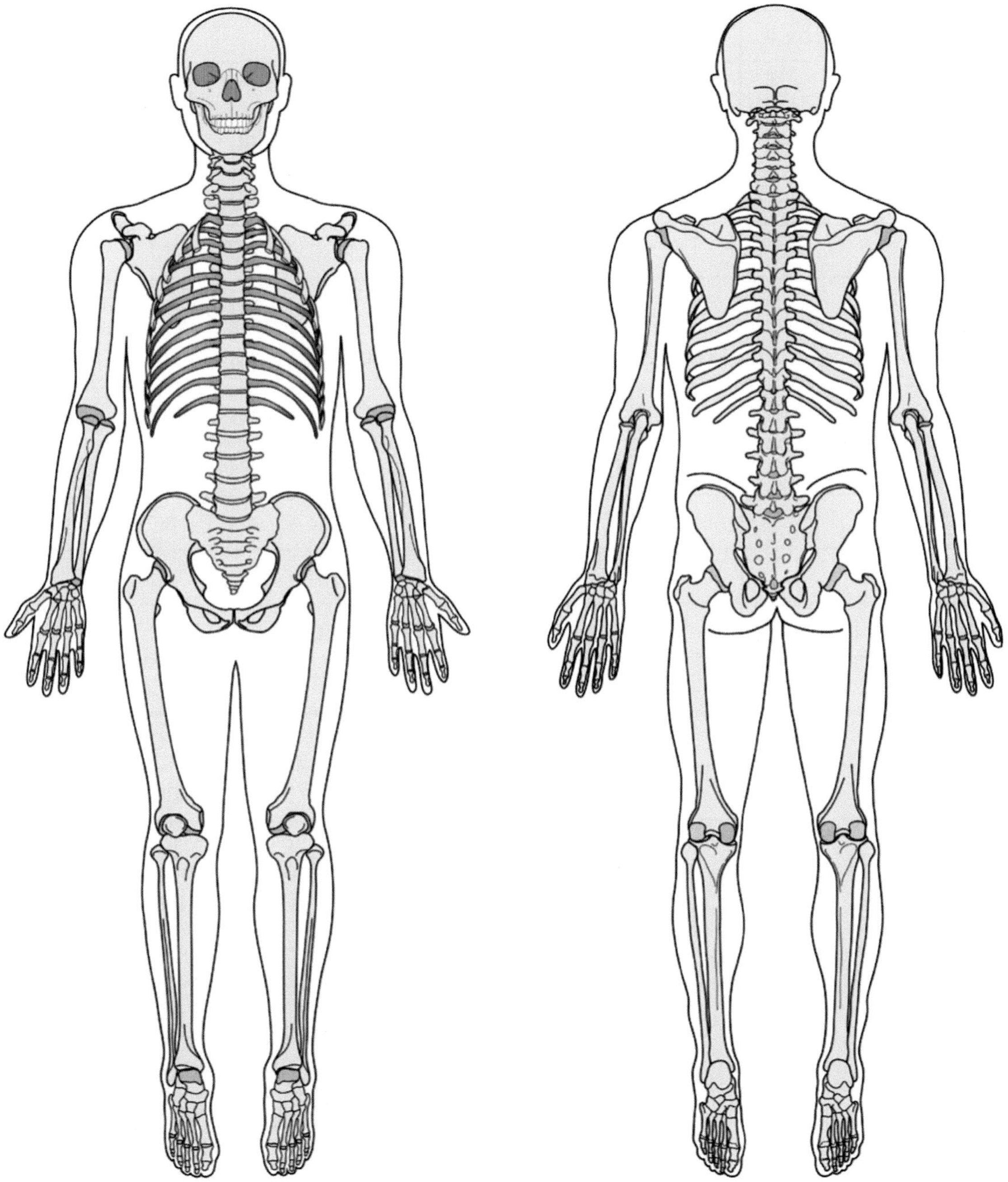

Page 2 of 3

Entomological Sample Collection Record
Use the following to record approximate number, preserved/live, type, and location number.

AF = Adult flies　　**LV** = Larvae　　**PU** = Pupae　　**P** = Preserved sample

AB = Adult beetles　　**EG** = Eggs　　**PC** = Pupal casings　　**L** = Live sample

Sample Log

Sample #	Approx #	PR/LV	Type	Location #
			☐ AF ☐ AB ☐ LV ☐ EG ☐ PU ☐ PC	
			☐ AF ☐ AB ☐ LV ☐ EG ☐ PU ☐ PC	
			☐ AF ☐ AB ☐ LV ☐ EG ☐ PU ☐ PC	
			☐ AF ☐ AB ☐ LV ☐ EG ☐ PU ☐ PC	
			☐ AF ☐ AB ☐ LV ☐ EG ☐ PU ☐ PC	
			☐ AF ☐ AB ☐ LV ☐ EG ☐ PU ☐ PC	
			☐ AF ☐ AB ☐ LV ☐ EG ☐ PU ☐ PC	
			☐ AF ☐ AB ☐ LV ☐ EG ☐ PU ☐ PC	
			☐ AF ☐ AB ☐ LV ☐ EG ☐ PU ☐ PC	
			☐ AF ☐ AB ☐ LV ☐ EG ☐ PU ☐ PC	
			☐ AF ☐ AB ☐ LV ☐ EG ☐ PU ☐ PC	
			☐ AF ☐ AB ☐ LV ☐ EG ☐ PU ☐ PC	
			☐ AF ☐ AB ☐ LV ☐ EG ☐ PU ☐ PC	
			☐ AF ☐ AB ☐ LV ☐ EG ☐ PU ☐ PC	
			☐ AF ☐ AB ☐ LV ☐ EG ☐ PU ☐ PC	
			☐ AF ☐ AB ☐ LV ☐ EG ☐ PU ☐ PC	
			☐ AF ☐ AB ☐ LV ☐ EG ☐ PU ☐ PC	
			☐ AF ☐ AB ☐ LV ☐ EG ☐ PU ☐ PC	
			☐ AF ☐ AB ☐ LV ☐ EG ☐ PU ☐ PC	
			☐ AF ☐ AB ☐ LV ☐ EG ☐ PU ☐ PC	
			☐ AF ☐ AB ☐ LV ☐ EG ☐ PU ☐ PC	
			☐ AF ☐ AB ☐ LV ☐ EG ☐ PU ☐ PC	

Page 3 of 3

APPENDIX D

Surface Recovery and Feature Excavation Forms

Controlled, effective, and efficient surface recovery and excavation of human remains in a forensic context are critical to any investigation. The expertise of a forensic archaeologist during surface recovery and excavation is invaluable in locating, excavating, and recording skeletal remains and ensuring that the maximum amount of information is recovered. When properly recorded, this information can help determine the date of deposition, the manner in which the remains were placed, and the relationship of any associated objects or surviving elements.

To assist with recording when using ground penetrating radar (GPR) in grid searches, the following form can be used to log profile data:

- GPR Profile Log

The following forms are designed as a focal point for recording surface recoveries and the grave feature. They are also designed to link with information recorded in other forms of documentation:

- Surface Recovery Record
- Feature Excavation and Recovery Record

In addition to the surface and excavation forms and visual skeletal inventories provided in Appendix A, a more detailed record of the positioning of remains may be necessary:

- Detailed Remains Positioning Record

The form is adapted from Bocquentin and Anton (2021:8) open-source files under the conditions of "be[ing] regularly reworked and improved, according to the needs of each anthropologist to meet the needs of each anthropologist and for the use of the greatest number of users." The example form is not intended for direct distribution or commercialization but rather the sharing of information to support best practices in an educational and professional setting. It is recommended that each user access the adaptive open-source file download and construct forms meeting their individual needs.

Electronic Reference for Adaptive Open-Source File Download

F. Bocquentin and M. Anton, "Visual inventories and field note templates for contextualized recording of human remains", *Bulletins et Mémoires de la Société d'Anthropologie de Paris* [Online], 33 (2) | 2021, Online since 28 September 2021. DOI: 10.4000/bmsap.7750

Example GPR Profile Log

Case #:	Date / Time:
Agency:	Location:
Operated by:	

Grid and Antenna Information

Grid dimensions: X= ____________ Y= ____________
Antenna: ______________ Velocity: ______________ Depth: ______________ n/s: ____________

GPR File Log

GPR File	X Start	X Stop	Y Start	Y Stop	Notes

Example Surface Recovery Record

Case #:	Date(s) of recovery:
Agency:	Location:
Excavated by:	

Method(s) of Locating Surface Feature

☐ Witness identification
☐ Visual surface search
☐ Accidental discovery
☐ HRD dog team
☐ Other:

Additional remarks:

Surface Feature Description

☐ Primary
☐ Secondary
☐ Fully Exposed
☐ Partially exposed

Partial exposure due to:

☐ Natural plant growth or detritus
☐ Purposeful concealment using:
☐ Burial erosion/exposure
☐ Aquatic pool or stream
☐ Other

Location of feature within scene:

Surface Feature #: ______________

Schematic of surface feature and surroundings:

N

Scale: 1:10 cm 1:20 cm

Remarks:

Final measures (cm)
Length: ____________________
Width: ____________________
Depth: ____________________
Surface elevation: __________
____

Page 1 of 2

Case #:	Date(s) of recovery:
Agency:	Location:
Excavated by:	

Method(s) of Recovery

☐ No excavation required
☐ Minor excavation required
☐ Excavation required
☐ Removal of plant growth and surface debris
☐ Removal of materials used for concealment
☐ Screening: ☐ Dry ☐ Wet ☐ Hand sort
Mesh size(s): ____________________

Position of Remains (if able to determine)

Orientation: ☐ East-west ☐ North-south ☐ North-east/South-west ☐ North-west/South-east
(Head first) ☐ West-east ☐ South-north ☐ South-west/North-east ☐ South-east/North-west

Position of face: ☐ Unknown ☐ Forward ☐ To left ☐ To right

General position: ☐ Extended ☐ Back ☐ Right side
☐ Flexed ☐ Chest ☐ Left side
☐ Tightly flexed ☐ Seated ☐ Unknown

Additional remarks:

Accompanying Documentation

☐ *Associated evidence from feature*
- ☐ No associated evidence recovered
- ☐ Field collection inventory ID list
- ☐ Associated evidence recovered
- ☐ Agency evidentiary ID list

☐ *Digital photography*
- ☐ Field photography log numbers: ____________________
- ☐ Agency photograph ID log numbers: ____________________

☐ *Survey/field drawings*
- ☐ Scene survey map
- ☐ Feature scale drawing
- ☐ Other scale drawing: ____________________
- ☐ Other scale drawing: ____________________

☐ *Soils/sediment data and samples*
- ☐ Stratigraphic profile form
- ☐ Stratigraphic layer descriptions
- ☐ Bulk soils/sediment sample numbers:

☐ *Botanical/entomological data and specimens:*
- ☐ Botanical collection record
- ☐ Entomological collection record

☐ *Skeletal inventory:*
- ☐ Visual skeletal inventory form(s): ____________________

Page 2 of 2

Example Feature Excavation and Recovery Record

Case #:	Date(s) of recovery:
Agency:	Location:
Excavated by:	

Method(s) of Locating Feature

☐ Witness identification	☐ Soil probe	☐ Burial erosion/exposure
☐ Visual surface search	☐ Shovel shining	☐ HRD dog team
☐ Geophysical survey	☐ Accidental discovery	☐ Other:

Additional remarks:

Method(s) of Recovery

☐ Hand trowel	*Screening*		*Approach used*
☐ Shovel and hand trowel	☐ Dry screen	Mesh size(s): ___________	☐ Direct excavation
☐ Backhoe	☐ Wet screen	Mesh size(s): ___________	☐ Grid unit
☐ Other:	☐ Hand sort		☐ Pedestal

Grave Feature

Grave orientation:

Schematic of grave outline and surrounding features:

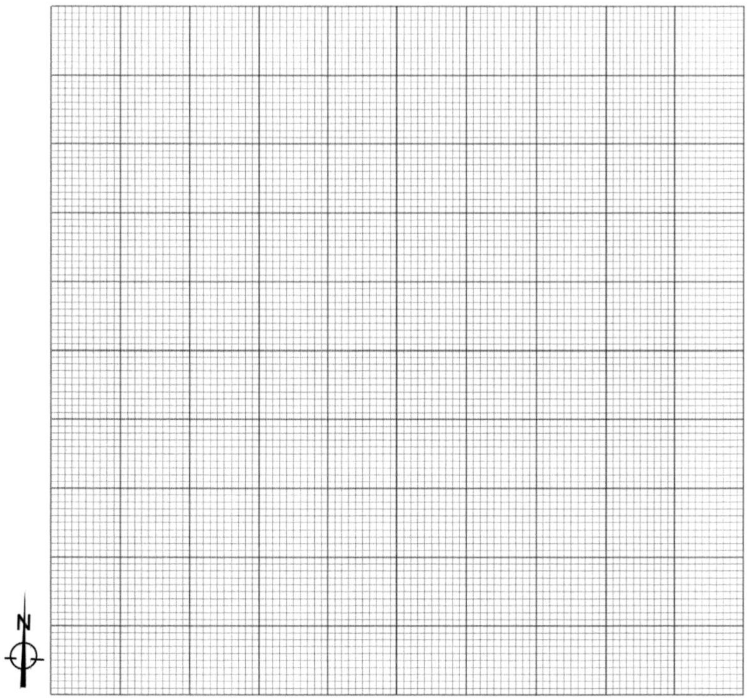

Scale: ☐ 1:10 cm ☐ 1:20 cm

Remarks:

Final measures (cm)

Length: ____________________

Width: ____________________

Depth: ____________________

Surface elevation: ___________

____

Page 1 of 2

Case #:	Date(s) of recovery:
Agency:	Location:
Excavated by:	

Type of Deposit

☐ Interment ☐ Cremation	☐ Primary ☐ Secondary ☐ Partial remains ☐ Indeterminate	☐ Single ☐ Double	☐ Plural ☐ Simultaneous ☐ Successive ☐ Indeterminate

Body Position

Orientation: (Head first)	☐ East-west ☐ West-east	☐ North-south ☐ South-north	☐ North-east/South-west ☐ South-west/North-east	☐ North-west/South-east ☐ South-east/North-west
Position of face:	☐ Unknown	☐ Forward	☐ To left	☐ To right
General position:	☐ Extended ☐ Flexed ☐ Tightly flexed	☐ Back ☐ Chest ☐ Seated	☐ Right side ☐ Left side ☐ Unknown	

Additional remarks:

Accompanying Documentation

☐ *Associated evidence from feature*
- ☐ No associated evidence recovered
- ☐ Associated evidence recovered
- ☐ Field collection inventory ID list
- ☐ Agency evidentiary ID list

☐ *Digital photography*
- ☐ Field photography log numbers: ____________________
- ☐ Agency photograph ID log numbers: ____________________

☐ *Survey/field drawings*
- ☐ Scene survey map
- ☐ Other scale drawing: ____________________
- ☐ Feature scale drawing
- ☐ Other scale drawing: ____________________

☐ *Soils/sediment data and samples*
- ☐ Stratigraphic profile form
- ☐ Bulk soils/sediment sample numbers:
- ☐ Stratigraphic layer descriptions

☐ *Botanical/entomological data and specimens:*
- ☐ Botanical collection record
- ☐ Entomological collection record

☐ *Skeletal inventory:*
- ☐ Visual skeletal inventory form(s): ____________________

Page 2 of 2

Example Detailed Remains Positioning Record

Case #:	Date(s) of recovery:
Agency:	Location:
Excavated by:	

SKULL

Exposed side: Anterior | Posterior | Superior | Inferior | Lateral right | Lateral left | Unknown

Joints:

Skull / Atlas	Articulated	Anatomical proximity	Disarticulated	▶
Atlas / Axis	Articulated	Anatomical proximity	Disarticulated	▶
Skull / Mandibule	Articulated	Anatomical proximity	Disarticulated	▶
Mandibule	Close	Open	Disarticulated	▶

Position : Primary | Secondary | Indeterminate

Observation : Preserved Headrest | Suspected Headrest | Other Constraints ▶

SPINE

Joints:

Cervical — Articulated | Anatomical proximity | Disarticulated ▶

Thoracic — Articulated | Anatomical proximity | Disarticulated ▶

Lumbar — Articulated | Anatomical proximity | Disarticulated ▶

Sacro-Cocc. — Articulated | Anatomical proximity | Disarticulated ▶

Exposed side ***Disjunctions***

Notes vertebral column

RIB CAGE

	Flattening:		***Lateral constraints:***	
Right side	Partial	Complete	Yes	No
Left side	Partial	Complete	Yes	No

Joints:

Right Rib-Vertebr. — Articulated | Anatomical proximity | Disarticulated ▶

Left Rib-Vertebr. — Articulated | Anatomical proximity | Disarticulated ▶

STERNUM

Exposed side:

Manubrium — Anterior | Posterior | Superior | Inferior | Lateral right | Lateral left

Body — Anterior | Posterior | Superior | Inferior | Lateral right | Lateral left

Joints:

	Right side			**Left side**		
Sternum/Clav.	Articulated	Anatomical proximity	Disarticulated	Articulated	Anatomical proximity	Disarticulated
Sternum/1st Rib	Articulated	Anatomical proximity	Disarticulated	Articulated	Anatomical proximity	Disarticulated
Sternum/Ribs	Articulated	Anatomical proximity	Disarticulated	Articulated	Anatomical proximity	Disarticulated

Open Source: Bocquentin and Anton, BMSAP 2021

Page 1 of 3

Case #:	Date(s) of recovery:
Agency:	Location:
Excavated by:	

	Right side	Left side
SHOULDER		
Position:		
Scapula	☐ Ant. ☐ Intermed. ☐ Lat.	☐ Ant. ☐ Intermed. ☐ Lat.
Clavicule	☐ Horizontal ☐ Intermed. ☐ Vertical	☐ Horizontal ☐ Intermed. ☐ Vertical
Humerus	☐ ____	☐ ____
	► ☐ Lateral Rotation ☐ Medial Rotation	► ☐ Lateral Rotation ☐ Medial Rotation
Lateral Constriction: (Shoulder)	☐ Yes ☐ No	☐ Yes ☐ No
Joints: *Scapula/Clavicule*	☐ Articulated ☐ Anatomical proximity ☐ Disarticulated	☐ Articulated ☐ Anatomical proximity ☐ Disarticulated
Scapula/Humerus	☐ Articulated ☐ Anatomical proximity ☐ Disarticulated	☐ Articulated ☐ Anatomical proximity ☐ Disarticulated
ELBOW		
Position:	► ☐ Extension	► ☐ Extension
	☐ Flexion : ☐ <90° ☐ =90° ☐ >90°	☐ Flexion : ☐ <90° ☐ =90° ☐ >90°
Localisation:		
Joints: *Humerus/Radius*	☐ Articulated ☐ Anatomical proximity ☐ Disarticulated	☐ Articulated ☐ Anatomical proximity ☐ Disarticulated
Humerus/Ulna	☐ Articulated ☐ Anatomical proximity ☐ Disarticulated	☐ Articulated ☐ Anatomical proximity ☐ Disarticulated
Radius/Ulna	☐ Articulated ☐ Anatomical proximity ☐ Disarticulated	☐ Articulated ☐ Anatomical proximity ☐ Disarticulated
	► ☐ Supination ☐ Pronation	► ☐ Supination ☐ Pronation
WRIST		
Position:	► ☐ Extension ☐ Flexion: ☐ <90° ☐ =90°	► ☐ Extension ☐ Flexion: ☐ <90° ☐ =90°
Joints: *Radius-Ulna/ Carpals*	☐ Articulated ☐ Anatomical proximity ☐ Disarticulated	☐ Articulated ☐ Anatomical proximity ☐ Disarticulated
Carpals	☐ Articulated ☐ Anatomical proximity ☐ Disarticulated	☐ Articulated ☐ Anatomical proximity ☐ Disarticulated
Carpals/ Metacarpals	☐ Articulated ☐ Anatomical proximity ☐ Disarticulated	☐ Articulated ☐ Anatomical proximity ☐ Disarticulated
Metacarpals/ Phalanges	☐ Articulated ☐ Anatomical proximity ☐ Disarticulated	☐ Articulated ☐ Anatomical proximity ☐ Disarticulated
HAND		
Position:	► ☐ Extension ☐ Flexion	► ☐ Extension ☐ Flexion
	► ☐ Palmar ☐ Dorsal ☐ Medial	► ☐ Palmar ☐ Dorsal ☐ Medial
	☐ Lateral ☐ Proximal ☐ Distal	☐ Lateral ☐ Proximal ☐ Distal
Localisation:		

Open Source: Bocquentin and Anton, BMSAP 2021

Page 2 of 3

Case #:	Date(s) of recovery:
Agency:	Location:
Excavated by:	

PELVIS

Joints:

	Right side	Left side
	☐ Closed ☐ Partially open ☐ Open	
Sacrum/Coxae	☐ Articulated ☐ Anatomical proximity ☐ Disarticulated	☐ Articulated ☐ Anatomical proximity ☐ Disarticulated
Pubis	☐ Articulated ☐ Anatomical proximity ☐ Disarticulated	☐ Articulated ☐ Anatomical proximity ☐ Disarticulated
Coxae/Femur	☐ Articulated ☐ Anatomical proximity ☐ Disarticulated	☐ Articulated ☐ Anatomical proximity ☐ Disarticulated
Hip	► ☐ Extension ☐ 90° ☐ Flexion	► ☐ Extension ☐ 90° ☐ Flexion
Femur:	► ☐ Lat. ☐ Med. ☐ Ant. ☐ Post. ► ☐ Lateral Rotation ☐ Medial Rotation	► ☐ Lat. ☐ Med. ☐ Ant. ☐ Post. ► ☐ Lateral Rotation ☐ Medial Rotation

KNEE

	Right side	Left side
Position:	► ☐ Extension ☐ Flexion : ☐ <90° ☐ =90° ☐ >90°	► ☐ Extension ☐ Flexion : ☐ <90° ☐ =90° ☐ >90°
Localisation:		
Joints: *Femur/Patella*	☐ Articulated ☐ Anatomical proximity ☐ Disarticulated	☐ Articulated ☐ Anatomical proximity ☐ Disarticulated
Femur/Tibia	☐ Articulated ☐ Anatomical proximity ☐ Disarticulated	☐ Articulated ☐ Anatomical proximity ☐ Disarticulated
Tibia/Fibula	☐ Articulated ☐ Anatomical proximity ☐ Disarticulated	☐ Articulated ☐ Anatomical proximity ☐ Disarticulated

FOOT

	Right side	Left side
Position:	► ☐ Extension ☐ Flexion ► ☐ Plantar ☐ Dorsal ☐ Medial ☐ Lateral ☐ Proximal ☐ Distal	► ☐ Extension ☐ Flexion ► ☐ Plantar ☐ Dorsal ☐ Medial ☐ Lateral ☐ Proximal ☐ Distal
Localisation:		
Joints: *Tibia-Fibula/Tarsals*	☐ Articulated ☐ Anatomical proximity ☐ Disarticulated	☐ Articulated ☐ Anatomical proximity ☐ Disarticulated
Tarsals	☐ Articulated ☐ Anatomical proximity ☐ Disarticulated	☐ Articulated ☐ Anatomical proximity ☐ Disarticulated
Tarsals/Metatarsals	☐ Articulated ☐ Anatomical proximity ☐ Disarticulated	☐ Articulated ☐ Anatomical proximity ☐ Disarticulated
Metatarsals/Phalanges	☐ Articulated ☐ Anatomical proximity ☐ Disarticulated	☐ Articulated ☐ Anatomical proximity ☐ Disarticulated

Open Source: Bocquentin and Anton, BMSAP 2021

Page 3 of 3

Soils Data and Sample Collection Forms

Soils and stratigraphy recording allows investigators to collect essential soils data efficiently and effectively when tagging soil samples and recording the soils found in the feature being excavated. This information is also useful in writing final reports and reconstructing the excavation process at a later date if needed.

The following are included:

- Flowchart for Feel Method of Soil Texturing
- Bulk Soils Sampling Tag
- Excavation Stratigraphic Profile Form
- Stratigraphic Layer/Soil Horizon Description Form

Feel Method of Soil Texturing

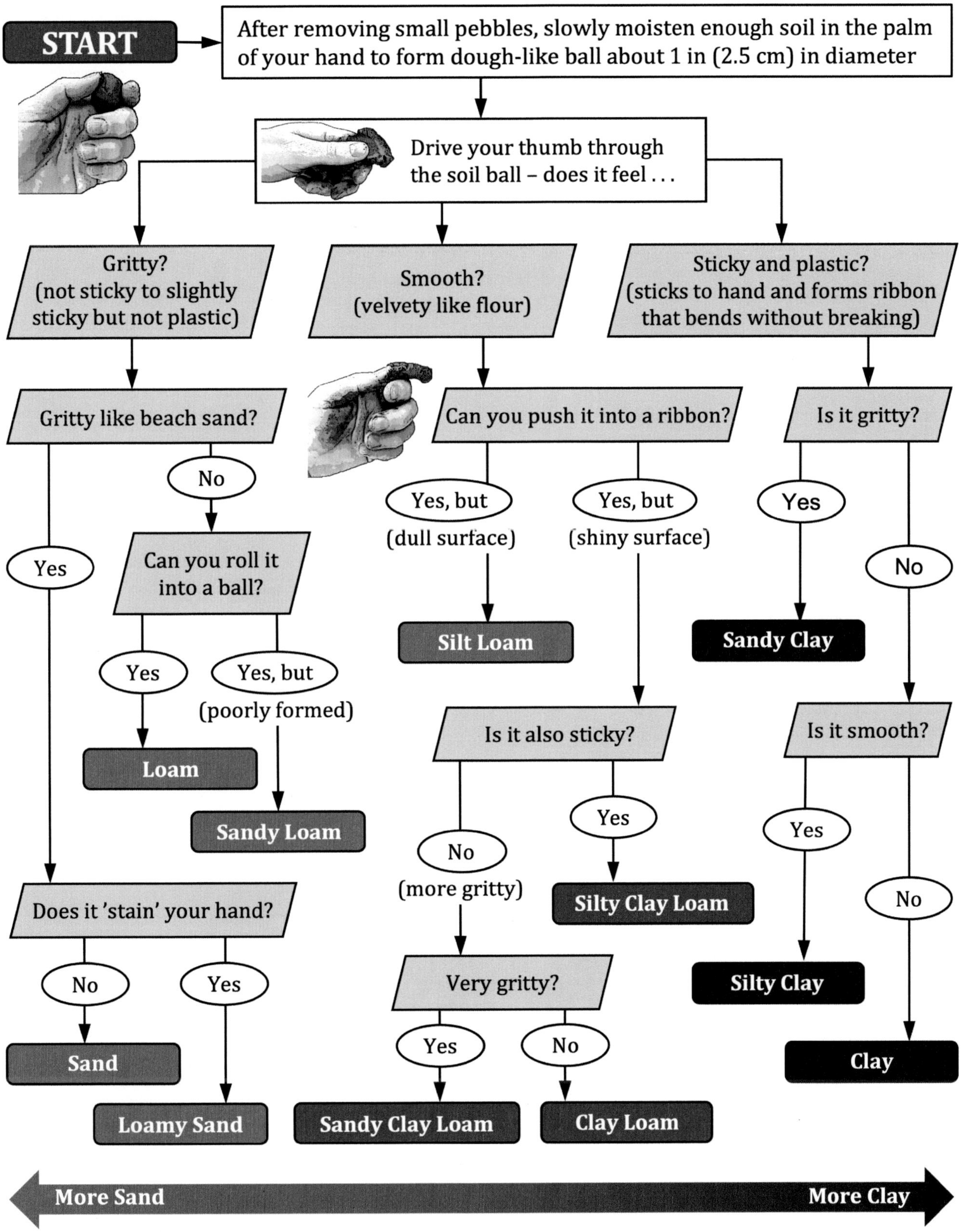

Example Bulk Soils Sample Tag

Soil Sample #:	Collected by:
Case #:	Date / Time:
Agency:	Location:
Excavator:	
Unit:	Level:
Material description:	

Example Excavation Stratigraphic Profile Form

Case #:	Date:
Agency:	Location:
Excavator:	
Unit ID:	☐ Shovel test ☐ Excavation

Layer #	Depth	Color	Texture	Notes

Soil sample tag #s:

Profile drawing / photo ID #s:

Example Stratigraphic Layer/Soil Horizon Description Form

Case #:	Date:
Agency:	Location:
Excavator:	
Unit ID:	Stratigraphic layer #:

LAYER COLOR: Munsell #: ☐ Dry ☐ Moist ☐ Wet

TEXTURE TESTS (with moistened soil)

Gritty/Smooth:	☐ loose	☐ weak	☐ friable	☐ firm	☐ hard	☐ cemented
Ball form:	☐ none	☐ weak	☐ fragile	☐ firm	☐ firm; stains	
Ribbon form:	☐ none	☐ slight	☐ stable	☐ sticky	☐ very gritty	
Ribbon plasticity:	☐ none	☐ slight bend	☐ bends easily	☐ gritty	☐ smooth	

INCLUSIONS (macroscopic view)

Rock type(s): ____________________

Average size: ____________________

Average shape: ____________________

Frequency: ____________________

DISTURBANCES

☐ Roots
☐ Animals
☐ Insects
☐ Human-induced

STRATUM BOUNDARIES / DEPOSITION

Distinctness:	☐ abrupt	☐ clear	☐ gradual	☐ diffuse
Topography:	☐ smooth	☐ wavy	☐ irregular	☐ broken
Deposition:	☐ naturally	☐ culturally	☐ mixed	☐ indeterminate

COMMENTS:

Evidence Inventory and Chain of Custody Forms

During search and recovery, field experts, such as forensic archaeologists, often work directly with Crime Scene Investigators, Death Investigators, or other forensic science technicians to document, collect, and preserve evidence meticulously from the scene for legal process and forensic analysis. Chain of custody is a detailed, documented process that tracks the handling of physical or digital evidence from collection to its presentation in court. It is crucial for establishing the evidence's authenticity and integrity by recording every person who handles it, along with the date, time, and purpose of each transfer.

The following forms are easily used during field search and/or recovery to maintain evidence control and custody records:

- Evidence Inventory Log
- Evidence Chain of Custody Form

Example Evidence Inventory Log

Case #:	Field Recovery #:
Agency:	Location:
Lead Investigator:	
CSI/tech:	Date/Time:

Items Collected in Field Recovery

Field #	CSI ID #	Description of Item(s)

Example Evidence Chain of Custody Form

Case #:	Field Recovery #:
Agency:	Location:
Date(s) of Recovery:	

Scene Lead Personnel

Lead Investigator: *Contact information:*	**Recovery Team Lead:** *Contact information:*

Evidence for Transfer/Transportation

Inventory ID list attached: ☐ Field ID # ☐ CSI Evidence #
Description of evidence being transferred:

Transfer/Transportation Custodians

Transfer from:	*Transfer to:*
Name:	Name:
Title:	Title:
Agency:	Agency:
Date/time:	Date/time:
Signature:	Signature:

GLOSSARY

active geophysical prospecting method: sends an induced signal into the ground by a transmitter and then measures the returning signal via a receiver to detect subsurface anomalies

acoustic shadow: an area where sound waves cannot be heard or seen due to an obstruction, often indicates a raised surface on side-scan sonar imagery

adipocere: soap- or wax-like insoluble fatty acids that form from slow hydrolysis of the body's fat during decomposition; forms best in an oxygen-free, humid environment, such as in wet ground or a sealed coffin or casket

adult: final, fully developed stage of an organism's life cycle

aerial imagery: photographs or digital images of the Earth's surface taken from airborne platforms like airplanes, drones, or satellites

aerial survey: examination of area of interest using helicopters, small aircraft, or remote-controlled drones

ala: wing-like structure

algae: a diverse group of aquatic organisms that use photosynthesis to produce energy, ranging from microscopic single-celled to large multicellular forms

algor mortis: postmortem cooling of the body as it loses heat to the surrounding environment

alveolus: angular cavity or pit

amalgam inlay: dental restoration containing a mixture of mercury with at least one other metal, such as silver, tin, or zinc; also known as a *filling*

American Academy of Forensic Sciences (AAFS): professional society for people in all areas of forensics and dedicated to the application of science to the legal process

American Board of Forensic Anthropology (ABFA): organization that certifies professionals recognized for their special qualifications in forensic anthropology

American Board of Forensic Entomology (ABFE): organization that certifies professionals recognized for their special qualifications in forensic entomology

amphibian: taxonomic class of cold-blooded vertebrate animal distinguished by moist, permeable skin that lacks scales, and an aquatic gill-breathing larval stage followed by a terrestrial lung-breathing adult stage

Analyst (A-ABFA): certified professionals recognized for their laboratory skills and fundamental knowledge in forensic anthropology and for meeting the standards set forth by the American Board of Forensic Anthropology

apical: toward the tip of the tooth root

apical foramen: small opening at tip of tooth root that allows blood and nerve supply to pass into root canal and pulp chamber

appendicular skeleton: bones of the shoulder girdle, pelvic girdle, and limbs

anemophilous plants: wind-pollinated plants

anomaly: nonspecific irregularity or feature detected using geophysical survey tools

antemortem: before death

anterior: toward the front

annual secondary growth: distinctive feature of woody plants that manifests as growth rings within their tissues

archaeology: study of past human societies through the recovery and analysis of the material culture, physical remains, and evidence of environmental interactions that they have left behind

articular surface: surface that comes into contact with another bone

articulation: location where two or more bones make contact, forming a joint (true articulation must have soft tissues connecting the bones; although some may use the term to describe undisturbed skeletal elements, it is more correct to describe the elements as being in *anatomical position*)

artifact: any portable object made, used, or modified by humans

associated evidence: objects that have some direct association with remains (e.g., clothing, personal items)

association: an object's relationship to other objects or features found within the same archaeological level or general location

association (principle of): archaeological principle presuming that objects found together within the same layer or feature were deposited at approximately the same time

auditory ossicles: irregular paired bones of the ears that consist of the incus (anvil), stapes (stirrup), and malleus (hammer); found within the temporal bones of the cranial vault

autogamous plants: self-pollinating plants

autolysis: chemical process that results in the destruction of tissues by intracellular enzymes within an organism

avian: characteristics pertaining to birds

axial skeleton: bones of the midline; includes skull, auditory ossicles, hyoid, ribs, and vertebral column

azimuth: projected horizontal angle measured from the center of a circle to a direction of interest; usually progressing from 0° to 360° in a clockwise fashion

azimuth control-point method: uses direct distance and 0° to 360° spherical coordinate system from a fixed point, or axis of the plane, for data point locations of objects when mapping

backfill: to refill a hole or excavation with the material that was taken out of it; also refers to the material itself

backhoe: heavy excavating equipment consisting of a digging bucket on the end of a two-part arm, which is typically mounted on a tractor or front loader

backsight: initial stadia rod reading taken on a point of known elevation (e.g., benchmark or datum), or a known intermediate traverse point from a previous survey

ball-socket vertebrae: joint articulation found in reptile vertebrae with the cranial side of the vertebra being concave and the caudal side being convex

baseline: an arbitrary transect reference line established for the purpose of mapping a larger area

baseline control-point method: uses direct distance and horizontal offsets of objects at a 90° angle from a baseline for data point locations of objects when mapping

bearing: measure of direction to a distant location or object, typically expressed in degrees or cardinal direction using a compass

benchmarks: precisely determined points of elevation or triangulation established by a government agency or licensed surveyor; typically stamped brass disks affixed to rock outcrops, bridges, buildings, sidewalks, or other prominent features

bilateral: on both sides

biological anthropology: study of the behavioral and biological aspects of humans, their extinct ancestors, and related nonhuman primates such as chimpanzees, gorillas, and monkeys

biological profile: estimation of the age, sex, ancestry, and stature for an unidentified individual based on analysis of skeletal features

biostratinomy: study of the environmental factors that affect organic remains between death and the final burial of the remains

bioturbation: process where living organisms disturb, mix, and rework soils and sediments

bloating: result of a production and accumulation of gases due to the uncontrolled growth of endogenous bacteria and fungi in the body; recognizable byproduct of decomposition

blow flies: flies of the family Calliphoridae that deposit their eggs in carrion, decomposing tissues, dung, and open wounds

botanical field press: portable tool used to collect and preserve plant specimens in the field by pressing and drying them

box screen: heavy-duty square frame with 1/4-inch steel mesh used for sifting through surface debris and soil removed from the excavation to recover materials that may otherwise be overlooked

buccal: surface of premolars and molars adjacent to the cheek

bulldozer: continuous tracked tractor equipped with a substantial blade used to push large quantities of soil during heavy construction excavation

burial: process of deliberately placing human remains in the ground and covering them

burial cut: characteristic of a grave indicated by the line of definition between the backfill sediment and the strata through which the grave has been dug; also known as a grave outline

burial depression: primary or secondary depression that forms over a burial because of soil compaction and/or decomposition

burial site: area disturbed during the process of burying a body

cadaver bag: non-porous bag designed to contain human remains; used for leakproof storage and transportation of remains

cadaver decomposition island: localized area of highly enriched soil directly beneath and surrounding a decomposing corpse; stained by fluids released during the decomposition process and often contains concentrations of fly larvae casings

calcination: disintegration of bone by heat; calcinated bone is typically grayish-white and crumbly in appearance

canal: tunnel-like channel

cancellous (trabecular) bone: light, porous interior structure of short bones, irregular bones, and ends of long and tubular bones

canine: pointed, cone-shaped tooth located between incisors and premolars in permanent dentition

carapace: top portion of a turtle shell

carpals: small, short bones of the wrist; each wrist consists of eight bones: scaphoid, lunate, triquetral, pisiform, trapezium, trapezoid, capitate, and hamate

carpometacarpus: middle long bone in the wing of a bird, formed by the fusion of the metacarpals and several carpal bones

carrion beetle: beetle from the family Silphidae that feeds on decaying organic matter

caudal: toward the tail of a quadruped

cementoenamel junction (CEJ): area where the enamel and cementum of a tooth meet; marks boundary between crown and root

cementum: hard tissue covering tooth root; provides attachment surface for periodontal ligament

cemetery: a designated and communal place specific to interment of remains of the dead

central-axis baseline: fixed transect line bisecting the area into halves; used for measuring offsets during mapping

cephalic: toward the head of a quadruped

cervical vertebrae: seven vertebrae that comprise the superior portion of the vertebral column; individually abbreviated as C1, C2, etc. with C1 (atlas) and C2 (axis) as the most superior

chaining pin: striped metal stake with a circular eye at one end and a point at the other (also known as a surveyor's arrow); used to temporarily mark a point and in constructing a grid or establishing a perimeter

chain of custody: system that documents handling of evidence and management where each item is tracked from initial recovery through presentation in court

clandestine grave: burial site used for the concealment and disposal of human remains in a grave

clavicle: S-shaped tubular paired bones, also known as the collar bones, found in the anterior of the shoulder girdle

clayey: soil made of very fine mineral particles that are sticky and plastic when wet; nutrient-rich and very smooth in texture

closed association: relationship among objects found together in a way suggesting they were deposited at the same time, like in a grave

close-up views: photographs that depict individual items or feature details to the exclusion of anything else, clearly showing any markings, defects, or other identifying features from all sides

coccyx: comprising four or five fused or unfused small bony elements found inferior to the sacrum; also known as the tailbone

Coleoptera: taxonomic order of insects comprising the beetles

compaction: reduction in volume or density of soil or sediments due to applied force

compression marks: marks are produced when an object is pressed against another object or material with sufficient force to leave an impression, usually as a negative contour variation of the object's surface

condyle: large, rounded articular projection

contamination: any transfer of material from one source to another that has the potential to damage, destroy, and/or compromise the forensic significance and context of an item, tool mark, or other form of evidence

context: an object's exact place in time and space and its association and relationship with other items or data (i.e., where it is, when it arrived, and how it got there)

contour lines: joined points of equal elevation on a map to show valleys, hills, and steepness of slopes in relation to a fixed reference point

control-point mapping: method of mapping concerned with determining the position of an object or feature in relation to a fixed known point; typically involves survey equipment when evidence is spaced out across a larger area

coprophiles: organisms that consume fecal matter, either their own or that of other species

coroner: public official who presides over investigations into unnatural deaths

cortical (compact) bone: smooth, dense outer layer of bone

clutter: small discontinuities that reflect energy but are not the target of the ground-penetrating radar geophysical survey

cranial skeleton: the skull (cranium and mandible) and hyoid

cranium: a skull without a mandible

cremation: process using intense heat to reduce a body rapidly to ashes and small bone fragments

cremains: resulting ash, fragmentary bone, and teeth from cremation process

cremulator: processing equipment used to reduce cremains to very small and non-distinguishable particles; designed to reduce the volume of the cremains for interment

crenulated margin: jagged or irregular edges where carnivores have removed bone

crest: sharp border or ridge

crown: visible portion of the tooth; covered by enamel

cusp: elevation on occlusal surface of tooth; primarily found on premolars and molars

cylinder: resulting modified bone shape when both ends of a long bone have been removed through gnawing

datum: a designated fixed point of reference for all elevation, depth, and angle measurements made during survey mapping and excavation

datum line: line set from the datum and extended across excavation to ensure a consistent and level reference when measuring elevation

deciduous teeth: the first set of teeth that develop; also known as primary or 'baby' teeth, with humans having an average of 20 deciduous teeth

declination: angular difference between true north and magnetic north for a given location; measured in degrees, minutes, and seconds

declination diagram: map feature that shows the angular relationship between true north, magnetic north, and grid north

Defense POW/MIA Accounting Agency (DPAA): agency within the U.S. Department of Defense whose mission is to recover unaccounted Department of Defense personnel listed as prisoners of war or missing in action from designated past conflicts, from countries around the world

dendrochronology: scientific study of growth ring patterns in woody plants to draw conclusions about age, origin, and historical climate conditions

dens: tooth-shaped projection

dental bridge: fixed or removable partial denture used to replace missing teeth; anchored to adjacent teeth by wires or permanent implants
dentin: softer core tissue of crown and root of tooth; surrounds pulp chamber
depth: vertical measure of how far an object is below a fixed reference point (e.g., datum)
detritivores: organisms that derive nutrients by feeding on decomposing organic material
diachronic: change over time
diaphysis: (*pl. diaphyses*) shaft of a long bone
diatoms: unicellular algae with uniquely patterned silica-based cell walls
Diplomate (D-ABFA): certified professionals recognized for their special qualifications in forensic anthropology and for meeting the standards set forth by the American Board of Forensic Anthropology
Diptera: taxonomic order of insects comprising the flies
disarticulated: relative location of skeletal elements that is inconsistent with anatomical positioning
Disaster Mortuary Operational Response Team (DMORT): experts in the fields of victim identification and mortuary services
dispersal: process of remains being spread widely away from the point of original deposition through a variety of taphonomic agencies
distal: end of bone furthest from the axial skeleton; toward posterior of the mouth for premolars and molars or lateral side for incisors and canines
disturbed grave: grave altered by either natural, human, or nonhuman actions at some point after the initial burial, but not necessarily moved to a new location; burial cut may also be marred by the same actions
dorsal: on the back of the hand or top of the foot in humans; toward the back of a quadruped
dry bone rodent gnawing: gnawing on dry, cortical bone, especially margins that fit easily into a rodent's mouth, that leaves behind sets of short, often overlapping, striations with U-shaped profiles
ectoparasite: external parasites that inhabit and feed on the surface of their host
edge polish: rounded appearance resulting from repeated gnawing in the same location; especially evident in thicker cortical bone
edge spade: short-handled digging tool with a small flat, square, sharpened blade; used in removing sod or very thin layers of soil from surface areas (e.g., shovel shining)
eggs: round or oval bodies laid by a female that provides protection and nutrients for offspring contained inside structure
electrical conductivity: a measure of how strongly a material conducts the flow of electrical current
electrical resistivity: a measure of how strongly a material opposes the flow of electrical current
electrical resistivity survey: active geophysical remote-sensing method that measures the electrical resistance of the subsurface; used to help identify subsurface features
electrical resistivity tomography (ERT): geophysical technique that measures the spatial distribution and contrast of electrical resistivity in the subsurface; data imaging helps identify subsurface features
electromagnetic (EM) induction meter: active geophysical survey tool that contains a transmitter and a receiver used to measure differences in the electrical conductivity of the ground
electronic distance measurement (EDM): surveying instrument system that measures the distance between two points by using electromagnetic waves to time how long it takes for a signal to travel to a reflector and back
electronic transit theodolite: a specialized optical survey instrument equipped with a precision telescope that measures both horizontal and vertical angles
elevation: vertical measure of how far an object is above (i.e., height) or below (i.e., depth) a fixed reference point (e.g., datum)
elevation plane: an imaginary horizontal flat surface that extends outward in all directions from a surveyor-designated fixed point of reference (e.g., datum)
enamel: hard, white mineral portion of the tooth; makes up majority of tooth crown
epicondyle: small projection superior to a condyle
epiphyseal growth plate: layer of cartilage between metaphysis and epiphysis that allows for growth in bone
epiphyseal line: remnant of epiphyseal growth plate in adult bones
epiphysis: (*pl. epiphyses*) end of bone separate from metaphysis during development; becomes fused when growth has ceased
etching: dissolution of a surface by acids; taphonomically associated with the growth and decay of plant material containing humic acid
ethanol (80%, ETOH): commonly known as ethyl alcohol; used in forensic entomology for killing adult specimens and long-term storage of adults, eggs, and larvae
ethyl acetate: commonly known as nail polish remover; fluid used in kill jar when collecting adult insect specimens
ethmoid: small irregular bone found in the superior portion of the nasal cavity; externally visible on the medial aspect of the eye orbit
evidence: everything used to demonstrate who is responsible for a criminal act
evidence marking tents: letter or number identifier placed near evidence during photography; also used as

letter and number baseline references in a grid to identify the position of a single grid square

excavation: controlled and systematic removal of soil and sediments to uncover remains and other forms of evidence

excavation spoil: soil dug up from an excavation or a grave cut during burial; may also be referred to as backfill

exhumation: legal recovery of remains from their official place of burial, often to identify unknown remains, recover a DNA sample from identified remains to identify a different set of unknown remains, or for further analysis, including trauma

extended position: burial position where an individual's legs form a 180° angle in relation to the trunk of the body

facet: smooth, flattened articular surface

feature: non-portable elements of a site that cannot be removed without altering or destroying their form, such as an animal burrow, posthole, ditch, trash pit, or built structure

femur: (*pl. femora*) paired long bones that make up the upper portion of the leg; also known as the thigh bone

ferrous: material containing iron

fibula: (*pl. fibulae*) paired long bones located on the lateral aspect of the lower leg when in standard anatomical position

field archaeology: on-site study and excavation of archaeological sites to examine and document evidence of past human activity and changes in societies over long periods

fish: cold-blooded aquatic vertebrate animal living in water, moving with the help of fins, and breathing with gills

fixative: solution used in forensic entomology to immediately stabilize a specimen's structure by preventing autolysis (enzymatic breakdown) and putrefaction (bacterial decay)

flat bones: bones that are thin, flat, usually somewhat curved, lacking a diaphysis and medullary cavity, such as cranial bones of the skull, ribs, sternum, and scapula

flexed position: burial position where an individual's legs form an angle of 90° or less in relation to the trunk of the body

flower: seed-bearing part of a plant, consisting of reproductive organs

folding meter stick: metric foldable ruler (also known as a carpenter's tape); used when drawing features and taking depth measurements

foramen: opening or hole passing through bone

foramen magnum: large opening found at the base of the cranium

forensic anthropology: the application of the science of physical anthropology and human osteology in a legal setting for the purpose of human identification

forensic archaeology: the application of standard archaeological principles and methods to locate and recover human remains and associated evidence within the context of a forensic investigation

forensic botany: a specialized field of study focusing on the examination of algae, fungi, and plants in relation to forensic investigations

forensic context: interrelated circumstances in which something of medicolegal significance occurs or is found, such as the association and relationship among skeletal remains, personal possessions, location of burial, and environment

forensic entomology: the scientific study of insects and their application in forensic investigations; occasionally broadened to include other arthropods such as spiders, centipedes, and scorpions

forensic odontology: the examination and evaluation of dental evidence in a legal setting

forensic palynology: a specialized branch of forensic botany that employs pollen and spores as crucial evidence in legal investigations

forensic pathology: application of principles of medicine in general and pathology to death investigations to determine cause of death and circumstances surrounding death

forensic photography: used to document carefully and thoroughly and visually preserve an accurate representation of the contextual relationships of evidence related to criminal investigations, legal proceedings, and scientific analysis

forensic taphonomy: evaluation and interpretation of the depositional context, discriminating between perimortem and postmortem modifications of the remains, and estimating postmortem interval

foresight: any stadia rod reading taken to establish the elevation of a new, unknown point

fossa: shallow depression

frass: dry, crumbly, brownish strands of adult beetle feces and masticated materials

frontal: large irregular bone found in the forehead region of the cranium

frontal (coronal) plane: plane that runs through body from head to feet, dividing body into front and back halves

frost heave: occurs when water in the soil freezes and expands, causing the upward or outward movement of the ground surface or objects within the ground

fruit: the fleshy product of a flowering plant that contains seeds

fungi: organisms that lack chlorophyll and feed on organic matter, thrive in both dry and moist environments, and reproduce through microscopic spores commonly dispersed by the wind

furcula: sternal element in a bird skeleton; also known as the wishbone

fused tibia-fibula: common anatomical feature in many nonhuman fauna, particularly those adapted for running locomotion, like birds, various small mammals, and some hoofed mammals

gastropods: a large class of invertebrates in the mollusk phylum that includes snails, slugs, and limpets

Geographic Coordinate System (GCS): spatial reference system that uses latitude and longitude coordinates for communicating positions on Earth's curved surface

Geographic Information System (GIS): computer-based system for capturing, storing, manipulating, analyzing, and displaying geographically referenced data

geological map: depicts rock formations, geological zones, and soil types across a landscape

geophysical survey: systematic collection of geophysical data to detect subsurface anomalies, which are recognized as localized areas of contrasting physical properties of materials (e.g., metal buried in soil)

geophysical prospecting: the study of locating and mapping hidden objects or features that are underground or underwater

Global Positioning System (GPS): satellite-based global navigation system that provides users with accurate location, velocity, and time information anywhere on or near Earth; utilizes the World Geodetic System (WGS84) as a standard reference

gnawing: reduction of hard fibrous materials through consistent chewing

gradient magnetometer: geophysical survey tool that measures small variations in the Earth's magnetic field through paired receivers; also known as a gradiometer

grave: feature in the ground where a body has been buried

grave outline: characteristic of a grave indicated by the line of definition between the backfill sediment and the strata through which the grave has been dug; also known as a burial cut

grid north: refers to the northward direction indicated by the north-south grid lines on a map

grid pattern: visual search method where individuals are positioned close enough to one another in a line so that their field of view overlaps as they move across the landscape in transects and then search the same area again in a direction perpendicular (shifting 90°) to the first search

grid survey: ensures entire area has been adequately searched, and areas between transect lines have not been missed during geophysical search

grid-system mapping: method of mapping concerned with laying out grid squares over the scene to control the work area and heavily localized areas of evidence are recorded in great detail

groove (sulcus): furrow on bone surface

ground-penetrating radar (GPR): active geophysical remote-sensing method that uses radar pulses to detect density anomalies in ground subsurface layers

grub: beetle larvae with soft bodies, legs, and hardened heads with pincer-like mandibles

height: vertical measure of how far an object is above a fixed reference point (e.g., datum)

height of instrument (HI): elevation of the line of sight of a survey instrument above a known datum

historic finds: materials related to the period of recorded history

homodont dentition: conical peg-like teeth of the same type, most often found in reptiles

horizontal (transverse) plane: plane that is perpendicular to median and frontal planes; divides body into upper and lower sections at any level

human remains detection (HRD) dog: air scent dog specially trained to alert to the generic scent of human decomposition from a dead body or tissue and fluid from a decomposed body and assisting in locating human bodies, body parts, and body fluids; also known as a cadaver dog

humerus: (*pl. humeri*) paired long bones that make up the upper arm

humus: dark, organic material that forms in soil when plants and animal matter decays

hyaline cartilage: cartilage tissue covering external articular surface of bone

hyoid: single U-shaped bone found inferior to the mandible; only bone in the human skeleton that does not articulate with another bone

hypoplastrons: bony elements that fuse together to form a turtle shell

incisal: biting and cutting surface of incisors and canines

incisor: flat, chisel-shaped tooth at the anterior of the mouth

indirect evidence: objects that provide a circumstantial relationship with remains (e.g., weapons, digging tools)

inferior: lower or below; toward the feet

infracranial skeleton: all skeletal elements below the skull and hyoid

innominate (os coxa): (*pl. os coxae*) large flat irregular paired bones, also known as the hip bones, located laterally in the pelvic girdle; provide an anchor for the legs

inside-out pattern: visual search method where the surface scene is first processed inwardly, then direction is reversed and it is processed outwardly after uncovering concentrated remains

***in situ*:** Latin phrase meaning *in the place*; used when remains and/or associated evidence are found in their original, undisturbed location or position

instars: stages where the outer layer of larval insect cuticle (exoskeleton) splits from the inner layers (endoskeleton) to allow for growth

International Commission on Missing Persons (ICMP): intergovernmental organization addressing issues of persons missing due to armed conflicts, violations of human rights, and natural disasters

International (FDI) system: standard dental numbering system of the *Fédération Dentaire Internationale*; based on numerical identifier for quadrant and tooth type in deciduous and permanent teeth

intrusions: disturbances that cut into previous deposits (e.g., a grave) and introduce materials from a different context or time sequence

intrusive search: use of destructive methods to locate clandestine graves, bodies deposited on the surface, and associated evidence; includes probing and coring the soil, digging test excavations and/or shovel shining, and using heavy equipment

irregular bones: bones with complex shapes that are not easily characterized in other classifications, such as the vertebrae, sacrum, and mandible

interment: the act of placing remains in a permanently designated location; usually accompanied with funeral rites

inurnment: process of burying or entombing cremated remains in an urn

KAA fixative: a solution used in forensic entomology for killing and preserving larval insect specimens (components of solution are listed in Table 9.4)

Kahle's solution: a solution used in forensic entomology for killing and preserving adult insects and preserving larvae (components of solution are listed in Table 9.4)

labial: surface of incisors and canines adjacent to the lips

lacrimal: small flat paired bones located on the medial aspect of the eye orbits; anatomically house the tear glands

larva: (*pl. larvae*) the immature form of an insect that emerges from the egg and develops prior to pupation; often referred to as a fly maggot or beetle grub

lateral: away from the midline

latitude: geospatial coordinate that specifies the north-south position of a point, measured in degrees from the equator (0°) to 90° north or 90° south

leaf litter: accumulating and decomposing plant parts on the ground surface

leaves: flattened, green organs in a plant that are specialized for photosynthesis

lichens: unique composite organisms formed through a symbiotic partnership between a fungus and a photosynthetic partner, typically a green alga or cyanobacterium

line (ridge): long, thin elevation with roughened surface

lingual: surface of the tooth adjacent to the tongue

livor mortis: postmortem gravitational pooling of the blood, causing purplish-blue coloration of the skin

loamy: soil made of a balanced mixture of sand, silt, and clay; nutrient-rich and crumbly in texture

long bones: bones that are considerably longer than they are wide with an elongated diaphysis and larger diameter epiphyses at both ends, such as the humerus and femur

longitude: geospatial coordinate that specifies the east-west position, measured in degrees from the Prime Meridian (0°) to 180° east or 180° west

lumbar vertebrae: five vertebrae that comprise the inferior portion of the vertebral column; individually abbreviated as L1, L2, etc. with L1 as the most superior and L5 as most inferior, articulating with the sacrum

macrobotanicals: plant material that is visible to the naked eye and typically does not require magnification for analysis

maggot: soft-bodied legless larva of a fly

magnetic locator: passive geophysical survey tool used to measure changes in magnetic fields surrounding buried ferromagnetic objects; also known as valve and box locators

magnetic north: direction in which the north end of a compass needle will point to the northern magnetic pole in response to Earth's magnetic field

magnetometer (MAG): passive geophysical remote-sensing tool used to measure small variations in the Earth's magnetic field caused by ferrous concentrations, burned soils and clays, and differences in the magnetic susceptibility of soils, stone, or decayed organic matter below the ground surface; capable of detecting magnetic field around metallic objects, such as weapons

mammal: taxonomic class of warm-blooded vertebrate animal distinguished by hair or fur, secretion of milk by females to feed young, and typically birth live young

mandible: single irregular bone also known as the lower jaw

marbling: greenish-blue discoloration of blood vessels visible through the skin during decomposition

maritime chart: depicts underwater formations and the depth of the sea floor

marrow: soft, fatty tissue found at the center of most bones

mass grave: consists of disarticulated remains or only articulated fragments (e.g., an ossuary); in forensic contexts, remains are often articulated due to less bioturbation and other forms of taphonomic disturbance over a shorter period

matrix: physical substance (e.g., soil, sediment) that surrounds and fills a space where evidence or remains are found

maxilla: (*pl. maxillae*) irregular paired bones that make up the upper jaw

medial: toward the midline

median (sagittal) plane: plane that runs through body from head to feet, dividing body into left and right halves

medical examiner (ME): medically qualified government appointed official who investigates deaths that occur under unusual or suspicious circumstances and performs postmortem examinations

medullary cavity: central cavity of bone that holds bone marrow

mesial: toward anterior of the mouth for premolars and molars or median plane for incisors and canines

metacarpals: five short tubular paired bones that form the palm of the hand; individually abbreviated as MC1, MC2, etc. with MC1 (base of the thumb) as the most lateral when in standard anatomical position

metal detector: passive geophysical survey tool that responds to metal that may not be readily apparent in subsurface layers

metaphysis: (*pl. metaphyses*) expanded, growth portion of a long bone found between the diaphysis and epiphysis

metapodial: bone in hoofed mammals formed from fusion of the third and fourth metacarpals or third and fourth metatarsals

metatarsals: five short tubular paired bones that form arch of the foot; individually abbreviated as MT1, MT2, etc. with MT1 (base of the big toe) as the most medial when in standard anatomical position

microbotanicals: plant materials that are not discernible to the naked eye and require magnification for proper examination and analysis

midrange views: photographs that focus on relationships among specific features or items of evidence and their surroundings; link objects depicted in close-up views to their environment depicted in overviews

minimum number of individuals (MNI): fewest possible number of individuals represented in an osteological assemblage

molar: broad, grinding teeth at the posterior of the mouth

monostatic antenna: antenna where the transmitter and receiver are contained within the same housing

mosses: non-vascular plants that form dense, green mats in moist, shady environments

multiple grave: consists of the remains of two or more individuals buried in the same feature at different times; often exhibits a combination of primary articulated remains and disturbed remains due to the process of reentering an existing grave to deposit additional remains

Munsell soil color book: commercially available color reference system consisting of a set of color chips that are matched with soil and an alphanumeric notation for the soil color hue (color family), value (lightness or darkness), and chroma (intensity)

mycology: scientific study of fungi

nasal: small flat paired bones that make up the bridge of the nose

nasal concha: (*pl. conchae*) small irregular paired bones located laterally in the nasal cavity

natural bristle brush: brush made of animal hair or hog bristles (also known as China bristle paint brushes)

necrology: study of the phenomena of death, involving determination of the moment of death and the different changes that occur in the tissues of the body after death

nganga: a ritual cauldron associated with Afro-Cuban religions; contain ritual artifacts that often include human and animal skeletal remains

non-ferrous: metal materials other than iron or steel

nonintrusive search: use of nondestructive methods to locate clandestine graves, bodies deposited on the surface, and associated evidence; includes visual searches, human remains detection dogs, and the majority of geophysical prospecting methods

North arrow: photographic marker for indicating north orientation in site plan view

notch: indentation at an edge

nutrient foramen: external opening of nutrient canal in bone; facilitates blood and nerve supply

oblique plane: any plane through the body that is not parallel or perpendicular to the other planes; divides body at an angle other than horizontal or vertical at any level

obstructed areas: landscape areas where a 360° field of vision is impeded by structures or natural features

occipital: large irregular flat bone that makes up the back and base of the cranial vault; foramen magnum feature located on this bone

occlusal: chewing or grinding surface of premolars and molars

offset: horizontal measurement taken at a right angle (90°) from a baseline

open areas: landscape areas where a 360° field of vision is not impeded by structures or natural features

open association: relationship among objects where simultaneous deposition is only assumed and not proven, like a knife found near a grave

orientation: cardinal direction in which the head lies in relation to the body's central axis; should be recorded in directional terms using a compass, natural features, or human-made structures

orienteering (baseplate) compass: simple navigation tool that consists of a rotating magnetic pointer, with one end marked for north, and a rotating degree dial, both supported by a handheld base plate with a sightline and directional markings; most often during outdoor activities but can also be used for simple mapping

orthophoto map: a geometrically corrected aerial or satellite image that has a uniform scale; also known as an orthoimage

osteology: anatomical study of the structure and function of the human skeleton, including individualized traits and pathology; used in the identification of human remains regarding age, sex, ancestry, stature, and health status

osteophagic: eating or chewing bones

overlay sheet: tracing sheet placed on top of a plan drawing to superimpose a record of a new layer of stratigraphy or evidence

overviews: photographs that capture the complete scene, showing layout and orientations, including major landmarks (e.g., landscape features, buildings, doors, trees and ground cover, grave)

palatine: small irregular paired bones that make up the posterior of the palate and floor of the nasal cavity

palmar: on the palm of the hand

Palo: Afro-Caribbean syncretic religion that routinely incorporates human skeletal remains in its rituals

parasitoids: insects that deposit their eggs within the bodies or pupae of other insects, allowing their larvae to consume the host from within as a nutrient source

parietal: large flat paired bones found on the superior portion of the cranium

passive geophysical prospecting method: uses a receiver that measures variations within the natural forces of the Earth (e.g., magnetic fields) that are generally produced by buried metallic objects or other detectable subsurface anomalies

patella: (*pl. patellae*) sesamoid bone, also known as the knee cap, found in the anterior of the knee joint

pedestal excavation: method of carefully exposing remains or specific items by leaving them *in situ* and supported by a column or pedestal of sediment, situating them higher in relation to the surrounding excavated area

pelvic girdle: consists of the sacrum, coccyx, and left and right innominate (os coxa); connects the axial skeleton to the lower limbs

penetrometer: a soil probe with a pressure gauge used to measure soil density

perimortem: at or around the time of death

periodontal ligament (PDL): soft tissue ligament holding tooth in tooth socket

periosteum: fibrous membrane covering the outer surface of bone

permanent teeth: second set of teeth that replace deciduous teeth during development; humans have an average of 32 permanent teeth

personal protective equipment (PPE): equipment used to minimize exposure to hazards that cause injury, illness, or contamination in work environment

perturbation: any event, natural or human-induced, that disrupts the normal structure of *in situ* soils and sediments

phalanges: (*sing. phalanx*) small tubular bones of the fingers and toes; a total of 14 phalanges per hand and foot, identified by position with five proximal, four intermediate (thumb and big toe lack an intermediate phalanx), and five distal phalanges

photogrammetry: the science of obtaining reliable measurements from photographs and digital imager

photography scale: metric measurement tool used to show the ratio of an object's depiction to its actual size; also, a color tool used to show any variations in color between an object's actual color and its depiction

phycology: the scientific study of algae

phyllids: small, leaf-like structures in mosses that absorb water directly

Physicians for Human Rights (PHR): nongovernmental organization that focuses on the health consequences of mass atrocities and human rights violations around the world

pit: tiny pocket or depression

plan drawing: two-dimensional 'bird's eye' (i.e., directly above) view of an object or area drawn to scale

planar surface: interfaces of stratigraphic horizons detected by a ground-penetrating radar during geophysical survey

plantar: on the sole of the foot

planning frame: 1-m square metal frame subdivided into 10-cm sub-squares using lines attached to the frame; used for mapping heavily localized areas of evidence

plant: organisms that cannot move voluntarily, have no sensory organs, and generally produce their own nutrients through photosynthesis; extended more broadly in forensics to encompass a diverse array of life forms, fungi, blue-green protists, red, green, and brown algae, diatoms, and certain bacteria

plastron: bottom portion of a turtle shell

platform excavation: method of carefully cutting into the horizontal area adjacent to the primary feature being excavated and creating a 'platform' from which to work safely

plumb bob (plummet): a pointed tip weight that suspends from a string; used as a vertical reference line when measuring depth within an excavation

pointing trowel: small excavation tool with a pointed, flat leaf-shaped metal blade (also known as a cement or bricklayer's trowel)

point source: small hyperbolic reflections due to smaller features detected using ground-penetrating radar

pollen: a fine, powdery substance produced by plants for reproduction

polyphydont dentition: teeth that are continuously replaced throughout life
portacath: small medical device placed under the skin to provide long-term access to a vein for treatments; also known as an injection port
position: relationship of legs, arms, and head to each other and to the trunk of the body
postdepositional: occurring after remains are deposited
posterior: toward the back
postcranial: all bones of quadruped skeleton except the skull
postmortem: after death
postmortem interval (PMI): amount of time between an organism's death and when it is examined forensically
prehistoric finds: materials related to the period prior to recorded history
premolar: bicuspid teeth located between canines and molars in permanent dentition; not found in deciduous dentition
preservative: solution used in forensic entomology to maintain a specimen in a stable, non-degraded state for long-term storage
primary datum: main fixed point of reference for all elevation and angle measurements made during survey mapping and excavation
primary grave: consists of the body in the location where it was originally deposited, and the context of the grave has not been disturbed
primary grave depression: forms as a result of natural compaction of the loose sediment that was placed over the body and settling after the release of gases and the collapse of the abdominal region during decomposition
primary surface site (or scatter): location where remains were originally placed; may include an abundance of skeletal remains still in relative anatomical position and/or the presence of a cadaver decomposition island
prismatic compass: hand-held surveying instrument that uses a prism to allow the user to simultaneously see the object being sighted and read the compass bearing from a circular, graduated scale
process: a bony projection
pronation: rotation of hand so palm faces posteriorly in standard anatomical position
prone: positioning where the body is facing down toward the ground
propylene glycol (99%): solution used in forensic entomology for preservation and long-term storage of hard- and soft-bodied specimens that may be used for DNA characterization
provenience: precise position of an object within the matrix; reflects its three-dimensional placement (i.e., north-south, east-west, and vertical positioning) at the site
proximal: end of bone closest to axial skeleton
pulp chamber: inner portion of tooth crown containing blood and nerve supply
puparium: (*pl. puparia*) hard, darkened, barrel-shaped case that forms from skin following the larval stage; protects final instar as it transforms into an adult insect
putrefaction: decomposition of animal proteins by bacterial flora that spread from the gastrointestinal tract
radius: (*pl. radii*) paired long bones located on the lateral aspect of the lower arm when in standard anatomical position
ramus: arm-like bar of bone
receiver (Rx): device that captures signal (e.g., electromagnetic waves) and converts them back into electrical signals
reel measuring tape: fiberglass metric measuring tape held on a hand reel; typically used in 20-, 50- or 100-m lengths when laying out grids in geophysical survey and when mapping larger areas of search and recovery
reference number line: line that is at a 90° angle to the baseline and is used to identify reference grid squares
reflection: nonspecific feature detected using ground-penetrating radar
reflection profile: representation of soil layers and subsurface features produced by a ground-penetrating radar system during geophysical survey
remains: collective term for human and nonhuman tissues recovered from a scene
remotely operated vehicle (ROV): free-swimming submersible craft used to perform underwater observation or other tasks; often deployed in waters by search and rescue personnel when it is not safe for divers to conduct searches
remote sensing: employing a set of non-invasive techniques (e.g., ground-penetrating radar, magnetometry, resistivity) to locate burials and other forms of evidence, guide excavation strategies, and minimize disturbance
reptile: taxonomic class of vertebrate animal distinguished by a body covered in scales or scutes, reliance on external sources for body heat, and typically laying soft-shelled eggs on land
reversal (principle of): archaeological principle presuming that natural causes or human activity has moved materials from one location and deposited them in another in reverse order
reverse degree dial: prismatic compass feature where 0–360° dial is labeled counterclockwise, which allows the user to read the correct degree of bearing directly from the compass
rib: paired, curved tubular and flat bones that make up the rib cage; individually identified by side (left

or right) and numbered from superior (rib #1) to inferior (rib #12)

rigor mortis: postmortem stiffening of muscles in the limbs due to chemical changes in the tissues

ringing: prominent horizontal bands of antenna noise seen in a reflection profile produced by a ground-penetrating radar

root (dental): portion of tooth embedded in jaw; covered by cementum

root (plant): part of a vascular plant that typically grows underground, anchoring the plant, absorbing water and dissolved minerals from the soil, and storing food

root canal: narrow end of pulp chamber at root end of tooth

sacrum: large irregular bone, comprising five fused bony elements, located at the base of the vertebral column and between the innominates in the pelvic girdle

sandy: soil made of larger, coarse particles that do not adhere or stick to one another; nutrient poor and gritty in texture

saprophytes: organisms that feed on dead or decaying organic matter

scale: map feature that indicates the relationship (i.e., ratio) between distance on a map and the corresponding distance on the ground

scapula: (*pl. scapulae*) large flat paired bones, also known as the shoulder blade, located in the posterior portion of the shoulder girdle; provide an anchor for the arms

scavengers: later-stage insect species that excel at scavenging, frequently consuming the larvae of other insects along with any residual human tissue

scene: area within a site where a specific activity took place

scent cone: concentration of scent dispersing through the environment

scent pool: concentration of scent either at the point of origin or trapped at a remote location

screening: process of sifting leaf litter and excavated soil through wire mesh to recover small bones and other forms of evidence

scutes: outer layer of keratinized pieces found on a turtle shell

searching: process of utilizing broad search methods during attempts at locating a site or scattered remains

search sweep: set distance or bounded subunit (e.g., line, lane, grid square, or zone) marked within the broader search area when conducting visual surface and geophysical searches

secondary datum: fixed point of reference needed for elevation and angle measurements in a portion of the site where the primary datum is not visible or easily accessible during mapping or excavation

secondary grave: consists of skeletal elements that have been removed from their original location of burial by human activity and then reburied in another location

secondary grave depression: forms within the primary grave depression due to additional soil compaction and soft tissue decomposition

secondary surface site (or scatter): location of remains after they have been moved from their primary or original place of deposition by natural, human, or nonhuman actions; often marked by the presence of partial elements or smaller proportions of skeletal remains

section drawing: cross-section view one would have if an imaginary vertical plane cut through a feature to show the scaled relationship between different layers of stratigraphy or details in object placement

sediment: transported or deposited particles or aggregates derived from rocks, soils, or biological material

sedimentation: process by which mineral particles and/or organic matter settle out of fluid and accumulate on a surface

seed: the small, hard part of a plant that contains a new plant embryo and its food supply, protected by a coat

semi-flexed position: burial position in which the angle of the legs is between 90° and 180° from the trunk

sesamoid bones: smaller, rounded bones that form within a tendon, such as the patella, and vary greatly in size

short bones: bones that are roughly cube-shaped, lacking a diaphysis, and contain mostly trabecular bone, such as the carpals and tarsals

shoulder girdle: consists of the left and right proximal humerus, scapula and clavicle; connects the upper limbs to the axial skeleton

shovel shining: invasive search method by removing thin layers of soil or sediment by keeping the back of a flat-bladed transfer shovel almost parallel with the ground surface; used to delineate the burial outline

shovel testing: a 'last resort' invasive search method utilizing small-scale test excavations (usually the width of a spade shovel) in an attempt to locate buried evidence or a grave outline

side-scan sonar: marine geophysical survey tool that uses sound waves to produce a graphic image of the seafloor surface or other water feature floor surfaces

silty: soil made of fine particles that are larger than clay but smaller than sand; nutrient-rich and smooth in texture

sinus: hollow area within a cranial bone

site: distinct spatial clustering of human activity

site plan: a detailed, scaled drawing that represents the horizontal layout of a site, including natural features, built structures, and limits of recovery areas and excavations, in relation to a fixed reference point (e.g., datum)

site processing: detailed searching after locating a site or scattered remains to delineate the extent of the site and to locate additional bones and associated evidence; may involve detailed clearing of the scene, mapping of remains and associated evidence, excavation of remains if needed, and collection of remains and associated evidence

skeletonization: refers to the complete decomposition of soft tissues and exposure of skeletal elements

sketch map: illustration not drawn to scale, but includes overall measurements of the surroundings and the location of evidence recovery areas in relation to landscape features or built structures (also known as a 'mud map')

skin slippage: separation of skin layers during decomposition

skull: the cranium and mandible

Society for American Archaeology (SAA): professional organization dedicated to the research, interpretation, and protection of the archaeological heritage of the Americas

soil: layer of generally loose mineral and/or organic materials that occurs in the land surface and usually hold liquid, gases, and biota

soil chemistry: types and amounts of chemical elements and compounds present in the soil; includes properties like soil pH, oxidation potential, and the capacity to store and supply essential nutrients

soil composition: proportions of different components (i.e., mineral particles, organic matter, water, and air, as well as living organisms) that make up soil

soil consistency: degree to which soil particles stick together and resist deformation or rupture

soil-coring probe: tool used to detect mixing in soil horizons by removing and examining a vertical core of soil

soil horizons: distinct layers with unique physical, chemical, and biological characteristics resulting from soil-forming processes

soil pH: measure of acidity or alkalinity in soil; significantly affects the preservation of materials

soil profile: arrangement of soil horizons

soil texture: relative proportions of sand, silt, and clay in a given amount of soil

soil texture classes: soil type based on the relative proportions of sand, silt, and clay (e.g., sandy loam, silty clay), which in turn determine a soil's physical characteristics

sonar: sound navigation and ranging to navigate, communicate, or detect objects

sphenoid: large complex irregular bone of the cranium forming the posterior and lateral aspects of the eye orbits

spine: relatively long, slender projection

spiral pattern: visual search method in which the searcher moves in decreasing concentric circles within a small search area (i.e., moving from the outer edges toward the center)

spore: asexual reproductive cell of organisms like fungi

stadia rod: graduated rod used to measure distance from the observation point (i.e., survey instrument) to a place where the rod is positioned; used to determine differences in elevation during survey mapping

standard anatomical position: body standing erect, face forward, feet together, arms slightly raised, palms of hands facing anteriorly

stem: part of a plant that serves as the main structural axis, supporting leaves, flowers, and fruits while transporting water, nutrients, and sugars between the roots and the rest of the plant

strata: (*sing. stratum*) layers of soil, sediment, and debris accumulating over time

stratigraphy: analysis of layered deposits to understand the chronological sequence of events and how they relate to human activity, environment, and site formation

sterile soil: any soil horizon in an excavation or within a burial site that does not contain evidence or data relevant to the specific incident under investigation

sternum: small flat bone comprising three fused or unfused bony elements (manubrium, sternal body, and xyphoid process); located at the midline of the chest and is the anterior anchor site for the ribs

strip (line) pattern: visual search method where individuals are positioned close enough to one another in a line so that their field of view overlaps as they move across the landscape in transects

subaerial weathering: process where exposed bones become sun-bleached from UV light and crack apart slowly over the course of years; timing is dependent upon many local environmental factors

subchondral bone: area of bone at joint covered by hyaline cartilage

submerged areas: areas underwater or covered by water on a regular or seasonal basis

superior: upper or above; toward the head

superposition (principle of): archaeological principle presuming more recent sediment layers are laid down on top of older ones and that the strata are found in a position like that of their original deposition; used to establish a relative chronology of strata and the artifacts and features they contain

supination: rotation of hand so palm faces anteriorly

supine: positioning where the body is facing up away from the ground

surface scatters: include remains situated either completely on the ground surface or partly exposed, with little or no effort of concealment

suture: joint between cranial bones

synsacrum: large number of fused vertebrae that form a solid skeletal connection between the axial skeleton, vertebrae, and pelvic girdle in a bird skeleton

taphonomic agencies: destructive forces that tend to alter remains

taphonomic effects: actual alterations occurring to the remains, which are produced by taphonomic agencies

taphonomy: the study of changes that biological organisms undergo between the time of death and the time of discovery of their remains; may be extended to include changes that happen to remains during and after their recovery

tarsals: small, short bones of the ankle; each ankle consists of seven bones: calcaneus, talus, navicular, 1st cuneiform, 2nd cuneiform, 3rd cuneiform, and cuboid

tarsometatarsus: distal long bone in the lower leg of birds, formed by fusion of tarsal and metatarsal bones

T-bar probe: metal bar probe used to detect variations in the density of subsurface soil layers

temporal: large flat irregular paired bones found on the sides of the cranium; contain the auditory ossicles

temporary datum: temporary point of reference needed for elevation and angle measurements in a portion of the site where the primary datum is not visible or easily accessible; must be mapped in relation to the primary datum prior to its removal

test pit: small-scale excavation using a spade shovel to assess the presence and depth of remains and associated evidence

thoracic vertebrae: 12 vertebrae that comprise the central portion of the vertebral column and articulate with the 12 pairs of ribs; individually abbreviated as T1, T2, etc. with T1 as the most superior

tibia: (*pl. tibiae*) paired long bones located on the medial aspect of the lower leg when in standard anatomical position

tibiotarsus: middle long bone in the lower leg of a bird, formed by fusion of the tibia and several tarsal bones

time since death (TSD): amount of time between an organism's death and its discovery

tool marks: impression or compression marks left by the contact of a tool on a surface

tooth furrows: gnaw marks that penetrate the cortical bone and are at least more than three times long as they are wide

tooth pits: gnaw marks that do not penetrate the cortical bone and have dimensions where their length is no more than three times their width (i.e., smaller, rounded, irregular marks)

tooth punctures: gnaw marks that penetrate the cortical bone and have dimensions where their length is no more than three times their width; may also include deeper marks in areas of cortical bone already exposed by gnawing

tooth scores (striations): gnaw marks that do not penetrate the cortical bone but are at least more than three times long as they are wide

topographic map: portrays natural and built surface features and contour lines for a detailed representation of the shape and elevation of the landscape

total station: advanced surveying instrument that integrates an electronic transit theodolite, an electronic distance measurement system, and a data collector and microprocessor

towfish: geophysical survey component containing a transmitter and receiver for use in side-scan sonar

transect: fixed path or lane along which individuals search for and mark occurrences of any possible evidence

transfer shovel: long- or short-handled digging tool with a flat, square, sharpened blade; used in moving soil from one location to another or when backfilling holes

translucent bone: characteristic of certain animal bones appearing transparent or semi-transparent; most often found in fish

transmitter (Tx): device that converts electrical signals into electromagnetic waves for transmission

traverse line: a sequence of connected survey lines, measured in azimuth and distance, that defines a path or establishes the location of points and features on the landscape

triangulation: involves the measure of the angles of a triangle

trilateration: involves the measure of the sides of a triangle; based on the calculation of the hypotenuse length (c^2) of a triangle when the length of the base (a^2) and one side (b^2) are known ($a^2 + b^2 = c^2$)

trochanter: large, blunt elevation for muscle attachment

true north: direction along the surface of the Earth that ends in the location of the North Pole, which is one end in the axis of the Earth's rotation; also known as geographic north

tubercle: small, round elevation with roughened surface

tuberosity: large, round elevation with roughened surface

tubular bones: bones that are shaped like long bones but significantly smaller in size, such as the metacarpals and metatarsals

turning point: survey point where both a foresight reading is taken from the first instrument position and a backsight reading is taken from the next instrument position

ulna: (*pl. ulnae*) paired long bones located on the medial aspect of the lower arm when in standard anatomical position

unilateral: on one side

United States Geological Survey (USGS): a non-regulatory science bureau within the U.S. Department of the Interior that studies landscapes and produces several series of topographic maps of the United States

Universal (National) system: standard dental numbering system used in North America; based on location in quadrant and alphabetical identifier for deciduous teeth and numerical identifier for permanent teeth

ventral: toward the chest of a quadruped

vertebra: (*pl. vertebrae*) irregular bones, extending from the cranium to the sacrum, that make up the cervical, thoracic, and lumbar regions of the spine

visual surface search: systematic and controlled search of an area involving a team of personnel walking through an area in transects to locate various types of forensic evidence on the ground surface or surface changes that could possibly indicate a clandestine burial

vomer: single small flat bone found in the midline of the nasal cavity

weathering: destruction of bone through natural mechanical and chemical forces in the environment

wet-bone rodent gnawing: gnawing on fresh bone to obtain fat inside of bones; leaves a scooped-out appearance into cancellous areas

woody plants: plants that have hard, fibrous cells beneath the outer bark layer; usually referred to as trees or shrubs

World Geodetic System (WGS84): reference coordinate system currently used by the Global Positioning System

zone search: search method where the total search area is divided into smaller zones or quadrants that are easily managed in a day or less

zooarchaeology: study of animal remains from archaeological sites to understand past human-animal relationships

zoogamous plants: animal-pollinated plants

zygomatic: irregular, flat paired bones of the face, also known as the cheekbones

INDEX

Note: **Bold** page numbers refer to tables, *italic* page numbers refer to figures.

C

D

G

I

J

K

L

M

N

O

T

U

V

W

Y

Z

For Product Safety Concerns and Information please contact our EU representative GPSR@taylorandfrancis.com Taylor & Francis Verlag GmbH, Kaufingerstraße 24, 80331 München, Germany

Batch number: 10740984

Printed by Printforce, the Netherlands